D1220874

Guide to the
Performing Arts
1960

compiled by

S. Yancey Belknap

Director, Archives of Dance-Music-Theatre
University of Florida
Gainesville, Florida

LIBRARY
OF
MOUNT ST. MARY'S
COLLEGE
EMMITSBURG, MARYLAND
WITHDRAWN

The Scarecrow Press, Inc.
New York   1962

ML
118
.G8
1960

Copyright 1962 by the
University of Florida Library

L. C. Card No. 60-7226

50225

PREFACE

This is the fourth annual index of the performing arts which began as
a supplement to Guide to the Musical Arts, 1953-1956. There are two
sections: the main body of the volume and a separate section for the
television arts. No attempt is made to cover the whole of the respec-
tive fields.

This index of domestic and foreign periodicals includes illustrations
arranged alphabetically just below the non-illustrative items. It is
designed to aid editors, producers and scholars, including college and
high-school students. Its form is non-technical and many dates and
biographical data are included.

Periodicals added are: American Composers Alliance Bulletin, Music
and Dance, New Theatre Magazine, Theatre Research, Tulane Drama
Review and Verdi.   Music and Musicians has been omitted.

ABBREVIATIONS

Ja	January	My	May	S	September
F	Febuary	Je	June	O	October
Mr	March	Jl	July	N	November
Ap	April	Ag	August	D	December

AP	action picture	n	number
engr	engraving	p	page
ens	ensemble	ph	photograph, photographer
hl	half length	por	portrait
il	illustrated	v	volume
lith	lithograph	wl	whole length

PERIODICALS

ACAB	American Composers Alliance Bulletin		
AM	American Music	Th Arts	Theatre Arts
CMJ	Canadian Music Journal	Th Notbk	Theatre Notebook
Chrys	Chrysalis	Th R	Theatre Research
GDC	Le Guide du Concert	TD	Toute la Danse
HF	High Fidelity	TDR	Tulane Drama Review
IM	International Musician	Ver	Verdi
J Rev	Juilliard Review	WM	World of Music
LaS	La Scala	WP	World Premières
MD	Music and Dance	WT	World Theatre
MEJ	Music Educators Journal		
MR	Music Review		
MC	Musical Courier		
Mus Q	Musical Quarterly		
NTM	New Theatre Magazine		
ON	Opera News		
Op	Opera		
OP, OpP	Opéra de Paris		
PlM	Players Magazine		
Spec	Spectacles		

A MENINA DAS NUMNES, opera
Villa-Lobos, Brazil note, Op
v 11 n 5 p 344 My'60
ABBIATI, FRANCO (1898-). Gli
anni del Ballo in Maschera.
Ver v 1 n 1 p 1-27 Ap'60; Ver
v 1 n 2 p 631-656 Ag'60
--- ---Libera Musica e Musica
di Stato. il La S n 127 p 7-11
Je'60
--- ---The years of Un Ballo in
Maschera (half page in English,
half in German). Ver v 1 n 1
p 231-278 Ap'60
ABBOTT, GEORGE, 1888-, pro-
ducer
His new musical, "Fiorello",
based on the late Fiorello H. La
Guardia, review. PLM v 36 n 5
p 107 F'60
ABRAMS, JEROME. Gallantry
and greed; I (the historical
background of La Forza del
Destino). il ON v 24 n 19 p 8-9
Mr 12'60
--- ---II (historical background
of La Tosca). il ON v 24 n 20
p 4-5 Mr 19'60
ACCADEMIA MUSICALE
CHIGIANA
Siena; July-September school;
opera notes. il ON v 25 n 6 p 29
D 17'60
L'ACADEMIE INTERNATIONALE
d'ETE
Nice; 1959 founded; notes. WM
n 5 p 105 O'60
---Two groups, phs. WM n 5
p 109 O'60
L'ACCADEMIA NAZIONALE DI
SANTA CECILIA
History; concerts. La S n 128
inset JL'60
---Stagione d'abbonamento
1960-61: 42 concerts; 25 con-
certi Sala dell'Academia: calen-
dario. La S n 132 inset N'60
ACCARDO, SALVATORE,
violinist
Berthoumieux, Serge. Criticism;
prodigious memory. GDC n 275
p 752 Je 3'60
ACCOMPANISTS

Garvey, David. Accompanists
anonymous. por J Rev v 7 n 1
p 6-7, 29 Winter 59-60
---Kagen, Sergius. Training ac-
companists at Julliard. J Rev
v 7 n 1 p 5, 14 Winter 59-60
ACCORDAILLES, dance
Dominique and Paul d'Arnot, AP
wl ph: Paris. TD n 94 p 16 Je'60
ACCORDION
Composers commissioned bv the
American Accordionists Associ-
ation. MC v 161 n 3 p 34 F'60
ACCORDION SYMPHONY
Ettore, Eugene, conductor of
Sano Accordion Symphony, ens
ph: NYC. IM v 58 n 10 p 32 Ap'60
ACHOT-HAROUTOUNIAN,
TANIA pianist
Note on Iranian, broadcasting in
Australia. MD v 51 n 6 p 14 D'60
ACHUCARRA, JOAQUIN
pianist
Paris concert review.
spanish. GDC n 265-6 p 527
MR 25'60
ACIS AND GALATEA, opera
Ens AP wl ph: University of
Alabama. ON v 24 n 10 p 2
Ja 9'60

ACOUSTICS
De Gaetani, Thomas. (A review of Sound In the Theatre
by Burris-Meyer and Mallory;
use of amplification under control.) J Rev v 7 n 3 p 11
Spring '60

---Gorman, Robert. (Variable
control of reverberation time
and intensity-ambiophonic
sound.) HF v 10 n 12 p 43-4
D'60

---Henderson, V. L. Acoustic
considerations at the O'Keefe
Centre, Toronto. drawings
CMJ v 4 n 4 p 25-32
Summer '60

---New Jersey plant, Paul
Weathers sound room:

1

(Acoustics)

speakers between "dead" and "live" parts of a room. HF v 10 n 6 p 97 Je'60

---Stagecraft Corporation, Peekskill, New York: acoustical shell for theatres, gymnasiums. MEJ v 47 n 1 p 11 S-O'60

ACROBATICS

Piat et Naudy, AP wl ph: Paris TD n 90 p 14 F'60

ACTING

Bergler, Edmund. On acting and stage fright. TDR v 4 n 3 p 159-164 Mr'60

---Brown, Ivor. (warning actors at present excess of "ham-avoidance", fear of expressing emotion.) WP v 11 n 9 p 1 Jl'60

---Fenichel, Otto. On acting. TDR v 4 n 3 p 148-159 Mr'60

---Morgan, Mona. Autobiographical acting (confusing to tell a young actor "Imagine you in his place"). PLM v 36 n 4 p 82-3 Ja'60

---The Naturalistic Theatre, an excerpt on the Moscow Art Theatre from Vsevolod Meyerhold's book. "On the Theatre, TDR v 4 n 4 p 134-47 My'60

---Summer theatres, US; how the actors fare. Th Arts v 44 n 6 p 14-6 Je'60

---Vejrazka, Vilezstav. The stage actor on television. WT v 9 n 4 p 337-340 Winter '60

ACTORS

Clurman, Harold. Actors: The image of their era. TDR v 4 n 3 p 38-44 Mr'60

---Highfill, Philip H. Actors' wills. Th Notbk v 15 n 1 p 7-15 Autumn '60

---Pitoëff, Georges, par Pierre Jean Jouve (other signed comments) portfolio Spec n 1 1960

---US; Notes on Actors Fund. Th Arts v 44 n 12 p 8 D'60

---France; small pictures of François Périer, Jeanne Moreau,

Claude Rich, Françoise Brion, Sophie Marin, Hubert Ginoux , Evelyne Rey, Serge Reggiani, Th Arts v 44 n 12 p 62 D'60

ADABACHE, OLGA, 1918 - , dancer

Dans le rôle de la Fée Carabosse, AP hl ph: Lido. TD n 98 p 11 D'60

ADAMOV, ARTHUR, 1908 - , writer

Esslin, Martin. The theatre of the absurd. TDR v 4 n 4 p 3-15 My'60

ADAMS, LLOYD, violin maker Notes by Theodore Salzman. IM v 58 n 11 p 21 My'60

ADDISON, ADELE, singer Por ph. HF v 10 n 10 p 76 O'60

ADELAIDE

Best, Michael. Adelaide Festival of Arts. MD v 50 n 8 p 10-11 F'60

--- ---Festival of Arts; critical comments. por MD v 50 n 10 p 15 Ap'60

---Sinclair, John. Adelaide Arts Festival. MD v 50 n 10 p 12-3 Ap'60

L'ADELCHI, film

Review; Manzoni, il La S n 133 p 86 D'60

ADIEW, BALLERINA, play Schleswig; Klaus Werner. WP v 12 n 3 p 39 D'60

LES ADIEUX, opera

A L'Opéra -Comique;texte et musique de Marcel Landowski critique. GDC n 285 p 162 O O 21'60

---Landowski, Marcel, Musique et livret; L'Opéra - Comique. il Op P n 19 p 53 1960

---Paris Opéra - Comique; music, Marcel Landowski. WP v 12 n 3 p 29 D'60

--- ---same bill, Volo di Notte. Op v 11 n 11 p 763 N'60

ADLER, HENRY (1919?). To hell with society (plays and theatre critics, Kenneth Tynan in particular, as reacting to politics and social adjustment

2

before art). TDR v 4 n 4
p 63-76 My'66
ADLER, KURT, 1905-, conductor
Notes on festival. il ON v 25 n 1
p 5 O 8'60
THE ADMIRABLE CRICHTON,
  play
Pitlochry, ens AP wl ph:M. Cox,
1960. WT v 9 n 3 p 293 Autumn
'60
ADRIANA LECOUVREUR,
  opera
San Carlo notes, il La S n 122
p 37 Ja'60
--- ---opening night; Tebaldi re-
placed; Olivero criticism. ON
v 24 n 11 p 26 Ja 16'60
---Act II; Giulietta Simionato as
the Princesse de Boullon, AP
wl ph: San Carlo. ON v 24 n 11
p 26 Ja 16'60
AFRIAT, NICOLE, pianist
Chamfray, Claude. Paris review. GDC n 259-60 p 405
F 12'60
THE ADVENTURES OF THE
  BRAVE SOLDIER SCHWEYK,
  play
Ens AP wl ph: Reussens, 1951.
WT v 9 n 1 p 26 Spring '60
ADVERTISING
Broadway's use of critics'
quotes. Th Arts v 44 n 12
p 14-5 D'60
AESTHETICS
Athens; Congrès International
d'Esthétique; le IV e. WP v 11
n 3 p 7 Ja'60
---Ballet to abstract music; re-
marks by Everett Helm on
Milloss in C ologne Opera. MR
v 21 n 3 p 244 Ag'60
---Brustein, Robert. Scorn not
the proscenium, critic. Th Arts
v 44 n 5 p 8-9 My'60
---Candida, Federico. IL
Mistero della Musica. La S
n 125 p 61-3 Ap'60
---Chekhov; issue devoted to
staging Chekhov, 23 producers
give artistic ideas. portfolio
WT v 9 n 2 Summer '60

---Farrington, C onor A. The
language of drama. TDR v 5 n 2
n 2 p 65-72 D'60
---Jacobs, Robert L. Music as
symbol; reflections on Mr.
Deryck Cooke's The Language
of Music. MR v 21 n 3 p 226-
236 Ag'60
---Keller, Hans. Wordless
functional analysis. MR v 21
n 1 p 73-76 F'60; same. MR
v 21 n 3 p 237-9 Ag'60
---(Lang, Paul Henry.)
Editorial on modern music composition: trends, 12-tone to
serialization, as an introduction to articles on the Seminar
in advanced Musical Studies
held at Princeton University.
Mus Q v 46 n 2 p 145 Ap'60
---Regner, Otto Friedrich.
(Germany today: the ballet
still "under the sway of Ex-
pressionism, a technical
breakaway" only.) WT v 9 n 3
p 230 Autumn '60
---Romanticism; British poets
as an influence on continental
composers: a study by Paul
Chancellor. Mus Q v 46 n 1
p 1-11 Ja'60
---Valency, Maurice. (On the
loss of meaning in art: "a
major disaster of our time".)
Th Arts v 44 n 8 p 8-9, 68
Ag'60
---Verdi's "vocal style". Ver
v 1 n 2 p 1027-9 Ag'60
AF GUDS NAADE, play
Copenhagen notes; Niels Locher.
WP v 12 n 3 p 27 D'60
L'AFFAIRE DREYFUS, play
Athens notes. Manolis Scoulou-
dis. WP v 11 n 5 p 9 MR '60
AFRICA
Genet, Jean, le premier au-
teur français a avoir su ex-
ploiter le "merveilleux"
africain. il Spec n 1 p 75-8
1960
---Glickman, Sylvia Foodim.
Letter on trip to Africa

3

(AFRICA)
(music recitals). J Rev v 7 n 1
p 21 Winter 59-60
---Jones, A. M. Studies in African Music (critically reviewed by Mieczyslaw Kolinski). Mus Q v 46 n 1 p 105-110 Ja'60
---Mann, Herbie, jazz musician, sent by US Department of State; notes. por IM v 58 n 9 p 21, 34 Mr'60
---Théâtre des Nations; Ensemble National de la Côte d'Ivoire. TD n 92 p 28 Ap'60
---Ensemble National de la Côte d'Ivoire, stilts, ens ph. Bernaud. WP v 11 n 7 p 1 My'60
---Ivory Coast, stilt dancers, AP wl ph: Pic. WT v 9 n 4 p 347 Winter '60
AFTER DINNER OPERA
Notes; Norman Myrvik, Francis Barnard, Jeanne Beauvais. il ON v 25 n 5 p 4 D 10'60
AGAMEMNON: play
Ens AP wl ph: Reussens, 1951. WT v 9 n 1 p 19 Spring '60
---Outdoors, Athens 1954, ens AP wl ph: Harissiadis. WT v 9 n 2 p 154 Summer '60
AGNES, SOLEDAD
Career sketch; b. Paris; reviews quoted. il TD n 93 p 23 My'60
AGNINI, ARMANDO 1885-1960, scenic designer
New Orleans; on stage champagne toast to Agnini's 50 years as a stage designer. MC v 161 n 1 p 24 Ja'60
---Notes; b. Naples. MC v 161 n 6 p 37 My'60
AGRICOLA: ALEXANDER, 1446-1506, composer
Lerner, Edward R. The "German" works of Alexander Agricola. Mus Q v 46 n 1 p 56-66 Ja'60
AH, WILDERNESS, play
Ens AP wl ph: NYC. Th Arts v 44 n 9 p 13 S'60
AHNEUS HA HATA, play
Lahti; Martti Kainulanen.

WP v 12 n 3 p 28 D'60
AIDA, opera
Covent Garden; Rita Gorr as Amneris fine; Louis Quilico good as Amonasro. Op v 11 n 8 p 580 Ag'60
---Dettmer, Roger. The first stereo Aida comes vested in grandeur (London; Vienna under Karajan). HF v 10 n 2 p 53-4 F'60
---Metropolitan; NYC review. MC v 162 n 6 p 15 D'60
---University of California's Greek Theater, directed by Dino Yannopoulos, William Christensen, choreographer; cast. MC v 161 n 3 p 38 F'60
---Verona Arena; décor, Pino Casarini; Gavazzeni; Guilio Bertola; choreography, Ria Legnani; La S n 129-30 p 37, 71 Ag-S'60
---Chicago Lyric Opera, the Triumph scene, ens AP wl ph: Sorensen. Op v 11 n 12 p 818 D'60
---Cincinnati Summer Opera as staged by Dino Yannopoulos, Triumphal scene on two levels, ens AP ph: Grauman Marks, MC v 162 n 4 p 6 O'60
---Veron A, the Triumph Scene, ens AP wl ph: Pagliarani, OP v 11 p 70 Autumn'60
--- ---2 ens AP wl phs. La S n 129-30 p 37 Ag-S '60
AIX-EN-PROVENCE
De Francesco, Silvano. Festival (1960). il La S n 129-30 p 40, 74 Ag-S '60
---Le Festival; reports. GDC n 284 p 132-3 O14'60
---Jolivet, André director of second year "Centre Français d' Humanisme Musical"; notes. WM n 3 p 57 Je '60
---Porter, Andrew. Opera reviews (6). Op v 11 p 31-4 Autumn '60
AIX-LES-BAINS
International Dance Festival, 1954 pm; notes on lighting by Yves-Bonnat. WT v 9 n 2 p 151-2

4

Summer '60
AKAKAMAS GREEK, play
Herbert; Afrique du Sud, ph:
Bruxelles. WP v 11 n 10 p 1
Ag '60
ALABAMA
Birmingham; The Valley Thea-
tre, notes. PlM v 36 n 6 p 121
Mr '60
ALADJEM, SILVIO, conductor
Montevideo; concerts of Ameri-
can composers; notes. MC v 161
n 3 p 46 F '60
ALASKA
Festival 1960 notes. MC v 161 n 7
p 6 Je '60
---Festival of Music; notes. IM
v 58 n 12 p 35 Je '60
---Fifth festival, Anchorage;
Verdi's Requiem, Robert Shaw.
ON v 25 n 2 p 5 O 29'60
---North Murray. Fifth year under
direction of Mary Hale; Rudolph
Ganz, a guest; Festival notes. MC
v 162 n 2 p 14 Ag '60
---Festival; community Orches-
tra and Chorus on stage, ph. MC
v 162 n 4 p 16 O '60
--- ---Julius Herford, director,
with guests, Rudolph Ganz and
Robert Shaw, small ph. MC v 162
n 2 p 14 Ag '60
ALBACH, BEN. Bibliographie
raisonnée du théâtre neerlandais. ThR v 2 n 2 p 88-98 1960
ALBENIZ, ISAAC, 1860-1909,
composer
Chambray, Claude. Fiche biographique (small por ph). GDC
n 255-6 p 323-4 '60
---De Fougères, Adalgisa Ramellini. Isaac Albeniz, 1860-1960.
por La S n 128 p 40-2 Jl '60
---Por ph; and with his family at
Nizza, ph. La S n 128 p 42 Jl '60
d'ALBERT, EUGENE FRANCIS
CHARLES, 1864-1932, com-
poser
Balogh, Erno. Sentimental realist (d'Albert, b. Glasgow). por
ON v 24 n 13 p 8-9 Ja 30'60
---Por ph: coll. E. Balogh. ON
v 24 n 13 p 9 Ja 30'60

ALCIBIADE, play
Athens notes; Georges Theotocas.
WP v 11 n 5 p 10 Mr '60
ALCINA, opera
London review of Royal Stock-
holm Opera. Op v 11 n 10 p 731-
6 O '60
---Messinis, Mario. Alcina;
Venice. La S n 125 p 48 Ap '60
---Teatro La Fenice review;
Joan Sutherland. Op v 11 n 4
p 284-5 Ap '60
---Ballet scene; and two singers,
phs: Venice. La S n 125 p 48
Ap '60
---Hallin, Margareta, as Alcina
with Ingvar Wixell as Ruggiero,
AP hl ph: Southern; also ens AP
wl ph: Stockholm Opera. Op v 11
n 10 p 714 O '60
---Thebom and Sinclair, AP wl
ph: Dallas Civic Opera. ON v 25
n 8 p 28 D 31'60
ALDEBURGH FESTIVAL
The Editor. Britten's "A Mid-
summer Night's Dream". Op
v 11 p 21-4 Autumn '60
---Notes on festival built by Bri-
tten and Peter Pears. Th Arts
v 44 n 5 p 18 My '60
---Unwin, Arthur. (Description of
this lovely music festival.) MD
v 51 n 2 p 14-5 Ag '60
ALDRICH, RICHARD STODDARD
(1902-).
My ten favorite plays, a list. Th
Arts v 44 n 3 p 71 Mr '60
ALEXANDER, opera
Bremen notes; Theodor Holter-
dorf. WP v 12 n 2 p 24 N '60
ALEXANDRA, opera
Avidom (1908-); première. MC
v 161 n 7 p 20 Je '60
ALEXANDROVITCH, GEORGES
pianist
Berthoumieux, Serge. Paris re-
view. GDC n 265-6 p 524 Mr 25'60
ALFANO, FRANCO 1876-, composer
Maione, Rino. Franco Alfano;
"Alfano è il solo successore di
Verdi in Italia". por La S n 122
p 48-9 Ja '60
---Left profile por ph; and small

5

(ALFANCO, FRANCO)
ph. La S n 122 p 49 Ja '60
THE ALFRED DELLER TRIO
NYC review; 16th to 18th cent-
ury music. MC v 161 n 3 p 28
F '60
ALFVEN, HUGO 1872-1960
composer
Debievre, Pierre. (Obituary.)
GDC n 278 p 842 Je 24'60
ALGAZI, M. L.
Por ph: F. Lyon. GDC n 279-
280 p 881 Jl 1'60
ALGERIA
Althouel, G. Lucie de Lammer-
moor (la troupe italienne);
Franco Patane, le maestro. GDC
n 261-2 p 437 F 26'60
---Giullermin, André. Music re-
port. GDC n 273 p 694 My 20'60
ALGIERS LITTLE THEATRE, 1930-
New Orleans; 30-years; notes.
Th Arts v 44 n 4 p 57 Ap '60
ALLAMISTAKEO, opera
Turin review of Viozzi's opera.
Op v 11 n 1 p 44 Ja '60
--- ---ens AP wl ph: Morris. Op
v 11 n 1 p 44 Ja '60
ALLARD, MARIA, 1742-1802,
ballerina
E Dauberval nell opera "Silvie",
AP wl print. La S n 129-30 p 23
Ag-S '60
ALLEGRA PIAZZETTA
(dell'Ara), ballet
Ens AP wl ph: Naples. La S
n 128 p 52 Jl '60
ALLEN, EDISON B. When jazz
began. il IM v 59 n 5 p 14-5 N'60
ALLERS, FRANZ, 1905-. (Inter-
view on eight-week visit to
Soviet Union as director of My
Fair Lady.) por IM v 59 n 2
p 10-1 Ag '60
---Por ph; also ensemble picture
with Russian orchestra players.
IM v 59 n 2 p 10 Ag '60
---With Soviet artists, ens ph:
Russia. MC v 162 n 1 p 11 Jl '60
ALLIO, RENÉ. (On staging chek-
hov; a French view.) il WT v 9
n 2 p 112-115 Summer '60
ALMANZOR, LUCETTE

Silvant, Jean. Chez Lucette
Almanzor. TD n 91 p 24 Mr '60
AMAHL AND THE NIGHT VISITORS,
opera
Fourth year; tour of 12 US cities
with original cast. AmM v 8 n 1
p 17 Ja '60
JES AMANTS CAPTIFS, opera
Bordeaux notes; Paul Guth;
music Pierre Capdeville. WP
v 11 n 10 p 3 Ag '60
---Première; Pierre Capdevielle,
score, libretto, Paul Guth; Bor-
deaux review. MC v 162 n 1
p 31 Jl '60
LES AMANTS IMPATIENTS, play
Budapest; Endre Illes; notes. WP
v 11 n 4 p 9 F '60
AMARA, LUCINE
As Micaela AP phs: Le-Blang.
ON v 24 n 14 F 6'60
AMATO OPERA
NYC notes. MC v 161 n 7 p 22
Je '60
--- ---Luisa Miller(1849); and
Un Giorno di Regno, version by
Robert Morris. ON v 25 n 3
p 20 N 19'60
AMBEI, ALBERTO CESARE. Com-
positori di Punta
(Pierre Boulez, Karlheinz Stock-
ausen). La S n 129-30 p 28-30
Ag-S '60
AMERICAN BALLET THEATRE
European tour itinerary. AmM
v 8 n 5 p 13 Je '60
---Goth, Trudy. Balletti U. S. A.
1960. il La S n 133 p 42-7 D '60
---Minsk, Kiev, Lvov, Leningrad
and Moscow; US government
sponsored. AmM v 8 n 8 p 10
S '60
---Munich; Festival de Ballets.
TD n 96 p 12 S-O '60
---NYC report. MD v 51 n 2 p 28
Ag '60
---Report. MC v 161 n 6 p 9 My'60
---Tour under ANTA; some de-
tails. AmM v 8 n 1 p 17 Ja '60
---Portfolio: Serrano and Bruhn
in Cullberg's "La Signora del
Mare";"Totem";"I Clowns";
"Commenti di un coreografo"

by Tudor; Balletti Orff, 5 AP wl
phs. La S n 133 p 42-7 D'60
AMERICAN CENTER: PARIS
Dance programs; notes. TD
n 97 p 2 N '60
THE AMERICAN COMMUNITY
THEATRE ASSOCIATION
Young, John Wray; The birth
of an organization. PlM v 36
n 8 p 184 My '60
AMERICAN COMPOSERS
ALLIANCE OFFICERS and
members list; also affiliated
and associate members. ACAB
v 9 n 2 cover 1960
AMERICAN EDUCATIONAL
THEATRE ASSOCIATION
Denver meeting; active leaders.
ThArts v 44 n 9 p 78 S '60
---Overseas Touring Committee
praised by Jerome Coray, direc-
tor, USO shows: letter. Th Arts
v 44 n 1 p 96 Ja '60
AMERICAN FEDERATION OF
MUSICIANS
Kenin, Herman D. The Inter-
national String Congress in Ok-
lahoma 1959. MEJ v 47 n 2
p 71 N-D '60
---Local 802 subsidy for (NYC)
Community Opera, Inc. per-
formances for children. ON
v 25 n 6 p 7 D 17'60
---Officers; business matters;
each issue a report. IM 1960
---Official business, reports,
officers, projects, lists of de-
faulters, of unfair employees.
IM 1960
---Official proceedings, Las
Vegas convention; IM v 59 n 2
Ag '60
---Scholarships, 83 in 1959 and
100 in 1960; details. IM v 58
n 12 p 5 Je '60
---Second annual String Congress,
Puerto Rico; plans and faculty.
il IM v 58 n 9 p 12-3, 37 Mr '60
---Second International AFM
String Congress in Puerto Rico;
plan. MEJ v 46 n 4 p 8 F-Mr '60
---Sixty-third convention, Las
Vegas; reports; pictures;

resolutions. IM v 59 n 1 Jl '60
---Sponsor and supporter of the
Second International String Con-
gress in Puerto Rico. WM n 3
p 57 Je '60
---Seeking 52-week contracts in
Lincoln Center; notes. MC
v 161 n 6 p 6 My '60
AMERICAN MUSIC CENTER
Commissions 1960-61: list of
composers. MC v 162 n 3 p 31 S '60
---Ford Foundation grant of
$210,000; list of orchestras par-
ticipating. MC v 161 n 1 p 25 Ja '60
---List of orchestras and com-
posers commissioned for each.
AmM v 8 n 10 p 12 N '60
AMERICAN MUSIC COUNCIL
Progress report on project plac-
ing young composers in second-
ary schools; 20 more to be ap-
pointed. AmM v 8 n 11 p 10
D '60
AMERICAN MUSIC FESTIVAL
NYC; 21st year; notes. IM v 58
n 9 p 45 Mr '60
AMERICAN NATIONAL THEATRE
and ACADEMY
Medals and prizes to $40,000
at annual meeting; notes. AmM
v 8 n 7 p 10 Ag '60
AMERICAN OPERA SOCIETY
Eighth season in Town Hall, NYC;
criticism. ON v 25 n 8 p 28
D 31'60
---NYC; La Voix Humaine, Den-
ise Duval's debut in USA; Les
Mamelles de Tirésias; reviews.
MC v 161 n 4 p 19 Mr '60
---Orfeo ed Euridice, concert
version; Simionato. MC v 162
n 6 p 18 D '60
---Les Troyens, the first com-
plete American performance
(concert form); Robert Lawrence
replacing Sir Thomas Beecham.
MC v 161 n 3 p 27 F '60
THE AMERICAN OPERA WORK-
SHOP
Busch, Hans. The American Op-
era Workshop. WM n 4 p 70-73
Ag ' 60
AMERICAN SYMPHONY LEAGUE

7

(AMERICAN SYMPHONY
LEAGUE)
St. Louis convention report of
American Symphony Orchestra
League. MC v 162 n 1 p 40
Jl '60
AMES, WILLIAM, composer
Première : Oboe Quartet (NYC
1960). ACAB v 9 n 3 p 26 1960
LES AMES MORTE, play
France; Arthur Adamov d'après
Nicolas Gogol, musique de
Claude Lochy. WP v 11 n 9
Jl '60
---D'après Gogol, Arthur Ada-
mov, Paris 1960, ens ph: Ber-
naud. WT v 9 n 2 p 161 Summer
'60
AMIEL, JOSETTE, dancer
Carandente, Giovanni. Succès
de Josette Amiel à l'Opéra de
Rome. TD n 94 p 27 Je '60
---Giselle à l'Opéra: "une ex-
cellente Giselle". TD n 96 p 22
S-O '60
---L'Opéra de Rome. il TD n 92
p 6-8 Ap '60
---As Giselle, Act I, AP wl ph:
Paris Opera. TD n 96 p 22
S-O '60
---In Cimento dell'Algegria
(Amiel) with Walter Zappolini,
AP wl ph: Rome Opera. TD n 95
p 20 Jl-Ag '60
---In Il Cimento dell'Allegria
(Milloss), AP wl phs: E. de
Rosen. TD n 92 cover, p 6 Ap '60
---With Peter Van Dijk in Le Lac
des Cygnes (Bourmeister), AP
wl ph: Paris Opera. OpP n 19
p 47 1960
LES AMIS DE LA MUSIQUE DE
CHAMBRE
Franchel, Blaise. Paris review;
pianist, Jean Martin, Elwood
Peterson, singer. GDC n 292
p 422 D 9'60
---Machuel, Dominique. Paris
review. GDC n 286 p 198 O 28'60
---Paris; two concerts. GDC
n 263-4 p 487, 488 Mr 11'60
---Paris concert, "consacrée à
Jacques Ibert". GDC n 295
p 490 D 30'60

---Andreoli, Arturo, composer,
ens AP wl ph: Bergama. La S
n 132 p 45 N '60
AMON AND TAMAR, opera
Israel Opera; Josef Tal, com-
poser. MC v 161 n 7 p 20 Je'60
L'AMORE DEI TRE RE, opera
Philadelphia comment. ON v 25
n 8 p 29 D 31'60
L'AMORE DELLE TRE MELAR-
ANCE, opera
San Carlo, Naples; review. La S
n 123 p 36 F '60
THE AMOROUS GOLDFISH, play
Folkestone; Michael Voisey;
notes. WP v 11 n 3 p 12 Ja '60
THE AMOROUS PRAWN, play
London notes; Anthony Kimmins
WP v 11 n 6 p 11 Ap '60
LES AMOURS DE ZELINDE ET
DE LINDOR, play
Paris notes; Stendahl d'après
Goldoni. WP v 11 n 8 p 6 Je '60
AMSTERDAM
Noske-Friedlaender, Leny.
Music report. MC v 161 n 5 p 33
Ap '60
---Reports on the recorded
music field. HF 1960
---Vereniging het Toneel-Museum.
ThR v 2 n 2 p.118 1960
AMY, GILBERT, composer
Première: Invention I (pour
flûte, vibraphone-xylorimba,
piano-celesta). GDC n 293-4
p 457 D 16'60
ANDA,GEZA, pianist
Berthoumieux, Serge. Paris re-
view. GDC n 271 p 626 My 5'60
ANDERSON; MARIAN, 1902-,
singer
Pugliese, Giuseppe. (As Ulrica).
Ver v 1 n 2 p 989 Ag '60
ANDERSON, MAXWELL, 1888-
1959, playwright
Cox, Martha Heasley. (Obitu-
ary.) PLM v 36 n 5 p 104 F '60
---With Behrman, Sherwood and
Rice hl ph. Th Arts v 44 n 9 p 21
S '60
ANDERSON, MICHAEL. Arnold
Wesker and the workers (theatre
for working class in Great
Britain). NTM v 2 n 1 p 2-6 O'60

--- ---The capital without a theatre (Cardiff). NTM v 1 n 2
p 4-7 Ja '60

THE ANDERSONVILLE TRIAL,
play
Bohle, Bruce. (Review.) Th Arts
v 44 n 3 p 12 Mr '60
---NYC notes; Saul Levitt. WP
v 11 n 6 p 5 Ap '60

ANDREA CHENIER, opera
Ashbrook, William.Background
with figures (Andrea Chénier).
ON v 24 n 21 p 4-5, 30 Mr 26'30
---Gambetta, Rosario. La Scala
review. GDC n 259-60 p 402
F 12'60
---La Scala criticism: Tebaldi
and Del Monaco. il La S n 123
p 33 F '60
--- ---review; Tebaldi, Del
Monaco, Bastianini. Op v 2 n 3
p 214-5 Mr '60
---Metropolitan cast; story;
background; décor bibliography;
discography; portfolio. ON v 24
n 21 Mr 26'60

ANDREANI, ISABELLE, singer
As Carmen, AP hl ph. OpP n ll
1960

ANDREOTTI, ROBERTO (1908-).
La tradizione parmense su
Gustavo III ed il Ballo in Mas-
chera. Ver v 1 n 2 p 799-804
Ag '60

ANDREWS, JULIE, 1935-, actress
As Guenevere in "Camelot", left
profile ph: Milton H. Greene.
Th Arts v 44 n 12 p 25 D '60
---Por ph: Houston Rogers. Th
Arts v 44 n 10 p 15 O '60

ANDREWS, ROBERT C.
scenic designer
List of twenty-two productions
found in "A Sadler's Wells scene
book", circa 1794 (two illustrations). Th Notbk v 15 n 2 p 59
Winter '60-61

ANDRIESSEN, HENDRIK, 1892-,
composer
Première: Symphonic Etude
(1959); Amsterdam notes. MC
v 161 n 5 p 33 Ap '60

ANGELES, VICTORIA de los
(1923). (On the role of Mélisande.) por ON v 24 n 11 p 15

Ja 16'60
---Gelatt, Roland. Victoria of the
angels. il HF v 10 n 9 p 36-39 S'60
---Machuel, Dominique. Paris re-
view. GDC n 274 p 724 My 27'60
---As Carmen, AP wl ph. Op v 11
n 2 p 83 F '60
---As Mélisande, AP hl ph: Mel-
ançon. ON v 24 n 11 p 17 Ja 16'60
---In La Traviata, AP wl ph: Angus
McBean. Op v 11 n 9 p 593 S '60
---In Madama Butterfly, AP wl ph:
Angus McBean. Op v 11 n 11
p 726 N '60
---In Manon at Covent Garden,
four AP phs: Donald Southern. Op
v 11 n 8 cover, p 577-8 Ag '60

ANGELICA, play
Torino 1960, ens AP wl ph: Tre-
visio. WT v 9 n 2 p 171 Summer '60

THE ANGELICUM, MILAN
Allorto, Riccardo, director; As-
canio in A lba review. Op v 11 n 1
p 42 Ja '60

ANGELINA, opera
See La Cenerentola

ANGELIQUE, opera
Mannes College; Jacques Ibert
score; notes. MC v 161 n 6 p 16
My '60

ANGIOLIERI, CECCO
Viviani, Alberto. Cecco Angio-
lieri dodecafonico Maledetto. il
La S n 133 p 31-41 D '60

ANHALT, ISTVAN, composer
Premiere: First Symphony
Montreal review. CMJ v 4 n 4
p 46-7 Summer '60

ANIARA, opera
Covent Garden review of Stockholm
Opera. H. K. MR v 21 n 4 p 324
N '60
---Criticism. WT v 9 n 2 p 174
Summer '60
---Hamburg; Günther Rennert.
"gave it all that it can possibly be
given"; libretto and music not up
to the subject. Op v 11 n 6 p 423-4
Je '60
---Koegler, Horst, Hamburg re-
view. ON v 24 p 28 Ap 16'60
---London review, Stockholm
Opera. Op v 11 n 10 p 712 O '60
---Notes; Vienna recording, Swe-
dish cast. HF v 10 n 3 p 32 Mr'60

(aniara)
---Ens AP wl ph: Hamburg Opera.
WM n 4 p 83 Ag '60
---Hamburg; the ballet scene;
Joan Carroll as the Blind Poetess
2 ens AP wl phs: Simon; Peyer.
Op v 11 n 6 p 423 Je '60
---Stockholm, 1959, ens AP wl
ph: Rydberg. WT v 9 n 2 p 176
Summer '60
---Stockholm Opera in London,
ens AP wl ph. Op v 11 n 10
p 711 O '60
ANN ARBOR FESTIVAL
Michigan; 67th year; Philadel-
phia Orchestra for 25th season.
MC v 161 n 3 p 18 F '60
ANNA CHRISTIE, play
Tel Aviv, 1957; ens AP wl ph:
Mirlin-Yaron. WT v 9 n 1 p 83
Spring '60
ANNA NERA, play
Modine notes; Giuseppe Patroni
Griffi. WP v 11 n 10 p 7 Ag '60
ANNUAL AMERICAN MUSIC
FESTIVAL
Twenty-first year; notes on 3
programs. AmM v 8 n 5 p 14
Je '60
ANSERMET, ERNEST, 1883-,
conductor
Right profile por ph. HF v 10
n 4 p 93 Ap '60
ANSIKTET, film
Pechter, William S. The light is
dark enough (Ingmar Bergman
and his films). TDR v 5 n 2 p 94-
101 D '60
ANTHONY, CHARLES, singer
As Jacquino in Fidelio, AP ph:
Melancon. ON v 24 n 15 F 13'60
ANTIGONE, play
Lyon, Raymond. Au Théâtre
National Populaire; GDC n 295
p 484 D '60
ANTIGONE SOUS L'OCCUPATION,
play
Athens notes; N. Pergialis. WP
v 12 n 1 p 6 O '60
ANTINE, RUTH VINITSKY,
pianist
London debut; notes. AmM v 8
p 10 O '60
ANTONIO
See Soler, Antonio Ruiz, 1921-,

dancer
APAKA, ALFRED, 1919-, singer
Review of Decca recording of his
Polynesian songs. HF v 10 n 8
p 73 Ag '60
APPLEBAUM, LOUIS, 1918-,
director
Stratford, Ontario: list of com-
posers at conference; subsidies;
programs. MC v 162 n 2 p 24
Ag '60
---With Oscar Shumsky and Leo-
nard Rose, hl ph: Stratford Fes-
tival, Ontario. IM v 58 n 11 p 16
My '60
APOLLON MUSAGETE
L'Opéra de Berlin, ens AP wl
ph. TD n 89 p 3 Ja '60
THE APOTHECARY, opera
Florence; Ensemble of Villa
Olmo; notes. MC v 161 n 6 p 34
My '60
L'AQUILA
Une società di concerti, trenta
concerti: L'Orchestra dell'Opera
di Montecarlo, etc. La S n 131
p 62 O '60
ARABELLA, opera
Metropolitan; NYC review. MC
v 162 n 6 p 15 D '60
ARCHITECTURE
Arena Theatre, Washington, D.C.
designed by Harry Weese after
listening to tape-recorded sug-
gestions from staff; notes on com-
pany and policy with model of new
building. Th Arts v 44 n 12 p 22
D '60
---Chicago's Auditorium Theatre;
rehabilitation; history; superb
acoustics. il HF v 10 n 2 p 51
F '60
---Civic theatre for today; Stephen
Joseph's ideas; Leicester's Civic
Theatre. NTM v 1 n 4 p 5-7 Jl'60
---Construction details of Nuffield
Theatre at University of South-
ampton. il Th Notbk v 14 n 4
p 115-118 Summer '60
---Darcante, Jean. (Need of theatre buildings, 300-400 seats,
inexpensive, all purpose "houses
of culture".) WP v 11 n 3 p 7
Ja '60
---De Gaetani, Thomas. Theatre

---De Gaetani, Thomas. Theatre architecture; how does it look from where you're sitting? drawings J Rev v 7 n 2 p 4-12 Spring '60

---Editorial on ultimate costs in building a "cheap theatre" instead of a "dear" one in English cities; upkeep and box-office involved. NTM v 1 n 3 p 3-4 Ap '60

---English, John. A new deal for the theatre; II (charts and description of experimental Arena Playhouse). NTM v 2 n 1 p 19-25 O '60

---George, Graham (Vancouver's Queen Elizabeth Theatre, 1954 to date; Jubilee Auditoria in Edmonton and Calgary, also begun 1954.) CMJ v 4 n 2 p 9-13 Winter '60

---Harrison, Wallace K. Steps to the opera house (his problems and approach for the new Metropolitan). il ON v 25 n 2 p 15-7 O 29'60

---India; conference on theatre construction; report. WP v 11 n 9 p 8 Jl '60

---Mandelli, Piero. A Salisburgo un nuovo gran Teatro d'Opera. il La S n 128 p 20-2 Jl '60

---Miller, James Hull. Why theatre architecture lags; Part I. PLM v 37 n 1 p 6 O '60

--- ---Part II. PLM v 37 n 2 p 30 N '60

---Neville, John. The actor's viewpoint (on theatre architecture and facilities; in favor of "in the round"). NTM v 2 n 1 p 7-11 O '60

---Philharmonic Hall, Lincoln Center; details of capacity and stage. AmM v 8 n 2 p 3 F '60

---Piper's Opera House, Virginia City, Nevada; details of construction. Th Notbk v 15 n 2 p 52-5 Winter '60-61

---Plan for University of Toronto's music building; "the rallying point for music in Canada". MD v 50 n 10 p 20 Ap '60

Salzburg's Festspielhaus; "the world's largest, most up-to-date opera stage". ON v 25 n 2 p 18 O 29'60

---Teatro Massimo in Palermo; notes; history. HF v 10 n 11 p 10, 12 N '60

---Theatrical; Berlin report; Paris 1961 conference on "Front Line Theatre"; Rio de Janeiro manual on theatre construction in process. WP v 11 n 3 p 7 Ja '60

---Washington, D. C. The National Cultural Center; architect, Edward Durrell Stone; plans, pictures. AmM v 8 n 4 p 1-5 Ap '60

---Wechsberg, Joseph. Salzburg's new Festspielhaus. il Op v 11 n 8 p 535-540 Ag '60

---Boise, Idaho; exterior view of little theatre, designed by A. L. Troutner, ph. Th Arts v 44 n 8 p 17 Ag '60

---Canterbury Cathedral, distance view, ph. HF v 10 n 10 p 49 O '60

---Cheltenham; the Opera House, exterior view; and a sketch of the Everyman Theatre to replace it, phs. NTM v 1 n 3 Ap '60

---Drawings of ancient and modern auditoria and opera houses by Thomas De Gaetani. J Rev v 7 n 2 p 4-14 Spring '60

---East Berlin: the Apollo Saal of rebuilt Berlin St aatsoper, ph: Jurgen Simon. Op v 2 n 3 p 187 Mr '60

---Facciata del Teatro di Reggio Emilia, ph. La S n 127 p 39 Je '60

---Genoa's Carlo Felice, view toward the stage, ph. ON v 24 n 22 p 13 Ap 2'60

---Hamburg Staatsoper, auditorium ph: Rheinlander. Op v 2 n 3 p 186 Mr '60

---Harvard: Loeb Drama Center, exterior ph. Th Arts v 44 n 5 p 55 My '60

---Interno del Teatro della Canobiana, Milano, 1840; il Teatro Carcano, 1830. La S n 128 p 13 Jl '60

---Leipzig Opera House, view of balcony and parquet seats, ph:

(Architecture)

Helga Wallmuller. Op v11 n 11 p 751 N'60

---Metropolitan Opera House at Lincoln Center for the Performing Arts: proposed entrance, ph: Ezra Stoller. MC v 161 n 3 p 19 F '60

---Monaco; looking from the opera stage toward audience, ph. La S n 127 p 43 Je '60

---Naples, Teatro di Corte 1954 reopening, from the stage, ph: Pariso, Op v 11 n 2 p 126 F '60

---The new Beethovenhalle, view toward the stage, ph. HF v 10 n 4 p 43 Ap '60

---Philharmonic Hall, Lincoln Centre; scale model, artist's rendering of exterior, of interior, and a sectional view, phs. AmM v 8 n 2 cover, p 5 F '60

---La Piccola Scala, auditorium and proscenium, ph: Piccagliani. Op v 2 n 3 p 186 Mr '60

---Prague; Pavillon du Belvedere, ph. GDC n 273 cover My 20'60

---Prisbram, Czechoslovakia, la Maison de la Culture, exterior ph. WP v 11 n 7 p 16 My '60

---Rome Sant'Andrea al Quirinale, interior where Sardou set act I of La Tosca, ph. Op v 11 n 4 p 263 Ap '60

---Salzburg's new Festival House, exterior and interior views, 2 phs. WM n 4 p 81 Ag '60

--- ---auditorium, foyers, and the stage, 4 phs. Op v 11 n 8 p 536-8 Ag '60

--- ---distance view and drawing of interior, 2 phs. La S n 128 p 20-1 Jl '60

---San Carlo in Milan; exterior view; the Royal box, 2 phs. ON v 25 n 7 p 22-3 D 24'60

---Théâtre American , New Orleans, 1822-1854, exterior view ph: Bettmann archive. ON v 25 n 5 p 23 D 10'60

---Theatre, Stratford, Ontario, designed by Guthrie and Mosievitch, for 2,000 people; notes and ph. NTM v 1 n 4 p 16-7 Jl'60

--- Il Teatro Comunale di Piacenza, from the stage, ph. La S n 123 p 40 F '60

--- Il Teatro Popolare Italiano, exterior ph. and scene from Adelchi (1960 play), phs: Frontoni. WT v 9 n 2 p 168 Summer '60

---Vienna State Opera, exterior view, ph. MC v 162 n 4 p 23 O '60

ARDEN, JOHN. The Reps and new plays, a writer's viewpoint. NTM v 1 n 2 p 23-6 Ja '60

ARENA STAGE

Washington, D. C. notes on policy; on new building by Harry Weese. il Th Arts v 44 n 12 p 22 D '60

ARENA THEATRE COMPANY

Scene from Pygmalian in Anthony Waller's setting; Topolski's setting; from the Little Foxes; from Crime Passionelle, 4 ens AP phs. NTM v 2 n 1 p 17-8 O '60

ARETINO, PIETRO, 1492-1556, playwright

Giovaninetti, Silvio. Pepe dell' Aretino, sale di Goldoni. il La S n 132 p 68-9 N '60

ARGENTINA

Arnosi, Eduardo. (La Gioconda; Forza del Destino; L'Andrea Chénier). La S n 131 p 71-2 O '60

--- ---Music report. La S n 123 p 81 F '60; La S n 124 p 75 Mr '60; La S n 125 p 95 Ap '60; La S n 127 p 70 Je '60; La S n 128 p 64 Jl '60; La S n 132 p 86 N '60; La S n 133 p 113 D '60

--- ---Teatro Colón (report). Op v 11 n 11 p 759 N '60

--- ---Teatro Colón's Tannhäuser; Hans Beirer in the title role; Gré Brouwenstign "a most wonderful Elisabeth". il Op v 11 n 12 p 823 D '60

---Benavente, Saulo. (on staging Chekhov in Argentina.) WT v 9 n 2 p 119 Summer '60

---Ponferrada, Juan-Oscar. Argentina theatre report. WT v 9 n 1 p 68-70 Spring '60

---Societies interested in theatre; Fédération argentine de Théâtre indépendent, the periodical "Revista", bi-mensuelle.

WP v 12 n 2 p 3 N '60
---Theatre development; list of playwrights. WT v 9 n 3 p 267, Autumn '60
---Theatre report. WP v 11 n 9 p 7 Jl '60; WP v 11 n 10 p 2 Ag ' Ag '60; WP v 12 n 1 p 3 O '60
---Cesar et Cleopatre, Shaw, ens AP ph: Buenos Aires. WP v 11 n 10 p 1 Ag '60
---Scene from: Historias para ser Contadas: from El Herrero y el Diablo, both Buenos Aires, phs: Chaure. WT v 9 n 3 p 268-9 Autumn '60
ARISTOCRATS OF SONG, chorus Child, Allen, director; 24 singers; Chicago note. MC v 162 n 6 p 23 D '60
---Small outdoor ph: Indiana. MC v 162 n 3 p 14 S '60
ARISTOTLE; The Poetics (Francis Fergusson's essay on Gerald F. Else's book on Aristotle's Poetics). TDR v 4 n 4 p 23-32 My '60
ARMA, PAUL Chamfray, Claude. Paul Arma, nous parle de son concerto pour Bande Magnétique. GDC n 293-4 p 455-6 D 16'60
DER ARME KONRAD (Völkel), opera Berlin; Jean Kurt Forest d'aprés le drame de Friedrich Wolf. WP v 11 n 4 p 11 F '60
---de J. K. Forst, AP ph: Berlin. WP v 11 n 4 p 1 F '60
ARMED FORCES ENTERTAIN- MENT BRANCH US Army; groups from universities and colleges sent to entertain American troops abroad; notes. IM v 58 n 12 p 45 Je '60
ARMISTEAD, HORACE. Fidelio sesign, Act II, scene 1, the dungeon (and other scenes). ON v 24 n 15 p 4 F 13'60
ARMSTRONG: WILLIAM A;(1882?-). (On use of the phrase "to produce".) Th Notbk v 15 n 1 p 39 Autumn '60
ARNE, THOMAS AUGUSTINE, 1710-1778, composer

Sadie, Stanley. The chamber music of Boyce and Arne. Mus Q v 46 n 4 p 425-36 O '60
ARNOLD, MALCOLM, 1921-, composer Fourth Symphony; BBC and Arnold; "shamelessly diatonic". MC v 162 n 6 p 30 D '60
ARNOSI, EDUARDO. Teatro Colón (notes). Op v 11 n 11 p 759 N '60
---See also Argentina
ARNOLD, PAUL (1909-). The Little Tailor, a one-act legend (text). TDR v 5 n 1 p 22-42 S '60
ARONOFF, MAX (1907-)- Orchestra and players (The new School of Music, Philadelphia, and its methods). MC v 161 n 3 p 14 F '60
ARRAU, CLAUDIO, 1903- pianist NYC review. MC v 161 n 1 p 37 Ja '60
ARRIGO, GIROLAMO, composer Première:Quarta Occasione;Festival d'Art d'Avant-Garde. GDC n 295 p 490 D 30'60
---Quarta Occasione (pour sept voix solistes et cinq instruments divers). GDC n 293-4 p 457 D 16'60
ARROYO, RAFAEL, pianist Paris;consacré à Albeniz. GDC n 269-70 p 599 Ap 22'60
ART Bilcke, Maruits. Les premiers abstraits belges. il WP v 11 n 4 p 8 F'60
---Discovolo, Antonio. L'usignolo. LaS n 128 p 18 Jl'60
---Rice, David Talbot. Byzance capitale de l'Art Byzantin. il WP v 11 n 3 p 7 Ja'60
---Zeshin, Shibata. Red Berry Plant and Butterfly, a laquer painting. ON v 24 n 24 cover Ap 16'60
---Arte etrusca Tarquinia. Tomba du leopardi (part. di un affresco). LaS n 132 cover N'60
---Biot;le Musée Fernand Léger, sculptured mural, ph. TD n 94 p 25 Je'60
---Botticelli. Particolare di un affresco botticelliano. LaS n 131

14

ASTAIRE, FRED, 1899-, dancer-
singer
And Adele, AP hl ph: NYC, 1931.
Th Arts v 44 n 9 p 25 S '60
---Right profile ph. HF v 10 n 1
p 82 Ja '60
ATANASOV, GEORGI, 1881-1931,
composer
Bulgarian criticism; Tsveta, au
opera on Turkish-occupied Bul-
garia. Op v 11 n 8 p 549 Ag '60
LE ASTUZIE FEMINILI, opera
A la Petite Scala de Milau; Cim-
arosa commentaire. DC n 263-4
p 484 Mr 11'60
---Piccola Scala; review. La S
n 124 p 27 Mr '60
---Sartori, Claudio. Piccola Sca-
la: cast and review. Op v 2 n 3
p 215 Mr 160
---Two AP phs: Piccola Scala.
La S n 124 p 27 Mr '60
ATKINS, CHET, guitarist
AP wl ph. IM v 58 n 11 p 5 My'60
ATKINSON, BROOKS (1894-). An-
atomy of newspaper criticism.
Th Arts v 44 n 4 p 8-9 Ap '60
---Ryan, Peter J. (comment.)
por Th Arts v 44 n 4 p 6 Ap '60
---Caricature by Al Hirshfeld. Th
Arts v 44 n 4 cover Ap '60
---Por ph: Carl Perutz. Th Arts
v 44 n 4 p 7 Ap '60
ATLANTICA, play
Helsinki; vers par Inkeri Kilpin-
en. WP v 11 n 4 p 4 F '60
ATONALISM
Mann, Thomas, in his novel Dok-
tor Faustus, a musician of atonal
school; criticism by Murray Sch-
afer. CMJ v 4 n 3 p 29-34
Spring '60
---Russell, George. (On jazz:
"jazz will by-pass atonality be-
cause jazz has its roots in folk
music and that is scale-based
music; jazz will be intensely
chromatic. You can be chromatic
and not be atonal"). IM v 59 n 3
p 35 S'60
---See also Twelve-Tone System
L'ATTAQUE DU MOULIN, opera
Rehearsal of Bruneau work, ens
AP ph. Op v 11 n 9 p 595 S '60

ATWELL, WINIFRED, pianist
West Indies pianist in Australia,
at the piano, ph. MD v 51 n 3 p 15
S '60
AU SOLEIL DU MEXIQUE (Rognoni),
operetta
Rennes review. GDC n 261-2 p 436
F 26'60
L'AUBERGE DU CHEVAL BLANC
(ORLANDI), operetta
Châletet; reprise par Maurice
Lehmann; Meray, Ernon, Thory.
TD n 98 p 5 D '60
---Le Bal des Insectes, ens AP wl
ph: Lido. TD n 98 cover D '60
AUBERT, LOUIS 1877-, composer
Premiere: Improvisation; Ida Presti
et Alexandre Lagoya à Gaveau.
GDC n 293-4 p 459 D 16'60
AUBERT, PAULINE, pianist
Oleg, Alexandre. Paris review.
GDC n 292 p 423 D 9'60
AUCLERT, PIERRE. Airs d'Oysans
(1936-8) (etudes musicales analy-
tiques). GDC n 288 p 269 N 11'60
AUNT EDWINA, play
London review (Charley's Aunt
trick). Th Arts v 44 n 4 p 16 Ap'60
AUS EINEM TOTENHAUS, opera
Mecklembourg, Janacek work, ens
AP wl ph. WP v 11 n 6 Ap '60
AUSTRALIA
Adelaide Festival; seminar for
composers; list of leaders. WM n 2
p 31 Ap '60
---The Australian National Eisted-
dfod, Canberra; adjudicators. MD
v 50 n 8 p 13 F '60
---APRA (Australian Performing
Right Association, Ltd.): a cata-
logue of Australian and New Zea-
land music; notes. MD v 51 n 5
p 8 N '60
---List of violinists and pianists to
appear in ABC concerts. MD v 50
n 9 p 15-6 Mr '60
---Lympany, Maura. Australia's
musical life. MC v 161 n 7 p 11
Je '60
---Mares, F. H. Theatre in Australia. NTM v 1 n 3 p 24-28 Ap'60
---Mladenov, Peter. Opera report.
Op v 11 n 7 p 474-5 Jl '60
---Opera and ballet at Silver Jubilee,

(Australia)
Arts Festival of the National Theatre Movement of Victoria; Gertrude Johnson, founder. por MD v 50 n 7 p 14 Ja '60
---Penberthy, James. (Survey of musical resources of West Australia; its isolation; the University.) MD v 51 n 3 p 12-3 S '60
---Perth; contest in composition; other notes. MD v 51 n 1 p 16 Jl '60
---Rees, Leslie. Theatre report. WT v 9 n 3 p 272-276 Autumn '60
---Sinclair, John. Mr. Tzipine's remarks on Melbourne critics. MD v 50 n 12 p 10-11 Je '60
---Tasmania; music notes. MD v 51 n 3 p 19 S '60
---Taxation on theatres. WP v 12 n 3 p 2 D '60
---The Telephone, Menotti, sung by Ronal Jackson and Glenda Raymond; Sidney Myer Music Bowl. MD v 50 n 10 p 19 por Ap '60
---Vaughan, Denis. (Suggestion, with list of able musical men in Australia, newspapers publish articles to bring criticism forward dropping unmeasured and rightening reviews.) MD v 51 n 2 p 13 Ag '60
---Wagner, W. Opera report. Op v 11 n 10 p 685 O '60
---West Australian Ballet Company (Kira Bousloff); notes. MD v 51 n 6 p 23, 30 D '60
---Downing, Desmonde. The Marriage of Figaro, ens AP wl ph: ABC-TV. WT v 9 n 4 p 331 Winter '60
---London Festival Ballet members: Wendy Barry, Jill Bathurst, Pixie Bevan, Joan Potter, Marilyn Burr, ens ph. MD v 50 n 9 p 31 Mr '60
---Travelling Theatre van, Arts Council, ph. WT v 9 n 3 p 275 Autumn '60
AUSTRALIAN BROADCASTING COMPANY
Chopin anniversary; list of performing artists. MD v 50 n 8 p 12 F '60
---Concert list: Ernest Llewellyn,

Sydney violinist; Ladislav Jasek (1930-) violinist; Thomas Matthews, violinist; Maurice Clare, violinist; and others. MD v 50 n 9 p 15-6 Mr '60
AUSTRALIAN UNESCO SEMINAR FOR COMPOSERS
Loughlin, George. (Report of Adelaide seminar at the Elder Conservatorium.) por MD v 51 n 2 p 16-7 Ag '60
AUSTRALIAN YOUTH ORCHESTRA
Notes. MD v 50 n 10 p 19 Ap '60
AUSTRIA
Brunner, Gerhard. (Music report.) MC v 161 n 7 p 16 Je '60
---Jeunesses Musicales; details of work with youth. ON v 24 n 20 p 14 Mr 19'60
---Mandelli, Piero. (Music reports.) La S n 131 p 67-8 O '60
---NYC concert of Austrian composers; Eric Simon, director; review. MC v 161 n 6 p 21 My '60
---Opera; Vienna Staalsoper, Volksoper, Graz (summer notes). Op v 11 n 11 p 760-1 N '60
---Theatre report. WP v 11 n 9 p 7 Jl '60
AUTIER, VICKY, singer
Review of record: Vive Paris. HF v 10 p 101 O '60
AUTOHARP
Cleator, Margaret. (Using the autoharp in a second-grade US school room.) MEJ v 47 n 1 p 103 S-O '60
AVAKIAN, LEOPOLD, violinist
Machuel, Dominique. Paris review; Iranien. GDC n 283 p 101 O 7'60
AVEVA DUE PISTOLE CON GLI OCCHI BIANCHI E NERI, play
Milan notes; Dario Fo. WP v 12 n 2 p 24 N '60
AVIOLITTOLOMA, play
Helsinki notes; Seere Salminen. WP v 11 n 10 p 2 Ag '60
AVSHALOMOV, JACOB, 19-, composer
Career sketch; b. Tsingtao, China; 1937 to US. AmM v 8 n 7 p 9 Ag'60
---Première: Of Man's Mortalitie; Berkshire Festival 1959, composer conducting. ACAB v 9 n 2 p 18 1960

16

---American, por ph: San Francisco. AmM v 8 n 7 p 9 Ag '60

AWARDS
Académie du disque français:
Grand Prix National du Disque
1961 (listes). GDC n 295 inset
D 30'60
---Académie Internationale: pal-
marès- GDC n 283 p 103 O 7'60
---Annual Leventritt award; list
of previous (since 1939) winners;
Jury list 1959; Malcolm Frager
(1935-) winner. AmM v 8 n 2 p 11
F '60
---The Avalon Foundation, $15,000
to the National Music League.
AmM v 8 n 3 p 18 Mr '60
---Bales, Richard, $1,200,the
Alice M. Ditson Annual Award.
AmM v 8 n 5 p 13 Je '60
---Benny, Jack: the Laurel-leaf
award from the American Com-
posers' Alliance; list of previous
winners. MD v 50 n 8 p 13 F '60
--- ---note. ACAB v 9 n 2 p 17
1960
---Binder, Peter, 1933-, winner
of Blanche Thebom award. ON
v 24 n 11 p 2 Ja 16'60
---Bing, Rudolf; Austria and Italy;
two decorations. AmM v 8 n 1
p 18 Ja '60
---Bressler, Charles, tenor, win-
ner of the Cercle de la Jeune
Critique's award. Théâtre des
Nations. AmM v 8 n 8 p 4 S '60
---Caston, Saul, conductor award
from National Music Council.
AmM v 8 n 11 p 10 D '60
---Cincinnati's American Opera
Auditions, winners: Arlene Saun-
ders, Constance Lambert, Geor-
ge Shirley and Spiro Malas. ON
v 25 n 3 p 6 N 19'60
---Cliburn, Van, to Juilliard
School, his alma mater: $5000
to set up annual award honoring
Mme. Rosina Lhevinne; notes.
MC v 161 n 3 p 49 F '60
---Croix de la Légion d'honneur:
Pierre Auclert et Jacques Dupont
(compositions). GDC n 288 p 260
N 11'60
---Eaves Costume Company

awards for regional theatre; win-
ners 1960. PlM v 37 n 2 p 27 N'60
---Faulkner, Barbara V. from the
National Association of Teachers
of Singing (US): $1,000 prize. ON
v 24 n 14 p 3 F 6'60 ;same. MEJ
v 46 n 4 p 12 F-Mr '60
---France; Le Courrier des Con-
servatoires; Mulhouse: Palmarès.
GDC n 285 p 176-7 O 21'60
--- ---Le 3e Concours de chant,
Romans; Concours International
de Vercelli; Mulhouse, Palmares.
GDC n 285 p 176-7 O 21'60
---Genève: 16 Français primés au
IXVIe Concours International d'Ex-
écution Musicale de Genève (liste).
GDC n 288 p 253 N 11'60
---Hayes, Helen, honorary Doctor
of Fine Arts from Southern Illinois
University. PlM v 37 n 1 p 4 O '60
---The International Opera Prize
(Recordi and Co.) to Jean-Pierre
Rivière for Pour un Don Quichotte.
ON v 25 n 5 p 7 D 10'60
---Juilliard School, NYC; honors list.
J Rev v 7 n 3 p 7 Fall '60
---Kirstein, Lincoln, from the Em-
peror of Japan; notes on award.
AmM v 8 n 10 p 12 N '60
---Kreisler, Fritz (1875-) honored
by the city of New York; notes. MC
v 161 n 3 p 21 F '60
--- La Légion d'Honneur: Lycette
Darsonval. TD n 89 p 30 Ja '60
---Levintritt award withheld; rea-
sons. MC v 162 n 5 p 4 N '60
---National Institute of Social Scien-
ces to Rudolf Bing; citation quo-
ted. ON v 25 n 8 p 7 D 31'60
---Oscar Espla Prize to Arnold
Kempkes; notes. WM n 4 p 78 Ag'60
---Princeton University to Laurence
Dilsner for high school teaching;
notes. MEJ v 47 n 1 p 8 S-O '60
---Prix de l'Universite de la danse
1969 Institut Choregraphique: liste.
TD n 95 p 20 Jl-Ag '60
---Les Prix du C onservatoire Na-
tional Supérieur de Musique; notes.
GDC n 283 p 102 O 7'60
---Le Prix Nadal to Ane Maria Ma-
tute, Barcelona, for "Primera Me-
moria". WP v 11 n 4 p 8 F '60

17

(Awards)
---Sarah Siddons award to Ruth Roman for her role in "Two For the Seesaw". Th Arts v 44 n 2 p 95 F '60
---Schang, Frederick C., Jr receiving Sweden's Royal Order of Vasa; notes. MC v 161 n 3 p 21 F '60
---Spain; Les Prix Nationaux des Théâtre: Antonio Buero Vallejo, Un sonador para un pueble; Luis Escobar, Elena Ossorio (list of other prize winners). WP v 11 n 3 p 1 Ja '60
---Tucker, Forrest, award "Theatre Man of the Year", Chicago's ANTA chapter.Th Arts v 44 n 4 p 66 Ap '60
---US; college and conservatory section; many reports. MC 1960
---US unions present awards to George V. Allen, Director of the US Information Agency, notes and ens ph. IM v 59 n 6 p 5 D '60
---Wolff, Stéphane. Les lauréates des " Voix d'Or"de Luchon à l'Opéra-Comique. GDC n 269-70 p 590 Ap 22'60
AXELSON, DORIS LANITA.
Grieg's unfinished opera (Peer Gynt; collaboration with B. Björnson). ON v 24 n 10 p 26 Ja 9'60
AYER, ANNE, singer
Career sketch; wife of Dr. Edward F. MacNichol. MC v 162 n 2 p 9 Ag '60
---Por phs. MC v 162 n 2 cover, p 9 Ag '60
AYLESFORD MAIDENS, play
Canada; Kay Hill. WP v 11 n 8 p 2 Je '60
AZALDEGUI, JUAN, 1925?-conductor
Sydney Royal Philharmonic appointment; b. Spain. MD v 51 n 6 p 12 D '60

B

BABBITT, MILTON (1916-). Twelve-tone invariants as compositional determinants. Mus Q
v 46 n 2 p 246-259 Ap '60
---Notes. AmM v 8 n 4 p 6 Ap '60
BABILÉE, JEAN, 1923-dancer with Gerard Ohn and Claire Sombert, ens AP wl ph. La S n 125 p 45 Ap '60
BABIN, VICTOR, 1908-, Pianist And Vitya Vronsky, duo-pianists, phs. MC v 162 n 6 cover, p 10 D '60
BABITZ, SOL (1911-). Violin views and reviews (series on technique). drawings IM 1960
BABOTCHKINE, BORIS (1904). (On staging Chekhov.)il WT v 9 n 2 p 115-6 Summer '60
BACCHELLI, RICCARDO (1891-). Verdi (on the genius of the composer, comparative criticism). Ver v1 n p 209-219 Ap '60
BACH, JOHANN SEBASTIAN(1685-1750). Ier concerto Brandebourgeois (1721): analyse par Pierrette Mari. GDC n 284 p 143-4 O 14'60
---Mendel, Arthur. Recent developments in Bach chronology. il Mus Q v 46 n 3 p 283-300 Jl'60
---Whittaker, W. Gillies(?-1944). The cantatas of Johann Sebastian Bach (book reviewed). MR v 21 n 2 p 157 My'60
---Facsimiles:Autograph title page of wrapper of the original parts of Bach's Cantata No. 21;3d page Cantata No. 182; pages from Traversiere I of St. John Passion;same No. II. Mus Q v 46 n 3 p 294 Jl'60
THE BACH ARIA GROUP
NYC review;Richard Lewis, soloist. MC v 161 n 4 p 19 Mr'60
BACH FESTIVAL
Singer, Samuel L. 275th Bach Festival, Bethlehem, Pennsylvania;review. MC v 161 n 7 p 4 Je'60
BACHELET, ALFRED, 1864-1944, composer
Chamfray, Claude. Fiche biographique. GDC n 289 p 304 N 18'60
BACHMAN, DR. HAROLD B., 1892-, director
Past presidents of the American Bandmasters' Association to direct in Chicago;notes. IM v 59 n 4 p 49 O'60

BACKX, LOUIS, pianist
Paris review. GDC n 293-4 p 461
D 16'60
BACQUIER, GABRIEL, singer
As Don Juan, several AP phs:
Paris Opéra. OpP n 19 p 29 '60
BAD HERSFELD FESTIVAL
Tenth year;notes. WM n 3 p 55
Je'60
BADEN LEHRSTÜCK, play
Brecht, Bertolt. Baden Lehrs-
tück, trans. Lee Baxandall. TDR
v 4 n 4 p 118-133 My'60
BADINGS, HENK, 1907-, composer
Opera commission from Dutch
government on refugee problem.
WM n 1 p 10 F'60
BAIGNÈRES, CLAUDE. Danse
classique et ballet moderne du
Lac des Cygnes à Pas de Dieux
(Kelly). OpP n 19 p 72 1960
BAILEY, JOHN, dancer
In Les Sylphides (Fokine), Nat-
ional Theatre Movement;Mel-
bourne notes. por MD v 50 n 9
p 24 Mr'60
BAIRD, TADEUSZ, 1928-, composer
Première:Expressioni varianti
(violin and orchestra);Warsaw.
WM n 1 p 10 F'60
---Warsaw;Four Essays For Or-
chestra;note. WM n 2 p 28 Ap'60
LE BAISER de la FÉE(MACMIL-
LAN), ballet
Guest, Ivor. (Notes on previous
versions;review of Covent Gar-
den première.) il MD v 50 n 11
p 27 My'60
BAKER, BUCK R. Request number
(personal narrative on playing
for the Dillinger Gang). IM v 59
n 3 p 12-3 S'60
BAKER, JOSEPHINE, 1906-, singer
Frattini, Angelo. Letter aperto a
Josephine Baker e a Gino Bram-
ieri. por LaS n 132 p 70-1 N'60
---And husband, Jo Bouillon in
recording of songs by RCA Vic-
tor. por HF v 10 n 4 p 75 Ap'60
---Por ph. LaS n 132 p 70 N'60
THE BALALAIKA SYMPHONIC
ORCHESTRA
NYC notes;Alexander Kutin, conducting. MC v 161 n 4 p 19 Mr'60

BALANCE A TROIS(BABILÉE),
ballet
Ens AP wl ph:Milan. LaS n 125
p 45 Ap'60
BALANCHINE, GEORGE, 1904-,
choreographer
CBS-TV commission:ballet on
story of Noah to Stravinsky mu-
sic. WM n 6 p 131 D'60
BALCH, JACK. Anatomy of a fail-
ure (A Loss of Roses). Th Arts
v 44 n 2 p 10-1 F'60
--- ---George C. Scott (1928-), actor. por Th Arts v 44 n 6 p 10-2
Je'60
--- ---A miracle named Patty (on
Patty Duke playing Helen Keller
in The Miracle). il Th Arts v 44
n 1 p 28-9 Ja'60
--- ---The openings (Broadway).
Th Arts v 44 n 1 p 14-6 Ja'60;
same. Th Arts v 44 n 2 p 14-6
F'60
LE BALCON, play
Paris notes;Jean Genet. WP v 11
n 10 p 3 Ag'60
---Richards, Stanley. (NYC review
of The Balcony.) PlM v 37 n 1
p 9 O'60
THE BALD SOPRANO, play
Ionesco, Eugène, author of the play,
stating his mental process in
this work;trans. Jack Undank.
TDR v 4 n 3 p 10-3 Mr'60
BALKANSKA, MARIA. Bulgaria
(Theatre). WT v 9 n 3 p 276-9
Autumn'60
BALL, LUCILE, 1911-, actress
Interview. Th Arts v 44 n 12 p 18
D'60
BALLAD ON OVERSEAS THEME,
play
Montreal notes;Frederic Spoerly.
WP v 11 n 7 p 3 My'60
BALLARD, STANLEY(1908?-). (A
speech against foreign tape in
US TV-films, otherwise Ameri-
can;Senate hearing.) IM v 59 n 3
p 9 S'60
BALLAUF, CHARLOTTE, ice dancer
AP wl ph. TD n 97 p 26 N'60
LA BALLATA della luna vagabonda
(SANJINA), ballet
Ens AP wl ph:Belgrade.   La S

(La Ballata)
n 133 p 67 D'60
BALLET
Australia;British Ballet Australasian Organization and National Dancing Association of Australia:1960 annual Conference;notes. MD v 51 n 1 p 27 Jl'60
--- ---Kathleen Gorham as Giselle;Borovansky Ballet. MD v 51 n 6 p 22 D'60
--- ---letters on recent performances of Victorian National Theatre Ballet as premature venture. MD v 50 n 11 p 28 My '60
--- ---the Royal Academy branch founded by Jennie Brenan and Francis Scully;list of famous Australian pupils. MD v 50 n 12 p 25 Je'60
---Belgrade;Ballata della luna vagabonda(Sanjina). La S n 133 p 67 D'60
---Berlin Festival notes on Ballet of Two Worlds;the Basle City Theater;Merce Cunningham and Carolyn Brown. MC v 162 n 6 p 32 D'60
---Campanini, Barbara;career sketch (b. Parma). il LaS n 124 p 9-13 Mr'60
---Cissan, Mill. Les russes à Paris;II. Les Ballets Russes. il TD n 95 p 29 Jl-Ag'60
---Cologne Opera;Milloss using abstract music for descriptive ballet;examples:La Sonate de L'Angoisse to Bartók;Tides to Stravinsky. MR v 21 n 3 p 244 Ag'60
---Cuba, Santiago;report by Aubrey Hitchins. MD v 51 n 2 p 27-8 Ag'60
---Dumesnil, René. La Dame aux Camelias d'Henri Sauguet(chorégraphie par Mme. Tatiana Gsovsky). il LaS n 128 p 24-5 Jl'60
---France;Ivor Guest reporting on trends and dancers. MD v 51 n 2 p 26 Ag'60
---Genova-Nervi;V Internazionale del Balletto;le cronache.

LaS n 129-30 p 65-8 Ag-S'60
---Ghis, André. Nice, Soirée de ballets. GDC n 263-4 p 481 Mr 11'60
---Goth, Trudy. Balletti U. S. A. 1960, 20. anno di vita "Balletto del Teatro". portfolio LaS n 133 p 42-7 D'60
--- ---Festival of Two Worlds, Spoleto; American Ballet Theatre; New American Ballet;operas. il LaS n 129-30 p 36, 70 Ag-S'60
--- ---Teatro Fenice e Broadway di New York. LaS n 127 p 30 Je'60
---Mexico's Ballet Concerto Company:El Reyecito, music by John Wilson. J Rev v 7 n 3 p 20 Fall'60
---Moore, Lillian. Unlisted ballets by Jean Georges Noverre. il Th Notbk v 15 n 1 p 15-20 Autumn'60
---New York City Ballet;new works; notes. Am M v 8 n 10 p 11 N'60
--- ---report. MC v 162 n 6 p 12 D'60
--- ---"Panamerica", eight ballets to Latin American music;review. MC v 161 n 4 p 46 Mr'60
---Norman, Elizabeth. Schubert's incidental music to Rosamunde. MR v 21 n 1 p 8-15 F'60
---Paris;deCuevas company's Sleeping Princess, revived by Robert Helpmann;soloists;review. GDC n 290 p 320 N 25'60
---Regner,Otto Friedrich. (Germany today.)WT v 9 n 3 p 227-232 Autumn'60
---Review of Massine's Fantasmi al Grand Hotel, La Scala. LaS n 125 p 43-4 Ap'60
---Reyna, Fernando. I Taglioni. il LaS n 132 p 30-6 N'60
---Rome;Milloss:Figliol prodigo di Sergieri Prokofief;Danses sacrée et profane di Debussy; Cimento dell'allegria. il LaS n 127 p 27, 55 Je'60
---Terry, Walter. American ballet. il Th Arts v 44 n 11 p 57-60 N'60
---Venice review of 3 ballets by Yugoslavian National Theatre at La Fenice;Dusanka Sifnios praised. MC v 161 n 5 p 32 Ap'60
---Vestris, Gaetano, 1728-1808;

20

Ferdinand R eyna's sketch. portfolio La S n 129-30 p 18-25 Ag-S '60
---West Australian Ballet (Kira Bousloff); successful tour. MD v 51 n 6 p 23, 30 D '60
---Boquet, Pierre-Jean. Mlle. Guimard, dessin en couleur. OpP n 19 cover 1960
---Dancer from Royal Danish, posed beneath bust of Auguste Bournonville, ph. Th Arts v 44 n 8 p 7 Ag '60
---Dirtl, Willy, and Paul Vondrak, AP ph: Bregenz. La S n 131 p 67 O '60
---Le Maure de Venise (Lifar), AP hl ph: Austria-Jonker. WP v 11 n 6 p 1 Ap '60
---Metropolitan Opera rehearsal under Tommy Andrew, ens AP ph: Melançon. ON v 24 n 20 p 2 Mr 19'60
---Portfolio of Vestris; scenes, costumes, portraits. La S n 129-30 p 20-6 Ag-S '60
---Tarantella, nel balletto di Salvatore Guida, AP wl ph: Metropolitan. La S n 125 p 54 Ap '60
---Wuppertal Theatre Ballets, ens AP wl ph. WP v 11 n 3 p 14 Ja '60
LE BALLET DE BERLIN-EST
Chapowalenco, Georges. (Report.) TD n 95 p 23-4 Jl-Ag '60
LE BALLET MEXICAIN
Paris; "comme un spéctacle d'amateur". TD n 97 p 23 N '60
LE BALLET NATIONAL FRANÇ-AISES (Douvai-Palau)
Douai, Jacques, dirécteur; Thérèse Palau. TD n 98 p 30 D '60
---Lyon, Raymond. Pour saluer Le Ballet National Français. GDC n 293-4 p 453 D 16'60
BALLET OF TWO WORLDS
New company by Herbert Ross and Nora Kaye under Belgian, Henriques Pimental; Nervi. MC v 162 n 1 p 34 Jl '60
---Two programs; Herbert Ross TD n 95 p 5 Jl-Ag '60
BALLET RAMBERT

Guest, Ivor. Letter from London, series. MD v 51 n 3 p 27 S '60
BALLETS MODERNES DE PARIS
Dominique et Françoise; review. il TD n 94 p 16-7 Je '60
BALLETTO NAZIONALE MESSI-CANO (Javier de Leon)
Several AP wl phs: Torino. La S n 132 p 48 N '60
UN BALLO IN MASCHERA, opera
Abbiati, Franco. Gli anni del Ballo in Maschera. Ver v 1 n 1 p 1-27 Ap '60
--- ---The years of Un Ballo in Maschera (English and German columns each page) Ver v 1 p 231-278 Ap '60
--- ---in Italian also). Ver v 1 n 2 p 631-656 Ag '60
---Andreotti, Roberto. The Parma tradition of Gustave III and Un Ballo in Maschera. Ver v 1 n 2 p 1090-1099 Ag '60
---Benois, Alessandro, e Nicola Benois. Scenografia verdiana e allestimenti scaligeri del Ballo in Maschera (a cura di Giovanni Cenzato). Ver v 1 n 1 p 90-108 Ap '60
---Editorial statement after the Gino Roncoglia criticism of "historical fussiness". threatening Verdi; criticism; purpose of Verdi Institute. Ver v 1 n 2 p reface Ag '60
---Flora, Francesco. Il Libretto. Ver v 1 n 1 p 44-72 Ap '60
--- ---(also German translation of this article). Ver v 1 n 1 p 305-353 Ap '60
--- ---Il Libretto; Act III. Ver v 1 n 2 p 662-678 Ag '60
---Gara, Eugenio. Il Camino dell 'opera in um secolo d'interpretazioni (English and German translations p 418-457). Ver v 1 n 1 p 112-133 Ap '60
--- ---II. Ver v 1 n 2 p 704-719 Ag '60
---Graf, Herbert, Regarding the staging of Un Ballo in Maschera. (German and Italian translation found p 413-17). Ver v 1 n 1 p 109-111 Ap '60
---Historical details of perfor-

(Un Ballo in Maschera)
mances 1861-1955, in reply to
a student of music's letter. Ver
v 1 n 2 preface Ag '60
---Mila, Massimo. Problems of
philology and interpretation concerning the score of Un Ballo in
Maschera; II. Ver v 1 n 2
p 957-976 Ag '60
---Pannain, Guido. L'Opera. Ver
v 1 n 1 p 73-89 Ap '60
--- ---II. Ver v 1 n 2 p 679-703
Ag '60
--- ---The opera (Verdi criticism,
German and English side by side).
Ver v 1 n 1 p 354-379 Ap '60
---Rome Opera; original libretto;
review. MC v 161 n 3 p 44 F '60
---Roncaglia, Gino. Riccardo or
Gustave III? ("historical fussiness is a restless woodworm";
"there is nothing in the music
that is Swedish, English or American"). Ver v 1 n 2 preface
Ag '60
---Royal Opera Stockholm at
Covent Garden; review. R. L. J.
MR v 21 n 4 p 323 N '60
---La Scala review. il La S n 127
p 23 Je '60
---Walker, Frank. Lettere inedite: contributo alla storia di un
Ballo in Maschera. Ver v 1 n 1
p 279-304 Ap '60
--- ---Unpublished letters: a
contribution to the history of Un
Ballo in Maschera. Ver v 1 n 1
p 28-43 Ap '60
--- ---Unveröffentlichte briefe.
Ver v 1 n 1 p 279-304 Ap '60
---Weaver, William. (Review of
Rome production, moved back
to Sweden, with Wakhevitch décor
under Wallman.) Op v 2 n 3
p 216-7 Mr '60
---Weerth, Ernest de. Rome
Opera review. ON v 24 n 17 p 28
F 27'60
---Bolshoi, 1891 décor: 6 settings
(I. Kukánov, F. Scenián and P.
Issanov), phs. Ver v 1 n 2 Ag '60
---Décor, a portfolio of settings:
Alessandro Benois (2); Nicola
Benois (2); Matislav Dobujinsky

(1); Carlo Ferrario (1); Ita Maximowna (1); Angelo Parravicini (1);
George Wakhevitch (2); Alfredo
Zurigo (1). Ver v 1 n 2 Ag '60
---The dwelling place of the sorceress, Act I, sc. 2; Carlo Ferrario, Teatro alla Scala, 1862;
Carlo Songa, 1903; Allessandro
Benois 1947, 3 stage sets, phs.
Ver v 1 n 1 p 592 Ap '60
---Focosi, A. (Ens AP wl ph:
print, Ricordi first edition). Ver
v 1 n 2 p 631 Ag '60
---Melodramme in tre atti, Musica
di Giuseppe Verdi da rappresentarsi al Teatro Apolli in Roma,
il Carnevale 1859. (The Libretto,
first edition, Ricordi), facsimile.
Ver v 1 n 1 p 304 Ap '60
---Paris Opéra, two scenes, phs.
OpP n 19 p 32 1960
---Stockholm Opera in London, ens
AP wl ph: Rogers. Op v 11 n 10
p 708 O '60
BALLOU, ESTHER WILLIAMSON,
composer
Première: A Passing Word (in
Washington 1960). ACAB v 9 n 3
p 26 1960
BALLROOM DANCING
Sydney's annual Ballroom Festival;
APRA Perpetual Trophy to Kevin
Gibson and Shirley Saunderson. MD
v 50 n 12 p 28 Je'60
---US;Recreational Dancing Institute;
Guy Lombardo, Lawrence Welk,
Les Brown, Louis Armstrong on
Advisory Board. IM v 58 n 12 p 21
Je'60
BALOGH, ERNO(1897-). Sentimental
realist, Eugène d'Albert(1864-1932).
por ON v 24 n 13 p 8-9 Ja 30'60
-- ---Voice of the teens:career of
Erich Wolfgang Korngold, 1897-
1957. por ON v 24 n 20 p 12-3
Mr 19'60
BALTIMORE
Mondawin Shopping Center housing
Baltimore Symphony;note. IM v 59
n 1 p 19 Jl'60
---Music report. MC v 161 n 5 p 20
Ap'60
---Series of chamber orchestra concerts(anonymous donor through

Goucher College) ; notes. AmM
v 8 n 7 p 4 Ag '60

BALTIMORE CIVIC OPERA
Faust cast. ON v 24 n 15 p 2
F 13'60

---Schauensee, Max de. Faust;
Richard Cross and others. ON
v 24 n 21 p 27 Mr 26'60

BANCROFT, ANNE, actress
NYC notes. Th Arts v 44 n 8 p 6
Ag '60

LE BANDIT DAVELIS, comedy
Athens notes; Traiforos-Yanna-
kopoulos. WP v 11 n 5 p 9 Mr '60

BANDS
Best New Band of 1960; notes on
competition; Jackie G leason,
honorary chairman; George V.
Clancy, project leader. por IM
v 59 n 2 p 9 Ag '60

---Bryan, Arthur H. Band instruments harbor germs (anti-
septic practices outlined). MEJ
v 46 n 5 p 84 Ap-My '60

---Barulli, Don. Gene Krupa,
1909-; his career. por IM v 58
n 10 p 10-11, 32-3 Ap '60

---College Band Directors National Association, US; schedule
of Chicago convention, December
1960. MEJ v 47 n 1 p 111-2
S-O '60

--- ---biennial convention in
Chicago report. portfolio MEJ
v 47 n 2 p 77 N-D '60

---Filas, Thomas. Something
for class C Band, please but
don't make it too hard. (thesis,
we are making it too easy in US
schools). MEJ v 47 n 1 p 85-6
S-O '60

---Gordon, Edgar B. Instrumental music in the pioneer days
(US band evolution). MEJ v 46
n 3 p 34, 37 Ja '60

---Jerden, Leonard. Have Tux
will swim (1938 incident in North
Dakota). IM v 59 n 5 p 16-7 N'60

---Maine; Le Montagnard Band in
66th year. IM v 59 n 2 p 46
Ag '60

---Mayer, Francis N. John Philip
Sousa, his instrumentation and
scoring. chart MEJ v 46 n 3

p 51-7 Ja '60

---Merrick, Joseph, pseud. Why
bands? (Small ensembles are also
valuable). MEJ v 46 n 5 p 66
Ap.-My '60

---Ode, James A. Army band opportunities. IM v 58 n 7 p 18 Ja'60

---Portable band shell; Casper City
Band, Wyoming, since 1889. IM
v 59 n 4 p 49 O '60

---Recordings reviewed: Mercury's
British Band Classics; Capitol's
Band of the Royal Marines. HF
v 10 n 2 p 75, 76 F '60

---Regular column on US band activities, "Bands Are for People".
IM 1960

---Rental Manuscript Library for
band music; details; Interlochen.
MEJ v 46 n 4 p 78 F-Mr '60

---Review of recording "The Sound
of a Marching Band: 120 cadence",
Medallion release. HF v 10 n 11
p 108 N '60

---Reynolds, George. You can't
beat the band. (historical notes,
US). il MEJ v 47 n 1 p 59-60, 62
S-O '60

--- ---Part II. MEJ v 47 n 2 p 90
N-D '60

---Salvation Army bands, 1878-
to date. MC v 162 n 6 p 2 D '60

---Santelmann, William F. The
art of band scoring. MC v 162 n 2
p 21 Ag '60

---US; Best Band Contest 1960;
notes. IM v 58 n 12 p 11 Je '60

--- ---ten top dance bands contest;
176 competing, US and Canada;
Detroit finals; notes. IM v 59 n 5
p 9 N '60

--- ---33 high school and college
bands for Festival Parade, Indian-
apolis; one and 3/4 miles per hour
marching. IM v 58 n 9 p 43 Mr '60

--- ---contest 1960; rules and prizes for The Best New Band. IM
v 59 n 3 p 9, 15 S '60

--- ---contest won by Jimmy Cook,
1925-and his Las Vegas Band (with
ensemble ph.) IM v 59 n 6 p 10
D '60

---Whear, Paul W. Problems of
the small college band. MEJ v 46

(Bands)
n 4 p 76, 78 F-Mr '60
---Carnegie Tech Kiltie Band, on stage, ph: US. MEJ v 47 n 2 p 90 N-D '60
---Dance bands, ens phs of Steve Laughery's 9-piece; Ray Alburn's 11-piece; Ronnie Drumm's 15 piece; Rod Aaberg's 15-piece; also Cobo Hall, Detroit where the US contest will be played; phs. IM v 59 n 5 p 10-1 N '60
---Leaders in the "Best Band Contest 1959", ens ph: Chicago. IM v 59 n 3 p 15 S '60
---Majorettes in uniform, ens AP ph: Tennessee. MEJ v 47 n 1 p 71 S-O '60
---Manitowoc Marine Band: 3 generations of Stechmessers, Herbert (64 yrs) Chester (42 and Gary (17), ens ph: US IM v 59 n 5 p 26 N '60
---Stewart, Carleton, president of the American Bandmasters Association, por ph: Iowa. MEJ v 47 n 1 p 73 S-O '60
BANHAM, MARTIN. Drama in the Commonwealth: Nigeria. NTM v 1 n 4 p 18-21 Jl '60
BANKHEAD, TALLULAH, 1903-, actress
AP hl ph. Th Arts v 44 n 9 p 13 S '60
BARABBAS, play
Ens AP wl ph: George Henri, 1956. WT v 9 n 1 p 13 Spring '60
BARATI, GEORGE, 1913-, conductor
Career notes; b. Hungary. por IM v 58 n 8 p 33 F '60
BARBER, SAMUEL, 1910-, composer
Première: Toccata Festival for Organ and Orchestra, Philadelphia Orchestra, soloist, Paul Callaway. IM v 59 n 5 p 24 N '60
---Vanessa, opera, review of Victor recording; notes on composer. CMJ v 4 n 2 p 46-7 Winter '60
---Por ph. MC v 162 n 6 p 16 D'60
DER BARBIER VON BAGDAD, opera

Bregenz; Cornelius work; criticism; one AP ph: Spang. Op v 11 p 75 Autumn '60
--- ---ens AP wl ph: Finke; also Sonja Draksler and Friederike Sailor, AP hl ph: Spang. Op v 11 p 74, 76 Autumn '60
IL BARBIERE DI SIVIGLIA, opera
Covent Garden; Act I ens AP wl phs: Southern, and others. Op v 11 n 7 p 503 Jl '60
---Ens AP wl ph: Covent Garden. WM n 4 p 83 Ag '60
---Ens AP wl ph: Bergamo. La S n 133 p 65 D '60
---Rubes, Jan, and Andrew Mac-Millan, ens AP wl ph: Canadian Opera. MC v 161 n 7 p 19 Je '60
---Paisiello (1740-1816) opera at the Schwetzingen Festival; notes. WM n 3 p 55 Je '60
---Paisiello's score; "larvae" of the same characters developed by Rossini. il Op v 11 n 5 p 352 My'60
---Teatro Piccola Scala; Paisiello; review. il La S n 125 p 46 Ap '60
---Ens AP wl ph: Schwetzingen Festival. WM n 4 p 83 Ag '60
BARBIERI, FEDORA, 1920-, singer
In Un Ballo, AP hl ph: Milan. La S n 127 p 23 Je '60
BARBIROLLI, SIR JOHN, 1899-, conductor
Chicago criticism. MC v 161 n 5 p 21 Ap '60
---Hallè Orchestra season; criticism. MR v 21 n 3 p 245-6 Ag '60
---Succeeding Stokowski in Houston but retaining some Hallé concerts; notes. MC v 162 n 6 p 4, 33 D '60
BARBIZET, PIERRE, 1922-, pianist
And Christian Ferras; Paris review. GDC n 278 p 849 Je 24'60
BARDHAN, SHANTI, dancer
Paris review; Bombay dancers; "d'un ballet dramatique de marionnettes vivantes". TD n 94 p 22 Je'60
BARDI, GIULIA
See Stahlmann, Sylvia, singer
BARE EN TAGSTEN, play
Copenhagen notes; Soya. WP v 11 n 5 p 2 Mr '60
BARFORD, PHILIP T; The early dances of Josef Lanner (1801-43).

MR v 21 n 2 p 114-120 My '60
--- ---Josef Lanner: a further
appraisal. MR v 21 n 3 p 179-185
Ag '60
--- ---Mahler: a thematic arche-
type. MR v 21 n 4 p 297-316 N'60
BARILLI, BRUNO (1880-1952).Ap-
punti inediti di Bruno Barilli su
Verdi; presentali da Gian Paolo
Minardi. Ver v 1 n 1 p 220-228
Ap '60
---Minardi, Gian Paolo. Fram-
menti Verdiani di Bruno Barilli.
Ver v 1 n 2 p 790-798 Ag '60
BARIONI, DANIELE, 1933-, singer
As Macduff, AP hl ph: Melançon.
ON v 24 n 9 p 17 Ja 2'60
---Por ph. ON v 24 n 18 p 29
Mr 5'60
BARLIN, ISRAEL
See Berlin, Irving
BARON, GUY, ?-1959, pianist
Note on British musician. GDC
n 259-60 p 388 F 12'60
BARON, SAMUEL, flutist
With Robert Conant, harpsichor-
dist; NYC review. MC v 161 n 4
p 37 Mr '60
BARRA, PEDRO DE LA
Chile; theatre notes. WT v 9 n 3
p 268 Autumn '60
BARRABAS, play
Barcelona notes; Joaquin Calvo
Sotelo. WP v 11 n 7 p 6 My '60
BARRAGE CONTRE LE PACIFIQUE,
play
Paris notes; Geneviève Serreau.
WP v 11 n 5 p 7 Mr '60
BARRAUD, HENRY, 1900-,
composer
Festival Henry Barraud à Théâtre
des Champs-Elysées. GDC n 290
p 320 N 25'60
---Paris review of Te Deum, Tra-
jan Popesco. GDC n 281-2 p 25
S 30'60
---Por ph: Lipnitzki. GDC n 288
cover N 11'60
BARRAULT, JEAN-LOUIS (1910-)
(On staging Chekhov.) il WT v 9
n 2 p 117-8 Summer '60
---Notes. WP v 12 n 3 p 4 D '60
---Notes on his position in the
French theatre. Th Arts v 44 n 12

p 63 D '60
---Paris subsidy; survey by Jean-
Pierre Lenoir. Th Arts v 44 n 1
p 24-5 Ja '60
---HL ph: Max Waldman. Th Arts
v 44 n 12 p 60 D '60
---In Tête d'Or with Alain Cuny, AP
hl ph: Pic. Th Arts v 44 n 1 p 22
Ja '60
THE BARRETTS OF WIMPOLE
STREET, play
Nielson, Margaret A. Teenagers
and the Barretts (details of a high
school production). il PlM v 37 n 3
p 58 D '60
---Omaha High School, ens AP wl
ph. PlM v 37 n 3 p 58 D '60
BARROW INTIMATE OPERA
SOCIETY
Notes. Op v 11 n 4 p 267 Ap '60
BARRYMORE, ETHEL,1879-1959,
actress
Notes. Th Arts v 44 n 10 p 26 O'60
---And Bruce McRae in Cousin Kate,
AP wl ph: 1903. Th Arts v 44 n 1
p 78 Ja '60
THE BARTERED BRIDE, opera
Osborne, Conrad L. Sung in Czech,
Prodana Nevesta, review of Artia
recording). HF v 10 n 9 p 65 S '60
BARTÓK, BÉLA (1881-1945). IIe
Quatuor (1915-7): analyse par Pier-
rette Mari. GDC n 290 p 335-6
N 25'60
---Forte, Allen. Bartok's "serial"
composition. Mus Q v 46 n 2 p 233-
245 Ap '60
BARTON, JUNE, 1936-, singer
Por ph: Australia. MD v 51 n 5
cover N '60
THE BARN THEATRE
Augusta, Maine, exterior ph. Th
Arts v 44 n 6 p 17 Je '60
BARZIN, LEON 1900-, conductor
Mari, Pierrette. L'Orchestre de
la Société Philharmonique de Paris.
GDC n 265-6 p 526 Mr 25'60
---Notes; b. Brussels. AmM v 8
n 1 p 9 Ja '60
---Small AP hl ph: London. AmM
v 8 n 1 p 7 Ja '60
BASEGGIO, CESCO, 1897-, actor
And Carlo Micheluzzi, AP wl ph
and scene from Goldoni's Sior

25

LIBRARY OF MOUNT ST. MARY'S COLLEGE EMMITSBURG, MARYLAND

(Baseggio, Cesco)
Nicoletto", ens ph. La S n 132
p 68-9 N '60
BASIE, COUNT, 1906-, Pianist
Feather, Leonard. Silver Ju-
bilee for Count Basie. il IM v 59
n 5 p 18-9 N '60
---Por ph; with Joe Williams, ph.
IM v 59 n 5 cover, p 18 N '60
BASNETT, ROBERTA, singer
Por ph: NTC. MC v 161 n 5 p 36
Ap '60
BASSETT, LESLIE, composer
Première: For City, Nation,
World (Buffalo, 1960). ACAB
v 9 n 3 p 26 1960
BASTIANINI, ETTORE, singer
Criticism. ON v 25 n 8 p 30
D 31'60
---As Andrea Chénier, AP hl ph:
La Scala. La S n 123 p 32 F '60
---As Carlo Gérard, AP ph: Le
Blanc. ON v 24 n 21 p 17
Mr 26'60
---As Count Di Luna, AP ph: Le
Blanc. ON v 24 n 17 p 17 F 27'60
BASTIEN, GINETTE, dancer
Bro, Yves. (sketch.) TD n 91
p 19 Mr '60
---Notes. il TD n 96 p 30 S-O'60
BATACLAN, play
Argentina notes; Felix M. Pelayo.
WP v 12 n 3 p 26 D '60
BATE, STANLEY, 1913-1959,
composer
Notes; b. Plymouth. MC v 161
n 6 p 37 My '60
BATH MUSIC FESTIVAL
Menuhin, Yehudi, and Ian Hun-
ter; notes. Th Arts v 44 n 5
p 18 My '60
---Report. WM n 3 p 55 Je '60
LES BÂTISSEURS D'EMPIRE,
play
Lyon, Raymond. Boris Vian's
Les Bâtisseurs d'Empire. GDC
n 255-6 p 321 Ja 15'60
---de Boris Vian, AP hl ph: Ber-
nand. WP v 11 n 4 p 1 F '60
LA BATTAGLIA, opera-comique
Schwetzingen; Gerhard Wimber-
ger. WP v 11 n 10 p 12 Ag '60
LA BATTAGLIA DI LEGNANO,
opera

Ugolini, Savarese e Washington,
AP hl ph: Venice. La S n 123
p 41 F '60
BAUERNPASSION, opera
Bad Hersfeld production, ens AP
wl ph. WM n 4 p 82 Ag '60
BAUME, EMILE, pianist
Notes. GDC n 255-6 p 283 Ja 15'60
---Paris review. GDC n 263-4 p 492
Mr 11'60
---Por ph. GDC n 255-6 cover
Ja 15'60
BAURRAUD, HENRY, composer
Notes; b. Bordeaux. GDC n 288
p 240 N 11'60
BAVARIAN RADIO ORCHESTRA
Hartmann, Karl Amadeus,
director; repertory notes. MC
v 161 n 7 p 16 Je '60
BAVEL, ZAMIR, 1929-, composer
Première: Israeli Rhapsody; note.
MC v 161 n 5 p 39 Ap '60
BAXANDALL, LEE. Bertolt
Brecht's J. B. (notes and an Eng-
lish translation of Baden Lehrs-
tuck). TDR v 4 n 4 p 113-133 My'60
BAYANIHAN PHILIPPINE COMPANY
Frattini, Angelo. Rapsodia delle
Filippine. il La S n 125 p 72-3
Ap '60
---NYC criticism; "theatrical vir-
tuosity". PLM v 36 n 4 p 83 Ja'60
---Paris, Théâtre des Nations; le
folklore philippin. TD n 93 p 15
My '60
BAYREUTH
Brunner, Gerhard. (Report, in-
cluding a new Ring, staged by
Wolfgang Wagner.) il MC v 162
n 3 p 2 S '60
--- ---Reviews: Meistersinger; The
Flying Dutchman; Lohengrin; Parsi-
fal. MC v 162 n 5 p 28 N '60
---The Festival Theatre, 1876;
features conceived by Wagner and
designed by Semper; in a survey
of theatres by Thomas De Gaetani.
J Rev v 7 n 2 p 9 Spring '60
---Opera reviews by William Mann,
John Warrack and The Editor Op
v 11 p 34-47 Autumn '60
---The Ring; criticism. R. L. J. MR
v 21 n 4 p 321-2 N '60
---Lohengrin, bridal chorus in

Act III; Act II of Götterdämmerung, two ens AP wl phs: Lauterwasser. Op v 11 p 45-6 Autumn '60

BEACH INSPECTOR AND THE MERMAID, ballet
West Australian Ballet, small AP ph. MD v 51 n 1 p 28 Jl '60

BEAN, DAVID, pianist
London press notes. AmM v 8 n 11 D '60

THE BEAR, play
Scenes: Bern (1954) and Praha (1954), 2 phs. WT v 9 n 2 p 141 Summer '60

BEATON, CECIL (1904-). Sets and costumes for "Saratoga", il Th Arts v 44 n 1 p 17 Ja '60

BEATRICE AND BENEDICT
American première by Little Opera Society; other notes. Op v 11 p 410 Je '60
---Little Orchestra Society; concert version of Berlioz work. ON v 24 n 24 p 27 Ap 16'60

LE BEAU DANUBE (MASSINE), ballet
Miskovich, Milorad, AP wl ph: Nervi. La S n 129-30 p 66 Ag-S'60

BEAUCHAMP, ALBERT (1921-).
Summary of conference April 28 on situation of music in France; many speakers summarized. GDC n 276 p 868-877 Jl 1'60
---Por ph. GDC n 279-280 p 880 Jl 1'60

BEAUMONT, TESSA
In le Barbier de Seville dûe à Leonide Massine, ens AP wl ph: Lido. TD n 96 p 28 S-O'60

THE BEAUX ARTS TRIO OF NEW YORK
Greenhouse, Bernard, cellist, Menahem Pressler, pianist, Daniel Guilet, violinist; London notes. AmM v 8 n 8 p 5 S '60

BECERRA SCHMIDT, GUSTAVO, 1924-, composer
Chile; Director of the Institute of Musical Extension; notes. WM n 1 p 9 F '60

BECHERINI, BIANCA Amenità e viaggi nella vita di Cherubini. il La S n 125 p 21-26 Ap '60

BECKER, JOHN J. Wallingford Riegger. ACAB v 9 n 3 p 13 1960

BECKET, play
Pryce-Jones, Alan.Anouilh review: Becket ou l'Honneur de Dieu. Th Arts v 44 n 12 p 9-10 D '60
---Cremer, Bruno, and Daniel Ivernel, AP wl ph. Th Arts v 44 n 1 p 23 Ja '60
---Montparnasse-Gaston Baty, Cremer and Ivernel, AP wl ph: Pic. Th Arts v 44 n 1 p 23 Ja '60
---Smith, Oliver, three sets and 5 costume sketches. Th Arts v 44 n 10 p 22-3 O '60

BECKETT, SAMUEL, 1906-, playwright
Esslin, Martin. The theatre of the absurd. TDR v 4 n 4 p 3-15 My'60
---Moore, John R. A farewell to something ("this negative universe" in Waiting For Godot). TDR v 5 n 1 p 49-60 S '60

BEDIN, PAULETTE, violinist
With Sylvaine Billier, pianist; Paris debut.GDC n 263-4 p 487 Mr 11'60

BEECHAM, SIR THOMAS (1879-).
Frederick Delius (book reviewed). MR v 21 n 2 p 151-154 My '60
--- ---(On Haydn's Salomon symphonies.) por HF v 10 n 5 p 61 My'60
---Chicago criticism. MC v 161 n 5 p 21 Ap '60
---Washington, D. C. notes. MC v 161 n 6 p 32 My '60
---With Victoria de los Angeles and Nicolai Gedda, hl ph: EMI. Op v 2 n 3 p 222 Mr '60

BEETHOVEN, LUDWIG VAN (1770-1827). Ier Quatuor en Fa Majeur: analyse par Pierrette Mari. GDC n 255-6 p 325-6 Ja 15'60
--- ---5e Symphonie en do mineur, opus 68: analyse par Pierrette Mari. GDC n 267-8 p 569 Ap 8'60
--- ---Xe Sonate pour piano et violon: analyse par Pierrette Mari. GDC n 288 p 271-2 N 11'60
---Berges, Ruth. The ideal beloved (Leonore in Fidelio; Beethoven's views on women). ON v 24 n 15 p 8-9 F 13'60
---Conly, John M. Reflections on a

27

(Beethoven)
goodly fellowship. HF v 10 n 4
p 34-6 Ap '60
---Darrell, R. D. Beethoven's
"Battle Symphony" (Maelzel and
his Panharmonicon, augmented
orchestra) and a review of Morton Gould's recording. HF v 10
n 8 p 55-6 Ag '60
---Landon, H. C. Robbins. It all
began in Bonn (Beethoven's early
life in Bonn, in Vienna). il HF
v 10 n 4 p 40-3 Ap '60
---MacArdle, Donald W. Beethoven and the Philharmonic Society
of London. MR v 21 n 1 p 1-7
F '60
--- ---Minor Beethoveniana II
(eight items discussed). Mus Q
v 46 n 1 p 41-55 Ja '60
---Marsh, Robert C. Beethoven's
cello music, complete and in
stereo (Deutsche Grammophon).
HF v 10 n 7 p 51 Jl '60
--- ---The Beethoven symphonies
in stereo (a discography). HF
v 10 n 4 p 44-5. 85-7 Ap '60
--- ---Beethoven's Symphonies:
Josef Krips and Lovro von Matacic,
conducting for Everest and Par-
liament respectively, the London
Symphony and the Czech Phil-
harmonic. HF v 10 n 9 p 64 S'60
---Pirie, Peter J. Toscanini and
Furtwängler, an empire divided
(Beethoven symphonic canon). HF
v 10 n 4 p 37-9 Ap '60
---Steichen, Dana; her book on
Countess von Erdödy as "Bee-
thoven's Beloved". ON v 24 n 15
p 26 F 13'60
---Temperley, Nicholas. Beetho-
ven in London concert life, 1800-
1850. MR v 21 n 3 p 207-214 Ag'60
---Truscott, Harold. Beethoven's
Fourth Piano Concerto; his violin
Concerto (analysis). MD v 50 n 7
p 8-11 Ja '60
---Maehler, Willibord. Beethoven
at 34, portrait. ON v 24 n 15 p 7
F 13'60
---A number of pictures in an
issue featuring Beethoven; portraits, birthplace, etc. HF v 10

n 4 Ap '60
---Signed portrait. La S n 125 p 80
Ap '60
BEGG, HEATHER, singer
In Il Trovatore, Carl Rosa Opera
in London. Op v 11 n 10 p 707 O'60
THE BEGGAR'S OPERA, play
Notes on oil painting by Robert
Smirke (1752-1845) of quarrel in
Newgate scene, played by Peachum
and Dowton, 1815; ph: coll. Mr. J.
O. F latter. Th Notbk v 14 n 4
p 132 Summer '60
THE BEGUINE
Perry, Charles. Modern drumming
(with music rolls). IM v 59 n 3 p 18-9
S '60
BEHAN, BRENDAN, 1923-, writer
London notes. PIM v 36 n 5 p 105
F '60
BEHAN, WILLIAM
Left profile por ph: Duncan Melvin.
Th Arts v 44 n 10 p 15 O '60
BEHRENS, EDITH. Bach for a cup
of coffee (Boris Goldovsky sketch).
por ON v 24 n 24 p 14-5 Ap 16'60
BEIRER, HANS, singer
As Siegmund, AP hl ph: Buenos
Aires. La S n 133 p 113 D '60
BEL CANTO
Franca, Ida. Manual of Bel Canto
(book reviewed by Conrad L. Os-
borne). ON v 24 n 22 p 28 Ap 2'60
---Kallman, Chester. (On the meaning
of bel canto; operas that vocally de-
lineate character.) ON v 25 n 7
p 9-13 D 24'60
---Vinci, Ernesto. (Comments on
Ida Franco's book "Manuel of Bel
Canto".) CMJ v 4 n 4 p 75-8
Summer '60
BELGIUM
Bourguignon, de, Francis. (Music
report.) MC v 161 n 7 p 15 Je '60
---Closson, Herman. Belgian art-
ists abroad. WT v 9 n 1 p 47-50
Spring '60
---Editorial: introduction to the
theatre in Belgium; note on bicep-
halism. WT v 9 n 1 p 3 Spring '60
---Guglielmi, Edoardo. Belgium,
music report. La S n 125 p 91
Ap '60
---Opera; Antwerp, Brussels, Liège.

Op v 11 n 12 p 827 D '60
---Piel, Emma. De Belgique; re-
naissance de L'Orchestre Nat-
ional. GDC n 287 p 233 N 4'60
--- ---Le concours international
de Quatuor à cordes de Liège; Un
Âge d'Or, le XVIe siècle; le 5e
contenaire de Gilles de Binche.
GDC n 284 p 134-5 O 14'60
---Theatre report. WP v 11 n 10
p 2 Ag '60
---The theatre; whole issue fea-
tures drama in Belgium. il WT
v 9 n 1 Spring'60
BELGRADE
Logar, Mihovil. Opera di Stato.
La S 1960
--- ---Opera di Stato di Belgrado
e Zagabria. il La S n 126 p 37
My '60
---Report; New York Phisharmonic
notes; Emil Gilels; other artists.
MC v 162 n 1 p 33 Jl '60
BELGRADE OPERA
In Khovanschina, two phs. Op v 11
n 9 p 633 S '60
BELINSKY, ISAI. The oboist looks
at his problems (technique). IM
v 59 n 4 p 34-5 O '60
BELL, LESLIE (1906-). Fragments.
CMJ v 4 n 3 p 89 Spring '60
BELLAMY, EDWARD; A super
steals the show (apple to balky
donkey bringing Farrar to the
footlights). ON v 24 n 13 p 13
Ja 30'60
LA BELLE, AU BOIS DORMANT
(Petipa-Nijinska-Helpmann)
Champs-Elysées; le Marquis de
Cuevas; Horacio Guerrico, la
supervision artistique; Raymond
de Larrain, la présentation dé-
corative; Hightower, Prokowsky,
Melikova, Adabache, Nicholas
Polajenko. il TD n 98 p 7-13 1960
---Silvant, Jean. En version inté-
grale par Cuevas. TD n 92 p 3
Ap '60
--- ---(Golovine as the Prince,
Liane Daydé as Princess Aurora;
criticism.) il TD n 98 p 12-3 D'60
---Théâtre des Champs-Elysées;
Cuevas company review. TD n 96
p 12-9 S-O'60

---review of de Cuevas Ballet.
GDC n 290 p 320 N 25'60
---Cuevas company; notes; port-
folio: Paris. TD n 98 p 7-11 D'60
LA BELLE DE CADIX
Chapallaz, Gilbert. Lausanne.
GDC n 267-8 p 554 Ap 8'60
LA BELLE HÉLÈNE, operetta
Paris, Théâtre Mogador; Geori
Boué "dazzling" as Helen; review.
Op v 11 n 6 p 420 Je '60
---See also Helen of Troy, opera
LA BELLE ROSE (CHIRIAEFF),
ballet
Les Grands Ballets Canadiens;
notes. WP v 11 n 4 p 1 F '60
BELLERI, MARGUERITE, singer
With Mr. Bing and friends at a
Metropolitan Opera party honoring
her 50 years in the chorus, ens ph:
Melançon. ON v 24 n 19 p 3 Mr12'60
BELLINI, VINCENZO, 1801-1835
Candida, Federico. Bellini senza
pace. La S n 129-30 p 56 Ag-S'60
---Matz, Mary Jane. (Bellini and
Malibran.) il ON v 24 n 17 p 8-9
F 27'60
---Porter, Andrew. Bellini's last
opera (I Puritani). por Op v 11
n 5 p 315-21 My '60
---Schiavoni. Lithograph portrait;
room in the Bellini Museum, Cat-
ania, ph: Consoli. ON v 24 n 17
p 8-9 F 27'60
BELLSON, LOUIS
And his drums, wl ph. IM v 59
n 5 p 13 N '60
BELMONT, ELEANOR R. (1879-).
A cause to celebrate (25 years of
the Metropolitan Opera Guild).
por ON v 25 n 1 p 9-13 O 8'60
---Accepting tray, enscribed with
the names of Metropolitan Opera
Guild, ens ph: Melançon. ON
v 25 n 3 p 7 N 19'60
---Por ph: Avedon, 1955. ON v 25
n 1 p 10 O 8'60
BELSHAZZAR, oratorio Graf,
Herbert; production at Indiana
University; review. ON v 24 n 12
p 26 Ja 23'60
---Final tableaux at Indiana Univ-
ersity, ens AP wl ph. ON v 24
n 12 p 28 Ja 23'60

BELT, BYRON, manager
Por ph:Chicago. MC v 162 n 1
p 22 Jl'60
BELVEDERE LAKE THEATRE
Central Park, NYC;ens ph:Geo.
E. Joseph. Th Arts v 44 n 8 cov-
er Ag'60
BENAVENTE, SAULO(1916-). (On
staging Chekhov in Argentina.)
il WT v 9 n 2 p 119 Summer'60
BENDER, HEINRICH, conductor
Munich notes. MR v 21 n 4 p 327
N'60
BENEDETTO, RENATO di. Tea-
tro San Carlo. il LaS n 122 p 37
Ja'60
--- ---Teatro San Carlo:L'Amore
delle Tre Melarance. il LaS
n 123 p 36-7 F'60
--- ---Teatro San Carlo di Nap-
oli. LaS 1960
BENFIELD, WARREN A. Special
problems of the orchestral bass
player. por IM v 58 n 8 p 18-9
F'60
BENJAMIN, ARTHUR, 1893-1960,
composer
Note on Sydney-born musician.
por MD v 50 n 10 p 17 Ap'60
---Notes. MC v 161 n 6 p 37 My'60
---Warrack, John. An appreciation.
por Op v 11 n 6 p 434 Je'60
BENNET, PHIL
Notes and por ph. IM v 59 n 5 p 34
N'60
BENNY, JACK, 1894-, singer
Awards;his benefit concerts have
brought in $1,900,000 for mu-
sicians' charities. IM v 58 n 10
p 28 Ap'60
BENOIS, ALESSANDRE(1870-) and
Nicola Benois (1901-). Design-
ing Verdi operas and the La
Scala productions of Un Ballo in
Maschera (German translation
side by side the English). Ver
v 1 n 1 p 380-412 Ap'60
--- ---Scenografia verdiana e
allestimenti scaligeri del Ballo
in Maschera (a cura di Giovan-
ni Cenzato). Ver v 1 n 1 p 90-
108 Ap'60
---Two settings for Un Ballo in
Maschera, Act III, scenes 1 and

3, two phs:Milan, 1947. Ver v 1 n 1
Ag'60
---Por ph:Michel Petit. TD n 92 p 11
Ap'60
BENOIS, NICOLA(1901-). Hansel and
Gretel for La Scala, ens AP ph:
Piccagliani. ON v 24 n 14 p 27 F
6'60
--- ---Sets for Un Ballo in Masch-
era:Zurich 1956 Act II, Act III
scene 3; Milan 1957 Act III scene
3, phs. Ver v 1 n 2 Ag'60
BENTLEY, ERIC (1916-). The ma-
king of a dramatist (1892-1903)
(Shaw). TDR v 5 n 1 p 3-21 S'60
---Two books on Brecht. TDR v 4
n 4 p 105-112 My '60
BENVENUTO CELLINI, opera
Cairns, David. Criticism of the
work and of BBC Broadcast. Op
v 11 n 9 p 651-2 S '60
BENZI, ROBERTO, 1939-, con-
ductor
Carmen at the Paris Opéra; notes.
ON v 24 n 14 p 26 F 6'60
BERG, ALBAN, 1885-1935,
composer
Hamburg; Lulu; and Wozzeck;
criticism. Op v 2 n 3 p 207 Mr'60
---NYC; memorial concert; review.
MC v 162 n 6 p 18 D '60
---Wolff, Stéphane. Au Théâtre des
Nations: Loulou d'Alban Berg.
GDC n 275 p 748 Je 3'60
BERG, GUNNAR, composer
Première: Jaffky's "; note. GDC
n 274 p 723 My 27'60
BERGAMO
Ballini, Marcello. Teatro Donizetti:
Il Pigmalione. il LaS n 132 p 45, 79
N'60
BERGANZA, TERESA, singer
As Rosina, two AP phs: Southern.
Op v 11 n 7 cover, p 505 Jl '60
BERGEN FESTIVAL
Plans. MC v 161 n 7 p 17 Je '60
BERGER, ARTHUR VICTOR (1912-).
String Quartet 1958 (analysis by
George Perle). Mus Q v 46 n 4
p 521-2 O '60
BERGEY, CAROL, singer
German contract. ON v 24 n 19
p 3 Mr 12'60
BERGES, RUTH. Mahler and the

30

great god Pan. por MC v 161 n 1 p 10-1, 37 Ja '60

---Schumann in Vienna. il MC v 162 n 5 p 10-12 N '60

---The ideal beloved (Beethoven's views on women and marriage). ON v 24 n 15 p 8-9 F 13'60

---The making of a hero: Parsifal. il ON v 24 n 23 p 8-9 Ap 9'60

---The tragic star of Hugo Wolf. por MC v 161 n 4 p 10-2 Mr '60

BERGHOF, HERBERT, actor
And others in the Andersonville Trial, ens AP hl ph: Friedman-Abeles. Th Arts v 44 n 2 p 18 F '60

BERGLER, EDMUND. On acting and stage fright. TDR v 4 n 3 p 159-164 Mr '60

BERGMAN, G. M. La grande mode des pantomimes à Paris vers 1740 et les spectacles d'optique de Servandoni. Th R v 2 n 2 p 71-81 1960

BERGMAN, INGMAR, 1918-, director
Pechter, William S. (On Bergman films; Ansiktet in particular, The Face). TDR v 5 n 2 p 94-101 D '60

BERGMANN, ROBERT. Le jazz est-il de musique contemporaine? TD n 93 p 29-30 My '60

---Le Jazz est-il de musique contemporaine? TD n 97 p 29-30 N '60

---II. La querelle de la Modernité. TD n 94 p 28-9 Je '60

BERGONZI, CÁRLO, singer
Career notes. il ON v 24 n 22 p 15, 29 Ap 2'60

---As Gabriele Adorno AP hl ph: Melançon; por ph. ON v 24 n 22 p 17, 29 Ap 2'60

---As Manrico, AP ph: Melançon. ON v 24 n 17 p 17 F 27'60

---E Floriana Cavalli, nella Forza del destino, AP wl ph: Roma. La S n 124 p 32 Mr '60

---Por ph; also frontispiece of first edition of Verdi's Macbeth (witches). La S n 133 p 69 D '60

BERIO, LUCIANO, 1925-, composer

Notes and facsimile "Tema". La S n 127 p 9 Je '60

---Première: Allelujah II (1956-58); Donaueschingen, 1959. MR v 21 n 1 p 80 F '60

---Tempi Concertati (Paris critique). GDC n 291 p 355 D 2'60

BERIOSOVA, SVETLANA, 1932-, ballerina
Munich criticism. TD n 96 p 11 S-O '60

BERKELEY
As a California music center; notes. MC v 161 n 6 p 29 My '60

BERMEL, ALBERT. Jean Vilar: unadorned theatre for the greatest number. TDR v 5 n 2 p 24-43 D'60

BERKSHIRE MUSIC CENTER
Dumm, Robert W. The opening concerts; Saarinen's acoustic canopy. MC v 162 n 2 p 3-4 Ag '60

---Summer school survey. WM n 5 p 105 O '60

---Twentieth year; program. WM n 3 p 57 Je '60

---Monteux, Pierre, rehearsing the orchestra; Lorna Cooke de Varon rehearsing the Tanglewood Choir, two phs: Lenox, Massachusetts. WM n 5 p 108 O '60

BERLIN
The Komische Oper: La Bohéme, review; Otello, review. Op v 11 n 2 p 143-5 F '60

---Music report. MC v 161 n 3 p 46 F '60

---Repertory, a list of ballets since 1949. TD n 89 p 21 Ja '60

---Staatsoper; Kosma's The Weavers of Lyon; The Poor Konrad; "musical substance negligible as its ideological tendency is dominant". Op v 2 n 3 p 206 Mr '60

BERLIN CHAMBER ORCHESTRA
Tour of 12 countries of Asia and Africa under Hans von Benda. WM n 1 p 9 F '60

BERLIN FESTIVAL
Brunner, Gerhard. Music report. MC v 162 n 6 p 31-3 D '60

---Gibelli, Vincenzo. Le Festwochen di Berlino Ovest. il La S n 132 p 50-1 N '60

---Notes: New York Philharmonic;

(Berlin Festival)
Boris Blacher's "Rosamunde Floris"; Ballet of Two Worlds. MC v 162 n 5 p 27-8 N '60
---Reviews. E. H. MR v 21 n 4 p 328-9 N '60
---Tenth year; notes. WM n 3 p 56 Je '60
BERLIN, IRVING, 1888-, composer
Por ph. Th Arts v 44 n 9 p 57 S '60
BERLINSKI, JACQUES, 1913-, conductor
Australian debut; b. Poland.MD v 51 n 6 p 11 D '60
BERLIOZ, (Louis) HECTOR, 1803-1869, composer
Friedheim, Philip. Radical harmonic procedures in Berlioz. MR v 21 n 4 p 281-296 N '60
---Roddy, Joseph. Berlioz's Grande Messe des Morts, Munch and the Boston Symphony recording. HF v 10 n 5 p 59-60 My '60
BERMUDA
Opera outdoors; the Chautauqua Opera Company; artists. MC v 162 n 4 p 31 O '60
BERNARDINI, PIERO. Musica leggera. La S n 125 p 64 Ap '60
BERNSTEIN, LEONARD, (1918-). The Joy of Music (book reviewed by Caryl D. Friend of the Juilliard Faculty). J Rev v 7 n 1 p 22 Winter 59-60
BERNSTEIN, SEYMOUR. Audiences expect more today. por IM v 59 n 6 p 32-3 D '60
BERRI, PIETRO. Puccini e il "Mal della pietra". il La S n 128 p 16-9 Jl '60
---Testimonianze e contributi elvetici su Paganini. il La S n 123 p 13-30 F '60
BERWALD, FRANZ ADOLF, 1796-1868, composer
The Little Orchestra: Sinfonia Singuliere. MC v 162 n 6 p 17 D '60
BERYOZKA RUSSIAN DANCE COMPANY
Boulimov, Vladimir. Le Ballet

"Berezka" en Italie. il TD n 97 p 5, 10 N '60
BESANÇON
Le VIIIe Festival de Besançon; report. GDC n 283 p 95-6 O 7'60
BESOEGSTID, play
Aarhus notes; Erik Rosthall. WP v 11 n 8 p 4 Je '60
BESOYAN, RICK (1924-). Little Mary Sunshine (complete text; NYC cast; 4 pictures). Th Arts v 44 n 12 p 27-56 D '60
BESSY, CLAUDE, dancer,
And Gene Kelly, ph: Paris Opéra. TD n 96 p 25 S-O '60
---As Venus in Pas de Dieux (Gene Kelly), Paris Opéra phs. OpP n 19 1960
---In Studio 60 (Bessy), ens AP wl ph: Paris. OpP n 19 p 69 1960
BEST, MICHAEL. Philistines and festivals (the program of the Australian Festival seeming to reflect "Business Tycoons"). MD v 50 p 10-11 F '60
THE BEST MAN, play
NYC notes; Gore Vidal. WP v 11 n 9 p 6 Jl '60
---NYC review; press notes. Th Arts v 44 n 6 p 58-9 Je '60
---Vidal, Gore. (notes on writing this play.) il Th Arts v 44 n 7 p 8-9 Jl '60
---Douglas, Melvyn, Leora Dana and Lee Tracy, AP hl ph: Friedman-Abeles. Th Arts v 44 n 5 p 58 My '60
---Two scenes; conference with playwright, Gore Vidal, phs: NYC. Th Arts v 44 n 7 p 8-9 Jl '60
BESTYMT, SYLVIA, 1955-, pianist
Chamfray, Claude. Paris concert. GDC n 265-6 p 527 Mr 25'60
BETTI, UGO (1892-1953). Preface to The Mistress. TDR v 5 n 2 p 13-4 D '60
----Religion and the theatre. TDR v 5 n 2 p 3-12 D '60
---McWilliam, G. H. Interpreting Betti. TDR v 5 n 2 p 15-23 D '60
BETTIS: VALERIE, 1920-, dancer
Small AP ph: John Lindquist. Th Arts v 44 n 11 p 65 N '60
THE BIBICAL ROAD, musical drama

32

Schönberg; criticism. MR v 21 n 1 p 21-22 F '60

BIBIENA, GIUSEPPE GALLI ? (1696-1757). Scena con "volo di putti", scena con "palazzo sopra le nubi", scena probabilmente di mano di un Bibiena. La S n 132 p 26-9 N '60

BIBLE, FRANCES, singer With Di Filippi after Gioconda in Miami, ph: Pineda. ON v 24 n 21 p 26 Mr 26'60

THE BIBLE Sheean, Vincent. The Bible and opera. ON v 25 n 4 p 9-12 D 3'60

BIBLIOGRAPHY Albach, Ben. Bibliographie raisonnée du théâtre neerlandais. Th R v 2 n 2 p 88-98 1960

---Book list of recent accessions Library of the Society for theatre Research. Th Notbk v 15 n 2 p 45 Winter 60-61

---Books and records for giving music experience to children with speech limitations. MEJ v 47 n 1 p 52 S-O '60

---Chalaupka, Christl. Austrian theses on theatre research (1953-58 university theses). Th R v 2 n 1 p 37-43 1960

---Edmunds, John, and Gordon Boelzner. Some Twentieth Century American Composers. New York Public Library. 1959. (review). MR v 21 n 4 p 337-8 N '60

---Freedley, George. Theatre Arts Bookshelf (reviews and lists). Th Arts 1960

---Fry, Christopher (1907-), a bibliography books and periodicals, arranged under general and specific criticism, by Bernice Larson Schear and Eugene C. Prater. TDR v 4 n 3 p 88-98 Mr '60

---Krummel, Donald W. Quarterly book-list (music arranged by languages). Mus Q 1960

---Lesure, François. RISM: Recueils imprimés XVIe-XVIIe siècles. WM n 2 p 29 Ap '60

---Music: list of new complete editions. WM n 1 p 7 F '60

---Opera; list of books on the opera, the composer, and the period, each issue ON 1960

---Periodicals; state music education periodicals and editors, addresses (51, USA). MEJ v 47 n 1 p 80 S-O '60

---Périodiques des arts du spectacle dans le monde: France; Belgium. Th R v 2 n 1 p 60-62 1960

---Recommended articles in national periodicals, each issue. WM 1960

---Stott, R. T oole. Circus and Allied Arts, v. II, a world bibliography (book reviewed by Tristan Rémy). Th Notbk v 15 n 2 p 68-9 Winter '60-61

---The theatre of the Southern United States from the beginnings through 1865. Th R v 2 n 3 p 163-174 1960

---Theatre; section "Books and Theatre 1959-60" which includes annotations on books and phonograph records. TDR v 4 n 4 p 149-157 My '60

BIDULE, fantaisie bouffe, Paris notes; Marc Cab and Jean Valmy; music, Jack Ledru. WP v 11 n 4 p 5 F '60

BIENVENU, LILY, pianist-composer with Lydia Karine, Sylyette Milliot: Paris review. GDC n 283 p 101 O 7'60

BIGGS, E. POWER, 1906-, organist Notes on his search for old American organs with five pictures. HF v 10 n 8 p 38-9 Ag '60

---Hl ph. HF v 10 n 3 p 95 Mr '60

BIGNEN, MAX, scenic designer Vienna criticism. ON v 24 n 19 p 26 Mr '60

BILLAUD, CHRISTIANE, pianist Paris review. GDC n 293-4 p 462 D 16'60

BILLON, HENRIETTE, 1918-, singer Notes. Th Arts v 44 n 10 p 25 O '60

BILLY LIAR, play London notes; Waterhouse and Hall. WP v 12 n 3 p 36 D '60

BINDER, PETER, 1933-, singer

(Binder, Peter)
Blanche Thebom Foundation
award. MC v 161 n 3 p 53 F '60
---London press notes. AmM v 8
n 11 p 12 D '60
---Notes; b. Philadelphia. AmM
v 8 n 10 p 9 N '60
---Por ph. AmM v 8 n 10 p 7 N'60
BINET, JEAN, 1893-1960,
composer
Notes; b. Geneva. MC v 161 n 6
p 37 My '60
BING, RUDOLPH (1902-)·Thoughts
for a twenty-fifth birthday (The
Metropolitan Opera Guild). por
ON v 25 n 1 p 14-5 O 8'60
---Millstein, Gilbert. Rudolf
Bing. Th Arts v 44 n 3 p 54-6
Mr '60
---And wife, accepting honor, ens
AP wl ph: Melançon. ON v 24
n 11 p 3 Ja 16'60
---Por ph: Roger Prigent. Th Arts
v 44 n 3 p 55 Mr '60
BINKERD, GORDON, composer
Premières; a list with place of
performance, all in 1959. ACAB
v 9 n 2 p 18 1960
THE BIRD IN LA PLATA, play
Thorsen; ens AP ph: Oslo. WP
v 12 n 1 p 4 O '60
BIRKAS, LILIAN, singer
In Salome; Rome Opera review.
La S n 127 p 27, 55 Je '60
BIRMAN, JOHN
Por ph: Australia. MD v 51 n 6
p 23 D '60
BIRMMGHAM, Alabama
Graham, Alice. Metropolitan;
concerts. MC v 162 n 1 p 24 Jl '60
--- ---Music report. MC v 161
n 5 p 29 Ap '60
---Symphony; Arthur Winograd
to succeed conductor Arthur
Bennett Lipkin; plans. MC v 161
n 5 p 29 Ap '60
BIRNIE, TESSA, pianist
New Zealand-born; world tour
notes. MD v 50 n 8 p 15 F '60
BISHOP, JOHN
Director of Adelaide's first
Festival of Arts; notes. por MD
v 50 n 10 p 12-3 Ap '60
---Por ph. MD v 50 n 9 p 17 Mr'60

BITSCH, MARCEL, 1921-,
composer
Notes; Divertissement in program
of Quintette Instrumental à vent
de Paris. GDC n 281-2 p 33
S 30'60
BIVIANO, JOE, accordionist
AP ph. IM v 59 n 1 p 15 Jl '60
BIZET, GEORGES 1838-1875,
composer
Klein, John W. Nietzsche's atti-
tude to Bizet. MR v 21 n 3 p 215-
225 Ag '60
BJELINSKI, BRUNO, composer
Première: Mediterranean Sym-
phony; at Zagreb. WM n 2 p 32
Ap '60
BJÖRLING, JUSSI, 1911-1960,
singer
Covent Garden in La Bohème;
criticism. Op v 11 n 5 p 363 My'60
---Death; Johan Jonato; Siar, Swe-
den. MD v 51 n 5 p 8 N '60
---Heart attack, March 15, at the
Metropolitan. ON v 24 n 24 p 3
Ap 16'60
---London comments; "the aristo-
crat of tenors". MC v 161 n 5 p 31
Ap '60
---Obituary. Op v 11 n 11 p 743-746
N '60
---Obituary; b. Sweden. por MC
v 162 n 4 p 20 O '60
---Recordings left at his death, un-
released. por HF v 10 n 11 p 71
N '60
---Schang, F. C. (Obituary.) ON
v 25 n 3 p 22 N 19'60
---As des Grieux, AP hl ph. Th Arts
v 44 n 3 p 49 Mr '60
---Por ph: Bruno. Op v 2 n 3 p 195
Mr '60
---Por ph and 6 AP phs. Op v 11 n 11
p 742-5 N '60
---Small por ph. HF v 10 n 10 p 67
O '60
---With his dog at his summer cot-
tage near Stockholm, page-size
ph: Roester I Radio. ON v 25 n 3 p 23
N 19'60
BLACHER, BORIS, 1903-, composer
Perle, George. (Criticism of Re-
quiem.) Mus Q v 46 n 4 p 525 O'60
THE BLACK SHIPS, opera

Osaka Festival revival; Koscak Yamada, composer. ON v 25 n 2 p 7 O 29'60

---Première; Osaka Festival; music by Koszak Yamada. MC v 162 n 1 p 33 Jl '60

BLACKWOOD, EASLEY, 1933-, composer
Career notes; b. Indiana. AmM v 8 n 10 p 16-7 N '60

---Lowens, Irving. (career notes; criticism of Washington première of Blackwood's String Quartet No. 2, op 6). Mus Q v 46 n 2 p 265-270 Ap '60

---Por ph. AmM v 8 n 10 p 18 N '60

BLAFFEN TEGEN DE MAAN, play
Arnheim notes; Dimitri Frenkel Frank. WP v 11 n 10 p 10 Ag '60

BLAISE, vaudeville
Paris; Claude Magnier. WP v 11 n 3 p 8 Ja '60

BLANCHART, PAUL (1897-) Le Théâtre des Nations et la recherche dramatique et scénique. il Th R v 2 n 1 p 16-25 1960

BLANKENBURG, HEINZ, singer
Notes; b. NYC. AmM v 8 n 8 p 5 S '60

BLANKENHEIM, TONI
And Pilarezyk in Lulu, AP hl ph: Peyer. ON v 24 n 18 p 2 Mr 5'60

BLAU, HERBERT. "Meanwhile, Follow the Bright Angels" (European stages seen by a California director) TDR v 5 n 1 p 89-101 S '60

BLIGH, N. M. Mirror curtains. il Th Notbk v 15 n 2 p 56 Winter '60-61

BLIN, ROGER, director
Paris notes. TDR v 5 n 1 p 91 S '60

BLIND MAN'S BUFF, play
Stratford, Canada; Alfred Euringer. WP v 12 n 1 p 3 O '60

BLITZSTEIN, MARC (1905-). Out of the cradle (the composer's story of producing "The Cradle Will Rock"). por ON v 24 n 15 p 10-11, 29 F 13'60

---Commission for opera on Sacco and Vanzetti. ON v 24 n 21 p 3 Mr 26'60

---Regina, opera; criticism of Columbia recording. CMJ v 4 n 2 p 49 Winter '60

BLOCH, ANDRE, 1873-1960, composer
Chamfray, Louis. Fiche biographique. GDC n 281-2 p 77 S 30'60

---Notes; b. Wissembourg, GDC n 283 p 94 O 7'60

BLOCH, ERNEST, 1880-1959, composer
Hart, Philip. The lapidary of Agate Beach: Ernest Bloch. por HF v 10 n 5 p 44-7 My '60

---Semini, C. F. Omaggio a Bloch. il La S n 122 p 50-4 Ja '60

BLOCH, JOSEPH (1880-). Westward to the East (tour notes and pictures). J Rev v 7 n 3 p 8-10 Fall '60

---In Japan, several phs. J Rev v 7 n 3 p 8-10 Fall '60

BLOMFIELD, GRAHAM, 1936-, composer
Notes; b. New Zealand. MD v 50 n 10 p 20 Ap '60

THE BLOOD OF GOD, play
Sastre's criticism. TDR v 5 n 2 p 125 D '60

BLOOD WEDDING, opera
Cologne review of Wolfgang Fortner work. Op v 11 n 8 p 557 Ag'60

BLOOMGARDEN, KERMIT, 1905-, producer
Hl ph: Friedman-Abeles. Th Arts v 44 n 10 p 15 O '60

BLUM, DANIEL (1900-). New faces become old favorites (1930s in US). Th Arts v 44 n 9 p 58-9 S '60

BLUTHOCHZEIT, opera
Fortner; ens AP wl ph: Dönitz, 1957. WT v 9 n 3 p 223 Autumn '60

BOBZIEN, KARL, flutist
With Margarethe Scharitzer; Paris review. GDC n 263-4 p 487 Mr 11'60

BODONI, GIOVAN BATTISTA, 1740-1813, court typographer
Notes on his volume, released after the Italian visit of Gustave III; Parma notes; Verdi's interest ar-

(Bodoni, Giovan Battista)
aroused. Ver v 1 n 2 p 1092-4
Ag '60
BOEHM, KARL, 1894-, conductor
At the Metropolitan; Wagner
success. MC v 161 n 3 p 23
F '60
BOELLMANN, LEON, 1862-
1897, composer
Chamfray, Claude. Fiche
biographique. GDC n 263-4
p 495-6 Mr 11'60
BOEPPLE, PAUL, choral
director
Left profile por ph: NYC. MC
v 161 n 1 p 36 Ja '60
---Left profile por ph: NYC.
MC v 161 n 7 p 24 Je '60
LA BOHÈME, opera
American première of Leon-
cavallo's work; NYC notes. ON
v 24 n 17 p 27 F 27'60
---Metropolitan; NYC review.
MC v 162 n 6 p 14 D '60
---Ens AP wl ph: Trieste. La S
n 122 p 38 Ja '60
---Komische Oper, the Café
Momus, ens AP wl ph: Simon.
Op v 11 n 2 p 143 F '60
---Panna e Poggi, AP hl ph:
Como. La S n 125 p 50 Ap '60
BOHLE, BRUCE. (NYC plays a
a report). Th Arts v 44 n 4
p 59-61 Ap '60
--- ---The openings (NYC's
critical box score and summary).
il Th Arts v 44 n 7 p 58-9 Jl'60
---same. Th Arts v 44 n 5 p 57-
8 My '60
--- ---Reviews: The Best Man;
Duel of Angels; Bye Bye Birdie;
A Second String; Viva Madison
Avenue and other NYC plays.
Th Arts v 44 n 6 p 58-9 Je '60
BOHM, KARL, 1894-, conductor
Criticism of his Dresden Opera
days. portfolio Op v 11 n 5
p 324-330 My '60
---Downes, Edward. Karl Bohm
the Met's specialist. HF v 10
n 3 p 54-5 Mr '60
---Por ph. HF v 10 n 3 p 54
Mr '60
---Por ph; and 14 pictures of

his Dresden Opera period. Op
v 11 n 5 p 324-330 My '60
BOHME, KURT, singer
Munich; as Osmin, AP hl ph:
Toepfer. Op v 11 n 10 p 701 O'60
BOITO, ARRIGO, 1842-1918,
librettist
Por ph. La Scala n 122 p 21
Ja '60
BOIZARD, GILLES, composer
Cantique du Printemps; remise
solennelle des Prix de Rome. GDC
n 291 p 354 D 2'60
BOKHARI, Z. A. (1904-) The com-
poser in Pakistan faces new pro-
blems. WM n 1 p 4-5 F '60
BOLET, JORGE, 1914-, pianist
At Piano recording for film,
Song Without End (Liszt), ens hl
ph: Christie. AmM v 8 n 3 p 7
Mr '60
BOLL, ANDRE (1896-). Othello,
review of Lifar's Le Maure de
Venise.) TD n 95 p 14, 18
Jl-Ag '60
---And Jacques Charon; La Locan-
diera, hl ph: Paris. OpP n 19
p 57 1960
BOLOGNA
Music report. La S n 123 p 67
F '60
BOLSHOI THEATRE
Décor 1891, Un Ballo in Masch-
era, opera, six settings (I. Ku-
kànov, F. Sceniàn, P. Issanov),
phs. Ver v 1 n 2 Ag '60
BOLT, ROBERT, 1924-,
playwright
Critical notes. WT v 9 n 3 p 292
Autumn '60
BONDEVILLE, EMMANUEL, 1898-,
composer
Dumesnil, René. L'Academie des
Beaux Arts elit Emmanuel Bond-
eville. por La S n 125 p 32-3
Ap '60
BONDON, JACQUES, composer
Paris; Théâtre National Popu-
laire, 12-tone compostion on the
planet Jupiter from science fic-
tion "La Cupole". MC v 161 n 5
p 32 Ap '60
---Première: La Coupole (critique).
GDC n 259-60 p 410 F 12'60

BONE, AUDREY EVELYN. Chopin in Britain. il MD v 50 n 11 p 12-3 My '60

BONNAT, YVES (1912-). The lighting of open-air performances. il WT v 9 n 2 p 149-157 Summer '60

BONSTELLE, JESSIE, 1870?-1932 Detroit theatre notes. Th Arts v 44 n 10 p 78 O '60

BOOKS

Abbiati, Franco. (Biography of Giuseppe Verdi discussed by Gino Roncaglia.) il LaS n 126 p 18-22 My '60

---Atlas de la Musique par Paul Corraer et Albert Vauder Linden (reviewed by Raymond Lyon). GDC n 293-4 p 446 D 16'60

---Baker's Biographical Dictionary of Musicians, revised by Nicolas Slonimsky. ON v 24 n 24 p 22 Ap 16'60

---Beecham, Sir Thomas. Frederick Delius (book reviewed). MR v 21 n 2 p 151-154 My '60

---Bentley, Eric. Two books Brecht. TDR v 4 n 4 p 105-112 My '60

---Burk, John N. Mozart and His Music (reviewed by Ann M. Lingg). ON v 24 n 20 p 30 Mr 19'60

---Della Corte, A. Alban Berg, Versuch einer Würdigung; Colloque International tenu à Wégimont, 1955; L'Organo, rivista di cultura organaria e organistica. La S n 131 p 36-7 O '60

--- ---(Forschungsbeiträge zur Musikwissenschaft; Horst Scharschuh.) La S n 132 p 53 N '60

--- ---In questo mese ha lette. La S 1960 or n 123 p 46-7 F'60

--- ---The language of music, Londra, Oxford University Press; Musick's Monument di Thomas Mace, Parigi; Im Konzertsaal Karikiert, München. La S n 128 p 34-5 Jl '60

--- ---The Sonata in the baroque Era, University of N. C. Press. LaS n 127 p 32-3 Je'60

---Dialects; Lewis Herman's Foreign Dialects, a Manual for Actors, Directors and Writers; note. PlM v 37 n 1 p 4 O '60

---A Dictionary of English Costume, 900-1900 by C. W. and P. E. Cunnington and Charles Beard (book review by Hal Burton) Th Notbk v 14 n 4 p 137-8 Summer '60

---Duval, J. H. Svengali's Secrets and Memoirs of the Golden Age, reviewed by Max de Schauensee. ON v 24 n 14 p 23 F 6'60

---Ernest, Earle. Three Japanese plays from the Traditional Theatre (reviewed by Shigetoshi Kawatake). Th R v 2 n 3 p 177-8 1960

---Fergusson, Francis. On Gerald F. Else's "Aristotle's Poetics: The Argument". TDR v 4 n 4 p 23-32 My '60

---Freedley, George. Theatre Arts Bookshelf (column of reviews followed by a list of theatre books briefly annotated). Th Arts 1960

---Fuchs, George. Revolution in the Theatre, condensed by Constance Connor Kuhn (book review by Norman Marshall). Th Notbk v 14 n 3 p 106 Spring '60

---Hartnoll, Phyllis. Theatre arts bookshelf. Th Arts v 44 n 1 p 87-8 Ja '60

---Hewitt, Barnard, editor. The Renaissance Stage, Documents of Serlio, Sabbattini and Furttenbach (reviewed by Richard Southern). Th Notbk v 14 n 3 p 102-4 Spring '60

---Hucher, Yves. L'Oeuvre de Florent Schmitt (review by Raymond Lyon). GDC n 293-4 p 446 D 16'60

---An International Vocabulary of Technical Terms, edited by Kenneth Rae and Richard Southern (book review by Norman Marshall. Th Notbk v 14 n 4 p 133-5 Summer'60

---Kerman's Opera as Drama; Spike Hughes' The Toscanini Legacy and other reviews. CMJ v 4 n 2 p 73-80 Winter '60

---Kindermann, Heinz. Theatregeschichte Europas, Band II: Renaissance; Band III: Barockzeit

37

(Books)

(reviewed by W. H. Bruford). Th
R v 2 n 3 p 175-7 1960

---Krummel, Donald W. Quarterly
book-list (music books, arranged in language groups). Mus Q
1960

---LaRue, Jan. Ars Nova and the
Renaissance by Hughes and Abraham (a book review of volume
three, New Oxford History of
Music). J Rev v 7 n 3 p 23 Fall
'60

---Leathers, Victor. British Enter-
tainers in France (book review
by I. K. F.). Th Notbk v 14 n 4
p 139 Summer'60

---Lorin, Michel. Three reviews:
Paul Pitton's La Musique et son
Histoire;Marguerite Long's Au
piano avec Claude Debussy;Pail-
lard's La Musique français classique. GCD n 278 p 841-2 Je 24
'60

---Lyon, Raymond. A review of
Claude Rostand's study of Liszt.
GDC n 285 p 169 O 21'60

--- ---Review of Wagner and Louis
II de Bavière-GDC n 281-2 p 69
S 30'60

--- ---(Reviewing Antoine Goléa's
La Musique dans la Société Eu-
ropénne.)GDC n 295 p 500 D 30
'60

---Malignon, Jean. Rameau (review).
GDC n 292 p 428 D 9'60

---Mouravieff, Larissa. Traite de
danse classique (critique). TD
n 97 p 23 N'60

---Music;brief, pointed reviews of
material both generally cultural
and specifically for teachers.
MEJ v 47 n 2 p 94-5 N-D'60

--- ---Frederick Werlé reviewing
books. MC v 161 n 3 p 54 F'60

--- ---signed reviews in regular
section, The Bookshelf. J Rev'60

---Nagler, A. M. Shakespeare's
Stage (reviewed by Walter Hod-
ges). Th Notbk v 14 n 3 p 104-5
Spring'60

---Opera and music books reviewed
by the Editor and others. Op '60

---Pincherle, Marc. An illustrated

history of music (review). ON v 24
n 16 p 22 F 20'60

---Priestley, J. B. The Story of the
Theatre (book review by Richard
Leacroft). Th Notbk v 14 n 3 p 108
Spring'60

---Puccianti, Anna, on Antonio Stradivari, Cremona 1959;reviewed by
Maria Pampanaro Cardini. il LaS
n 125 p 35-8 Ap'60

---Puccini by Mosco Carner (review). ON v 24 n 24 p 22 Ap 16'60

---Recent books on Shakespeare,
notes on five (Barber, Kökeritz, Lev-
in, Nagler, essays). Th R v 2 n 2
p 115-6 1960

---Regular column of reviews:books
on music, criticism, education,
people, arts. HF 1960

---Reviews:Famous Puccini Operas
by Spike Hughes;Instrumental Music by David G. Hughes;Leonhard-
House, The Foundations and Prin-
ciples of Music Education, and
others. MR v 21 n 3 p 250-7 Ag'60

---Reviews, signed, each issue. Op'60

---Roche, Maurice. Monteverdi (review by Raymond Lyon). GDC n 284
p 136 O 14'60

---Rostand, Claude. La musique Al-
lemande (reviewed by Raymond
Lyon). GDC n 288 p 264 N 11'60

---Rousselot, Léone. Le Chant, "acte
réflexe" (review by Raymond Lyon).
GDC n 287 p 236 N 4'60

---Rubbra, Edmund. Counterpoint
(reviewed). MR v 21 n 2 p 148-150
My'60

---Samuel, Claude. Prokofiev (review
by Lyon). GDC n 286 p 203 O 28'60

---Scholarly reviews of music criticism, of biography, of scores and
records. MR 1958-60

---Steichen, Dana. Beethoven's Beloved (book review by David Hall).
J Rev v 7 n 1 p 24 Winter 59-60

--- ---Beethoven's Beloved (Count-
ess Marie von Erdödy), reviewed by
Fred Grumfeld. ON v 24 n 15 p 26
F 13'60

---Stevens, Risë in a biography by
Kyle Crichton, "Subway to the Met",
reviewed by Gustl Breuer. ON v 24
n 14 p 22 F 6'60

38

---Stravinsky and Robert Craft in "Platonic-dialogue technique"; criticism of Stravinsky at work. ON v 24 n 11 p 30 Ja 16'60

---Střĺbný, Adeněk. Les pièces historiques de Shakespeare(reviewed by Jaroslav Polorný). Th R v 2 n 2 p 113-5 1960

---Suck, Friedrich. Memorial editions (music). WM n 3 p 52-3 Je '60

---Supitchitch, Ivo. La musique expressive. vol. I Presses Universitaires de France (review by Raymond Lyon). GDC n 289 p 293 N 18'60

---Theatre and kindred subjects including reference material for teachers; reviews PlM 1960

---Theatre books, signed reviews, each issue. NTM 1960

---Vita di Emilio Nicola von Reznicek, Gegen den Strom (Zurigo); review.LaS n 129-30 p 45 Ag-S'60

---Wickham, Glynne. Early English stages, 1300 to 1660. vol. I. 1300-1576 (reviewed by Pierre Sadron). Th R v 2 n 2 p 109- 112 1960

---Worsthorne, Simon Towneley. Venetian opera in the Seventeenth Century (book reviewed by J. Isaacs). Th R v 2 n 1 p 44-6 1960

---Zillig, Winifried. Variationen Ueber Neue Musik (book review by Everett Helm). Mus Q v 46 n 3 p 381-3 Jl '60

BOOTH, SHIRLEY, 1907-, actress
And Sidney Blackmer, AP wl ph: Vandamm. Th Arts v 44 n 2 p 13 F '60

BORDEAUX
Bertin, Audré. La Jiive; Lakmé (reviews). GDC n 255-6 p 306 Ja 15'60

---Festival (XIe) de Bordeaux; Les Amants Captifs de Pierre Capdevielle; Stéphane Wolff critique. GDC n 275 p 749 Je 3'60

BORG, KIM. Interview on his career. por ON v 24 n 12 p 14 Ja 23'60

---As the Count in Figaro, AP

hl ph: Melançon. ON v 24 n 12 p 17 Ja 23'60

BORGE, VICTOR, 1909-, pianist
Notes. Th Arts v 44 n 10 p 24 O'60

---At piano, AP ph. Th Arts v 44 n 10 p 24 O '60

BORGIOLI, DINO, 1891-1960, singer
Tributes; Erik Aitken, Ivor Newton and the Editor. Op v 11 p 747-750 N '60

---Por ph and as Alfredo in La Traviata, AP hl ph. Op v 11 n 11 p 747, 749 N '60

BORI, LUCREZIA, 1889-1960, singer
Contents of her will. MC v 162 n 1 p 10 Jl '60

---Grazzini, Jennie. Letter (the funeral of Lucrezia Bori in Valencia). il ON v 25 n 7 p 6 D 24'60

---Obituary. Op v 11 n 7 p 497 Jl '60

---Obituary; b. Valencia. MC v 161 n 7 p 10 Je '60

---Schauensee, Max de. (Obituary.) il ON v 25 n 1 p 26-7 O 8'60

--- ---(Review of record by International Record Collectors Club.) ON v 25 n 8 p 32 D 31'60

---Valencia; funeral procession leaving the cathedral, ph: J. Cabrelles Sigüenza. ON v 25 n 7 p 6 D 24'60

---As Cio-Cio-San, AP wl ph. ON v 25 n 1 p 27 O 8'60

---As Goose Girl in Königskinder, AP wl ph. Op v 11 n 7 p 496 Jl'60

---Coaching La Rondine, her last role, with Licia Albanese, ph. ON v 24 n 14 p 3 F 6'60

---With Botta in Mascagni's Iris, AP wl ph: White. ON v 24 n 13 p 5 Ja 30'60

BORIS GODUNOV, opera
Athens; Andreas Paridis directing, décor J. Stefanellis; a success; cast. Op v 11 n 7 p 485 Jl'60

---La Scala; Nicolai Ghiaurov e Renato Ercolani; Gloria Lane nel Dimiter Usunof; two AP hl phs. La S n 125 p 43 Ap '60

---Metropolitan; NYC review.

(Boris Godunov)
MC v 162 n 6 p 14 D '60
---Athens, ens AP wl ph. Op v 11
n 7 p 485 Jl '60
---Frankfurt; coronation scene,
ens AP wl ph: Englert. Op v 11
n 10 p 693 O '60
BORODIN, ALEXANDER, 1833-
1887, composer
Lloyd-Jones, David. Borodin in
Heidelberg. il Mus Q v 46 n 4
p 500-508 O '60
---With other Russian chemists,
ens ph: Heidelberg, 1860; also
page from his Scherzo in E for
piano duet, facsimile. Mus Q
v 46 n 4 p 500-1 O '60
BOROVANSKY, EDWARD, 1902-
1959, director
Career notes; b. Czechoslovakia.
MD v 50 n 7 p 32 Ja '60
---Page-size por ph. MD v 50 n 7
p 26 Ja '60
THE BOROVANSKY BALLET
(Van Praagh)
Hutton, Geoffrey W. (Giselle in
in Melbourne; Kathleen Gorham,
Robert Pamie and as Queen of
the Wilis, Marilyn Jones; review.)
MD v 51 n 6 p 22 D '60
--- ---Melbourne review; Coppelia.
MD v 51 n 5 p 22 N '60
---Repertory notes. MD v 51 n 2
p 24 Ag '60
---Sydney; "Journey to the Moon"
(Grinwis); review. MD v 50 n 7
p 27 Ja '60
---Sydney criticism. MD v 50 n 10
p 26 Ap '60
---Tour notes; repertory. MD
v 51 n 1 p 27 Jl '60
---Van Praag, Peggy, Artistic
Director; Edward Borovansky,
founder, death December 1959.
MD v 50 n 7 p 27 Ja '60
---same. MD v 50 n 9 p 26 Mr '60
BORTNYANSKY, J. K., 1751-
1825, composer
Seaman, Gerald. D. S. Bortny-
ansky (1751-1825). MR v 21 n 2
p 106-113 My '60
BORUSIAK, MARCEL, composer
Divonne winner: 300, 000 francs
with 6 months at the hotel to

compose "Canto pour 12 instru-
ments" for the Festival. GDC
n 281-2 p 66 S 30'60
BOSCHI, HELENE, pianist
And Germaine Mounier; Paris re-
view. GDC n 276 p 786 Je 10'60
BOSQUET, GUY
As David in fight with Goliath, ens
AP wl ph. OpP n 19 p 18 1960
BOSTON
Dumm, Robert W. Boston music
reports. MC 1960
---Norton, Elliot. Theatre USA:
Th Arts v 44 n 5 p 53-6 My '60
---Opera report. Op v 11 n 9 p 614
S '60
---Strasfogel, Ian. Opera report.
ON v 24 n 18 p 26 Mr 5'60
BOSTON CONSERVATORY
Report. MC v 161 n 4 p 43 Mr'60
BOSTON OPERA GROUP
Caldwell, Sarah, director; tour-
ing Offenbach's Voyage To the
Moon. ON v 24 n 18 p 2 Mr 5'60
---Opera Group, Inc. under Sarah
Caldwell; notes. Op v 11 n 8 p 545
Ag '60
BOSTON SYMPHONY ORCHESTRA
Australia; notes on tour. MD v 50
n 9 p 9 Mr '60
---Critical reviews. MC 1960
---Darrell, R. D. The jauntiest
maestro: Fiedler of the Pops (the
Boston Symphony without a dozen
first-desk men). il HF v 10 n 5
p 38-40 My '60
---Dumm, Robert W. (Report.) MC
v 161 n 7 p 34 Je '60
---Eight-week tour of the Far East;
itinerary. AmM v 8 n 4 p 16 Ap'60;
same. MC v 161 n 6 p 7 My '60;
same. WM n 1 p 9 F '60
---Japan; news report of 30 day tour.
MC v 162 n 1 p 11 Jl '60
---NYC; two reviews. MC v 161 n 3
p 25 F '60
--- ---William Steinberg; Munch with
cellist, Piatigorsky. MC v 161 n 4
p 15, 18 Mr '60
---Third tour abroad under US gov-
ernment; Aaron Copland to aid
Munch and Burgin. AmM v 8 n 2
F '60
---With Ruggiero Ricci, violinist;

relayed directly from Boston via the transatlantic telephone cable to BBC Home Service. Am M v 8 n 1 p 9 Ja'60

BOSTON UNIVERSITY
Music report. MC v 161 n 3 p 52 F'60

BOSWORTH, ARTHUR FERDI-NAND, ?-1959, impresario
Career notes. por MD v 51 n 1 p 23 Jl'60
---Por ph:London. MD v 51 n 1 p 23 Jl'60

BOTIAUX, GUSTAVE, singer
Notes. GDC n 259-60 p 375 F 12 '60
---Por ph:André Gardé. GDC n 259 cover F 12'60

LE BOUFFON AMOUREUX
Marseille;Claire Sombert et Michel Bruel, AP wl ph:Lido. TD n 91 p 9 Mr'60

BOULANGER, LILI, 1893-1918, composer
Chamfray, Claude. Fiche biographique. GDC n 291 p 368 D 2'60
---Paris;Clairières dans le Ciel played by sister, Nadia Boulanger. GDC n 281-2 p 33 S 30'60

BOULEZ, PIERRE, 1926-, composer
Ambesi, Alberto Cesare. Compositori di Punta. LaS n 129-30 p 28-30 Ag-S'60
---Donaueschingen 1959;Hans Keller reporting. MR v 21 n 1 p 79 F'60
---Golea, Antoine. Rencontres avec Pierre Boulez (review by Pierre Saucier). CMJ v 4 n 3 p 85 Spring '60
---New York Philharmonic:"Improvisation sur Mallarmé I"; review. MC v 161 n 6 p 17 My'60
---Notes. HF v 10 n 4 p 11 Ap'60

BOULT, SIR ADRIAN, 1889-, conductor
Hallé Orchestra;Beethoven's Missa Solemnis with quartet (Monson, Joyce, Galliver and Standen). MR v 21 n 3 p 245 Ag'60

BOURGAULT-DUCOUDRAY, LOUIS ALBERT, 1840-1910, composer
Chamfray, Claude. Fiche biogra-phique. GDC n 293-4 p 472 D 16'60

BOURGEAT, MARCELLE. Les connaissances et les pré-occupations d'un professeur de danse. TD n 94 p 23-4 Je'60

LE BOURGEOIS GENTILHOMME, play
Falk, Eugene H. Molière the indignant satirist. TDR v 5 n 1 p 73-88 S'60

LE BOURGEOIS GENTILHOMME, opera
Gambetta, Rosario. La Scala review. GDC n 274 p 719 My 27'60
---La Scala;Marie Sabouret, AP wl ph;ens ph. LaS n 126 p 31 My'60

BOURMEISTER, VLADIMIR
Informal wl ph:Paris Opéra-OpP n 19 p 46 1960

BOURNAY, JEAN de. La musique enregistrée, serie. TD 1960

BOURRÉE FANTASQUE(BALAN-CHINE), ballet
London Festival Ballet, staged by Una Kai;notes. Am M v 8 n 7 p 6 Ag'60

BOUSLOFF, KIRA, director
West Australian Ballet;dancers, repertory 1960 in Perth. MD v 51 n 1 p 28-9 Jl'60

BOWEN, KENNETH, 1933-, singer
Winner in Liverpool contest. Op v 11 n 7 p 456 Jl'60

BOWMER, ANGUS L. , director
US tour;notes. PlM v 36 n 7 p 149 Ap'60

A BOY WAS BORN
Britten première at Dartington; notes. MR v 21 n 1 p 82 F'60

BOYCE, WILLIAM, 1710-1779, composer
Sadie, Stanley. The chamber music of Boyce and Arne. Mus Q v 46 n 4 p 425-436 O'60

BOYDEN, DAVID D. (1910-). The missing Italian manuscript of Tartini's Traite des Agremens. Mus Q v 46 n 3 p 315-328 Jl'60

BOZZA, EUGENE. Le Chant de la Mine (études musicales analytiques). GDC n 257-8 p 365 Ja 29'60

BRAGAGLIA, ANTON GIULIO, 1890-1960, director
Giovaninetti, Silvio. (Obituary.)

41

(Bragaglia)
La S n 129-30 p 31 Ag-S '30
BRAGGIOTTI, MARIO, 1905-,
  composer
At piano playing his score for
The Princess to Jo Anna the cho-
reographer, and Roger Furse,
the designer, ens ph: London.
AmM v 8 n 7 p 7 Ag '60
BRAHMS, JOHANNES, 1833-1897,
  composer
Goldsmith, Harris. Kreisler re-
issued, Szigeti anew, review of
Brahms Violin Concerto by Angel,
by Mercury. HF v 10 n 3 p 60-1
Mr '60
---Por ph. HF v 10 n 2 p 58 F '60
BRAILOWSKY, ALEXANDRE,
  1896-, pianist
Bruyr, José. Integrale de Chopin.
GDC n 265-6 p 525 Mr 25'60
---Paris; VIe Concert Chopin.
GDC n 271 p 627 My 5'60
--- ---reviews. GDC n 267-8
p 556, 560 Ap 8'60
BRAMIERE, GINO
Frattini, Angelo. Lettere aperto
a Joséphine Baker e a Gino Bram-
ieri. por La S n 132 p 70-1 N'60
---Laughing ph. La S n 132 p 71
N '60
BRAND, play
Ibsen, 1928, Georges Pitoëff,
AP wl ph. Spec n 1 p 34 1960
BRANT, HENRY DREFUSS, 1913-,
  composer
New York Philharmonic: "Anti-
phony One"; orchestra in 5 parts
of the hall; review. MC v 161 n 6
p 17 My '60
---Premières: Atlantis (Pough-
keepsie 1960); The Fire Garden
(NYC 1960). ACAB v 9 n 3 p 27
1960
LE BRAVE SOLDAT SWEIK, play
de Lewis Allan d'après Jaroslav
Hasek, ens ph: Berlin-Est. WP
v 11 n 5 p 1 Mr '60
BRAZIL
Kovacs, Roberto. Rio de Janerio;
opera. ON v 25 n 5 p 30 D 10'60
---Obry, Olga. (Theatre report.)
il WT v 9 n 4 p 352-4 Winter '60
---Opera notes. Op v 11 n 7 p 476

Jl '60
---Opera repertory 1960. Op v 11
n 5 p 344 My '60
---Philadelphia, St. Monica's
Church, under Anselmo Inforzato:
rediscovered church music of
Brazilian composers 200 years ago.
MC v 161 n 6 p 26 My '60
---Sao Paolo; opera notes. Op v 11
n 11 p 762 N '60
---Symphony orchestra forming for
Brasilia. MC v 162 n 4 p 30 O'60
---Richards, Stanley. Theatre in
Brazil (the theatre school under
Martim Goncalves at University
of Bahia, as well as notes on São
Paulo and Rio). PlM v 37 n 3 p
p 57-8 D '60
---Theatre report. WP v 11 n 6 p 1
Ap '60
---Scene from A Raposa e as Uvas,
ens ph: Carlos. WT v 9 n 3 p 270
Autumn '60
BRECHT, BERTOLT, 1898-1956,
  playwright
Baxandall, Lee. Bertolt Brecht's
J. B. (Das Badener Lehrstück
vom Einverständnis, as trans-
lated by Baxandall, with notes).
TDR v 4 n 4 p 113-133 My '60
---Bentley, Eric. (On Willett's
The Theatre of Bertolt Brecht;
and Esslin's Brecht.) TRD v 4
n 4 p 105-112 My '60
---Esslin, Martin, The Theatre of
the absurd. TRD v 4 n 4 p 3-15
My '60
---Karsch, Walter. German drama
today. WT v 9 n 3 p 203-12
Autumn '60
---Paris review; La Résistible
Ascension d'Arturo Ui. GDC
n 290 p 323 N 25'60
---Scene from Die heilige Johanna
der Schlachthöfe; from Die Ges-
chichte der Simone Machard, ens
AP wl phs: Germany. WT v 9 n 3
p 203-4 Autumn '60
BREGENZ
Riemens, Leo. Opera reviews:
Wiener Blut; Der Barbier von
Bagdad. il Op v 11 p 73-6
Autumn '60
BREL, JACQUES, singer

Notes on Belgian chansonnier; Columbia recording. por HF v 10 n 12 p 87 D '60

DE BREMER STADSMUZIKANTEN (Rebel), ballet
Amsterdam notes. WP v 11 n 4 p 11 F '60

BRENNAN, EILEEN, actress
In Little Mary Sunshine (Harrison), AP wl ph: Friedman-Abeles. Th Arts v 44 n 12 p 29 D'60; same. Th Arts v 44 n 9 p 67 S'60

BRENNAN, WALTER, pianist
Paris review. GDC n 259-60 p 408 F 12'60

BRENNECKE, WILFRIED, Chopin and Polish Music; impressions of a visit to Warsaw. WM n 2 p 26-28 Ap '60

BRENTA, GASTON
Bruyr, José. Gaston Brenta, "Musicien belge" (critique). GDC n 290 p 329 N 25'60

BREUER, ROBERT. The court jester. ON v 24 n 12 p 8, 31 Ja 23'60

BRIEN, ALAN. London, a city in a state of flux. il Th Arts v 44 n 4 p 14-6 Ap '60

BRIENHOLT, VERNA, and Irene Schoepfle. Music experience for the child with speech limitations. MEJ v 47 n 1 p 45-6, 48, 50 S-O '60

LE BRIGAND, play
Budapest notes; Moricz and Thurzo. WP v 11 n 5 p 12 Mr'60

BRITISH BROADCASTING COMPANY
Glock, William, new music director; details of programs. WM n 1 p 10 F'60

BRITTEN, BENJAMIN, 1913-, composer
Brown, David. Britten's three canticles. MR v 21 n 1 p 55-65 F'60
---Première: Cantata Accademica-Carmen Basiliense; Basle note. MC v 162 n 5 p 25 N'60
---Première of opera, A Midsummer Night's Dream, at Aldeburgh Festival: review. MC v 162 n 2 p 22 Ag'60

---Conducting, small ph. HF v 10 n 3 p 59 Mr'60
---Portfolio of six pictures including a portrait, phs: Aldeburgh, England. WM n 5 cover, p 107 O'60
- ---With James Pease, Sir David Webster, Claire Watson, backstage at "Peter Grimes", ph. AmM v 8 n 11 p 9 D '60
---With singers, rehearsal of Britten's A Midsummer Night's Drean, opera, ens hl ph; Allegro. Op v 11 n 12 p 797 D '60

BRITTON, DONALD, music teacher
Melbourne notes. MD v 50 n 11 p 18 My '60

BROADCAST MUSIC, INC.
Seventh annual "Concert Music, USA"; statistics, and survey. 1959 AmM v 8 n 6 p 7 Jl '60
---Survey on modern music, US and Canada; report. WM n 5 p 104 O '60

BROADWAY CHAPEL PLAYERS
The Bible Salesman by Jay Thompson in folk idiom, Negro boy. ON v 24 n 23 p 28 Ap 9'60

BROADWAY GRAND OPERA ASSOCIATION
Il Trovatore cast. ON v 24 n 21 p 3 Mr 26'60

BROCKETT, O. G. The theatre of the Southern United States from the beginnings through 1865: a bibliographical essay. Th R v 2 n 3 p 163-174 1960

BRODIE, PAUL, saxophonist
NYC review. MC v 162 n 6 p 43 D '60

BRONSON, HOWARD C., 1889-1960
Obituary notes. MEJ v 46 n 4 p 14 F-Mr '60

BRONSTEIN, ROBERT, conductor
Chamfray, Claude. Orchestre Philharmonique de la R. T. F. et Choeurs de l'Universitaire de Paris. GDC n 292 p 423 D 9'60

BROOK, PETER (1925-). Extrait d'une interview donnée. par Peter Brook au journal "L'Express" de Paris; théâtre contemporain.) WP v 12 n 1 p 4 O '60

BROOKE, MRS. FRANCIS, 1723-1789, critic

43

(Brooke)
Needham, Gwendolyn B . Mrs.
Francis Brooke: dramatic critic
Th Notbk v 15 n 2 p 47-52
Winter 60-61
BROOKING, JACK (1927?). The
declamatory theatre of France;
Part I. PlM v 37 n 2 p 31 N'60
--- ---Part II. PlM v 37 n 3 p 56
D '60
--- ---The motley theatre of It-
aly; Part II. PlM v 37 n 1 p 8-9
O '60
BROOKLYN OPERA COMPANY
La Bohème, fourth production;
review. MC v 162 n 2 p 25 Ag'60
---Notes; Janice Matisse in Car-
men. ON v 25 n 5 p 30 D 10'60
---La Traniata; Cavalleria Rus-
ticana and Pagliacci. MC v 161
n 6 p 36 My '60
BROOKS, VAN WYCK (1886-). Hu-
neker in retrospect. HF v 10 n 12
p 38-41 D '60
BROTHIER, JEAN-JACQUES
With Michel Roux, Georges
Pretre, Bérthe Monmart, Alain
Vanzo, ens ph: Erlanger de Ro-
sen. GDC n 257-8 cover Ja 29'60
BROTT, ALEXANDER, 1915-,
composer
Three Astral Visions; "sheer
hokum". CMJ v 4 n 2 p 38
Winter '60
BROUWENSTIJN, GRÉ, 1915-,
singer
In Fidelio; Frankfurt praise. Op
v 2 n 3 p 207 Mr '60
---And Randolph Symonette in
Tiefland, AP wl ph: Particam,
1957. ON v 24 n 13 p 8 Ja 30'60
BROWN, CHARLES (1898-). Deuxième Symphonie (1957) (études
musicales analytiques). facsimiles GDC n 261-2 p 445 F 26'60
---3e Quatuor à Cordes(études
musicales analytiques). GDC n 277
p 823 Je 17'60
---Trio pour cordes, violon-alto-
cello(études musicales analy-
tique). GDC n 269-270 p 600
Ap 22'60
---Première: Deuxieme Symphonie; a la radio. GDC n 265-6

p 522 Mr 25'60
---Première: Le Troisième Qua-
tuor à Cordes; Paris commentaire.
GDC n 285 p 164 O 21'60
BROWN, DAVID. Britten's Three
Canticles. MR v 21 n 1 p 55-65
F '60
BROWN, DAVID A. 1943-, pianist
Merriweather Post Contest win-
ner. MC v 161 n 7 p 30 Je '60
BROWN, HARRY JOHN, 1926-,
conductor
Milwaukee Symphony conductor.
MC v 161 n 5 p 39 Ap '60
BROWN, IVOR (1891-). After Che-
khov. WP v 11 n 9 p 1 Jl '60
--- ---Where to perform (trend to
the arena stage best be curbed by
architects to the extent that plays
may be acted on proscenium type
stage at times). WP v 11 n 10 p 1
Ag '60
BROWN, TOM, 1913?-, director
Australia; manager of the Trust
Opera Company, por ph. MD v 51
n 3 p 14 S '60
BROWNE, E. MARTIN (1900-).
Britain's bonanza of the byways
(festivals at Bath,Aldeburgh, King's
Lynn and others). il Th Arts v 44
n 5 p 18-20 My '60
BROWNING, JOHN, 1935-, pianist
Chicago criticism. MC v 161 n 6
p 27 My '60
---Notes; honors; b. Denver. IM v
v 58 n 7 p 37 Ja '60
---With Erich Leinsdorf in a record-
ing session, hl ph: Capitol Records.
AmM v 8 n 9 p 9 O'60
BROWNLEE, JOHN (1901-). Making
the opera workshop work; Man-
hattan School of Music. MC v 162
n 4 p 8 O '60
---As Don Alfonso in Cosi fan tutte,
AP wl ph: NYC. MC v 162 n 4 p 8
O '60
BRUBECK, DAVID WARREN (1920-).
The Dave Brubeck Quartet (analy-
sis of "Jazz Impressions of Eur-
asia"). MD v 50 n 9 p 10-13 Mr'50
---Por ph. MD v 50 n 9 p 11 Mr'60
BRUCKNER, ANTON (1824-1896).
VIIe Symphonie: analyse par Pie-
rrette Mari. GDC n 281-2

p 79-80 S 30'60
BRUMAIRE, JACQUELINE,
  singer
As Marguerite with Albert Lance
as Faust, AP hl phs: Paris Opéra.
OpP n 19 p 26-7 1960
BRUNEAU, ALFRED, 1857-1934,
  composer
Hl ph; and two scenes from his
operas. Op v 11 n 9 p 595-99
S '60
BRUNNER, GERHARD. Vienna
music reports. MC 1960
BRUSCANTINI, SESTO
As Ford, AP hl ph: Glyndebourne.
Op v 11 n 8 p 543 Ag '60
BRUSSELS
Müller, Liesel. Opera ON v 25
ON v 25 n 5 p 29 D 10'60
---Music notes. La S n 123 p 79
F '60
---Opera at the Monnaie under
Huismans; report. Op v 11 n 1
p 30 Ja '60
---Youth music center, called
"Pierrot Lunaire"; notes. WM
n 6 p 131 D '60
BRUSTEIN, ROBERT (1927-).
Scorn not the procenium, critic.
Th Arts v 44 n 5 p 8-9 My '60
--- ---The memory of heroism
(essay on Greek tragedy as con-
trasted with the present "socio-
logical world-view".) TDR v 4
n 3 p 3-9 Mr '60
BRUYR, JOSE, Hommage à Ar-
thur Honegger. GDC n 289 p 288
N 18'60
--- ---Les amis du guide; inédiles
GDC n 265-6 p 523 Mr 25'60
BUCHOLZ, HORST, actor
US debut in "Cheri", NYC com-
ment. PlM v 36 n 4 p 86 Ja '60
BUCQUET, MARIE-FRANÇOISE,
  pianist
Paris review. GDC n 290 p 322
N 25'60
BUDAPEST
Lebow, Howard, (Musical con-
ditions.) J Rev v 7 n 3 p 3-6
Fall '60
---Szöllösy, András. Teatro
dell'Opera. il La S 1960

BUDAPEST HUNGARIAN BALLET
  (Solymossy)
Melbourne-based; notes. MD v 51
n 3 p 28 S '60
BUDAPEST OPERA
Kristof, Karoly. Report. ON v 24
n 23 p 28 Ap 9'60
BUDAPEST QUARTET
Marsh, Robert C. The early quar-
tets, Beethoven anew (Columbia
release). HF v 10 n 1 p 61-2 Ja'60
BUENAVENTURA, ENRIQUE.
Bird's-eye view of the Latin Am-
erican theatre. WT v 9 n 3 p 265-
271 Autumn '60
---Colombia; honors. WP v 11 n 6
p 7 Ap '60
BUENOS AIRES
Cebreiro, J. B. Teatro Colón
(Norma less good than The Love
of Three Oranges). Op v 11 n 2
p 139 F '60
---Firas, Leopold H. Music notes.
MC v 161 n 1 p 27 Ja '60; same.
MC v 161 n 5 p 33 Ap '60; same.
MC v 162 n 6 p 32-3 D '60
--- ---Teatro Colon: opera and
ballet report. MC v 162 n 1 p 31
Jl '60
---La Giocanda, opera; review of
American singers (Udovick, Mig-
non Dunn, Aldo Protti, Norman
Scott), Carlos Cillario, conducting.
MC v 162 n 3 p 26 S '60
---New Magazine, Revista de Tea-
tro. WP v 12 n 3 p 3 D '60
---Pascal, Marie. Chaos at the
Colón: Lucia di Lammermoor,
Rigoletto, La Tosca; Norma. ON
v 24 n 9 p 30 Ja 2'60
---Teatro Colón 1960 repertory.
Op v 11 n 5 p 342 My '60
---Valenti Ferro, Enzo. Contem-
porary music in Buenos Aires.
WM n 5 p 104 O'60
---Santa Juana de America, small
AP ph. WP v 12 n 2 p 3 N '60
BÜHRMANN, DR. MAX, 1904-,
  director
York Festival; Chinese Shadow
Plays, report by George Speaight.
Th Notbk v 15 n 1 p 35 Autumn '60
BUKER, ALDEN. The status of

45

(Buker)
music therapy. MEJ v 46 n 5
p 62, 64 Ap-My '60
BULGARIA
Balkanska, Maria. Season 1959-
60, theatre. il WT v 9 n 3 p 276-
9 Autumn '60
---Logar, M. Music report. La S
n 133 p 113 D '60
---Music notes. La S n 123 p 79
F '60
---Sagaeff, L. (Reports on music,
on publications, on artists ab-
road.) WM n 6 p 130 D '60
---Theatre report. WP v 11 n 9 p 8
Ag '60; same. WP v 12 n 1 p 3
O '60
---Scene from Sisyphee et la Mort,
Bourgas, ph: 1959; scene from
Liubow Yarovaja, Sofia, ph: 1959.
WT v 9 n 3 p 279 Autumn '60
BULL, JOHN, 1563-1628, composer
Dart, Thurston. Search for the
real John Bull (in music archives
of the New York Public Library).
MD v 51 n 3 p 20 S '60
BUNDERVOET, AGNELLE, pianist
Et orchestre de chambre Paul
Kuentz; Paris criticism. GDC
n 259-60 p 408 F 12'60
BURCHIELLI
Por (? sec. XVI). n 131 p 14 O'60
DIE BÜRGSCHAFT, opera
Weill, ens AP wl ph: Heinz Kos-
ter, 1957. WT v 9 n 3 p 215
Autumn '60
BURKE, ANTHONY, dancer
Partnering Fonteyn, AP wl ph:
Sadler's Wells. MD v 50 n 12 p 24
Je '60
BURKE, JAMES, cornet-trumpet
soloist
Por ph. MEJ v 46 n 5 p 37 Ap-My
'60
BURKHARDT, HERMAN, bass
player
Career notes. IM v 58 n 8 p 30
F '60
BURNETT, CAROL, actress
In Once Upon a Mattress, AP wl
ph: Friedman-Abeles. Th Arts
v 44 n 1 p 71 Ja '60
BURST OF SUMMER, play
Melbourne Little Theatre; Oriel

Gray. WP v 11 n 7 p 2 My '60
---Melbourne Little Theatre, ens
AP wl ph: 1960. WT n 9 n 3 p 274
Autumn '60
BURT, FRANCIS, composer
Première: Volpone, opera; Gün-
ther Rennert, director. WM n 3 p 56
Je '60
BUSCH, FRITZ (1890-1951). Letter
declining in 1948 to be present at
the 400th anniversary of the Dresden Opera House. Op v 2 n 3 p 180
Mr '60
---Schmiedel, Gottfried. Fritz Busch and the Dresden Opera. il Op
v 2 n 3 p 175-181 Mr '60
---Por ph. and his Dresden musi-
cal days, nine phs. Op v 2 n 3
p 175-181 Mr '60
BUSCH, HANS (1907-). The American Opera Workshop. WM n 4
p 70-72 Ag '60
--With Elizabeth Schwarzkopf, hl
ph: London. AmM v 8 n 1 p 7 Ja'60
BUSONI, FERRUCCIO, 1866-1924,
composer
Selden-Goth, Giselda. Un severo
vaglio degli ultimi quartetti bee-
thoveniani (scoperta di un inedito
di Busoni). facsimile La S n 123
p 21-3 F '60
---Scoperta di un inedito di Busoni
(? Lugen Lymo). La S n 123 p 21
F '60
BUSSOTTI, SYLVANO, composer
Description of "Five Piano Pieces
for David Tudor (1959)" as played
by Tudor, NYC. MC v 161 n 7 p 26
Je '60
---Notes and facsimile "Notazione
per piano". La S n 127 p 10 Je '60
BYE BYE BIRDIE (Champion),
musical
NYC notes; press comments. Th
Arts v 44 n 6 p 59 Je'60
---NYC review. PlM v 37 n 1 p 9
O'60
---The Telephone Hour, ens ph. Th
Arts v 44 n 6 p 7 Je'60
---Van Dyke, Dick, and Chita Rivera,
AP wl ph: Friedman-Abeles. Th
Arts v 44 n 5 p 59 My'60
BYRNE, M. ST. CLARE. The ear-
liest Hamlet prompt book in an

an English library. facsimiles
Th Notbk v 15 n 1 p 21-31 Autumn'60

C

CADA NOCHE MUERE JULIETA,
play
Mexico; Federico S. Inclán. WP
v 11 n 7 p 13 My '60
THE CAFARELLI OPERA COMPANY
PANY
Cleveland notes. MC v 162 n 4
p 19 O '60
CAGE, JOHN (1912-). Indetermin-
acy (a recording of 90 anecdotes
backed by assorted sound). CMJ
v 4 n 3 p 55-6 Spring '60
--- ---The 25-year Retrospective
Concert (a recording produced
by George Avakian and reviewed
by Milton Wilson). CMJ v 4 n 4
p 54 Summer '60
---Frankenstein, Alfred. In re-
trospect, the music of John Cage.
por HF v 10 n 4 p 63 Ap '60
---Première: Theatre Piece; notes.
MC v 161 n 6 p 36 My '60
THE CAGE IN THE TREE, play
Chicago Community Theatre, ens
ph. Th Arts v 44 n 2 p 85 F '60
CAGNEY, JAMES, 1904-, actor
In Penny Arcade, ens AP wl ph:
1930. Th Arts v 44 n 9 p 61 S '60
CALENDAR
Each issue, listing of theatre
events with notes on the product-
ions. Th Arts 1960
CALIFORNIA
Helm, Everett, (Music report.)
MR v 21 n 3 p 240-1 Ag '60
CALIGULA, play
NYC review of Camus' play. Th
Arts v 44 n 4 p 59 Ap '60
CALLAS, MARIA Meneghini,
1923-, singer
EMI recording 1952 to date; Wal-
ter Legge: "and never a cross
word". HF v 10 n 5 p 26 My '60
---Epidauros, Norma reviewed.
il Op v 11 p 76, 78 Autumn '60
---In Norma; Epidaurus out-door
theatre. notes. ON v 25 n 2 p 20
O 29'60

---As Anna Bolena, La Scala
1957, AP hl ph: Piccagliani. Op
v 2 n 3 p 191 Mr '60
---Por drawing. Op v 11 n 8 p 525
Ag '60
CALLAWAY, PAUL, conductor
Washington, D. C. honor. il ON
v 24 n 12 p 2 Ja 23'60
CALVE, EMMA, 1858-1942, singer
As Carmen, AP hl ph. ON v 25 n 8
p 10 D 31'60
IL CALZARE D'ARGENTO, opera
Pizzetti, Ildebrando; Cartelloni
notes. La S n 133 p 116 D '60
CAMELOT, musical
Lerner-Loewe show based on
King Arthur; notes. Th Arts v 44
n 12 p 25-6 D '60
---Première in Toronto; review.
MC v 162 n 5 p 29 N '60
CAMINITO THEATRE
Argentina, founded 1959: note.
WT v 9 n 1 p 68 Spring '60
CAMINO REAL, play
NYC notes. Th Arts v 44 n 7 p 59
Jl '60
---Revival at St. Marks Play-
house, ens AP wl ph: Sam Shaw.
Th Arts v 44 n 7 p 61 Jl '60
CAMPANINI, BARBARA ?-1799,
ballerina
Reyna, Ferdinando. La Barbarina,
croce e delizia. il La S n 124 p 9-
13 Mr '60
---Detta la"Barbarina", un ritratto
di Rosalba Carriera (1743). La S
n 124 Mr '60
IL CAMPIELLO, opera
Turin review. Op v 11 n 2 p 147
F '60
CAMPO, FRANK, composer
Première: String Trio, Op 22;
notes on The Musical Art Quartet.
MC v 161 n 6 p 35 My '60
CAMPOGALLIANI, ETTORE,
conductor
Reggio Emilia; notes. La S n 131
p 65 O '60
CAMPERA, ANDRE (1660-1744).
Idoménee (études musicales an-
alytiques). GDC n 290 p 334
N 25'60
---Chamfray, Claude. Fiche bi-
ographique. GDC n 261-2 p 447-8

(Campera)
F 26'60
CAMUS, ALBERT (1913-1960).
  Why I work in the theatre. Th
  Arts v 44 n 12 p 58-9, 70-1 D'60
  ---Por ph: Henri Cartier-Bresson.
  Th Arts v 44 n 12 p 58 D '60
  ---With J. L. Barrault, hl ph. WP
  v 11 n 4 p 7 F '60
CANADA
  Beckwith, John. Notes on some
  new music heard on CBS Radio.
  CMJ v 4 n 2 p 37-9 Winter '60
  ---The Canada Council and na-
  tional subsidy of music; a sur-
  vey. IM v 58 n 12 p 18-9 Je '60
  ---Canadian League of Composers;
  Louis Applebaum, director, of
  conference in Stratford. WM n 3
  p 55 Je '60
  --- ---Stratford, International
  Conference of Composers; Henri
  Dutilleux reporting. WM n 6
  p 131 D '60
  ---The Canadian Music Library
  Association; Montreal report.
  CMJ v 5 n 1 p 52 Autumn '60
  ---Docherty, Ian. (Vancouver
  opera reviews.) Op v 11 n 10
  p 687, 691 O '60
  ---George, Graham. Three Canadian concert-halls (Vancouver,
  Edmonton and Calgary.) CMJ
  v 4 n 2 p 4-13 Winter '60
  ---Hartt College of Music, Hartford; un premier festival de musique canadienne. CMJ v 4 n 2
  p 35-7 Winter '60
  ---Heinze, Sir Bernard. Report
  on Canada's musical development
  (19 orchestras, a four months
  survey under the Canada Council).
  por MD v 51 n 3 p 8-9 S '60
  ---Hugo, Reg. (On music festivals
  in Canada; a counter-argument
  to a previous negative article.)
  CMJ v 4 n 4 p 33-7 Summer '60
  ---International Conference of
  composers, Stratford, Ontario;
  report. CMJ v 5 n 1 p 4-16
  Autumn '60
  ---International folk music conference in Quebec 1961. WM n 6
  p 130 D '60

  ---Kemp, Hugh. Canadian tele-
  vision drama. PlM v 36 n 4 p 81-2
  Ja '60
  ---Kines, Thomas. (On positive
  values of music festivals.) CMJ
  v 4 n 4 p 37-40 Summer '60
  ---The music festival controversy;
  Sir Ernest MacMillan, Boris Rou-
  bakine, Minuetta Kessler, Victor
  Kerslake, Geoffrey Payzant, Soeur
  Marie de St-George Antoine. CMJ
  v 5 n 1 p 30-8 Autumn '60
  ---Music festivals; letter from
  Richard W. Cooke on costs and
  management of Canadian Music
  Festivals. CMJ v 4 n 2 p 87-8
  Winter '60
  ---New music by Canadian com-
  posers; criticism of Harry Som-
  ers, Jean Papineau-Couture,
  François Morel, Otto Joachim.
  CMJ v 5 n 1 p 62-7 Autumn '60
  ---Notes on national theatre center.
  Th R v 2 n 3 p 183 1960
  ---Payzant, Geoffrey. The com-
  petitive music festivals. CMJ v 4
  n 3 p 35-46 Spring '60
  ---Ross, Malcolm, editor. The
  Arts in Canada: a Stock-Taking
  at Mid-Century (review by George
  Falle). CMJ v 4 n 3 p 81 Spring '60
  ---Schabas, Ezra. (Music report.)
  MC v 161 n 7 p 19 Je '60 ; same.
  MC v 162 n 5 p 29 N '60
  ---Theatre reports. WP v 11 n 4
  p 1, 7 F '60; same. WP v 11 n 6
  p 7 Ap '60; same. WP v 11 n 6 p 7
  Ap '60;same. WP v 11 n 8 p 8 Je'60;
  same. WP v 11 n 9 p 7 Jl '60;
  same. WP v 11 n 10 p 8 Ag '60; WP
  v 12 n 1 p 3 O '60; WP v 12 n 3 p 4
  D '60
  ---Weaver, J. Clark. Canada On
  Stage, a collection of one-act plays,
  edited by Stanley Richards (book
  review). PlM v 37 n 2 p 35 N '60
  ---Les trois désires de Coquelicot
  (Aslani), small ph. WP v 12 n 3
  p 4 D '60
CANADIAN OPERA COMPANY
  Kidd, George. Report. Op v 11
  n 4 p 271 Ap '60
  ---Krehm, William. Season 1959-
  1960: The Love of Three Oranges;

48

;La Forza del Destino;The Merry Wives of Windsor;notes. CMJ v 4 n 4 p 48-51 Summer'60
---Notes. ON v 24 n 16 p 3 F 20'60
---In Love of the Three Oranges; La Forza del Destino, two ens AP wl phs:Gray. Op v 11 n 4 p 272 Ap'60
CANDIDA, FEDRICO. Il mistero della musica. LaS n 125 p 61-3 Ap'60
CANGALOVIC, MIROSLAV, 1921-, singer
Monte Carlo criticism; "highly reminiscent of C haliapin". Op v 11 n 5 p 355 My '60
CANIGLIA, MARIA, 1906-, singer Career sketch; b. Naples. il ON v 24 n 21 p 9 Mr 26'60
---As Tosca AP wl ph: Rome. ON v 24 n 21 p 9 Mr 26'60
CANNON, HERBERT, director Por ph: ABC, Australia. MD v 51 n 3 p 17 S '60
CANTATAS
Drinkwater, David. The Cantatas of Johann Sebastian Bach by W. Gillies Whittaker (a book review). J Rev v 7 n 2 p 18 Spring '60
---Whittaker, W. Gillies(?-1944). The Cantatas of Johann Sebastian Bach (book reviewed). MR v 21 n 2 p 157-8 My '60
---Wienandt, Elwyn A. Das Licht scheinet: two settings by K. H. Graun. MR v 21 n 2 p 85-93 My'60
CANTE FLAMENCO
Review of recording, Manolo Caracol in 26 flamenco songs; history by Professor Manuel Garcia Matos. HF v 10 n 6 p 81 Je '60
CANTICUM MUSICUM
NYC; old-time music, seven artists. MC v 162 n 6 p 35 D '60
CANTICUM SACRUM
Vienna under Herbert von Karajan; review. MC v 161 n 5 p 30 Ap '60
EL CANTO DE LA CIGARRA, play Madrid notes; Alfonso Paso. WP v 11 n 7 p 6 My '60
CAPDEVIELLE, PIERRE, 1906-, composer
Career notes. GDC n 275 p 735 Je 3'60

---Première: Concerto; played by Agnelle Bundervoet and the National Orchestra, Manuel Rosenthal, conducting; Paris. GDC n 279-80 p 890 Jl 1'60
---Por ph: Joyeux. GDC n 275 cover Je 3'60
CAPRI, ANTONIO (1901-). Ottant 'anni di Ildebrando Pizzetti. il La S n 129-130 p 9-17 Ag-S '60
--- ---La pianistica di Chopin. il La S n 126 p 9-17 My '60
--- ---Testimonianza di Pergolesi. il La S n 132 p 24-29 N '60
CAPRICCIO, opera
Vienna review; Schwarzkopf "at her ravishing best". ON v 25 n 1 p 23 O 8'60
---Wechsberg, Joseph. Vienna review. Op v 11 n 7 p 475 Jl '60
---University of Southern California, ens AP wl ph: Maria Jeanette. ON v 24 n 17 p 26 F 27'60
CAPRICHOS (ROSS), ballet
Ens AP wl ph: Sharland, Th Arts v 44 n 11 p 58 N '60
LE CAPTAINE FRACASSE, opera
Wolff, Stéphane. An Théâtre de l'Ile-de-France. GDC n 273 p 693 My 20'60
THE CAPTIVE, opera
Wishart, composer; première at Barber Institute of Fine Arts, Birmingham, June 1960. Op v 11 n 10 p 683 O '60
CARACALLA BATHS
Teatro dell'Opera di Roma: Terme di Caracalla, 2 luglio-4 settembre 1960; calendar; maestri concertatori e direttori. La S n 128 inset Jl '60
CARAMOOR FESTIVAL
British music for 1960; notes. AmM v 8 n 5 p 12 Je '60
CARANDENTE, GIOVANNI. Succès de Josette Amiel à l'Opéra de Rome. TD n 94 p 27 Je '60
CARBONARI, VIRGILIO
With Eduardo DeFilippo in "Il Barbiere" of Paisiello, AP hl ph: Piccola Scala. La S n 125 p 46 Ap'60
CARDEN, GEORGE, choreographer
Notes on "Once Upon a Mattress", Melbourne; and on "Fantasy On Ice". MD v 50 n 8 p 28 F '60

CARDEW
  Première: Autumn '60; notes.
  GDC n 293-4 p 458 D 16'60
CARDILLAC, opera
  Wuppertal; details of a fine Hindemith revival Op v 11 n 6
  p 425 Je '60
---Hindemith; ens AP wl ph: Ursula Knipping, 1959. WT v 9 n 3
  p 216 Autumn '60
--- ---ens AP wl ph: U. Knipping,
  Wuppertal. WP v 11 n 10 p 1
  Ag '60
CARDINI, MARIA PIMPANARO.
  Antonio Stradivari and the Cremona Schools of Music. La S
  n 125 p 34-8 Ap '60
THE CARETAKER, play
  London notes; Harold Pinter.
  WP v 11 n 10 p 15 Ag '60
CAREY, MARGARETTA. Music
  for the educable mentally retarded. MEJ v 46 n 4 p 72, 74
  F-Mr '60
CARIMINA. An introduction to
  Spanish dancing. MD v 50 n 8
  p 31 F '60
CARINE, CRIS, dancer
  With Vassili Sulich in modern
  ballet by George Reich, AP wl
  ph: Paris. TD n 93 p 27 My '60
CARL ROSA OPERA
  London reviews: Faust; The Barber of Seville; Il Trovatore; La
  Bohème; Don Giovanni. Op v 11
  n 10 p 705-9 O '60
CARLES, MARC. Variations pour
  orchestre (études musicales analytiques). GDC n 292 p 429 D 9'60
---Paris; la Ire audition des variations Symphoniques. GDC
  n 295 p 487 D 30'60
CARMEN, opera
  Covent Garden notes; Gloria Lane.
  Op v 11 n 1 p 68 Ja '60
---Cushing, Mary Walkins. (The
  role of Carmen as interpreted by
  Calvé and others.) ON v 24 n 14
  p 4-5 F 6'60
---Metropolitan; Jane Rhodes of
  the Paris Opéra, Nikola Nikolov
  as Don Jose. MC v 162 n 6 p 16
  D '60
--- ---NYC review. MC v 162 n 6

p 15 D '60
--- ---cast; story; articles; décor
  notes; bibliography; discography;
  portfolio. ON v 24 n 14 F 6'60
---NYC Opera; Gloria Lane; Jean
  Sanders; both good. MC v 162 n 6
  p 16 D '60
---Osborne, Conrad L. Beecham's
  Carmen, a definitive statement
  (Capitol records reviewed). HF
  v 10 n 2 p 54-5 F '60
---Paris Opéra review; "more
  work into this production than had
  been heaped on any opera in France
  during this century". Op v 11 n 2
  p 141-2 F '60
--- ---Notes; moved to the Opéra,
  new production under Raymond
  Rouleau. ON v 24 n 14 p 26 F 6'60
---Reviews: Sete; and at Nice. GDC
  n 263-4 p 480-1 Mr 11'60
---La Scala criticism. il La S
  n 124 p 30 Mr '60
---In Santiago, Chile, ens AP hl
  ph: Revista Ercilla. ON v 24 n 9
  p 28 Ja 2'60
---L'Opéra de Paris, 1959; ens
  AP wl ph: Bernand. WT v 9 n 1
  p 76 Spring '59
--- ---portfolio: 1960. OpP n 19
  p 7-11 1960
---Two AP wl phs: Teatro alla
  Scala. La S n 124 p 29 Mr '60
CARMEN (PETIT), film
  Petit and Jeanmaire, AP wl ph.
  TD n 96 p 31 S-O '60
CARMINA BURANA, opera
  Munich; ens AP wl ph: Betz. Op
  v 11 p 57 Autumn '60
LE CARNAVAL DES ANIMAUX
  Decca; Beatrice Lillie, Julus Katchen and Gary Graffman plus a
  lion in the London Zoo. HF v 10
  n 5 p 26 My '60
CARNEGIE HALL, NYC
  Bought by NYC for five million;
  details of future plans and uses.
  MC v 162 n 1 p 4 Jl '60
---Schulze, Richard, and his wife,
  launch drive to save Carnegie Hall;
  outline of his plan by E. Lucretia
  Sisley. MC v 161 n 3 p 19 F '60
---State of New York law signed by
  Governor to save demolition. MC

50

v 161 n 6 p 4 My '60

CARRÈRE, CLAUDINE, pianist
Louvet, Michel. Paris review.
GDC n 295 p 495 D 30'60

CARROLL, DAVID, band leader
And orchestra in Latin American
recording (Mercury) "Latin Percussion". por HF v 10 n 12 p 89
D '60

CARTAS CREDENCIALES, play
Madrid notes; Joaquin Calvo So-
tello. WP v 11 n 7 p 7 My '60

CARTER, ELLIOTT (1908-). Germany (review of Der Tod des
Grigori Rasputin and Lady Macbeth of Mzensk). Mus Q v 46 n 3
p 367-8 Jl '60

--- ---Shop talk by an American
composer. Mus Q v 46 n 2 p 189-
201 Ap '60

---Goldman, Richard Franko.
(Carter's Second String Quartet;
analysis.) Mus Q v 46 n 3 p 361-
3 Jl '60

---Première: le Deuxième Quatu-
or; Le Quatuor Juilliard; Besançon. GDC n 283 p 95 O 7'60

CARTER, GAYLORD, organist
Por ph. IM v 59 n 1 p 11 Jl '60

CARTERI, ROSANNA
Por ph: Ferri. Op v 2 n 3 p 195
Mr '60

CARUSO: ENRICO, 1873-1921,
singer
Weerth, Ernest de. (A hat for
Dorthy Benjamin who became
Mrs. Caruso.). ON v 24 n 9 p 8
Ja 2'60

---As Canio, AP ph: DuPont. MC
v 161 n 3 p 8 F '60

---Clowning with a tennis racket,
ph. ON v 25 n 8 p 9 D 31'60

CARVALHO, ELEAZAR DE, 1915-,
conductor
Guaratingueto; Brazilian school-
with-festival similar to Tanglewood. MD v 50 n 8 p 16 F '60

CARVER, ROBERT, 1487-1546?,
composer
Collected works, edited by Denis
Stevens (review by Sylvia W.
Kenney). Mus Q v 46 n 3 p 383-5
Jl '60

CASADESUS, JEAN, 1927-, pianist

Notes. GDC n 278 p 831 Je 24'60

---At the piano, ph. GDC n 278
cover Je 24'60

CASADESUS, ROBERT, 1899-,
pianist
Berthoumieux, Serge. Paris review. GDC n 273 p 689 My 20'60

---Cleveland criticism. MC v 162
n 6 p 26 D '60

---Goldsmith, Harris. (Columbia's
Casadesus discs: Beethoven, Bach
and Casadesus, the composer.) por
HF v 10 n 4 p 62-3 Ap '60

CASALS, PABLO, 1876-, cellist
Criticism. IM v 59 n 1 p 21 Jl'60

---The Fourth Annual Festival Casals;
notes. IM v 58 n 12 p 6 Je '60

---University of California class;
auditions by tape recording and
live. AmM v 8 n 1 p 17 Ja '60

---Portrait; and AP ph. IM v 59
n 1 cover, p 21 Jl '60

---Receiving life membership in
American Federation of Musicians,
ens ph: NYC. IM v 58 n 12 p 6 Je'60

---With Alexander Schneider and
Rudolf Serkin, ens hl ph: Clemens
Kalischer. MC v 162 n 2 p 10 Ag'60

CASALS FESTIVAL 1960
Notes; guest soloists. AmM v 8
n 9 p 13 O '60

LA CASAMENTERA, play
Montevideo, 1959; ens AP wl ph:
Teatro Solis. WT v 9 n 2 p 186
Summer '60

CASELLA, ALFREDO (1883-1947).
(Le quattro lettere: vito Reali).
La S n 123 p 24-5 F '60

---Raeli, Vito. Casella's letters.
La S n 122 Ja '60

---DeChirico. Alfredo Casella. LaS
n 123 p 25 F '60

CASEY, JOHN
See O'Casey, Sean, 1880

CASINO D'ENGLISH
Ballets 1960 de Milroad Misko-
witch; notes. TD n 95 p 27 Jl-Ag '60

EL CASO DE PEDRO VENTURA, play
Queretaro, Mexico; Federico S.
Inclan. WP v 11 n 5 p 13 Mr '60

CASS, RICHARD, pianist
NYC review. MC v 161 n 6 p 18
My '60

---Por ph. MC v 161 n 6 p 21 My'60

51

CASSADO, GASPAR
Lyon, Raymond. Dialoghi pour violoncelle et orchestre, Orchestre National. GDC n 286 p 196 O 28'60
---Mari, Pierrette. Gaspar et Chieko Cassado à Gaveau. GDC n 293 p 463 D 16'60
CASSEL, WALTER, 1910-, singer
As Kurvenal, AP hl ph:Melançon. ON v 24 n 10 p 17 Ja 9'60
CASSIANI(TSOUCALA), opera
Athens notes;Georges Sklavos. WP v 11 n 5 p 10 Mr'60
CASTALDO, JOSEPH, composer
Première:Epigrams;"cerebral rather than heartfelt music". MC v 161 n 6 p 26 My'60
CASTELLANI, FRANCO, actor
As Hamlet, AP ph:Italy. Th Arts v 44 n 4 p 55 Ap'60
CASTELLI, CHRISTIANE
And Albert Lance in La Tosca, AP wl ph. OpP n 19 p 12 1960
CASTÉRÈDE, JACQUES. Suite en trois mouvements(etudes musicales analytiques). GDC n 267-8 p 565 Ap 8'60
---Jourdan-Morhange, H. Paris; Société Nationale. GDC n 265-6 p 522 Mr 25'60
---Mari, P. Envois de Roma, serie; Aubin et l'Orchestre National de la R. T. G. et des Choeurs:Castérède. GDC n 271 p 629 My 5'60
CASTIGLIONI, NICCOLO, composer
Première:Aprèsludes;Cologne notes. Mus Q v 46 n 4 p 519-21 O'60
CASTIGLIONI, VITTORANGELO. LaScala reviews. il LaS n 124 p 27-31 Mr'60 ; series 1960
CASTLE IN SWEDEN, play
Paris, 1960, ens AP wl ph:Bernand. WT v 9 n 2 p 158 Summer '60
CATALDO, ANTONIO. La cantina musicale di via Giambologna (Renzo Tozzi). il LaS n 123 p 27 F'60
LA CATHÉDRALE DE CHARTES
Bruyr, José. Sept. siècles (critiques). GDC n 288 p 259-60

N 11'60
CAUGHT DEAD, musical
Birmingham, Alabama; notes. MC v 161 n 5 p 29 Ap '60
CAVALIERI, LINA, singer
Notes. ON v 24 n 13 p 7 Ja 30'60
---Por ph: Mishkin. Op v 24 n 13 p 6 Ja 30'60
CAVALIERI DI EKEBU
Trieste notes (and one scene, ph.) La S n 122 p 38 Ja '60
CAVALLERIA RUSTICANA, opera
Metropolitan cast; story; décor notes; bibliography; discography; portfolio. ON v 24 n 13 Ja 30'60
CAVALLI, FLORIANA, singer
In Der Rosenkavalier, AP wl ph: Catania. La S n 127 p 29 Je '60
---In Francesca da Rimini, ens AP wl ph: Rome. La S n 128 p 30 Jl '60
THE CAVE OF SALAMANCA, play
Cervantes Saavedra, Miguel de (1547-1616). The Cave of Salmanca, trans. by Edwin Honig. Chrys v 13 nos. 1-4 1960
CAZDOZ, JOAN, dancer
AP wl ph: M. Petit. TD n 95 p 15 Jl-Ag '60
CELIBIDACHE, SERGIU, 1912-, conductor
Florence notes. MC v 161 n 6 p 33 My '60
CELLETTI, RODOLFO. Jenny Lind, usignolo svedese. il La S n 124 p 14-19 Mr '60
CELLIER, ALEXANDRE, 1883-, organist-composer
Lyon, Raymond. Entreetien avec Alexandre Cellier. GDC n 276 p 778-9 Je 10'60
---Mari, Pierrette. Les 50 ans d'organiste d'Alexandre Cellier: concert. GDC n 276 p 786 Je 10'60
THE CENCI, opera
London review. Op v 11 n 1 p 60 Ja '60
LA CENERENTOLA, opera
Sadler's Wells review. Op v 2 n 3 p 233 Mr '60
---Sadler's Wells review. Op v 11 n 12 p 847 D '60
---Vienna review. Op v 11 n 1 p 29-30 Ja '60

---Vienna; Dr. Guenther Rennert, producer; note. MC v 161 n 1 p 26 Ja '60

---Sadler's Wells; Cinderella arrives at the ball, ens AP wl ph: Rogers. ON v 24 n 13 p 26 Ja 30'60

CENSHOSHIP
Spain; 227 spanish intellectuals protest to their government; notes. WP v 12 n 3 p 3 D '60

---Verdi and the Vatican over Un Ballo in Maschera. Ver v 1 n 2 p 817 Ag '60

LES CENT VIERGES, operetta
Marseille; commentaire par Jean Abel. GDC n 257-8 p 353 Ja 29'60

CENTRAL CITY OPERA
Colorado notes. Op v 11 n 11 p 756 N '60

CENTRAL PARK, NYC
Enlarged program; new theatre; notes. MC v 162 n 5 p 33 N '60

CENTRE FRANÇAIS D'HUMANISME MUSICAL
Jolivet, André, director; Aix-en-Provence plans for second year. WM n 3 p 57 Je '60

CENTRO SPERIMENTALE DI CINEMATOGRAFIA
Italian school, two-year program open to foreign students. PlM v 37 n 1 p 9 O '60

CENZATO, GIOVANNI
Ricordi di Orio (Vergani). il LaS n 132 p 54-7 N '60

LE CERCLE CULTUREL DE ROYAUMONT
Program notes; list of authorities. TD n 93 p 15 My '60

LE CERCLE DE CRAIE CAUCASIEN
Brecht par le Berliner Ensemble, Théâtre des Nations, ens AP wl ph. Th R v 2 n 1 p 25 1960

LE CERCLE MUSICAL DE PARIS
Belliard, Maxine; Pierrette Mari; Claudia Barreau. GDC n 276 p 787 Je 10'60

CERULLI, DOM. Jack Teagardeu. il IM v 58 n 7 p 12-3 Ja '60

CERVANTES SAAVEDRA, MIGUEL DE (1547-1616). The
Cave of Salamanca, translated by Edwin Honig. Chrys v 13 nos. 1-4 1960

CEZARY BARYKA, play
Lublin notes; Janusz Warminski. WP v 11 n 6 p 9 Ap '60

CHACUN, MADELEINE, pianist
Louvet, Michel. Paris concert. GDC n 274 p 726 My 27'60

CHAILLEY, JACQUES: 1910-, composer
Paris concert: Hommage à Jacques Chailley; Jacques Feschotte. GDC n 276 p 785 Je 10'60

CHAKIRIS, GEORGE, singer
With Lady Crosfield, hl ph: London. AmM v 8 n 3 p 7 Mr '60

CHALICE OF ANTIOCH
Ph: Cloisters 1950. ON v 24 n 23 p 13 Ap 9'60

CHAMBER MUSIC
Adelaide; James Whitehead and Lance Dossor, cello and piano; Ladislav Jasek and Clemens Leske, Kreutzer Sonata; the Sydney Sinfonietta fine. MD v 50 n 11 p 11 My '60

---Boston; notes. MC v 161 n 3 p 41 F '60

---Chailley, Marie-Therese, and Nicole Rolet de Casteele; Paris notes. GDC n 276 p 787 Je 10'60

---Chamfray, Claude. Le 400e Concert des Amis de la Musique de Chambre: française. GDC n 275 p 755 Je 3'60

--- ---Trio Pasquier et Jean-Pierre Rampal. GDC n 293-4 p 463 D 16'60

---Chicago; several reviews. MC v 161 n 4 p 29 Mr '60

---Chicago Chamber Orchestra; notes. MC v 162 n 6 p 24 D '60

---Chicago notes, including the Pro Musica Society; the Chicago Piano Quartet; the Festival String Quartet; and others. MC v 161 n 5 p 22 Ap '60

---Fauré, Gabriel; criticism by Gustave Samazeuilh. GDC n 289 p 289-92 N 18'60

---Garvey, David. (On accompanying; at highest level, chamber music.) J Rev v 7 n 1 p 6-7 Winter 59-60

(Chamber Music)

---Hindemith's music; his theory and his practice with a chart by Victor Landau of exceptions and violations. MR v 21 n 1 p 38-54 F '60

---Ideal for stereo, editorial. HF v 10 n 6 p 33 Je '60

---Jourdan-Morhange, H. Quatuor Loewenguth; Paris; commentaire (2). GDC n 291 p 357, 358 D 2'60

---Karlsruhe review of l'Orchestre de Chambre de Nancy. GDC n 261-2 p 444 F 26'60

---Liège; International Quartet Competition; notes. MC v 162 n 2 p 8 Ag '60

---Los Angeles; Roth Quartet in Beethoven Festival; notes. MC v 161 n 6 p 28 My '60

---Malvern, Australia; Allegri Chamber Music Club, two reviews. MD v 50 n 12 p 20 Je '60

---Mari, Pierrette. Ensemble Sylvie Spycket (critique). GDC n 255-6 p 310 Ja 15'60

---Milan, Orchestra di camera dell'Angelicum; Riccardo Allorto; calendario. La S n 131 inset O '60

---Nine brief new reports; quartets. IM v 59 n 5 p 32 N '60

---Oleg, A. (Fernand Caratgé and others; Paris.) GDC n 289 p 298 N 18'60

---L'Orchestre de chambre de la R. T. F., dir. Pierre Capdevielle; Paris review. GDC n 281-2 p 45 S 30'60

---L'Orchestre de chambre de Valenciennes; Eugène Bozza, leur chef. GDC n 271 p 627 My 5'60

---Paris; Concerts de chambre de Paris; Paul Kuentz. GDC n 287 p 229 N 4'60

--- ---le Quatuor Loewenguth et le Quatuor Stross; review. GDC n 269-70 p 596 Ap 22'60

--- ---Orchestre de chambre de Nantes, Trajan Popesco; review. GDC n 279-80 p 893 Jl 1'60

--- ---Orchestre de chambre de Versailles; review. GDC n 261-2 p 441 F 26'60

--- ---Orchestre de chambre

Paul Kuentz. GDC n 292 p 424 D 9'60

--- ---Orchestre de la Sarre, Karl Ristenpart; solistes. GDC n 269-70 p 597 Ap 22'60

--- ---Quatuor Italien; review. GDC n 271 p 626 My 5'60

--- ---Quatuor Pascal; cycle Gabriel Faure et les musiciens français, une semaine de concerts. GDC n 257-8 p 359 Ja 29'60

--- ---Société Nationale de Musique; Quatuor Pascal; Liliane Caillon, violinist; Lily Laskine, harpist. GDC n 261-2 p 439 F 26'60

--- ---review; Le Triptyque and R. T. F.: Quintette Instrumental a vent de Paris; Ensemble Instrumental de la R. T. F., with Paul Derenne and Nadia Boulanger. GDC n 281-2 p 33-4 S 30'60

---Poore, Charles Prescott. Mexico; Musica da Camera series, 19th season, under Aurelio Fuentes on Sunday mornings. MC v 162 n 5 p 27 N '60

---Ramat-Gan Chamber Orchestra; conductor, Franklin Choset; notes. MC v 161 n 7 p 20 Je '60

---Sadie, Stanley. The chamber music of Boyce and Arne. Mus Q v 46 n 4 p 425-36 O '60

---Spoleto 1960; list of groups to play chamber music programs. MC v 161 n 5 p 33 Ap '60

---Sydney; The Andrew Hoffman String Quartet; notes. MD v 50 n 12 p 20 Je '60

---Trio pour Cordes de Charles Brown; Paris concert. GDC n 278 p 847 Je 24'60

---Twelve brief news reports; quartets, concerts, artists. IM v 59 n 6 p 40, 51 D '60

---US; The Curtis String Quartet; The Eastman String Quartet; notes. MC v 161 n 4 p 25 Mr '60

---Washington, D. C.; notes on the Budapest Quartet and others. MC v 161 n 6 p 32 My '60

CHAMBER ORCHESTRA OF STUTTGART

Paris; Karl Munchinger; review by Claude Chamfray. GDC n 255-6

p 310 Ja 15'60
CHAMBER 110, play
Montreal notes;Jacques Bobet.
WP v 11 n 7 p 4 My'60
CHAMFRAY, CLAUDE. Musique
de films. GDC 1960
---Première:Altitude, CBS Symphony under Charles Houdret;
notes. CMJ v 4 n 4 p 44 Summer
'60
LA CHANCE de MAROULA, revue
Athens notes;Yannoukakis. WP
v 12 n 1 p 8 O'60
A CHANCE IN the DAYLIGHT,
play
Cheltenham notes;Leonard Smith.
WP v 11 n 10 p 15 Ag'60
CHANCELLOR, PAUL. British
bards and continental composers. Mus Q v 46 n 1 p 1-11 Ja
'60
CHANG, YI-AN, pianist
Notes. b. Shanghi, to US 1941. Am
M v 8 n 3 p 9 Mr'60
CHANGE FOR THE ANGEL, play
London notes;Bernard Kops. WP
v 11 n 8 p 11 Je'60
CHANNING, CAROL(1921-). (On
mixing comedienne act with one
of nude girls, Las Vegas comment.)Th Arts v 44 n 10 p 77 O'60
LA CHANSON du MAL-AIMÉ(J. J.
ETCHEVERRY), ballet
A l'Opéra-Comique;Claude Bessy et Attilio Lubis, AP wl ph:
Michel Petit. TD n 89 p 28 Ja'60
LE CHANT de la MINE, oratorio
Berthoumieux, Serge. Paris review of Eugène Bozza's work.
GDC n 265-6 p 523 Mr 25'60
CHANTEAU, THERESE, pianist
Bruyr, José. Review. GDC n 267-8
p 558 Ap 8'60
CHANTEREAU, FRANÇOISE
AP wl ph:France. TD n 94 p 19
Je'60
LES CHAPEAUX, play
Athens notes;Manthos Crispis.
WP v 11 n 7 p 10 My'60
CHAPLIN, SIDNEY, 1927-, actor
Marries dancer, Noelle Adam
(1935-) in Long Island. MD v 50
n 10 p 28 Ap'60
CHAPOWALENCO, GEORGES. Fes-

tival de ballets, Munich. TD n 96
p 11-2 S-O'60
LE CHAR ÉTERNITÉ, play
Buenos Aires notes;André Lizarraga. WP v 11 n 9 p 1 Jl'60
CHARBONS ARDENTS, play
Budapest;Geza Molnar. WP v 11
n 10 p 5 Ag'60
CHARLOT al CIRCO
Ens AP wl ph:All'Olimpia. LaS
n 124 p 55 Mr'60
CHARPENTIER, GUSTAVE, 1866-
1956, composer
Demarquez, Suzanne. A l'Opéra,
concert de gala en commémoration
du Centenaire de la Naissance de
Gustave Charpentier;l'air de
Louise. GDC n 293-4 p 457 D 16'60
---Dumesnil, René. Nostalgie de
Montmarte. il LaS n 132 p 39-41
N'60
---Por ph;scenes of Montmarte.
LaS n 132 p 39-41 N'60
CHARPENTIER, JACQUES
Première:Etudes Karnatiques;
criticism. GDC n 274 p 726 My 27
'60
CHARPENTIER, MARC-ANTOINE,
1634-1704, composer
Hitchcock, H. Wiley. (Three recordings by Pathé reviewed). Mus Q
v 46 n 1 p 114-6 Ja'60
CHARPENTIER, RAYMOND. Sonate
pour alto et piano(études musicales analytiques). GDC n 271 p 631
My 5'60
CHASE, MARIAN, director
Drama and dance as therapy;Washington notes. Th Arts v 44 n 12
p 21 D'60
LA CHASTE SUZANNE
Billiet, Jacques. A la Gaité-Lyrique;Germaine Roger. GDC n 284
p 137 O 14'60
CHASTENET, ANDRÉ. Considérations générales sur le Théâtre
Lyrique en France. GDC n 277
p 813 Je 17'60
CHATEAU en SUÈDE, play
Paris notes;Françoise Sagan. WP
v 11 n 7 p 8 My'60
---Ens AP wl ph:Paris. WP v 11
n 7 p 8 My'60
LA CHATTE métamorphosée en
55 femme, operetta

(La Chatte)
Ansonia Opera Circle, NYC, under "The Lady Was a Kitten"; notes. ON v 24 n 21 p 28 Mr 26'60
THE CHAUTAUQUA OPERA
Howell, John Daggett, director;repertory, conductors. MC v 162 n 4 p 19 O'60
CHAUVET, GUY, singer
Paris criticism. GDC n 267-70 p 590 Ap 22'60
CHAUVIRÉ, YVETTE, 1917-, ballerina
AP wl ph. La S n 128 p 59 Jl '60
---In La Dame aux Camélias (T. Gsovsky), AP wl ph: Paris Opéra. OpP n 19 p 45 1960
CHAVEZ, CARLOS, 1899-
Goldman, Richard Franko. Review of recording of 3 works: Sinfonia India; Sinfonia de Antihona; Sinfonia Romantica. Mus Q v 46 n 3 p 396-8 Jl '60
---Lyon, Raymond. Carlos Chavez et Henryk Szeryng avec L'Orchestre Philharmonique de la R. T. F. GDC n 284 p 128 O 14'60
---Paris review of Orchestre Philharmonique de la R. T. F. under Chavez; his 4th Symphonie in the program. GDC n 281-2 p 31-2 S 30'60
CHAYEFSKY, PADDY, 1923-, playwright
Por ph. Th Arts v 44 n 7 p 18 Jl '60
CHAYNES, CHARLES. Concerto pour trompette et orchestre de chambre (études musicales analytiques). GDC n 259-60 p 412 F 12'60
CHEATHAM, ADOLPHUS "DOC", jazz trumpet
Notes; b. Nashville. IM v 58 n 9 p 34 Mr '60
---Por ph. IM v 59 n 3 p 22 S '60
CHEESEMAN, PETER. Repertory in Derby (history of the Derby playhouse, its attempt to attract youth). il NTM v 2 n 1 p 15-19 O '60
CHEKHOV, ANTON, 1860-1904, playwright
The Chekhov Centenary in the

U. S. S. R. WT v 9 n 2 p 100 Summer '60
---In what style should Chekhov be staged? Replies from 23 producers, world-wide symposium. il WT v 9 n 2 p 111-148 Summer '60
---Kanters, Robert. Le docteur Tchékhov. por Spec n 1 p 9-10 1960
---Markov, Pavel. New trends in the interpretation of Chekhov. portfolio WT v 9 n 2 p 101-110 Summer'60
---Pitoëff, Georges (comment 1939: Tchékhov est peu connu en France). Spec n 1 p 5 1960
---Pitoëff, Sacha. La confidance en L'homme de Tchékhov. WP v 11 n 3 p 1, 7 Ja '60
---Towarnicki, Frédéric de. Quand Paris découvre Tchékhov. il Spec n 1 p 11-21 1960
---And brother Nikolaï, wl ph: 1883. Spec n 1 p 6 1960
--L'Oncle Vania, acte III, ens AP wl ph: Moscow, 1899. Spec n 1 p 12 1960
---Por ph. WP v 11 n 3 p 1 Ja'60
---Two phs. La S n 129-30 p 26 Ag-S '60
---Various productions, a portfolio. WT v 9 n 2 p 107-110 Summer '60
---With Lidia Iavorskaïa, actress, and Tatiana Chtchepkina-Koupernid, writer, page-size wl ph: 1894. Spec n 1 p 8 1960
THE CHELSEA OPERA GROUP
Tenth anniversary; Don Giovanni. Op v 2 n 3 p 198 Mr '60
CHELTENHAM FESTIVAL OF BRITISH CONTEMPORARY MUSIC
Report. WM n 3 p 56 Je '60
CHEMLA, TEDDY. Nouvelles de la guitare; II. ses possibilités et ses limites. GDC n 287 p 235 N 4'60
---III. Tonalités lui convenant le mieux. GDC n 289 p 294 N 18'60
LE CHENE ET LE TILLEUL, opéra-ballet
Paris; Inghelbrecht, composer; review. GDC n 295 p 486 D 30'60
CHENETTE, LOUIS. (On music

curricula in US schools.) MEJ
v 47 n 1 p 83-4 S-O'60
CHER MENTEUR, play
Kilty play, ens ph: Paris WP v 12
n 2 p 4 N '60
CHERCHE PARTENAIRE (Reich),
ballet
France; music, Henri Betti. WP
v 12 n 1 p 4 O '60
CHERRY BLOSSOM FESTIVAL,
operetta
Canada, Regina; vegetables in
fantasia for childre. PlM v 37 n 1
O '60
THE CHERRY ORCHARD, play
Chekhov as interpreted in Russia.
il WT v 9 n 2 p 101-106 Summer
'60
---Costa production, 1946, AP wl
ph: Roma. WT v 9 n 2 p 125
Summer '60
---Denmark 1958, ens AP wl ph:
Gunnar Graham. WT v 9 n 2 p 136
Summer '60
---Moscow Art Theatre, 1958; ens
AP wl ph: Paris. WT v 9 n 2
p 104 Summer '60
---Ens ph: Montana State Univer-
sity. PlM v 36 n 7 cover Ap '60
---Renaud-Barrault, 1955, ens
AP wl ph: Bernand. WT v 9 n 2
p 118 Summer '60
CHERUBINI, LUIGI, 1760-1842,
composer
Becherini, Bianca. Amenità e
viaggi nella vita di Cherubini
(Quatrelles L'Epine). il La S n 125
p 21-6 Ap '60
---Bruyr, José. Hommage à Cher-
ubini. GDC n 288 p 253 N 11'60
---Chamfray, Claude. Fiche biographique. GDC n 278 p 858 Je 24
'60
---Selden, Margery Stomme. The
first romantic? (Influence of Cherubini on European composers).
por ON v 24 n 15 p 12-3 F 13'60
---Dumont, M. Un ritratto (1792).
also caricatura di Alfred Turcas
in un acquarello. La S n 125 p 25-
6 Ap '60
---Tomb of Cherubini: Vincenza
Cinque, Macori and Duval, small
ph. La S n 133 p 105 D '60

CHEVALIER, MAURICE, 1888-,
singer
Notes. Th Arts v 44 n 10 p 25 O'60
LE CHEVALIER A LA ROSE, opera
Salzbourg; notes. TD n 96 p 27
S-O '60
CHEVALLEY, SYLVIE. Recherches
théâtrales: thèses de doctorat sou-
tenues et en préparation dans les
Universitiés de France 1944-1959.
Th R v 2 n 2 p 99-108 1960;same.
Th R v 2 n 3 p 141-162 1960
UN CHEVEU SUR L'OREILLER,
play
Argentina; Carlos Carlino. WP
v 11 n 10 p 1 Ag '60
CHEVILLARD, CAMILLE, 1859-
1923, composer
Chamfray, Claude. Fiche biog-
raphique. GDC n 287 p 239 N 4'60
---Ferte, Armand. Camille Chev-
illard (critical sketch). GDC
n 263-4 p 477-8 Mr 11'60
CHIARMELLO, GIANCARLO,
composer
Italy; Antiphons for baritone and
wind ensemble. Mus Q v 46 n 3
p 376 Jl '60
CHICAGO
Auditorium Theatre; rehabilitation
notes; view toward stage. HF v 10
n 2 p 51 F '60
---Chicago Concerts, Inc. ; two
series: Lists. MC v 162 n 1 p 21
Jl '60
---Dettmer, Roger. Lyric Opera
report. il Op v 11 n 1 p 26-9 Ja'60
---Devries, Dosha. (Music report.)
MC v 161-2 1960
CHICAGO CHAMBER ORCHESTRA
Kober, Dieter, conductor; notes.
MC v 161 n 3 p 37 F '60
CHICAGO CONCERTS, INC.
Belt, Byron; new impresario;
notes. MC v 161 n 6 p 26 My '60
CHICAGO FINE ARTS QUARTET
Members; 28 concerts; notes. IM
v 59 n 6 p 40 D '60
CHICAGO LYRIC OPERA
Repertory 1960. Op v 11 n 5 p 342
My '60
---Seven-week season; list of sin-
gers; repertory. AmM v 8 n 6
p 12 Jl '60

CHICAGO SYMPHONY
Contemporary selections under
Fritz Reiner; guest conductors.
AmM v 8 n 9 p 11 O '60
---Mayer, Martin. Dr. Reiner's
orchestra (manner with the or-
chestra; the hall; administration).
il HF v 10 n 2 p 38-41, 110 F '60
---Reiner, Fritz; recent programs
of the 69-year old orchestra. MC
v 161 n 3 p 35-6 F '60
---Report; conductors, Hendl, Vo-
tto, Shaw and Rosbaud. MC v 162
n 6 p 23 D '60
---Reviews; Igor Markevitch; Fritz
Reiner. MC v 161 n 4 p 28 Mr '60
---The 69th season; critical notes.
MC v 161 n 6 p 27 My '60
CHICAGOLAND MUSIC FESTIVAL
Notes. MC v 161 n 6 p 8 My '60
CHIDORI, play
Tokyo notes; Tanaka Chikao. WP
v 11 n 5 p 13 Mr '60
--- ---ens AP wl ph: 1959. WT v 9
n 1 p 89 Spring '60
CHIFRINE, NISSON. (On staging
Chekhov.) WT v 9 n 2 p 123
Summer '60
CHILDREN'S MUSIC CENTER
Publications; Los Angeles notes.
MEJ v 47 n 1 p 18 S-O '60
CHILDRENS OPERA GROUP
Mr. Postwhistle, opera, by Peter
Openshaw; cast for Fromley. Op
v 11 n 5 p 335 My '60
CHILDREN'S THEATRE
Allen, John. The young audience
(on children's theatres and com-
plications). NTM v 1 n 3 p 12-4
Ap '60
---Colombia; three groups at the
4th Festival of Bogota. WP v 12
n 1 p 4 O '60
---The Enchanted Forest, music
Ian Richardson, play Anthony Wood
Woodhall; notes. WP v 11 n 6 p 12
Ap '60
---Flanders, 1954; Do As You Like
in the Land of Your Whims, ens
ph: Segers. WT v 9 n 1 p 61
Spring '60
---Holloway, Sister Marcella M.
Play writing can be fun. PlM v 36
n 5 p 102 F '60

---Silver Springs, Maryland, the
adventure Theatre; notes. PlM
v 36 n 5 p 97 F '60
---Ward, Winifred. Children's
theatre: help wanted. il Th Arts
v 44 n 8 p 53-8 Ag '60
---Way, Brian. Plays for children.
NTM v 2 n 1 p 25-30 O '60
---Wichita, Kansas, Children's
Theatre; notes. PlM v 36 n 5 p 97
F '60
---US; productions listed by the-
atre, title, with director. PlM
1960
---Van Vlaenderen, Michel. A
children's theatre in Flanders.
WT v 9 n 1 p 58-61 Spring '60
---Portfolio of six plays in the US.
Th Arts v 44 n 8 p 54-5 Ag '60
CHILE
Cruz Coke, Carlos. Santiago
opera; the Italian cycle. ON v 24
n 9 p 28-9 Ja 2'60
---Theatre; Stanley Richards on
his trip to Chile, on Chilean the-
atre. PlM v 36 n 8 p 186 My '60
---Le Dialogue des Carmélites,
ens AP wl ph: Universidad de
Chile. WP v 12 n 3 p 1 D '60
---La Barra, de, Pedro, por ph:
Universidad de Chile; also 2 scenes
from his work. PlM v 36 n 8 p 187
My '60
---Theatre conference group ph:
Santiago. WP v 12 n 2 p 4 N '60
CHINESE SHADOW PLAYS
Speaight, George. Chinese shadows
(puppet plays). Th Notbk v 15 n 1
p 35 Autumn '60
CHINNER, NORMAN, 1909-,
conductor
The Seasons, oratorio; Melbourne
review. MD v 50 n 7 p 17 Ja '60
CHITRALEKHA, play
New Delhi 1959, ens AP hl ph:
Indraprastha Theatre. WT v 9 n 2
p 167 Summer '60
CHOPIN, FREDERIC, (1810-1849).
Concerto No. 2 en fa mineur Op.
21: analyse par Pierrette Mari. GDC
n 259-60 p 417-8 F 12'60
---Bone, Audrey Evelyn. Chopin in
Britain. MD v 50 n 11 p 12-3 My'60
---Brennecke, Wilfried. Chopin and

58

Polish music; impressions of a visit to Warsaw. WM n 2 p 26-28 Ap '60
---Capri, Antonio. La pianistica di Chopin. il La S n 126 p 9-17 My '60
---Chamfray, Claude. Célébration à Paris du cent cinquantenaire de Chopin: un Comité national: Malroux; Couve de Murville; Jox; Jaujard; Sedoux; Picon. GDC n 265-6 p 521 Mr 25'60
--- ---Le cent cinquantenaire de Chopin est célébré à l'Opéra: Marguerite Long, le programme du premier concert auquel participa Chopin à Paris en 1832; review. GDC n 269-70 p 601 Ap 22'60
---Della Corte, A. In questo mese ha letto: Correspondance de Frédéric Chopin, ed. Richard-Masse, Parigi. La S n 127 p 32 Je '60
---Dumesnil, René. Hommage a Chopin. por La S n 131 p 26-7 O'60
---Glinski, Countess Delfina; notes; painting by Barrias reproduced. MC v 162 n 6 p 28 D '60
---Mari, Pierrette. A la radio, concert Chopin par six prix internationaux. GDC n 267-8 p 564 Ap 8'60
---Pratt, Ross. Chopin in Britain (1837, 1848). CMJ v 5 n 1 p 24-9 Autumn '60
---Batt. Chopin leaving his last concert; plaque in London commemorating first concert at 99 Eaton Place, ph. MD v 50 n 11 p 12, 13 My '60
---Calco della mano sinistra; 2 facsimiles, autografo, lettera e Polonaise in fa minore; in un disegno a matita dell'amica George Saud. La S n 126 p 9-12 My '60
---Por; cast of left hand. La S n 131 p 26-7 O '60
CHOPIN PIANO COMPETITION, WARSAW
History of international piano contest; previous winners listed; 1960 Maurizio Pollini (1942-); hurdles. MD v 50 n 10 p 16 Ap '60
---Warsaw report; also First

International Musicological Chopin Congress. WM n 2 p 26-7 Ap '60
CHORAL MUSIC
Brooklyn College fourth festival of Baroque Choral Music. MC v 161 n 6 p 34 My '60
---San Diego State College; Roger Wagner, director; session on choral music from Gregorian to contemporary. IM v 58 n 9 p 43 Mr '60
---See also choruses, cantatas
A CHOREOGRAPHER COMMENTS (Tudor), ballet
Juilliard School, 4 ens AP wl phs; Impact. J Rev v 7 n 2 p 17 Spring '60
CHOREOGRAPHY
Vestris, Gaetano, 1728-1808, career sketch. il La S n 129-30 p 18-25 Ag-S '60
---Four small phs: Fosse; Robbins; Champion; Kidd. Th Arts v 44 n 11 p 66 N '60
CHORUSES
Australia; massed choirs under Boyd Dawkins; Song of Australia Centenary concert. MD v 50 n 7 p 13 Ja '60
--- ---The Luton Girls' Choir; notes. MD v 50 n 7 p 17 Ja '60
---Australian Boys Choir list. MD v 50 n 10 p 20 Ap '60
---Bertini, Garry, founder 1955 "Chorale Israélienne Rinat"; Paris notes. GDC n 285 p 166 O 21'60
---Boston productions; notes. MC v 161 n 6 p 30 My '60
---Brasseur, Elisabeth; chorale, une serie de concerts, Cantates de Bach. GDC n 269-70 p 599 Ap 22'60
---Brooklyn Philharmonic Choral Society; Brahms' German Requiem; notes. MC v 161 n 3 p 33 F '60
---The Canby Singers; an evening of 16th and 17th century unaccompanied choral music; NYC review. MC v 161 n 5 p 36 Ap '60
---The Cappella Russian Male Chorus under Nicholas Afonsky with soloist, Nicolai Gedda; NYC review. MC v 161 n 4 p 17 Mr '60
---Castil. Chorale Montjoie; Paris.

59

(Choruses)

GDC n 277 p 817 Je 17'60

---Chicago; Vytis, male chorus; note. ON v 24 n 24 p 3 Ap 16'60

---Chicago Symphony Orchestra Chorus under Margaret Hillis; review. MC v 161 n 5 p 21 Ap'60

---Chile; Coros Polifonicos, notes. IM v 58 n 7 p 14 Ja '60

---Cleveland Orchestra Chorus (200) under Robert Shaw in L'Enfance du Christ; notes. MC v 161 n 4 p 31 Mr '60

---Johnston, D onald W. Choirs, choruses, chorales. MC v 161 n 1 p 36 Ja '60

---Myers, G ordon. Organizing a community chorus. MEJ v 46 n 4 p 68, 70 F-Mr '60

---Netherlands Chamber Choir under Felix de Nobel; 18 singers; NYC review. MC v 161 n 5 p 37 Ap '60

---Obernkirchen Children's Choir under Edith Moeller; NYC review. MC v 161 n 3 p 28 F '60

---Orchestre et choeurs Trajan Popesco; Paris review. GDC n 281-2 p 25-8 S 30'60

---Paris, canadian singers under the name "Les Disciples de Massenet de Montreal". GDC n 279-80 p 893 Jl 1'60

--- ---Don Cossacks; review. GDC n 259-60 p 405 F 12'60

--- ---Eglise de Pentemont: Chorale de Pentemont, Eddy Oelschlager; 200e anniversaire de Cherubini. GDC n 291 p 359 D 2'60

---Petits Chanteurs de Saint-François-de-Salles; Paris review. GDC n 267-8 p 556 Ap 8'60

---Polish Singers Alliance; NYC review. MC v 162 n 6 p 37 D '60

---Rodda, Ramona Strang. How does your choir sound? (Junior High School emphasis). MEJ v 46 n 3 p 60-63 Ja '60

---Roger Wagner Chorale with Los Angeles Symphony: Messiah (Bärenreiter edition); notes. MC v 161 n 3 p 37 F '60

---Schola Cantorum under Hugh Ross; 50th anniversary program.

MC v 161 n 7 p 23 Je '60

---Le Triptyque and Le Madrigal de la R. T. F. , dir. Jean-Paul Kreder; Paris review. GDC n 281-p 51-2 S 30'60

---Valence; Chorales protestantes, under Pierre Bégou; notes. GDC n 273 p 696 My 20'60

---St. Paul's Cathedral Boys' Choir with Leonard Bernstein at the piano, ens ph: London 1959. AmM v 8 n 11 p 7 D '60

DAS CHRISTELFLEIN, opera Munich cast. Op v 11 n 5 p 348 My '60

CHRISTIE, JOHN, 1882-, director Glyndebourne notes. MR v 21 n 3 p 249 Ag '60

---Talk on Glyndebourne at the week-end course on "Opera-Classical, Romantic and Modern". Op v 11 n 6 p 405 Je '60

CHRISTINE (HOLM), musical NYC notes. Th Arts v 44 n 7 p 59 Jl '60

CHRISTOPHER SLY, opera Eastwood, Thomas, composer; criticism of London's R oyal Court Theatre production under Colin Graham. Op v 2 n 3 p 226-7 Mr '60

CHRISTMAS
Freedley, George. Theatre Arts Bookshelf (a review column of several longer reviews with a further list attached). Th Arts v 44 n 12 p 6-7 D '60

---Honnegger's "Cantate de Noel"; Pierre Mollet, les enfants, les choeurs, chef Ansermet; Paris "Festival Honegger". GDC n 291 p 357 D 2'60

---Music on stereo tapes: a discography. HF v 10 n 12 p 105 D '60

---Music publishers and special music for Christmas available; large bibliography. MC v 162 n 3 p 15-8 S '60

---Opera, 90-minute, "Golden Child"; Paul Engle librettist and Philip Bazanson, an Iowa composer. MEJ v 47 n 2 p 12 N-D '60

---Paris; Noël dans les eglises.

GDC n 293-4 p 440-2 D 16'60
---Poem, Christmas greetings
by (Hope E. Stoddard). IM v 59
n 6 p 42 D '60
---Recording suitable for gifts,
by Herbert Kupferberg. HF v 10
n 12 p 45-6 D '60
CHRISTMAS EVE, opera
Rimsky-Korsakov at Zurich; re-
view. ON v 24 n 22 p 27 Ap 2'60
CHRISTOFF, BORIS, 1918-,
singer
With Symphony of the Air under
Julius Rudel; review. MC v 161
n 4 p 16 Mr '60
---In Boris Godunov, AP wl ph:
La Scala. La S n 125 p 44 Ap '60
---Por ph. MC v 162 n 5 p 22 N'60
CHURCH MUSIC
Les Archives Sonores de la Mus-
ique Sacrée, Lumen company of
France recording; details. HF
v 10 n 6 p 18 Je '60
---Broder, Nathan. Music of the
American Moravians (Columbia
releases reviewed). HF v 10 n 6
p 57-8 Je '60
---Castaldo, Joseph, score, and
John Shoemaker, libretto, of
"sacred cantata, Flight " on
Christ's Crucifixion and Resurre-
ction; "shocking". MC v 162 n 1
p 23 Jl'60
---Gradenwitz, Peter. The relig-
ious works of Arnold Schönberg.
MR v 21 n 1 p 19-29 F'60
---Jourdan-Morhange, H. Semain-
es de musique sacrée. GDC
n 290 p 322 N 25'60
---Louvet, Michel. Concert his-
toric, Eglise St. Gervais; les
Choeurs Richard-Waldy; Jean
Ver-Hasselt, organiste (premiè-
res, commentaire). GDC n 291
p 361 D 2'60
---Machaut, G. de. Messe "Notre-
Dame" (commentaire par J. Rol-
lin). GDC n 292 inset D 9'60
---Marcello: Psalm XVIII, Psalm
XV; Carissimi: Judicuum extre-
mum. and others; review of
Westminster recordings. Mus Q
v 46 n 1 p 122-4 Ja '60
---Mari, Pierrette. Messe en si,

Oratoire du Louve; H. Hornung,
un chef chorale; solistes. GDC
n 279-80 p 891 Jl 1'60
---NYC report. MC v 161 n 1 p 36
Ja '60
---Paris; Heures musicales de
Saint-Severin; review. GDC n 277
p 819 Je 17'60
--- ---La Société des Chanteurs de
Saint-Eustache: Messe en si de J-
S-Bach. GDC n 269-70 p 598
Ap 22'60
--- ---L'Orchestre et choeurs Tra-
jan Popesco en L'Eglise Saint-Ger-
main-des-Prés: Te Deum de Henry
Barraud; Psaume 129 de J. J. Grun-
enwald; Requiem op. 48 de Gabriel
Fauré. GDC n 281-2 p 25-8 S 30'60
--- ---Many reviews of special pro-
grams in the churches. GDC 1960
--- ---concert; Père Chéry, les
Petits Chanteurs de Saint-Louis;
Edith Briand, singer. GDC n 269-
70 p 599 Ap 22'60
--- ---reviews: La Passion Selon
Saint Matthieu (Bach), Fritz Wer-
ner and La Chorale H. Schutz;
then at Saint-Eustache, La Pas-
sion Selon Saint Jean, R. P. Martin.
GDC n 271 p 629-30 My 5'60
---Torah cantillation in the Reform
synagogue; notes on "Bibical Chant"
by A. W. Binder. MEJ v 46 n 3 p 82
Ja '60
---Wilson, Leonard. New choral
church music. CMJ v 4 n 4 p 61-5
Summer '60
---Yearbook for Liturgy and Hymn-
ology, volume 4; notes. WM n 4
p 78 Ag '60
CICCOLINI, ALDO
Chamfray, Claude. Paris review.
GDC n 293-4 p 461 D 16'60
---Paris review. GDC n 257-8
p 358 Ja 29'60
CILEA, FRANCESCA, 1866-1950,
composer
Marchetti, Arnaldo. A dieci anni
dalla sua scomparsa. La S n 133
p 78-9 D '60
---At the piano; at the Radio Roma,
1950, 2 phs. La S n 133 p 78-9
D '60
CIMENTO DELL'ALLEGRIA

61

(Cimento)
Milloss ballet; Josette Amiel e
Walter Zapolini, AP wl ph:Rome
Opera. LaS n 127 p 27, 55 Je'60

CINCINNATI
Humphreys, Henry S. May Festival review. MC v 161 n 7 p 4
Je'60
--- ---Music report. MC v 161
n 6 p 32 My'60
--- ---Music report:Don Quix-
ote;Don Giovanni, opera;con-
certs. MC v 162 n 6 p 22 D'60
--- ---Opera notes:La Sonnambula with Roberta Peters;Car-
men with Gloria Lane; La Traviata with Mary Costa. MC
v 162 n 2 p 13 Ag'60
---Johnen, Louis John. Music report. MC v 161 n 1 p 24 Ja'60;
same. MC v 161 n 3 p 43 F'60;
---Music Festival, 1873 to date;
notes. IM v 58 n 11 p 23 My'60
---Salome in a double bill with
Peter Grimes;Fausto Cleva
notes. MC v 162 n 3 p 11 S'60

THE CINCINNATI MAY FESTI-
VAL
Forty-third;notes. Am M v 8
n 3 p 18 Mr'60

CINCINNATI SUMMER OPERA
Dietz, Betty A. (Summary.)ON
v 25 n 1 p 23-4 O 8'60
---Repertory plans 1960. MC
v 161 n 6 p 6 My'60
---Summary 1960 season. Op v 11
n 10 p 684 O'60
---Thirty-ninth season;notes. Am
M v 8 n 6 p 13 Jl'60

CINCINNATI SYMPHONY
ORCHESTRA
Beethoven's Ninth;criticism;
list of soloists under Max Rudolf. MC v 161 n 6 p 32 My'60
---Contemporary repertory under director, Max Rudolf;
guest conductors. Am M v 8
n 9 p 13 O'60
---Rudolf, Max, conducting;notes.
MC v 161 n 3 p 43 F'60

CINEMA
See   Moving Pictures

CIRCUS
Matthews, William H. , Jr. Big

Top Americana(notes on Shelburne,
Vermont;on Pownal, Vermont;on
Peru, Indiana). PlM v 36 n 5 p 116
F'60
---Stott, R. Toole. Circus and Allied
Arts, a world bibliography, vol. II
(reviewed by Tristan Rémy). Th
Notbk v 15 n 2 p 68-9 Winter'60-61

LE CIRQUE d'HIVER
Wolff, Stéphane. Les frères Boug-
lione;ballet by André-René Bertin from Herodiade. GDC n 257-8
p 357 Ja 29'60

CIVIC CONCERT SERVICE
Vichey, Luben, president; annual
meeting. il MC v 162 n 6 p 7 D '60
---Annual conference, several
group phs: NYC. MC v 162 n 6
p 7 D '60

CILILIZATION MISUNDERSTOOD,
play
Bulgaria, Théâtre de Pleven, set
by G. Karakachev, ph: 1959. WT
v 9 n 3 p 276 Autumn '60

CALFLIN, AVERY, 1898-, composer
NYC notes on Recitativo, Aria and
Stretta, the Joseph Eger Players.
MC v 161 n 7 p 25 Je '60

CLANCY, RUSSELL. And a cartridge in a pear tree (his home installation of electronic music with
5 pictures). HF v 10 n 3 p 50-3,
130 Mr '60

CLAPHAM, JOHN. The progress
of Dvořák's music in Britain. MR
v 21 n 2 p 130-139 My '60

CLARION CONCERTS
NYC reviews; Newell Jenkins, conductor; soloists. MC v 161 n 4 p 19,
20 Mr '60
---US première: Scarlatti's Il Martirio di Saint 'Orsolo. AmM v 8
n 2 p 18 F '60

CLARK, FRANCES ELLIOTT (1860-
1958). (Excerpts from her letters
when in Europe.) MEJ v 46 n 5
p 25, 69-73 Ap-My '60
---Cooke, James Francis. (A memorial symposium.) il MEJ v 46 n 5
p 20-25 Ap-My '60
---Por ph. MEJ v 46 n 5 p 19
Ap-My '60

CLARKE, HENRY LELAND, 1907-,
composer

Premières: Freedom, Thy Holy Light (in Los Angeles 1960); Two Wedding Voluntaries (Maine 1960); ACAB v 9 n 3 p 28 1960
---Verrall, John. Henry Leland Clarke (with a check list of works). ACAB v 9 n 3 p 2-8 1960
LA CLE DES SONGES, ballet
Amiel, Josette, anu Attilio Labis, AP wl ph: L'Opéra-Comique. OpP n 19 p 64 1960
CLEMENS, HANS, 1885-1959, singer
Notes; b. Germany; d. Colorado. MC v 161 n 1 p 6 Ja '60
CLEMENS NON PAPA, JACOBUS 1500-1556, composer
American Institute of Musicology; masses now completed (criticism). Mus Q v 46 n 3 p 390-393 Jl '60
CLEVELAND
Reports: Summer Pops under Cleveland Orchestra, 16 concerts; Georges Georgescu as guest conductor 2 concerts for the Cleveland Orchestra; ballet companies. MC v 162 n 5 p 23 N '60
---Spaeth, Arthur. Theatre, Cleveland (Karamu, C leveland Play House, Western Reserve's Eldred Players, Lakewood Little Theatre and others). Th Arts v 44 n 1 p 76-7, 83 Ja '60
---Widder, Rose. Berea Bach Festival; Cleveland concerts. MC v 162 n 1 p 24 Jl '60
---Music report. MC v 161 n 4 p 31 Mr '60; same. MC v 161 n 5 p 24 Ap '60; same. MC v 161 n 6 p 30 My '60; same. MC v 162 n 6 p 26 D '60
THE CLEVELAND ORCHESTRA
Concerts; soloists. MC v 162 n 6 p 26 D '60
---Contemporary repertory listed; premières marked. AmM v 8 n 9 p 12 O '60
---Forty-second season notes. MC v 161 n 7 p 33 Je '60
---reviews (3) George Szell, conducting, Maureen Forrester and Ernst Haefliger; Henryk Szeryng, violinist; Leon Fleisher. MC v 161 n 4 p 16, 17 Mr '60

---Reviews; plans. MC v 161 n 5 p 24 Ap '60
CLEVELAND PHILHARMONIC ORCHESTRA
Grossman, Karl, conductor; notes. MC v 161 n 7 p 33 Je '60
CLEVELAND WOMEN'S ORCHESTRA
Schandler, Hyman, founder-director; 25th year; notes. MC v 161 n 6 p 30 My '60
CLIBURN, RILDIA O'BRYAN
Tribute to Steinway (facsimile) with photograph of Van, her son, at the keyboard, she standing. MEJ v 46 n 5 p 1 Ap-My '60
CLIBURN, VAN, 1935-, pianist
Award established at Juilliard: Mme. Rosina Lhevinne (sketch of her career). J Rev v 7 n 1 p 14-5 Winter 59-60
---Chicago criticism. MC v 161 n 6 p 26 My '60
---Interview. il ON v 24 n 21 p 12-3 Mr 26'60
---Juilliard award established by Mr. Cliburn: Mme. Rosina Lhevinne Award. AmM v 8 n 4 p 17 Ap '60
CLIFFORD, MAY, pianist
Career notes; Australian. por MD v 50 n 9 p 16 Mr '60
CLINT, LUKE, scenic designer
Notes; list of scenes painted for Sadler's Wells circa 1818 (two illustrations). Th Notbk v 15 n 2 p 61 Winter '60-61
CLOCHE DE MON COEUR (MOULIN), musical
Paris notes. WP v 11 n 3 p 6 Ja '60
CLOCKWISE, play
Ens AP wl ph: Sheldon Secunda. Th Arts v 44 n 1 p 27 Ja '60
CLOONAN, RICHARD T.
Theatre USA, series: Detroit. il Th Arts v 44 n 10 p 62-65 O '60
CLOSSON, HERMAN (1901-). Belgian artists abroad. WT v 9 n 1 p 47-50 Spring '60
CLURMAN, HAROLD EDGAR (1901-). A definition (on criticism of the living theatre). TDR v 4 n 4 p 32 My '60

63

(Clurman)
--- ---Actors: the image of their era. TDR v 4 n 3 p 38-44 Mr '60
--- ---The paradox of the French stage. il Th Arts v 44 n 12 p 64-5, 78 D '60
--- ---(The Theatre Group and other projects of the 1930s.) Th Arts v 44 n 9 p 15-8 S '60
---AP ph. Th Arts v 44 n 7 p 52 Jl '60

COCK A DOODLE DANDY, play London, 1959; ens AP wl ph: Gur Gravett. WT v 9 n 1 p 92 Spring '60

COCTEAU, JEAN (1889-). Hommage à Gérard Philipe. Spec 1 p 44 1960
---Picasso and Stravinsky, drawing. ON v 25 n 5 p 11 D 10'60

COE, RICHARD L. (1916-). Theatre Washington. il Th Arts v 44 n 12 p 21-4, 73 D '60

COELHO DE FREITAS, LEDA, singer
Paris debut, la cantatrice brésilienne. GDC n 267-8 p 557 Ap 8'60

COHN, JAMES, composer
Prize for symphony, competition by Italiana Diffusione. MC v 162 n 3 p 31 S '60

COKE, ROGER SACHEVERELL, 1912-, composer
Mitchell, Donald. The Cenci (review of Coke's opera, Scala Theatre, London). Op v 11 n 1 p 60 Ja '60

COLBRAN, ISABELLA ANGELA, 1785-1845, singer
Schmidt. Colbrau, portrait painted 1817 in role of Saffo, ph: La Scala Museum. ON v 25 n 7 p 27 D 24'60

COLBERT, CLAUDETTE (1905-). My ten favorite plays: list. Th Arts v 44 n 7 p 68 Jl '60

COLE, WENDELL (1914-). The nineteenth century stage at Piper's Opera House (Virginia City, Nevada). Th Notbk v 15 n 2 p 52-55 Winter 60-61

COLEMAN, EMILY. The Metropolitan Opera. il Th Arts v 44 n 3 p 34-5 Mr '60

COLERIDGE, SAMUEL TAYLOR, 1772-1834, poet
Fogle, Richard Harter. Coleridge on dramatic illusion. TDR v 4 n 4 p 33-44 My '60

COLLEGIUM MUSICUM of BOSTON
Geiringer, Karl, director: Haydn's Orlando Paladino. ON v 25 n 8 p 7 D 31'60

COLLIER, MARIE, singer
London criticism. Op v 11 n 1 p 64 Ja '60

COLLIN, IRENE, dancer
Wolff, Stéphane. (Obituary notes.) GDC n 274 p 718 My 27'60

COLLINS, RUDY, 1937-, jazz drummer
Born NYC; note. IM v 58 n 9 p 34 Mr '60

COLOGNE
Worthington, Randall. Music report: Electrola company; Electronic Music Studio at Westdeutscher Rundfunk; Opera House. por HF v 10 n 5 p 24 My '60

COLOGNE MUNICIPAL OPERA
Criticism: Wozzeck; The Fiery Angel; The Death of Grigori Rasputin; Blood Wedding; The Nightingale with L'Enfant et les Sortilèges; ballet notes also. MR v 21 n 3 p 243-4 Ag '60

COLOMBIA
Theatre report. WP v 11 n 6 p 7 Ap '60; same. WP v 11 n 9 p 7 Jl '60; same. WP v 12 n 1 p 4 O'60
---Cristobal Colon de Ghelderode, ens ph: Bogota. WP v 12 n 1 p 4 O '60

COLOMBO, GIANLUIGI
Paganini as a pianist. La S n 127 p 12-3 Je '60

COLOMBO, VERA, singer
E Mario Pistoni in "Serenade", AP wl ph: La Scala. La S n 124 p 31 Mr '60

COLUM, PADRAIC (1881-). Theatre, Dublin. Th Arts v 44 n 2 p 24-5 F '60

COLUMBIA ARTISTS MANAGEMENT
Opening of CAMI building in NYC, portfolio, including Judson Concert Hall, phs. MC v 162 n 5 p 5 N '60

COLUMBIA BROADCASTING
COMPANY
Commission to Balanchine and
Stravinsky for music-dance work
for TV. AmM v 8 n 6 p 14 Jl '60
COLZANI, ANSELMO, singer
Metropolitan debut.MC v 161 n 6
p 16 My '60
COLUMBUS, opera
Ekg at Munich's Cuvilliéstheater;
notes and two scenes. Op v 11 n 7
p 485 Jl '60
COMBAT (DOLLAR), ballet
Labis, Atilio, et Claude Bessy.
TD n 94 p 19 Je '60
LE COMÉDIE-FRANÇAISE
Blau, Herbert. (Notes on his Eu-
ropean theatre tour.) TDR v 5 n 1
p 93-5 S '60
---Brookings, Jack. The declama-
tory theatre of France; Part I.
PlM v 37 n 2 p 31 N '60
---The Malraux Plan in reforming
the Comédie Française. Th Arts
v 44 n 12 p 61 D '60
COMÉDIENS ROUTIERS
French section of the National
Theatre of Belgium; under Huis-
man brothers; notes. WT v 9 n 1
p 26 Spring '60
THE COMEDY OF ERRORS, play
Rotterdam, 1960; also scene from
Amsterdam 1960 production, phs:
Lemaire en Wennink; Particam.
WT v 9 n 2 p 172-3 Summer '60
COMMEDIA DELL'ARTE
Pantalone and Zanni serenading,
AP wl painting, fresco 1576 at
Trausnitz. Th R v 2 n 3 p 129 1960
---Harlequin, ph: La Scala Museum;
Daumier's Crispin et Scapin. ON
v 25 n 7 p 11 D 24'60
COMMEDIA umana (Massine), ballet
Fracci, Carla, ens AP wl ph: Ner-
vi. La S n 129-30 p 65 Ag-S '60
COMMUNAL THEATRE OF ANT-
WERP
The Dutch section of the National
Theatre of Belgium; notes on
administration. WT v 9 n 1 p 28-
29 Spring '60
COMMUNION FOR SHADOWS, play
Winnipeg notes; Joseph Mauro. WP
v 11 n 8 p 3 Je '60

COMMUNITY CONCERTS, INC.
Goldin, Milton. Commerce, concerts and critics. MEJ v 46 n 6
p 37, 39, 42 Je-Jl '60
---NYC; 33rd meeting. il MC v 162
n 6 p 11 D '60
---Thirty-third annual conference,
portraits and groups, phs: NYC.
MC v 162 n 6 p 11 D '60
COMPETITIONS
The Academy of Vocal Arts, Philadelphia: a Broadcast Auditions,
a scholarship as prize. ON v 24
n 12 p 3 Ja 23'60
---Australia; ABC concerto and
vocal contests, 1961 rules. MD
v 51 n 3 p 17 S '60
--- ---Music in the South Street
contests; notes. MD v 51 n 3
p 15-6 S '60
--- ---Wangaratta Choral Competition; judges; winners. MD
v 50 n 8 p 12 F '60
---Australian Musical Association,
London: competition open to Australia.-born and those residing
as much as 5 years; instrumentalists and vocalists. MD v 50
n 7 p 13 Ja '60
---Avis de Concours: Vienne, the
35e festival de la Société International pour la Musique Contemporaine; Grenoble; Bourse de
voyage, Paris. GDC n 284 p 141
O 14'60
---Bands; The Best New Band Contest 1960; notes on prizes; rules.
il IM v 59 n 3 p 9, 15 S '60
---Bayonne; Bourges. GDC n 288
p 262 N 11'60
---Bolzano; la dodicesima edizione
del concorso pianistico "Ferruccio
Busoni"; primo premio; il secondo
Agustin Anievas e James Mathis;
la giuria. La S n 131 p 66 O '60
---Broadcast Music, Inc. ; Student
Composers Awards; details. CMJ
v 4 n 2 p 42 Winter '60
---Bruyr, José. Concours d'inter-
prétation de la mélodie française.
GDC n 265-6 p 505 Mr 25'60
---Chapallaz, Gilbert. Genève: Le
concours international d'execution.
GDC n 286 p 209 O 28'60

(Competitions)

---Column "Castings and Contests", giving details of many musical contests. MC 1960

---Concorso Ricordi: Pour un Don Quichotte, Jean-Pierre Rivière, Randal Lemoine. La S n 133 p 116 D '60

---Le Concours de Rome; report by Pierrette Mari. GDC n 281-2 p 62 S 30'60

---Concours et palmarès: Barcelone; Vienna; Paysbas; Toulouse; Ricordi, the Jury. GDC n 288 p 265 N 11'60

---Concours Ginette-Neveu; Paris report. GDC n 273 p 691 My 20'60

---Concours international de piano Reine Elisabeth: reports. GDC n 279-80 p 894 Jl 1'60

--- ---list of winners. MC v 161 n 7 p 15 Je '60

---Concours Noémie Pérugia: le jury; Mlle. Renou, une première mention; Paris. GDC n 269-70 p 594 Ap 22'60

---Dandenong Festival, pianists; Australian notes. MD v 50 n 9 p 18 Mr '60

---Details on Nantes; Strasbourg; Liège; Budapest; Belgique. GDC n 295 p 501 D 30'60

---East Melbourne; composition contests under Guild of Australian Composers; winners. MD v 50 n 11 p 19 My '60

---Ford Foundation, 32 awards to theatre people. PlM v 36 n 8 p 177 My '60

---France; concours et palmarès: Cambrai; Nevers; Saint-Etienne. GDC n 289 p 302-3 N 18'60

--- ---partie officielle: Nancy; Lorient; Toulouse; Aix-en-Provence; guitare concours. GDC n 290 p 332-3 N 25'60

---Genève; 34 jures pour le concours international, 16e. GDC n 271 p 631 My 5'60

---Gershwin Memorial Contest; 16th year notes. MC v 161 n 5 p 8 Ap '60

---Grand Prix Musicale de la Ville de Paris 1960: details.

GDC n 267-8 p 547 Ap 8'60

---Guitare, notre concours de composition. GDC n 290 p 333 N 25'60

---Gutman, John. Metropolitan; National Council auditions; survey of last decade winners. ON v 25 n 4 p 21 D 3'60

---International String Congress sponsored by the American Federation of Musicians. MEJ v 47 n 2 p 71 N-D '60

---Music; a list with details of many composition and performance contests, "Awards and Competitions" regular column. MEJ 1960

--- ---contests: rules, addresses, column, Awards and Competitions. MEJ 1960

--- ---many contests with details MC v 162 n 1 p 6 Jl '60

--- ---"Avis de Concours". GDC 1960

---National Federation of Music Clubs: 16 year-round scholarships; details. IM v 58 n 9 p 43 Mr '60

---The 1960 Queen Elisabeth of Belgium International Music Competition; list of US prize-winners, AmM v 8 n 5 p 12 Je '60

---1961 Casals International Violoncello Competition; financed by private concert, home of Mr. and Mrs. David Rockefeller; notes. AmM v 8 n 10 p 13 N '60

---Paris; Concours national de Musique (liste). TD n 93 p 19 My '60

--- ---Grand Prix Musical du Conseil Général de la Seine (compositeur de musique français domicilié dans les limites du Department de la Seine); jury. GDC n 281-2 p 73 S 30'60

--- ---notes on Marguerite Long-Jacques Thibaud International Competition: pianists and violinists; notes. IM v 59 n 4 p 27 O'60

---Payzant, Geoffrey. The competitive music festivals (Canada). CMJ v 4 n 3 p 35-46 Spring '60

---Penfold, Dorothy. Twelfth

Hartwell Eisteddfod (Australia).
MD v 50 n 7 p 18 Ja '60
---Premio Paganini; Genova: I
premio Stuart Canin (USA) II
premio Siegfried Gawriloff (Ger-
mania) III Liliane Caillon (Fran-
cia). La S n 124 p 61 Mr '60
---Prince Rainier III of Monaco
Musical Composition Prize;
1960 first year; notes. MC v 161
n 1 p 8 Ja '60
---Prix de Rome; la salle de con-
férences du Louvre; M. Decaris;
"tout cela dans le grand tradition
du vénérable Institut de France-
remise Solennelle"; Gilles Boizard. GDC n 291 p 354 D 2'60
---Ricordi and Company, one act
opera, and a chamber opera;
notes. MD v 50 n 8 p 13 F '60
---Rules, dates, places. MC v 161
n 7 p 14 Je '60
---Selected list, open to all musicians, each issue. WM 1960
---Singing; Royal Liverpool Philharmonic Society's International
Singers Competition ; winners;
editorial on problems of training.
Op v 11 n 7 p 456 Jl '60
--- ---sixth "Chant de Toulouse";
and Bucharest the second "George Enesco Competition". Op
v 11 n 1 p 48 Ja '60
--- ---Toulouse France; list of
winners. ON v 25 n 6 p 7 D 17'60
---US; Naumberg Foundation expanding aid; details and leaders.
MC v 161 n 6 p 11 My '60
--- ---bands; report of 1960 contest with 5 bands pictured; Jimmy
Cook, 1912-leader in Las Vegas
first prize. IM v 59 n 6 p 10-1, 15
D '60
--- ---dance bands; Detroit finals;
notes. il   IM v 59 n 5 p 9-10
N '60
---Violinists, violists, violoncell-
ists by the Walter W. Naumberg
Foundation; awards, rules, judges, address. AmM v 8 n 6 p 10
Jl '60
---Les Voix d'Or: 1956 to date,
notes; 1960 at Vichy. GDC n 271
p 621 My 5'60

--- ---à Vichy. GDC n 267-8 p 547
Ap 8'60
---Melbourne "Sun" Aria finalists
on stage, ens ph: Sun. MD v 51 n 5
p 16 N '60
COMPOSERS
Australian UNESCO Seminar for
Composers, 1960; report by
chairman, George Loughlin. por
MD v 51 n 2 p 16-7 Ag '60
---Composers Forum; NYC report.
MC v 161 n 7 p 39 Je '60
---Composers Forum; a San Fran-
cisco; report. MC v 161 n 3 p 38
F '60
---Composers Showcase; NYC, Cir-
cle In the Square; John Cage pre-
mière; Henry Cowell; David Tudor;
Beaux Arts Quartet. MC v 161
n 6 p 36 My '60
---First International Composers'
Conference at Stratford, Ontario,
1960; plan. MEJ v 46 n 4 p 8 F-
Mr '60
COMPOSERS FACSIMILE EDITION
NYC; serviceable and inexpensive
reproduced modern music; note.
ACAB v 9 n 2 p 18 1960
COMPOSITION
Mari, Pierrette. Au Conservatoire
National Supérieur: concours de
composition. GDC n 283 p 98 O 7'60
---The Young Composers Project:
12 high schools, US; 12 young com-
posers in residence via Ford Found-
ation. MEJ v 46 n 6 p 72 Je-Jl '60
LE COMTE ORY, opera
Budapest; Maria Gyurkovics e
Jozsef Réti; Gyorgy Melis 2 phs.
La S n 126 p 38 My '60
CONCERTGEBOUW ORCHESTRA
Amsterdam season; conductors,
high lights. MC v 161 n 5 p 33
Ap '60
CONCERTO (SKIBINE), ballet
Skibine, George, and Marjorie
Tallchief, AP wl ph: L'Opéra
Comique. OpP n 19 p 62 1960
CONCERTO BAROCCO (BALANCHINE),
ballet
Ens AP wl ph: Roger Wood. Th
Arts v 44 n 11 p 60 N '60
CONCERTO IN BES (VINCENT)
ballet

(Concerto)
Pays-Bas; music, Vivaldi. WP
v 12 n 1 p 9 O '60
LES CONCERTS DE MIDI
Bruyr, José; le fameux cabaret
d'avant-grade: le Groupe des
Six. GDC n 267-8 p 561 Ap 8'60
---Chailley, Jacques, directeur;
serie; Simone Rist, Jean Mal-
raye, Marcel Vigneron, singers;
review. GDC n 267-8 p 558
Ap 8'60
CONCRETE MUSIC
Abbiati, Franco. Libera Musica
e Musica di stato. il La S n 127
p 7-11 Je '60
---Luening, Otto. (Book review of
Prieberg's Musica ex Machina.)
J Rev v 7 n 3 p 24 Fall '60
---See also Electronic Music
CONDON, EDDIE, 1905-, band-
leader
On concert stage, in a night club,
two small phs. HF v 10 n 5 p 36
My '60
CONDUCTING
Cleveland Orchestra fellowships
(Kulas Foundation) for two young
conductors. IM v 59 n 1 p 20 Jl
'60
---Piastro, Mishel. The concert
master as conductor. por IM
v 58 n 7 p 22 Ja '60
CONDUCTORS
Besançon; Le Concours des
Jeunes Chefs d'Orchestre. GDC
n 283 p 96 O 7'60
---Hallé Society list; notes on
fine programs. MR v 21 n 3
p 245-6 Ag'60
---Murphy, James F. Student
conductors for high schools, a
musical resource. MEJ v 46 n 5
p 47-8 Ap-My '60
---Paris, Festival Beethoven,
Concerts Lamoureux: Bernard
Haitink, Pierre Dervaux, Georges Prêtre; notes. GDC n 289
p 295 N 18'60
CONE, EDWARD T (1917-). Analysis today. Mus Q v 46 n 2
p 172-188 Ap '60
CONLY, JOHN M. Eye and ear
story (stereophonic phonography

vs. TV monophony, a parlor dis-
cussion). HF v 10 n 10 p 41 O'60
---Reflections on a goodly fellow-
ship (Beethoven). por HF v 10 n 4
p 34-6 Ap '60
THE CONNECTION, play
Critical note on Jack Gelber prize
play. WT v 9 n 2 p 190 Summer'60
CONNER, NADINE, 1913-, singer
Notes. il ON v 24 p 3 Ap 16'60
CONRAD, DODA, singer
Paris review. GDC n 255-6 p 311
Ja 15'60
LE CONSERVATOIRE NATIONALE
D'ART DRAMATIQUE
American view of France's acting
school. PlM v 37 n 2 p 31 N '60
THE CONSUL, opera
NYC Opera; Patricia Neway; cri-
ticism. MC v 161 n 4 p 14 Mr '60
--- ---revival with Patricia Neway,
original Magda; not as moving as
at first but a landmark of Ameri-
can opera. ON v 24 n 19 p 28
Mr 12'60
CONTE CRUEL (SKIBINE), ballet
Paris Opéra review; Delerue,
music; settings by Delfau. MC
v 161 n 3 p 44 F '60
CONTE SANS NOM, play
Athens; Jacques Campanellis;
notes. WP v 11 n 4 p 8 F '60
CONTEMPORARY BAROQUE
ENSEMBLE
NYC review. MC v 162 n 5 p 31
N '60
COOKE, DERYCK. The Language
of Music (Robert L. Jacobs dis-
cusses this book in an essay, "
"Music as symbol".) MR v 21 n 3
p 226-236 Ag '60
COOKERLY, JACK, organist
At the organ, ph. IM v 59 n 5 p 7
N '60
COPENHAGEN
Kolodin, Irving. Including the
Scandinavian (singers). il Th Arts
v 44 n 3 p 46 Mr '60
COPLAND, AARON, 1900-, composer
Boston Symphony; "joyously fear-
less programs". MC v 161 n 3
p 41 F '60
---England; notes on lectures and
conducting. AmM v 8 n 5 p 5 Je'60

---London concert, conducted by the composer; nothing later than 1926. MC v 161 n 7 p 13 Je '60
---Mason, Colin. (On Piano Fantasy.) AmM v 8 n 2 p 19 F '60
---Notes on his compositions which he is conducting in Europe. AmM v 8 n 4 p 8, 10 Ap '60
---Notes on recent activities. AmM v 8 n 11 p 10 D '60
---Tour itinerary. WM n 3 p 56 Je '60
---Por ph. AmM v 8 n 4 p 9 Ap'60
---Por ph. MC v 162 n 6 p 18 D '60

COPYRIGHT
Copyright Law Symposium number 10, Columbia University Press (book review). IM v 58 n 11 p 32 My '60
---Haensel, Carl. Copyright in opera and drama (Germany). WT v 9 n 3 p 245-8 Autumn '60
---Symposium number, Columbia University Press; essays include tape recording, photocopying, jukebox exemptions, etc. MEJ v 46 n 3 p 80 Ja '60

CORELLI, FRANCO, 1924? -, singer
As Chénier in Giordano opera; Genoa criticism; also Monte Carlo success in Turandot. Op v 11 n 5 p 354, 356 My '60

CORELLI, JEAN. Le ballet Allemand. il TD n 89 p 17-9 Ja '60

CORENA, FERNANDO, 1917? -, singer
As Dr. Dulcamara, AP hl ph: Eugene Cook. ON v 25 n 7 p 20 D 24'60
---Por ph. ON v 25 n 7 p 33 D 24'60

CORNEILLE, THOMAS (1625-1709) Medée, tragedie; la musique de M. Charpentier (as performed 1693 at the Academie Royale de Musique, Paris, the libretto as published by Christophe Ballard, 1693, in French). Chrys v 13 nos 5-8 1960

CORNELL, KATHERINE, 1898-, actress
Por ph. Th Arts v 44 n 9 p 13

S '60
CORONATION OF POPPEA, opera
See L'Incoronazione di Poppaea, opera

DER CORREGIDOR, opera
Wiesbaden; Act I AP ph. Op v 11 p 67 Autumn '60

CORTE, ANDREA DELLA (1883-).
In questo mese ha lette (Carteggio Nietzsche Wagner); Dialogues des vivants, André Maurois. La S n 122 p 42-3 Ja '60
--- ---In questo mese ha letto (seriale). La S 1960

CORTES, ANTONIO
Authentique Gitan, Flamenco par Yves Silvant. por TD n 92 p 22-3 Ap '60

CORTES, RAMIRO, composer
Première: Guitarra, Three Spanish Songs (NYC 1960). ACAB v 9 n 3 p 28 1960

COSAS DE PAPA Y MAMA, play
Madrid notes; Alfonso Paso. WP v 11 n 9 p 3 Jl '60

COSI fan tutte, opera
The Editor. (This Salzburg production and the Bayreuth Lohengrin "worth the long journey"; Rennert's production in the Landes theater.) il Op v 11 p 51-2 Autumn '60
---Niki-kai Company; Tokyo review; Takehisa Kinoshita, director. ON v 24 n 20 p 26 Mr 19'60
---Salzburg; Guenther Rennert staging and Carl Boehm, conducting to commedia dell'arte style; notes. MC v 162 n 4 p 27 O '60
---Gérard, Rolf. Designs, six photographs: Sedge LeBlanc. PlM v 36 n 6 p 130-2 Mr '60
---Hartt Opera Theatre, ens AP wl ph: Hartford, Conn. MC v 162 n 3 p 17 S '60
---Hintlesham; ens AP wl ph: Hawker Films. Op v 11 p 69 Autumn'60
---Salzburg, 1960; ens AP wl ph: Ellinger. WM n 5 p 110 O '60

COSMOPOLITAN OPERA
Rich, Alan. San Francisco's Cosmopolitan Opera: Turandot with Nilsson; a poor Boris; other notes. ON v 24 n 24 p 27-8 Ap 16'60

(Cosmopolitan)
San Francisco; liquidation. Op
v 11 n 10 p 685 O '60
COSTA, JEAN, organist
Louvet, Michel. Paris review.
GDC n 288 p 257 N 11'60
COSTA, ORAZIO (1911-). (On
staging Chekhov; Italian view-
point.) il WT v 9 n 2 p 124-5
Summer ''60
COSTON, HERBERT. Sean
O'Casey: prelude to playwriting.
TDR v 5 n 1 p 102-112 S '60
COSTUME
Chain mail; how to knit chain
mail by Edmund Chavez. il PlM
v 37 n 2 p 34 N '60
---Contemporary clothes, illus-
trated each issue. La S 1960
---Opera, Thaïs, in Naples; Vir-
ginia Zeani in "grotesque outfit"
" forgetting that it was Thaïs'
nudity which enticed the cenobite''.
ON v 24 n 14 p 26 F 6'60
---Armisted, Horace. Florestan,
costume sketch, Fidelio, ph:
Melançon. ON v 24 n 15 p 22
F 13'60
---Band dress, University of
Iowa, marching style, concert
style, 2 phs. MEJ v 46 n 4 p 51
F-Mr '60
---La Belle au Bois Dormant,
The International Ballet (Cuevas);
designer, Raymond de Larrain,
8 phs: Lido. TD n 98 p 7-11 D'60
---Faust; Méphisto, wl ph: Paris
Opéra. OpP n 19 1960
---Harlequin; Marcello Moretto
as Harlequin, hl ph: Milan. MC
v 161 n 4 p 15 Mr '60
--- ---wl ph: La Scala Museum.
ON v 25 n 7 p 11 D 24'60
---Job, character in outdoor Bib-
ical play, Kentucky; 2 phs. PlM
v 36 n 7 p 158 Ap '60
---Kiltie Band costume of Carnegie Institute of Technology:
concert style; marching style,
2 phs. MEJ v 46 n 3 p 35 Ja '60
---Motley. Martha, for the Metropolitan, 3 costume drawings.
ON v 25 n 1 p 17 O 8'60
---Oberlin, Russell, prince in

The play of Daniel, AP wl ph:
Denis de Marney. Op v 11 n 8
p 574 Ag '60
---Oedipus Rex, Sadler's Wells,
ens ph: Sim. ON v 24 n 23 p 26
Ap 9'60
---Portfolio of television plays and
opera, many countries. WT v 9 n 4
Winter '60
---Purdue University band costume,
marching style, military style, phs.
MEJ v 46 n 5 p 33 Ap-My '60
---Turandot; Teatro alla Scala,
several AP phs. La S n 126 p 30
My '60
---Turkish; Boehme as a comic
Turk; also a noble Turk, phs: A.
Madner. ON v 24 n 24 p 4-5
Ap 16'60
COUNCIL ON LIBRARY RESOURCES,
INC.
Grant to the International Federa-
tion on Library Associations
(IFLA). $95, 420 to promote
uniformity in cataloguing. Th R
v 2 n 2 p 128 1960
A COUNTRY SCANDAL, play
NYC review of Chekhov.   Th Arts
v 44 n 7 p 58 Jl '60
---Chekhov play, Greenich Mews,
NYC, ens AP ph. Th Arts v 44 n 7
p 60 Jl '60
COUPS DE ROULIS, musical
Reims review. GDC n 267-8
p 551 Ap 8'60
COURET, GABRIEL, régisseur
général
Paris Opéra; with René Bianco,
hl ph. OpP n 19 p 25 1960
COURLANDER, HAROLD
Folkways records, editor, ph.
HF v 10 n 6 p 44 Je '60
COURTNEY, RICHARD. British
theatre; report from London. PlM
v 36 n 5 p 105 F '60
COURVILLE, XAVIER DE
with Rampal and Veyron-Lacroix;
"Micropéra" program. GDC n 286
p 198 O 28'60
COVENT GARDEN OPERA
Barker, Frank Granville. (Reviews
of Der Rosenkavalier, Salome; note
on Carmen.) ON v 24 n 16 p 28-30
F 20'60

---Editorial: new booking scheme, complaints and answer from the management. Op v 11 n 11 p 728 N '60

--- ---repertory, on costs. Op v 11n 3 p 174 Mr '60

--- ---Sgr. Gobbi's withdrawal from Macbeth, with hesitancy by the administration to refund extra price on tickets. Op v 11 n 5 p 314 My '60

---Goodwin, Noël. (Report of operas; 1959 deficit of $68,500.) MC v 161 n 3 p 45 F '60

---Opinion (in letters) on opera in English, pro and con; on imported or British singers. Op v 11 n 2 p 127-130 F '60

---Reviews:Aïda;Cavalleria Rusticana and Pagliacci, Jon Vickers. il Op v 11 n 2 p 150, 153-4 F'60

--- ---Cavalleria Rusticana;Pagliacci;La Traviata;Tales of Hoffmann;Lucia di Lammermoor; Turandot. Op v 11n 3 p 225, 231 Mr'60

--- ---Cavalleria Rusticana;Pagliacci;The Mastersingers of Nuremberg. Op v 11 n 4 p 300-1 Ap'60

--- ---La Bohème. Op v 11 n 9 p 644 S'60

--- ---La Bohème;Aïda;Macbeth (cast and full review). il Op v 11 n 5 p 363, 367-9 My'60

--- ---La Sonnambula;Der Rosenkavalier;Il Barbiere di Sigviglia;Carmen. Op v 11 n 12 p 848, 850-1 D'60

--- ---La Traviata;Il Barbiere di Siviglia;Aïda;Elektra. Op v 11 n 7 p 502-6, 508-9 Jl'60

--- ---Macbeth;Parsifal;The Trojans. il Op v 11 n 6 p 438-47 Je'60

---Report. portfolio Op v 11 n 3 p 195-7 Mr'60

---Statistics of 1959-60:list of singers with number of appearances;producers;repertory with casts. Op v 11 n 8 p 540-1 Ag'60

COWAN, HARRIETTE, singer
Mari, Pierrette. Paris review.

GDC n 291 p 361 D 2'60

COWARD, NOEL, 1899-, playwright
Por ph. Th Arts v 44 n 9 p 57 S'60

COWELL, HENRY(1897-). A note on Wallingford Riegger. ACAB v 9 n 3 p 14-5 1960

---Première:Symphony No. 12(Houston 1960). ACAB v 9 n 3 p 29 1960

COWL, JANE, 1890-1950, actress
Hl ph. Th Arts v 44 n 9 p 57 S'60

THE CRADLE WILL ROCK, opera
Blitzstein, Marc. (His story of the first production of his opera which deals with unionism in the steel industry.) por ON v 24 n 15 p 10-1 F 13'60

---(Merkling, Frank.) New York City Opera; "lies somewhere between opera and a Harvard Hasty Pudding show; embarrassed its original sponsor, the Federal Theatre Project". ON v 24 n 19 p 27 Mr 12'60

---New York City Opera; "inspired by the school of Kurt Weil's Three-Penny Opera", "rather threadbare" jazz idion; notes. MC v 161 n 4 p 14 Mr '60

--- ---review. Op v 11 n 5 p 340 My '60

---Review; NYC Opera. il La S n 126 p 36 My '60

CRAIG, DON, conductor
Por ph. MEJ v 47 n 2 p 74 N-D'60

CRAS, JEAN, 1879-1932, composer
Chamfray, Claude. Fiche biographique. GDC n 274 p 730 My 27'60

CREMONA, TRANQUILLO.
Melodia (in copertina). La S n 123 cover F '60

IL CRESCENDO, one-act opera
Cherubini work; Florence notes. MC v 162 n 5 p 42 N '60

CRESPIN, REGINA, singer
As Fedra, AP hl ph: La Scala. La S n 123 p 31 F '60

---As the Marschallin, AP wl ph. Guy Gravett. Op v 11 n 12 cover D '60

CRESTON, PAUL, 1906-, composer
Ankara contract: lectures and conducting. MC v 161 n 5 p 39 Ap '60

LE CRI DE L'ENGOULEVENT, play
Montreal notes; Guy Dufresne. WP

71

(Le Cri)
v 11 n 6 p 1 Ap '60

CRITICISM

The adjudicator; discussion of imported judges for Canadian music competitions. CMJ v 4 n 3 p 43-5 Spring '60

---African music; a critical review of A. M. Jones' book, Studies in African Music. Mus Q v 46 n 1 p 105-10 Ja '60

---Ashbrook, William. (Fidelio) ON v 24 n 15 p 4-5 F 13'60

--- ---(The Flying Dutchman.) ON v 24 n 18 p 6-7 Mr 5'60

---Atkinson, Brooks. Anatomy of newspaper criticism. il Th Arts v 44 n 4 p 8-9 Ap '60

---Australia; music criticism controversy stirred by Georges Tzipine, visiting conductor. MD v 51 n 1 p 10-13 Jl '60

---Baignères, Claude. Creation of ballets at the Opéra and at the Opéra-Comique: Pas de Dieux, Gershwin and Gene Kelly; Daphnis and Chloe, Ravel and Skibine; Dame aux Camélias, baroque. OpP n 19 p 72 1960

---Un Ballo in Maschera; several critics found in issue devoted to this opera; Herbert Graf suggesting a return to the original locale, the Swedish Court of Gustave III. Ver v 1 n 1 Ap '60

---Barilli, Bruno. Unpublished notes on Verdi with a preface by Gian Paolo Minardi (German translation also). Ver v 1 n 1 p 616-629 Ap '60

---Bernstein, Seymour, pianist on the audience of today. por IM v 59 n 6 p 32-3 D '60

---Betti, Ugo, on religious drama; motives which "contaminate". such plays; disappointment in their pure dramatics. TDR v 5 n 2 p 3-12 D '60

---Bjoerling, Jussi, 1911-1960; F. C. Schang's memoir. por ON v 25 n 3 p 22 N 19'60

---British press quoted on US performers and composers, including Charles Ives. AmM v 8 n 1 p 19 Ja '60

---Britten, Benjamin; his canticles examined by David Brown. MR v 21 n 1 p 55-65 F '60

--- ---opera, A Midsummer Night's Dream: analysis by Donald Mitchell. Op v 11 n 12 p 797-801 D '60

----Brooks, Van Wyck. James Huneker. por HF v 10 n 12 p 38-41 D '60

--- Brustein, Robert, Scorn not the procenium, critic ("whole controvery . . . an elaborate evasion of the real problems of our theatre, shifting attention to purely formal condiderations when . . .). Th Arts v 44 n 5 p 8-9 My '60

---Camus, Albert. Why I work in the theatre. por Th Arts v 44 n 12 p 58-9, 70-1 D '60

---Chamfray, Claude. La musique de film au festival de la recherche de la R. T. F. GDC n 283 p 99-100 O 7'60

---Clurman, Harold. The paradox of the French stage (class differences more startling than American; interested in fine words, strong literary tradition). Th Arts v 44 n 12 p 64-5 D '60

---The composer-performer relationship, theme of a 5-day Paris conference under International Music Council, UNESCO; brief viewpoints; list of speakers. WM n 6 p 123-6 D '60

---Cone, Edward T. Analysis today. Mus Q v 46 n 2 p 172-188 Ap '60

---Conly, John M. Beethoven, reflections on a goodly fellowship. por HF v 10 n 4 p 34-6 Ap '60

--- ---Musical suggestion box (results of questionaire to well-known music men as to what recordings they feel need to be made). HF v 10 n 1 p 42 Ja '60

---Daniélou, Alain. The importance of the preservation of the traditional musical culture in Oriental countries. WM n 1 p 2-4 F '60

---Dodo, pseud. Malignita. La S 1960

---Dumnesnil, René. Hommage a Chopin. il La S n 131 p 26-7 O'60

---Dunn, Brian. The pattern of musical life in Britain. MD v 51 n 6 p 16-9 D '60
---The duty of the Institute of Verdi Studies; part answer to the criticism of Gino Roncaglia preceding this editorial. Ver v 1 n 2 preface Ag '60-
- -- Editorial on critics: on effect upon New Opera Company. Op v 11 n 6 p 386 Je '60
---English, John. A new deal for the theatre; I. (new small stages to fit "the subtle techniques" demanded of live theatre as a result of cinema, radio, TV). il NTM v 1 n 4 p 13-8 Jl '60
--- ---II. il NTM v 2 n 1 p 19-25 O '60
---Esslin, Martin. The theatre of the absurd. TDR v 4 n 4 p 3-15 My '60
---European theatre today seen by Herbert Blau of San Francisco's Actor's Workshop on a Ford grant; comments on the English Beatnik, the European attempt to become American, many such observations. TDR v 5 n 1 p 89-101 S'60
---Fabbri, Diego. (On theatre problems.) WP v 11 n 4 p 1, 7 F '60
---Fergusson, Francis. On Gerald F. Else's "Aristotle's Poetics: the Argument". TDR v 4 n 4 p 23-32 My '60
---Feydeau, Georges, 1862-1921; suffering and punishment in his dramatic works. TDR v 5 n 1 p 117-126 S '60
---Film score of Georges Auric for "Le Testament d'Orphée"; Cocteau. GDC n 267-8 p 566 Ap 8'60
---France; André Chastenet on Le Théâtre Lyrique en France. GDC n 277 p 813 Je 17'60
---Freud, Sigmund. Psychopathic characters on the stage. TDR v 4 n 3 p 144-8 Mr '60
---Fry, Christopher. Comedy. TDR v 4 n 3 p 77-9 Mr '60
---Fund-raising theatre parties; $8 million NYC, one of five

theatre tickets; agents in NYC, Ivy Larric and Leonore Tobin; what theatre people really think of such audiences. Th Arts v 44 n 3 p 20, 22 Mr '60
---Geddo, Angelo. Il comico nella musica applicata. il La Scala n 122 p 22-27 Ja '60
--- ---L'umore dei decadenti nel solco dell'esperienza pittorica (portfolio of modern paintings included). La S n 131 p 20-5 O '60
---Glyndebourne; comments by The Editor (Harold Rosenthal). Op v 11 p 11-14 Autumn '60
---Goldin, Milton. Commerce, concerts and critics: the organized audience plan reviewed (with a study of taste and repertory). MEJ v 46 n 6 p 37, 39 Je-Jl '60
---Granados, Enrique; criticism. il La S n 123 p 51-4 F '60
---Hammerstein, Oscar, II. The book had better be good. Th Arts v 44 n 11 p 18-9, 70 N '60
---Helm, Everett, on the "new" music trends since World War II; Kranichstein, for example. HF v 10 n 8 p 43-4, 92 Ag '60
---Ionesco, Eugène. My thanks to the critics; "drama reviewing is important only to the extent to which it can arouse interest in a work". il Th Arts v 44 n 10 p 18-9 O '60
---Jacobs, Robert L. Music as symbol; reflections on Mr. Deryck Cooke's The Language of Music. MR v 21 n 3 p 226-236 Ag '60
---Japanese music; criticism by Ikuma Dan, composer of opera, "Yu-Zuru". WM n 2 p 31 Ap '60
---Keating, John. To quote or not to quote (discussion of a Broadway phenomenon: quoting critics in advertising). Th Arts v 44 n 12 p 14-5, 76 D '60
---Keller, Hans. Wordless functional analysis: the second year and beyond-I ("new method of intra-musical analysis"). MR v 21 n 1 p 73-76 F '60
--- ---II. MR v 21 n 3 p 237-239 Ag '60

(Criticism)

---Kupferberg, Herbert. The pick of ''60 (records for Christmas choices). HF v 10 n 12 p 45-6 D '60

---Le Nô; introduction aux traites de Zeami. WP v 12 n 1 p 2 O '60

---Leningrad Symphony Orchestra in London (for the German label DGG) also concerts; comments. HF v 10 n 12 p 12, 14 D '60

---Lingg, Ann M. Meet Fricka (Wotan's wife). ON v 24 n 16 p 6-7 F 20'60

---Liviabella, Lino. Dove va la musica? portfolio La S n 124 p 20-5 Mr . 60

---London; letter from Walter Legge, husband of Elizabeth Schwarzkopf, on why he refused tickets to London music critics. MD v 50 n 12 p 13 Je'60

---Luparello, Maria Ada. Fiori nell'incanto sonoro. La S n 131 p 47-50 O '60

---McCleery, Albert. Theatre's debt to television. WT v 9 n 4 p 318-24 Winter '60

---McElroy, George. (A comparison of Wagner and Verdi.) ON v 25 n 8 p 17-20 D 31'60

--- ---The fortunes of fate(discussion of ''fate stories''; reconciliation of pagan ''fate'' with monotheism). Op v 24 n 19 p 4-7 Mr 12'60

---McKee, J. N. The symphonic element in opera. MR v 21 n 1 p 30-37 F '60

---Mahler; Philip T. Barford on a pentatonic archetype. MR v 21 n 4 p 297-316 N '60

---Marsh, Robert C. Beethoven symphonies in stereo (criticism with list of recordings after each). HF v 10 n 4 p 44-5, 85-7 Ap '60

---Marshall, Norman. Are stage plays suitable for TV? WT v 9 n 4 p 301-12 Winter '60

---Migliorini, Louis. (Letter on comparison of singers.) HF v 10 n 3 p 8 Mr '60

---Mila, Massimo. Problem di filologia e d'interpretazione

intorno alla partitura del Ballo in Maschera (English and German translations p 458-493). Ver n 1 n 1 p 133-156 Ap '60

---Mingus, Charles, 1922-, as a jazz composer; his NYC Jazz Workshop. por IM v 59 n 6 p 24-5 D '60

---Mitropoulos, Dimitri, and Verdi, Mario Medici's tribute. Ver v 1 n 2 preface Ag '60

---Morgan, Mona. Autobiographical acting. PlM v 36 n 4 p 82-3 Ja '60

---Music as diplomacy; comments on US artists sent abroad by US government; list. IM v 58 n 7 p 11, 14 Ja '60

---Music in Australia; statements in the controversy over devastating and ignorant critics by Dr. Nicolai Malko, by Adrian Bendall, President of the Musicians Union. MD v 51 n 2 p 10-13 Ag '60

--- ---Hungary; Kodály's style as an influence on composers; new trends. Mus Q v 46 n 4 p 525-35 O '60

--- ---Niccolo Paganini as a critic (Zdenek, Vyborny,trans. Willis Wager). Mus Q v 46 n 4 p 468-481 O '60

--- ---summer courses evaluated by question-and-answer; including Berkshire and National Music Camp (US) and notable European summer schools. WM n 5 p 105-6 O '60

--- ---today; not all contemporary music is avantgardiste; report of composers conference at Stratford, Ontario. CMJ v 5 n 1 p 4-16 Autumn '60

---Musical criticism in England in the 19th century discussed by E. D. Mackerness; ''chastity of mind'', the key words, the oratorio the ideal. CMJ v 4 n 2 p 14-24 Winter '60

---Nettl, Paul (On exoticism in dramatic music.) il ON v 24 n 24 p 4-7 Ap 16'60

---Nölter, Wolfgang. (On growing operatic uniformity; West Berlin and Hamburg same cast for Tristan.)

Op v 11 n 4 p 278 Ap'60
---Novak, Benjamin J., and Gladys
R. Barnett. Are music and science compatible? MEJ v 46 n 6
p 44, 46 Je-Jl'60
---O'Casey, Sean. (On opinions in
plays; on foolish present.-day playwrights who deplore the audience).
Th Arts v 44 n 5 p 20-2 My '60
---O'Neill as compared to other
playwrights (Strindberg, Shakespeare, Hauptmann); von Holfmann-
sthal finds O'Neill "a little too direct". TDR v 5 n 1 p 169-173 S'60
---Opera; Friedrich Schultze on the
"crisis" in opera repertory; lists
points to be considered; narrow
repertories of some great houses;
list of composers to be produced.
WP v 11 n 8 p 1, 7 Je '60
--- ---1950-1960; selected criticism
upon the 10th anniversary of the
London periodical, Opera; useful
and compact view of the decade.
Op v 11 n 2 p 107-26 F '60
--- ---Part 2; Opv 11n 3 p 184-194
Mr '60
--- ---repertory at Covent Garden;
comparisons; costs Opv 11n 3 p 174
Mr '60
--- ---reviewers; Mary Watkins
Cushing on the Fourth Estate. il
ON v 24 n 21 p 6-8 Mr 26'60
--- ---Verdi and Italy; excerpts
from Bruno Barilli which catch the
Verdi scene (presented in English,
in German, in Italian by Gian Paolo
Minardi). Ver v 1 n 2 Ag '60
---Oriental music; paper by Tran
Van Khé on the emotional approach
of the performer. WM n 6 p 127-8
D '60
---Paris: extraits de la critique Parisienne a la création 1921, L'Oncle
Vania, 1929 Les Trois Soeurs, Tchékhov. il Spec n 1 p 13-21 1960
--- ---séance April 28 1960 on the
situation of music in France, arranged by the Guide du Concert
and le Comité National de la Musique; distinguished speakers are
summarized. portraits GDC n 279-
80 p 868-888 Jl 1'60
---Pakistan's need as seen by Z. A.

Bokhari; a Western musician to
live permanently there, welding
Ragas and harmony into a "new"
music. WM n 1 p 5 F '60
---Perkins, Francis D. The critical "chain gang" (old New York's
hectic coverage of simultaneous
concerts). MC v 161 n 5 p 11 Ap'60
---Petit, Pierre. Les droits du
répertoire (Paris). OpP n 19 p 48
1960
---Pirie, Peter J. A reprieve for
romanticism (music). HF v 10
n 10 p 48-50, 130 O '60
---Pitoëff, Georges; extensive
criticism, signed, with a large
portfolio. Spec n 1 1960
---Pizzetti, Ildebrando. Giuseppe
Verdi, meister des theaters. Ver
v 1 n 2 p 1013-1038 Ag '60
---I Puritani: Chorley quoted in
Thirty Years' Musical Recollec-
tions; T. C. Cax in Musical recollec-
tions; of the last half century; The
Times 1848 on Jenny Lind's Elvira.
Op v 11 n 5 p 322 My '60
---Restout, Denise. Wanda Landowska. portfolio HF v 10 n 10
p 42-47 O '60
---Riegger, Wallingford; critical
articles ; signed tributes; check-
list and a discography. ACAB v 9
n 3 1960
---Robertazzi, Mario. Un modo di
raccontare la musica. La S n 132
p 58-61 N '60
---Rousselot, Léonne. Le Chant,
"acte refleve" (book reviewed by
Raymond Lyon). GDC n 287 p 236
N 4'60
---Samazeuilh, Gustave. La Mu-
sique de chambre de Gabriel
Fauré. GDC n 289 p 289-292
N 18'60
---Sastre, Alfonso. Drama and
society (tragedy as an instrument
of torture; on The Death of a
Salesman; Theatre of Magic and
Theatre of Anguish. TDR v 5 n 2
p 102-10 D '60
---Schafer, Murray. Two musicians
in fiction (Jean Christoph by Romain
Rolland; Doktor Faustus by Thomas
Mann). CMJ v 4 n 3 p 23-34 Spring'60

LIBRARY
OF
MOUNT ST. MARY'S
COLLEGE
EMMITSB...

(Criticism)

---Schauensee, Max de Puccini and Paris. ON v 25 n 5 p 17-9 D 10'60

---Schonberg, Arnold, as a self-critic; letters quoted; final Credo "I believe in the eternal supremacy of melodic conception and in the forswearing of the pure intellect at the cost of sincere inspiration". MC v 161 n 5 p 19 Ap '60

---Schwarz, Alfred. The allegorical theatre of Hugo von Hofmannsthal (1874-1929). TDR v 4 n 3 p 65-76 Mr '60

---Serialism, its extents and limits discussed by Ernst Krenek. il Mus Q v 46 n 2 p 210-232 Ap '60

---Sharp, William L. A play: scenario or poem. TDR v 5 n 2 p 73-84 D '60

---Shaw; Eric Bentley on Shaw's growth as a dramatist. TDR v 5 n 1 p 3-21 S '60

---Silvant, Jean. La danse et le sport. portfolio TD n 93 p 6-12 My '60

--- ---Place de la danse dans la vie au XXme siecle, dédiée à Serge Lifar. TD n 97 p 14-5, 18 N '60

---Silverberg, Robert. Music for people marooned on Mars (criteria: meaning below the surface, good performance, sonic quality). HF v 10 n 9 p 49-50 S '60

---Sion, Georges. Belgium, theatrical radar receiver (French section). WT v 9 n 1 p 35-47 Spring'60

---Slocum, Paul. Players on record (a column reviewing content and performance of phonograph recorded plays). PIM 1960

---(Stoddard, Hope E.) William Kincaid, flutist for 39 years with the Philadelphia Orchestra; interview. por IM v 58 n 11 p 12-3 My '60

---Stravinsky, Igor. The Firebird's first flight. il HF v 10 n 6 p 34-6 Je '60

--- ---NYC concerts; Les Noces (1923); and "Movements";

"Stravinsky is now a follower". MC v 161 n 3 p 26, 28, 29 F '60

---Summer theatre, US; as originally conceived; as now run; article by John S. Wilson. il Th Arts v 44 n 6 p 14-6 Je '60

---Sutherland, Joan, 1928-, singer; career sketch. portfolio Op v 11 n 10 p 675-682 O '60

---Taylor, Deems. What is American opera? (Definition, trends). ON v 25 n 6 p 9-11, 30 D 17'60

---Tchaikovsky by the composer, Russell Smith. HF v 10 n 3 p 48-9, 123 Mr '60

---Tenth anniversary issue of Opera: signed messages from officials, artists, editors; some comments include opera criticism as well as good wishes. Op v 11 n 2 p 85-103 F '60

---Theatre architecture; Walter Gropius 1927, quoted; types and purposes explored by Thomas De Gaetani with his own drawings. J Rev v 7 n 2 p 4-12 Spring '60

---Theatre for the "working class"; but the proponents seem not to notice the laboring class is now different (in Great Britain) which makes the argument of trades union obligation for culture less fresh. NTM v 2 n 1 p 2-6 O '60

---Trumpet; signed quotations from famous trumpeters, more than 20 technical suggestions. IM v 58 n 10 p 22-3 Ap '60

---Tzipine, Georges, conducting the Victorian Symphony in Melbourne; his remarks against the Australian newspaper critics arouse controversy. por MD v 50 n 12 p 10-11 Je '60

---US music; press quotations from Great Britain a frequent feature. AmM 1960

---Valency, Maurice. (On the loss of meaning in art.) Th Arts v 44 n 8 p 8-9, 68 Ag '60

---Verdi on Palestrina. Ver v 1 n 2 p 1021 Ag '60

--- ---Macbeth; Boris Goldovsky and Siobhan McKenna during an intermission radio broadcast of

of Metropolitan's Macbeth. Th
Arts v 44 n 3 p 38-9 Mr '60

--- ---Un Ballo in Maschera (the
score) by Guido Pannain. Ver v 1
n 1 (also n 2) 1960
---Walker, Frank. L'Abandonnée,
eine vergessene romanze. facsimiles Ver v 1 n 2 p 1069-1076
Ag '60
---Warnke, Frank J. The happy
ending (Figaro). ON v 24 n 12
p 4-5 Ja 23'60
---Warren, Leonard, 1911-1960;
roles (25) during his 21 Metropolitan seasons; criticism by Philip
L. Miller. il Op v 11 n 6 p 397-
403 Je '60
---Webster, Margaret. (Her view
of trends in British theatre; the
"reps".) Th Arts v 44 n 11 p 22-4,
71 N '60
---Wechsberg, Joseph. The beloved
critic: a fairy tale. Op v 11 n 2
p 104-6 F '60
---Wolff, Stéphane. (What the con-
servatories give the young musician.) GDC n 259-60 p 397 F 12'60
---Worner, Karl H. Parsifal at
Bayreuth; "diametrically opposed
to Richard Wagner's ideas, laid
down in the score". CMJ v 4 n 4
p 19-24 Summer '60
---Young, John Wray. A community
theatre quiz. portfolio Th Arts v 44
n 8 p 16-20 Ag '60
---Zavadski, Youri. Theatre in
Russia (philosophy of Soviet "real-
ization of man's spiritual progress").
WP v 11 n 5 p 1, 7 Mr '60
CROCHET, EVELYN, pianist
Boston criticism. MC v 161 n 3
p 41 F '60
CROLLA, HENRI, 1920-1960,
guitarist
Obituary; his career. GDC n 288
p 261 N 11'60
CROSS, RICHARD, 1937-, singer
Baltimore notes. ON v 24 n 21
p 28 Mr 26'60
CRUT, MAURICE
and André Terasse, violin and
piano; Paris review. GDC n 255-6
p 313 Ja 15'60

CSLOWIEK Z GLOXA, play
Lodz notes; Janusz Warminski.
WP v 12 n 3 p 34 D '60
CUBA
Wilhelm, Hermann. (Report of
opera repertory; "future is bright".)
Op v 11 n 8 p 549 Ag '60
LOS CUERVOS ESTAN DE LUTO,
play
Mexico notes; Hugo Arguelles.
WP v 11 n 10 p 8 Ag '60
CUEVAS, MARQUIS GEORGES DE
1886-1961
Left profile ph. TD n 98 p 7 D'60
CUIDADO CON LAS PERSONAS
FORMALES, play
Valencia notes; Alfonso Paso. WP
v 11 n 5 p 4 Mr '60
CULSHAW, JOHN. (London's new
philosophy of recording, fewer but
better records.) HF v 10 n 10 p 65
O '60
CULTURAL EXCHANGE PROGRAM
See The President's Special In-
ternational Program for Cultural
Presentations
CUNNINGHAM: MERCE, 1915-,
choreographer
Goth, Trudy. Teatro Fenice e
Broadway di New York. il La S
n 127 p 30 Je '60
---In "Changeling", AP wl ph:
Venice. La S n 127 p 30 Je '60
CURTIN, PHYLLIS. On being Susan-
nah (in Carlisle Floyd's opera).
AmM v 8 n 3 p 11-12 Mr '60
---As Salome, Cincinnati Summer
Opera, ens AP wl ph: Eugene
Cook. Op v 11 n 10 p 684 O '60
---With Carlisle Floyd, composer,
Hl ph. AmM v 8 n 3 cover Mr '60
---With Risë Stevens, Surovy and
Cook, ph: Wagner-International.
ON v 24 n 17 p 3 F 27'60
CURTIS, LOUIS WOODSON, 1885-
1960
Obituary. por MEJ v 46 n 4 p 104
F-Mr '60
CURTIS STRING QUARTET
Ens ph: Bethlehem, Pa. MC v 161
n 3 p 14 F '60
CUSHING, MARY WATKINS. A com-
plexity of gypsies (the role of Car-
men as it has been interpreted).

(Cushing)
ON v 24 n 14 p 4-5 F 6'60
--- ---Mooncalves (Cherubino, Octavian, Frederick in Mignon, Oscar in A Masked Ball). ON v 24 n 12 p 6-8 Ja 23'60
--- ---The fourth estate (on reviews of opera). il ON v 24 n 21 p 6-8 Mr 26'60
--- ---The good companions (in opera librettos, the servants and confidantes). ON v 24 n 10 p 6-7, 30 Ja 9'60
CYCLE GABRIEL FAURE
Paris concerts. GDC n 257-8 p 359-362 Ja 29'60
CYRANO DE BERGERAC, play
Le Petit Théâtre du Vieux Carre, ens AP wl ph: New Orleans. Th Arts v 44 n 4 p 58 Ap '60
---Old Vic, Bristol, ens AP wl ph: Desmond Tripp. NTM v 1 n 1 O '59---Shoroku and Isuzu, AP phs: Tokyo, 1960 WP v 12 n 3 p 1, 4 D '60
CYRANO DE BERGERAC (PETIT), Guest, Ivor. (criticism of Paris and London casts.) MD v 50 n 7 p 30 Ja '60
---Two ens AP wl phs. MD v 50 n 7 p 31 Ja '60
CZECHOSLOVAKIA
Eckstein, Pavel. Spettacoli d'opera in Cecoslovacchia. il La S n 129-130 p 42, 78 Ag-S '60
---Machek, J.-V. Lebl. Theatre report. WT v 9 n 1 p 70-72 Spring '60
---Opera; notes from Bratislava, Brno, Liberec, Olomouc. Op v 11 n 11 p 762 N '60
---Theatre report. WP v 11 n 6 p 7 Ap '60; same. WP v 11 n 7 p 8 My '60
---Wörner, Karl H. (On creative musical activity today.) Mus Q v 46 n 4 p 509-517 O '60
CZERWENKA, OSKAR, singer
Career sketch; b. Linz. ON v 24 n 15 p 14 F 13'60
---As Rocco in Fidelio, AP phs: Melançon. ON v 24 n 15 F 13'60
CZIFFRA, GYORGY, 1921-, pianist

Jourdan-Morhange, Hélène. Paris review. GDC n 261-2 p 440 F 26'60

D

DALE, WILLIAM, pianist
Notes; University of Florida and Yale; London concert. AmM v 8 n 5 p 9 Je '60
DALLAPICCOLA, LUIGI, 1904-, composer
Dialoghi pour violoncelle et orchestre, National Orchestra; critique GDC n 286 p 196 O 28'60
---Directing his music at the New School For Social Research NYC; criticism. MC v 161 n 3 p 43 F'60
---Variations for Orchestra; as orchestrated 1954; Strasburg Festival première. MC v 162 n 3 p 25 S '60
---Hl ph. La S n 124 p 23 Mr '60
DALLAS
Festival second year; opening Dallas Theater Center; Dallas Civic Opera notes. MC v 162 n 5 p 22 N '60
---Kalita Theatre; Paul Baker report. Th Arts v 44 n 11 p 78 N '60
---State Fair concerts; note. IM v 58 n 12 p 31 Je '60
DALLAS CIVIC OPERA
Askew, Rual. (The Civic Opera in its third year, successful with and without Callas; "Nicola Rescigno had the Dallas Symphony sounding like the best orchestra in the world".) Op v 11 n 2 p 137 F '60
---Griffith, Katherine. Callas from the chorus (performance notes for Lucia, Barber of Seville and Medea). ON v 24 n 11 p 12 Ja 16'60
---Kelly, Lawrence, director; Franco Zeffirelli, décor designer and stage director; criticism of fourth season. ON v 25 n 8 p 28 D 31'60
---Opera report. Op v 11 n 9 p 615 S '60; same. Op v 11 n 11 p 756 N '60
---Il Barbiere di Siviglia, ens AP wl ph: Mazziotta. Op v 11 n 2 p 138 F '60
DALLAS SYMPHONY

Inter-American interests; Paul Kletzki auditioning in Latin America for 1960-61 season. IM v 59 n 4 p 23 O '60

DALIBOR, opera
Smetana; davanti alla Cattedrale di San Vito, ens Ap ph: Prague. La S n 129-30 p 42 Ag-S '60

DALIS, IRENE, singer, 1925-, Career notes; b. California. AmM v 8 n 3 p 8 Mr '60
---Ap hl ph: Metropolitan. ON v 25 n 6 p 21 D 17'60
---As Brangäne, several AP phs: Melançon. ON v 24 n 10 Ja 9'60
---As Fricka, hl ph: Melançon. ON v 24 n 16 p 6 F 20'60
---Hl ph: Melançon. ON v 24 n 12 p 2 Ja 23'60

DALSKABATY, VILLAGE COUP-ABLE, play
Prague notes; Jan Drda. WP v 11 n 6 p 15 Ap '60

DALVIT, LEWIS, conductor
AP hl ph. MC v 161 n 7 p 25 Je '60

DAMASE, J. M., composer
Première: Farandale Service du Musique Légère de la R. T. F. GDC n 295 p 486 D 30'60

LA DAME AUX CAMELIAS (TA-TIANA GSOVSKY), ballet
Dumnesnil, René. (Review.) il La S n 128 p 24-5 Jl '60
---Paris Opéra review; Henri Sauguet music. MC v 161 n 5 p 31 Ap '60; same. OpP n 19 p 44 1960; same. TD n 91 p 13 Mr '60
---Royal Danish Ballet notes. TD n 94 p 14 Je '60
---Two AP phs; Henri Sauguet, composer, left profile ph. La S n 128 p 24-5 Jl '60

DIE DAME UND DAS EINHORN (ROSEN), ballet
Ens ph: H. Giessner 1953. WT v 9 n 3 p 231 Autumn '60

THE DAMNATION OF FAUST
Cambridge University review; an analysis really. Op v 11 n 5 p 373-5 My '60

DAN, IKUMA (1924-). (On music in Japan.) WM n 2 p 31 Ap '60

DANCE
Baignères, Claude. Danse classique et ballet moderne du Lac des Cygnes à Pas de Dieux (Kelly). OpP n 19 p 72 1960
---Bell, Fritz. Dance in the drama course (Las Vegas). PlM v 36 n 7 Ap '60
---Geddo, Angelo. Il comico nella musica applicata. il La Scala n 122 p 22-27 Ja '60
---Idla, Ernst and 100 young Swedish dancers on US tour, "Symphony of the World" show. MC v 161 n 3 p 21 F '60
---The Institute of International Education (Ford Foundation Grant): list of 5 dancers brought to USA to study. AmM v 8 n 9 p 15 O '60
---Lanner, Josef (1801-43) as a writer of dance music. MR v 21 n 2 p 114. 120 My '60
---Russia; training class had 40 piece orchestra the day Franz Allers visited. IM v 59 n 2 p 10 Ag '60
---Tassart, Maurice. Françoise et Dominique. GDC n 274 p 719 My 27'60
---US; Recreational Dancing Institute; aims. il IM v 58 n 8 p 8 F '60
---Vienna criticism of Katherine Dunham; of Jerome Robbins' company. MC v 161 n 5 p 30 Ap '60
---A Baoule Adjemele dance, Ivory Coast Company, ens AP wl ph: Pic. WT v 9 n 4 p 349 Winter '60
---Kola, Macedonia, Yugoslavia, ens AP wl ph: Mrs. Levi. WM n 4 p 84 Ag '60
---Stick Dance, Jaen, Spain, ens AP wl ph: Kennedy. WM n 4 p 84 Ag '60
---See also Ballet

DANCE-HISTORY AND CRITICISM
Diaghilev Ballet in Paris 1909. il TD n 90 p 5-10 F '60
---Moore, Lillian. Unlisted ballets by Jean Georges Noverre. il Th Notbk v 15 n 1 p 15-20 Autumn '60

DANCE FILMS
Aznavour, Charles, script; Marcel Martin, producer; Pierre

(Dance Films)
Lacotte, choreographer; Josette Clavier. TD n 92 p 28 Ap '60
---Chants d'Haiti, Max de Vaucorbeil; Paris. TD n 90 p 24 F'60
---Cuba; Soviet films shown in Santiago, "one-week festival" reported by Aubrey Hitchens. MD v 51 n 2 p 28 Ag '60
---Films ballets soviétiques. TD n 98 p 23 D '60
---Le Rossignol et l'Empereur de Chine; Jean Corelli, Claude Catulle; Rosella Hightower notes. TD n 92 p 12 Ap'60
DANCE NOTATION
Abbie, Margaret. Dance notation (notes from 1450 to Benesh System). MD v 51 n 5 p 27, 29 N '60
THE DANCE OF DEATH, play
Pryce-Jones, Alan. (Review of Strindberg.) por Th Arts n 44 n 11 p 8 N '60
DANDELOT, GEORGE, 1895-, composer
"Trois poèmes de Ginette Bonvalet"; Hélène Bouvier qui chante. GDC n 257-8 p 359 Ja 29 '60
DANIEL-LESUR (1908-). Colomb de Donant, musique de film. (commentaire). GDC n 259-60 p 413 F 12'60
DANIELOU, ALAIN, 1907-
See Sharan, Shiva, 1907-
DANILOVA, ALEXANDRA, 1907-, choreographer
With John Gutman of the Metropolitan, hl ph: Melançon. ON v 24 n 19 p 2 Mr 12'60
D'ANNUNZIO, GABRIELE (1863-1938).
Lettere inedite a Zacconi. La S n 129-30 p 49-55 Ag-S '60
DANS L'OMBRE DES CORBEAUX
Anvers notes; Mark E. Tralbaut. WP v 11 n 5 p 15 Mr '60
DANTONS TOD, opera
Ens AP wl ph: Graz Opera. Op v 11 n 11 p 761 N '60
---Ens AP wl ph: Wassner. Op v 11 n 9 p 621 S '60
DANZA, ballet
Première: Bavarian State Opera; using Werner Egk's

Variations on a Caribbean Theme; Munich. WM n 2 p 32 Ap '60
DAPHNE, opera
American première of Strauss by the Little Orchestra Society; review. MC v 162 n 5 p 14 N '60
---The Little Orchestra Society; American première of Strauss; cast. Op v 11 n 12 p 817 D '60
---NYC Opera; criticism. ON v 25 n 3 p 20 N 19'60
DAPHNIS ET CHLOE (SKIBINE), ballet
Rayet and Lucien Duthoit, AP wl ph: Pairs Opéra. OpP n 19 p 42 1960
DARCANTE, JEAN (1910-).
Une liberte debile. WP v 12 n 3 p 1 D '60
--- ---Letter from the Secretary General, ITI. WP v 11 n 10 p 7 Ag '60
---Por ph. WP v 12 n 3 p 1 D '60
DARLING, ERIK, 1934-, folk singer
Career notes; with the Weavers; banjo player. por HF v 10 n 12 p 48-50 D '60
DARMSTADT
International Summer Courses for Modern Music; 1960 notes. WM n 3 p 57 Je '60
---Kranichsteiner Institut; notes on courses for new music. WM n 5 p 105 O '60
---Programs at a congress on "Historical Forces and Historismus in Contemporary Music Life"; notes. WM n 2 p 32 Ap '60
---Wörner, Karl H. (Report of recent International Vacation Courses for New Music with general summation of trends.) Mus Q v 46 n 2 p 270-275 Ap '60
---Members of the staff; a seminar on use of the harp in new music, 2 phs: Ludwig. WM n 5 p 109 O '60
DARRAS, GENEVIEVE, pianist
Chamfray, Claude. Paris review. GDC n 273 p 692 My 20'60
DARRE, JEANNE-MARIE, pianist
Chamfray, Claude. Paris review. GDC n 295 p 491 D 30'60

---Paris review. GDC n 261-2
p 443 F 26'60
DARRELL, ROBERT DONALDSON
(1903-). The tape deck (regular
column of critical reviews). HF
1960
DARSONVAL, LYCETTE, 1912-,
ballerina
Studio notes. il TD n 97 p 17 N'60
DA SILVA, HOWARD, 1909-, actor
AP hl ph. Th Arts v 44 n 10 p 24
O'60
DAVID, GYULA, 1913-, composer
Critical notes. Mus Q v 46 n 4
p 532 O'60
DAVIDSON, LOUIS, trumpeter
Small por ph. IM v 58 n 12 p 7
Je'60
DAVIES, PETER MAXWELL,
composer
Première:Prolation;Royal Liv-
erpool Orchestra under John
Carewe. MC v 162 n 6 p 30
D'60
DAVIS, DONALD, actor
In Krapp's Last Tape, AP hl
ph. Th Arts v 44 n 3 p 13 Mr'60
DAVIS, IVAN, 1931-, pianist
Notes. IM v 59 n 4 p 38 O'60
---Winner of Franz Liszt Piano
Competition;Texas. MEJ v 47
n 1 p 28 S-O'60
---Winner of Liszt Award, NYC;
details;b. Texas. MC v 161 n 6
p 4 My'60
---Left profile por ph:Texas. Am
M v 8 n 5 p 7 Je'60
DAVIS, JACKIE, organist
Por ph. IM v 58 n 11 p 15 My'60
DAVIS, MICHAEL, 1936-, violinist
NYC notes. MC v 161 n 1 p 20
Ja'60
---AP hl ph:US. MC v 161 n 1 p 15
Ja'60
DAVIS, RICHARD. Sergei Lyapu-
nov(1859-1924). MR v 21 n 3
p 186-206 Ag'60
DAVY, GLORIA, 1932-, singer
In Aïda;debut at Covent Garden
with comment and one ph. Op
v 11 n 7 p 509 Jl'60
---Notes. Por ON v 25 n 8 p 4
D 31'60
DAYDE, BERNARD, 1921-, designer

With Spanish dancer, Antonio, hl
ph. TD n 94 p 10 Je'60
DAYDE, LIANE, 1932-, ballerina
Avec Michel Renault;60,000 kil-
omètres;La Princess Aurora
chez Cuevas. il TD n 97 p 12-3
N'60
---Munich;"la grand triomphatrice
du Festival de Ballets". TD n 96
p 11 S-O'60
---Princess Aurora, Serge Golo-
vine, Prince Charmant, AP wl ph:
Lido. TD n 98 p 12 D'60
DE AMICIS, EDMONDO(1846-1908).
Giuseppina Verdi-Strepponi. Ver
v 1 n 2 p 1057-1068 Ag'60
DEAN, WINTON(1916-). Alcina at
Covent Garden, Stockholm Op-
era. Op v 11 n 10 p 713-6 O'60
DEAR LIAR, play
Based on Shaw's correspondence
with Mrs. Patrick Campbell, play
liked in US (except NYC audience).
PlM v 37 n 1 p 10 O'60
---NYC notes;Shaw letters. WP v 11
n 9 p 6 Jl'60
THE DEATH of a SALESMAN, play
Sastre, Alfonso, on this play. TDR
v 5 n 2 p 107-8 D'60
---Théâtre National de Belgique,
ens AP wl ph:Bernand, 1952. WT
v 9 n 1 p 31 Spring'60
DEBAAR, ANDRÉ
With Christiane Lenain in Made-
moiselle Jaïre, AP hl ph:Omnia.
WT v 9 n 1 p 12 Spring'60
DeBANFIELD, RAFFAELLO, com-
poser
Career notes;b. London;opera,
Lord Byron's Love Letter, Col-
umbia recording reviewed. CMJ
v 4 n 2 p 45 Winter'60
DEBIERA HABER OBISPAS, play
Mexico;Rafael Solana. WP v 11
n 5 p 14 Mr'60
DEBIÈVRE, PIERRE. Hommage à
Jules Gressier et André Bloch.
GDC n 283 p 94 O 7'60
DEBUSSY, CLAUDE(1862-1918).
Quatuor à cordes(études musical-
es analytiques). GDC n 288 p 268
N 11'60
---Criticism. ON v 24 n 11 p 14
Ja 16'60

(Debussy)
---Dietschy, Marcel. The family and childhood of Debussy. il Mus Q v 46 n 3 p 301-314 Jl '60
---Images: analyse par Pierrette Mari. GDC n 286 p 207-8 O 28'60
---Portrait of his mother; one of his father. Mus Q v 46 n 3 p 310 Jl '60
---Thiele, Ivan. Drawing of Claude Debussy, 1913. ON v 24 n 11 p 9 Ja 16'60
DECKER, HERMINE D. The author? Who's that? PlM v 37 n 1 p 7 O '60
DÉCOR
Armistead, Horace. Fidelio for the Metropolitan; notes. il ON v 24 n 15 p 22 F 13'60
--- ---Pélleas et Mélisande for the Metropolitan: notes and portfolio. ON v 24 n 11 p 20-1 Ja 16'60
---Beaton, Cecil. (notes on his décor for musical, Saratoga.) il Th Arts v 44 n 1 p 17 Ja '60
---Benois, Alessandro, e Nicola Benois. Scenografia verdiana e allestimenti scaligeri del Ballo in Maschera. Ver v 1 n 1 p 90-108 Ap '60
---Brothier, Jean-Jacques. Butterfly (interviewed on décor by Michel Lorin; Paris). GDC n 255-6 p 303 Ja 15'60
---Chekhov; issue devoted to staging Chekhov; 23 producers give artistic ideas with many pictures. WT v 9 n 2 Summer '60
---Dallas; notes on Franco Zeffirelli mounting operas; scenery flown from Palermo, from Venice, from Milan. ON v 25 n 8 p 28 D 31'60
---Fox, Frederick. Andrea Chénier for the Metropolitan; notes and portfolio. ON v 24 n 21 Mr 26'60
--- ---Tosca for the Metropolitan; notes. il ON v 24 n 20 p 21 Mr 19 '60
---Fox, William. Simon Boccanegra for the Metropolitan; notes and portfolio. ON v 24 n 22 p 22 Ap 2'60
---France; notes on present-day theatre designers. Th Arts v 44 n 12 p 79 D '60

---Gérard, Rolf. Carmen designs for the Metropolitan. il ON v 24 n 14 p 22 F 6'60
--- ---Décor notes on Cavalleria Rusticana; and Pagliacci for the Metropolitan. ON v 24 n 13 Ja 30'60
---"High-fidelity mural" with "uncanny power to dissolve tensions", Blazer Associates. HF v 10 n 3 p 111 Mr '60
---Kerz, Leo Parsifal settings for the Metropolitan; notes and portfolio. ON v 24 n 23 p 21 Ap 9'60
---Larrain, Raymond. La Belle au Bois Dormant, de Cuevas ballet notes. GDC n 290 p 320 N 25'60
---Larson, Orville K. Rolf Gérard's scene design for opera. PlM v 36 n 6 p 130-2 Mr '60
---Lyric Opera of Chicago's The Flying Dutchman: sets borrowed from Rome, "the shipping expenses seemed hardly worth while " (picture of ship and Nilsson). MC 161 n 1 p 21 Ja '60
---Magon, Jero. Projected scenery. PlM v 36 n 7 p 164 Ap '60
---Messel, Oliver. Le Nozze di Figaro for the Metropolitan; notes. il ON v 24 n 12 p 23 Ja 23'60
---Motley. Il Trovatore sets for the Metropolitan. ON v 24 n 17 p 23 F 27'60
--- ---Il Trovatore for the Metropolitan; criticism. il Op v 11 n 1 p 24-5 Ja '60
---Nagasaka, Motohiro. Madama Butterfly settings for the Metropolitan 1958; notes and portfolio. ON v 24 n 24 p 21 Ap 16'60
---Nagler, A. M. (on Craig and Hofmannsthal, on staging "Das gerettete Venedig.") Th R v 2 n 1 p 12-3 1960
---Neher, Caspar; notes on Macbeth 1959 for the Metropolitan. il ON v 24 n 9 p 23 Ja 2'60
---Otto, Ted. Tristan und Isolde for the Metropolitan; criticism. il ON v 24 n 10 p 22-3 Ja 9'60
--- ---Metropolitan notes, two phs.

Op v 11 n 2 p 133 F '60
---Reinking. Prince Igor for Vienna Staatsoper; "impressive projections". Op v 11 n 5 p 343 My '60
--- ---Stage setting (Germany) since 1945.WT v 9 n 3 p 249-258 Autumn '60
---Rosenfeld, Sybil. A Sadler's Wells scene book (seven illustrations included). Th Notbk v 15 n 2 p 57-62 Winter '60-61
---Verman, E. Tom Payot, WP v 11 n 5 p 8 Mr '60
---Wieber, Jean; notes from Rennes. GDC n 257-8 p 354 Ja 29'60
---Andrews, Robert C. Two designs: Column Street; Iwanowna (from a Sadler's Wells Scene book). Th Notbk v 15 n 2 Winter '60-61
---Un Ballo in Maschera, La Scala; Act I, sc. 2 dwelling of the soceress by Carlo Ferrario (1862), by Carlo Songa(1903), by Alessandro Benois (1947), 3 sets. Ver n 1 n 1 p 592 Ap '60
--- ---opera portfolio of 18 settings by various designers, phs. Ver v 1 n 2 Ag '60
---Bauer-Ecsy, Leni. Set for opera, Volpone, by Francis Burt; Stuttgart 1960.WT v 9 n 3 cover Autumn '60
---Bayreuth; Das Rheingold, final scene; Lohengrin, Act II ens phs: Bayreuth. MC v 162 n 3 p 2 S'60
---Beaton, Cecil. Saratoga, musical; set act I, the French Market in New Orleans; costume drawings; Beaton and his mother in Wiltshire; one ens AP wl ph: Beaton. Th Arts v 44 n 1 p 17-21 Ja '60
--- ---Sets and costumes for "Saratoga" (musical), 10 pictures. Th Arts v 44 n 1 p 17-20 Ja '60
---Berman, Eugene. La Forza del Destino settings for the Metropolitan, portfolio: Melançon. ON v 24 n 19 Mr 12'60
---Bibiena, Giuseppe Galli.

Scena con "volo di putti", scena con "palazzo sopra le nubi"; scena probabilmente di mano di un Bibiena. La S n 132 p 26-29 N '60
---Bignens, Max. Der Zar lässt sich photographieren, ens AP wl ph: Günter Englert. WT v 9 n 2 p 163 Summer '60
---Bozzettoper Il Malato immaginario di Jacopo Napoli, ph: Naples. La S n 127 p 28 Je '60
---Brulin, Tone. Mariken van Niemeghen, play, ph: Reussens, 1951. WT v 9 n 1 p 25 Spring '60
---Brunet, Maurice. Médeé, décor for Paris Opéra, 3 sets, phs. OpP n 19 p 30 1960
---Bury, John. Major Barbara, set for Coventry, ph. NTM v 1 n 1 O '59
---Buzzati, Dino. Fantasmi al Grand Hotel, ballet set design, ph: La Scala. MC v 161 n 4 p 34 Mr'60
---Cane, Joseph. Androcles and the Lion for the Glyndebourne Children's Theatre, ph: Angus McBean. NTM v 1 n 3 p 14 Ap '60
---Costumi di Caramba per Fra Gherardo, drawings La S n 129-30 p 17 Ag-S '60
---Cristini, C. M. Design for The Love of Three Oranges Act III, s scenes 1 and 3, San Carlo; ph. Op v 2 n 3 p 216 Mr '60
---La Dame aux Camélias, Genève 1921, ph. Spec n 1 p 29 1960
---Dayde, Bernard. Dessin pour "Jugando al toro (Antonio); also Quartsilunu (Harald Lauder), phs. TD n 94 p 10-1 Je '60
--- ---Le Lac des Cygnes; Munich ph; TD n 91 p 17 Mr '60
---Dmitriev, V. The Three Sisters, setting, Moscow Art Theatre, 1940. WT v 9 n 2 p 102 Summer '60
---Eckart, William, and Jean. Costume and set design for "Fiorello", musical; set design for "Mister Johnson"; for Damn Yankees"; for "The Golden Apple, phs. Th Arts v 44 n 7 p 56-7 Jl '60
--- ---Scenic design and lighting. portfolio Th Arts v 44 n 7 p 55-7, 67 Jl '60

Décor)
---Elson, Charles. The Flying
Dutchman for the Metropolitan,
portfolio: Melançon. ON v 24 n 18
Mr 5'60
---Francis, André. Pas de Dieux
(Gene Kelly), Paris Opéra phs.
OpP n 19 1960
---Fritzsche, Max. The Petrified
Forest, play set, Bochum 1954.
WT v 9 n 3 p 250 Autumn '60
---Greenwood, Thomas, the Elder.
Two designs, water-colour sket-
ches, Gothic exteriors (1777), ph:
Victoria and Albert Museum. Th
Notbk v 15 n 1 Autumn '60
---Grieve, John Henderson (1770-
1845). Three stage designs: Red
Gothic; Philip and His Dog (2).
Th Notbk v 15 n 2 Winter '60-1
---Jones, Robert Edmond. Henry
VIII, eight set designs (never used
as Billy Rose canceled the pro-
duction), phs. PlM v 37 n 3 p 52-4
D '60
---Jürgens, Helmut. Die tote Stadt,
ph: Betz, 1955. WT v 9 n 3 p 251
Autumn '60
---Kern, Ronald C. Two designs by
the elder Thomas Greenwood in
1777. plates Th Notbk v 15 n 1
p 31-2 Autumn '60
---Kingshill, Jane. Act I design for
Les Malheurs d'Orphee, ph: John
Vickers. Op v 2 n 3 p 182 Mr '60
---Kodály's Háry János as produced
at Juilliard Opera Theater, 6 ens
AP phs: Impact. J Rev v 7 n 2
cover, p 26 Spring '60
---Lanc, Emile. La Malle de Pam-
éla, ph: Bruxelles, 1955. WT v 9
n 1 p 15 Spring '60
--- ---La Plage aux Anguilles, setting, ph; Hella. WT v 9 n 1 p 17
Spring '60
---Larrain, Raymond de. La Belle
au Bois dormant, International
Ballet (Cuevas) several costumes
and a rideau. TD n 96 cover, p 14-
5 S-O '60
--- ---hl ph and pictures of his costumes and sets for "La Belle au
Bois Dormant", International Ballet (Cuevas), 8 phs: Lido. TD n 98

p 7-11 D '60
---Lenneweit, H. W. Die Frauen
von Trachis, set ph: Ilse Buhs,
1959. WT v 9 n 3 p 252 Autumn '60
---Malclès, Jean-Denis. Becket ou
l'Honneur de Dieu, ph: Bernand,
1959. WT v 9 n 1 p 77 Spring '60
---Martin, Denis. Bearskin, a play
by Paul Willems for the Belgian
National Theatre, 1951; color ph.
WT v 9 n 1 cover Spring '60
---Maximowna, Ita. Le Diable et
le Bon Dieu, set ph: Ilse Buhs,
1952. WT v 9 n 3 p 253 Autumn '60
---Mertz, Franz. Oedipus; set ph:
Cartharius, 1952. WT v 9 n 3 p 253
Autumn '60
---Mielziner, Jo. The Gang's All
Here, two settings, Act I sc. 2 and
Act II sc. 1 phs: Peter Juley. Th
Arts v 44 n 11 p 51 N '60
---Motley. Sets for 21 Trovatore,
the Metropolitan, phs: Melançon.
ON v 24 n 17 F 27'60
---Neher, Caspar. Ballo in Maschera,
ph: Heinz Köster, 1956. WT v 9 n 3
p 254 Autumn '60
---O'Hearn, Robert. Costume sketch
for Dr. Dulcamara in L'Elisir d' Am-
ore, ph: Louis Melançon; also set-
ting. ON v 25 n 7 p 18 D 24'60
---Peynet. Les Noces de Jean-
nette, sets for Paris Opéra, several
phs. OpP v 19 p 58-61 1960
---Piscator, Erwin. The Crucible,
ph: Tübingen, 1954. WT v 9 n 3
p 254 Autumn '60
---Pitkin, William. Invitation to a
March, set design. Th Arts v 44
n 10 p 15 O '60
---Portfolio: ballet in Germany.
TD n 89 Ja '60
---Reinking, Wilhelm. Kabale und
Liebe, set ph: Heinz Köster, 1955.
WT v 9 n 3 p 255 Autumn '60
---Renard, Raymond. Capitaine
Bada, play setting, ph: Cayet, 1956.
WT v 9 n 1 p 42 Spring '60
---Ristich, Dusan. L'uccello di fu-
oco (Kostich), Belgrade ph. La S
n 127 p 31 Je '60
---Roethlisberger, Max. Christmas
Eve, revival at Zurich, ens AP wl
ph: Baur. ON v 24 n 22 p 27 Ap 2'60

84

---Rychtarik, Richard. The Magic Flute, Metropolitan set, ph: 1940. ON v 25 n 1 p 16 O 8'60
---San Carlo: set for Fedora, opera; set for L'Amore delle Tre Melarance, phs: Naples. La S n 123 p 36-7 F '60
---Scaioli, Alberto. Scena per Debora e Jaele (Pizzetti). La S n 129-30 p 17 Ag-S '60
---Set for "Clandestine on the Morning Line", Washington, D. C. Th Arts v 44 n 7 p 17 Jl '60
---Set for Il protagonista di Kurt Weill, ph: Naples. La S n 127 p 28 Je '60
---Sokolic, Dorian. The Ohrid Legend (Kirbos), ballet, ph: Rijeka, 1957. WT v 9 n 4 p 375 Winter '60
---Stanic, Dusan. The Tower of Babylon, comedy, ens ph: Beograd 1958. WT v 9 n 4 p 370 Winter '60
---Strzelecki, Zenubiusz. The Sea Gull (1959) set, Warsaw. WT v 9 n 2 p 143 Summer '60
---Svoboda, Jan. Setting for The Sea Gull, Prague, 1960. WT v 9 n 2 cover Summer '60
---Television settings (a number of sets and scenes from TV plays, giving scenic artist, title of production, country and date). WT v 9 n 4 Winter '60
---Tintori, Silvano. Macbeth of Bloch, 4 sets, phs. La S n 122 p 51-4 Ja '60
---Topolski, Feliks. Man and Superman, arena setting ph: Lacey. NTM v 2 n 1 p 18 O '60
---Tosi, Piero. Uncle Vanya, sets, 1955, 3 phs: Bosio. WT v 9 n 2 p 120 Summer '60
---Van Nerom, Jacques. De Bruid in de Morgen, setting, ph: O. V. Brugge. WT v 9 n 1 p 18 Spring'60
--- ---Setting for Le Cocu Magnifique, ph: Brugge. WT v 9 n 1 p 9 Spring '60
--- ---Setting for play, Sur la Terre comme au Ciel, ph: O. V. Brugge, 1958. WT v 9 n 1 p 40

Spring '60
---Wagner operas; original sets side by side with recent Bayreuth settings, 8 phs. Op v 11 n 11 N'60
---Wakhevitch. Macbeth for Covent Garden, three sets. Op v 11 n 4 p 255 Ap '60
---Waller, Anthony. Pygmalion, arena setting ph; Lacey. NTM v 2 n1 p 18 O '60
---Walter, Paul. La Forza del Destino, setting for closing scene, Teatro Colón, ph: Homero. Op v 11 n 11 p 759 N '60
---Zeffire lli, Franco. Cavallerica Rusticana, Covent Garden, ens AP wl ph: Houston Rogers. Op v 11 n 2 p 153 F '60
--- ---Lucia de Lammermoor, Paris Opéra 1960, 1 phs. OpP n 19 p 24 1960
--- ---Alcina set and two smaller phs: Giacomelli. Op v 11 n 4 p 286 Ap '60
DE COSTER, CYRUS C. (1914-). Alfonso Sastre. TDR v 5 n 2 p 121-132 D '60
DEFENSE DE DOUBLER, play Paris notes; Dominique Nohain. WP v 11 n 4 p 6 F '60
DE FERRA, GIAMPAOLO. Teatro Verdi di Trieste: Oro del Reno; Walkiria. La S n 123 p 39 F '60
DE FILIPPO, EDUARDO, director AP hl ph: Italy. Th Arts v 44 n 4 p 54 Ap '60
DE FOUGERES, ADALGISA RAMELLINI. Isaac Albeniz, 1860-1960. por La S n 128 p 40-2 Jl'60
DE FRANCESCO, SILVANO. Aix-en-Provence 1960. il La S n 129-30 p 40, 74 Ag-S '60
DE GAETANI, THOMAS. Theatre architecture. drawings J Rev v 7 n 2 p 4-12 Spring '60
DEGAS, HILAIRE GERMAN EDGAR (1834-1917). La scuola di danza; la ballerina, 3 paintings. La Scala n 122 p 23-4, 26 Ja '60
DEGEILH, CLAUDINE AP wl ph: Biro. TD n 96 p 24 S-O '60

DE HONDEN, play
Amsterdam; Tone Brulin. WP
v 12 n 3 p 34 D '60
DELACROIX, FERDINAND VICTOR
EUGÈNE (1798-1863). Chopin
por. La S n 126 p 15 My '60
DELANNOY, MARCEL, 1898-,
composer
Demarquez, Suzanne. Abraham
et l'Ange; review of première.
GDC n 276 p 789 Je 10'60
DELIUS, FREDERICK, 1863-1934,
composer
Beecham, Sir Thomas. Frederick
Delius (book reviewed). MR v 21
n 2 p 151-154 My '60
DELLA CASA, LISA, 1919-, singer
As the Countess in Figaro, AP
phs: Melançon ON v 24 n 12 Ja 23
'60
De LUCIA, FERNANDO, 1860-1925,
singer
Schauensee, Max de. (Career
sketch; involvements with Caruso).
por ON v 24 n 20 p 10-1 Mr 19'60
DEL MONACO, MARIO, 1915-,
singer
San Carlo criticism. ON v 25 n 8
p 30 D 31'60
---And Giulietta Simionato in the
Trojans, AP wl ph: Milan. La S
n 128 p 26 Jl '60
---As Samson, AP wl phs. OpP
n 19 p 22, 23 1960
---In Andrea Chénier, AP wl ph:
La Scala. La S n 123 p 33 F '60
---E Leonie Rysanek in "Otello",
AP wl ph: La Scala. La S n 22 p 34
Ja '60
LA DEMANDE EN MARIAGE, play
Athens; Basile Ziogas. WP v 11
n 7 p 10 My '60
DEMARQUEZ, SUZANNE (1899-).
La semaine symphonique, serie;
Paris. GDC 1960
--- ---Premières auditions; Palais
de Chaillot "Musique d'Aujourd'hui":
le breton Jean Durbin "Première
suite d'Alain Fournier"; L'archi-
lecte Xenakis "Metastasis"; Louis
Saguer's Seis Cantares de F. Gar-
cia Lorca; Maurice le Roux's le
Cercle des Métamorphoses: T. N. P.
et R. T. F. GDC n 295 p 485 D 30'60

--- ---France; music reports.
MC v 162 n 1 p 31-2 Jl '60
---Thème Oriental, pour flûte
seule; commentaire. GDC n 257-
8 p 359 Ja 29'60
DEMBAUGH, WILLIAM, singer
Notes. ON v 24 n 22 p 2 Ap 2'60
DE MILLE, CECIL, 1881-1959,
director
Por ph. Th Arts v 44 n 8 back
cover Ag '60
DEN KORTE DAG ER LANG NOK,
play
Copenhagen notes; Karl Bjarnhof.
WP v 11 n 7 p 4 My '60
DENMARK
Hedman, Frank. Music (records
in particular). HF v 10 n 7 p 24,
26 Jl '60
---Royal Danish Ballet; 3 nouveaux
ballets: Vivaldi Concerto (Alfred);
Noces de Sang (Londres 1953);
Pierre et le Loup (Larsen-Prokof-
ieff). TD n 93 p 21 My '60
---Theatre report. WP v 11 n 5 p 2
Mr '60; same. WP v 12 n 1 p 4
O '60
DENS, MICHEL
And Liliane Berton in Les Noces
de Jeannette, opera, several AP
phs: Paris Opéra. OpP n 19
p 60-1 1960
DE QUINTO, JOSÉ MARIA, producer
Spain; with Alfonso Sastre, dramatist,
report on Committee for Theatrical
Realism (GTR). WP v 12 n 3 p 4
D '60
DERBY PLAYHOUSE
Cheeseman, Peter, its manager
on history, repertory, problems
of audience; now a fortnightly re-
pertory theatre. il NTM v 2 n 1
p 15-19 O '60
LA DERNIÈRE BANDE, play
Paris notes; Samuel Beckett. WP
v 11 n 8 p 5 Je '60
DERWENT, CLARENCE (1884-1959).
Has fun gone from the theatre? WP
v 11 n 5 p 7 Mr '60
DESCOMBEY, MICHEL, dancer
As Eros in Pas de Dieux (Gene
Kelly), several AP phs: Paris
Opéra. OpP n 19 1960
---In Qarrtsiluni (Lander), ens AP

wl ph: Paris Opéra. OpP n 19
p 44 1960

DESPORTES, YVONNE, composer
Première: Sonate (flûte, saxo,
voix, percussion-clavier et
piano); Paris. GDC n 257-8
p 360 Ja 29'60

DESSAGNES, GONTRAN, composer
Première: Fantaisie Concertante
pour deux guitares et orchestre;
commentaire par Suzanne Demarquez. GDC n 285 p 161 O 21'60

DETROIT
Belle Isle Concert Banol under
Leonard B. Smith; notes. IM
v 58 n 12 p 31 Je '60
---Cloonan, Richard T. Theatre
USA: Detroit. portfolio Th Arts
v 44 n 10 p 62-5 O '60
---Gilbert, Ernest J. Metropoli-
tan Opera. MC v 162 n 1 p 25
Jl '60
--- ---Music report. MC v 161
n 4 p 31 Mr '60; same. MC v 161
n 6 p 31 My '60
---Nine scenes from local play
groups, phs. Th Arts v 44 n 10
p 63-4 O '60

DETROIT OPERA THEATRE
Resident group; conductor,
Valter Poole and first-chair men
of Detroit Symphony; notes. IM
v 59 n 5 p 23-4 N '60

DETROIT SYMPHONY ORCHESTRA
Gilbert, Ernest J. (Paul Paray
notes; acoustics in Ford Auditorium.) MC v 161 n 1 p 23 Ja '60

DEVANT LES RIVAGES ÉTRAN-
GERS, play
Budapest notes; Anna Barnassin.
WP v 11 n 8 p 8 Je '60

DEVI, AMALA, dancer
Notes and AP wl ph: M. Petit.
TD n 90 p 19 F '60

DE VITO, GIACONDA, violinist
Notes. por MD v 50 n 9 p 16
Mr '60
---Por ph. MD v 50 n 9 p 16
Mr '60

DEVON FESTIVAL
British notes. Th Arts v 44 n 5
p 20 My '60

DEVRIES, GABRIELLE, violinist

Paris; with Nadine Desouches.
GDC n 275 p 754 Je 3'60

DE YOUNG, RICHARD B. ,?-1960
Obituary. MC v 161 n 3 p 20
F '60

LE DIABLE BOITEUX
Françaix, Jean (1912-). Paris
review. GDC n 284 p 127 O 14'60

DIAGHILEV, SERGE, 1872-1929,
impresario
La saison russe à Paris Ier mai
1909; numero spécial "Le Theatre".
il TD n 90 p 5-10 F '60

DIAMOND, DAVID, 1915-, composer
The World of Paul Klee, symphonic
work based on pictures (listed) of
Klee; notes. WM n 2 p 32 Ap '60

DIANA ESTÁ COMUNICANDO,
play
Madrid notes; José Lopez Rubio.
WP v 11 n 9 p 4 Jl '60

THE DIARY OF A MADMAN, opera
Sadler's Wells review. il Op v 11
n 6 p 442-3 Je '60
--- ---New Opera; two scenes AP
wl phs: Dominic. Op v 11 n 6
p 445 Je '60

DIAZ LARROQUE, ERNESTO,
singer
Paris; and Adolfo Mindlin. GDC
n 275 p 754 Je 3'60

LO DICIAMO ALL'ONOREVOLE?
drama
Ens AP wl ph. La S n 124 Mr '60

DIDO AND AENEAS, opera
Aix; preceded by La Senna Fes-
teggiante; notes. Op v 11 p 32-3
Autumn '60
---Britten-Handel première at
Aix-en-Provence; review. MC
v 162 n 3 p 24 S '60
---Aix-en-Provence; Berganza,
ens AP wl ph: Serge Lido. MC
v 162 n 3 p 25 S '60
---Steffek e Teresa Berganza, AP
hl ph: Aix-en-Province. La S
n 129-30 p 40 Ag-S '60

DIETSCHY, MARCEL. The family
and childhood of Debussy. Mus Q
v 46 n 3 p 301-314 Jl '60

DI FILIPPI, ARTURO, 1900?-,
director
Miami Opera Guild under

(Di Filippi)
Di Filippi; report. por ON v 24
n 21 p 26 Mr 26'60
DI GIACOMO, SALVATORE 1860-
1934, author
Riva, Ubaldo. La Musica nelle
poesie di Salvatore Di Giacomo.
il La S n 133 p 48-55 D '60
---Por ph. and several informal
phs. La S n 133 p 49-55 D '60
DILLEY, HARRY, trumpeter
Por ph. IM v 59 n 1 p 19 Jl '60
DINGES, SUSAN S. (Experiment
in childrens acting at University
of Kansas City.) PlM v 36 n 8
p 185 My '60
DINNY AND THE WITCHES, play
Cherry Lane, ens AP wl ph: Av-
ery Willard. Th Arts v 44 n 1
p 88 Ja '60
DISCOGRAPHIES
Disques parles et disques pour
enfants. GDC n 292 p 412-4
D 9'60
---Pugliese, Giuseppe. Die sch-
llplattensammlung(Un Ballo). Ver
v 1 n 1 and n 2 Ap '60 and Ag '60
THE DISENCHANTED, play
Schulberg, Budd, and Harvey
Breit. (Complete text of the play,
NYC cast and 6 illustrations). Th
Arts v 44 n 8 p 21-47 Ag '60
A DISTANT BELL, play
Review. Th Arts v 44 n 3 p 14
Mr '60
DI STEFANO, GIUSEPPE, 1921-,
singer
Schauensee, Max de. (Philadel-
phia's la Bohème and other opera
notes.) ON v 24 n 16 p 27 F 20'60
---E il direttore del San Carlo di
Lisbona (Bohème) ph. La S n 126
p 68 My '60
DIVONNE-LES-BAINS
Jourdan-Morhange, H. Festival
de Divonne; Marcel Borusiak's
"Canto pour 12 Instruments". GDC
n 281-2 p 66 S 30'60
DIXMIER, DENYSE, pianist
Castil. Review. GDC n 275 p 753
Je 3'60
DIXTUOR A VENT DE PARIS
Chamfray, Claude. Paris review.
GDC n 292 p 424 D 9'60

DJAMILEH, opera
Bizet criticism; performance by
Thomas Scherman's Little Or-
chestra Society, NYC. ON v 24
n 11 p 28 Ja 16'60
DOBBS, MATTIWALDA, 1925-,
singer
Moscow criticism. Op v 11 n 3
p 218 Mr '60
---NYC review; "her coloratura
among the most beautiful today".
MC v 161 n 3 p 29 F '60
---Conversing in Moscow with
Galina Vishnevskaya, hl ph: Hurok.
ON v 24 n 18 p 11 Mr 5'60
DOBIAS, CHARLES, violinist
Notes; b. Czechoslovakia. por
IM v 59 n 5 p 37 N '60
DOBIÁŠ, VACLAV, 1909-, composer
Critical notes. Mus Q v 46 n 4 p 510
O '60
DOBUJINSKY, MATISLAV(1875-1957).
Un Ballo in Maschera, setting for
Metropolitan opera 1943, Act III
scene 3, ph. Ver v 1 n 2 p 1015
Ag '60
LE DOCTEUR VARJU, play
Budapest notes; Endre Vesze. WP
v 11 n 5 p 11 Mr '60
DOCTOR FAUST, opera
London; concert version Doktor
Faust; review. Op v 11 n 1 p 62
Ja '60
---La Scala review. La S n 126 p 31
My '60
---Di Busoni; Margherita Roberti;
Dino Dondi, 2 AP hl phs. La S
n 126 p 32 My '60
---La Scala; Busoni work, Act II,
ens AP wl ph: Piccagliani. Op v 11
n 6 p 427 Je '60
DODANE, CHARLES, composer
Première: La Messe à capella;
Besançon notes. GDC n 283 p 95
O 7'60
DODECAPHONY
See Twelve Tone System
DODO, pseud. Malignità (seriale).
La S 1960
DOHNANYI, ERNST VON 1877-
1960, composer
Obituary. MC v 161 n 4 p 7 Mr '60
DER DOKTOR UND DIE TEUFEL,
play

Wüppertal;notes. WP v 11 n 3 p 3 Ja'60
---Wüppertal, 1959;ens AP wl ph: Sorani. WT v 9 n 1 p 78 Spring '60;same. WT v 9 n 3 p 235 Autumn'60
LA DOLCE VITA, film
Music criticism;Fellini. GDC n 278 p 840 Je 24'60
DOLIN, ANTON, 1904-, director
With Serge Lifar and John Gilpin in "Bonaparte à Nice", hl ph. TD n 96 p 25 S-O'60
DOLIN, SAMUEL, composer
Symphony No. 2 under Susskind, CBS radio review. CMJ v 4 n 2 p 38 Winter'60
DOLORES, operetta
Lyon;Le Miracle de la Femme par Henri Gheon. WP v 11 n 8 p 7 Je'60
DOM JUAN, ou le Festin de Pierre
Nelson, Robert J. The unreconstructed heroes of Molière. TDR v 4 n 3 p 19-28 Mr'60
DON CAMILLO, play
Athens notes;Sotiris Patatzis d'après le roman de Guareschi. WP v 11 n 5 p 9 Mr'60
DON CARLOS, opera
Berlin State Opera, ens AP wl ph. Op v 11 n 12 p 831 D'60
---Jurinac and Resnik, AP wl ph: Ellinger. ON v 25 n 2 p 23 O 29 '60
---Metropolitan;ens AP wl ph:LeBlanc, 1951. Op v 11 n 2 p 115 F'60
DON GIOVANNI, opera
Broder, Nathan. A notable Don from Deutsche Grammophone. HF v 10 n 1 p 62 Ja'60
--- ---(Two Angel recordings reviewed;Birgit Nilsson;Joan Sutherland.)HF v 10 n 11 p 77 N'60
---Mann, William. Glyndebourne. Op v 11 p 14-6 Autumn'60
---Metropolitan;Karl Boehm, conducting;Herbert Graf, production;Berman décor;Cesare Siepi, Roberta Peters. MC v 161 n 3 p 24 F'60
---NBC Opera review. MC v 161

n 6 p 16 My'60
---Newman, Ernest. (Letter on this opera.) MR v 21 n 1 p 78 F'60
---Rome, Teatro dell'Opera;review. LaS n 124 p 32 Mr'60
---Salzburg;Karajan, Schuh and Otto; Leontyne Price as Donna Anna "ideally fitting into this weirdly baroque night-scene". Op v 11 p 49 Autumn'60
---Washington, D. C. under Paul Callaway, staged by Robert Merrill;review. MC v 161 n 3 p 39 F'60
---Bacquier e Panerai, AP hl ph: Aix-en-Provence. LaS n 129-30 p 40 Ag-S'60
---Glyndebourne, three scenes, Joan Sutherland, Geraint Evans, five AP phs:Guy Gravett. Op v 11 p 14-5 Autumn'60
---Wuppertal, ens AP ph:Kurt Saurin. WT v 9 n 3 p 258 Autumn'60
DON JUAN, opera
Meissner, Jean de. A l'Opéra, reprise de Don Juan. GDC n 292 p 419 D 9'60
---Portfolio:Paris Opéra. OpP n 19 p 28-9 1960
DON PASQUALE, opera
L'Opéra-Comique review;4 dancers mime next scene during musical interlude. ON v 24 n 19 p 26 Mr 12'60
---Turin review;Italo Tajo "one of his finest achievements". Op v 11 n 1 p 43 Ja'60
DONAUESCHINGEN FESTIVAL
Criticism. E. H. MR v 21 n 4 p 329-31 N '60
---Strobel, Heinrich, director; notes. WM n 6 p 131 D '60
DONDI, DINO, singer
Teseo in Fedra, AP wl ph: Sa Scala. La S n 123 p 32 F '60
DONEUX, EDGAR, conductor
Dijon notes. GDC n 289 p 299 N 18'60
DON PASSOS, JOHN (1896-) and Paul Shyre. USA (text of the play, NYC cast and 3 scenes). Th Arts v 44 n 6 p 23-50 Je '60
DORATI, ANTAL, 1906-, conductor
Minneapolis Symphony resignation; Ormandy 1931-36; Mitropoulos

(Dorati)
1937-49; Dorati 1949-1960. IM
v 58 n 7 p 8 Ja '60

DOUAI, PAUL. (Address before
the meeting April 28 on the situation of French music; followed by
discussion: Raphaël Cuttoli, Jean
Malraye, Manuel Recasens and
others.) GDC n 279-80 p 878-887
Jl 1'60
---Por ph: F. Lyon. GDC n 279-
280 p 881 Jl 1'60

DOUBRAVA, JAROSLAV, 1909-,
composer
Notes. Mus Q v 46 n 4 p 511 O'60

DOUGLAS, KIRK 1916-, actor
Por ph. Th Arts v 44 n 10 p 83
O '60

DOUGLAS, MELVIN, 1901-, actor
Millstein, Gilbert. (Career sketch; b. Macon, Georgia, as Melvyn
Edouard Hesselberg.) por Th Arts
v 44 n 1 p 30-3 Ja '60

DE DOUX DINGUES, comedy
Paris notes; Michel André d'après
Joseph Carole. WP v 11 n 8 p 6
Je '60

DOWD, RONALD, singer
As Oedipus AP wl ph: David Sim.
Op v 2 n 3 cover Mr '60
---As Tannhauser, AP hl ph: David
Sim. Op v 11 n 2 p 158 F '60

DOWIS, JEANEANE, pianist
NYC debut reviewed. MC v 161
n 1 p 17 Ja '60

DOWNES, EDWARD (1911-). Bay-
reuth's cosmos. ON v 25 n 2 p 23
O 29'60
---Karl Bohm, the Met's Mozart-
Strauss-Wagner specialist. por
HF v 10 n 3 p 54-5, 128 Mr '60

DOWNING, ROBERT. J. B.'s
journeys (various productions beginning with Yale 1958). Th Arts
v 44 n 2 p 29 F '60

DRAGON, CARMEN, conductor
Notes. AmM v 8 n 5 p 8 Je '60

DRAKE, ALFRED, 1914-
And Wynn Murray in Babes In
Arms, AP hl ph: 1937. Th Arts
v 44 n 9 p 61 S '60

DRAMA
Arden, John. The Reps and new
plays, a writer's viewpoint.

NTM v 1 n 2 p 23-6 Ja '60
---Australia; Leslie Rees reporting. WT v 9 n 3 p 272-6 Autumn'60
---Balch, Jack. The openings. Th
Arts v 44 n 2 p 14-16 F '60
---Buenaventura, Enrique. Bird's-
eye view of the Latin American
theatre. il WT v 9 n 3 p 265-271
Autumn '60
---Brustein, Robert. The memory
of heroism (Greek tragedy translated for today by Richmond Latti-
more and David Grene, an essay).
TDR v 4 n 3 p 3-9 Mr '60
---Camus, Albert. Why I work in
the theatre. por Th Arts v 44
n 12 p 58-9, 70-1 D '60
---Cervantes Saaverdra, Miguel
de (1547-1616). The Cave of Salamanca. Chrys v 13 nos. 1-4
1960
---Clurman, Harold. The paradox
of the French stage. Th Arts v 44
n 12 p 64-5 D '60
---Corneille's Medée (the libretto
published 1693 by Christophe Ballard, in French, here reprinted as
faithfully as possible). Chrys v 13
nos. 5-8 1960
---Dumur, Guy. Jean Genet, parabole et parodie. il Spec n 1 p 75-8
1960
---Freedley, George. Plays first
produced off Broadway, June 1,
1959-May 31, 1960; Part I (through The Meeting). PlM v 37 n 2
p 32-3 N '60
--- ---Part II. PlM v 37 n 3 p 54-5
D '60
---Gassner, John. Playwrights of
the period (1930's in US). Th Arts
v 44 n 9 p 19, 26 S '60
---Gianoli, Luigi. La prosa al Ger-
olamo; atti unici di Parise, Gaipa
e Bertoli. il La S n 124 p 52-3
Mr '60
---Giovaninetti, Silvio. Giorgio
Prosperi's "La congiura"; Picnic"
William Inge. il La S n 127 p 48-
9 Je '60
--- ---Giovaninetti per la prosa.
La S 1960
--- ---Lavinia tra i dannati. La S
n 123 p 60-1 F '60

90

--- ---La legge attende; Guglielmo Giannini commenta. La S n 128 p 46-7 Jl '60
--- ---Pepe dell' Aretino, sale di Goldoni. il As S n 132 p 68-9 N '60
---Hill, Lucienne. Translated from the French (comment on method and aim in translation). Th Arts v 44 n 2 p 69 F '60
---Huisman, Jacques. Libéralisme esclavagiste. WP v 12 n 1 p 1 O '60
---Inquiry into television drama; list of international specialists questioned with resumes of replies (1) can all plays be televised (2) what treatment to adapt (3) what new shifts of interest to make up losses. WT v 9 n 4 p 313-317 Winter '60
---Ionesco, Eugène, confessing The Bald Soprano, play, arose from the "automatic quality of language" in an English primer and was transmuted into "a kind of universal petty bourgeoise" drama. TDR v 4 n 3 p 10-3 Mr'60
---Keating, John. New Dramatists Committee (Michaela O'Hara, 1948, started free tickets, craft discussions, production observance, reading his play, rehearsed readings). Th Arts v 44 n 7 p 17, 20, 63 Jl '60
---Kernodle, George R. Seven medieval theatres in one social structure. Th R v 2 n 1 p 26-36 1960
---Kitto, H. D. F. International Student Drama Festival (Bristol). NTM v 1 n 2 p 14-7 Ja '60
---Lilar, Suzanne. The sacred and the profane in the work of Belgian dramatists. portfolio WT v 9 n 1 p 4-22 Spring '60
---List of playwrights who can translate foreign works: language, name, country of his origin (18 countries). WP v 11 n 3 p 2 Ja '60
---London reviews. Th Arts v 44 n 4 p 14-6 Ap '60

---Lyon, Raymond. Le théâtre Paris notes on "Le Théâtre de la Cité de Villeurbanne"; on Le Comédie de L'Est. GDC n 278 p 851 Je 24'60
---Munich report. Th Arts v 44 n 4 p 14-6 Ap '60
---New Orleans report. il Th Arts v 44 n 4 p 57-8 Ap '60
---O'Casey, Sean. The Drums of Father Ned (complete text). Th Arts v 44 n 5 p 23-52 My '60
---One-man show; Bernard Sobel's comments with names and pictures. Th Arts v 44 n 10 p 24-6 O '60
---Panel discussion of repertory; Dr. Glynne Wickham, chairman. NTM v 1 n 1 p 23-7 O '59
---Paris; notes on plays 1959-60; on 1960-61. il Th Arts v 44 n 12 p 67, 74 D '60
---Richards, Stanley. On and Off Broadway (review column). PlM 1960
---Sartre, Jean-Paul. Un texte inédit (Conférence sur le Théâtre, Paris, 1960). por WP v 11 n 9 p 1, 7 Jl '60
---Shakespeare; reports from US, Brazil, Denmark, France on dates and plays first performed (world research ITI). WP v 12 n 3 p 2 D '60
--- ---complete under George Rylands (Cambridge for Decca; details). HF v 10 n 5 p 33 My '60
---Taylor, Samuel, with Cornelia Otis Skinner. The Pleasure of his Company (text of play, NYC cast 1958 and pictures). Th Arts v 44 n 4 p 22-52 Ap '60
---Texts of plays; Brobury Pearce Ellis on how a scholar of the theatre might consider various texts; Shakespeare and Tennessee Williams as examples. TDR v 5 n 1 p 113-6 S '60
---Theatre Arts Magazine 1948-1959: play scripts published with date and cost of back numbers. Th Arts v 44 n 1 p 90 Ja '60
---Towarnicki, Frédéric de Quand

(Drama)
Paris découvre Tchékhov. portfolio Spec n 1 p 11-21 1960
---Trewin, J. C. United Kingdom. il WT v 9 n 3 p 290-3 Autumn '60
---US; summer theatres (160), mostly commercialized now; the "package show"; glamor in the festivals. WT v 9 n 3 p 294-6 Autumn '60
---World calendar: US(Broadway, regional), then by place with information and dates. Th Arts 1960
---Dramatists: Theodore Apstein, Robert Anderson, Louis A. Lippa, George Hamlin, ens ph. Th Arts v 44 n 7 p 19 Jl '60

DRAMA-HISTORY AND CRITICISM
Bentley, Eric (1916-). The making of a dramatist (Bernard Shaw). TDR v 5 n 1 p 3-21 S '60
---Falk, Eugene H. Molière the indignant satirist: Le Bourgeoise gentilhomme. TDR v 5 n 1 p 73-88 S '60
---Farrington, Conor A. The language of drama (both audience and actors wish poetry returned to the stage). TDR v 5 n 2 p 65-72 D '60
---Klarmann, Adolf D. Friedrich Duerrenmatt and the tragic sense of comedy. TDR v 4 n 4 p 77-104 My '60
---Fry, Christopher. Comedy. TDR v 4 n 3 p 77-9 Mr '60
---Glenville, Peter. The history play (a problem for modern dramatists; "melodrama and beau geste inacceptable to a modern audience"). il Th Arts v 44 n 10 p 22-3 O '60
---Kaula, David. On Noh drama. TDR v 5 n 1 p 61-72 S '60
---McWilliams, G. H. Interpreting Betti. TDR v 5 n 2 p 15-23 D '60
---Nelson, Robert J. The unreconstructed heroes of Molière. TDR v 4 n 3 p 14-37 Mr '60
---O'Casey, Sean: his years before playwriting by Herbert Coston. TDR v 5 n 1 p 102-12 S '60

---Sastre, Alfonso. Drama and society; I. Tragedy as an instrument of torture; II. on the Death of a Salesman; III. Theatre of Magic and Theatre of Anguish. TDR v 5 n 2 p 102-110 D '60
--- ---criticism of his dramas by Leonard C. Pronko. TDR v 5 n 2 p 111-120 D '60
---Schwarz, Alfred. The allegorical theatre of Hugo von Hofmannsthal (1874-1929). TDR v 4 n 3 p 65-76 Mr '60
---Sharp, William L. A play: scenario or poem. TDR v 5 n 2 p 73-84 D '60
---Stephenson, Robert C. Farce as method. TDR v 5 n 2 p 85-93 D '60
---Strindberg's "Dream Plays"; criticism by John R. Milton. TDR v 4 n 3 p 108-116 Mr '60

DRAMA-TWENTIETH CENTURY
Adler, Henry. To hell with society. TDR v 4 n 4 p 53-76 My '60
---Blau, Herbert. (On the stage today in London and Paris.) TDR v 5 n 1 p 89-101 S '60
---The college musical; John S. Wilson on its history. il Th Arts v 44 n 8 p 48-52 Ag '60
---Esslin, Martin. The theatre of the absurd (a "grotesquely heightened picture", criticism of Beckett, Adamov, Ionesco, Brecht, etc.). TDR v 4 n 4 p 3-15 My '60
---Fowlie, Wallace. New plays of Ionesco (1912-) and Genet (1910-). TDR v 5 n 1 p 43-8 S '60
---France; articles by Albert Camus; Jean-Pierre Lenoir, Harold Clurman. il Th Arts v 44 n 12 D '60
---Karsch, Walter. German drama today. WT v 9 n 3 p 203-12 Autumn '60
---Popkin, Henry. The plays of Tennessee Williams. TDR v 4 n 3 p 45-64 Mr '60
---Valency, Maurice. (On the loss of meaning", a major disaster", in art.) Th Arts v 44 n 8 p 8-9, 60 Ag '60
---Vilar, Jean. (On attempt of T. N. P. to get audience to think for themselves.)

WP v 12 n 2 p 1, 3 N '60
---Voices of the 20th century; a
review of recording of many people, Henry Fonda linking the ar-
ray. PlM v 36 n 6 p 139 Mr '60
---Wesker, Arnold. (On repertory
theatre, on the "New Drama".)
NTM v 1 n 3 p 5-7 Ap '60
---Plays to illustrate Maurice Valency's article on the loss of
meaning in art: scene from the
Balcony picturing the world as a
brothel; Rhinoceros, men turn
into animals; Death watch, prison
life; Endgame, live in ash cans;
Donald Davis in the mono-drama,
Krapp's Last Tape; waiting for
Godot, six AP phs. Th Arts v 44
n 8 p 10-11 Ag '60

DRAMA IN UNIVERSITIES AND
  COLLEGES
A. and M. University of Tallahassee, Florida; Creative Children's Theatre, notes. Th Arts
v 44 n 8 p 56 Ag '60
---Banham, Martin. (Theatre at
University College, Ibadan, Nigeria; repertory.) NTM v 1 n 4
p 18-21 Jl '60
---Brandt, George, and actors
in a discussion: university drama.
NTM v 1 n 1 p 17-20 O '59
---Brown, M. Charleen. Theatre
training on the campus. PlM v 36
n 7 p 166 Ap '60
---Catholic University, Washington, D. C.; notes. Th Arts v 44
n 12 p 22 D '60
---Cornell University; fifteenth
conference of New York Community Theatre Association. Th Arts
v 44 n 12 p 70 D '60
---Hulsopple, Bill G. Theatre in
Southeast Missouri. PlM v 36 n 5
p 106-7 F '60
---Johnston, Denis. The college
theatre-why? Th Arts v 44 n 8
p 12-3, 69 Ag '60
---Knudsen, Hans. The university
drama department (Germany). WT
v 9 n 3 p 262-4 Autumn '60
---Pennsylvania State University;
Five O'Clock Theatre notes. Th
Arts v 44 n 12 p 70 D '60

---Princeton University; notes. Th
Arts v 44 n 11 p 72 N '60
---Savage, Prof. George. American colleges and universities and
the professional theatre. NTM v 1
n 1 p 8-12 O '60
---The Thespians of Loyola University, 1860-; present activities.
Th Arts v 44 n 4 p 58 Ap '60
---Tulane in New Orleans; report.
Th Arts v 44 n 4 p 58 Ap '60
---US; plays and directors arranged
in "See For Yourself" and "App-
lause" columns, college and high
school separate. PlM 1960
---University of Chile; theatre report by Stanley Richards, il PlM
v 36 n 8 p 186-7 My '60
---University of Detroit; repertory
theatre. Th Arts v 44 n 10 p 78
O '60
---University of Panama, theatre
1959; Frank McMullen, founder,
under International Educational
Exchange Program; notes. Th
Arts v 44 n 6 p 68 Je '60
---University of Southampton;
Richard Southern on the new theatre building. il NTM v 1 n 4 p 21-
4 Jl '60
---Valency, Maurice. Flight into
lunacy (this Columbia University
professor explores "the loss of
meaning in art, a major disaster
of our time"). Th Arts v 44 n 8
p 8-9, 68 Ag '60
---Wickham, Glynne. Campus The-
atre, Inc. (a European observes a
Washington convention of the Am-
erican Educational Theatre Associ-
ation; his suggestions for betterment).
NTM v 1 n 3 p 28-30 Ap '60
---Wilson, John S. Musicals: the
old college try. portfolio Th Arts
v 44 n 8 p 48-52 Ag '60
---Emerson College; Love for Love,
AP ph: Boston. Th Arts v 44 n 5
p 55 My '60
---Howard University; Countée
Cullen's version of Medea, ens
AP ph: Robt. H. McNeil. Th Arts
v 44 n 12 p 23 D '60
---Kinderspiel, ens AP wl ph: Boston
University. Th Arts v 44 n 5 p 54

(Drama in universities(
My '60
---La Barra, Pedro de, por ph:
Universidad de Chile; 2 other
pictures, plays. PlM v 36 n 8
p 187 My '60
---Musicals: US college portfolio.
Th Arts v 44 n 8 p 48-50 Ag '60
---Scenes from: The Raft of the
Medusa (Weslyan University);
John Brown's Body (Yale); Romeo
and Juliet (Long Beach State Col-
lege); Private Life of the Master
Race (Hunter College); Love's
Labour's Lost (Carnegie Tech);
and The Skin of our Teeth (St.
Mary's, Indiana), six ens AP
phs: USA. Th Arts v 44 n 8 p 14-
5 Ag '60
---The Skin of our Teeth (St. Mary
Mary's, Indiana), six ens AP
phs: USA. Th Arts v 44 n 8 p 14-
5 Ag '60
---Tufts Arena Theatre in Kanin's
Rashomon, ens AP wl ph: Boston.
Th Arts v 44 n 5 p 54 My '60
THE DRAMATURG
Skopnik, Günter. Der dramaturg.
WT v 9 n 3 p 233-8 Autumn '60
DRAPER, RUTH, 1884-1956,
actress
Richards, Stanley. The Art of
Ruth Draper (book review of bi-
ography and anthology of 35 mono-
logues). PlM v 37 n 2 p 38 N '60
DRAUSSEN VOR DER TÜR, play
Peiser, Gerd, and Edda Weide-
mann, AP hl ph: H. Köster,
1957. WT v 9 n 3 p 206 Autumn'60
THE DREAM OF PETER MANN,
play
Edinburgh notes; Bernard Kops.
WP v 12 n 1 p 15 O '60
DRESDEN
As a recording center for Strauss;
Karl Böhm. HF v 19 n 11 p 26, 28
N '60
THE DRESDEN OPERA
Schmiedel, Gorrfried. Ernst von
Schuch and the Dresden Opera.
portfolio Op v 11 n 1 p 7-15
Ja '60
---Schmiedel, Gottfried. Fritz
Busch and the Dresden Opera.

il Op v 2 n 3 p 175-181 Mr '60
--- ---Karl Böhm and the Dresden
Opera. Op v 11 n 5 p 324-330
My '60
---Schuch, Ernst von, and the
theatres he conducted in; scenes
and artists in his career. Op v 11
n 1 p 7-14 Ja '60
---Böhm, Karl, por ph. and sing-
ers during his regime (14) phs.
Op v 11 n 5 p 324-30 My '60
DREW, JOHN, 1853-1927, actor
Clurman, Harold. Actors: The
image of their era. TDR v 4 n 3
p 38-44 Mr '60
DRIVER, TOM F Strength and
weakness in Arthur Miller. TDR
v 4 n 4 p 45-52 My '60
DRON, MARTHE, 1878-1960,
pianist
Obituary; b. Nancy. GDC n 285
p 160 O 21'60
DRUCKER, STANLEY, clarinettist
Notes; b. Brooklyn. IM v 59 n 5
p 36 N '60
DRUKTENIS, ADELE, singer
Por ph; Chicago. MC v 161 n 6
p 28 My '60
THE DRUMS OF FATHER NED,
play
O'Casey, Sean. (Text of play,
drawing of a set by Gardner Lea-
ver, cast 1959 Lafayette(Indiana)
Little Theatre). Th Arts v 44 n 5
p 23-52 My '60
DRUMS UNDER THE WINDOWS,
play
NYC; O'Casey with Martyn Green
and Dana Elcar. Th Arts v 44
n 12 p 12 D '60
DUBLIN
Colum, Padraic. Theatre, Dub-
lin. Th Arts v 44 n 2 p 24-5 F'60
---Grand Opera Society; repertory
notes. Op v 2 n 3 p 202 Mr '60
DUBOIS, P. -M. -, 1910? -, composer
Première: Mademoiselle Julie;
Service du Musique Légère, R. T. F.
GDC n 295 p 486 D 30'60
DUBROVNIK
Eleventh summer festival; notes.
WM n 3 p 55 Je '60
---Festival notes. WP v 11 n 3
p 7 Ja '60

---Logar, Mihovil. En plein
air. il La S n 131 p 34-5 O'60
---Wood, Peggy. (Notes.) Th Arts
v 44 n 12 p 17 D '60
---Four scenes, Palazzo Ducale.
La S n 131 p 34 O '60
---Tirena, ens AP wl ph: Vilko
Zuber, 1958. WT v 9 n 4 p 374
Winter '60
LA DUCHESSE DE LANGEAIS,
play
Fink and Wussow, AP ph: Rudolf
Betz, 1959. WT v 9 n 3 p 234
Autumn '60
DUCHOW, MARVIN. The inter-
national conference of composers
at Stratford (Ontario). CMJ v 5
n 1 p 4-16 Autumn '60
I DUE BARONI, opera
Affelder, Paul. Siena; Bruno Rig-
acci directing artists from Picco-
la Scala. ON v 25 n 6 p 29 D 17'60
---AP wl ph: Siena. ON v 25 n 6
p 29 D 17'60
---Siena; ens AP wl ph: APC. Op
v 11 n 10 p 695 O '60
DUEL OF ANGELS, play
Fry's adaptation of Girandoux's
Pour Lucrèce; review. Th Arts
v 44 n 6 p 58 Je '60
---Leigh, Vivien, John Merivale,
Peter Wyngarde, ens AP wl ph.
Th Arts v 44 n 6 p 61 Je '60
DUERRENMATT, FRIEDRICH,
1921-, author
Klarmann, Adolf D. Friedrich
Duerrenmatt and the tragic sense
of comedy. TDR v 4 n 4 p 77-104
My '60
DUKAS, PAUL (1865-1935). La
Péri (poème dansé): analyse par
Pierrette Mari. GDC n 261-2
p 449 F 26'60
DUKE, PATTY, 1948?-, actress
Balch, Jack. (Interview with girl
playing the young Helen Keller
and her mentor, John Ross.) il
Th Arts v 44 n 1 p 28-9 Ja '60
---As Helen Keller in The Miracle
Worker, AP wl ph: Philippe Hals-
man. Th Arts v 44 n 1 cover Ja'60
--- ---2 AP phs. Th Arts v 44 n 1
cover, p 26 Ja '60
DULLIN, CHARLES, 1885-1949,

director
Report of honors, his importance;
L'Association Charles Dullin,
Paris. WP v 11 n 4 p 7 F '60
DUMESNIL, RENÉ (1879-). La
Dame aux Camelias, ballet d'Hen-
ri Sauguet. il La S n 128 p 24-5
Jl '60
--- ---Hommage à Chopin. il La S
n 131 p 26-7 O '60
--- ---Nostalgie de Montmarte. il
La S n 132 p 39-41 N '60
--- ---La vie musicale en France:
L'Académie des Beaux Arts elit
Emmanuel Bondeville. por La S
n 125 p 32-3 Ap '60
--- ---La vie musicale en France;
une profitable leçon de gout (Rich-
ard Wagner). La S n 129-30 p 32-3
Ag-S '60
--- ---Wanda Landowska et les
dimanches de Saints-Leu-La-
Forêt. La S n 133 p 80 D '60
DUMONT-DUREAU, JANINE,
singer
Paris review; Françoise Doreau
and Roger Loewenguth also. GDC
n 261-2 p 439 F 26'60
DUMUR, GUY. Jean Genet, parabole
et parodie. il Spec n 1 p 75-8 1960
DUNLOP, LIONEL. People; Joan
Sutherland. il Op v 11 n 10 p 675-
682 O '60
DUNN, MIGNON, singer
In costume, ph. ON v 25 n 5 p 4
D 10'60
DUPRE, MARCEL (1886-). L'ex-
écutant (opening of the Congrès du
Conseil International de la Musique).
GDC n 286 p 193 O 28'60
---Lyon, Raymond. Review. GDC
n 276 p 788-9 Je 10'60
DURBIN, JEAN. Première suite
d'Alain Fournier (études musicales
analytiques). GDC n 292 p 429
D 9'60
DURAND, LIONEL (1921?-1961).
Opera, Paris. Th Arts v 44 n 3
p 42-3 Mr '60
DURANTE, JIMMY 1893-, comedian
And Merman in Red, Hot and Blue,
AP hl ph: 1936. Th Arts v 44 n 9
p 64 S '60
DUSSEK, JOHANN LADISLAUS,

95

(Dussek)
1960-1812, composer
(Lang, Paul H.) Review of re-
cording by Society of Forgotten
Music. Mus Q v 46 n 1 p 118-120
Ja '60
DUTCH THEATRE MUSEUM
Amsterdam note. WT v 9 n 2
p 174 Summer '60
DUTILLEUX, HENRI, 1916-,
Notes; b. Angers. GDC n 283
p 80 O 7'60
---Première: la second Symphon-
ie; Besançon; notes. GDC n 283
p 95 O 7'60
---Première: Second Symphony;
Boston Symphony commission;
"Munch's euphanasy" for French
works. MC v 161 n 3 p 41 F '60
---Por ph: Richard de Grab. GDC
v 283 cover O 7'60
DUVAL, DENISE, singer
American Opera Society; Les
Mamelles de Tirésias; then La
Voix Humaine; reviews. Op v 11
n 7 p 471-2 Jl '60
---Jourdan-Morhange, H. Le livre
d'or de Paris-Inter. GDC n 269-
70 p 596 Ap 22'60
---In La Voix Humaine. AP ph:
Edinburgh. Op v 11 p 63 Autumn'60
---In Vol de Nuit, opera ens AP wl
ph: Pairs Opéra. OpP n 19 p 55
1960
---Por ph: Paris; facsimile ex-
cerpts from the vocal score of
La Voix Humaine; Cocteau's set
design. Op v 11 n 8 p 530-4 Ag'60
DUVAL, FRANCA
As Mirandoline, La Locandiera,
AP hl ph: Paris; ens AP wl phs.
OpP n 19 p 56-7 1960
DVOŘÁK ANTONIN, 1841-1904,
composer
Clapham, John. The progress of
Dvořák''s Music in Britain. MR
v 21 n 2 p 130-139 My'60
DYGAT, ZYGMUNT, pianist
Paris notes. GDC n 288 p 258
N 11'60

E

EAMES, EMMA, 1865-1952,

singer
Por ph: Byron coll. ON v 25 n 5
p 24 D 10'60
EARHEART, WILL, 1871-1960
Obituary notes. MEJ v 46 n 5
p 10 Ap-My '60
EATON, QUAINTANCE. The
National Cultural Center, Wash-
ington, D. C. drawing ON v 24
n 21 p 10 Mr 26'60
---With James Browning, hl ph:
NYC; also notes on her forth-
coming "Opera Caravan". ON
v 25 n 7 p 4 D 24'60
EBERT, PAUL. Shakespeare
smash hit (Julius Caesar at Oak-
ridge, Tennessee). il PlM v 36
n 4 p 78 Ja '60
ECKART, WILLIAM, 1920-,
scenic designer
Por ph. Th Arts v 44 n 7 p 56
Jl '60
---Costume and set disigns for
"Fiorello", musical; set designs
for "Mister Johnson", for "Damn
Yankees", for The Golden Apple,
phs. Th Arts v 44 n 7 p 56-7 Jl'60
L'ECOLE NATIONALE DE MUSIQUE
DE VERSAILLES
Lorin, Michel. (Review.) GDC
n 259-60 p 411 F 12'60
L'ECOLE SUPERIEURE D'ETUDES
CHOREGRAPHIQUES
Silvant, Jean. Une ecole de danse
à Paris. TD n 96 p 3-5 S-O'60
EDDISON, ROBERT(1908-). Capon
and Goodman's Fields (description
from a rough pencil sketch made
by William Capon, being a "hy-
pothetical reconstruction" of 1741
period). facsimile Th Notbk v 14
n 4 p 126-132 Summer '60
EDINBURGH FESTIVAL
Beaux Arts Trio (first visit) and
Juilliard Quartet; notes. MC v 162
n 5 p 28 N '60
---Opera; Falstaff fine; I Puritani
less so; triple bill, Il Segreto di
Susanna, Voix Humaine, Arlecchino;
notes. ON v 25 n 2 p 20 O 29'60
---Plans for 1960. MD v 51 n 2 p 14
Ag '60
---Porter, Andrew. Opera reviews.
Op v 11 p 62-4 Autumn '60

---Program notes;premières.
WM n 3 p 56 Je'60
EDUCATION
Aftreth, Orville B. The princi-
pal's role in the music program.
MEJ v 46 n 3 p 41-3 Ja'60
---Albertson, Marjorie. We not only teach music, we also teach
children. MEJ v 46 n 4 p 99-103
F-Mr'60
---The American Academy in
Rome:fellowships $3,000. MC
v 162 n 2 p 8 Ag'60
---Assenine, Serge. L'Ecole chor-
egraphique de Moscou. il TD
n 98 p 16-7 D'60
---Bailey, Bryan. Building the
young audience (methods used
at Coventry's Belgrade Theatre
to interest school children in
drama). NTM v 1 n 2 p 18-21
Ja'60
---Berger, Kenneth. What music
can do. MEJ v 46 n 4 p 97 F-Mr
'60
---Bourgeat, Marcelle. Les con-
naissances et les préoccupa-
tions d'un professeur de danse.
TD n 94 p 23-4 Je'60
---Carey, Margaretta. Music for
the educable mentally retarded.
MEJ v 46 n 4 p 72, 74 F-Mr'60
---Chance, Varner M. Follow-up
program(in school music, US).
MEJ v 46 n 3 p 46, 48 Ja'60
---Cologne;first summer course
at State College of Music;notes.
WM n 3 p 57 Je'60
---Cox Jane Carlon. Music in the
junior high school special cur-
riculum. MEJ v 46 n 5 p 58, 60
Ap-My'60
---Dance studios in Paris;Jean
Silvant's estimate with criti-
cism. TD n 96 p 3-5 S-O'60
---Dartington, England;report of
1959 music school. MR v 21 n 1
p 81-2 F'60
---Eastman School of Music:mu-
sic degree with a minor in hu-
manities;notes. MC v 161 n 3
p 49 F'60
---L'Ecole du danse du Théâtre
du Châtelet, Paris. il TD n 96

p 20-1 S-O'60
---Ernest, Karl D. The general
music program (US schools, with
a program report form of aid to
teachers). MEJ v 46 n 3 p 19-20
Ja'60
--- ---The report of the general
music program (as considered at
Atlantic City Meeting 1960 of the
MENC). MEJ v 46 n 6 p 21-3
Je-Jl'60
---European schools run by US
Army;music co-ordinator, Max
T. Krone's survey. il MEJ v 46
n 3 p 21-3 Ja'60
---Faculty notes on leaders of the
Second String Congress, Puerto
Rico:Roy Harris;Warren A. Ben-
field;Rafael Druian, Johana Har-
ris, Sidney Harth, Teresa Harth,
Frank Houser, Louis Krasner,
William Lincer, Lorne Munroe,
Theodore Salzman Jesus Maria
Sanroma, Abraham Skernick. IM
v 58 n 9 p 37 Mr'60
---France; Pierre Lefèvre's Ecole
Supérieure d'Art Dramatique in
Strasbourg, founded by Michel
Saint-Denis;" most impressive
in France". PlM v 37 n3 3 p 56
D '60
---Gehrkens, Karl Wilson. The
development of a college cur-
riculum in music education (at
Oberlin). MEJ v 47 n 2 p 31-4
N-D '60
---Gray, Justin. Music education
and creativity. MEJ v 46 n 4 p 58,
62 F-Mr '60
---The Harp; Carlos Salzedo; Sum-
mer Harp Colony in Maine; notes.
MC v 161 n 6 p 43 My '60
---Horn, Dorothy D. Music theory
for high school students. MEJ
v 46 n 3 p 74-5 Ja '60
---Hungary; music by Howard Le-
Bow. J Rev v 7 n 3 p 6 Fall '60
---Johnston, Denis. The college
theatre-why? il Th Arts v 44 n 8
p 12-3 Ag '60
---Jourdan-Morhange, H. Poulenc
au cours d'interpretation de Marcelle Gerar; Paris. GDC n 274
p 725 My 27'60

(Education)
---Kerman, Joseph. The place of music in basic education. MEJ v 46 n 5 p 43-6 Ap-My '60
---Krone, Max T. Guides to Musical Experience (as adopted by US Army Dependents' Schools in Europe 1959). il MEJ v 47 n 2 p 48-9, 52-5 N-D '60
---Lamers, William M. The two kinds of music. MEJ v 46 n 4 p 36-8 F-Mr '60
---Ling, Stuart J. Toward real musical literacy (in US). MEJ v 46 n 5 p 52, 54 Ap-My '60
---Lundin, Robert W. Musical learning and reinforcement theory. MEJ v 46 n 4 p 46, 48-9 F-Mr '60
---McCutcheon, Marjorie F. (Junior high school music curricula, a patchwork.) MEJ v 47 n 1 p 87 S-O '60
---Marple, Hugo D. The challenge of the Conant report to music education. MEJ v 47 n 2 p 35-6 N-D '60
---Metropolitan Opera Guild's full-tuition scholarship plan; details. MC v 161 n 1 p 8 Ja '60
---The Metropolitan Opera Student Performance; a summary of repertory and audiences. ON v 24 n 18 p 1 Mr 5'60
---Metropolitan Opera Unit to sing in schools. MC v 162 n 6 p 4 D'60
---Michigan, Interlochen Music Camp. il La S n 131 p 31-3 O'60
---Music; auditions for US Army and Navy musicians reveal educational lacks; details by James A. Ode on band men, both recruits and draftees. IM v 58 n 7 p 18 Ja '60
--- ---Australia; conservatory and school notes; examiners and awards. MD 1960
--- ---Bronxville, New York, program of lecture series for young listeners; Jean Calvert Scott on preparation to listen, on type of programs. MEJ v 46 n 3 p 31-2 Ja '60
--- ---curricula in US schools;

Louis Chenette. MEJ v 47 n 1 p 83-4 S-O '60
--- ---Great Britain; report on press criticism by musicians on antiquated teaching; comment. MC v 161 n 5 p 30-1 Ap '60
--- ---how boys were kept in music class at time of voice change; methods explained by Frederick J. Swanson. MEJ v 46 n 4 p 50, 53-4 F-Mr '60
--- ---notable summer schools, US and Europe. WM n 5 p 105 O '60
--- ---publications, large bibliography for teachers, supervisors, etc. MEJ v 47 n 2 p 92-3 N-D '60
--- ---summer schools, including notes on Dartington Hall under William Glock. WM n 3 p 57 Je'60
--- ---teacher; training time laid out (general culture, basic music, musical performance, professional education) in percentages, as outlined by the National Association of Schools of Music; this is part of an article by Robert W. House on the role of fine arts in the preparation fo teachers. MEJ v 47 n 2 p 39-40, 43 N-D '60
---Naumberg Foundation, competitions for young instrumentalists; notes. IM v 59 n 1 p 20 Jl '60
---Nice; International Summer Academy under the Ministry of Cultural Affairs; faculty list, including Serge Lifar for dance. WM n 2 p 33 Ap '60
---Opera; In-Service course for NYC teachers arranged by Metropolitan Opera Guild and the Board of Education (NYC). ON v 24 n 19 p 1 Mr 12'60
--- ---audiences; how the Metropolitan and continental opera companies bring in young audiences. Op v 11 n 10 p 672 O '60
--- ---US; work of the American Opera Workshop; Indiana University as an example. WM n 4 p 70-72 Autumn '60
---Orchestra players as trained in The New School of Music, Philadelphia; article by the director,

Max Aronoff. MC v 161 n 3 p 14
F '60
---Paris; École Normale; cours
d'interprétation Noémie Perugia.
GDC n 295 p 496 D 30'60
---Phelps, Roger P. Research in
music education. MEJ v 46 n 6
p 51-3 Je-Jl '60
---pour un Baccalauréat Artistique,
par L. Dulau. GDC n 295 p 503
D 30'60
---Schwartz, Will. The universities, guardians of our musical
heritage. MEJ v 47 n 1 p 41-3
S-O '60
---Slocomb, Don B. Make way
for music (a Texas school superintendent speaks in detail). MEJ
v 47 n 2 p 70 N-D '60
---Stockholm Opera School; two-
year course, nine students. Op
v 11 n 4 p 266 Ap '60
---Stratford, Connecticut; theatre
course of study in 5-week school
program; note. PlM v 36 n 7
p 149 Ap '60
---Sur, William R. Music for teen-
agers (schools might offer general elective in upper grades;
ensemble experience for the less
talented also). MEJ v 47 n 2
p 62, 64 N-D '60
---Tallmadge, William H. Teaching improvisation (in schools).
MEJ v 47 n 2 p 58-60 N-D '60
---Teen-Age Summer Guide; note.
PlM v 36 n 8 p 179 My '60
---Theatre; Pennsylvania State
University's Mateer Playhouse.
PlM v 36 n 7 p 159 Ap '60
--- ---the Windsor Camp Theatre,
Lenox, Massachusetts, founded
3 years ago by James Hall for
teen-agers; ballet, acting, music,
art. il Th Arts v 44 n 6 p 21-2
Je '60
---Ulano, Sam. Approach to practical drumming ("must be well
versed in all styles"). IM v 58
n 10 p 19 Ap '60
---US project for upper 20 percent
students; music curricula de-
tailed by William C. Hartshorn.
MEJ v 47 n 1 p 33-6 S-O '60

---University of British Colum-
bia, Summer School of Music;
Dr. Welton Marquis; details.
CMJ v 4 n 3 p 50 Spring '60
---Vilar, Jean. (On the attempt
for ten years to educate the ad-
herents of the Théâtre National
Populaire.) WP v 12 n 2 p 2, 3
N '60
EDWIGE, play
Montreal; Maurice Gagnon; notes.
WP v 11 n 4 p 1 F '60
EGK, WERNER, 1901-, conductor-
composer
American première of his Inspec-
tor General, composer conducting
at NYC Center; William Ball, stage
director. MC v 162 n 5 p 16 N '60
---Influence of romanticism; com-
ments. WT v 9 n 3 p 218 Autumn'60
---Première: Variations on a Cari-
bbean Theme; Freiburg. WM n 2
p 32 Ap '60
EGYPT
Termon, M. Sauvons les temples
d'Égypte. WP v 11 n 4 p 8 F '60
EHRLING, SIXTEN, 1918-, conductor
Resignation as conductor of Stock-
holm Opera; Michael Gielen re-
placing. Op v 11 n 8 p 565 Ag '60
EHRMANN, A.
And Recasens, hl ph: F. Lyon.
GDC n 279-180 p 880 Jl 1'60
THE EIFFEL TOWER
And Paris, ph: Greff. ON v 25 n 5
p 19 D 10'60
EINER VON UNS, play
Stuttgart notes; Michael Mansfeld.
WP v 12 n 3 p 39 D '60
EISENBERT, NORMAN. Stereo in-
tegration steps up. charts HF v 10
n 10 p 51-53, 131 O '60
EISENSTADT OGGI
Viandante, Il. Provincia del Bur-
genland; Haydn. il La S n 133 p 77
D '60
THE ELDER STATESMAN, play
San Miniato, 1959; ens AP wl
ph: Locchi. WT v 9 n 1 p 87
Spring '60
ELECTRA, play
Mexico notes. WP v 11 n 10 p 7
Ag '60
ELECTRA, opera

(Electra)
Hofmannsthal, Hugo von; 1874-
1929; critical notes by A. M. Nat-
ler. Th R v 2 n 1 p 9-10 1960
ELECTRONIC MUSIC
Beckwith, John. Notes on new
music heard on CBS Radio (Istvan
Anhalt, Hugh LeCaine, Nether-
land Henk Badings). CMJ v 4 n 2
p 37-8 Winter '60
---Chamfray, Claude. Paul Arma,
nous parle de son "Concerto pour
Bande Magnétique". GDC n 293-4
p 455-6 D 16'60
---Cologne; I. S. C. M. ; various composers mentioned. MR v 21 n 3
p 242 Ag '60
---Demarquez, Suzanne. Première
biennale de la recherche. GDC
n 279-80 p 891 Jl 1'60
---Krenek, Ernst. Extents and
limits of serial techniques. il
Mus Q v 46 n 2 p 210-232 Ap '60
---Luening, Otto. (Review of Prieberg's Musica Ex Machina.)
J Rev v 7 n 3 p 23 Fall '60
---Paris; several comments; Maurice Kagel; pianist A. Kontarsky
and others. GDC n 259-60 p 411
F 12'60
---Publishing house for new types
of music set up by Aldo Bruzzich-
elli in Italy. MC v 162 n 1 p 30
Jl '60
---Russia; Shostakovich on lack of
Russian interest in electronic mu-
sic; Los Angeles report. MC v 161
n 1 p 23 Ja '60
---Salzman, Eric. (Visit to the elec-
tronic synthesizer at the Columbia-
Princeton Music Center, NYC; sur-
vey of other efforts in this field.)
il HF v 10 n 8 p 40-42 Ag '60
---Ussachevsky, Vladimir. Notes
on "A Piece for Tape Recorder".
Mus Q v 46 n 2 p 202-209 Ap '60
ELGAR, SIR EDWARD, 1857-1934,
composer
Chamfray, Claude. Fiche biogra-
phique. GDC n 257-8 p 367-8
Ja 29'60
ELIAS, ROSALIND, singer
As Fenema in Nabucco, AP hl ph:
Melançon. ON v 25 n 4 p 20 D 3'60

ELIOT, THOMAS STEARNS, 1888-,
author
Farrington, Conor A. The language
of drama. TDR v 5 n 2 p 65-72
D '60
ELISA, opera
Teatro della Pergola di Firenze;
Gabriella Tucci. il La S n 127
p 26 Je '60
---Tucci, Gabriella, 2 AP phs:
Firenze. La S n 127 p 26 Je '60
L'ELISIR D'AMORE, opera
Metropolitan; cast; notes on com-
poser, décor, story. il ON v 25
n 7 D 24'60
---Metropolitan; Guarrera and Eli-
sabeth Söderström, ens AP wl ph:
Eugene Cook; and other action phs.
ON v 25 n 7 D 24'60
---La Scala; Gobbi, Carosio and
Tagliavani, ens AP wl ph: Wood.
Op v 11 n 2 p 108 F '60
ELIZABETHAN THEATRE TRUST
Australia; editorial on opera; pro-
gress under Dr. Karl Rankl. MD
v 50 n 11 p 7 My '60
---Phillips, Linda. Melbourne; Aus-
tralian première of Salome, Joan
Hammond in the title role. il MD
v 50 n 11 p 8-9 My '60
ELLIS, BROBURY PEARCE. "The
true originall copies" (on Shakes-
peare texts and for modern exam-
ple, texts of The Glass Menagerie;
how a scholar might view and eval-
uate). TDR v 5 n 1 p 113-6 S '60
ELMAN, MISCHA, 1891-, violinist
NYC review. MC v 161 n 4 p 19
Mr '60
EMMANUEL, MAURICE, 1938-,
composer
Machuel, Dominique. Hommage;
Jacques Chailley, René Dumesnil,
etc. GDC n 255-6 p 310 Ja 15'60
THE EMPEROR JONES, opera
Taylor, Deems. (Comment.) ON
v 25 n 6 p 11, 30 D 17'60
EMPIRE STATE FESTIVAL
McConnell, Hughes. Peter Ibbetson;
Katya Kabanova. ON v 25 n 2 p 22
O 29'60
---New York report. MC v 162 n 2 p 11
Ag '60
---1960 plans. AmM v 8 n 5 p 13 Je'60

---Report; Peter Ibbetson, opera, reviewed. il Op v 11 n 11 p 752-3 N '60

L'EMPRISE (SANDERS), ballet
L'Opéra-Comique; Georges Delerue notes. MC v 161 n 6 p 33 My '60

--- ---music, Georges Delerue; décor François Ganeau; Claire Sombert et Youly Algaroff. TD n 92 p 15 Ap '60

---Sombert, Claire, and Youly Algaroff, AP wl ph: Paris. OpP n 19 p 63 1960

THE ENCHANTED FOREST, play
Birmingham Repertory, for children by Anthony Woodhall. WP v 11 n 6 p 12 Ap '60

L'ENFANT DE LES SORTILÈGES, ballet
Ravel in a critical article by Luigi Guadagnino. La S n 126 p 24-8 My '60

---Ogéas, Françoise and Nadine Sautereau (la Princess), AP wl ph: Paris Opéra. OpP n 19 p 43 1960

ENGEL, LEHMAN (1910-). The singer on Broadway. MC v 162 n 1 p 9-10 Jl '60

---Left profile por ph: NYC. MC v 162 n 1 p 9 Jl '60

ENGLISH, JOHN. A new deal for the theatre; I (live theatre in mid-twentieth century dramatic practice). NTM v 1 n 4 p 13-8 Jl '60

--- ---II (the 20th century arena theatre similiar to the classical Greek theatre, in size close to Elizabethan; notes on 12 years use with charts). NTM v 2 n 1 p 19-25 O '60

ENNOR, VALMAI, dancer
Career notes; b. Melbourne. por MD v 50 n 10 p 27 Ap '60

DIE ENTFUHRUNG AUS DEM SERAIL, opera
Ens AP wl ph: Hamburg. Op v 11 n 1 p 39 Ja '60

ENTREMONT, PHILIPPE, 1935-, pianist
Career notes. MD v 50 n 9 p 3 Mr '60

---Por ph. MD v 50 n 9 cover Mr '60

L'EPÉE DE DAMOCLES, play
Moscow notes; Nazim Khikmet. WP v 11 n 4 p 14 F '60

EPIDAUROS
Demos, Jean. Norma with Callas. Op v 11 n 76, 78 Autumn '60

EPISODES (BALANCHINE), ballet
Helm, Everett. (Criticism, New York City Ballet.) MR v 21 n 3 p 241 Ag '60

EPSTEIN, FAITH, 1943-, pianist
NYC review. MC v 161 n 7 p 26 Je '60

EPSTEIN, LONNY, 1885-, pianist
Career notes; small ph. J Rev n 7 n 1 p 15 Winter 59-60

EQUIPMENT
Details of Steinway piano service to American pianists; construction notes. HF v 10 n 3 p 44-5 Mr '60

---Fowler, Charles. A mike or two around the house (extra uses; selections). HF v 10 n 11 p 60-3 N '60

---Freas, Ralph. Change in High Fidelity's equipment reports: goods from the dealer's shelves, no comment from the manufacturer. HF v 10 n 4 p 33 Ap '60

---High Fideltiy Equipment reports, a consumer's guide. HF 1960

---Home electronic music installation as developed by Russell Clancy. il HF v 10 n 3 p 50-3 Mr '60

---Music devices to aid teachers; to keep instruments right; to record scores on tape, etc. MEJ 1960

---Osborne, Conrad L. High Fidelity. ON v 25 n 3 p 26 N 19'60

---Zide, Larry. Stereo cartridges have personalities. HF v 10 n 5 p 41-3 My '60

ERIK XIV, play
Lyon, Raymond. August Strindberg au T. N. P. Chaillot; "très bon spectacle". GDC n 261-2 p 446 F 26'60

ERKEL, FERENC, composer, 1819-1893
Por drawing. La S n 133 p 111 D '60

DIE ERMORDUNG CAESARS, opera

(Die Ermordung Caesars)
Essen. WP v 11 n 3 p 3 Ja '60
ERNANI, opera
Del Monaco and Rossi-Lemeni,
Act II, ens AP wl ph: Naples 1960.
ON v 25 n 8 p 30 D 31'60
ERNEST IN LOVE, play
NYC; new version of Wilde; review.
Th Arts v 44 n 7 p 58 Jl '60
---Ens AP ph. Th Arts v 44 n 7
p 60 Jl '60
ERNST, KARL D. The general music program. MEJ v 46 n 3 p 19-20 Ja '60
--- ---The report of the general music program (as considered at Atlantic City Meeting 1960 of MENC). MEJ v 46 n 6 p 21-3 Je-Jl '60
---Por ph. MEJ v 46 n 4 p 35 F-Mr '60
ERNSTER, DEZSO, singer
As Hunding AP ph: Melançon. ON v 24 n 16 p 17 F 20'60
ERROR OF JUDGEMENT, play
England; Alan Peters and Campbell Singer. WP v 11 n 9 p 14 Jl '60
ERWARTUNG, monodrama
New Opera Company, London; Schoenberg notes. MC v 161 n 7 p 13 Je '60
--- ---review. Op v 11 n 6 p 439 Je '60
DIE ERWECKUNG DER PIA CAMERON, play
Wuppertal notes; Max Zweig. WP v 12 n 3 p 40 D '60
ESCANDE, MAURICE-RENÉ, 1892- Administrator of the Comédie-Française, por ph: Max Waldman. Th Arts v 44 n 12 p 60 D '60
EL ESCARABAJO, play
Buenos Aires, ens AP wl ph. WP v 11 n 4 F '60
ESPLA, OSCAR (1889-). Veillée d'armes de Don Quichotte (études musicales analytiques). GDC n 285 p 174 O 21'60
---Paris notes on "Don Quijote Velando las armas". GDC n 288 p 254 N 11'60
ESSLIN, MARTIN. The theatre of the absurd. TDR v 4 n 4 p 3-15

My '60
ETHNOLOGICAL DANCE
Jones, A. M. Studies in African Music (Nyayito, the funeral dance and such discussed). Mus Q v 46 n 1 p 105 Ja '60
ETIENNE, CLAUDE, 1917-, actor
In L'Affaire Pinedus, ens AP wl ph: Hella. WT v 9 n 1 p 38 Spring'60
ETO, TOSHIYA, 1927-, violinist
Por ph. HF v 10 n 4 p 72 Ap '60
THE ETON CHOIRBOOK
Harrison, Frank L. editor (review by Sylvia W. Kenney). Mus Q v 46 n 1 p 111-13 Ja '60
ETUDES CHORÉGRAPHIQUES (LIFAR), ballet
Paris notes; music, Schumann. WP v 11 n 10 p 10 Ag '60
EUGENE ONEGIN, opera
Sarroca, Suzanne, and Gabriel Bacquier, AP hl ph: Paris. OpP n 19 p 52 1960
---Two AP phs: Belgrade. La S n 125 p 56 Ap '60
EURIDICE, opera
Boboli Gardens, ens AP wl ph: Marchiori. Op v 11 n 9 p 635 S'60; same. Op v 11 p 20 Autumn '60
EURYANTHE, opera
Actors' Opera; NYC review. MC v 161 n 7 p 22 Je '60
---NYC; Actors' Opera; note. Op v 11 n 7 p 472 Jl '60
EURYDICE AND ORPHEUS, opera
New York City Opera, ens AP wl ph: Fred Fehl. ON v 25 n 3 p 18 N 19'60
EVANS, GERAINT, singer, 1922-, and Marilyn Horne in Wozzeck, AP hl ph: C. M. Jones, San Francisco. ON v 25 n 3 p 17 N 19'60
---As Falstaff, AP hl ph: Glyndebourne. Op v 11 n 8 p 542 Ag '60
EVANS, MAURICE, 1901-, actor
Por ph: 1935. Th Arts v 44 n 9 p 57 S '60
EVERYMAN THEATRE, CHELTENHAM
Wood, Cyril. A playhouse for Cheltenham. il NTM v 1 n 3 p 18-23 Ap '60
EWELL, TOM, 1909-, actor
In "A Thurber Carnival", AP wl

ph: NYC. Th Arts v 44 n 5 p 7
My '60
THE EXCEPTION AND THE RULE,
play
Derby Playhouse, ens AP wl ph:
Raymonds. NTM v 2 n 1 p 15 O'60
THE EXCURSIONS OF MR. BROUC-
CEK, opera
Koegler, Horst. Munich review.
il ON v 2 n 3 p 209 Mr '60
---Munich, two ens AP wl phs: Ru-
dolf Betz. Op v 2 n 3 p 208 Mr'60
EXPERIMENTAL OPERA THEATRE
OF AMERICA
Auditions under Renato Cellini;
notes. MC v 161 n 1 p 8 Ja '60
---List of 19 winners, NYC audi-
tions. MC v 161 n 5 p 45 Ap '60
---New Orleans; 1960 Spring Fes-
tival. MC v 161 n 6 p 26 My '60
EXPLOSION RETARDÉE, play
Bucarest notes; Paul Everac. WP
v 11 n 9 p 12 Jl '60
EXPRESSIONAL DANCE
Australia; The Modern Ballet
Group; ex-Dunham dancer, Anto-
nio Rodriques. MD v 51 n 2 p 24
Ag '60
--- ---Vija Vetra and groups at
Prahan. MD v 51 n 3 p 32 S '60
---Geddo, Angelo. Il comico nella
musica applicata. il La Scala
n 122 p 22.-27 Ja '60
---Germany today; Jooss, Wigman,
T. Gsovsky, Y. Georgi, Gustav
Blank, Milloss, Erich Walter,
Werner Ulbrich, Nika Nilanowa;
notes. WT v 9 n 3 p 230-2 Autumn
'60
---Krokover, Rosalyn. (On Martha
Graham company.) MC v 161 n 6
p 9 My '60
---Paris; Paulina Ossona at the
American Student and Artist Cen-
ter; criticism. TD n 94 p 6 Je'60
---Tamiris, Helen, and Daniel Na-
grin. The Spartan life of Modern
dance. il Th Arts v 44 n 11 p 61-
5, 72 N '60
---Juilliard School of Music, port-
folio: Impact. J Rev v 7 n 2 p 16-
7 Spring '60
---Studio; studi preparatori, 2 AP
phs. La Scala n 122 p 25, 27 Ja'60

---Vetra, Vija, AP wl ph: Victoria,
Australia. MD v 51 n 6 p 32 D '60
EYER, RONALD. To the manner
born (Haydn). por ON v 24 n 12
p 10-1 Ja 23'60
EYLE, FELIX, orchestra manager
Interview with the manager of
Metropolitan's orchestra; b. Lvov;
on the work; on rehearsing. il ON
v 24 n 14 p 10-1 F 6'60
EYMAR, JACQUELINE, pianist
Criticism. GDC n 267-8 p 535
Ap 8'60
---Et le Troi Kehr; review. GDC
n 295 p 492 D 30'60
---Lyon, Raymond. (career notes;
b. Nice.) GDC n 292 p 417 D 9'60
---Por ph. TD n 94 p 12 Je '60
---Por ph: Hrand. GDC n 267-8
cover Ap 8'60
EYSSERIC, NICOLE, pianist
Concerts Choteau series; notes.
GDC n 293-4 p 459 D 16'60
THE EZZOLIED
Burkhard, Willy(1900-1955), com-
poser for Ezzo's Gesang c. 1060
(1927 work); Johann Nepomuk
David (1895-); première notes.
WM n 4 p 7 Ag '60

F

FABIUS, BRUNO, pianist
Paris review. GDC n 273 p 690
My 20'60
FABBRI, DIEGO (1911-). On the-
atre problems. WP v 11 n 4 p 1, 7
F '60
---Left profile por ph. WP v 11 n 4
p 1 F '60
FABBRI, MARISA, actress
AP hl ph. La S n 126 p 53 My '60
---AP hl ph: Milan. La S n 122
p 61 Ja '60
FACE OF A HERO, play
NYC notes. Th Arts v 44 n 12
p 12 D '60
---Robert L. Joseph. WP v 12 n 3
p 38 D '60
FADIMAN, CLIFTON (1904-). Be-
hind the scenes (a tribute to the
Metropolitan Opera Guild from
Texaco's Roving Reporter). ON

(Fadiman)
v 25 n 1 p 16-7 O8'60
THE FAIRY QUEEN, opera
Hitchman, Percy J. (Purcell's opera produced by the University of Nottingham; review; sketches of scenery and 3 ens AP wl photographs.) Th Notbk v 14 n 3 p 92-99 Spring '60
THE FAIRY QUEEN (JOOSS), opera
Schwetzingen review. Op v 11 p 69 Autumn '60,
FAISANDIER, GERARD, bassoonist
Chamfray, Claude. Paris; the bassoon as a solo instrument; pianist, Eléonore Kraemer. GDC n 259-60 p 409 F 12'60
FALK, EUGENE H. (1913-). Molière the indignant satirist: Le Bougeois gentilhomme. TDR v 5 n 1 p 73-88 S '60
FALKNER, (DONALD) KEITH, 1900-, singer
Appointed director of Britain's Royal College of Music, leaving Cornell University. ON v 24 n 17 p 3 F 27'60
--- With pupil, Carol Elder, and pianist, Robert B. Meikle, ph: Cornell University. AmM v 8 n 5 p 7 Je '60
FALL OF THE CITY, opera
Peabody, Baltimore; James Cohn, composer. Op v 11 n 7 p 472 Jl '60
--- ---1937 work with The Old Maid and the Thief, Menotti supervising the latter. MC v 161 n 5 p 20 Ap '60
FALLA, MANUEL DE (1876-1946). Nuits dans les jardins d'Espagne (études musicales analytiques). GDC n 273 p 699 My 20'60
FALSTAFF, opera
Glyndebourne 1960 compared with 1957 and 1958; the role of Ford. MR v 21 n 3 p 249-250 Ag '60
--- Leipzig review; Joachim Herz, producer; "assurance of style". Op v 11 n 5 p 347 My '60
LA FANCIULLA DEL WEST, opera
Verona Arena; cast; review. LaS n 129-130 p 71 Ag-S '60

--- San Francisco Opera; Act 3 ens AP wl ph: C. M. Jones. Op v 11 n 12 p 821 D '60
--- Verona; Act 3, ens AP wl ph: Irifoto. Op v 11 p 71 Autumn '60
LOS FANTASMAS DE MI CEREBRO, play
Barcelona notes; Gironella and Manegat. WP v 11 n 5 p 4 Mr'60
FANTASMI AL GRAND HÔTEL (MASSINE), ballet
La Scala notes; Luciano Chailly, music, Dino Buzzati and Luciana Novaro. TD n 92 p 16 Ap '60
--- Music by Luciano Chailly; notes. La S n 125 p 43-4 Ap '60
--- Première Teatro all Scala. MD v 50 n 12 p 27 Je '60
--- Ens AP wl ph: Milan. TD n 92 p 17 Ap '60
THE FANTASTICKS
Ens AP wl ph: NYC. Th Arts v 44 n 7 p 60 Jl '60
THE FANTASY TRAIN
Frattini, Angelo. (Review). il La S n 123 p 62-3 F '60,
LE FANTÔME DE L'OPÉRA, pseud. (Notes on l'Opéra-Comique; comments on the Paris Opéra, series). GDC n 255-6 p 302 Ja 15'60
FANTÔMES AU GRAND HOTEL (MASSINE), ballet
See Fantasmi al Grand Hotel (Massine, ballet FARKAS,
FARKAS, FERENC, 1905-, composer
Critical notes on Hungarian composers. Mus Q v 46 n 4 p 525-35 O '60
FARKAS, PHILIP, principal hornist
Notes. IM v 58 n 8 p 37 F '60
FARLOW, TAL, guitarist
Hl ph. IM v 58 n 12 p 27 Je '60
FARMER, ART, 1928-, trumpeter
Cerulli, Don. Art Farmer; b. Iowa. IM v 59 n 2 p 18-9 Ag '60
--- Left profile por ph; also AP hl ph. IM v 59 n 2 cover, p 18 Ag '60
FARMER, HENRY GEORGE(1882-). Voltaire as music critic. MR v 21 n 4 p 317 N '60
FARO, ANTONIO JOSÉ. Rio de Janeiro: operas. Op v 11 n 7 p 476 Jl '60
FARRAR, GERALDINE, 1882-,

singer
As Cio-Cio-San, AP ph. MC
v 161 n 3 p 11 F '60
---As Nedda, AP ph. ON v 24 n 13
p 12 Ja 30'60
---wl ph. ON v 25 n 8 p 10 D 31'60
FARRELL, EILEEN, 1910-, singer
Osborne, Conrad L. A voice
close to perfection (Angel; Columbia releases). por HF v 10
n 1 p 64 Ja '60
---Review of record of popular
songs wrongly labeled: "I've Got
a Right To Sing the Blues". HF
v 10 n 10 p 103 O '60
---As La Gioconda with Irene Kramarich, her mother, La Cieca,
AP hl ph: Chicago Lyric. MC
v 161 n 1 p 21 Ja '60
FARRINGTON, CONOR A. The
language of drama. TDR v 5 n 2
p 65-72 D '60
FASSETT, JAMES HAROLD. Tea-
tro Farnese, Parma (need of a
Verdi repertory, under Istituto
di Studi Verdi). Ver v 1 n 2
preface Ag '60
FAURE, GABRIEL (1845-1925). 2e
Quatuor de Fauré: analyse par
Pierrette Mari. GDC n 265-6
p 529-30 Mr 25'60
--- ---Requiem, op. 48 (analyse;
critique de Trajan Popesco à
Paris 1960). GDC n 281-2 p 26-7
S 30'60
---Mari, Pierrette. Festival
Faure de Foix. GDC n 279-80
p 895 Jl 1'60
---Samazeuilh, Gustave. La mus-
ique de chambre de Gabriel
Fauré; GDC n 289 p 289-92
N 18'60
FAUST, opera
Metropolitan; Elisabeth Soed-
erstroem; criticism. por MC
v 161 n 1 p 12 Ja '60
---Portfolio: Paris Opéra 1960.
OpP n 19 p 25-7 1960
FAYRFAX, ROBERT (1464-1521).
Collected works. I. The Masses
(book review by Margaret E.
Lyon. Mus Q v 46 n 4 p 543-546
O '60
FEATHER, LEONARD GEOFFREY

(1914-). Jazz, pastime or pro-
fession? IM v 59 n 6 p 12-3 D'60
FEDERAL COMMUNICATIONS
COMMISSION
Reply 1960 on use of foreign
tapes dubbed to American-made
films. IM v 59 n 3 p 42 S '60
LA FÉDÉRATION FRANÇAISE
DE DANSE
Congrès, l'Hotel de Ville de
Vincennes: report. TD n 96 p 24
S-O '60
FEDORA, opera
Lyric Opera of Chicago; review.
ON v 25 n 7 p 28 D 24'60
---Milan; Giordano; notes. il LaS
n 131 p 29, 59 O '60
FEDRA, opera
La Scala review; Pizzetti. La S
n 123 p 31-2 F '60
---Pizzetti music d'Annunzio
libretto; Régine Crespin; review
of La Scala production. Op v 2 n 3
p 212-14 Mr '60
---La Scala, Act I ens AP wl ph:
Piccagliani. Op v 2 n 3 p 214
Mr '60
FEIST, ROBERT, conductor
Note. ON v 25 n 6 p 7 D 17'60
FELSENSTEIN, WALTER (1901-).
A propos d'un Théâtre universel.
WP v 11 n 10 p 1 Ag '60
---Bernheimer, Martin. (East
Berlin's Komische Oper; director
and his aims.) portfolio ON v 25
n 6 p 12-5 D 17'60
---Por ph. WP v 11 n 10 p 1 Ag'60
LA FEMME DOIT CRAINDRE
LE MARI, play
Athens notes; Georges Tzavellas.
WP v 11 n 5 p 8 Mr '60
UNE FEMME QUI DIT LA VERITE,
play
Paris notes; André Roussin. WP
v 12 n 1 p 5 O '60
LA FENICE
Matz, Mary Jane. Great opera
houses: La Fenice. ON v 25 n 8
p 22-6 D 31'60
---Stagione lirica 1959-60- La S
n 122 inset Ja '60
---Exterior view 1792; interior ph:
1957. ON v 25 n 8 p 23, 24
D 31'60

FENICHEL, OTTO. On acting.
TDR v 4 n 3 p 148-159 Mr '60
FERGUSSON, FRANCIS (1904-).
On The Poetics (an essay review
of Gerald F. Else's "Aristotle's
Poetics: the Argument"). TDR
v 4 n 4 p 23-32 My '60
FERNALD, JOHN (1905-). (On
staging Chekhov; English view-
point.)il WT v 9 n 2 p 126-7
Summer '60
FERNANDI, EUGENIO, singer
As Ismaele in Nabucco, AP hl
ph: Melançon. ON v 25 n 4 p 20
D 3'60
---As Mario Cavaradossi, AP hl
ph: Melançon. ON v 24 n 20 p 17
Mr 19'60
FERRARIO, CARLO (1833-1907).
Un Ballo in Maschera, opera La
Scala setting Act III, scene 3,
1862, ph. Ver v 1 n 2 Ag '60
FERRAS, CHRISTIAN, 1933-
violinist
AP hl ph. MC v 162 n 6 p 34
D '60
FERRER, JOSE VICENTE, 1912-,
producer
In Gianni Schicchi; Santa Fé suc-
cess. Op v 11 n 11 p 758 N '60
---Santa Fe Opera, Gianni Schicchi
in English; notes. MC v 162 n 2
p 4 Ag '60
---As Gianni Schicci, ens AP wl
ph: Perry, Sante Fe. ON v 25
n 1 p 25 O 8'60
---Por ph: 1936. Th Arts v 44 n 9
p 61 S '60
FERRERO, MARIO (1922-). (On
staging Chekhov; Italian view-
point.) il WT v 9 n 2 p 130
Summer '60
FERTE, ARMAND. Camille Chev-
illard, 1859-1923. GDC n 263-4
p 477-8 Mr 11'60
FESCHOTTE, JACQUES. Jeu de
Noel, Carl Orff "Ludus de Nato
Infante Mirificus", l'Opéra de
Stuttgart à Stuttgart. GDC n 295
p 488-9 D 30'60
FESTA, CONSTANTIUS (1490-1545).
Hymni per totum annum, edited
by Glen Haydon (critically reviewed by Alexander Main.

Mus Q v 46 n 1 p 102-4 Ja '60
FESTIVAL BALLET (DOLIN).
See London Festival Ballet
FESTIVAL DE LA RECHERCHE
Demarquez, Suzanne. Pierre
Schaeffer et son groupe(1960).
GDC n 277 p 816 Je 17'60
--- ---Première biennale de la
recherche. GDC n 283 p 99
O 7'60
IL FESTIVAL DI NERVI
Avant le 5e; Ariodante Borelli
de l'Ente Manifestzioni Genovesi;
huits ballets. il TD n 92 p 5
Ap '60
FESTIVAL OF TWO WORLDS
See - - - - Spoleto
THE FESTIVAL QUARTET
Boston; list and praise. MC v 161
n 4 p 32 Mr '60
FESTIVAL RIOPLATENSE DE
TEATRO INDEPENDIENTE
Montevideo report; groups listed
and plays. WP v 11 n 9 p 8 Jl '60
FESTIVALS
Aix-en-Provence; reviews of
opera and concerts. MC v 162 n 3
p 24-5 S '60
---Australia; notes on 13th Annual
Hartwell (Victoria) Eisteddfod;
on the Toora Music and Speech
Festival; Four Choirs.MD v 51 n 2
p 19 Ag '60
--- ---talk of a Commonwealth
Art Festival. MD v 51 n 1 p 17
Jl '60
---Bach Festival, Bethlehem,
Pennsylvania. MC v 161 n 7 p 4
Je '60
---Barcelona; Festival de Danse;
Claude Giraud; notes. TD n 92
p 13 Ap '60
---Bergamo; Festival Autunnale
dell'opera Lirica, Teatro delle
Novità: calendario. La S n 131
inset O '60
---Berne; Salzbourg; Stockholm;
Helsinki. GDC n 273 p 681 My 20
'60
---Bulgaria; Fourth Festival of
Bulgarian Music, several places
over several months; report by L.
Sagaeff. WM n 6 p 130 D '60
---Butcher, Harold. Santa Fe

Festival, fourth season. MC v 162 n 2 p 4 Ag '60

---Canada; on the controversy as to their value; Sir Ernest Macmillan and others. CMJ v 5 n 1 p 30-8 Autumn '60

---Cannes; notes. TD n 93 p 5 My '60

---Casals Festival, 4th; Puerto Rico notes. MC v 161 n 6 p 11 My '60

---Chambéry; Fêtes du Centenaire du reattachement de la Savoie la France. TD n 92 p 13 Ap '60

---Chapowalenko, Georges. 3 Festivals: Salzburg. TD n 98 p 24-6 D '60

---Cincinnati May Festival, review. MC v 161 n 7 p 4 Je '60

---Cole, Charles. Festival of American Music of the Eastman School of the University of Rochester. MC v 161 n 7 p 6 Je '60

---Cologne; 34e Festival mondial. WP v 11 n 6 p 8 Ap '60

---Dapilly, Jacques. Le Lude, les fastueuses soirées au Bord du Loir. GDC n 283 p 96 O 8'60

---Demarquez, Suzanne. Festival de Strasbourg. GDC n 281-2 p 65 S 30'60

---Divonne-les-Bains; notes and 1960 criticism; Marcel Borusiak, winner. GDC n 281-2 p 66 S 30'60

---Dubrovnik; report by Logar Mihovil. il La S n 131 p 34-5 O '60

---Europe; Austria and Britain. il Th Arts v 44 n 5 inset My '60

--- ---guide, arranged by countries. Th Arts v 44 n 5 p 62-5 My '60

---Evian; program notes. TD n 95 p 22 Jl-Ag '60

---Il Festival di Lucerna; programa. La S n 131 p 71 O '60

---5e Festival de Ballets de Nervi; Leonide Massine. por TD n 95 p 11 Jl-Ag '60

---France; notes on many. MC v 161 n 7 p 15 Je '60

---Les Gilles de Binche, ens ph: Lebrun. WT v 9 n 1 p 67 Spring'60

---Gisors 1961; notes. TD n 95 p 21 Jl-Ag '60

---Graf, Milan. De Yougoslavie; la rencontre de Dubrovnik. GDC n 287 p 232 N 4'60

---Gravier, Albert. Festival de Lyon-Fournière (le Ballet National hongrois, l'Orchestre Philharmonique de Lyon; Isaac Stern, etc.). GDC n 285 p 173 O 21'60

---Hairs, M. L. Floralies Gantoises; aux origines du Tableau de Fleurs Flamand. il WP v 11 n 6 p 8 Ap '60

---Haulot, Arthur. Theatre in the streets (Walloon region of Belgium, processions, etc.) WT v 9 n 1 p 62-67 Spring '60

---Holland; Portugal; Chimay. GDC n 275 p 745 Je 3'60

---Huesgen, Elsa M. Gutenberg Festival in Mainz. MC v 161 n 3 p 47 F '60

---Hugo, Reg. (Counter-argument on Canadian music festivals from the president of the Federation of Canadian Music Festivals.) CMJ v 4 n 4 p 33-7 Summer '60

---Italy; reports. MC v 162 n 1 p 30 Jl '60

--- ---theatre report by Giacinto Giancola. WT v 9 n 3 p 288-9 Autumn '60

---Japan; several reported. MC v 162 n 1 p 33 Jl '60

---Kines, Thomas. (On positive values in Canadian music festivals.) CMJ v 4 n 4 p 37-40 Summer '60

---Kitto, H. D. F. International Student Drama Festival (Bristol). NTM v 1 n 2 p 14-7 Ja '60

---List 1960 over the world with dates. MC v 161 n 6 p 14-5 My'60

---Lorin, Michel. Saison et festival de Vichy. GDC n 277 p 810 Je 17'60

---Loyola Community Theatre, host to 15th annual Chicago Drama Festival of the National Theatre Conference. PlM v 36 n 4 p 73 Ja '60

---Maggio Musicale Fiorentino, XXIII 1960. il La S n 128 p 28-9 Jl '60

---Mari, Pierrette. Le Centenaire du Rattachement de la Savoie à la France: Fête de l'Edelweiss, Fête de la Neige, Régates sur les lacs, etc.; Musique à Aix-les-Bains, Evian, Mégève, Chambéry, Annecy.

(Festivals)
GDC n 267-8 p 567 Ap 8'60
--- ---Le VIIIe Festival de Besançon;cinq oeuvres contemporaines inédites. GDC n 283 p 95 O 7'60
---Melbourne;Beethoven Festival; The Victorian Symphony under Dr. Karl Rankl;notes. MD v 50 n 7 p 8 Ja'60
--- ---Four Choir Festival. MD v 51 n 5 p 9 N'60
---Mennesson, Félix. 20e festival de Lyon-Fourvière. GDC n 277 p 811 Je 17'60
---Menton;Le XIe Festival, full report by Pierrette Mari. GDC n 281-2 p 66-7 S 30'60
---Moravian music in Bethlehem, Pennsylvania. MC v 162 n 4 p 11 O'60
---Munich;directeur du ballet de l'Opéra National Bavarois, Heinz Rosen:Festival de Ballets. TD n 96 p 11-2 S-O'60
--- ---Edinburgh;1961 plans. Op v 11 n 12 p 840 D'60
--- ---Monaco;Lucerne;Lyon-Fourviere;Vichy;Dubrovnik. GDC n 274 p 714, 722 My 27'60
---Music at the Vineyards, third year at Saratoga, California, the Paul Masson Winery;notes. MC v 162 n 2 p 15 Ag'60
---1960 schedules in Europe. Op v 11 n 1 p 52 Ja'60
---Osaka;review. Op v 11 n 9 p 629 S'60
---Paris;Un Festival d'Art d'Avant-Garde:Arrigo's Quarta Occasione;Gilbert Amy's Invention I;Cardew's Autumn 60. GDC n 293 p 457 D 16'60
---Payzant, Geoffrey. The competitive music festivals (Canada). CMJ v 4 n 3 p 35-46 Spring'60
---Penberthy, James. Festival of Perth, 1961. MD v 51 n 6 p 9, 14 D'60
---Peninsula Music Festival (Wisconsin);repertory under Thor Johnson;concerts and opera. MC v 162 n 4 p 18 O'60
---Place, music director, orch-

estra, date, soloists:Stratford, Ontario;Chautauqua Institute, New York;Vancouver Festival;Aspen Festival;Casals Festival. IM v 58 n 11 p 19 My'60
---Prades, Xe;Beaugency VIIIe. GDC n 271 p 620 My 5'60
---Red Rocks Festival, Colorado notes. MC v 162 n 2 p 25 Ag'60
---Reports:Monaco;Metz;Aix. GDC n 284 p 130-3 O 14'60
---Saint-Benoit-sur-Loire;Divonnes-les-Bains;Festival de Baalbeck;Festival de Jazz d'Antibes et Juan-les-Pins;Vichy, 3 semaines. GDC n 276 p 777, 780 Je 10'60
---San Carlo Opera;XIII Estate Musicale:chorus, ballet orchestra under Ettore Gracis;new arena described. MC v 162 n 3 p 26 S'60
---The Schütz Festival;Dresden notes;since 1955-WM n 4 p 77 Ag'60
---Seaman, Julian. May Music Festival (67th), Ann Arbor, University of Michigan;reviews. MC v 161 n 7 p 8 Je'60
---Siena;annual;Italian music reviews;Guido Chigi Seracini. il LaS n 129-30 p 38 Ag-S'60
---Split;notes. MC v 162 n 1 p 33 Jl'60
---US;Canada;place and date, some repertory in the lists. Th Arts v 44 n 6 p 6, 71 Je'60
--- ---jazz festivals. IM v 58 n 12 p 12-3 Je'60
---Vichy;Xme Festival;program. TD n 95 p 16 Jl-Ag'60
---Walter, Franz. The growth of international festivals. WM n 3 p 50-1 Je'60
---Whitehead, Robert. American festival fundamentals. portfolio Th Arts 44 n 6 p 51, 63 Je'60
---Wiesbaden International Festival; Vienna State Opera;Teatro Massimo Opera and Wiesbaden State Opera;repertory. MC v 162 n 1 p 34 Jl'60
---Winters, Ken. Europe (music report). CMJ v 5 n 1 p 39-44 Autumn '60
---Wood, Peggy. Festivals:true and false. Th Arts v 44 n 12 p 16 D'60

---World; city, dates, plays and authors, ballets, opera, etc. in form of a chart. WP v 11 n 8 p 2 Je '60

--- ---city, dates, plays and authors, including opera, ballet, etc. WP v 9 n 11 p 2 Jl '60

---Portfolio of events abroad. Th Arts v 44 n 5 My '60

---Prague Spring Festival musical performance in Belvedere Gardens, audience and stage, ph. WM n 4 p 83 Ag '60

FETLER, PAUL
Notes on "Contrasts for Orchestra". MC v 161 n 6 p 31 My '60

FÉVIER, HENRY, 1875-1957, composer
Chamfray, Claude. Fiche biographique. GDC n 285 p 175 O 21 '60

FEYDEAU, GEORGES (1862-1921).
Going to Pot, adapted by Norman R. Shapiro (text). TDR v 5 n 1 p 127-168 S '60

---Shapiro, Norman R. Suffering and punishment in the theatre of Georges Feydeau. TDR v 5 n 1 p 117-126 S '60

FEZANDAT, MICHEL, printer
Heartz, Daniel. Parisian music publishing under Henry II: A propos of four recently discovered guitar books. il Mus Q v 46 n 4 p 448-467, O '60

LA FIANCÉE VENDUE, opera
Liège; Smetana cast; review. GDC n 265-6 p 518 Mr 15'60

FIDELIO, opera
Ashbrook, William. (Criticism of the work.) il ON v 24 n 15 p 4-5 F 13'60

---Metropolitan; Karl Boehm conducting; Jon Vickers as Florestan. MC v 161 n 3 p 24 F '60

--- ---cast; story; criticism; décor notes; discography; bibliography; portfolio. ON v 24 n 15 F 13'60

--- ---review. il Op v 11 n 5 p 339 My '60

---Au Palais Garnier; Hans Knappertsbusch. GDC n 276 p 784 Je 10'60

---Act I, closing moments, ens AP wl ph: Helga Wallmüller. Op v 11 n 12 p 808 D '60

---Ens AP wl ph: Rome; Branka Stilinovich, AP wl ph. La S n 128 p 31 Jl '60

---Paris Opéra; José Beckmans décor, 5 phs. OpP n 19 p 33-5 1960

FIDELMAN, DAVID. Amplifier ratings, fact and fantasy. HF v 10 n 9 p 47. 48, 108 S '60

FIEDLER, ARTHUR, 1894-, conductor
Darrell, R. D. The jauntiest maestro: Fiedler of the Boston Pops. il HF v 10 n 5 p 38-40 My '60

THE FIERY ANGEL, opera
Cologne review. Op v 11 n 8 p 557 Ag '60

--- ---made one acutely conscious of the inherent differences between concert and stage music". MR v 21 n 3 p 243 Ag '60

---Goldman, Richard Franko. (Review of Prokofiev recorded by Westminster.) Mus Q v 46 n 1 p 124-6 Ja '60

---London première. WM n 3 p 57 Je '60

---Venice 1955, ens AP wl ph: Giocomelli. Op v 2 n 3 p 188 Mr '60

FIESTA, opera
Mannes College; short Milhaud score; notes. MC v 161 n 6 p 16 My '60

LA 58e SECONDE, play
Bucarest notes; Dorel Dorian. WP v 11 n 9 p 12 Jl '60

FIGAROS HOCHZEIT
See Nozze di Figaro

THE FIGHTING COCK, play
NYC press comment. Th Arts v 44 n 2 p 16 F '60

--NYC review. PlM v 36 n 5 p 110 F '60

---Two ens AP wl phs: NYC; also as "L'Hurluberlu", Paris scene. Th Arts v 44 n 2 p 70-72 F '60

FIGUEIREDO, GUILHERME
(1915-). Une pièce et son auteur a travers le monde. WP v 11 n 6

(Figueiredo)
p 1 Ap '60
THE FIGURE IN THE CARPET
(BALANCHINE), ballet
Ens ph: NYC MC v 161 n 6 p 9
My '60
LA FILLE MAL GARDÉE (ASHTON),
ballet
Guest, Ivor. (London review, Roy-
al Ballet.) MD v 50 n 9 p 27
Mr '60
---Covent Garden review. MC v 161
n 5 p 31 Ap '60
LA FILLE MAL GARDÉE (DAU-
BERVAL), ballet
Vestris, Auguste, AP wl ph. LaS
n 129-30 p 24 Ag-S '60
FILM MUSIC
Chamfray, Claude. Bal des Adi-
eux; Franz Liszt. GDC n 295
p 497 D 30'60
--- ---La Dolce Vita, music by
Fellini; Nino Rota; Georges De-
lerue; Philippe de Broca. GDC
n 278 p 840 Je 24'60
--- ---La musique de film au Fes-
tival de la Recherche de la R. T. F.
GDC n 283 p 99-100 O 7'60
--- ---Musique de films. GDC
n 259-60 p 413 F 12'60
---Cocteau, Jean; list of his films;
notes on Georges Auric music
for "Le Testament d'Orphée";
criticism. GDC n 267-8 p 566
Ap 8'60
---Les Etoiles du Midi, music by
Maurice Jarre.Pourquoi? GDC
n 271 p 630 My 5'60
---Françaix, Jean, music in Dialogues des Carmélites (L. Bruck-
Berger and Ph. Agostini); notes.
GDC n 279-280 p 897 Jl '60
---Herrmann, Bernard. Composing for the screen.AmM v 8 n 4
p 12 Ap '60
--- ---career sketch; notes on
film scores. por AmM v 8 n 1
p 15-16 Ja '60
---Kenin, Herman D. (Testimony
as President of American Federation of Musicians before Federal Communications Commission
on US films for TV, "deceptive
use of foreign canned music".

IM v 58 n 8 p 5, 41-2 '60
---Korngold, Erich Wolfgang,
1897-1957; career sketch. por
ON v 24 n 20 p 13 Mr 19'60
---Pastorale d'Automne, musique
Yves Baudrier; La bataille du
Rail; notes. GDC n 288 p 260
N 11'60
---Popov, music for "Le Poème
de la Mer"; critical notes. GDC
n 287 p 230 N 4'60
---Prodromidès, music for "Le
Voyage en Ballon"; critical
notes. GDC n 287 p 230 N 4'60
---Rózsa, Miklós, score for Ben
Hur, 1960 version for MGM;
critical notes by Charles Reid.
HF v 10 n 1 p 22 Ja '60
---Sauguet, Henri, pour "Tu es
Pierre"; commentaire. GDC
n 257-8 p 366 Ja 29'60
---Thiriet, Maurice, pour "Les
Veux de l'Amour "de Denys de
La Patelière; commentaire par
Claude Chamfray. GDC n 257-8
p 366 Ja 29'60
---Tiomkin, Dimitri, score for
"The Alamo", San Antonio Sym-
phony première. MC v 162 n 5
p 25 N '60
---Vertes Demeures, Villa-Lobos
"une musique luxuriante"; Colomb
de Dunant, commentaire. GDC
n 265-6 p 521 Mr 25'60
---Vlad, Roman, music for "Les
Mystères d'Angkor"; criticism.
GDC n 287 p 230 N 4'60
LE FILS RIVAL, opera
Bortnyansky (1751-1825); criti-
cism. MR v 21 n 2 p 107-8 My'60
FINE ARTS QUARTET
Chicago reviews. MC v 162 n 5
p 21 N '60
---Sorkin, Leonard, Abram Loft,
Irving Ilmer, George Sopkin; BBC.
AmM v 8 n 8 p 6 S '60
---Ens AP wl ph: Chicago.IM v 59
n 6 p 40 D '60
FINE ARTS SOCIETY, 1906-
Detroit note. Th Arts v 44 n 10
p 78 O '60
FINEL, PAUL
As Don José, Carmen, AP wl ph:
Paris Opéra. OpP n 19 p 10 1960

110

FINIAN'S RAINBOW, musical
Revival NYC, ens AP wl ph:
Alix Jeffry. Th Arts v 44 n 7
p 61 Jl '60
FINLAND
Buckbee, George. (Music report.)
MC v 161 n 7 p 17 Je '60
---Theatre; 34 houses, 5631 per-
formers; report on drama fare.
il WT v 9 n 3 p 280-2 Autumn'60;
same. WP v 11 n 7 p 8 My '60;
same. WP v 12 n 2 p 4 N '60
FINNEY: ROSS LEE, 1906-,
composer
Première: String Quintet; Wash-
ington review. Mus Q v 46 n 1
p 76-9 Ja '60
FINNEY, DR. THEODORE M.,
1902-, musician
Por ph: Pittsburg. MC v 162
n 6 p 42 D '60
LA FINTA SEMPLICE, opera
Hastings, Baird, translator and
conductor of the Mozart Festival
Orchestra; Boston notes. MC
v 162 n 4 p 16 O '60
FIORELLO, musical
Review, PlM v 36 n 5 p 107 F'60
---Slocumb, Paul. Players on
record. PlM v 36 n 5 p 110 F'60
---Ens AP wl ph: Friedman-Ab-
eles. Th Arts v 44 n 2 p 17 F'60
---Scene "Unfair", ens AP wl ph.
Th Arts v 44 n 3 p 63 Mr '60
FIORILLO, ALEXANDER, 1940-,
pianist
Note. MC 161 n 1 p 35 Ja '60
THE FIREBIRD, ballet
Stravinsky, Igor. Firebird's
first flight. il HF v 10 n 6 p 34-6
Je '60
---Paris, 1910; the wedding scene,
ens AP wl ph. HF v 10 n 6 p 35
Je '60
FIRKUSNY, RUDOLF, 1912-,
pianist
Career notes; Czechoslavia to
US 1938. AmM v 8 n 3 p 9 Mr'60
FISCHER, EDWIN, 1886-1960,
pianist
Note; b. Basle. MD v 50 n 10
p 20 Ap '60
---Obituary notes. MC v 161 n 4
p 7 Mr '60

FISCHER, JOSEPH A; 1900-
1960, publisher
Obituary. MC v 162 n 5 p 42
N '60
FISCHER-DIESKAU, DIETRICH,
1925-, singer
Criticism; Wozzeck in Berlin.
Op v 11 n 4 p 276 Ap '60
---In Arabella; della Casa as
Arabella; criticism. Op v 11
n 8 p 548-9 Ag '60
---As Falstaff, Munich, AP hl
ph: Betz. Op v 11 p 61 Autumn'60
---Por ph. HF v 10 n 7 p 49 Jl '60
---With Paul Klecki, conductor
hl ph: Japanese Radio. WM n 6
p 135 D '60
FITZGERALD, ELLA, 1918-,
singer
Wilson, John S. (Singing Ger-
shwins; Norman Granz direct-
ing her "toward the melodious
heart of the popular repertory".)
HF v 10 n 1 p 63-4 Ja '60
---Por ph. HF v 10 n 1 p 63 Ja'60
FITZGERALD, GERALD (1898?-).
Carmen for posterity (Conchita
Supervia, 1895-1936). ON v 24
n 14 p 8-9 F 6'60
FIVE FINGER EXERCISE, play
Shaffer, Peter. Labels aren't
for playwrights (press comments
also page 16) Th Arts v 44 n 2
p 20-1 F '60
---Bedford, Brian, Michael Bryant
and Jessica Tandy, AP hl ph: Fred
Fehl; two other scenes, Th Arts
v 44 n 2 p 21-3 F '60
FLACHOT, REINE, violinist
Paris; Deuxième concert Katcha-
turian. GDC n 271 p 627 My 5'60
FLAGELLO, EZIO, 1931-, singer
As Paolo Albiani in Simon Boc-
canegra, AP ph: Melançon. ON
v 24 n 22 p 17 Ap 2'60
FLAGSTAD, KIRSTEN, 1895-,
singer
As Isolde, AP hl ph. Th Arts
v 44 n 3 p 48 Mr '60
THE FLAMING ANGEL
See The Fiery Angel, opera
FLANAGAN, WILLIAM, composer
Première: A Concert Ode (Detroit
1960). ACAB v 9 n 3 p 29 1960

FLEMISH NATIONAL THEATRE
The Studio; Herman Teirlinck's
influence in 1947 founding. WT
v 9 n 1 p 51-54 Spring '60
FLEURS DE SODOME, play
Athens notes; J. Coundouris.
WP v 12 n 1 p 6 O '60
DER FLIEGENDE HOLLANDER
See The Flying Dutchman, opera
FLIGHT, sacred cantata
Castaldo, Joseph, composer
Temple University Festival;
"words shocking" by John Shoe-
maker", a follower of James
Joyce"; review. MC v 162 n 1
p 23 Jl '60
FLOR STRING QUARTET
Small ph. IM v 58 n 8 p 37 F'60
FLORA, FRANCESCO. Il Libretto
(Ballo in maschera). Ver v 1 n 1
p 44-72 Ap '60
--- ---Act III. Ver v 1 n 2 p 662-
678 Ag '60
FLORALIES GANTOISES
Festival, 2 flower pictures shown
as inspiration for exposition:
Jean Breughel de Velours, Dan-
iel Seghers, 2 phs. WP v 11 n 6
p 8 Ap '60
FLORENCE
Music report. La S n 122 p 65
Ja '60
---Palazzo Vecchio, salone dei
cinquecento, Stagione sinfonica
1960-61, Ottobre-Aprile; calen-
dario. La S n 133 inset D '60
--- ---stagione sinfonica 1960-61,
9 Ottobre-9Aprile: calendario.
La S n 132 inset N '60
---Selden-Goth, Gisella. Music
report. MC v 161 n 1 p 26 Ja '60;
same. MC v 161 n 6 p 33 My '60
FLORENCE, play
Montreal notes; Michel Dube.
WP v 12 n 3 p 27 D '60
FLORESCO, ARTA, singer
Paris; Legation de Roumanie.
GDC n 289 p 297 N 18'60
FLORIDA
Dale, William, graduate of Univ-
ersity of Florida and Yale; Lon-
don concerts. AmM v 8 n 5 p 9
Je '60
---DiFilippi, Arturo, director and

founder of Miami Opera Guild;
Gioconda. por ON v 24 n 21 p 26
Mr 26'60
---Florida Symphony Orchestra
contest for young pianists; details.
MC v 162 n 3 p 10 S '60
---Gainesville; The Teen Theatre;
notes. PlM v 37 n 2 p 27 N '60
---Jones, Joela (1946-), Miami
pianist
star at Eastman School's festival;
pupil of José Echaniz. MC v 161
n 7 p 6 Je '60
---Nikolaidi, Elena, teaching in
Tallahassee at Florida State
University. por ON v 25 n 8 p 4
D 31'60
---The Opera Guild of Greater
Miami 20th year); singers. Op
v 11 n 10 p 684 O '60
---St. Petersburg;Alfredo Antonini,
conducting, Virgil Fox at the
organ; notes. MC v 161 n 1 p 25
'60
--- ---Charles F. Rice and the
Derby Lane Band;notes. IM v 58
n 12 p 31 Je'60
---Sarasota Concert Band under
Arthur W. Rohr;notes and out-
door ph. IM v 59 n 1 p 32 Jl'60
--- ---Ascolo Theatre:notes on the
Turnau Opera Players. ON v 24
n 17 p 3 F 27'60
---Winter Park;Bach Festival, 25th
year reviewed. MC v 161 n 5 p 20
Ap'60
---Casciolo, Frank, President of
Local 655 AFM, accepting award
from Roy Oliver, Miami Univer-
sity, ph. IM v 58 n 9 p 45 Mr'60
---Derby Lane Band of St. Peters-
burg, ens ph. IM v 58 n 12 p 31
Je'60
FLORIDA THEATRE CONFERENCE
Notes. PlM v 36 n 7 p 170 Ap'60
FLORIDA THEATRE FESTIVAL
Daytona;Ken Parker, playwright,
speaker;Maurice Geoffrey, chair-
man. PlM v 37 n 1 p 4 O'60
---Geoffrey, Maurice;Daytona notes.
PlM v 36 n 8 p 177 My'60
---Sponsored by the Florida Thea-
tre Conference;Maurice Geoffrey;
Daytona notes. Th Arts v 44 n 9

112

p 79 S'60
FLOWER DRUM SONG, musical
NYC review. PlM v 36 n 8 p 183
My'60
DIE FLUT, opera
British première of Blacher,
Group Eight performance. Op
v 11 n 5 p 363 My'60
---Notes. Op v 2 n 3 p 182 Mr'60
THE FLYING DUTCHMAN, opera
Covent Garden notes. MR v 21
n 4 p 327 N'60
---Gerken, Eva. (Tales of pro-
longed wandering, of eternal
punishment facinated Wagner.)
il ON v 24 n 18 p 4-5 Mr 5'60
---Metropolitan Opera cast;story;
criticism;décor;bibliography;
discography and portfolio. ON
v 24 n 18 Mr 5'60
--- ---Thomas Skippers, conduc-
ting. MC v 161 n 3 p 24 F'60
---Wagner production at Bayreuth,
Act 3, ens AP wl ph. Op v 11 n 36
Autumn'60
FO, DARIO, playwright
Giovaninetti, Silvio. (Notes.) il
LaS n 131 p 52-3 O'60
FOGLE, RICHARD HARTER(1911-)
Coleridge on dramatic illusion.
TDR v 4 n 4 p 33-44 My'60
LA FOIRE d'EMPOIGNE, play
Ens ph:The Hague. WP v 12 n 1
p 1 O'60
FOLDES, ANDOR, 1915-, pianist
Mari, Pierrette. Paris;Dean
Dixon, le chef, l'Orchestre Na-
tional:Andor Foldes. GDC n 255
p 319 Ja 15'60
FOLK DANCING
Boulimov, Vladimir. Le Ballet
Berezka en Italie. il TD n 97 p 5
N'60
---International Folk Music Coun-
cil, Vienna report. WM n 5 p 102
O'60
---Pryma, Roma;Paris recital;
ukrainienne. TD n 98 p 31 D'60
---Danze popolari "Lado", ens AP
wl ph:Zagreb. LaS n 125 p 94
Ap'60
FOLK MUSIC
Archives being formed under
International Music Council
113

(UNESCO); Jack Bornoff. MC v 161
n 6 p 13 My'60
---Critical notes on new recordings.
HF 1960
---Fondé le Comité National de la
Musique, Le Ballet National Fran-
çais (Jacques Douai-Thérèse Pa-
lau);quatre ans. GDC n 293-4 p 453
D 16'60
---Philippine Music Educators Group;
report. MEJ v 46 n 3 p 6 Ja'60
---Picken, Laurence. 13th annual
conference of the International
Folk Music Council held in Vienna.
WM n 5 p 101-2 O '60
---Randal, Edward L. (survey of
recordings, jazz to ballads.) HF
v 10 n 5 p 90 My '60
---Russia, compiler and annotator,
Henry C owell; "Folk Music of the
U. S. S. R. " HF v 10 n 9 p 85 S '60
---Shelton, Robert. Folk-ways,
700discs; Moe Asch. por HF v 10
n 6 p 42-4 Je '60
--- ---The Weavers, American
folk-song group (history of 4 sin-
gers). il HF v 10 n 12 p 48-50
D '60
---Szabolcsi, Bence. Bausteine zu
einer Geschichte der Melodie (Bu-
dapest book reviewed at length). P.
T. B. MR v 21n 4 p 339-342 N '60
---US groups sent abroad also con-
tact authentic folk music, notes.
IM v 58 n 7 p 11 Ja '60
---Bergen Festival, ens AP wl ph.
MC v 161 n 7 p 17 Je '60
FOLK SONGS
Folklore Canadien, review of re-
cording by the Chorale of l'Univer-
sité Saint-Joseph under Rev. Fa-
ther Neil Michaud. CMJ v 4 n 3
p 51-2 Spring '60
---Panama; the mejorana as typical
ballad; several examples, music
and words. CMJ v 4 n 3 p 4-22
Spring '60
FONDA, JANE, 1938-, actress
With her father, Henry Fonda, hl
ph: Max Waldman; in There Was
a Little Girl, four facial studies.
Th Arts v 44 n 3 cover, p 10-11
Mr '60
FONTEYN, MARGOT, 1919-,ballerina

(Fonteyn)
Career sketch; b. Reigate as
Peggy Hookman, il MD v 50 n 11
My '60
---E Michael Somes in "Le Peri",
AP wl ph: La Scala. La S n 124
p 31 Mr '60
FORD AUDITORIUM
Exterior ph: Detroit. IM v 59 n 4
p 12 O '60
FORD FOUNDATION
Composers-in-residence project;
Robert Washburn reporting from
Elkhart, Indiana, on a full year
devoted to music composition with
student groups to work with him.
MEJ v 47 n 1 p 108 S-O '60
---See also Subsidies
FORREST, EDWIN, 1806-1872,
actor
Clurman, Harold. Actors: the im-
age of their era. TDR v 4 n 3 p 38-
44 Mr '60
FORRESTER, MAUREEN
Fleming, Shirley. A contralto
without compulsions. HF v 10 n 7
p 12, 14 Jl '60
---Fleming, Shirley. A contralto
without compulsions (notes on her
Mahler specialty also). por HF
v 10 n 7 p 12 Jl '60
FORT WORTH
Martha, opera review. MC v 161
n 1 p 24 Ja '60
---Martha, opera; Warenskjold and
Gonzales, AP wl ph: C. E. Royer.
ON v 25 n 3 p 13 N 19'60
---Operas: Manon and Il Trovatore;
Irving Guttman of Canada producer,
Rudolf Kruger, conductor. Op v 11
n 7 p 472 Jl '60
---Saxe, Serge. Martha. Op v 2 n 3
p 200 Mr '60
--- ---Music report. MC v 161 n 3
p 39 F '60
--- ---Music report. MC v 161 n 6
p 31 My '60
FORT WORTH SYMPHONY
Review. MC v 161 n 6 p 30 My '60
FORTE, ALLEN. Bartok's "serial"
composition. Mus Q v 46 n 2 p 233-
245 Ap '60
THE 49th COUSIN, play
NYC notes; Florence Lowe and

Caroline Francke. WP v 12 n 3
p 38 D '60
LA FORZA DEL DESTINO, opera
Historical background. ON v 24
n 19 p 8-9 Mr 12'60
---Metropolitan Opera cast; story;
background articles; décor notes;
bibliography; discography; port-
folio. ON v 24 n 19 Mr 12'60
--- ---review. MC v 161 n 4 p 13
Mr '60
---Rome; Floriana Cavalli, Carlo
Bergonzi; review. il La S n 124
p 32 Mr '60
---Genoa; Act 2, scene 2, ens
AP wl ph: Leoni. Op v 11 n 6
p 428 Je '60
---Portfolio: Melançon. ON v 24
n 19 Mr 12'60
FOSS, LUKAS, 1922-, composer
Concerto for Improvising Solo
Instruments; played by Philadel-
phia Orchestra in NYC; criticism.
MC v 162 n 5 p 17 N '60
---Première: Introductions and
Goodbyes; libretto by Meuotti;
played by Philharmonic, nine
minutes. MC v 161 n 7 p 23
Je '60
---"Time Cycle" by the NY Phil-
harmonic; review. MC v 182 n 5
p 31 N '60
FOSSE, BOB, 1927?-, chareographer
Hl ph: Pat Ferrier. Th Arts v 44
n 11 p 66 N '60
FOSTER, SIDNEY, pianist
NYC review. MC v 161 n 1 p 13
Ja '60
FOURNIER, MONIQUE, pianist
Paris; Canadian's debut. GDC
n 286 p 197 O 28'60
FOURNIER, MARGUERITE
Por ph. La S n 131 p 43 O '60
FOURNIER, Pierre
Bruyr, José. Paris review.
GDC n 274 p 723 My 27'60
FOWLER, CHARLES (1920?). Are
you cheating yourself on speakers?
charts HF v 10 n 9 p 40-42 S'60
--- ---Mozart as you motor (tape
recorder operated on car battery
by means of an inverter; remote
control from trunk). HF v 10 n 6
p 40-1 Je '60

FOWLIE, WALLACE (1908-). New plays of Ionesco (1912-) and Genet (1910-). TDR v 5 n 1 p 43-8 S'60

FOX, LEVI. The Shakespeare Birthplace Trust; Stratford-on-Avon's new library and headquarters (scale model shown). Th Notvk v 14 n 3 p 90-91 Spring '60

FRA DIAVOLO, opera
Philopera Circle review. Op v 11 n 8 p 583 Ag '60

---Ens AP wl ph: Bernard Hales. Op v 11 n 8 p 583 Ag '60

FRACCI, CARLA, 1936?-, dancer
E Carmen Puthod nel balletto "Fantasni al Grand Hotel", wl ph: La Scala. La S n 124 p 30 Mr '60

---E Piero Columella, wl ph: La Scala. La S n 122 p 34 Ja '60

FRAGER, MALCOM, 1935-, pianist
Award: first prize 1960 Queen Elisabeth of Belgium. AmM v 8 n 5 p 12 Je '60

---Career notes. AmM v 8 n 2 p 11 F '60

---Fleming, Shirley. (Winner of both Leventritt and Queen Elisabeth of Belgium contests; quoted; his first recording session.) HF v 10 n 12 p 24 D '60

---Leventritt Award winner, notes. MEJ v 46 n 4 p 18 F-Mr '60

---Premier Laureat 1960 Brussels International Music Competition: sketch. AmM v 8 n 6 p 8 Jl '60

---Prize: Queen Elisabeth of Belgium, International Music Competition; notes on American from St. Louis. WM n 4 p 78 Ag '60

---Arriving Idlewild Airport with trophy, ph: 1960. MC v 162 n 2 p 2 Ag '60

---At the piano. hl ph. AmM v 8 n 2 p 9 F '60

---With Queen Elisabeth of Belgium, hl ph: 1960. AmM v 8 n 6 p 9 Jl '60

FRANCAIX, JEAN (1912-). Concerto pour clavecin et orchestre (études musicales analytiques). GDC n 288 p 266 N 11'60

--- ---Concerto pour piano et orchestre (1936) (études musicales analytiques). GDC n 289 p 301 N 18'60

FRANCE
Avis de concours; partie officielle. GDC n 281-2 p 73-5 S 30'60

---Boll, André. Opera (short report). WT v 9 n 1 p 74 Spring '60

---Brookings, Jack. The declamatory theatre of France; Part I. PlM v 37 n 2 p 31 N '60

--- ---Part II. PlM v 37 n 3 p 56 D '60

---Clurman, Harold. The paradox of the French stage. il Th Arts v 44 n 12 p 64-5 D '60

---Colloque, Avril 28, 1960: sur la situation du monde musical en France; participaient à cette séance (liste). GDC n 279-80 p 868-877 Jl 1'60

---Concerts dans nos Provinces (regular section of reviews). GDC 1960

---Création de la Section français des Bibliothèques-Musées des Arts du Spectacle. Th R v 2 n 2 p 119 1960

---Demarquez, Suzanne. Théâtre des Nations; French festivals. MC v 161 n 7 p 14 Je '60

---Dumur, Guy. Jean Genet, parabole et parodie. portfolio Spec n 1 p 75-8 1960

---Editorial: La Grève des Théâtres Lyriques Nationaux. GDC n 263-4 p 473 Mr 11'60

---La Fédération Française de Danse: congrès, l'Hotel de Ville de Vincennes. TD n 96 p 24 S-O '60

---French National Music Committee with Paris setting up Les Semaines Musicales de Paris; history and report 1960. WM n 6 p 122-3 D '60

---L'Institut International du Théâtre: report. WP 1960

---Lenoir, Jean Pierre. French theatre under the Fifth Republic. por Th Arts v 44 n 12 60-3 D '60

---Mignon, Paul-Louis. (Critical report on drama.) il WT v 9 n 2 p 158-160 Summer '60

--- ---France (drama report).

(France)
WT v 9 n 1 p 74-6 Spring '60;
same. WT v 9 n 3 p 282-5
Autumn '60;same. WT v 9 n 4
p 356-8 Winter '60
---Music report. La S n 122 p 77
Ja '60; same. La S n 123 p 74-5
F '60
--- ---Music reports: Alger; Bay-
onne et Côte Basque; Belfort;
Saint-Donat; Nimes. GDC n 277
p 821-2 Je 17'60
---Alger; Beauvais; Mulhouse;
Nancy; Saint-Amand; Valence.
GDC n 273 p 694-6 My 20'60
--- ---Alger; Bordeaux; Colmar;
Dijon; Sete; Strasbourg. GDC
n 278 p 853-4 Je 24'60
--- ---Alger; Lorient; Rennes;
Troyes. GDC n 275 p 757-8 Je
3'60
--- ---Alger; Lyon; Pau; Annecy.
GDC n 279-80 p 896 Jl 1'60
--- ---Alger; Nantes; Brive. GDC
n 276 p 792 Je 10'60
--- ---Alger; Perpignan; Bourges.
GDC n 284 p 139 O 14'60
--- ---Annecy; Nantes; Dijon.
GDC n 289 p 299 N 18'60
--- ---Belfort; Bourges; Perpignan;
Valenciennes. GDC n 290 p 326-8
N 25'60
--- ---Besançon; Lyon; Orléans.
GDC n 292 p 426-7 D 9'60
--- ---Caen; Toulouse; Romans.
GDC n 274 p 727 My 27'60
--- ---Marseille; Perpignan;
Bourges. GDC n 275 p 750 Je3'60
--- ---Nancy; Marseille; Belfort.
GDC n 277 p 814 Je 17'60
--- ---Nimes; Reims; Lyon; Mar-
seille; Rennes; Agde. GDC n 269-
70 P 591-3 Ap 22'60
--- ---Pergignan; Marseille; Dijon;
Metz; Reims. GDC n 271 p 623-4
My 5'60
--- ---Rennes; Dijon. GDC n 287
p 231 N 4'60
--- ---Rouen Perpignan. GDC
n 274 p 721 M̄y 27'60
--- ---Saint-Etienne; Alger. GDC
n 281-2 p 67-8 S 30'60
--- ---Toulouse; Sete; Grenoble;
Nice; Bordeaux; Reims;

Marseille; Liège. GDC n 263-4
P 480-483 Mr 11'60
--- ---Toulouse; Mulhouse; Mar-
seille. GDC n 273 p 687-8
My 20'60
---Musique en France (advance
calender by place, artists and
programs). GDC 1960
---Opera notes: Bordeaux; Lyons.
Op v 11 n 1 p 32 Ja '60
--- ---Paris Opéra; Bordeaux;
Besançon; Toulouse. Op v 11 n 12
p 827-8 D '60
---Recherches théâtrales: thèses
de doctorat, soutenues et en pré-
paration dans les Universitiés de
France, 1944-1959. Th R v 2 n 3
p 141-162 1960
---Repertory notes from Bordeaux;
Lyons; Marseilles; Reims; Rouen.
Op v 11 n 5 p 344-5 My '60
---Reyna, Ferdinando. Music re-
ports. La S 1960
---Spectacles Lyrique: calendar.
GDC 1960
---Stein, Elliott. (The new Julien
administration; effect at Opéra
and at Opéra-Comique.) Op v 11
n 2 p 139-142 F '60
---Theatre reports. WP 1960
---La vie musicale en Alsace; Belfort; Valence; Calais; Saint-Etienne;
Toulon; Clermont-Ferrand. GDC,
n 293-4 p 464-5 D 16'60
---Wolff, Stéphane. Les Directeurs
français se penchent sur le Théâtre
lyrique_les buts essentiels de l'Union des Directeurs-Animateurs de
la Décentralisation artistique nationale. GDC n 273 p 685 My 20'60
--- ---Notes on Bordeaux, Marseilles, Strasbourg. Op v 2 n 3
p 203 Mr '60
FRANCO, JOHAN, 1908-, composer
Premières: Songs of the Spirit
(NYC 1960); Bugle Song (Virginia
1960); Suite No. 2 for Organ (NYC
1960). ACAB v 9 n 3 p 30 1960
---Premières, three in 1959; place
and performance notes. ACAB v 9
n 2 p 20 1960
FRANÇOIS, SAMSON, 1924-, pianist
McMullen, Roy. (Paris interview.)
HF v 10 n 8 p 20 Ag '60

---Paris review. GDC n 257-8 p 362 Ja 29'60

FRANÇOISE ET DOMINIQUE, dancers
Rentrée à Paris. il TD n 93 p 16 My '60

FRANK, CLAUDE, pianist
Por ph. AmM v 8 n 2 p 9 F '60

FRANKE, PAUL
As Spoletta in Tosca, AP hl ph: Melançon. ON v 24 n 20 p 17 Mr 19'60

FRANKS, DOBBS. New Orchestra of New York (the story of Franks and Gregory Millar's new venture). pors MD v 51 n 5 p 24-5 N '60
---Career notew. por MD̄ v 51 n 5 p 26 N '60

FRANKS, LAURIE, singer
Career notes. MD v 51 n 6 p 26 D '60
---Por ph. MD v 51 n 6 p 26 D'60

FRASCONI, ANTONIO(1919-). Verdi portrait, wood-cut. ON v 25 n 8 cover D 31'60
LO frate 'nnamorato, opera Jesi;Piccola Scala notes. Op v 11 n 11 p 768 N'60
---Piccola Scala, Act I, ens AP wl ph:Piccagliani. Op v 11 n 8 p 562 Ag'60
---Misciano e Fiorenza Cossotto, AP hl ph:Milan;Franzini e Pedani, AP hl ph. LaS n 128 p 27 Jl '60

FRATTINI, ANGELO(1896-). Da "Porgy and Bess" a "The fantasy train". il LaS n 123 p 62-3 F'60
--- ---Lettere aperte a due vecchi amici. por LaS n 122 p 62-3 Ja'60
--- ---Lettere aperto a Josephine Baker e a Gino Bramieri. por LaS n 132 p 70-1 N'60
--- ---Per le riviste;malgrado tutto, "Arrivano i nostri". La S n 127 p 50-1 Je'60
---Right profile por ph;and AP hl ph. LaS n 122 p 62-3 Ja'60

FRAZZONI, GIGLIOLA, singer
Criticism. Op v 11 n 5 p 354 My '60

FREAS, RALPH. The coming breakthrough in tape(home service

1970);interview with Dr. Peter Goldmark. por HF v 10 n 3 p 46-7 Mr'60
---How many revolutions can we afford?(Customers discouraged by fast stereo changes.) HF v 10 n 9 p 35 S'60

FREE AND EASY, musical
Piel, Emma. Brussels review;comparison with Porgy and Bess;Harold Arlen, costumes Jed Mace. GDC n 257-8 p 356 Ja 29'60

FREEDOMLAND
NYC;Paul Lavalle, musical director; notes. IM v 59 n 4 p 35 O'60

FREEDLEY, GEORGE(1904-). Plays first produced off Broadway, June 1, 1959-May 31, 1960:list by title, playwright, place and date;Part I. PlM v 37 n 2 p 32-3 N'60
--- ---Part II. PlM v 37 n 3 p 54-5 D'60
--- ---Theatre Arts Bookshelf (reviews in depth, followed by an annotated list of more than 20 other theatre titles). Th Arts v 44 1960
--- ---(Theatre books:MacDougall's Isadora;An International Vocabulary of Technical Terms in Eight Languages; and ten others.) Th Arts v 44 n 4 p 67-9 Ap'60
--- ---Theatre Subject Headings (book form, subject headings used in the Theatre Collection of New York Public Library). PlM v 37 n 1 p 4 O'60
---As instructor in the first course in theatre librianship in 1959;Mr. Freedley's awards as Curator of the Theatre Collection, New York Public Library. Th R v 2 n 1 p 59 1960
---Theatre course;first of its kind; NYC notes. PlM v 36 n 6 p 121 Mr '60

DER FREISCHUTZ, opera
Guildhall School of Music; review. Op v 11 n 7 p 513 Jl '60
---Osborne, Conrad L. (Weber: reviews of Electrola and of Deutsche Grammophon releases.) HF v 10 n 12 p 60-1 D '60

FREMAUX, LOUIS, conductor
Por ph: Harcourt. GDC n 281-2

(Frémaux)
p 36 S 30'60

FRETWELL, ELIZABETH, singer
As Violetta, AP hl ph: Rogers.
Op v 11 n 11 p 781 N '60

FREUD, SIGMUND (1856-1939).
Psychopathic characters on the
stage, trans. Henry Alden Bunker. TDR v 4 n 3 p 144-8 Mr '60

FRICKER, PETER RACINE, 1920-,
composer
Third Symphony; London Philharmonic Pritchard; "thoughtful, well-
wrought". MC v 162 n 6 p 30
D '60

FRICSAY, FERENC, 1914-
Hl ph. La S n 132 p 78 N '60

FRIEDHEIM, PHILIP. Radical
harmonic procedures in Berlioz.
MR v 21 n 4 p 281-296 N '60

FRIEDMAN, GERARD, singer
Paris criticism. GDC n 278
p 848 Je 24'60

FRIS, MARIA
With Rainer Kochermann, AP
wl ph: Frankfort. TD n 89 p 14
Ja '60

FRISCO BELLES, opera
Wehner, George, composer;
Brooklyn première note. ON
v 24 n 15 p 2 F 13'60

FRISKIN, JAMES, 1886-, pianist
Notes; b. Glasgow. AmM v 8 n 5
p 10 Je '60

FROM DEATH TO MORNING,
cantata
Alexander, Leni, Chilean composer; critical note from Cologne. Mus Q v 46 n 4 p 524 O '60

FROM THE HOUSE OF THE DEAD,
opera
Dresden; Janček reviewed. Op
v 11 n 6 p 422 Je '60

FROMM, PAUL (1906-). The
Princeton Seminar: its purpose
and promise. Mus Q v 46 n 2
p 155-158 Ap '60

---His Fromm Music Foundation
of Chicago; 1952 to date. AmM
v 8 n 4 p 15 Ap '60

FROMM MUSIC FOUNDATION
Chicago; founded 1952 by Paul
Fromm; four-fold program.
AmM v 8 n 4 p 15 Ap '60

---Princeton University seminar,
program. WM n 2 p 33 Ap '60

---US and foreign composers commissioned: list. WM n 1 p 10 F'60

FROMONT-DELUNE, JEANNE,
1885-1960, violinist
Obituary; b. Ransart. GDC n 277
p 810 Je 17'60

FRY, CHRISTOPHER (1907-). Comedy. TDR v 4 n 3 p 77-9 Mr '60

---Lecky, Eleazer. Mystery in the
plays of Christopher Fry. TDR
v 4 n 3 p 80-7 Mr '60

---Schear, Bernice Larson, and
Eugene G. Prater. A bibliography on Christopher Fry. TDR
v 4 n 3 p 88-98 Mr '60

FRY, PETER
Israel; Peter Fry's Ensemble;
notes. WP v 12 n 3 p 4 D '60

FUCHS, JOSEPH, 1905-, violinist
Career notes; b. NYC. AmM v 8
n 3 p 6 Mr '60

---AP hl ph. MC v 162 n 6 p 27
D '60

FUGLEN I LA PLATA, play
Norway; Magne Thorsen. WP
v 12 n 1 p 9 O '60

FULLER, ALBERT
And Paul Wolfe, duo harpsichor-
dists; NYC review. MC v 161 n 1
p 16 Ja '60

FULLERTON, CHARLES A.
Wolfe, Irving. Rural school
music missionary (with portrait
photograph and 2 groups of Iowa
school pupils). MEJ v 46 n 5
p 26-28 Ap-My '60

FUNKE, LEWIS (1912-). The
Phoenix Theatre, NYC; seventh
season. il Th ARts v 44 n 1 p 72-
3, 84 Ja '60

FURTWANGLER, WILHELM, 1886-,
Pirie, Peter J. Toscanini and
Furtwängler, an empire divided
(Beethoven symphonic canon). HF
v 10 n 4 p 37-9 Ap '60

FUSCHI, OLEGNA, pianist
With Artur Rubinstein, ph: Warsaw. MC v 162 n 1 p 34 Jl '60

G

THE GAG, play

118

Sastre criticism. TDR v 5 n 2 p 124 D '60

GAILLARD, MARIUS-FRANÇOIS composer
Chamfray, Claude. Sonate pour Piano (critique). GDC n 255-6 p 318 Ja 15'60

GALASSI-BERRA, GIANCARLO, playwright
Hl ph: Italy. Th Arts v 44 n 4 p 54 Ap '60

GALGEVJERGET, play
Aalborg notes; Leck Fischer. WP v 11 n 6 p 3 Ap '60

GALILEI, VINCENZO, 1520-1591, composer
Palisca, Claude V. Vincenzo Galilei and some links between "pseudo-monody" and monody. Mus Q v 46 n 3 p 344-360 Jl '60

GALLERY CIRCLE THEATRE, 1948-
New Orleans; notes. Th Arts v 44 n 4 p 57 Ap '60

GALLI, PIETRE. pianist
Paris review. GDC n 278 p 754 Je 3'60

GALLI-ANGELINI, GABRIELLA, pianist
With Jacqueline Tolmer; Paris review. GDC n 265-6 p 523 Mr 25'60

GALLINI, NATALE. Note sull'Otello. il La Scala n 122 p 13-21 Ja '60

GALLO, FORTUNE, 1878-, impresario
Career notes. il ON v 24 n 17 p 10-1 F 27'60
---At the organ, ph. ON v 24 n 17 p 10 F 27'60

GAMETSUI YATSU, play
Tokyo notes; Kikuta Kazuo. WP v 11 n 5 p 13 Mr '60
---de Kikuta, ens ph: Tokyo. WP v 11 n 5 p 1 Mr '60

THE GANG'S ALL HERE, play
Lawrence, Jerome, and Robert E. Lee. The Gang's All Here (text, sets, NYC cast). il Th Arts v 44 n 11 p 26-56 N '60
---Several phs: Friedman-Abeles. Th Arts v 44 n 11 N '60

GANZ, RUDOLPH (1879-). Letter.

MD v 50 n 10 p 2 Ap '60
---Notes. MD v 51 n 6 p 19 D '60
---Weds Esther Goodman LaBerge; notes. MC v 161 n 3 p 18 F '60
---And wife, formerly Esther La- Berge, hl ph. MD v 51 n 6 p 19 D '60

GARA, EUGENIO (1888?-) Il cammino dell'opera in un secolo d'interpretazioni. Ver v 1 n 1 p 112-133 Ap '60
--- ---II. Ver v 1 n 2 p 704-719 Ag '60

GARBATO, ENZIO. Una vita dolorosa (Richard Wagner). il LaS n 129-30 p 46-8 Ag-S '60

UN GARÇON D'HONNEUR, play
Paris notes; Antoine Blondin and Paul Guimard. WP v 11 n 7 p 9 My '60

GARDEL, MAXIMILIEN, 1741- 1787, choreographer
Por print. La S n 132 p 31 N '60

GARDEN, MARY, 1877-, singer
As Cleopatra AP hl ph. ON v 25 n 8 p 10 D 31'60

GARFI, TINA
e Flaviano Labò, AP hl ph: Catania. La S n 126 p 35 My '60

GARNER: ERROLL, 1923-, jazz musician
Cerulli, Dom. Erroll Garner (estimate as musician; personality sketch.) por IM v 58 n 9 p 16-7 Mr '60

GARTSIDE, ROBERT, singer
London notes; b. St. Louis. AmM v 8 n 9 p 6 O '60

GARVEY, DAVID. Accompanists anonymous. por J Rev v 7 n 1 p 6-7, 29 Winter 59-60

GASSMAN, VITTORIO, 1922-, actor
With Giulio Basetti, AP hl ph: Italy. Th Arts v 44 n 4 p 55 Ap'60

GASSNER, JOHN (1903-). Playwrights of the period (1930s in US). Th Arts v 44 n 9 p 19, 26 S '60

GATTI-CASAZZA, GIULIO, 1869- 1940
Cushing, Mary Watkins. (1908- 1935, Metropolitan Opera; memories of music critic for the Herald Tribune.) por ON v 25 n 3

(Gatti)
p 10-1 N 19'60
---Por ph: Mapleson coll. ON
v 25 n 3 p 10 N 19'60
GAUTHIER, JUDITH, 1846-1917,
poet
Janni, Guido. Wagner's idyl in
the days of "Parsifal". La S
n 127 p 14-7 Je '60
GAY ROSALINDA, operetta
Australia; Beatrice Oakley, dir-
ecting; dance list. MD v 51 n 1
p 27 Jl '60
LA GAZZETTA, opera
Naples review. La S n 132 p 47
N '60
---Ens AP wl ph: Naples. La S
n 132 p 47 N '60
GEBERT, ERNST, conductor
Orchestra re-named for the Cal-
ifornia city as host; notes. IM
v 59 n 9 p 50 D '60
GEDDA, NICOLAI, 1927-, singer
Kupferberg, Herbert. All-purpose
tenor. HF v 10 n 8 p 45-6 Ag '60
---As Hoffmann, AP hl ph Th Arts
v 44 n 3 p 49 Mr '60
---Por ph: Douglas Glass. HF
v 10 n 8 p 45 Ag '60
GEDDO, ANGELO. Il comico nella
musica applicata. il La Scala
n 122 p 22-27 Ja '60
--- ---L'umore dei decadenti nel
solco dell'esperienza pittorica.
il La S n 131 p 20-5 O '60
GEE, GEORGE 1895-1959,
comedian
Obituary. MD v 50 n 9 p 19 Mr'60
GEHMAN, RICHARD What makes
(David Merrick run. il Th Arts
v 44 n 11 p 15-17, 69 N '60
GEHRKENS, KARL WILSON. The
development of a college curri-
culum in music education (the
Oberlin course for training music teachers). MEJ v 47 n 2
p 31-4 N-D '60
GELATT, ROLAND. Music makers (a frequent column on people
and events in record making).
HF 1960
---Victoria of the Angels. il HF
v 10 n 9 p 36-39 S '60
GELENG, INGVELDE. Germany

(theatre report). il WT v 9 n 2
p 162-164 Summer '60
GELLER, HERB, saxophonist
Hl ph. IM v 58 n 12 p 22 Je '60
GENET, JEAN, 1910-, playwright
Dumur, Guy. Jean Genet, para-
bole et parodie. il Spec n 1 p 75-8
1960
---Fowlie, Wallace. New plays of
Ionesco and Genet. TDR v 5 n 1
p 43-8 S '60
GENEVA
Music notes. La S n 123 p 79 F'60
GENNARI, PIERO. Teatro Comun-
ale di Piacenza. La S n 123 p 40
F '60
GENNARO, PETER, choreographer
AP ph: NYC. Th Arts v 44 n 10
p 17 O '60
GENOA
Carlo Felice, the restored opera
theatre. il ON v 24 n 22 p 12-3
Ap 2'60
---Reviews; V Festival Internazion-
ale del Balletto, Genova-Nervi.LaS
n 129-30 p 65-8 Ag-S '60
---Teatro comunale dell'Opera,
37a Stagione sinfonica al Teator
Carlo Felice direttori, pianisti,
violinisti: calendario. La S n 132
inset N '60
GENOUSIE, play
Lyon, Raymond. Au T. N. P. ré-
camier "Genousie" de René de
Obaldia. GDC n 284 p 135 O 14'60
---Paris notes; René de Obalda.
WP v 12 n 2 p 21 N '60
---Théâtre National Populaire, ens
AP wl ph: Bernand. WT v 9 n 4
p 358 Winter '60
GEOFFREY, MAURICE
Director of First Florida Theatre
Festival; Daytona notes. Th Arts
v 44 n 9 p 77-8 S '60
---Note. PlM v 36 n 6 p 123 Mr '60
GEORGE, GRAHAM. Three Canad-
ian concert-halls(Vancouver, Ed-
monton, Calgary). CMJ v 4 n 2
p 4-13 Winter '60
GERARD, ROLF, 1910?-, scenic
designer
Larson, Orville K. Rolf Gérard's
scene design for opera (Cosi for
tutte designs, 6 pictures). PlM

v 36 n 6 p 130-2 Mr '60
GERGANNA: OPERA
The Narodna Opera in Plovdiv;
notes. Op v 11 n 8 p 549 Ag '60
GERKEN, EVA. The restless and
the damned (The Flying Dutch-
man). ON v 24 n 18 p 4-5
Mr 5'60
GERMANY
Cologne; deux nouveaux ballets.
TD n 93 p 22 My '60
---Corelli, Jean. Le ballet Alle-
mand. il TD n 89 p 17-9 Ja '60
---East; theatre notes. WP v 11
n 4 p 1 F '60; same. WP v 11 n 7
p 1 My '60; same. WP v 11 n 8
p 7 Je '60; same. WP v 11 n 10 p 1
Ag '60
---Geleng, Ingvelde. Germany
(theatre report). WT v 9 n 1
p 78-80 Spring '60; same. WT
v 9 n 2 p 162-164 Summer '60
---Group-singing; expansion of the
movement; notes. WM n 4 p 78
Ag '60
---Koegler, Horst. Opera notes:
Berlin, Staatsoper, also Städtis-
che Oper; Cologne (longer sur-
vey). Op v 11 n 1 p 32-3 Ja '60
--- ---The Städtische Oper (criti-
cism of administration; of the
Berlin debut of Wieland Wagner,
Tristan); Berlin Staatsoper also.
Op v 2 n 3 p 203, 206 Mr '60
---Korn, Barbara. (Music report.)
MC v 161 n 7 p 16 Je '60
---Music report. La S n 133 p 111
D '60
---Opera; Rosamunde Floris, a
Blacher opera; Erwin Piscator,
Berlin staging; other operas in
various cities. Op v 11 n 12
p 828-830 D '60
---forecasts for 1960-61. Op v 11
n 9 p 619-20 S '60
---notes: Aachen; Augsberg; Ber-
lin; Bremen; Cassel; Essen; Fr-
ankfurt; Gelsenkirchen; Hamburg;
Hanover; Nuremberg; Karlsruhe;
Wiesbaden. Op v 11 n 4 Ap '60
---Berlin; Cologne; Dresden; Ham-
burg; Stuttgart; Wuppertal. Op
v 11 n 6 p 420-5 Je '60
---Berlin, Städtische Oper,

Staatsoper, Komische Oper;
Darmstadt; Düsseldorf; Frankfurt;
Halle; Hamburg; Hanover; Karl
Marx Stadt; Leipzig; Mainz; Munich, Theater am Gärtnerplatz, Cu-
villiés theater, Staatsoper; Nurem-
burg. Op v 11 n 7 p 478-485 Jl'60
---Berlin's Städtische; Bielefeld;
Bremen; Cologne; Dessau; Düsse-
ldorf- Duisberg; Leipzig; Mannheim;
Munich; Stuttgart. Op v 11 n 8
p 553-9 Ag '60
---Cologne; Dortmund; Dresden;
Düsseldorf; Leipzig; Mannheim;
Munich; Regensburg; Wiesbaden.
il Op v 11 n 5 My '60
---Perle, George. (Criticism of
contemporary music with report
of 34th World Music Festival of
the International Society for Contemporary Music, Cologne.) Mus Q
v 46 n 4 p 517-525 O '60
---Silvant, Jean. La danse en Allemagne. il TD n 89 p 6-15 Ja '60
---Steyer, Ralf. Frankfurt; Fidelio
on revolving stage with Gré Brouwenstijn. Op v 2 n 3 p 207 Mr '60
---Summer music courses, Württ
emberg, Germany; notes. WM n 5
p 105 O '60
---Theatre; issue featuring German
theatre, various angles, signed
articles. WT v 9 n 3 Autumn '60
---Vecchio-Verderame, Angelo.
Music report. La S n 124 p 70-1
Mr '60; La S n 125 p 93 Ap '60;
La S n 126 p 69-70 My '60;La S
n 128 p 60 Jl '60;La S n 129-30
p 76-7 Ag-S '60
---West; theatre report. WP v 11
n 6 p 1 Ap '60; WP v 11 n 9 p 7
Jl '60;WP v 11 n 10 p 2 Ag '60;
WP v 12 n 2 p 1 N '60; WP v 12 n 3
p 3 D '60
---Wölfing, Siegmund. Opera re-
ports from Hamburg and Leipzig;
notes from other cities. il Op v 11
n 1 p 38-41 Ja '60
---Klaus Storlebeker de Küba,
East Germany, dark ens ph: Klaus
Marschke. WP v 11 n 8 p 7 Je '60
GERSHWIN, GEORGE (1898-1937).
Ira Gershwin, pen sketch. Th
Arts v 44 n 2 p 79 F '60

(Gershwin)
---Chamfray, Claude. Fiche
biographique. GDC n 265-6
p 528 Mr 25'60
---At the piano, right profile ph.
La S n 132 p 60 N '60
---Por ph; with Ira Gershwin, ly-
ricist, and DuBose Heyward in
Boston, ph: Vandamm; scene
from Porgy and Bess, ph: ANTA.
ON v 24 n 20 p 6-8 Mr 19'60
DAS GERETTETE VENEDIG, play
Nagler, A. M. Hugo von Hofmann-
nsthal and theatre. Th R v 2 n 1
p 10-3 1960
GERMANICO SUL RENO
Machinerie avec décorations
(from Worsthorne's Venetian
Opera in the 17th Century). Th R
v 2 n 1 p 26 1960
DIE GESCHICTE DER SIMONE
MACHARD, play
Ens AP wl ph: 1957, Frankfurt.
WT v 9 n 3 p 203 Autumn '60
GESELLSCHAFT IM HERBST,
play
Mannheim notes; Tankred Dorsi.
WP v 12 n 1 p 12 O '60
GESENSWAY, LOUIS
Première: Ode to Peace, Phila-
delphia Orchestra; commissioned
by Edward Benjamin of Greens-
boro, North Carolina. IM v 59
n 4 p 39 O '60
GESENSWAY, LOUIS
Première: Ode to Peace, Sym-
phonic poem; Philadelphia
MC v 161 n 6 p 26 My '60
GHITALLA, ARMANDO
With his trumpet, Boston Sym-
phony, ph. MEJ v 46 n 4 p 59
F-Mr '60
GIAIOTTI, BONALDO
As High Priest in Nabucco, AP
hl ph: Melançon. ON v 25 n 4 p 20
D 3'60
GIANCOLA, GIACINTO. Italy
(theatre). il WT v 9 n 3 p 286-290
Autumn '60;same. WT v 9 n 2
p 168-170 Summer '60
GIANNINI, VITTORIO (1903-). Ad-
dress to Juilliard Convocation:
the spirit in music.). J Rev v 7
n 1 p 8 Winter 59-60

---Première: Divertimento No. 2
for Orchestra; La Jolla, Califor-
nia. J Rev v 7 n 3 p 19 Fall '60
---Première: Fourth Symphony;
dedicated to Jean Morel; notes.
J Rev v 7 n 2 p 13 Spring '60
---With Irene Jordan, singer of
his "The Medead", hl ph. MC
v 162 n 5 p 31 N '60
GIANOLI, REINE, pianist
Bruyr, José. Review. GDC
n 267-8 p 558 Ap 8'60
GIBSON, R. D.
Director of the firm of J. and W.
Chester, Ltd., publishers. MD
v 51 n 1 p 20 Jl '60
GIBSON, WILLIAM, 1914-, play-
wright
Por ph. Th Arts v 44 n 7 p 19
Jl '60
GIELGUD, SIR (Arthur) JOHN,
1904-, actor
One-man show of Shakespeare.
"Ages of Man". Th Arts v 44 n 10
p 24 O '60
---As Hamlet with Judith Anderson,
AP hl ph: 1936. Th Arts v 44 n 9
p 13 S '60
GIESEN, EDNA
Por ph: NYC. MC v 161 n 1 p 6
Ja '60
A GIFT OF FURY, play
Ens AP wl ph: San Francisco.
Th Arts v 44 n 3 p 59 Mr '60
GILBERT AND SULLIVAN
Hughes, Gervase. The music of
Arthur Sullivan (book reviewed
by Arthur Jacobs). Op v 11 n 5
p 362 My '60
---NYC Center; staged by Dorothy
Raedler; The Mikado and The
Pirates of Penzance reviewed.
MC v 162 n 5 p 15 N '60
---New York CityCenter, new
group formed for Gilbert and Sull-
ivan; notes. ON v 25 n 7 p 7
D 24'60
---Review of London's release of
Pinafore. HF v 10 n 6 p 62 Je '60
---Santa Fé; The Gondoliers under
Martyn Green; notes. Op v 11 n 11
p 758 N '60
GILDER, Rosamund (1900-). Jottings
on long runs. WT v 9 n 4 p 366-8

Winter '60
---USA (theatre report). il WT
v 9 n 2 p 188-192 Summer '60;
same. WT v 9 n 3 p 294-6
Autumn '60
GILELS, EMIL, 1916-, pianist
Boston criticism; "mallet-like
aggression that while superb with
full orchestra at forte rather
perforates Schubert and Schumann". MC v 161 n 5 p 29 Ap '60
---Louvet, Michel. Paris review;
"prince du piano". GDC n 265-6
p 526 Mr 25'60
---NYC criticisms. MC v 161 n 4
p 15, 18 Mr '60
GILLESPIE, DIZZY, guitarist
and Les Spann, AP ph: US. IM
v 58 n 11 p 21 My '60
GILMAN, LAWRENCE, critic
Por ph: Pinchot, NYC. ON v 24
n 21 p 7 Mr 26'60
GIMPEL, BRONISLAV, violinist
and Jakob Gimpel, pianist; notes.
AmM v 8 n 4 p 8 Ap '60
GINNER, RUBY. Gateway to the
dance (book review by Joan Law-
son). Th Notbk v 15 n 1 p 36
Autumn '60
LA GIOCONDA, opera
Miami review; Frances Bible.
ON v 24 n 21 p 26 Mr 26'60
GIONO, JEAN (1895-). Homère.
WP v 11 n 8 p 1, 7 Je '60
GIORDANO, UMBERTO, 1867-
1948, composer
Por dedicated to Illica, ph. La S
n 133 p 59 D '60
UN GIORNO DI REGNO, opera
American première; Amato Opera
Theatre. Op v 11 n 8 p 545 Ag '60
GIOVANGILI, ORAZIO COSTA
See Costa, Orazio, 1911-
GIOVANINETTI, SILVIO (1901-).
Da Manzoni a Gibson a Montanelli.
il La S n 133 p 86-7 D '60
--- ---Giovaninetti per la prosa.
il La S 1960
--- ---Polemica spenta. il Sa S
n 122 p 60-1 Ja '60
GIOVINEZZA (DANTZIG), ballet
Ostende notes. WP v 11 n 3 p 10
Ja '60
THE GIRLS IN 509, play

Gallery Circle Theatre, ens AP
wl ph: New Orleans. Th Arts
v 44 n 4 p 58 Ap '60
GISELLE (CORALLI), ballet
Daydé, Liane, et Michel Renault,
Moscow. il TD n 95 p 13 Jl-Ag'60
---Hutton, Geoffrey W. Borovansky
Ballet 1960. MD v 51 n 6 p 22
D '60
---Royal Ballet: criticism of
Annette Page and Ronald Hynd;
of Lynn Seymour. MD v 50 n 10
p 27 Ap '60
---Chauviré, Yvette, et Youly
Algaroff, Act I, ens AP wl ph:
Moscow. TD n 98 p 27 D '60
GISH, DOROTHY, 1898-, actress
Por wl ph: 1932. Th Arts v 44
n 9 p 60 S '60
GIUDITTA, opera
Honegger ; Anna Maria Rota, ens
AP wl ph: Rome. La S n 125
p 49 Ap '60
GIULIO CESARE, opera
Frankfurt; Leonardo Wolovsky
as Caesar, ens AP wl ph: Englert.
Op v 11 n 7 p 479 Jl '60
GLANVILLE-HICKS, PEGGY,
composer
Première: Drama for Orchestra
(NYC 1960). ACAB v 9 n 3 p 30
1960
GLAZEN MUREN (KAESEN), ballet
Amsterdam notes. WP v 11 n 8 p 9
Je '60
GLEASON, JACKIE, 1916-, comedian
With committee sponsoring contest
for "Best Dance Band of 1960", ens
ph: NYC. IM v 58 n 11 p 7 My '60
---With Eileen Herlie in Take Me
Along, musical, ens AP wl ph:
NYC. Th Arts v 44 n 7 p 13 Jl'60
GLENVILLE, PETER. A larger
slice of life (the history play.). il
Th Arts v 44 n 10 p 22-3 O'60
GLI ARCANGELI NON GIOCANO
AL FLIPPER, play
Milan; Dario Fo, music by Fio-
renzo Carpi. WP v 11 n 4 p 9
F '60
GLORIANA, opera
Covent Garden 1952, ens AP wl
ph: Wood. Op v 11 n 2 p 119 F'60
LES GLORIEUSES, play

(Les Glorieuses)
Paris notes;André Roussin. WP
v 12 n 1 p 5 O'60
---Roussin, ens AP wl ph:Paris.
WP v 12 n 1 p 4 O'60
GLUPIEC I INNI, play
Katowice;Jerzy Broszkiewicz.
WP v 12 n 3 p 35 D'60
GLYNDEBOURNE OPERA
Brewster, Patricia. Spring week-
end at Glyndebourne. il Op v 11
n 6 p 403-6 Je'60
---Caplat, Moran, General Mana-
ger;Vittorio Gui and Dr. Günther
Rennert;notes. Op v 11 n 4 p 305
Ap'60
---Edinburgh reviews. ON v 25 n 2
p 20 O 29'60
---In Iolanthe(review of Angel re-
cording). HF v 10 n 8 p 72 Ag'60
---Opera reviews preceded by
comments by Günther Rennert,
Head of Production;by Vittorio
Gui, Head of Music;The Editor on
the operas;William Mann on Don
Giovanni;Andrew Porter on Cen-
erentola. il Op Autumn'60
---Reviews:I Puritani;Falstaff. MC
v 162 n 2 p 22 Ag'60
--- ---I Puritani,under Bryan Balk-
will;Falstaff and Rosenkavalier.
MR v 21 n 3 p 247-50 Ag'60
---Season 1960 under Gui and Ren-
nert "both international figures
for each of whom Glyndebourne is
merely one commitment among
many";criticism of Don Giovanni
and Die Zauberflöte. MR v 21 n 4
p 326-7 N'60
---Portfolio 1960 phs: Guy Gravett.
Op v 11 Autumn '60
---Principals for I Puritani: Joan
Sutherland, Nicola Filacuridi,
Ernest Blanc and Giuseppe Modes-
ti, portrait phs. Op v 11 n 5 p 323
My '60
---Singers: Bruscantini as Ford,
GeraintEvans as Falstaff; Regina
Sarfaty as Octavian, AP phs. Op
v 11 n 8 p 542-3 Ag '60
---Sutherland, Joan, and John Ken-
tish in Bellini's "I Puritani", AP
wl ph. WM n 4 p 82 Ag '60
GLYNDEBOURE'S CHILDRENS

THEATRE
Androcles and the Lion, pro-
ducer, John Allen, décor, Joseph
Cane, ens AP wl ph: Angus Mc-
Bean. NTM v 1 n 3 Ap '60
GLOCK, WILLIAM 1908-,
New music director, BBC; innova-
tions Third Programme. WM n 1
p 10 F '60
GO BACK FOR MURDER, play
London notes; Agatha Christie.
WP v 11 n 9 p 13 Jl '60
A GOAT IN CHELM, opera
Binder, A. W. ; NYC. ON v 24
n 22 p 3 Ap 2'60
GOBBI, CLOTHILDE, 1856-1960
Obituary. ON v 25 n 8 p 32
D 31'60
GOBBI, TITO, singer
San Francisco praise. MC v 162
n 5 p 22 N '60
---As Falstaff, AP wl ph. La S
n 125 p 83 Ap '60
---E Italo Tajo in Don Goivanni,
AP hl ph: Roma. La S n 124 p 32
Mr '60
GOBEL, BODIL, singer
Machuel, Dominique. Concert
d'échange; Copenhagen's Gobel
in Paris; Finn Reiff, organist;
Per Bokelund, violinist. GDC
n 293-4 p 461 D 16'60
GOBERMAN, MAX
Founder-director of the Library
of Recorded Masterpieces; com-
plete-Vivaldi in process. HF v 10
n 1 p 59 Ja '60
---Por ph. HF v 10 n 3 p 78 Mr '60
GOEB, ROGER, composer
Première: Iowa Concerto (Iowa
1960). ACAB v 9 n 3 p 30 1960
GOING TO POT, play
Feydeau, Georges. Going to
Pot, adapted by Norman R. Sha-
piro (text). TDR v 5 n 1 p 127-
168 S '60
GOLDBERG, SYZMON, 1909-,
violinist
Notes; b. Poland; Aspen Festival,
artist-in-residence. AmM v 8
n 5 p 8 Je '60
GOLDEN, HARRY. More than
nostalgia. ON v 24 n 9 p 9
Ja 2 '60

GOLDEN FLEECING, play
NYC notes; Lorenzo Semple, Jr.
WP v 11 n 4 p 3 F '60
GOLDIN, MILTON. Commerce,
concerts and critics: the organ-
ized audience plan. MEJ v 46
n 6 p 37, 39 Je-Jl '60
GOLDMAN, RICHARD FRANKO
(1911-). A History of Western
Music by Donald Jay Grout (a
book review). J Rev v 7 n 3 p 11
Fall '60
--- ---New York; report on Lenox
String Quartet at the New School,
3 premières aided by the Fromm
Music Foundation. Mus Q v 46
n 1 p 71-6 Ja '60
--- ---The Main Stream of Music
by Donald Francis Tovey (a book
review). J Rev v 7 n 1 p 9
Winter 59-60
--- ---The Memoirs of Lorenzo
Da Ponte (a book review). J Rev
v 7 n 2 p 18 Spring '60
--- ---New York (Elliott Carter's
Second String Quartet; de Menasce).
Mus Q v 46 n 3 p 361-367 Jl '60
--- ---(On Stravinsky's recent
work, première of Double Canon;
Epitaphium; Movememts for
Piano and Orchestra (1958-59);
criticism.) Mus Q v 46 n 2
p 260-264 Ap '60
--- ---The music of Wallingford
Riegger. ACAB v 9 n 3 p 15-6
1960
GOLDOVSKY, BORIS (1908-). Tou-
ring the opera. MC v 162 n 4
p 15 O '60
--- ---and Siobhan McKenna. (An
intermission feature, Metropo-
litan Opera radio broadcast CBS;
Macbeth.) Th Arts v 44 n 3 p 38-
9 Mr '60
---Career sketch; b. Moscow.
por ON v 24 n 24 p 14-5 Ap 16'60
---Por at 17 years; at the Micro-
phone, ph: Kalisher. ON v 24
n 24 p 14-5 Ap 16'60
---Por ph. MC v 162 n 4 p 15
O '60
GOLDOVSKY OPERA THEATRE
In Rigoletto, ens AP wl ph: Boston. Th Arts v 44 n 3 p 32 Mr '60

GOLDSAND, ROBERT, 1911-,
pianist
NYC review. MC v 161 n 1 p 14
Ja '60
LA GOLETA THEATRE
Argentina; note. WT v 9 n 1 p 68
Spring '60
GOLEYZOVSKY, KASSIAN
Illoupina, Anna. Moscow, un
concert chorégraphique. TD n 96
p 9-10 S-O '60
GOLOS, GEORGE S. Some Slavic
predecessors of Chopin. Mus Q
v 46 n 4 p 437-447 O '60
GOLSCHMANN, VLADIMIR, 1893-,
conductor
Kerr, Russell. (Interview; b.
Paris.) por. MC v 161 n 3 p 15
F '60
---Por ph. HF v 10 n 2 p 64 F '60
GONCALVES, MARTIM, director
Por ph: University of Bahia,
Brazil. PlM v 37 n 3 p 57 D '60
GONZALEZ VERGEL, ALBERTO.
(On staging Chekhov; Spanish view-
point.) WT v 9 n 2 p 146 Summer'60
GOODVYE CHARLIE, play
NYC notes; George Axelrod. WP
v 11 n 6 p 5 Ap '60
--- ---NYC review. PlM v 36 n 7
p 165 Ap '60
GOODBYE TO NUMBER 6, play
Adelaide notes; Alex Symons.
WP v 11 n 9 p 2 Jl '60
GOODBYE TO THE CLOWN,
opera
Laderman, Ezra, composer;
NYC première. ACAB v 9 n 3
p 10 1960
---Neway Opera Theatre; NYC
première of Laderman's work.
Op v 11 n 8 p 545 Ag '60
GOODMAN, BENNY
With court dancers in Bankok,
wl ph: ANTA. IM v 58 n 8 p 10
F '60
GOODMAN, GERALD, harpist
NYC review. MC v 161 n 1 p 17
Ja '60
GORDON, EDGAR B. Instrumental
music in the pioneer days (US).
MEJ v 46 n 3 p 34, 37 Ja '60
GORDON, EMANUEL L. 1921-1960
Obituary. IM v 58 n 9 p 8 Mr '60

GORDON, RUTH, 1896-, actress
Por ph. Th Arts v 44 n 9 p 13
S'60
GORIN, IGOR, 1909-, singer
Melbourne notes. MD v 50 n 7
p 16 Ja'60
---In costume with Orlando Bar-
era, hl ph:El Paso. MC v 161 n 6
p 30 My'60
GORLIER, SIMON
Heartz, Daniel. Parisian music
publishing under Henry II: A pro-
pos of four recently discovered
guitar books. Mus Q v 46 n 4
p 448-467 O'60
GORTCHAKOV, NICOLAI. Vakh-
tangov (les premiers contacts
entre le maître et ses élèves).
WP v 11 n 7 p 1, 7 My'60
GOSSE de PARIS(AZNAVOUR)
Festival de Cannes;notes. TD n 93
p 5 My'60
GOTH, TRUDY. A New York:Bal-
letti Filippini;Balletti Israeliani;
Balletti Polacchi. il LaS n 123
p 42-4 F'60
--- ---20₀anno di vita "Balletto
del Teatro". il La S n 133 p 42-7
D '60
GÖTTERDÄMMERUNG, opera
Vienna; "a gigantic oratorio"
stripped down by Herbert von Kar-
ajan; review. ON v 25 n 1 p 22
O 8'60
---Vienna; impressive; Karajan
kept orchestra loud; criticism. Op
v 11 n 8 p 547 Ag '60
---Bayreuth, 1960; ens AP wl ph:
Lauterwasser. WM n 5 p 110 O'60
GOUSSEAU, LELIA, pianist
Paris review. GDC n 259-60
p 407 F 12'60
GOÛT DE MIEL, play
de Shelagh Delaney, ens ph: Ber-
nand. WP v 11 n 7 p 1 My '60
GRACE ENCORE POUR LA TERRE,
play
Liège, 1957; ens AP wl ph: Wado.
WT v 9 n 1 p 46 Spring '60
GRACIA HOSOKAWA, opera
Cimatti, Vincenzo, 1880-, compo-
ser; première May 1960 in Japan.
Op v 11 n 10 p 695 O '60

GRADENWITZ, PETER (1910-).
The religious works of Arnold
Schönberg. MR v 21 n 1 p 19-29
F '60
GRAF, HERBERT (1903-). Regard-
ing the staging of Un Ballo in Mas-
chera (suggests return to original
locale, the Swedish Court of Gus-
tave III). Ver v 1 n 1 p 109-111
Ap '60
--- ---(Restoration of Teatro Far-
nese in Palma: neglect of backstage
area in original plan likely to prove
a future disadvantage to operatic
use.) Ver v 1 n 2 preface Ag '60
GRAFFMAN, GARY, 1928-, pianist
Los Angeles debut. MC v 161 n 5
p 23 Ap '60
---Repertory; European tour. AmM
v 8 n 2 p 6 F '60
GRAHAM, MARTHA, 1900-, dancer
Capezio Award; citation. MD v 50
n 10 p 28 Ap '60
---Juilliard School notes on Capezio
Dance Award, William Schuman
presenting it. J Rev v 7 n 1 p 12
Winter 59-60
---Worland, Tommy. (Report of
Graham company in NYC.) MD
v 51 n 2 p 29 Ag '60
---As Clytemnestra with partner,
AP ph. MC v 161 n 6 p 9 My '60
---In Alcestis, AP wl ph. La S
n 128 p 64 Jl '60
GRAN TEATRO DEL MUNDO, play
Calderon, Einsiedeln, Schweiz
1955, outdoor lighting, ens AP
WL ph: W. E. Baur. WT v 9 n 2
p 155 Summer '60
GRANADA FESTIVAL
Ninth annual Festival of Music
and Dance; report by Maurice
Faulkner, MC v 162 n 1 p 33-4
Jl '60
---Ens ph. WM n 3 cover Je '60
GRANADOS, ENRIQUE 1867-1916,
composer
Langhi, Ugo Ramellini. Ricordi
di un "Prince Charmant" della
musica spagnola. il La S n 123
p 51-4 F '60
---Por ph; Goyescas, ens AP ph.
La S n 123 p 52-3 F '60
GRAND KABUKI THEATRE

Richards, Stanley. (NYC comment.)
PlM v 37 n 2 p 46 N '60
LA GRANDE DUCHESSE DE GER-
OLSTEIN, opera
Notes and ph: Paris TV. Op v 11
n 12 p 829 D '60
GRANDJANY, MARCEL, 1891-,
harpist
Review of Capitol recording. HF
v 10 n 5 p 85 My '60
GRANT PARK, CHICAGO
Summer music series. MC v 161
n 7 p 30 Je '60
GRAUN, CARL HEINRICH, 1704-
1759, composer
Wienandt, Elwyn A. Das Licht
scheinet; two settings by K. H.
Graun. MR v 21 n 2 p 85-93 My'60
GRAVEY, FERNAND (1905-). Per-
formers' rights. WT v 9 n 4
p 341-3 Winter '60
GRAY, JUSTIN. Music education
and creativity. MEJ v 46 n 4
p 58, 62 F-Mr '60
GRAZ OPERA
Repertory comment; Pique Dame.
MC v 161 n 5 p 30 Ap '60
GREAT BRITAIN
Chancellor, Paul. British bards
and continental composers. Mus Q
v 46 n 1 p 1-11 Ja '60
---Clapham, John. The progress
of Dvořák's music in Britain. MR
v 21 n 2 p 130-139 My '60
---The Council for Theatre Pre-
servation; Th Notbk v 14 n 3 p 77-78
Spring '60
---Dunn, Brian. The pattern of mu-
sical life in Britain. MD v 51 n 6
p 16-9 D '60
---Festivals. Th Arts v 44 n 5
p 18-20 My '60
---Hall, W. Glenvil, M. P. The
Labour Party and the provincial
theatre. NTM v 1 n 1 p 5-7 O '59
---London conference on "Music in
Britain, today and Tomorrow".
WM n 5 p 104 O '60
---Mackerness, E. D. Music and
moral purity in the early Victorian
era. CMJ v 4 n 2 p 14-24 Winter'60
---Moody, John. The Arts Council
and theatre finance. NTM v 1 n 1
p 21-3 O '59

---Music report. La S n 122
p 78 Ja '60
---Opera news. Op v 11 1960
---Opera notes: Sadler's Wells;
English Opera Groups; Cam-
bridge University Musical Soc-
iety. Op v 11 n 1 p 23 Ja '60
--- ---Covent Garden; Handel
Opera Society; Kentish Opera
Group; Royal Academy of Music;
Oxford University Opera Club;
Promenade Concerts; Welsh Na-
tional Opera. Op v 11 n 7 p 470-1
Jl '60
--- ---Covent Garden; Sadler's
Wells; New Opera Company; Revi-
val Opera Company; Barrow In-
timate Opera Society; Bath Opera;
Bristol Opera School; Kent Rural
Music School; Sheffield Singers'
Grand Opera Society; Opera For
All Tour. Op v 11 n 4 p 267-8
Ap '60
--- ---Covent Garden; Sadler's
Wells; Revival Opera Company;
Philopera Circle; Cherubini Bi-
centenary celebration; Chester
Opera Group. Op v 11 n 6 p 407
Je '60
---Pratt, Ross. Chopin in Britain
(1837 and in 1848). CMJ v 5 n 1
p 24-9 Autumn '60
---Russell, Sir John W. A Tory
and the provincial drama (what
the Conservative Political Centre
offers). NTM v 1 n 2 p 11-4 Ja'60
---Stacey, Roy. The amateur theatre.
PlM v 36 n 8 p 192 My '60
---Theatre report. WP v 11 n 7 p 8
My '60
---Theatre research facilities; the
British Museum; the habit of
"Grangerising". Th Notbk v 14
n 3 p 74-5 Spring '60
---Treves, Piero. Music reports.
La S 1960
---Trewin, J. C. (Theatre report.)
il WT v 9 n 1 p 90-92 Spring '60;
same. WT v 9 n 2 p 182-186
Summer '60; same. WT v 9 n 4
p 364-6 Winter '60
---University theatres; Bristol;
Southampton; functions discussed
in editorial. Th Notbk v 14 n 4

(Great Britain)
p 110-111 Summer 1̃60
---Webster, Margaret. (Observations on trend of British theatre; the "reps".) Th Arts v 44
n 11 p 23-4, 71 N '60
---Wesker, Arnold. (On the obligation of the Trade Union Congress to work for a workers' drama; with editorial discussion of
this plea.) NTM v 2 n 1 p 2-6
O '60
GREATER TRENTON SYMPHONY
Roebling, Mrs. Mary G, president, with conductor, Nicholas
Harsanyi and singer, Licia Albanese, hl ph: New Jersey. MC
v 161 n 3 p 40 F '60
GREECE
National Opera repertory. Op
v 11 n 12 p 836 D '60
---Paris review of dance group,
Panegris, under Dora Straton.
il TD n 94 p 6 Je '60
---Theatre: visitors; native theatre
and opera notes. WP v 11 n 4
p 7 F '60
--- ---report. WP v 11 n 5 p 2
Mr '60; same. WP v 11 n 8 p 8
Je '60; same. WP v 12 n 2 p 4
N '60
GREEK TRAGEDY
Brustein, Robert. The memory
of heroism (contrasting Greek
tragedy with our view of a "soc-
iological world"; praise for Latt-
imore-Grene's "The Complete
Greek Tragedies"). TDR v 4 n 3
p 3-9 Mr '60
GREEN, MARTYN, 1899-, actor
And George Brenlin in Drums
Under the Windows, AP hl ph:
Martha Swope. Th Arts v 44 n 12
p 11 D '60
THE GREEN PASTURES: play
Harrison, Richard B., as De
Lawd, with Alonzo Fenderson as
Moses, AP hl ph: NYC. Th Arts
v 44 n 9 p 12 S '60
GREENBERT, NOAH, director
Robinson, J. W. The Play of
Daniel produced by The New York
Pro Musica. Th Notbk v 15 n 1
p 33-34 Autumn '60

---Left profile por ph. and the
New York Pro Musica, ens AP wl
ph. Am M v 8 n 5 cover Je'60
GREENE, LEON, singer
And Patricia Kern in Merrie Eng-
land, AP hl ph:Angus McBean. Op
v 11 n 9 p 646 S'60
GREENICH VILLAGE, U. S. A.,
revue
Notes. Th Arts v 44 n 12 p 12 D'60
GREENWILLOW, play
NYC notes;Frank Loesser. WP
v 11 n 9 p 5 Jl'60
---Ens AP wl ph:Friedman-Abeles.
Th Arts v 44 n 5 p 59 My'60
GRESSIER, JULES, ?-1960, con-
ductor
Notes;Roubaisien d'origine. GDC
n 283 p 94 O 7'60
LA GRÈVE des AMOUREUX, com-
edy
Paris notes;Roger Feral. WP v 11
n 4 p 6 F'60
DIE griechische PASSION
Martinu;Zurich note. Op v 11 n 10
p 696 O'60
GRIEG, EDVARD, 1843-1907,
composer
Axelson, Doris Lanita. Grieg's
unfinished opera (Peer Gynt, col-
laborating with B. Björnson). ON
v 24 n 10 p 26 Ja 9'60
GRIEVE, JOHN HENDERSON, 1770-
1845, scenic designer
List of scenes painted for Sadler's
Wells circa 1814 (three illustra-
ted). Th Notbk v 15 n 2 p 61 Win-
ter '60-61
GRIFFITH, KATHERINE. The ex-
pressive silences (Peléas et Mé-
lisande). ON v 24 n 11 p 6-7 Ja
16'60
GRIMES, TAMMY, 1935?-, singer
Keating, John. Tammy Grimes.
por Th Arts v 44 n 11 p 20-2 N'60
---Por ph:Milton H. Greene. Th
Arts v 44 n 11 p 21 N'60
GRISELDA, opera
Teatro Massimo Bellini di Catan-
is. il LaS n 127 p 29 Je'60
GRISI, GIULIA, 1811-1869, singer
E Mario (Marquis, Giovanni da
Candia);89 lettere di Giuseppe
Mazzini.LaS n 125 p 27-31 Ap'60

---Moglie del tenore Mario (il marchese Giovanni de Candia) in un ritratto di Emery Walker. LaS n 125 p 29 Ap'60

GRJEBINA, IRINA, dancer
Les Ballets Ukrainiens;Paris. il TD n 98 p 22 D'60

LE GROS MALIN, play
Athens notes;Tsiforos and Vassiliadis. WP v 12 n 3 p 30 D'60

GROSZ, MIKULAS, 1915-, violinist
Born in Czechoslovakia;1952 NYC. Am M v 8 n 5 p 5 Je'60
---Chicago criticism. MC v 161 n 5 p 22 Ap'60

THE GROUP THEATRE
NYC in the 1930's, several ens AP wl phs. Th Arts v 44 n 9 p 16 S'60

GROUPE de MUSIQUE ALGORITH-MIQUE de PARIS
Demarquez, Suzanne. Promoteurs: Pierre Barbaud, Roger Blanchard, Jeanine Charbonnier (reports of research). GDC n 283 p 100 O 7'60

GRUENWALD, J. J. Psaume 129 pour Choeurs, Orchestre et Orque (1958); Paris critique, Trajan Popesco 1960. GDC n 281-2 p 26 S 30'60

GRUMIAUX, ARTHUR, violinist
Et Orchestre National, H. Schmidt-Isserstedt, directeur; review. GDC n 261-2 p 443 F 26'60 .

GRÜMMER, ELISABETH, singer
Career sketch. por HF v 10 n 7 p 20 Jl '60
---Worthington, Randall: Cologne; interview. por HF v 10 n 7 p 20 Jl '60

GRUNFIELD, FRED. The great American opera (Porgy and Bess). il ON v 24 n 20 p 6-9 Mr 19'60

GRUNOR-HEGGE, ODD, director
Norwegian National Opera; Flagstad retiring. Op v 11 n 11 p 769 N '60

GUADAGNINO, LUIGI. Teatre Raveliano. il La S n 126 p 24-28 My'60

GUADAGNO, ANTON, director
Seattle; New York Opera Festival. MC v 161 n 3 p 39 F '60

IL GUARANY, opera
R io de Janiero notes. Op v 11 n 7 p 476 Jl '60

GUARD, BILLY, public relations man
Hl ph: Metropolitan. ON v 24 n 21 p 6 Mr 26'60

GUARNIERI, CAMARGO (1907-). Deuxième Sonate, 1955 (études musicales analytiques). GDC n 257-8 p 346 Ja 29'60
---Jourdan-Morhange, H. Corréa de Avezedo; singer, Kleusa de Pannafort. GDC n 269-70 p 595 Ap 22'60

GUARRERA, FRANK: 1923?-, singer
Critical report of interview in which the singer tells how he prepares an opera role. ON v 25 n 7 p 14-5 D 24'60
---As Escamillo, AP hl ph: Leblang, ON v 24 n 14 p 17 F 6'60
---As Macbeth, AP hl ph: B oeh. ON v 25 n 1 p 25 O 8'60
---As Simon Boccanegra AP phs: Melançon, ON v 24 n 22 Ap 2'60
--- ---AP hl ph: Harry C. Schumer. ON v 25 n 7 p 15 D 24'60

GUERRERO, ABERTO, 1886-1959
Beckwith, John. (In memoriam.) CMJ v 4 n 2 p 33-5 Winter '60

GUEST, IVOR (1920-) French ballet (report). MD v 51 n 2 p 26 Ag '60
--- ---Le Baiser de la Fée (Macmillan); review of Covent Garden première. il MD v 50 n 11 p 27 My '60
--- ---Letter from London, a series. MD 1960
--- ---Maurice Bejart's company at Sadler's Wells Theatre. MD v 50 n 12 p 28 Je '60
--- ---Petit's Cyrano de Bergerac MD v 50 n 7 p 30 Ja '60
--- ---Zizi Jeanmaire, London's Royalty Theatre notes. MD v 51 n 6 p 29 D '60
---Por drawing. MD v 50 n 7 p 30 Ja '60

GUI, VITTORIO (1885-). Glyndebourne. Op v 11 p 7-10 Autumn'60
---Glyndebourne, ens AP ph: Guy Gravett. Op v 11 p 9 Autumn '60

LE GUIDE DU CONCERT FÊTE
Colloque du 28 avril 1960: de célébrer le cinquantième

(Le Guide)
anniversaire du "Guide du Concert:" séance du matin; séance
de l'apprèsmidi. GDC n 279-80
p 865-877 Jl 1'60
---Silvant, Jean. Son cinquantenaire. TD n 94 p 12 Je '60
GUILIANO, JUAN
Et Hélène Traïline, dans Combat (de Banfield), AP wl ph. TD
n 92 p 10 Ap '60
GUIMARD, MADELEINE, 1743-
1816, dancer
Boquet, Pierre-Jean. Mlle. Gui-
mard, dessin. OpP n 19 cover
1960
GUISE, J. M.
Et Adolfo Mindlin; Paris review
by Castil. GDC n 261-2 p 441
F 26'60
GUITAR
Chemla, Teddy. Nouvelles de la
guitare: Georges Auric, Jean
Rivier, Jean Jacques Grunen-
wald, Alexandre Tansman (com-
mentaire). GDC n 285 p 170
O 21'60
--- ---II l'écriture pour guitare.
GDC n 286 p 202 O 28'60
--- ---II. ses possibilités et ses
limites. GDC n 287 p 235 N 4'60
--- ---III. Tonalités lui convenant
le mieux. GDC n 289 p 294
N 18'60
--- ---IV. Les harmoniques. GDC
n 293-4 p 470 D 16'60
---Classical guitar on college
level; Washington University
course. IM v 58 n 9 p 43 Mr '60
---First International Guitar Festival; 500 from 23 countries to
Greenwood Lake, New York. MC
v 162 n 2 p 7 Ag '60
---Heartz, Daniel. Parisian music publishing under Henry II: A
propos of four recently discovered guitar books. il Mus Q v 46
n 4 p 448-467 O '60
---How to compose for the guitar
without being a guitarist; details
of a contest (1) interprétation (2)
composition; Paris rules given
and address. GDC n 285 p 171-2
O 21'60

---Paris; I. Presti and A. Lagoya,
review. GDC n 261-2 p 441
F 26'60
---Title pages of four recently dis-
covered books of guitar pieces by
Guillame Morlaye, Paris, Michel
Fezandat, printer; lady playing a
four-course guitar, 16th century
engraving; the Paduane Chant
d'Orlande; facsimiles. Mus Q
v 46 n 4 p 450-3 O '60
GULBENKIAN FOUNDATION
Portugaliae Musica; mid-16th cent-
ury to mid-nineteenth coverage of
publication; notes. WM n 1 p 10
F '60
GUSTAVE III, KING OF SWEDEN
His murder as basis for theatre
pieces; Scribe; Verdi. Ver n 1
n 1 p 398-9 Ap '60
GUTHRIE, TYRONE, 1900-, actor
Edinburgh Festival, his creation
of a theatre from a church hall;
similar structure in Stratford's
Festival Theatre, Ontario (pic-
tured). NTM v 1 n 4 p 16-7 Jl'60
---Directing, ph. Th Arts v 44 n 7
p 52 Jl '60
GUTTOVEGGIO, JOSEPH
See Barber, Samuel
GYPSIES
Hungarian State Gypsy Orchestra,
Notes. IM v 58 n 7 p 11 Ja '60
GYPSY BARON, operetta
Metropolitan notes. ON v 24 n 9
p 3 Ja 2'60
  Ens AP wl ph: Melançon. ON
v 24 n 9 p 2 Ja 2'60
---Metropolitan, Act 3 ens AP wl
ph: Melançon. Op v 2 n 3 p 199
Mr '60
GYRING, ELIZABETH, composer
Premières: Two Pieces for Piano;
Adagio for Clarinet and String
Quartet (NYC 1960); Fantasy No. 4
(NYC 1960). ACAB v 9 n 3 p 30
1960

H

HAAHUONE, play
Helsinki notes; Lauri Kokkonen.
WP v 12 n 3 p 29 D '60
HÁBA, ALOIS, 1893-, composer

His position among Czech composers. Mus Q v 46 n 4 p 514 O '60

HABIMAH THEATRE
Israel report. WP v 12 n 3 p 4 D '60

HACKENBERG, KURT. Some notes on organization (in German theatre). WT v 9 n 3 p 199-202 Autumn '60

HAEBLER, INGRID, pianist
Clarion Concerts; NYC review. MC v 161 n 1 p 16 Ja '60
---Paris debut of Austrian; notes. GDC n 295 p 487 D 30'60

HAEFLIGER, ERNEST
Machuel, Dominique. Paris concert, Haefliger and Jacqueline Bonneau. GDC n 276 p 787 Je 10 '60
---Por ph. MC v 161 n 4 p 16 Mr '60

HAENSEL, CARL (1899-). Copyright in opera and drama (Germany). WT v 9 n 3 p 245-8 Autumn '60

HAENSEL, PETER. The special role of the publisher (in German theatre). WT v 9 n 3 p 239-244 Autumn '60

HAGER, PAUL, director
Vienna productions of opera; "the reverse principle to that of Bayreuth". ON v 24 n 19 p 26 Mr 12'60

HAINAUX, RENÉ. Editorial (on Chekhov; interpretation of roles in 50 years; the new trends in scenic design as applied to Chekhov plays). WT v 9 n 2 p 99 Summer ' 60
--- ---(Editorial on relation of theatre and television.) WT v 9 n 4 p 299 Winter '60
--- ---Editorial to introduce issue, featuring present German theatres. WT v 9 n 3 p 195 Autumn '60

HAIRS, M. L. Aux origines du tableau de fleurs Flamand; 24e Exposition Internationale quinquennale de Fleurs ,"Floralies Gantoises". WP v 11 n 6 p 8 Ap '60

HAITI

Danse Petro, ens AP wl ph. WP v 11 n 7 My '60
---Invocation of the Gods in the Haitian Voodoo cult, ens AP wl ph: Pic. WT v 9 n 4 p 351 Winter'60

HAITINK, BERNARD, 1930-, conductor
Concertgebouw Orchestra; with Eugen Jochum. MC v 161 n 5 p 33 Ap '60
---Por ph: Amsterdam. HF v 10 n 7 p 56 Jl '60

HALASZ ,KALMAN, 1919-, composer
Notes. Mus Q v 46 n 4 p 531 O'60

HALE, UNA
As Antonia, AP hl ph: Houston Rogers. Op v 2 n 3 p 232 Mr '60

HALLÉ SOCIETY
(Boulton, John.) Critical report of the season; list of conductors, of soloists. MR v 21 n 3 p 244-6 Ag '60

HAMBLETON, T. EDWARD (1911-). The Phoenix Theatre, NYC (interview on its seven seasons). il Th Arts v 44 n 1 p 72-3 Ja '60
---With Stuart Vaughan, hl ph: NYC. Th Arts v 44 n 1 p 70 Ja'60

HAMBLY, GAVIN. Opera in 19th century life and literature. Op v 11 n 11 p 738-741 N '60

HAMBURG OPERA
Nölter, Wolfgang. (Criticism; repertory.) Op v 2 n 3 p 207-8 Mr '60

HAMILTON, CHICO, drummer
Behind his drums, AP ph. IM v 58 n 12 p 17 Je '60

HAMILTON, DAVID, dancer-choreographer
Modern dance teacher in California. por MD v 51 n 3 p 27 S '60

HAMLET, play
Byrne, M. St. Clare. The earliest Hamlet prompt book in an English library. facsimiles Th Notbk v 15 n 1 p 21-31 Autumn '60
---Freud, Sigmund. Psychopathic characters on the stage; trans. Henry Alden Bunker. TDR v 4 n 3 p 144-8 Mr '60
---Sweden; Alf Sjoberg production; review. WP v 11 n 9 p 8 Jl '60
---Cooke, George Frederick.

(Hamlet)
(Chester, 1785, his prompt
book: 5 facsimiles with hand-
written comments). Th Notbk
v 15 n 1 Autumn '60
---Ens AP ph: Dubrovnik 1959.
WP v 11 n 3 p 7 Ja '60
---Prague, 1959; ens AP wl ph:
Svoboda. WT v 9 n 1 p 73 Spring
'60
---Toyoko Hall, the Bungakuza
Troupe, ens AP wl ph. Th R v 2
n 2 p 65 1960
HAMLET, opera
Stein, Elliott. Lille review of
Thomas' Hamlet. Op v 11 n 9
p 618 S '60
HAMMERSTEIN, OSCAR, II
(1895-1960). The book had better
be good. Th Arts v 44 n 11 p 18-
9, 70 N '60
---Harry, S. J. The partnership
of Rodgers and Hammerstein.
AmM v 8 n 3 p 14 Mr '60
---Obituary. MC v 162 n 3 p 9
S '60
---Por ph: Charles Thill. Th Arts
v 44 n 11 p 18 N '60
HAMMOND, PAUL, dancer
Por ph. MD v 50 n 10 p 28 Ap'60
HANDEL FESTIVAL
Halle; Otto and Theophano; Ime-
neo; reviews. Op v 11 n 7 p 480-
1 Jl '60
HANDEL OPERA SOCIETY
Reviews; Hercules; Radamisto.
il Op v 11 n 9 p 641-4 S '60
A HAND OF BRIDGE opera
Mannes College; Samuel Barber
score; notes. MC v 161 n 6 p 16
My '60
HANDEL, GEORGE FREDERIC,
1685-1759, composer
Books reviewed; Winton Dean's
Handel's dramatic Oratorios and
Masques; Flower's biography;
and other works on the composer
or by him. MR v 21 n 2 p 159-
162 My '60
---La Rue, Jan. Handle's Clarinet.
MR v 21 n 3 p 177-8 Ag '60
HANEY, CAROL, 1924?-, actress
With Warren Beatty in A Loss of
Roses, AP wl ph: Friedman-

Abeles. Th Arts v 44 n 2 p 13
F '60
HANSBERRY, LORRAINE (1930-).
A raisen in the sun (text of play,
NYC cast, portfolio). Th Arts
v 44 n 10 p 27-58 O '60
--- ---(On the Negro in American
theatre.) Th Arts v 44 n 10 p 9-
11, 69 O '60
HANSBERRY, RICHARD, trombonist
Career notes. por IM v 58 n 8 p 31
F '60
HANSEL AND GRETEL, opera
Cook, Daniel. Christmas at La
Scala. il ON v 24 n 14 p 26 F 6'60
---La Scala notes. il La S n 122
p 36 Ja '60
---La Scala, Cossotto and Scotto,
AP wl ph: Piccagliani. Op v 2
n 3 p 211 Mr '60
HANSON, HOWARD (1896-, Cultiva-
ting a climate for creativity. MEJ
v 46 n 6 p 28-30 Je-Jl '60
---Award: Huntington Hartford
Foundation Award; notes. J Rev
v 7 n 2 p 20 Spring '60
---Festival of American Music at
the Eastman School; his views;
review. MC v 161 n 7 p 6 Je'60
---Riker, Charles C. Howard Han-
son, outdoor man. por MC v 161
n 4 p 9 Mr '60
---Two hl phs. MC v 161 n 4
cover, p 9 Mr '60
HAPSBURG DOUBLE EAGLE
Drawing. ON v 24 n 20 cover
Mr 19'60
HARASIEWICZ, ADAM, pianist
Mexico; criticism. MC v 161
n 5 p 32 Ap '60
HARBISON, JANCIE, pianist
Chicago criticism. MC v 161 n 6
p 28 My '60
HARMONICA
Schackner, Alan. Chromatic
harmonica, a new orchestral
color. il IM v 58 n 19 p 12-3, 29
Ap '60
HARMONY
Hentoff, Nat. New directions in
jazz. IM v 59 n 3 p 14-5 S '60
---Sessions, Roger. Problems
and issues facing the composer
today. Mus Q v 46 n 2 p 159-171

Ap '60

HARP COLONY OF AMERICA
Salzedo, Carlos, and harpists,
ens ph: Camden, Maine. MC
v 162 n 3 p 29 S '60

HARPISTS
Geliot-Domange, Huguette; Paris
concert. GDC n 267-8 p 557
Ap 8'60
---Grandjany, Marcel; notes.
J Rev v 7 n 2 p 13 Spring '60

HARPSICHORD
Paris; à la mémorie de Wanda
Landowska: Aimée Van de Wiele,
Rampal et Morelli. GDC n 293-4
p 462 D 16'60

HARRELL, LYNN, 1944-, cellist
Merriweather Post Winner. MC
v 161 n 7 p 30 Je '60

HARRELL, MACK, 1910-1960,
singer
Kagen, Sergius. Mack Harrell
(obituary). por J Rev v 7 n 2 p 15
Spring '60
---Obituary b. Texas. MC v 161
n 3 p 20 F '60

HARRIS, ROY, 1898-, composer
Notes; director of 2nd String
Congress, Puerto Rico. IM v 58
n 9 p 37 Mr '60
---Close-up ph. MEJ v 47 n 1 p 77
S-O '60

HARRISON, LOU, composer
Yates, Peter. Lou Harrison (with
checklist of compositions). ACAB
v 9 n 2 p 2-7 1960

HARRISON, WALLACE K. Steps
to the opera house ("it should
have both dignity and gaiety" says
the chief architect of the new Metropolitan). il ON v 25 n 2 p 15-7
O 29'60

HARRY, HUBERT, pianist
Oleg, Alexandre. Paris criticism.
GDC n 288 p 257 N 11'60

HARRY, S. J. The partnership of
Rodgers and Hammerstein. AmM
v 8 n 3 p 14 Mr '60

HARSANYI, TIBOR, 1898-1954,
composer
Career notes Divertimento in
Paris program 1960. GDC n 281-
2 p 46 S 30'60

HARSHAW, MARGARET, 1912?-,
singer
Career notes; b. Philadelphia.
AmM v 8 n 8 p 3 S '60
---As Kundry, AP ph; LeBlang.
ON v 24 n 23 p 17 Ap 9'60
---Por ph. AmM v 8 n 8 cover
S '60

HART, MOSS, 1904-, playwright
Por ph. Th Arts v 44 n 7 p 2
Jl '60

HART, PHILIP. Ernest Bloch, a
memoir. por HF v 10 n 5 p 45-7
My '60

HARTH, SIDNEY
Career notes teacher at 2nd
String Congress, Puerto Rico.
IM v 58 n 9 p 37 Mr '60

HARTMANN, KARL AMADEUS,
1905-, composer
Por; painting. La S n 127 p 8
Je '60

HARTMANN, RUDOLF, 1900-,
director
Munich interview; b. Ingolstadt.
por ON v 24 n 21 p 14 Mr 26
'60
---Directing a rehearsal at Bay-
erische Staatsoper, ens ph. Op
v 11 n 12 p 841 D '60

HARTNOLL, PHYLLIS. Theatre
arts bookshelf (reviews including
Dr. Richard Southern's Change-
able Scenry and Bertram Joseph's
The Tragic Actor). Th Arts v 44 n 1
p 87-8 Ja '60

HARTSHORN, WILLIAM C. Music
for the academically talented. MEJ
v 47 n 1 p 33-6, 54 S-O '60

HARY JÁNOS, opera
Juilliard review. il ON v 24 n 24
p 26 Ap 16'60
---US première; review of Juilliard
staff. MC v 161 n 5 p 14 Ap '60
---Juilliard Opera Theater, 6 ens
AP wl phs: Impact. J Rev v 7 n 2
cover, p 26-7 Spring '60

HASKIL, CLARA, 1895-, pianist
Chamfray, Claude. (Review with
career notes.) por GDC n 295
p 499 D 30'60
---Et Arthur Grumiaux, review by
Pierrette Mari. GDC n 293-4
p 461 D 16'60
---Left profile por ph. GDC n 295

(Haskil)
cover D 30'60
HASQUENOPH, PIERRE. Huit
inventions pour piano (études
musicales analytiques). GDC
n 269-70 p 600 Ap 22'60
HASTINGS, BAIRD, director
Mozart Festival Orchestra, Boston; note. ON v 25 n 8 p 7 D 31'60
HAUBENSTOCK-RAMATI, ROMAN,
composer
Notes and facsimile"Decisions".
La S n 127 p 11 Je '60
---Première: Petite Musique de
Nuit (1958); Donaueschingen,
1959. MR v 21 n 1 p 80 F '60
HAUBIEL, CHARLES, 1892-
composer
Symphonic saga, "Pioneers";
Los Angeles notes. MC v 161 n 6
p 43 My '60
HAUGER, GEORGE. When is a
play not a play? (on ballet, opera
and theatre mixtures). TDR v 5
n 2 p 54-64 D '60
HAULOT, ARTHUR (1913-). The-
atre in the streets (Walloon region
of Belgium, processions, etc.).
WT v 9 n 1 p 62-67 Spring '60
HAUT-PEROU, play
Argentina; Andrés Lizarraga.
WP v 12 n 2 p 18 N '60
HAVANA
Csonka, Paul, conductor, Erik
Santemaria, stage director and
singers, Ana Menendez and Maria
Teresa Carrillo, ens hl ph. Op
v 11 n 8 p 550 Ag '60
HAVET OG MENNESKENE, play
Denmark notes; Kaj Munk. WP
v 11 n 6 p 2 Ap '60
HAVUKKA-AHON AJATTELIJA,
play
Helsinki notes; Veikko Huovinen.
WP v 11 n 4 p 4 F '60
HAYDN, FRANZ JOSEPH (1737-
1809). Symphonie dite "Des Jou-
ets"(analyse par Pierrette Mari).
GDC n 292 p 431-2 D 9'60
---Eyer, Ronald. To the manner
born (a study of Haydn in the field
of opera). por ON v 24 n 12 p 10-
1 Ja 23'60
---Goberman, Max, in Vienna

recording Haydn symphonies ex-
actly as written; also Vivaldi; re-
port by Kurt Blaukopf. HF v 10
n 12 p 14, 16 D '60
---Marsh, Robert. Haydn's Salo-
mon symphonies, Beecham and
the Royal Ph7lharmonic. por HF
v 10 n 5 p 60 My '60
---New editions discussed: Lo
Speziale, edited by Helmut Wirth;
Kanons, edited by Otto Erich Deu-
tsch; Il Mondo della luna. MR v 21
n 2 p 164-5 My '60
---Randall, J. K. Haydn: string
Quartet in D major, op. 76, no. 5
MR v 21 n 2 p 94-105 My '60
---Il Viandante. Eisenstadt Oggi.
il LaS n 133 p 77 D '60
HAYS, LEE, 1914-, folk singer
Notes on the Weavers. por HF
v 10 n 12 p 49 D '60
HE WHO KEEPS HIS WORD, play
Gomas, Dias, author; ens ph:
São Paolo. WP v 12 n 3 D '60
HEARTBREAK HOUSE, play
NYC review; cast. PlM v 36 n 4
p 86 Ja '60
HEARTZ, DANIEL. Parisian music
publishing under Henry II: A Pro-
pos of four recently discovered
guitar books. il Mus Q v 46 n 4
p 448-467 O '60
HEATER, CLAUDE, singer
Notes. por ON v 25 n 6 p 5
D 17'60
---Notes; b. California. MC v 162
n 6 p 28 D '60
HEER RANJAH, play
New Delhi 1959, ens AP wl ph:
Fine Arts Theatre. WT v 9 n 2
p 166 Summer '60
HEIDSIECK, ERIC, pianist
Paris notes. GDC n 295 p 487
D 30'60
---With Orchestre de la Société
des Concerts du Conservatoire,
dir. André Vandernoot; Paris re-
view. GDC n 278 p 849 Je 24'60
HEIFETZ, JASCHA, 1901-, violinist
Concert at UN Assembly Hall, NYC;
notes. MC v 161 n 1 p 5 Ja '60
---Goldsmith, Harris. Heifetz plays
Sibelius' Concerto (record review
of Heifetz-Hendl compared to

Spivakovsky-Hannikainen, Everest and Ricci). HF v 10 n 10 p 70 O'60
---Small ph. HF v 10 n 10 p 70 O'60
HEILER, INGRID, harpsichordist
Paris review. GDC n 288 p 259 N 11'60
HEINE, HEINRICH, 1797-1856, critic
Nymphenberger Verlag de Munich:"Ciel, Enfer et Tricot"(le poète Heine et le ballet). TD n 93 p 16 My'60
HEINRICH, JULIA, 1880?-1919, singer
Career sketch;German-American soprano. Op v 11 n 10 p 699 O'60
HEINRICH VIII und seine FRAUEN, play
Ens AP wl ph:Kiehl, Berlin, 1958. WT v 9 n 3 p 210 Autumn'60
HEINRICH SCHÜTZ FESTIVAL
Thirteenth;Stuttgart notes. WM n 3 Je'60
---See also Stuttgart
HEINZE, SIR BERNARD(1894-). Report on Canada's musical development. por MD v 51 n 3 p 8-9 S'60
---Director of New South Wales Conservatorium of Music;Canada note. MD v 50 n 10 p 20 Ap'60
HELEN OF TROY, opera
Boston;review by William Allin Storrer of "an almost total artistic failure". Op v 11 n 10 p 683 O'60
HELFFER, CLAUDE, pianist
Paris review. GDC n 261-2 p 442 F 26'60
HELLO OUT THERE, play
Mechelen, 1958;setting by Francis Purnelle, ph:Cluytens, 1958. WT v 9 n 1 p 54 Spring'60
HELLO OUT THERE, opera
Première note;NYC 1953. Op v 11 n 11 p 786 N'60
---Ens AP wl ph:A. D. Hewitt. Op v 11 n 9 p 615 S'60
HELM, EVERETT(1913-). Jugoslavia (an account of a musical journey). Mus Q v 46 n 1 p 88-94 Ja'60

--- ---Letter on America. MR v 21 n 3 p 240-1 Ag'60
--- ---The dwindling racket (avant garde in music). HF v 10 n 8 p 43-4 Ag'60
--- ---The performer(a full report of the Congress of the International Music Council of UNESCO, Paris 1960). WM n 6 p 123-5 D'60
HÉLOISE, play
Review. PlM v 36 n 8 p 193 My'60
HENDERSON, CEDRIC "SKITCH", conductor
Por ph. Am M v 8 n 2 p 9 F'60
---Small ph. MC v 161 n 6 p 36 My'60
HENDERSON, V. L. Acoustic considerations at the O'Keefe Centre (Toronto). drawings CMJ v 4 n 4 p 25-32 Summer'60
HENDL, WALTER, 1917-, conductor
Kerr, Russell. (Career sketch.) MC v 162 n 2 p 6 Ag'60
---Informal hl ph:D. S. Druzinsky. MC v 161 n 7 cover Je'60
HENRY, ROBERT, pianist
London notes;b. Soochow, China. Am M v 8 n 9 p 10 O'60
HENRY IV
Part II at the Phoenix Theatre, NYC notes. Th Arts v 44 n 6 p 59 Je'60
HENRY V, play
Central Park, NYC; ens AP wl ph: G. E. Joseph, 1960. WT v 9 n 3 p 294 Autumn'60
HENTOFF, NAT. The expansion of jazz playing opportunities. IM v 58 n 12 p 12-3 Je'60
--- ---New directions in jazz. il IM v 59 n 3 p 14-5 S'60
HENZE, HANS WERNER, 1926-
Criticism. WT v 9 n 3 p 224 Autumn'60
---Criticism on operas. Op v 11 n 8 p 553, 556 Ag'60
---Première:"Antifone per il Festival de Salisburgo" under Herbert von Karajan. WM n 3 p 57 Je'60
---Right profile por ph. LaS n 127 p 10 Je'60
HEPBURN, KATHERINE, actress
Por ph:Friedman-Abeles. Th Arts v 44 n 6 cover Je'60
HERACLES, play
Ristic, Dusan. Set used in Narodno

135

(Heracles)
Pozoriste, Beograd, 1959, color
ph. WT v 9 n 4 cover Winter'60
HERCULES, opera
Handel Opera Society, ens AP
wl ph:Vaughan Jones. Op v 11 n 9
p 642 S'60
HERIOT, ANGUS. Emile Zola as
librettist. il Op v 11 n 9 p 595-99
S'60
HERMANTIER, RAYMOND
With Muriel Chaney in A chacun
selon sa Faim, AP hl ph:1950. WT
v 9 n 1 p 16 Spring'60
HÉRODIADE, opera
Historical notes on Massenet's
opera. ON v 25 n 4 p 11 D 3'60
HEROS et son MIROIR(SPAREM-
BLEK), ballet
Enghien notes;music, Kelemen. WP
v 12 n 1 p 3 O'60
HERRMANN, BERNARD(1911-). Com-
posing for the screen. Am M v 8 n 4
p 12 Ap'60
---Career sketch;b. NYC. Am M v 8
n 1 p 15-6 Ja'60
---Por ph. Am M v 8 n 1 p 15 Ja'60
HERZER, CLIFFORD, pianist
Notes;b. Albion, Michigan. Am M
v 8 n 9 p 7 O'60
HESS, MYRA, 1890-, pianist
Boston criticism. MC v 161 n 6
p 30 My'60
---Chicago criticism. MC v 161
n 5 p 21 Ap'60
---NYC review. MC v 161 n 4 p 17
Mr'60

L'HEURE ESPAGNOLE
Ravel's intention; comic opera
1907. por La S n 126 p 24-6
My '60
---Paris Opéra: Spectacle Ravel,
ens AP ph. OpP n 19 p 42 1960
L'HEUREUX STRATAGEME, play
Lyon, Raymond. Au T. N. P.
Chaillot; Marivaux. GDC n 257-8
p 366 Ja 29'60
---de Marivaux, ens AP wl ph:
Bernand. WP v 11 n 6 p 7 Ap'60
---Théâtre National Populaire,
1960, ens AP wl ph. WT v 9 n 2
p 160 Summer '60
HIDAKA, SUMIKO, singer
Tokyo; her Gilda. ON v 24 n 16

p 30 F 20'60
HIDALGO, JUAN, 1927-, composer
Barcelona; "Musica abierta"
group modeled after the Domaine
Musical, Paris. WM n 4 p 76
Ag '60
THE HIGHEST TREE, play
NYC notes; Dore Schary. WP v 11
n 4 p 4 F '60
HIGHFILL, PHILIP H. Actors'
wills. Th Notbk v 15 n 1 p 7-15
Autumn '60
HIGHTOWER, ROSELLA, 1920-,
ballerina
In La Belle au Bois Dormant, In-
ternational Ballet, ens AP wl ph:
Lido. TD n 98 p 11 D '60
HILL, ALFRED, 1871-1960,
composer
Obituary of "New Zealand" com-
poser; b. Melbourne. MD v 51
n 5 p 8 N '60
HILL, EDWARD BURLINGAME
1872-1960, composer
Career notes; b. Cambridge, Mass.
GDC n 284 p 122 O 14'60
---Obituary; b. Cambridge, Mass.
MC v 162 n 2 p 7 Ag '60
HILL, LUCIENNE. Translated
from the French. Th Arts v 44
n 2 p 69 F '60
HILL, MARTHA. The Art of Mak-
ing Dances by Doris Humphrey
(a book review). J Rev v 7 n 1
p 9 Winter 59-60
HILL, WEST T., JR. Famous
American theatres, series; Mac-
auley's Theatre in Louisville. il
Th Arts v 44 n 2 p 92-5 F '60
HINDEMITH, PAUL, 1895-,
composer
Criticism. WT v 9 n 3 p 217-8
Autumn '60
---Criticism; guest conductor,
Philharmonic, NYC. MC v 161
n 5 p 15 Ap '60
---Landau, Victor. Paul Hindemith,
a case study in theory and practice.
MR v 21 n 1 p 38-54 F '60
HINES, JEROME, 1921-, singer
As Banquo, AP hl ph: Melançon.
ON v 24 n 9 p 17 Ja 2'60
---As Gurnemanz in Parsifal AP
ph: Melançon. ON v 24 n 23 p 17

Ap 9'60
---As King Mark, AP hl ph: Melançon. ON v 24 n 10 p 17 Ja 9'60
---As Padre Guardiano AP ph: LeBlang. ON v 24 n 19 p 17 Mr 12'60
---As Wotan, AP phs: Melançon. ON v 24 n 16 F 20'60
---As the Landgrave in Tannhäuser, AP hl ph: LeBlang. ON v 25 n 6 p 21 D 17'60
HINGLE, PAT
In scenes from "J. B. " several AP phs: NYC. Th Arts v 44 n 2 F '60
HINTLESHAM FESTIVAL
Dunlop, Lionel. Così fan tutte. il Op v 11 p 68 Autumn '60
HIRSCHFELD, AL. Brooks Atkinson, caricature. Th Arts v 44 n 4 cover Ap '60
UNE HISTOIRE de BRIGANDS, comedy
Paris notes: Jacques Deval. WP v 11 n 4 p 5 F '60
HITCHINS, AUBREY. Teaching in Cuba, Santiago's Ballet School of Pro-Arte de Oriente. MD v 51 n 2 p 27-8 Ag '60
HITCHMAN, PERCY J. The Fairy Queen at Nottingham (including 3 AP wl phs: University of Nottingham). Th Notbk v 14 n 3 p 92-99 Spring '60
HOEBECKE, JEAN-MARIE, composer
Première: Divertissement sur un thème russe (pour quintette à vent); Gaveau. GDC n 285 p 165 O 21'60
HOFFMAN, GRACE, singer
Notes. AmM v 8 n 4 p 8 Ap '60
HOFFMAN, JERRY, 1934-impresario
NYC notes. MC v 161 n 3 p 48 F'60
HOFFMANN, William J., JR. The holyday tradition (Parsifal on Good Friday). ON v 24 n 23 p 6 Ap 9'60
HOFMANNSTHAL, HUGO VON (1874-1929). Eugene O'Neill; trans. Barrett H. Clark. TDR v 5 n 1 p 169 S '60
---Nagler, A. M. Hugo von Hofmannsthal and theatre. Th R v 2 n 1 p 5-15 1960
---Schwarz, Alfred. The allegorical theatre of Hugo von Hofmann-

sthal. TDR v 4 n 3 p 65-76 Mr '60
HOING, CLIFFORD, violin maker
High Wycombe, England; notes. MD v 50 n 11 p 15 My '60
HOLBROOK, HAL, actor
In Mark Twain Tonight, AP wl ph: 1959. WT v 9 n 1 p 94 Spring '60
HOLIDAY ON ICE, ice show
Review. il TD n 97 p 26-7 N '60
HOLLAND
Noske-Friedlaender, Leny. (Music report.) MC v 161 n 7 p 18 Je '60
---Riemens, Leo. Opera at the Holland Festival. il Op v 11 p 25-8 Autumn '60
--- ---Opera report. Op v 11 n 7 p 486-7 Jl '60
--- ---Opera reports: Amsterdam; Enschede. Op v 11 n 1 p 41-2 Ja '60
---Reviews. MC v 162 n 3 p 23-4 S '60
---The Stichting Gaudeamus of Bilthoven; notes. WM n 4 p 78 Ag '60
HOLLOWAY, SISTER MARCELLA M. Playwriting can be fun. PlM v 36 n 5 p 102 F '60
HOLLOWAY, STANLEY, actor
AP hl ph. Th Arts v 44 n 10 p 24 O '60
HOLLYWOOD BOWL
Wolf, Arthur. Varied season. MC v 162 n 1 p 25 Jl '60
HOLST, GUSTAV THEODORE, 1874-1934, composer
Letters between Holst and Vaughan Williams (book review). MR v 21 n 2 p 154-5 My '60
THE HOLY DEVIL, opera
Nabokov work for the Louisville Philharmonic Society, 1958; one act less than version called Rasputin's End. ON v 24 n 19 p 32 M 12'60
L'HOMME A L'OMBRELLE BLANCHE
Paris notes; Charles Charras, music, Louis Bessieres. WP v 11 n 10 p 4 Ag '60

137

L'HOMME CLANDESTIN, play
Paris notes; Anna Langfus. WP
v 11 n 5 p 8 Mr '60
LES HOMMES, play
Vialar; Georges Pitoëff, ens AP
wl ph: 1931. Spec n 1 p 33 1960
HONEGGER, ARTHUR (1892-1955).
Amphion (études musicales analytiques). GDC n 288 p 266
N 11'60
--- ---Cantate de Noël (études
musicales analytiques). GDC
n 288 p 268 N 11'60
--- ---Horace victorieux (études
musicales analytiques). GDC
n 271 p 631 My 5'60
--- ---Judith (études musicales
analytiques). GDC n 257-8 p 364
Ja 29'60
--- ---Le Symphonie (études mu-
sicales analytiques). GDC n 288
p 267 N 11'60
--- ---Pacific 231; J. Rollin's
commentaires pour 48e leçon,
serie. GDC n 290 inset N 25'60
--- ---Sonate pour alto et piano:
analyse par Pierrette Mari. GDC
n 275 p 761-2 Je 3'60
---Rostand, Claude. King David
at the Paris Opéra (resumé in
English of the history of the work).
OpP n 19 p 76 1960
---Por ph: Lipnitzki. GDC n 293-4
cover D 16'60
HONIG, EDWIN, trans. The Cave
of Salamanca by Miguel de Cer-
vantes Saavedra. Chrys v 13
Nos. 1-4 1960
L'HONNEUR EST EN CAUSE, play
Athens notes; Nicos Katiforis.
WP v 12 n 3 p 30 D '60
HOOVER, KATHLEEN O'DONNELL.
Pergolesi: a brief life, 1710-1736.
por ON v 24 n 12 p 9 Ja 23'60
---Her work toward an opera mus-
eum for the Metropolitan. il ON
v 24 n 19 p 14-5 Mr 12'60
HOPF, HANS, singer
As Tannhäuser, AP hl ph: Rudolf
Betz. ON v 25 n 6 p 21 D 17'60
HOPKINS, JOHN, conductor
Australian notes. MD v 51 n 6
p 12 D '60
HORNE, LENA, 1917-, singer

Hl ph. HF v 10 n 3 p 89 Mr '60
HORNE, MARILYN, singer
In Wozzeck at Gelsenkirchen, ens
AP wl ph: Kurt Saurin-Sorant. ON
v 25 n 8 p 14 D 31'60
---Warnke, Frank J. (Marilyn
Horne, California interview.) ON
v 25 n 8 p 14, 32 D 31'60
HOROWITZ, VLADIMIR, 1904-,
pianist
Marsh, Robert C. Beethoven
piano sonatas in stereo (review).
por HF v 10 n 4 p 61-2 Ap '60
THE HOSTAGE, play
Behan, Brendan; NYC report.
Th Arts v 44 n 9 report. Th Arts
v 44 n 9 p 8 S '60
---Pryce-Jones, Alan. (Review.)
il Th Arts v 44 n 11 p 8 N '60
L'HOTE NOCTURNE, play
Ostrava; L. Askenazy. WP v 11
n 8 p 13 Je '60
HOTTER, HANS, 1909-, singer
As Thomas Becket; "part made to
order for his powerful personality";
Vienna Staatsoper in German. Op
v 11 n 6 p 413 Je '60
---As Wotan, AP wl ph: Bayreuth.
Op v 11 n 11 cover N '60
HOUGHTON, NORRIS. (On staging
Chekhov; US viewpoint.) WT v 9
n 2 p 130-1 Summer '60
HOUSE, ROBERT W. The role of
fine arts in the preparation of
teachers. MEJ v 47 n 2 p 39-40
N-D '60
THE HOUSE ON CRISTO STREET,
play
Chicago Community Theatre, ens
AP ph. Th Arts v 44 n 2 p 85
F '60
HOUSEWRIGHT, DR. WILEY L.
author
Need for a National Music Research
Foundation.) MC v 162 n 5 p 34
N '60
HOUSTON
Barbirolli, Sir John, principal
conductor of the Houston Sym-
phony 1961-2. MC v 162 n 6 p 33
D '60
---Die Walkure; Walter Herbert,
director; Jerome Hines as Wotan;
cast notes. Op v 11 n 4 p 271 Ap'60

HOUSTON GRAND OPERA ASSO-
CIATION
Holmes, Ann. (Report on Carmen;
other notes.) ON v 24 n 18 p 26
Mr 5'60
HOUSTON SYMPHONY
Contemporary repertory; list.
AmM v 8 n 10 p 15 N '60
HOVHANESS, ALAN, 1911-
composer
Career sketch; b. Somerville,
Massachusetts. por AmM v 8 n 4
p 13-14 Ap '60
---Commission from Tokyo Sym-
phony; notes. AmM v 8 n 7 p 10
Ag '60
---Meditation on Orpheus; criticism.
Mus Q v 46 n 4 p 552 O '60
----Notes on his Japanese visit.
ACAB v 9 n 3 p 9 1960
---Première: Blue Flame; San
Antonio, 1959. ACAB v 9 n 2
p 21 1960
---Premières (3): Madras Sonata;
Alleluia; Nagooran (all in India
1960). ACAB v 9 n 3 p 31 1960
HOWAT, ROBERT, pianist
Boston criticism. MC v 161 n 4
p 32 Mr '60
LOS HUESPEDES REALES, play
Monterrey notes; Luisa Josefina
Hernandez. WP v 11 n 5 p 15
Mr '60
EL HUEVO, play
de F. Marceau; Théâtre El Buho,
ens AP ph: Bogota. WP v 11 n 9
p 7 Jl '60
HUFFMAN, WALTER SPENCER,
1902-, composer
Première: March, Chorale and
Variations; Washington review.
Mus Q v 46 n 1 p 79-80 Ja '60
LES HUGENOTS, opera
Wolff, Stéphane. Dominique Ple-
ssis vous parle - - -(entretien).
GDC n 276 p 782 Je 10'60
HUGHES, PATRICK CAIRN. No-
body calls him Willie now (Sir
William Walton). il HF v 10 n 9
p 43-46, 116 S '60
---The swan who could laugh (Gio-
acchino Rossini). HF v 10 n 7
p 38-40, 84 Jl '60

HUGHES, SPIKE. An introduction
to Verdi's Macbeth (with 12 pic-
tures). Op v 11 n 4 p 247-256
Ap '60
---Career notes. Op v 11 n 4
p 305 Ap '60
HUGHIE, play
Stockholm, 1958; Allan Edwall
and Bengt Eklund AP ph: Beata
Bergström. WT v 9 n 2 p 177
Summer '60
HUGO, REG. (On Canadian music
festivals.) CMJ v 4 n 4 p 33-7
Summer '60
HUGON, GEORGES, 1904-, composer
Notes; b. Paris. GDC n 281-2
p 51 S 30'60
HET HUIS DER SCHIMMEN (CARTER)
Amsterdam notes. WP v 11 n 4 p 11
F '60
HUISMAN, JACQUELINE
In Une Femme qu'a le Coeur trop
petit, ens AP wl ph: Cayet. WT
v 9 n 1 p 8 Spring '60
HUISMAN, JACQUES. Libéralisme
esclanagiste. WP v 12 n 1 p 1 O'60
---Por ph. WP v 12 n 1 p 1 O '60
HUISMAN, MAURICE, director
Royal Opera House ph: Brussels.
ON v 25 n 5 p 29 D 10'60
LE HUITIEME JOUR, play
Argentina notes; Alberto de Zava-
lia. WP v 12 n 2 p 18 N '60
HULL, HENRY, actor
And Reneice Rehan in Tobacco
Road, AP wl ph. Th Arts v 44
n 9 p 12 S '60
HULL, DR. ROBERT, conductor
With Gina Bachauer and her hus-
band, Alec Sherman, wl ph; Fort
Worth. MC v 161 n 3 p 39 F '60
HUNEKER, JAMES GIBBONS, 1860-
1921, critic
Brooks, Van Wyck. Huneker in
retrospect (career sketch, philoso-
phy, impact on America). por HF
v 10 n 12 p 38-41 D '60
HUNGARY
Lebow, Howard. Report from Hun-
gary. il J Rev v 7 n 3 p 3-6 Fall'60
---Los Angeles: Hungarian musicians
Georg Solti, Janos Starker and
Miklos Rozsa; review. MC v 161

(Hungary)
n 6 p 28 My '60
---Music report. La S n 122 p 86
Ja '60; same. La S n 123 p 79
F '60
---Szollosy, Andras. Music report.
La S n 133 p 111 D '60
---Theatre report. WP v 11 n 7 p 8
My '60; same. WP v 11 n 9 p 7
Jl '60; same. WP v 11 n 10 p 8
Ag '60; same WP v 12 n 1 p 4
O '60
---Weissman, John S. Hungary;
Budapest Music Weeks (with criti-
cism on contemporary composers
and trends). Mus Q v 46 n 4
p 525-35 O '60
HUNGER OF A GIRL, play
Australia notes; George Kerr.
WP v 12 n 3 p 26 D '60
HUNTINGTON HARTFORD FOUND-
ATION
California; artists colony. MR
v 21 n 3 p 240 Ag '60
HURLEY, LAUREL, 1927-, singer
As Marzelline in Fidelio, AP hl
ph: Melançon. ON v 24 n 15 p 17
F 13'60
HURLUBERLU
Giovaninetti, Silvio. (notes.)
La S n 125 p 70 Ap '60
HURNÍK, ILYA, 1922-, composer
Notes; b. Silesia. Mus Q v 46
n 4 p 513 O '60
HUSFRUE, play
Norway; Tormod Skagestad. WP
v 12 n 1 p 9 O '60
HUTCHINSON, NEIL, musical
director
Australia; career notes; Executive
Director of the Elizabethan The-
atre Trust. MD v 50 n 8 p 12
F '60
HUTTON, GEOFFREY W.,
journalist
Por ph. MD v 50 n 9 p 25 Mr '60

I

ICELAND
Première of Molière's Georges
Dandin; notes. WP v 12 n 2 p 3
N '60

L'IDIOTE, play
Paris notes; Marcel Achard. WP
v 12 n 2 p 20 N '60
IDOMÉNÉE, opera
Demarquez, Suzanne. Recon-
stitution et réalisation de Renée
Viollier, tragédie lyrique en 5
actes d'André Campra. GDC
n 292 p 420 D 9'60
I'D RATHER BE RIGHT, musical
Ens AP wl ph: 1937. Th Arts v 44
n 9 p 24 S '60
IDYLLE A CAPRI (FOYE), operetta
Liège review; music, Nico Dostal;
René Tobelli, staging; Suzanne Dei-
lhes and Henri Guy "dans l'ambiance
hollywoodienne". GDC n 257-8 p 356
Ja 29'60
IGLÉSIS, ROGER. First steps in
television for the stage producer.
WT v 9 n 4 p 325-336 Winter '60
IKEDA, YOKO, pianist
Paris debut. GDC n 273 p 689
My 20'60
ILLICA, LUIGI, 1857-1919, librettist
Castell'Arquato; un busto in bronzo,
opera dello scultore Nardo Paiella.
La S n 131 p 65 O '60
---Morini, Mario. Simoni e Illica
associati per un libretto. il La S
n 133 p 56-61 D '60
---In military dress, hl ph: 1915;
with Arturo Toscanini in Milan,
hl ph; wl ph. La S n 133 p 57, 59, 61
D '60
---Por ph: 1890. La S n 122 p 31
Ja '60
ILLINOIS OPERA GUILD
Auditions; prizes. ON v 25 n 1 p 7
O 8'60
ILS NE PORTENT PAS LE BLACK-
TIE, play
Ens AP ph: São-Paulo. WP v 11
n 7 My '60
ILS SAVENT CE QUE L'AMOUR,
play
Budapest notes; Miklos Hubay. WP
v 11 n 5 p 11 Mr '60
I'M TALKING ABOUT JERUSALEM,
play
Coventry notes; Arnold Wesker.
WP v 11 n 10 p 13 Ag '60
IMBRIE, ANDREW, 1921-, composer

Dahl, Ingolf. Review of String Quartets Nos. 2 and 3, played by the California and by the Walden Quartets; record. Mus Q v 46 n 1 p 120-22 Ja '60

IMPASSE DE LA FIDELITE (LURIO), musical
Paris notes; music, Jean Pierre Mottier. WP v 12 n 2 p 20 N '60

IMPRESSARIO, opera
Australian National Theatre; cast. MD v 51 n 1 p 21 Jl '60

IMPROVISATION
Its role in Oriental and Arabian music; its recent re-entry into Western music (report of 5-day Paris conference under International Music Council on the composer-performer relationship). WM n 6 p 125-6 D '60
---Lukas Foss Ensemble; "only the parts for members of the orchestra written, framework for the Ensemble to improvise". IM v 59 n 5 p 23 N '60
---Margot, Yves. Les petits secrets de l'improvisation. GDC n 275 p 759 Je 3'60
---Tallmadge, William H. Teaching improvisation (school children, once they acquire a few fundamental techniques, teach themselves). MEJ v 47 n 2 p 58-60 N-D '60

IN THE DROUGHT, opera
Joubert, John, composer; the New Opera Workshop, Sadler's Wells. Op v 11 n 2 p 150 F '60

LOS INCAS
Urpi, Alma, and Paul d'Arnot; Paris review by Claude Chamfray. GDC n 255-6 p 314 Ja 15'60

L'INCORONAZIONE di POPPAEA, opera
Hamburg, ens AP wl ph: Peyer. Op v 11 n 1 p 38 Ja '60

INDIA
Kellet, Brian. Shakespeare through sun, rain and earthquake. WP v 12 n 2 p 1, 4 N '60
---Khosla, G. S. India (theatre report.) il WT v 9 n 2 p 165-6 Summer '60

---Paris, Théâtre des Nations; Little Ballet Troupe de Bombay; Shanti Bardhan. TD n 94 p 22 Je'60
---Theatre report. WP v 11 n 8 p 8 Je '60; same WP v 11 n 9 p 8 Jl '60; same WP v 12 n 1 p 4 O'60

INDIANA
Edleman, Robert S. Southern Indiana's experiment (TV). PlM v 36 n 7 p 161-2 Ap '60
---Peru; Circus Americana. PlM v 36 n 5 p 117 F '60

INDIANA UNIVERSITY
Opera Theater; its scope and purposes. il WM n 4 p 71-72 Autumn'60

LOS INDIOS ESTABAN CABREROS, play
Buenos Aires, 1958; ens AP wl ph: Chaure. WT v 9 n 1 p 70 Spring '60

INDRANI, dancer
Note; daughter of Ragini Devi, dancer of India also. il MD v 50 n 8 p 30 F '60

L'INFIDELTA DE LUSA, opera
Budapest revival. ON v 24 n 12 p 26 Ja 23'60
---Royal Festival Hall; Haydn review. Op v 11 n 12 p 853 D '60

INGE, WILLIAM, 1913-, playwright
Hillman, Ronald. Mateer Playhouse (Pennsylvania) and Inge's one-act plays. PlM v 36 n 7 p, 58 Ap '60
--- Por ph: Roderick MacArthur, Th Arts v 44 n 2 p 12 F '60;same Th Arts v 44 n 7 p 18 Jl '60

INGHELBRECHT, D. E. (1880-) and G. Le Chêne et le Tilleul, opéra-ballet en 2 actes et 4 tableaux d'apres la Fontaine (ètudes musicales analytiques). GDC n 291 p 367 D 2'60

INGLIS, JEANNE
Obituary. GDC n 288 p 261 N 11'60

INGRAM, JOHN, composer
Melbourne teacher; Symphonic Overture, a London award. por MD v 51 n 3 p 19 S '60

INHERIT THE WIND, play
Ens ph: Little Theatre of the Rockies. PlM v 36 n 8 cover My '60

THE INSPECTOR-GENERAL, opera
Gambetta, Rosario. A la Scala

(The Inspector)
de Milan. GDC n 273 p 687
My 20'60
---Lubiana, Teatro dell'Opera;
review. LaS n 124 p 37 Mr'60
---NYC Opera;criticism. Op v 11
n 12 p 816 D'60
---Teatro Piccola Scala;review.
LaS n 126 p 33 My'60
---NYC Center, ens ph:Friedman-
Abeles. MC v 162 n 5 p 16 N'60
---Two ens AP wl phs:Piccola
Scala. LaS n 126 p 33 My'60
THE INSTITUTE OF VERDI
STUDIES
Medici, Mario. (List of people
and newspapers expressing an
interest.) Ver v 1 n 2 preface
Ag'60
INSTRUMENTATION and ORCH-
ESTRATION
Comparative instrumentation of
nine Sousa scores, four suites
and five marches;article by
Francis N. Mayer. MEJ v 46 n 3
p 51-7 Ja'60
INTER-AMERICAN EXCHANGE
PROJECT
Methods to be used. WM n 1 p 8
F'60
INTER-AMERICAN MUSIC FES-
TIVAL
Second;1961 plans in Washington.
WM n 2 p 31 Ap'60
---Washington;twelve composers
from eight countries commis-
sioned for April 1961 festival:
list. Am M v 8 n 6 p 14 Jl'60
INTERLOCHEN NATIONAL
MUSIC CAMP
See National Music Camp
INTERMEZZO, opera
Munich;review. Op v 11 n 58-9
Autumn'60
---Steffek and Prey as Christine
and Robert Storch, AP wl ph:
Betz. ON v 25 n 2 p 21 O 29'60
---Strauss, the Skat game scene,
ph: Betz. Op v 11 p 59 Autumn'60
INTERNATIONAL BALLET du
MARQUIE de CUEVAS
At 75, the Marquis "has decided
to disband the company which has
cost two million pounds sterling".

MD v 51 n 5 p 29 N '60
---La Belle au Bois Dormant
(Petipa) au Théâtre des Champs-
Elysées, October 19; critique. TD
n 96 p 12-9 S-O '60
---Munich report. TD n 90 p 20
F '60
---Paris review of the Sleeping
Princess (Petipa-Helpmann). GDC
n 290 p 320 N 25'60
---Silvant, Jean. Chez Cuevas. il
TD n 91 p 21 Mr '60
INTERNATIONAL CONFERENCE
OF COMPOSERS
Stratford, Ontario, 1960; notes.
CMJ v 4 n 2 p 43 Winter '60
---report. MC v 162 n 5 p 29 N '60
--- ---report by Marvin Duchow.
CMJ v 5 n 1 p 4-16 Autumn '60
--- ---Josef Tal, Hugh Le Caine,
Edgard Varèse, Otto Luening and
Vladimir Ussachevsky, Luciano
Berio, ens hl ph: Peter Smith.
CMJ v 5 n 1 p 7 Autumn '60
INTERNATIONAL CULTURE EX-
CHANGE
American National Theatre and
Academy: list of musicians sent
abroad, countries visited and year,
orchestras, chamber ensembles
and soloists 1956-Dec 1959; article
on music as diplomacy. IM v 58
n 7 p 10-11, 14, 34 Ja '60
INTERNATIONAL FEDERATION
FOR THEATRE RESEARCH
Advantages of membership. Th R
v 2 n 1 p 64 1960
---Members list. Th R v 2 n 3 p 180
1960
---Paris, June 1961 meeting; re-
ports from centers. Th R v 2 n 3
p 181-5 1961
---Publications; Paris 1961; Venice
centre at Casa Goldoni. Th Notbk
v 15 n 2 p 42-3 Winter 60-61
---Stockholm 1960, Drottningholm
Court Theatre; symposia; business;
two performances. Th R v 2 n 3
p 133-5 1960
---Vienna 1959 meeting: report;
officers. Th R v 2 n 2 p 69-70 1960
INTERNATIONAL FEDERATION OF
ACTORS, 1951-
Notes on actors'rights, especially

LES INVAINCUS, play
Athens; Thanassis Costavaras.
WP v 11 n 7 p 10 My '60
IONESCO, EUGENE (1912-). My
thanks to the critics. il Th Arts
v 44 n 10 p 18-9 O '60
--- ---The avant-garde theatre.
TDR v 5 n 2 p 44-53 D '60
--- ---The tragedy of language:
how an English primer became
my first play. TDR v 4 n 3 p 10-
13 Mr '60
---Esslin, Martin. The theatre
of the absurd. TDR v 4 n 4 p 3-
15 My '60
---Fowlie, Wallace. New plays
of Ionesco and Genet. TDR v 5
n 1 p 43-8 S '60
---Por ph: Bernand; three scenes
from three productions of "Rhin-
oceros", phs. Th Arts v 44 n 10
p 18-9 O '60
IPHIGENIE in TAURIS, play
Dubrovnik 1956, outdoor light-
ing, ens AP wl ph:Toso Dabac.
WT v 9 n 2 p 156 Summer'60
IRIS, opera
Rio de Janeiro;title role, Clara
Marise;review. Op v 11 n 10
p 686 O'60
IRISCHE LEGENDE, opera
Egk;ens AP wl ph:Peyer. WT
v 9 n 3 p 217 Autumn'60
IRMA LA DOUCE, musical
NYC;music, Marguerite Mon-
not;Elizabeth Seal, only woman
role. MD v 51 n 5 p 26 N'60
IRVING, ROBERT, 1913-, conduc-
tor
Small ph. HF v 10 n 3 p 66 Mr'60
ISRAEL
Bat-Kol, new music publication;
the Tel Aviv address. MEJ v 47
n 1 p 127 S-O'60
---Gamzu, Haïm. Israel (theatre
report). WT v 9 n 1 p 80-4 Spring
'60
GRADENWITZ, PETER. (Music
report.) MC v 161 n 7 p 20 Je'60
---Music report. LaS n 122 p 86
Ja'60;same. LaS n 126 p 71 My
'60;same. LaS n 127 p 69 Je'60
---Piattelli, Heinke. Music report;

LaS n 124 p 74 Mr'60;same. LaS
n 129-30 p 77 Ag-S'60;same. LaS
n 133 p 109 D'60
---Two dance ens phs:NYC. LaS
n 123 p 43 F'60
ISRAEL NATIONAL OPERA
Notes. MC v 161 n 7 p 20 Je'60
ISRAEL PHILHARMONIC
Metropolitan Opera House;review
also Carnegie Hall concerts. MC
v 162 n 5 p 17, 30 N'60
INSTITUTO di STUDI VERDANI
Labroca, Mario. Il Patrocinio del
consiglio internazionale della
Musica. Ver v 1 n 1 Ap'60
---Medici, Mario. L'Instituto di
Studi Verdiani. Ver v 1 n 1 preface
Ap'60
See also Institute of Verdi Studies
IT HAPPENED IN IRKUTSK, play
Criticism. WT v 9 n 2 p 178 Sum-
mer'60
L'ITALIANA in ALGERI, opera
Ens AP wl ph:Dubrovnik. LaS
n 129-30 p 76 Ag-S'60
---Ens AP ph:Palermo. LaS n 124
p 67 Mr'60
---Scattola, Carlo, and Supervia, AP
wl ph:Turin, 1925. Op v 11 n 1 p 22
Ja'60
ITALY
Abbiati, Franco. Libera musica e
musica di stato (the extremists
are entrenched in state art?). LaS
n 127 p 7-11 Je'60
---Brookings, Jack. The motley thea-
tre (survey). PlM v 36 n 8 p 188
My'60
--- ---Part II. PlM v 37 n 1 p 8-9
O'60
---Employees of all opera houses
strike in protest of low government
support of opera. MC v 161 n 3 p 21
F'60
---Giancola, Giacinto. Italy (theatre
report). WT v 9 n 1 p 84-6 Spring
'60;same. WT v 9 n 2 p 168-170
Summer'60;same. (festivals in-
cluded in report). WT v 9 n 3 p 286
Autumn'60
---Music notes. MC v 161 n 7 p 18
Je'60
---Music reports:Milan;Bologna;

Venice; Firenze; Trieste; Parma;
Bolzano; Arezzo; Catania; Salerno.
LaS F'60
--- ---Milan; Rome; Torino; Genova;
Naples; Trieste; Venice; Vincenza;
Bolzano; Salerno; Palermo. LaS
n 124 p 59-68 Mr'60
--- ---Reggio Emilia; Pesaro-Fano;
Arezzo; Bolzano; Salerno, etc. LaS
1960
---Opera; notes from Adria, Genoa,
Florence; Lucca; Milan; Naples; Tu-
rin; La Scala 1960-61; Reggio Em-
ilia; Venice; Trieste (repertory).
Op v 11 n 12 p 837-9 D'60
--- ---Bari; Brescia; Catania; Gen-
oa; Mantua; Venice. Op v 11 n 4
p 282-5 Ap'60
--- ---some reviews: Milan; Bari;
Catania; Genoa; Rome. Op v 11 n 6
p 425-30 Je'60
---Opera reports: Milan; Catania;
Genoa; Pisa; Turin. Op v 11 n 7
p 489-90 Jl'60
--- ---Milan; Como; Naples; Rome;
Venice. Op v 11 n 8 p 559-564
Ag'60
---RAI; programmi sinfonici; opere
liriche. LaS 1960
---Rodden, Philip. Milan; Bologna;
Modena; Parma; Trieste; Turin. Op
v 11 n 2 p 147-8 F'60
--- ---Opera reports: Rovigo; Turin.
Op v 11 n 1 p 43-4 Ja'60
---Rosselini, Renzo. (Opera today.)
ON v 24 n 21 p 15, 32 Mr 26'60
---Sartori, Claudio. Opera reports:
Bologna; Leghorn; Milan (longer
notes). Op v 11 n 1 p 42 Ja'60
---Selden-Goth, Gisella. Festival
fare. MC v 162 n 1 p 30 Jl'60
---Sorbello, Uguccione Ranieri di.
Italy; hope and hard times (thea-
tre survey). Th Arts v 44 n 4 p 53-
56 Ap'60
---Theatre report. WP v 11 n 10
p 8 Ag'60; same. WP v 12 n 3 p 4
D'60
---Vercelli; Le Xe Concours Inter-
national de Musique et de Danse.
J. B. Viotti. TD n 90 p 15 F'60
ITURBI, JOSÉ, 1895-, pianist
At the piano, AP hl ph. MC v 161
n 3 back cover F'60

IVANOV, play
Maly Teatr, Moskva, 1960, ens AP
wl ph. WT v 9 n 2 p 115 Summer'60
---Théâtre d'Aujourd'hui, Paris,
1957, ens AP wl ph: Bernand. WT
v 9 n 2 p 114 Summer'60
IVES, CHARLES, 1874-1954,
composer
Carter, Elliott. (His reply to the
question, "what do you think of
Charles Ives now?") Mus Q v 46
n 2 p 198-200 Ap'60
---Criticism, London Times. Am M
v 8 n 9 p 20 O'60
---Frankenstein, Alfred. Ives' Sec-
ond Symphony, Bernstein and New
York Philharmonic (review of
Columbia record). HF v 10 n 11
p 75-6 N'60
---Première: Lincoln, the Great
Commoner (NYC 1960). ACAB v 9
n 3 p 32 1960
IWAKI, conductor
AP ph: Japanese Radio Orchestra.
WM n 6 p 134 D'60

J

JACOBS, ARTHUR (1922-). Two
operas new to London (Les Malheurs
d'Orphée of Milhaud and Die Flut
of Blacher). il Op v 2 n 3 p 182-3
Mr '60
JACOBS, ROBERT L. (1904-). Mu-
sic as symbol; reflections on Mr.
Deryck Cooke's The Language of
Music. MR v 21 n 3 p 226-236
Ag '60
JACOB'S PILLOW
Building campaign notes; also Ted
Shawn's letter. MD v 50 n 8 p 2,
30 F '60
JAKACS, JENO, composer
Première: Semiseria; Cincinnati
Symphony under Max Rudolf. MC
v 161 n 1 p 24 Ja '60
JANIS, BYRON, 1928-, pianist
Bruyr, José. Paris criticism.
GDC n 295 p 494 D 30'60
---Notes; b. Pittsburgh. AmM v 8
n 9 p 6 O '60
JANNI, GUIDO. Wagner's idyl
(Judith Gauthier) in the days of
Parsifal. La S n 127 p 14-7 Je '60

JAPAN

Concert halls;notes by Joseph Bloch, pianist, on tour. J Rev v 7 n 3 p 8-10 Fall'60

---Dan, Ikuma. (On music in Japan.) WM n 2 p 31-2 Ap'60

---Kawatake, Toshio. Shakespeare in the Japanese theatre. Th R v 2 n 2 p 82-7 1960

---Kaula, David. The Noh drama (history;comparison to Kabuki). TDR v 5 n 1 p 61-72 S'60

---Kelly, Merle I. (Letter from Japan on music teaching in Missionary school.) il J Rev v 7 n 2 p 28 Spring'60

---Malm, William P. Japanese Music and Musical Instruments (book notes). MEJ v 46 n 3 p 10 Ja'60

---Martin, Burton E. (Opera report.)ON v 25 n 7 p 29 D 24'60

--- ---Rigoletto review. ON v 24 n 16 p 30 F 20'60

---Le Nô;introduction aux traites de Zeami (Gallimard). WP v 12 n 1 p 2 O'60

---Opera;Younger Opera Group; Nobuko Hara Opera Research Group;Fujiwara Opera Company; brief notes. Op v 11 n 10 p 695-6 O'60

---Paris recital of Japanese students at the Conservatoire National Supérieur;names;review. GDC n 265-6 p 525 Mr 25'60

---Shingo, Endo. Japan(theatre report). WT v 9 n 1 p 86-90 Spring '60

---Theatre report. WP v 11 n 5 p 2 Mr'60;same. WP v 11 n 7 p 8 My '60;same. WP v 11 n 9 p 8 Jl'60; same. WP v 12 n 2 p 4 N'60;same. WP v 12 n 3 p 4 D'60

---Tircuit, Heuwell. Festivals:Modern Music Festival and chamber music festival at Karuizawa;Osaka Festival. MC v 162 n 1 p 33 Jl'60

---Tokyo;Fujiwara Opera;the Niki-Kai Opera;the Japanese Broadcasting Company;opera. Op v 11 n 9 p 629 S'60

---Niki-Kai;Così fan tutte, ens

AP wl ph:Hasegawa. ON v 24 n 20 p 26 Mr 19'60

---Symphony Orchestra of the Japanese Radio, 3 phs. WM n 6 p 134-135 D'60

JAPAN PHILHARMONIC ORCHESTRA

Under Akeo Watanabe, six-week US tour under Cultural Exchange. Am M v 8 n 6 p 13 Jl'60

JÁRDANYI, PÁL, 1920-, composer Post-war Hungarian composers; notes. Mus Q v 46 n 4 p 530 O'60

DES JARDINS, MARGUERITE, singer

Toronto in Otello;note. ON v 25 n 6 p 28 D 17'60

JARO, ANTONIO JOSÉ. Rio de Janeiro:opera. Op v 11 n 10 p 686-7 O'60

JARRE, MAURICE, 1899?-, composer Strasbourg criticism of "Paix dans les Brisements". GDC n 281-2 p 65 S 30'60

JASON et MÉDÉE(NOVERRE), ballet Vestris, Gaetano, ens AP wl engr, 1781, Boydell. Th Notbk v 15 n 1 p 20 Autumn'60

JAZZ MUSIC

Allen, Edison B. When jazz began. il IM v 59 n 5 p 14-5 N'60

---ANTA list of jazz ensembles sent abroad;reception by various nations recorded and attendance in Asia and Africa. il IM v 58 n 8 p 10-1 F'60

---Archive of New Orleans Jazz, Tulane University;notes. IM v 59 n 5 p 15 N'60

---Basie;Leonard Feather on Count Basie's 25th anniversary as a band leader. por IM v 59 n 5 p 18-9 N'60

---Bergmann, Robert. Le jazz, est-il de musique contemporaine? TD n 97 p 29-30 N'60

--- ---Le Jazz. TD n 93 p 29-30 My '60

--- ---Part II. La querelle de la Modernité. TD n 94 p 28-9 Je'60

---Boston;jazz training at Berklee School of Modern Music. MC v 161 n 5 p 29 Ap'60

---Brubeck, Dave. (On "Jazz Impressions of Eurasia".)por MD v 50

146

n 9 p 10-1 Mr'60
---Cerulli, Dom. Jack Teagarden
(1905-). il IM v 58 n 7 p 12-3 Ja
'60
--- ---Jerry Mulligan. il IM v 59
n 4 p 18-9 O'60
---Collegiate Jazz Festival, Notre
Dame 1960;report;North Texas
State winner. il IM v 58 n 11
p 9 My'60
---Feather, Leonard. Jazz, pastime
or profession? IM v 59 n 6 p 12-3
D'60
---Garner, Erroll, 1923-;sketch.
por IM v 58 n 9 p 16-7 Mr'60
---Hentoff, Nat. Charles Mingus
(1922-) as composer, bassist and
leader (critical comparison with
others). por IM v 59 n 6 p 24-5
D'60
--- ---The expansion of jazz playing opportunities. IM v 58 n 12
p 12-3 Je'60
--- ---New directions in jazz. il
IM v 59 n 3 p 14-5 S'60
---Jazz For Juniors, phonorecord
by Roulette;review. MEJ v 46 n 3
p 13 Ja'60
---Jones, Kelsey. Reviewing three
new books on jazz (Ulanov;Sha-
piro and Paul's That Crazy American Music). CMJ v 4 n 2 p 83-5
Winter'60
---Krupa, Gene, 1909-;career story.
por IM v 58 n 10 p 10-1, 32-3 Ap
'60
---Lewis, John;criticism;on con-
trapuntal style. por HG v 10 n 10
p 54-6 O'60
---List of musicians toured by the
US Government and the countries
they visited. IM v 58 n 7 p 34 Ja
'60
--Mann, Herbie (Excerpts from
his African trip as a jazz musician sent by the US State Department.) por IM v 58 n 9 p 21, 34
Mr'60
---Mehegan, John. The Art of Jazz,
essays, edited by Martin T. Wil-
liams(a book review). J Rev v 7 n 1
p 23 Winter 59'60
---Monthly coverage of jazz recordings;John S. Wilson's notes.

HF 1960
---Stuart, Walter. Jazz improvising
for all instruments, series. IM 1960
---Tiger Rag:its component parts
by Nick LaRocca. IM v 59 n 5 p 12
N'60
---Wilson, John S. Is jazz too re-
spectable? HF v 10 n 5 p 34-7 My'
60
---King Phumiphol of Thailand, Ben-
ny Goodman and Herman Kenin,
two phs:NYC. IM v 59 n 2 p 14 Ag
'60
---North Texas State College Lab
Band, winner at Collegiate Jazz
Festival at Notre Dame 1960, ens
ph. IM v 58 n 11 p 9 My'60
JAZZ CONCERT(BALANCHINE-BO-
LENDER- MONCION-TARAS), ballet
Also list of scores used. Am M v 8
n 10 p 11 N'60
JAZZ-NOCTURNE(SHOOK), ballet
Rotterdam;music, Alex Philipse.
WP v 11 n 3 p 11 Ja'60
J. B. , play
MacLeish, Archibald. (Complete
text;portfolio, cast and notes.)Th
Arts v 44 n 2 p 29-64 F'60
---Portfolio of NYC production;scene
from Münster, from San Miniato,
Italy, also. Th Arts v 44 n 2 F'60
JEANMARIE, ZIZI, 1924-, dancer
Guest, Ivor. (London notes;Rain (Pe-
tit). MD v 51 n 6 p 29 D'60
JEANNE d'ARC au BUCHER, opera
Martin, Burton E. Tokyo review;M.
Kusabue in the title-role of Honeg-
ger work. il ON v 24 n 9 p 15, 28
Ja 2'60
JEFFORD, BARBARA, 1930-, actress
London criticism. WT v 9 n 2 p 182
Summer'60
JEFFRIES, WALTER. People;41. Bir-
git Nilsson. il Op v 11 n 9 p 607-12
S'60
JELINEK, HANNS, 1901-, composer
Redlich, Hans F. Hanns Jelinek(b.
Vienna). MR v 21 n 1 p 66-72 F'60
JELLICOE, ANN. (Interview on her
plays, on glamour and excitement
suited for today and sort of play a
"working-class" audience would
enjoy, etc.)NTM v 1 n 4 p 25-8 Jl
'60

147

JENS, SALONE, actress
and Roy Poole in The Balcony,
AP wl ph: Arnold Newman. Th
Arts v 44 n 4 p 60 Ap '60
JENUFA, opera
Chicago Lyric review. Op v 11
n 1 p 26 Ja '60
---Holland Festival review. Op
v 11 p 28 Autumn '60
JEPTHA, oratorio
Stuttgart company at the Paris
Opéra. Op v 11 n 2 p 140 F '60
JERITZA, MARIA, 1887-
As Marietta in Die tote Stadt,
AP hl ph: Tschidel. ON v 24
n 20 p 13 Mr 19'60
JESSONDA, opera
Cassel revival of Spohr work;
cast. Op v 2 n 3 p 206 Mr '60
JEU DE NOEL
Stuttgart; Carl Orff's "Ludus de
Nato Infante Mirificus"; critique.
GDC n 295 p 488-9 D 30'60
JEU SENTIMENTAL (COMBES)
Strasbourg notes. TD n 92 p 28
Ap '60
LES JEUNESSES MUSICALES
Aix-les-Bains; French section
host. WM n 3 p 57 Je '60
---Belgian Section opening a music
camp; notes. WM n 3 p 57 Je '60
---Formosa; 615 members, notes;
also Belgian Congo Section's rep-
ort. WM n 2 p 32 Ap '60
---Mayer, Sir Robert. (On various
national branches and their mus-
ical youth activities.) ON v 24
n 20 p 14, 32 Mr 19'60
---Weikersheim; German Section:
staff list. WM n 3 p 57 Je '60
---Wismeyer, Ludwig. The Musi-
cal Youth of the World in Berlin
(15th congress reported). WM
n 5 p 98-100 O '60
---World Congress (the 15th) in
Berlin; notes. WM n 4 p 77 Ag'60
LES JEUNESSES MUSICALES du
CANADA
The International Federation of
Musical Youth, Canadian section;
Mt. Orford, Canadian section;
Mt. Orford, Canada, notes. WM
n 4 p 78 Ag '60
---Papineau-Couture, Jean. Salle

de concert du Camp JMC. CMJ
v 5 n 1 p 50 Autumn '60
LES JEUXD'ENFANTS SONT FAITS,
play
Moncton, Canada; Jean Gavroche.
WP v 11 n 8 p 2 Je '60
JEUX DES DAMES, musical
Paris review. GDC n 295 p 484
D 30'60
JOACHIM, HEINZ. The composers
(in Germany today). WT v 9 n 3
p 213-226 Autumn '60
JOAN DE ZARISSA (MANDRICK-
ROSEN), ballet
Trofimova, Natacha, and Heino
Hallhuber, AP wl ph: Lido. TD
n 92 p 26 Ap '60
JOB, play
Fletcher, Winona L. Kentucky's
Pine Mountain State Park Summer
Theatre; success of drama'Job. "
PlM v 36 n 7 p 158 Ap '60
JOE ET CIE, play
Pitoëff, 3 AP phs. Spec n 1 p 25,
34, 37 1960
JOFFREY, ROBERT, choreographer
Company list; tour notes. MD v 50
n 9 p 31 Mr '60
---The Robert Joffrey Ballet; Jacob's
Pillow, then Chautauqua. MC v 162
n 2 p 29 Ag '60
JOHANNESEN, GRANT, 1921-,
pianist
London recital; b. Salt Lake City.
AmM v 8 n 9 p 10 O '60
JOHNEN, LOUIS JOHN, 1899-1960
Obituary; b. Cincinnati. MC v 161
n 3 p 20 F '60
JOHNSON, GERTRUDE, 1894-,
director
The National Theatre Movement of
Victoria: Silver Jubilee Arts Festi-
val, St. Kilda; 2 operas and 3 bal-
lets; notes. MD v 50 n 7 p 14 Ja '60
---Por ph. MD v 50 n 7 p 14 Ja '60
JOHNSON, HARRIETT. Demitasse
Verdi(Fredrik A. Chramer's puppet
opera theatre in Chicago). il ON
v 24 n 17 p 12-3, 31 F 27'60
JOHNSON, OSIE, drummer AP ph.
IM v 59 n 1 p 27 Jl '60
JOHNSON, ROBERT C. Ensemble of
singers from Le Nozze di Figaro,
drawing. ON v 24 n 12 cover Ja 23'60

148

JOHNSON, THOR, 1913-, conductor
Por ph. MC v 161 n 1 p 22 Ja '60
JOHNSTON, DENIS (1901-). The college theatre-why? Th Arts v 44 n 8 p 12-13, 69 Ag '60
--- ---That's show business. Th Arts v 44 n 2 p 82-3 F '60
LES JOIES DE LA FAMILLE, play Paris notes; Philippe Hériat. WP v 12 n 2 p 21 N '60
JOLIVET, ANDRÉ (1905-). Concertino pour trompette, orchestre à cordes et piano (études musicales analytiques). GDC n 290 p 334 N 25'60
--- ---2e Symphonie (études musicales analytiques.) GDC n 289 p 300 N 18'60
---Career notes. GDC n 289 p 272 N 18'60
---Film, Pickpocket; criticism. GDC n 261-2 p 444 F 26'60
---French première: IIe Symphonie; notes. GDC n 265-6 p 524 Mr 25'60
---Music for Skibine's "Ombres Lunaires", ballet; criticism. GDC n 277 p 812 Je 17'60
---Por ph: Serge Lido. GDC n 289 cover N 18'60
JOLLY'S PROGRESS, play NYC notes; Lonnie Coleman. WP v 11 n 6 p 4 Ap '60
---review; Pygmalion using Negro girl in Southern town. PlM v 36 n 6 p 137 Mr '60
JONES, "PHILLY" JOE, drummer Beside his drums, AP ph. IM v 59 n 5 p 31 N '60; same. IM v 58 n 10 p 33 Ap '60
JONES, REUNALD, 1910-, trumpeter Small por ph: NYC. IM v 58 n 12 p 7 Je '60
JONES, ROBERT EDMOND, 1887-1954, scenic designer Larson, Orville K. Robert Edmund Jones'Henry VIII (with 8 designs, never produced). PlM v 37 n 3 p 52-4 D '60
---Designs (8) for mounting Henry VIII (never used as Billy Rose canceled the production). phs.

PlM v 37 n 3 p 52-4 D '60
JORDAN, IRENE, 1919-, singer Notes. ON v 25 n 4 p 5 D 3'60
---With Vittorio Giannini, hl ph: Whitestone. ON v 25 n 4 p 5 D 3'60
JOSEPH, STEPHEN. Forward to 1890 (discussion of modern civic theatres, needed size and procenium or "flexible" discussed). NTM v 1 n 4 p 5-7 Jl '60
JOST, MACK, pianist Melbourne review. MD v 50 n 7 p 17 Ja '60
JOUBERT, JOHN, 1927-, composer Première: Piano Concerto, Hallé concert; Iso Elinson under George Weldon. MR v 21 n 1 p 82 F '60
JOURDAN-MORHANGE, HELENE, violinist Paris concert review. GDC n 276 p 786 Je 10'60
UNE JOURNEE EXTRAORDINAIRE, play Budapest notes; Laszlo Tabi. WP v 11 n 9 p 8 Jl '60
JOURNEY TO THE MOON (GRINWIS), ballet Borovonsky Ballet; review. MD v 50 n 7 p 27 Ja '60
---Sydney criticism; "the less said the sooner it can be expunged from the (Borovovansky) repertoire". MD v 50 n 8 p 26 F '60
JOUVE, PIERRE JEAN (1887-). Mémoire de Pitoëff. il Spec n 1 p 22-4 1960
JOVICZKY, JOZSEF, singer E Rozsi Delly in Tristano e Isotta, AP wl ph: Budapest. La S n 122 p 40 Ja '60
JUCKER, RAMA, 1936-, violinist Paris review. GDC n 257-8 p 361 Ja 29'60
JUDAS MACCABAEUS, opera Little Orchestra Society; notes. ON v 24 n 11 p 3 Ja 16'60
JUDD, WILLIAM M. On trends: more contests; more summer work; lack of concert halls in US; tax structure prohibitive; audiences not artists difference between city and provinces. MC v 162 n 1 p 13 Jl '60

JUEGO Y DANZA DE LA COQUE-
TA Y DON SIMON, play
Zaragoza notes; Jose Maria Pe-
mán. WP v 11 n 5 p 3 Mr '60
JUGANDO AL TORO(ANTONIO),
ballet
Antonio-Halffter-Bernard Daydé;
notes. il TD n 97 p 21 N '60
---Ballet Espagnol à l'Alhambra;
musique, Cristobal Halffter. GDC
n 285 p 163 O 21'60
JUGOSLAVIA
Contemporary music picture as
seen by Everett Helm. Mus Q
v 46 n 1 p 88-94 Ja '60
---Logar, Mihovil. Lubiana; Du-
brovnik. La S n 129-30 p 76 Ag-S
'60
---Music reports. La S 1960
JUILLIARD SCHOOL OF MUSIC
Alumni News, a regular column;
important notes for a study of mu-
sic in this century. J Rev 1960
---Award: Mme. Rosina Lhevinne;
scholarship: Rodgers and Hammer-
stein; notes. J rev v 7 n 1 p 14-5
Winter 59-60
---Faculty Activities, a regular
news column. J rev 1960
---Soviet composers' visit: Dr.
Boris Yarustovsky, Konstantin
Dannkevitch, Fikret Amirov, Tik-
hon Krennikov, Dmitri Shostako-
vich and Dmitri Kabalevsky; notes.
portfolio J Rev v 7 n 1 p 10-1
Winter 59-60
---Boston Chapter, ens phs. and
Los Angeles, concert alumni,
Daniel Pollack, Richard and Ade-
line Leshin, phs. J Rev v 7 n 2
p 3 Spring '60
JUILLIARD SCHOOL ORCHESTRA
Morel, Jean, conducting; Joseph
Fuch, Norman Dello Joio, William
Schuman, several phs. J Rev v 7
n 1 cover, p 20 Winter 59-60
JUILLIARD STRING QUARTET
Historical notes; repertory in
England. AmM v 8 n 4 p 10 Ap'60
---Machuel, Dominique. Paris re-
view. GDC n 273 p 690 My 20'60
---NYC review. MC v 161 n 5 p 36
Ap '60
---On tour: list of concert stops.

J Rev v 7 n 3 p 12-3 Fall '60
---Tour 40 cities, in 13 countries.
J Rev   v 7 n 2 p 13 Spring '60
---Budapest; wl phs. J Rev v 7 n 2
cover, p 12-3 Fall '60
---Cohen, Isidore, Robert Mann,
Raphael Hillyer and Claus Adam,
ens ph. AmM v 8 n 4 p 9 Ap '60
LA JUIVE, opera
Riemens, Leo. On Ghent revival
(one scene shown). Op v 11 n 5
p 343-4 My '60
JULES CÉSAR, play
Théâtre de France, ens AP wl
ph: Bernand. WT v 9 n 4 p 357
Winter '60
JULIEN, A. M.
See Maistre, Aman, 1903-
JULIUS CAESAR, play
Oakridge, Tennessee, review.
PlM v 36 n 4 p 78 Ja '60
---Arles, 1954, outdoors; Yves
Bonnat lighting, ens AP wl ph:
Bernand. WT v 9 n 2 p 151
Summer '60
---Tachkent; ens AP wl ph: Usbekski
Teatr Dram. WT v 9 n 4 p 362
Winter '60
---See also Jules César, play
JULLIEN, LOUIS ANTOINE, 1812-
1860, bandmaster
New York 1853-4; his stunts. MEJ
v 47 n 1 p 59 S-O '60
LA JUMENT DU ROI, comedy
Paris; Jean Canolle; notes. WP v 11
n 3 p 7 Ja '60
JURINAC, SENA, 1921-, singer
As Octavian, AP hl ph: Houston
Rogers. Op v 11 n 1 p 65 Ja '60
---In Le Nozze di Figaro, AP hl
ph. La S n 127 p 25 Je '60

K

KABELÁČ, MILOSLAV, 1908-,
composer
Critical notes. Mus Q v 46 n 4
p 511 O '60
KABOS, ILONA, 1902-, pianist
Surrounded in London by her
American pupils, ens ph.   AmM
v 8 n 3 p 7 Mr '60
KABUKI
The Center Theatre, NYC; notes.

150

Th Arts v 44 n 9 p 77-8 S '60
KADOSA, PAL, 1903-, composer
Critical notes. Mus Q v 46 n 4
p 527 O '60
KAGEN, SERGIUS (1909-). Mack
Harrell (1909-1959?). por J Rev
v 7 n 2 p 15 Spring '60
---Training accompanists at Juill-
iard. J Rev v 7 n 1 p 5, 14
Winter 59-60
---Por right profile ph. J Rev v 7
n 1 p 5 Winter 59-60
KAHN, ELSIE
Carmen, Paris Opéra, phs. OpP
n 19 p 8 1960
KAHN, ERICH ITOR, 1905-, com-
poser
Smith, Russell. Erich Itor Kahn
(with a check-list of compositions).
ACAB v 9 n 2 p 8-12 1960
KAI, UNA
With Charles Dickson and his
Festival Ballet dancers, ready to
rehearse Balanchine's Bourée Fant-
asque, ens WL ph: London. AmM
v 8 n 7 p 7 Ag '60
KAISER, GEORG(1878-1945). Der
Protagonist; trans. H. F. Garten.
TDR v 5 n 2 p 133-144 D '60
KALLIR, LILIAN, pianist
Career notes; b. Prague. AmM
v 8 n 3 p 4 Mr '60
---Por ph. AmM v 8 n 3 p 4 Mr'60
KALLMAN, CHESTER. The beau-
tiful and sharp-witted (bel canto and
opera buffa explained). ON v 25 n 7
p 9-13 D 24'60
THE KAMARU THEATRE
Lyric repertory under Herman
Wolfes. MC v 162 n 4 p 19 O'60
KAMELIADAMEN (RALOV), ballet
Copenhagen notes. WP v 11 n 8
p 4 Je '60
KAMERI THEATRE
Israel notes. WP v 12 n 3 p 4
D '60
KAMINSKI, JOSEF, composer
Première: Variations for English
Horn and Strings; Israel. MC v 161
n 7 p 20 Je '60
KANDA, AKIKO, dancer
AP wl ph: Spoleto. La S n 129-30
p 36 Ag-S '60
KANTERS, ROBERT. Le docteur

Tchékhov. por Spec n 1 p 9-10
1960
KARAJAN, HERBERT VON, 1908-,
conductor
Vienna; criticism of his operas.
Op v 11 n 8 p 547-8 Ag '60
---AP hl ph. La S n 132 p 78 N'60
KARSCH, WALTER (1906-). Ger-
man drama today. WT v 9 n 3
p 203-212 Autumn '60
KARSAVINA, TAMARA, 1885-,
ballerina
Five small AP phs. in article on
Les Ballets Russes. TD n 95
p 29 Jl-Ag '60
KARTUN, LEON, pianist
Machuel, Dominique. Paris re-
view. GDC n 263-4 p 491 Mr 11'60
KASEMETS, UDO. John Weinzweig
(1913-, Canadian composer). check-
list CMJ v 4 n 4 p 4-18 Summer'60
KASSEL MUSIC FESTIVAL
Program notes. WM n 3 p 56 Je '60
KATIMS, MILTON, 1909-, conduc-
tor
Career notes. AmM v 8 n 11 p 4
D '60
---Por ph: Seattle. AmM v 8 n 11
cover D '60
KATYA KABANOVA, opera
American première: review of
Empire State Festival near Bear
Mountain. ON v 25 n 2 p 22
O 29'60
---Sadler's Wells review. Op v 11
n 1 p 63 Ja '60
---Sadler's Wells; Marie Collier
and William McAlpine, AP hl ph.
Op v 11 n 1 p 64 Ja '60
KATZ, GEORGE, pianist
Awards: Fulbright; Naumberg;
Viotti Prize; London debut. AmM
v 8 n 5 p 8 Ja '60
KAUFMAN, GEORGE S. , 1889-,
producer
Directing, ens ph. Th Arts v 44
n 7 p 52 Jl '60
KAULA, DAVID. On Noh drama.
TDR v 5 n 1 p 61-72 S '60
KAUNAS OPERA
Repertory. Op v 11 n 4 p 286
Ap '60
KAWATAKE, SHIGETOSHI (1889-).
Shakespeare in the Japanese

(Kawatake)
theatre. Th R v 2 n 2 p 82-87 '60
KAYE, MARY, guitarist
With brother, Norman Kaye, and
accordionist Frankie Ross, ens
ph; por ph. also IM v 58 n 8
cover, p 15 F '60
KAYE, NORA, 1920-, ballerina
AP wl ph: Spoleto. TD n 95 cover
Jl-Ag '60
KEATING, JOHN (1919?-). A
bridge for young playwrights. WP
v 12 n 3 p 1 D '60
--- ---Interview with Margaret
Sullivan. Th Arts v 44 n 2 p 26,
28 F '60
--- ---Jason Robards, Jr. por Th
Arts v 44 n 4 p 10-2 Ap '60
--- ---A marathon named Merman.
il Th Arts v 44 n 9 p 62-3 S '60
--- ---New Dramatists Committee,
a bridge for young playwrights.
Th Arts v 44 n 7 p 17, 20, 63 Jl'60
--- ---The 1960-61 season on
Broadway. il Th Arts v 44 n 10 p 12-
17 O '60
--- ---(The problem of theatre
party and fund-raising audiences
in NYC.) Th Arts v 44 n 3 p 20, 22
Mr '60
--- ---Tammy Grimes. por Th Arts
v 44 n 11 p 20-2 N '60
--- ---To quote or not to quote
(using critic's comments in adver-
tising Broadway plays; special to
NYC in this era). Th Arts v 44
n 12 p 14-5, 76 D '60
---Por ph: Roderick MacArthur.
Th Arts v 44 n 10 p 16 O '60
KEENE, CONSTANCE, 1923-,
pianist
Notes on European repertory; Mrs.
Abram Chasins in private life. AmM
v 8 n 4 p 11 Ap '60
KEHIET, NIELS, dancer
AP wl ph: Denmark. TD n 93 p 24
My '60
KELLER, HANS (1919-). The new
in review; Donaueschingen 1959.
MR v 21 n 1 p 79-80 F '60
--- ---Wordless functional analysis:
the second year and beyond-I. MR
v 21 n 1 p 73-76 F '60
--- ---II. MR v 21 n 3 p 237-9 Ag '60

KELLER, HELEN, 1880-
Por ph: George Ham. Th Arts
v 44 n 8 p 2 Ag '60
KELLET, BRIAN. Shakespeare
through sun, rain and earthquake
(India). WP v 12 n 2 p 1, 4 N '60
KELLY, GENE, 1912-, dancer
At the Paris Opéra; notes and
an action picture. TD n 95 p 23
Jl-Ag '60
---With Richard Blareau, Paris
Opéra podium scene, ph. OpP
n 19 p 35 1960
KELLY, ROBERT, composer
Première: Toccata for Marimba
and Percussion Ensemble (Illinois
1960). ACAB v 9 n 3 p 32 1960
KEMPFF, WILHELM, 1895-,
pianist
Chamfray, Claude. Paris review.
GDC n 255-6 p 315 Ja 15'60
---Paris review. GDC n 275 p 752
Je 3'60
KENIN, HERMAN D. (1902-). In-
ternational String Congress spon-
sored by the American Federation
of Musicians. MEJ v 47 n 2 p 71
N-D '60
--- ---(Testimony before Federal
Communications Commission,
Washington, D. C. on "deceptive
use of foreign canned music".)
IM v 58 n 8 p 5, 41-2 F '60
---In Washington; in Brussels at
International Confederation of
Unions, several phs. IM v 58 n 8
p 4, 7 F '60
--- ---with legislators on the im-
portation of "illegal music" to the
US, several phs. IM v 58 n 10
p 5-6 Ap '60
THE KENTISH OPERA GROUP
Repertory notes. Op n 2 n 3 p 198
Mr '60
KENTON, STAN, 1912-, composer
Receiving $1000check from officials
of AFM, hl ph. IM v 59 n 4 p 7 O'60
KENTUCKY OPERA ASSOCIATION
Von Bomhard, Moritz, director,
on leave to Hamburg Opera. ON
v 25 n 7 p 7 D 24'60
KERMAN, JOSEPH. The place of
music in basic education. MEJ
v 46 n 5 p 43-6 Ap-My '60

KERN, RONALD C. Two designs by the elder Thomas Greenwood in 1777. Th Notbk v 15 n 1 p 31-32 Autumn '60

KERNODLE, GEORGE R. (1907-). Seven medieval theatres in one social structure. Th R v 2 n 1 p 26-36 1960

KEROGLY, opera
Baku; Mamedov in the title role, ens AP wl ph. Op v 11 n 1 p 46 Ja '60

KERR, RUSSELL. What price a career in music? What besides talent? MC v 162 n 1 p 7, 35 Jl '60

KERSLAKE, VICTOR (On Canada's music festivals.) CMJ v 5 n 1 p 35 Autumn '60

KESSLER, MINUETTA. (On Canada's music festivals.) CMJ v 5 n 1 p 34 Autumn '60

KESSLER, WALTER, oboist
Career notes; b. Tulsa. por IM v 58 n 8 p 31 F '60

KETELBY, ALBERT, 1875-1959, composer
Notes; b. Birmingham; d. Isle of Wight. MC v 161 n 1 p 6 Ja'60
---Obituary. MD v 50 n 9 p 19 Mr '60

KETTINGREACTIE, play
Pays-Bas; Max Croiset. WP v 11 n 10 p 9 Ag '60

KHATCHATURIAN, ARAM, 1903-, composer
Paris program; criticism of Katchaturian and of the pianist, Jacqueline Eymar. GDC n 267-8 p 563 Ap 8'60

KHOSLA, G. S. India (theatre report.) il WT v 9 n 2 p 165-6 Summer '60

KHOVANSTCHINA, opera
Venice criticism; Yugoslavian National Theatre at La Fenice. MC v 161 n 5 p 32 Ap '60

THE KILLDEER, play
Toronto notes; James Reany. WP v 11 n 5 p 2 Mr '60

KINCAID, WILLIAM (1897-). (His opinions on Stokowski as a conductor; on other conductors; on the Philadelphia Orchestra, 39

153

years). IM v 58 n 11 p 12-3 My'60
---Por ph: Philadelphia. IM v 58 n 11 p 12 My '60

KINES, THOMAS. (On Canadian music festivals, positive values stated by the president of the Ottawa Music Festival Association.) CMJ v 4 n 4 p 37-40 Summer '60

KING, LARRY, organist
With Sir William McKie, hl ph: London. AmM v 8 n 8 p 7 S '60

THE KING AND I, musical
Woman's College of the University of North Carolina, ens AP wl ph. PlM v 37 n 1 cover O '60

KING LEAR, play
Moscow, ens AP wl ph: 1960. WT v 9 n 4 p 361 Winter '60

KING LEAR, opera
Medici, Mario. Letters about King Lear (Verdi). Ver v 1 n 1 p 1039-1056 Ag '60

THE KING'S HENCHMAN, opera
Taylor, Deems. (On his own opera, The King's Henchman, and on American opera in general.) ON v 25 n 6 p 9-11 D 17'60

KIRCHNER, LEON, 1919-, composer
Première: Second String Quartet; NYC review. Mus Q v 46 n 1 p 73-4 Ja '60

KIRGHIZ OPERA
History; present repertory; review of Toktogul, opera with fine chorus parts, by Georgi Polyanovsky. Op v 11 n 4 p 289 Ap '60

KIRKPATRICK, RALPH, 1911-, harpsichordist
NYC; baroque "Cook's tour". MC v 161 n 3 p 29 F '60

KIRSTEN, DOROTHY (1917-). Interview, backstage at the San Francisco Opera. por ON v 25 n 1 p 18 O 8'60
---On horseback, as "La Faniculla del West", ph: San Francisco. LaS n 133 p 115 D '60

KITT, EARTHA, 1928-, actress
Critical comment on Jolly's Progress. Th Arts v 44 n 2 p 15 F'60

KLARMANN, ADOLF D. (1904-)
Friedrich Duerrenmatt and the tragic sense of comedy. TDR v 4 n 4 p 77-104 My '60

KLEBE, GISELHER, 1926-,
Comment. WT v 9 n 3 p 222
Autumn '60
---Première: The Murder of Cae-
sar, one-act opera; Essen notes.
MC v 161 n 3 p 47 F '60
---Wörner, Karl H. (Die tödlichen
Wünsche, opera, taken from Bal-
zac's la Peau de chagrin.) Mus Q
v 46 n 1 p 81-2 Ja '60
KLECKI, PAUL 1900-, conductor
And Maurizio Pollini, pianist with
the Orchestre National; Paris re-
view. GDC n 273 p 691 My 20'60
KLEES, JAY. Organizing an opera
audience. Op v 11 n 10 p 671-3
O '60
KLEIN, JOHN W. Nietzsche's atti-
tude to Bizet. MR v 21 n 3 p 215-
225 Ag '60
KLEPPER, WALTER MIHAIL,
composer
Première: Symphony No. I, In
Memoriam; Bucharest. WM n 5
p 104 O '60
KLOBUCAR, BERISLAV, conductor
Right profile por ph. La S n 124
p 73 Mr '60
KLOOSE, HANS-OTTO, singer
In Fledermaus; promise. Op v 2
n 3 p 207 Mr '60
DIE KLUGE, opera
Phillips, Linda. The Wise Woman,
Hobart première; Walter Stiasny,
conducting, Kurt Hommel, produc-
er, décor by Ronald Sinclair. MD
v 50 n 11 p 14 My '60
KNEPPER, JAMES, 1927-, trom-
bonist
Notes; b. Los Angeles. IM v 58
n 9 p 34 Mr '60
THE KNIGHTS OF THE ROUND
TABLE, play
The Playhouse, AP ph: San Fran-
cisco. Th Arts v 44 n 3 p 60 Mr'60
KNOX, SIR ROBERT, 1890-, director
Por ph. MD v 50 n 7 p 14 Ja '60
KNUDSEN, HANS (1886-). The
university drama department
WT v 9 n 3 p 262-264 Autumn '60
KOBER, DIETER, conductor
Por ph: Seymour. MC v 162 n 6
p 24 D '60
KOBIETA W TRUNDNEJ SYTUACJI,

play
Poland; Marek Domanski. WP v 12
n 1 p 10 O '60
KOCZIAN, JOHANNA VON, actress
In "A Clever Fool", AP ph: Munich.
Th Arts v 44 n 4 p 19 Ap '60
KODALY, ZOLTAN, 1882-, com-
poser
London visit. WM n 3 p 56 Je '60
---Married Sara Peceli (1939-).
MC v 161 n 3 p 34 F '60
KOEGLER, HORST. Düsseldorf-
Duisberg; opera review. Op v 11
n 11 p 764-5 N '60
--- ---Opera reviews. Op 1960
KOGAN, LEONID, 1924?-, violinist
Chicago review. MC v 162 n 5 p 21
N '60
KOGAN, MISCHA
Williams, Vernon G. Ten years
achievement in chamber music
(in Melbourne). il MD v 50 n 7
p 12-3 Ja '60
KOHON, HAROLD, violinist
Notes. IM v 59 n 5 p 36 N '60
KOHS, ELLIS, 1916-, composer
With Louis Kaufman, violinist,
and Dr. John Vincent, small ph:
Los Angeles. MC v 162 n 2 p 18
Ag '60
KOLODIN, IRVING (1908-). Includ-
ing the Scandinavian (singers of
world statue developed in Copen-
hagen and in Stockholm; with cri-
ticism). portfolio Th Arts v 44
n 3 p 46-7 Mr '60
KONER, PAULINE, dancer
AP wl ph: Barbara Morgan, Th
Arts v 44 n 11 p 61 N '60
KÖNIG HIRSCH, opera
Henze; ens AP wl ph: Heinz Kös-
ter, 1956. WT v 9 n 3 p 225
Autumn '60
KOOREE AND THE MISTS, ballet
Music by James Penberthy; re-
view of West Australian Ballet.
MD v 51 n 1 p 28-9 Jl '60
KOPS, BERNARD, playwright
WL ph. La S n 122 p 60 Ja '60
KORCZAK UND DIE KINDER, play
Scene Staatstheater, Kassel, 1960
ph: Nehrdich. WT v 9 n 3 p 209
Autumn '60
KORN, RICHARD, 1908-, conductor

Por ph: NYC. MC v 161 n 6 p 32 My '60

KORNGOLD, ERICH WOLFGANG, 1897-1957, composer
Career sketch; b. Brno; US citizen 1943. ON v 24 n 20 p 12-3 Mr 19'60
---Notes; b. Brno, Moravia. AmM v 8 n 9 p 7 O '60

KORTE, KARL, composer
NYC notes on Oboe Quintet. MC v 161 n 7 p 25 Je '60

KOUN, KAROLOS. (On staging Chekhov; Greek viewpoint.) il WT v 9 n 2 p 132-3 Summer '60

THE KOUSSEVITSKY FOUNDATION
List of grants for new compositions. AmM v 8 n 6 p 14 Jl '60

KOZUCH, THADDEUS, pianist
Criticism. GDC n 274 p 725 My 27'60

KRACHMALNICK, JACOB, violinist
Cleveland return. AmM v 8 n 10 p 13 N '60

KRAEHENBUEHL, DAVID, 1923-, composer
American première of Epitaphs Concertant'àt Chautauqua under Walter Hendl. MC v 162 n 1 p 24 Jl '60

KRALL, HEIDI, singer
Hl ph: Newmann. ON v 24 n 9 p 3 Ja 2'60

KRAUSE, HORST, dancer
and Diane Mansart in The Nutcracker, AP wl ph: Hanover. TD n 89 p 17 Ja '60

KRAUSE, TOM, 1935-, singer
Finland; note. MC v 161 n 7 p 17 Je '60

KRAUSS, ALFREDO, singer
In La Sonnambula, AP hl ph. LaS n 125 p 45 Ap '60

KREDIT BEI NIBELUNGEN, play
Potsdam notes; Fritz Kuhn. WP v 11 n 8 p 11 Je '60
---Ens AP wl ph: Potsdam. WP v 11 n 8 Je '60

KREISLER, FRITZ, 1875-, violinist
Por ph. MC v 161 n 3 p 10 F '60

KREMS, AUSTRIA
Symposium for Old Music (Gothic and Renaissance) under J. Mertin

of Vienna; program. WM n 2 p 31 Ap '60

KRENEK, ERNST (1900-). Extents and limits of serial techniques. il Mus Q v 46 n 2 p 210-232 Ap '60
--- ---Sestina (his analysis of his own composition). Mus Q v 46 n 2 p 223-4 Ap '60
---Notes; honors. WM n 3 p 56 Je '60
---Por ph: Lengemann. WM n 6 p 136 D '60

KRIPS, JOSEF, 1902-, conductor
Career since 1947; notes. HF v 10 n 4 p 12, 14 Ap'60

KRITZ, KARL, conductor
Career notes;b. Vienna. IM v 58 n 9 p 36 Mr'60

KROKOVER, ROSALYN. New York City Ballet. MC v 162 n 6 p 12 D'60
--- ---Three companies offer new dance productions. MC v 161 n 6 p 9 My'60

KROLL QUARTET
NYC review. MC v 162 n 6 p 36 D'60

KRONE, MAX T. (1901-). Freundschaft Durch Musik (US schools in Europe surveyed by the co-ordinator of music). MEJ v 46 n 3 p 21-3 Ja'60
--- ---Guides to Musical Experience (as adopted 1959 school year by US Army Dependents'Schools in Europe). il MEJ v 47 n 2 p 48-9 N-D'60

KRONENBERGER, LOUIS(1904-). The fifties:patchwork progress (US theatre). Th Arts v 44 n 1 p 10-11 Ja'60

KRUGER, RUDOLF, conductor
Career notes;b. Berlin. IM v 58 n 9 p 36 Mr'60

KRUPA, GENE, 1909-, jazz drummer
Cerulli, Dom. (Career sketch 1921 to date.) por IM v 58 n 10 p 10-1 Ap'60
---Several phs. IM v 58 n 10 cover, p 10 Ap'60

KRUYSEN, BERNARD, singer
With John Blot;Paris review. GDC n 290 p 322 N 25'60

KUAN HAN-CHING, c. 1180-1260
Peking;celebration of the 700th
anniversary of Kuan Han-ching;
review. Th R v 2 n 1 p 48 1960
---A scene from the Canton oper-
atic version;Ma Shih-tseng in the
title role, ens AP wl ph. Th R
v 2 n 1 p 25 1960
KUBELSKY, BENJAMIN
See Benny, Jack, 1894-, singer
KUCHTA, GLADYS, singer
Notes;b. Chicopee, Massachusetts.
Am M v 8 n 5 p 5 Je'60
KUENTZ, PAUL
Bruyr, José. Paris;Orchestre de
Chambre Paul Kuentz. GDC n 289
p 297 N 18'60
---Orchestre de chambre;Suzanne
Demarquez's Rhapsodie lyrique
pour violon et orchestre, etc. GDC
n 287 p 229 N 4'60
KUIBYSHEV OPERA
Parker, Ralph. History of the op-
era and present work under Anatol
Pikar. Op v 11 n 4 p 1289 Ap '60
KULIG, play
Katowicz. Wybicki. WP v 12
n 3 p 35 D '60
KUNGSHOLM OPERA THEATRE
View toward performance; view
below stage where the puppeteers
work, phs: Chicago. ON v 24 n 17
p 12-3 F 27'60
KUNST, DR. JAAP, 1891-, musi-
cologist
President of the International Folk
Music Council; note. WM n 1 p 8
F '60
KUPFERBERG, HERBERT. All-
purpose tenor, Nicolai Gedda
(1927-). por HF v 10 n 8 p 45-6
Ag '60
--- ---Giulietta Simionato, a mezzo
who delights in being a mezzo. por
HF v 10 n 2 p 49-50, F '60
DER KURASSIER SEBASTIAN, play
und sein Sohn; Ens AP wl ph: Ilse
Buhs, Berlin, 1958. WT v 9 n 3
p 205 Autumn '60
KURKA, ROBERT, 1921-1957, com-
poser
His opera, Schweik; career notes
of Czech origin from Illinois;"stands
near Martinu". Op v 11 n 5 p 346

My '60
KURTAG, GYÖRGY, 1926-, com-
poser
Critical notes on a group of Hun-
garian composers. Mus Q v 46 n 4
p 534 O '60
DIE KURVE, play
Lübeck notes; Tankred Dorst.
WP v 11 n 10 p 13 Ag '60
KUYPER, GEORGE ADRIAN, 1899-,
impresario
Hollywood Bowl and Southern Cal-
ifornia Symphony Association;
notes. MC v 161 n 3 p 38 F '60
KYO-MAI, play
Tokyo; Hojo Hidejo. WP v 11 n 9
p 9 Jl '60
KYOJIN DENSETSU, play
Tokyo notes; Abe Kobo. WP v 11
n 9 p 10 Jl '60

L

LABEY, MAURICE (1875?-). 4e
Symphonie (études musicales an-
alytiques). GDC n 274 p 728
My 27'60
LABIS, ATTILIO, dancer
As David, ens AP ph. OpP n 19 p 19
1960
---Dans la Danse devant l'Arche, le
Roi David (Charrat) à l'Opéra, AP
wl ph: Paris. TD n 98 p 21 D '60
---E Josette Amiel dans La Clef des
Songes, AP wl ph: Michel Petit. TD
n 98 p 28 D '60
LABROCA, MARIO (1896-). Die Sch-
irmherrschaft des Internationalen
Rates der Musik: Das Institut für
Verdi-Studien. Ver v 1 n 1 preface
Ap '60
--- ---Il Patrocino del consiglio in-
ternazionale della musica. Ver v 1
n 1 Ap '60
LE LAC DES CYGNES (BOURMEIS-
TER), ballet
Lyon, Raymond. Review Paris
Opéra. GDC n 295 p 483 D 30'60
---Maitre de Ballet du Théâtre Stan-
islavsky de Moscou: à l'Opéra de
Paris, 4 actes. TD n 97 p 2 N '60
---Paris Opéra notes. OpP n 19
p 46 1960
LE LAC DES CYGNES (ROSEN)
156

Munich, ballet report. il ballet
TD n 91 p 16-7 Mr '60
LACOTTE, PIERRE, dancer
With Josette Clavier in Gosse de
Paris, AP wl ph: Cannes. TD
n 93 p 5 My '60
LADERMAN, EZRA, composer
Première: Sextet for Winds and
Double Bass (Bronxville 1960).
ACAB v 9 n 3 p 32 1960
LADY FROM THE SEA (CULL-
BERG), ballet
American Ballet Theatre; NYC
première; based on Strindberg
play. PlM v 37 n 1 p 10 O '60
---Serrano and Fernandez, AP
wl ph: American Ballet Theatre.
MC v 161 n 6 p 9 My '60
LADY MACBETH OF MZENSK,
opera
Carter, Elliott. (Review of Sho-
stakovitch work at Cologne.)
Mus Q v 46 n 3 p 367-8 Jl '60
---Koegler, Horst. Düsseldorf
production. il ON v 24 n 9 p 14
Ja 2'60
---Düsseldorf production; history
of the work; "Shostakovich's veto
too late". Op v 11 n 1 p 33-5
Ja '60
---Düsseldorf, two AP phs: Hess.
Op v 11 n 1 p 35 Ja '60
THE LADY'S NOT FOR BURNING,
play
Bibliography. TDR v 4 n 3 p 95
Mr '60
---Bruxelles, 1952; ens AP wl ph:
Belgo-Presse. WT v 9 n 1 p 36
Spring '60
LAESTADIUS, LARS-LEVI. (On
staging Chekhov; Swedish view-
point.) il WT v 9 n 2 p 133-4
Summer '60
LAFON, MADELINE, 1923-,
dancer
In La Dame aux Camélias (T.
Gsovsky), AP wl ph: Paris Opéra.
OpP n 19 p 45 1960
---With her maître, Elvira Roné;
with Peter Van Dijk in Swan Lake;
as "Merle" in Peter and the Wolf
(TV), 3 AP phs. TD n 94 p 13
Je '60
LA FONTAINE, JEAN DE, 1621-95

His fables, especially "Renard et
les Raisins", discussed by Guilher-
ne Figueiredo as world art, "travers
le monde". WP v 11 n 6 p 1 Ap '60
LAJTHA, LÁSZLÓ, 1891-, com-
poser
Criticism. Mus Q v 46 n 4 p 528
O '60
LAKMÉ, opera
Philadelphia Grand Opera revival;
notes, ON v 24 n 22 p 26 Ap 2'60
LALAUNI, LILA, pianist-composer
Career notes. GDC n 269-70
p 575 Ap 22'60
---Paris criticism; also her own
première "Petite Suite". GDC
n 276 p 788 Je 10'60
---Por ph. GDC n 269-270 cover
Ap 22'60
LALO, EDOUARD, 1823-1892,
composer
Schulz, Gisa. A Northern legend:
Le Roi d'Ys (with career sketch
of composer). ON v 24 n 14 p 12, 31
F 6'60
---Por ph: Culver. ON v 24 n 14
p 12 F 6'60
LAING, HUGH, 1914-, dancer
In Tudor choreography, AP wl
ph. La Scala n 122 p 22 Ja '60
LA MARCHINA, ROBERT, cellist
Notes; b. NYC. IM v 59 n 5 p 37
N '60
LAMARE, JEAN-YVES. Un collo-
que des jeunes travailleurs intell-
ectuels. GDC n 278 p 843 Je 24'60
LAMASSE, ALETH, violinist
Paris criticism. GDC n 288 p 258
N 11'60
LAMBERT, RAYMOND, 1903-,
pianist
Sydney notes. MD v 51 n 6 p 12
D '60
LAMERS, WILLIAM M. (1900-).
The two kinds of music (school
music). MEJ v 46 n 4 p 36-38
F-Mr '60
LAMMERS, GERDA, singer
In Elektra; Covent Garden review.
il Op v 11 n 7 p 509 Jl '60
THE LAMOUREUX ORCHESTRA
Boston criticism. MC v 161 n 6
p 29 My '60
---NYC review; Igor Markevitch;

157

(The Lamoureux Orchestra)
"concerned with putting a fine lacquer on the music". MC v 161 n 5 p 15 Ap '60
---Paris; Concerts Lamoureux, Festival Beethoven: Bernard Haitink (hollandais); Pierre Dervaux; Geofges Prêtre; notes. GDC n 289 p 295 N 18'60
---Washington, D. C. notes. MC v 161 n 6 p 32 My '60
LAMY, MARCEL
E il maestro Vincenzo Cinque, hl ph: Paris. La S n 124 p 69 Mr '60
LANCE, ALBERT, singer
In La Tosca, two AP phs. OpP n 19 p 12, 14 1960
LANDAU, VICTOR. Paul Hindemith, a case study in theory and practice. MR v 21 n 1 p 38-54 F '60
LANDER, HARALD, 1905-, choreographer
Rio de Janiero; success in mounting ballets and training dancers. il TD n 97 p 24, 29 N '60
LANDER, HAROLD. Lincoln's touring partnership (Loughborough, Scunthorpe, Rotherham and the Lincoln Theatre Company). NTM v 1 n 4 p 8-12 Jl '60
THE LANDLADY, play
Ens AP wl ph: Paris. WP v 12 n 3 D '60
LANDON, H. C. ROBBINS (1926?-). It all began in Bonn (Beethoven's early life in Bonn; his playing for Mozart in Vienna; study with Haydn). il HF v 10 n 4 p 40-3, 106 Ap '60
--- ---The Red Priest of Venice (Antonio Vivaldi). il HF v 10 n 8 p 30-35 Ag '60
LANDOWSKA, WANDA, 1897-1959, harpsichordist
Dumesnil, René. Wanda Landowska et les dimanches de Saints-leu-la-Forêt. La S n 133 p 80 D '60
---Restout, Denise. Mamusia; vignettes of Wanda Landowska. il HF v 10 n 10 p 42-47, 136 O '60
---Portfolio of 14 pictures. HF v 10 n 10 cover, p 42-47 O '60
LANE, GLORIA, 1930?-, singer
London criticism of her Carmen

Op v 11 n 1 p 68 Ja '60
---As Carmen, AP hl ph: Covent Garden. Op v 11 n 1 p 68 Ja'60
---In Carmen head-dress, hl ph: NYC. MC v 162 n 6 p 31 D '60
LANG, PAUL HENRY (1901-). Editorial on modern music compositions; the aesthetics beneath "serialization". Mus Q v 46 n 2 p 145-154 Ap '60
LANG, PEARL, dancer
NYC concert; list of Juilliard dancers in her group. J Rev v 7 n 1 p 12 Winter 59-60
---AP wl ph: Peter Basch. Th Arts v 44 n 11 p 65 N '60
LANGDON, MICHAEL, singer
As Ochs, AP hl ph: London. Op v 11 n 12 p 849 D '60
LANGHI, UGO RAMELLINI.
Ricordo di un "Prince Charmant" della musica spagnola. (Enrique Granados). il La S n 123 p 51-4 F '60
LANNER, JOSEF, 1801-1843, composer
Barford, Philip T. The early dances of Josef Lanner. MR v 21 n 2 p 114-120 My '60
--- ---Josef Lanner: a further appraisal. MR v 21 n 3 p 179-185 Ag '60
LAPARRA, RAOUL, 1876-1943, composer
Chamfray, Claude. Fiche biographique. GDC n 267-8 p 568 Ap 8'60
LAPEYRETTE, KETTY,?- 1960, singer
Obituary notes. Op v 11 n 12 p 839 D '60
LAREDO, JAINE, 1941-, violinist
Notes on London debut; b. Bolivia. AmM v 8 n 3 p 6 Mr '60
---Por ph. HF v 10 n 7 p 52 Jl'60
LA ROCCA, D. JAMES (NICK), 1889-
Career notes; Italian family in New Orleans. por IM v 59 n 5 p 14-5 N '60
---Por ph: Larry Karl. IM v 59 n 5 p 14 N '60
LARRAIN, RAYMOND DE , scenic designer
La Belle au Bois Dormant, Cuevas notes. TD n 96 p 12-9 S-O '60

---La Belle au Bois dormant: le rideau d'avant-scène du dernier tableau; Nereide; Dame de la Reine; Chevalier de la Fée aux Etoiles; Le Prince de France: décor phs. TD n 96 cover, p 14-5 S -O '60

LARRIEU, MAXENCE, flutist
Machuel, Dominique. Lea Roussel-Maxence Larrieu; Paris. GDC n 267-8 p 562 Ap 8'60

LARROQUE, DIAZ, singer
With Adolfo Mindlin; Paris criticism. GDC n 269-70 p 598 Ap 22'60

LARSON, ORVILLE K. Robert Edmond Jones' Henry VIII (with 8 designs never produced, phs.) PlM v 37 n 3 p 52-4 D '60

LA RUE, JAN (1918-). Handel''s clarinet. MR v 21 n 3 p 177-8 Ag '60

LA RUE, PIERRE DE, ?-1518, composer
Chansons; Album de Marguerite d'Austriche; Martin Picker analyzes these unidentified songs and includes some facsimile pages. Mus Q v 46 n 3 p 329-343 Jl '60
---Superius part of "Pour ung jamais", facsimile Brussels Bibl. Roy. Mus Q v 46 n 3 p 343 Jl '60

THE LAST JOKE, play
London notes; Enid Bagnold. WP v 12 n 3 p 36 D '60

THE LAST TEMPTATIONS, play
Helsinki; ens AP wl ph: Unho, 1959. WT v 9 n 3 p 282 Autumn '60

LAS VEGAS
City travel sketch; AFM convention plans there; "more live musicians employed per capita than any other city in the world". il IM v 58 n 9 p 11 Mr '60

LATIN AMERICA
Buenaventura, Enrique. Bird's-eye view of the Latin-American theatre. il WT v 9 n 3 p 265-271 Autumn '60

LATIN AMERICAN DANCE
Eloury, Faly-Hao, Rock-Conga, le Bamba. TD n 95 p 25 Jl-Ag'60
---Paris; chants et de Danses d'Amerique latines; à la salle du conservatoire TD n 90 p 18 F '60

LATIN AMERICAN MUSIC
Centers in several countries set up to select artists to appear with the Dallas Symphony Orchestra; $1000 plus expenses. MC v 162 n 3 p 5 S '60
---Eastman School's departure from Festival of American Music to include Latin-American; review. MC v 161 n 7 p 6 Je '60

LAUGHTON, CHARLES, 1899-, actor
Hl ph: 1931. Th Arts v 44 n 9 p 60 S '60

LAURENT, JEAN
Liége; Xme Gala chorégraphique. TD n 97 p 2 N '60

LAUSANNE
Sénéchaud, Marcel. Lausanne; opera report. Op v 11 n 12 p 838 D '60

LAUWERYNS, GEORGES
Career notes; "un chef de théâtre". GDC n 263-4 p 482 Mr 11'60

LAVELLE, PAUL, director
NYC; Freedomland music man, por ph. IM v 59 n 4 p 35 O '60

LAVINIA TRA i DANNATI, play
Notes on Anna Proclemer and Giorgio Albertazzi. por La S n 123 p 60-1 F '60

LAWLER, VANETT (1904-). Music education as a profession. por IM v 58 n 9 p 18-9 Mr '60

LAWRENCE, JEROME, (1915-). and Robert E. Lee. The Gang's All Here (text, two sets and 3 scenes, phs; NYC cast). Th Arts v 44 n 11 p 26-56 N '60

LAWRENCE, ROBERT. Wagner's eunuch (criticism of Kundry; of Klingsor). ON v 24 n 23 p 4-5 Ap 9'60

LAWS, HUBERT, JR.
With flute, ph. J Rev v 7 n 3 p 21 Fall '60

LAWTON, DOROTHY, 1875-1960, librarian
Obituary; b. Bournemouth, England. MC v 161 n 4 p 7 Mr '60

LAZARE, play
Argentina notes; Martha Lehman.

159

(Lazare)
WP v 12 n 3 p 26 D '60
LEACH, RICHARD P. West side
story: New York City in 1964
(as projected by Lincoln Center's
Assistant Director of booking
attractions). ON v 25 n 2 p 13-14
O 29'60
LEADER OF THE HOUSE, play
Liverpool notes; Nigel Balchin.
WP v 11 n 6 p 13 Ap '60
LEAVER, GARDNER. Margaret
Sullavan, four drawings. Th Arts
v 44 n 2 p 27 F '60
LEBERTRE, NINON, dancer
With Van Dijk in le Peau de Cha-
grin; with Michel Rayne in Pellé-
as et Mélisande, two AP wl phs:
Paris. Op P n 19 p 67-8 1960
LEBESQUE, MORVAN. Les ren-
dez-vous de Gérard Philipe. il
Spec n 1 p 47-52 1960
LEBOW, HOWARD. Report from
Hungary. por J Rev v 7 n 3 p 3-6
Fall '60
LECKY, ELEZZER (1903-). Mys-
tery in the plays of Christopher
Fry. TDR v 4 n 3 p 80-7 Mr '60
LEDDY, J. F. The threshold of a
new age (Canada and US as free
countries; assessment of that
today). por MEJ v 47 n 1 p 37-40
S-O '60
LE DIZES, MARYVONNE, violin-
ist
And pianist, Maarten Bon; Paris
review. GDC n 283 p 100 O 7'60
LEDUC, MICHEL, 1917-, profes-
seur
Wolff, Stéphane. En Bavardant
avec Michel Leduc; Marseilles.
por GDC n 275 p 747 Je 3'60
LEE, ALYNE DUMAS, singer
Chicago notes. MC v 162 n 6
p 24 D '60
LEE, CANADA, 1907-1952, actor
In The Duchess of Malfi, AP wl
ph: Vandamm. Th Arts v 44 n 10
p 11 O '60
LEFEBURE, YVONNE (Elise),
1898-, pianist
Career notes. GDC n 291 p 337
D 2'60
---La Croix de la Légion

d'Honneur; aussi concert à Yvonne
Lefebure; Institut Néerlandais,
Paris. GDC n 257-8 p 360 Ja 29'60
---Paris criticism. GDC n 295 p 491
D 30'60
---Por ph: Lipnitzki. GDC n 291
cover D 2'60
LE FRANÇOIS, RENÉE, singer
Paris review; Emy Chardon and
Robert Salvat assisting. GDC
n 261-2 p 439 F 26'60
LeGALLIENNE, EVA, 1899-, actress
With Joseph Schildraut in Liliom,
AP wl ph:NYC, 1932. Th Arts v 44
n 9 p 17 S'60
LEGAY, HENRY, singer
Mennesson, Felix. Eugene Oneguine
et Henry Legay à l'Opéra-Comique.
GDC n 267-8 p 550 Ap 8'60
THE LEGEND of the INVISIBLE CITY
of KITEZH, opera
Rome review of Rimsky-Korsakov.
Op v 11 n 8 p 563 Ag'60
LEGGE, WALTER. (On London mus-
ical critics of the moment.)HF v 10
n 8 p 24 Jl'60
---Notes on his tiff with the music
critics of London. MC v 161 n 7
p 13 Je'60
LA LEGGENDA della città invisi-
ble, opera
Scotto, Renata, e Galié, AP wl ph:
Rome. LaS n 128 p 30 Jl'60
LEGGIO, CARMEN, saxophonist
With instrument, ph. IM v 58 n 12
p 35 Je'60
LEGINSKA, ETHEL, 1883-, composer
Première:Three Victorian Portraits, NYC. MC v 161 n 1 p 35 Ja'60
LEGISLATION
US;notes on attempts to subsidize
the National Symphony Orchestra
and other such art endeavors. IM
v 58 n 12 p 45 Je'60
--- ---Pelly Bill to ban foreign recordings as sound track for otherwise American TV or motion picture film;notes. IM v 58 n 12 p 5
Je'60
--- ---President Herman D. Kenin,
of American Federation of Musicians on "deceptive use of foreign
canned music"; his testimony before Federal Commission. IM

160

v 58 n 8 p 5, 41-2 F '60
--- ---Congress; H. R. 11043 to
correct "evasion of federal law"
on importing foreign musicians
to play at sub-standard fees; also
"wet-back" tapes of foreign music
produced by those "ineligible to
enter US" in person; notes. IM
v 58 n 10 p 5 Ap '60
LEGNANI, EMILIO SIOLI. Raro
cimelio manzoniano. facsimiles
La S n 122 p 44-6 Ja '60
LEHMANN, LILLI, 1848-1929,
singer
Hl ph. MC v 161 n 3 p 11 F '60
LEHMANN, LOTTE, 1885-, singer
Chicago, hl ph: Sorensen. Op v 11
n 11 p 757 N '60
LEHMANN, WILFRED, 1929-,
violinist
Career notes. MD v 51 n 2 p 12
Ag '60
LEICESTER'S CIVIC THEATRE
Milliard, H. L. (The Theatre
Society and the City Council on
plans for a civic theatre.) NTM
v 1 n 3 p 9-11 Ap '60
LEINSDORF, ERICH, 1912-, con-
ductor
Parsifal at the Metropolitan; cri-
ticism. Op v 11 n 6 p 409 Je '60
LEIPZIG OPERA
The building described by Sieg-
mund Wölfing; Alan Bush on opera
events; and a review of the new
Meistersinger by Ossia Trilling.
Op v 11 n 12 p 802-811 D '60
---Exterior of the Opera House,
ph: Helga Wallmüller; two inter-
ior views. Op v 11 n 12 p 802-5
D '60
LEMENI, NICOLA ROSSI
See Rossi-Lemeni, Nicola, 1922-,
singer
LEMMON, JACK, 1925-, actor
Por ph: Murray Laden. Th Arts
v 44 n 10 p 14 O '60
LENGYEL, ATTY, violinist
And Gabrielle Lengyel, Paris re-
view. GDC n 287 p 228 N 4'60
---Paris review: Atty Lengyel and
Gabrielle, pianist. GDC n 273
p 689 My 20'60
LENINGRAD SYMPHONY

London notes; Dimitri Shostakovich in person for his Cello Concerto, played by Rostopovich. MC
v 162 n 6 p 30 D '60
---London recording notes. HF v 10
n 12 p 12 D '60
---Paris reviews by Dominique Ma-
chuel, by Serge Berthoumieux.
GDC n 285 p 165 O 21'60
---With conductor, Eugen Mra-
vinsky, ens ph. also his por ph.
WM n 6 p 134-5 D '60
LENOIR, JEAN-PIERRE. French
theatre under the Fifth Republic.
Th Arts v 44 n 12 p 60-3 D '60
--- ---Paris: past, present, pro-
spective. il Th Arts v 44 n 12
p 67, 74 D '60
--- ---Theatre, Paris. Th Arts
v 44 n 1 p 24-5 Ja '60
--- ---Theatre, Prague. portfolio
Th Arts v 44 n 8 p 57-60 Ag '60
LENOX STRING QUARTET
Goldman, Richard Franko. New
York (premières: Sessions' Quin-
tet, Kirchner's Second String Quar-
tet, Krenek's Sixth String Quartet;
and Babbitt's Composition for
Four Instruments, 1948). Mus Q
v 46 n 1 p 71-76 Ja '60
LEPIANKIEWICZ, JULIUS, pianist
Paris review; Polish pianist. GDC
n 273 p 691 My 20'60
LERNER, EDWARD R. The "German" works of Alexander Agricola
(1446-1506). Mus Q v 46 n 1 p 56-
66 Ja '60
LEROUX, XAVIER, 1863-1919,
composer
Chamfray, Claude. Fiche biographique. GDC n 269-70 p 602
Ap 22'60
LESSEL, FRANCISZEK, 1780-1838,
composer
Golos, George S. Some Slavic predecessors of Chopin. Mus Q v 46
n 4 p 437-447 O '60
LESTRUD, VERNON. The playwright's the thing (getting new
playwrights). PlM v 36 n 6 p 132
Mr '60
LESUR, DANIEL (1908-). Ouver-
ture pour un Festival (études musicales analytiques). GDC n 263-4

(Lesur)
p 494 Mr 11'60
LESURE, FRANÇOIS (1923-). A
step toward a general inventory
of ancient music: International
Inventory of Music Sources (mu-
sic prior to 1800 in libraries).
WM n 2 p 29 Ap '60
LETTRE MORTE, play
Criticism. Th Arts v 44 n 12
p 74 D '60
---Paris notes; Robert Pinget. WP
v 11 n 8 p 5 Je '60
LETTRES D'AMOUR, play
Bucarest notes; Virgil Stoenscu.
WP v 11 n 9 p 11 Jl '60
LEUR JOUR, play
Prague, 1959; AP ph: Svoboda.
WT v 9 n 1 p 72 Spring '60
LEVY, MICHEL-MAURICE, 1883-,
composer
Chamfray, Claude. DeBetove à
Michel-Maurice Lévy. GDC n 273
p 684 My 20'60
LEVENTRITT AWARD
Twelve semi-finalists 1960; 5
American; list. AmM v 8 n 6 p 8
Jl '60
LEWIS, EARLE, 1885-1959
Noble, Helen. (Career sketch of
Metropolitan box office manager
since 1908; b. NYC.) por ON
v 24 n 10 p 8 Ja 9'60
LEWIS, JOHN, 1912?-, composer
Schuller, Gunther A. John Lewis
on the modern jazz beachhead.
HF v 10 n 10 p 54-56 O '60
---Two phs: Clemens Kallischer.
HF v 10 n 10 p 54, 56 O '60
LEWIS, RICHARD, 1914-, singer
As Ottavio, AP hl ph: Guy Gra-
vett. Op v 11 p 16 Autumn '60
LEWIS, ROBERT (1921?-). A
point of view and a place to prac-
tice it (thesis that we need today
a place like The Group Theatre
1931-41 to train theatre people.)
Th Arts v 44 n 4 p 62-3 Ap '60
---Directing Kim Stanley and
Horst Buchholz, ph. Th Arts
v 44 n 7 p 52 Jl '60
LEWIS, STEPHEN. (On his play
"Sparrers Can't Sing".) il NTM
v 2 n 1 p 12-5 O '60

LEWISOHN STADIUM
Concluding programs of the 43rd
season: notes. MC v 162 n 3 p 11
S '60
---Prize winners, medals from the
Mayor of New York City: Malcolm
Frager, Sara Blum; Stuart Canin,
Jaime Laredo, Ivan Davis; programs.
MC v 162 n 2 p 11 Ag '60
---Reports. MC v 162 n 1 p 21 Jl'60
LHEVINNE, ROSINA, 1880-, pianist
Citation by Juilliard School and her
reply il J Rev v 7 n 2 p 24-5
Spring '60
---Notes. por J Rev v 7 n 1 p 15
Winter 59-60
---With Dr. Arthur Wolf (Los Ange-
les) and George Kuyper, director of
Hollywood Bowl, hl ph: L. A. Con-
servatory. MC v 161 n 4 p 40 Mr'60
LIBRETTOS
Beaumarchais, author of the satires,
The Barber of Seville and The Marr-
iage of Figaro; real name Pierre
Augustin Caron; other notes. ON
v 24 n 12 p 8 Ja 23'60
---Cudworth, Charles. (On good and
bad opera translators.) HF v 10 n 11
p 53-5 N '60
---Flora, Francesca. The libretto
(Un Ballo in Maschera). Ver v 1 n 1
p 305-353 Ap '60
--- ---Il Libretto (Un Ballo in Masche-
ra); Act III. Ver 1 n 2 p 662-678
Ag '60
---Germany today; comment. WT
v 9 n 3 p 222 Autumn '60
---Heriot, Angus. Emile Zola as
librettist. il Op v 11 n 9 p 595-
99 S '60
---McElroy, George. The unhappy
fella; I (Tristan and similar legends).
ON v 24 n 10 p 4-5, 29 Ja 9'60
--- ---II. ON v 24 n 11 p 4-5
Ja 16'60
---McKee, J. N. The symphonic
element in opera. MR v 21 n 1
p 30-37 F '60
---Morini, Mario. Ojetti, libretti-
sta per una volta. il La Scala n 122
p 28-32 Ja '60
---Operas dealing with revolution-
ary struggles; Paul Nettl's survey.
ON v 24 n 15 p 6-7 F 13'60

---Rigotti, Domenico. Cechov librettista mancato. il La S n 129-30 p 26-7 Ag-S '60
---Sedwick, Frank. (Il Trovatore; sources.) ON v 24 n 17 p 4-5 F 27'60
---Stevenson, Florence. Without prescription (poisoning in librettos; famous poisoners). ON v 24 n 22 p 14, 32 Ap 2'60
---Valency, Maurice. Flight into lunacy ("stories, no matter how fantastic, must make sense"). ThArts v 44 n 8 p 8-9, 68 Ag '60
---Whetstone, George A. Libretto by Zola (notes on his several opera librettos). ON v 24 n 18 p 13, 30 Mr 5'60

HET LICHTE HUIS, play
Flanders, 1949; ens AP wl ph: Segers. WT v 9 n 1 p 60 Spring '60

LIDART, NORA. Serge Lifar à Athènes. il TD n 97 p 6-8 N'60

LIEBESLIEDER WALTZ (BALANCHINE), ballet
Note. AmM v 8 n 10 p 11 N '60

LIEBL, KARL, singer
Career notes; b. Bavaria. il ON v 24 n 18 p 15 Mr 5'60
---As Erik in The Flying Dutchman, AP phs: Melançon. ON v 24 n 18 Mr 5'60
---As Parsifal AP ph: Melançon. ON v 24 n 23 p 17 Ap 9'60

DAS LIED VON DER ERDE
Mahler; Fischer-Dieskau, Murray Dickie, Paul Kletzki in EMI studios; notes. HF v 10 n 6 p 12 Je '60
---Roddy, Joseph. Mahler recordings, Angel and Columbia reviews. HF v 10 n 12 p 59-60 D '60

LIÈGE
Ledain, Freddy. La Fiancée vendue; La Malibrau. GDC n 265-6 p 518 Mr 25'60

LIFAR, SERGE, 1905-, choreographer
À la Sorbonne. TD n 92 p 14 Ap '60
---Lidart, Nora. A Athènes. il TD n 97 p 6-8 N '60

LIFE WITH FATHER, play
Ens AP wl ph: 1939. Th Arts v 44 n 9 p 12 S '60

LIGABUE, ILVA, singer
As Donna Elvira, AP hl ph: Guy Gravett, Glyndebourne. Op v 11 n 11 p 750 N '60; same. Op v 11 cover Autumn '60

LIGETI, GYÖRGY, 1923-, composer
Cologne; "Apparitions" for orchestra; review. MR v 21 n 3 p 242-4 Ag '60
---Notes. Mus Q v 46 n 4 p 531 O '60

LIGHTING
Bonnat, Yves (1912-). The lighting of open-air performances. il WT v 9 n 2 p 149-157 Summer '60
---Echart, William, and Jean. Scenic design and lighting. portfolio Th Arts v 44 n 7 p 55-7, 67 Jl '60
---Open-air; Aix-les-Bains 1956: one construction and one audience, ph. WT v 9 n 2 p 150 Summer '60

LA LIGNE DE SANG, play
Arnold, Paul; Paris review. GDC n 281-2 p 64 S 30'60
---Paris notes; Paul Arnold. WP v 12 n 1 p 4 O '60

LILAR, SUZANNE. The sacred and the profane in the work of Belgian dramatists. portfolio WT v 9 n 1 p 4-22 Spring '60

LILLIE, BEATRICE, 1998-, comedienne
Recording spoken commentary for Decca; notes on Peter and the Wolf, on Le Carnaval des animaux. HF v 10 n 5 p 24 My'60
---AP hl ph. Th Arts v 44 n 9 p 56 S '60

THE LILY OF KILLARNEY, opera
Bristol Opera School review. Op v 11 n 7 p 512 Jl '60

THE LILY-WHITE BOYS, play
London notes; Harry Cookson. WP v 11 n 6 p 13 Ap '60

LIMON, JOSÉ, 1908-, dancer
Arnosi, Eduardo. Teatro Colón. il La S n 132 p 89 N '60
---South American tour, 3-months, US government sponsor. AmM v 8 n 6 p 14 Jl '60

LIMPUS, JOHN, singer
Australian; London death notice.
MD v 50 n 8 p 15 F '60
LINCOLN CENTER FOR THE PER-
FORMING ARTS
Details of plan; Philharmonic Hall
in particular. il AmM v 8 n 2
p 3-5 F '60
---Facts to date in a chart form;
plans 1964 discussed by Richard
P. Leach. ON v 25 n 2 p 13-4
O 29'60
---Orchestra pit gift $100,000
from James Donahue in memory
of Frank W. Woolworth, his grand-
father. ON v 25 n 2 p 7 O 29'60
---The problem of building a the-
atre company discussed by Robert
Whitehead as similar to a festival
establishment. Th Arts v 44 n 6
p 64 Je '60
---Progress report; 76 percent
funds in hand, 90 percent demolition done. ON v 24 n 10 p 3
Ja 9'60
---Scope of the project; the Philharmonic Hall. IM v 59 n 4 p 13
O '60
---Student Program; rehearsal by
the Philharmonic for 1,000 school
children. ON v 25 n 4 p 7 D 3'60
---Architect Max Abramovitz with
scale model of Philharmonic Hall,
ens 'ph: NYC. AmM v 8 n 2
cover F '60
---Glass-walled colonade, "modern
monumental" style ph: Ezra Stoller. ON v 25 n 2 cover O 29'60
---Arches over plaza, ph. ON v 25
n 7 p 1 D 24'60
---Rockefeller, John D., 3rd, beside model for the new Metropolitan, ph: Serating. ON v 25 n 2 p 8
O 29'60
---Several building-in-progress
phs: Allen Vogel. ON v 25 n 5
p 12-3 D 10'60
LIND, JENNY, 1820-1887, singer
Celletti, Rodolfo. Jenny Lind, usignolo svedese. il La S n 124
p 14-19 Mr '60
---In roles, small colored pictures,
Op v 11 n 2 cover F '60
---Several portraits. La S n 124

p 15-7 Mr '60
---Lindholm, Ingvar, composer
US première: Ritornello; criticism
from Cincinnati. MC v 161 n 3
p 43 F '60
LING, STUART J. (1918-). Toward
real musical literacy (US). MEJ
v 46 n 5 p 52, 54 Ap-My '60
LINGG, ANN M. Great opera houses.
ON v 25 n 4 p 22-27 D 3'60
--- ---Great opera houses: New Or-
leans. il ON v 25 n 5 p 22-5
D 10'60
--- ---Meet Venus (in Wagner's
opera, Tannhauser). il ON v 25
n 6 p 17-9 D 17'60
--- ---Queen of tears (Wilhelmine
Schroder-Devrient's influence up-
on Wagner) por ON v 24 n 18 p 8-9
Mr 5'60
--- ---Tristan arrives (NYC 1886).
ON v 24 n 10 p 12-3 Ja 9'60
LIPKIN, ARTHUR BENNETT,
conductor
Alabama; note on retirement. por
ON v 25 n 6 p 5, 7 D 17'60
---Notes. MC v 161 n 1 p 25 Ja '60
LIPP, WILMA, 1925-, singer
As Eurydice; Vienna notes. MC
v 161 n 3 p 47 F '60
LIPTON, MARTHA, 1915-, singer
As Countess di Coigny, AP ph:
Melançon. ON v 24 n 21 p 17
Mr 26'60
LISBON
Crowther, Richard. Lohengrin
and Don Giovanni: performance
notes; Mârouf produced by Mar-
cel Lamy. il Op v 11 n 6 p 430-1
Je '60
---Crowther, Richard. Opera re-
views: Wolf-Ferrari's Il Camp-
iello, "superbly performed"; Boi-
to's Mefistofele; Macbeth; La Bo-
hème; Cenerentola. Op v 11 n 8
p 564 Ag '60
---Teatre Nacional de San Carlos:
repertory. ON v 24 n 22 p 2
Ap 2'60
---Teatro Nacional de S. Carlo,
temporada de opera do ano de
1961, Janeiro-Abril; calendario.
La S n 133 inset D '60
---Il Campiello, ens AP wl ph:

164

Luis Mendes. Op v 11 n 8 p 565 Ag '60

LISITSIAN, PAVEL, baritone
Chicago review. MC v 161 n 6 p 27 My '60
---Metropolitan debut, role of Amonasro; critical notes. MC v 161 n 5 p 14 Ap '60
--- ---criticism. MC v 161 n 4 p 18 Mr '60

LISZT, FERENCZ (FRANZ) 1811-1886. Messe de Gran (études musicales analytiques). GDC n 267-8 p 565 Ap 8'60
---The film, "Virtuoso Franz Liszt as Composer" discussed as teaching material; rental address, Teaching Film Custodians, NYC. MEJ v 47 n 2 p 45-6 N-D'60
---Franz Liszt Sesquicentennial Committee, US; leaders in piano contest; prize money from director of Liszt film, William Goetz. MD v 50 n 8 p 13 F '60
---Goldsmith, Harris. The Liszt Piano Sonata; review of Leon Fleisher, Epic. HF v 10 n 9 p 63-4 S '60
---Right profile by Lehmann; calco della mano d'estra. La S n 126 p 14, 16 My '60

LITTLE BALLET OF BOMBAY
Paris; la légende de Ramavana "deguisés en marionettes, les mains sans doigts, les masques - - -" GDC n 274 p 719 My 27'60

THE LITTLE BOURGEOIS, play
Buenos Aires, 1959; ens ph. WT v 9 n 1 p 71 Spring 60

LITTLE MARY SUNSHINE (RAY HARRISON), musical
Besoyan, Rick (1924-). Little Mary Sunshine (complete text, NYC cast and 4 pictures). Th Arts v 44 n 12 p 27-56 D '60
---NYC review. PlM v 36 n 5 p 110 F '60
---Brennan, Eileen, Arthur Hunt and John McMartin, ens AP wl ph: Friedman-Abeles. Th Arts v 44 n 2 p 19 F'60
---Several photographs, including John Aniston and John McMartin as American Indians, phs:

Friedman-Abeles. Th Arts v 44 n 12 p 54 D '60

THE LITTLE ORCHESTRA SOCIETY
NYC; Bewald's Sinfonia Singuliere; Jean Francaix's opera, Le Diable Boiteux. MC v 162 n 6 p 17 D'60
--- ---review; Hans Schwieger, guest conductor; John Sebastian, harmonicist. MC v 161 n 4 p 20 Mr '60
---Vietnam, concert in acoustical shell in Jardin Botanique of Saigon, ens ph: ANTA IM v 58 n 7 p 11 Ja '60

THE LITTLE TAILOR, play
Arnold, Paul (1909-). The Little Tailor, a one-act legend (text). TDR v 5 n 1 p 22-42 S '60

LITTLE THEATRE OF ALEXANDRIA
Virginia; revivals of 18th century plays; notes. Th Arts v 44 n 12 p 24 D '60

LITTLEFIELD, JOAN. Sadler's Wells reviews. ON v 24 n 23 p 26 Ap 9'60

LITURGICAL MUSIC
See Church music

LITVINNE, FELIA, 1860-1936, singer
Weerth, Ernest de. Scenes from an enchanted life: 5. Felia Litvinne and the Gay Nineties. por ON v 24 n 10 p 9 Ja 9'60

LIVIABELLA, LINO(1902-). Dove va la musica? (facsimile signatures of contemporary composers with criticism). il La S n 124 p 20-5 Mr '60

LLOYD, NORMAN, 1909-, composer
Première: Walt Whitman Overture; Goldman Band. J Rev v 7 n 3 p 19 Fall '60

LLOYD-JONES, DAVID. Borodin in Heidelberg. il Mus Q v 46 n 4 p 500-508 O '60

LA LOCA DE LA CASA, play
Gaidos, B. Perez, author; ens AP wl ph: Madrid. WP v 12 n 3 D '60

LA LOCANDIERA, opera bouffe
Boll, André, d'après Goldoni; music, Maurice Thiriet; première notes. OpP n 19 p 56-7 1960

(La Locandiera)
- - -Opéra-Comique notes. WP
v 12 n 3 p 29 D '60
- - -Paris commentaire; André
Boll "découpé " la Commedia de
Goldoni, Jean Solar textes à
chanter; Maurice Thiriet, Musi-
que; cast and review. GDC n 288
p 255 N 11'60
- - -Première; L'Opéra-Comique
note. Op v 11 n 11 p 763 N '60
- - -Two scenes; Franca Douval as
Mirandoline, AP phs: Paris. OpP
n 19 p 56-7 1960
LOCATELLI, PIETRO, 1695-1764,
composer
Boyden, David D. Review of Con-
certi Grossi recorded by I Musi-
ci. Mus Q v 46 n 3 p 399-405 Jl
'60
LOCK UP YOUR DAUGHTERS,
play
Mermaid Theatre, Puddle Dock,
ens AP wl ph: Fox. NTM v 1 n 1
p 15 O '59
LOCKSPEISER, EDWARD (1905-)
An introduction to Poulenc's "La
Voix Humaine". il Op v 11 n 8
p 527-534 Ag '60
THE LODGER, opera
Tate, Phyllis; première notes.
Op v 11 n 9 p 648 S '60
- - -Tate, Phyllis, work, ens AP
wl ph: London. Op v 11 n 9 p 648
S '60
A LODGING FOR THE BRIDE,
play
London notes; Patrick Kirwan.
WP v 11 n 10 p 15 Ag '60
LOESSER, FRANK, 1910-, compos-
er
Career sketch; b. NYC. por AmM
v 8 n 5 p 11 Je '60
LOEVBERG, AASE NORDMO,
singer
As Elsa, AP hl ph. Th Arts v 44
n 3 p 49 Mr '60
- - -As Sieglinde, AP ph: Melançon.
ON v 24 n 16 p 17 F 20'60
LOEWE, FREDERICK (1904-). In-
terview; career notes; his scores
for musicals.) MC v 162 n 1 p 8
Jl '60
- - -Por ph: Karsh. MC v 162 n 1

cover Jl '60
LOGAN, JOSHUA, 1908-, producer
Directing, ph. Th Arts v 44 n 7
p 53 Jl '60
LOGAR, MIHOVIL (1902-) Teatro
dell'Opera de Zagabria. il La S
n 123 p 45 F '60
LA LOGEUSE, play
Paris notes; Jacques Audiberti.
WP v 12 n 2 p 21 N '60
LOGOTHETIDIS, BASILE, 1898-,
actor
Por ph. WP v 11 n 7 p 7 My '60
LOHENGRIN, opera
The Editor. Bayreuth reviews;
"superbly conducted by Lorin
Maazel who in the first opera of
his career already displayed pro-
digious talent". Op v 11 p 46-7
Autumn '60
LOIRE, RENE, director
Théâtre Charles-de-Rochefort;
notes on Eugene Oneguine and Le
Plumet du Colonel. GDC n 274
p 718 My 27'60
LONDON, GEORGE, 1921-, singer
As Golaud in Pelléas, AP hl ph:
Melançon. ON v 24 n 11 p 17
Ja 16'60
- - -As the Flying Dutchman, AP
phs: Melançon. ON v 24 n 18
Mr 5'60
LONDON
American musical artists; many
making London debuts. AmM 1960
- - -Brien, Alan. City in a state of
flux. il Th Arts v 44 n 4 p 14-6
Ap '60
- - -Courtney, Richard. (Behan in
London; The Aspern Papers; One
More River.) PlM v 36 n 5 p 105
F '60
- - - - - -London theatre (several re-
views). PlM v 37 n 2 p 28 O '60
- - -Editorial: prospects for the
opening season; changes in audience
taste. Op v 11 n 10 p 664 O '60
- - -Goodwin, Noël. England new
opera productions and American
works in London spring. MC v 161
n 7 p 13 Je '60
- - - - - -Music report. MC v 161 n 3
p 44-5 F '60; same. MC v 161 n 5
p 30-1 Ap '60

---Group Eight in opera at St. Pancras Hall: The Tide; The Sorrows of Orpheus; Il Mondo della Luna; review. il Op v 11 n 5 p 363, 367-8 My '60

---Reports on recorded music in column, notes from Abroad. HF 1960

---Temperley, Nicholas. Beethoven in London concert life, 1800-1850. MR v 21 n 3 p 207-214 Ag '60

LONDON BRIDGE THEATRE
Historical sketch, 1833-. maps Th Notbk v 14 n 4 p 119-122 Summer '60

LONDON CHILDREN'S THEATRE
Way, Brian. Plays for children. NTM v 2 n 1 p 25-30 O '60

LONDON MORNING (COWARD), ballet
Teatro Colón, Festival Ballet, ens AP wl ph. La S n 128 p 64 Jl '60

LONDON FESTIVAL BALLET
Bologna review. il La S n 123 p 38 F '60

---Zagreb notes. il La S n 123 p 45 F '60

LONG, MARGUERITE, 1874-, pianist
Mari, Pierrette. L'Académie de piano Marguerite Long. GDC n 276 p 790 Je 10'60

---Paris criticism. GDC n 267-8 p 561 Ap 8'60

THE LONG DREAM, play
Ens AP hl ph: NYV. Th Arts v 44 n 3 p 15 Mr '60

THE LONG VIEW, play
Birmingham notes; Lewis Grant Wallace. WP v 12 n 1 p 14 O '60

LOOK ON TEMPESTS, play
London notes; Joan Henry. WP v 11 n 8 p 12 Je '60

LOPEZ, PILAR, 1912-, dancer
Silvant, Yves. À Bobino. TD n 91 p 20 Mr '60

LOS ANGELES
Wolf, Arthur W. music report. MC v 161 n 4 p 30 Mr '60; MC v 161 n 5 p 23 Ap '60; MC v 161 n 6 p 28 My '60; MC v 162 n 6 p 22 D '60; --- --- (Russian

composers visiting; notes.) MC v 161 n 1 p 23 Ja '60

LOS ANGELES OPERA COMPANY
Wolf, Arthur W. (Estimate of the group.) MC v 161 n 6 p 28 My '60

LOS ANGELES PHILHARMONIC
Contemporary repertory; list. AmM v 8 n 10 p 15 N '60

A LOSS OF ROSES, play
Balch, Jack. Anatomy of a failure. Th Arts v 44 n 2 p 10-11, 16 F '60

THE LOST SHEEP, play
Bristol notes; R. H. Ward. WP v 11 n 10 p 16 Ag '60

LOUCHEUR, RAYMOND (1899-) 2e Symphonie)études musicales analytiques). GDC n 225-6 p 322 Ja 15'60

---Notes; b. Tourcoing; his "Portraits" in program in Paris 1960. GDC n 281-2 p 35 S 30'60

LOUGHLIN, GEORGE
Director of the Melbourne University Conservatorium, por ph. MD v 51 n 5 p 9 N '60

LOVE IN BATH
Handel; Sir Thomas Beecham's project; notes. HF v 10 n 11 p 24 N '60

LOVE FOR THREE ORANGES, opera
Colón Theatre; Prokofief under Feruccio Calusio; Buenos Aires première; notes. MC v 161 n 1 p 27 Ja '60

---Weaver, William. (Review of Molinairi-Pradelli production in Naples.) Op v 2 n 3 p 215 Mr '60

---Indiana University, ens AP wl ph. WM n 4 cover Ag '60

LOVELLO, TONY, accordonist
AP ph. IM v 59 n 5 p 47 N '60

LOVELOCK, DR. WILLIAM
Career sketch; music critic in Brisbane. MD v 50 n 11 p 18 My'60

LOW, HENRIETTA BAKER, 1869-1960.
Notes. MEJ v 46 n 5 p 12 Ap-My '60

LOWENS, IRVING (1916-). Washington, D. C.; the Kroll Quartet with Alan Shulman, cellist, introducing Ross Lee Finney's String Quintet. Mus Q v 46 n 1 p 76-9 Ja '60

--- ---(Easley Blackwood's String Quartet No. 2, op. 6). Mus Q v 46 n 2 p 265-270 Ap '60

LOWRY, W. McNEIL (1913-).

(Lowry)
Report of 5-year study by the Ford Foundation on the art needs of the US; symphony data quoted to NYC symposium of symphony players. IM v 59 n 3 p 40-1 S'60
---Program director of the Ford Foundation with Herman Kenin and Frederic R. Mann of Philadelphia's Robin Hood Dell, ens ph. IM v 59 n 3 p 9 S '60

LUALDI, ADRIANO, 1887-, composer
Left profile drawing. La S n 127 p 7 Je '60

LUCCA, FRANCESCO 1802-1872, editor
Morini, Mario. Naso fino di Giovannina (Strazza). il La S n 128 p 7-15 Jl '60

LUCCIONI, JOSÉ, singer
As Samson, AP hl ph. OpP n 19 p 23 1960

LUCERNE FESTIVAL
Faulkner, Maurice. Report; 100 symphony players assembled from all Swiss orchestras; program notes. MC v 162 n 4 p 29 O '60

LUCIA DI LAMMERMOOR, opera
Covent Garden review;Joan Sutherland; André Turp; John Shaw. Op v 2 n 3 p 236 Mr '60
---Koegler, Horst. Stuttgart production, remarkable for its singing; Ruth-Margret Pütz as Lucia, Josef Traxel as Edgardo. Op v 11 n 6 p 424 Je '60
---Law, Richard. Paris Opéra rebiew; Joan Sutherland's triumph; Zeffirelli décor. Op v 11 n 6 p 418 Je '60

LUCIO MANLIO L'IMPERIOSO
Della Corte, A. In questo mese ha letto. La S n 126 p 42 My '60

LUCRETIA, opera
Warrack, John. Aldeburgh review. Op v 11 p 24 Autumn '60
---Finale, ens AP wl ph: Rome. La S n 125 p 49 Ap '60

LUDAS MATYI, ballet
Hungary; folklore, 2 ens AP wl ph: Budapest. La S n 128 p 32 Jl '60

LE LUDE
Dapilly, Jacques. Les Fastueuses soirees au Bord du Loir (description of the fête; music and scenic). GDC n 283 p 96 O 7'60

LUDWIG, CHRISTA, 1928?-, singer
As Cherubino, AP hl ph: Wiesbaden. Op v 11 p 64 Autumn '60
---As Dorabella, Lyric Opera of Chicago, AP hl ph: Sorenson. Op v 11 n 1 p 28 Ja '60

LUDWIG II, film
Wagner, Richard, seen in this film; notes; one scene. ON v 24 n 16 p 28 F 20'60

LUENING OTTO (1900-). Musica ex machina: On the Relationship of Music and Technology by Fred K. Prieberg (a book review by a director of Columbia-Princeton Electronic Music Center). J Rev v 7 n 3 p 24 Fall '60

LUISA MILLER, opera
NYC; Town Hall cast of the Amato Opera Theatre. Op v 11 n 7 p 472 Jl '60

LUISILLO, dancer
Silvant, Yves. Lusillo et son théâtre de la danse espagnole. il TD n 98 p 19 D '60

LUKE, GUTHRIE, pianist
Note; b. NYC. AmM v 8 n 4 p 11 Ap '60

LULU, opera
Frankfurt review. Op v 11 n 4 p 277 Ap '60
--- ---two ens AP wl phs: Englert. Op v 11 n 4 p 277 Ap '60

LUMIERES SUR LE MONDE, cantata
Première at Aix-en-Provence; Peretti cantata to music by Georges Delerue; Paris Opéra artists. MC v 162 n 3 p 25 S '60

LA LUNA, opera
San Carlo, Naples; Orff review. La S n 127 p 56 Je '60

LUNA DE MIEL PARA DIEZ, play
Mexico; Felipe Santander. WP v 11 n 5 p 15 Mr '60

LA LUNA EN UN CHAL ARCO IRIS, play
Teatro Universitario, Montevideo, 1959, ens AP wl ph. WT v 9 n 2 p 187 Summer '60

LUNDIN, ROBERT W. Musical learning and reinforcement theory. MEJ v 46 n 4 p 46, 48-9 F-Mr '60

LUPARELLO, MARIA ADA. Fiori nell'incanto ponoro. drawings. La S n 131 p 47-50 O '60

LUTE
Newman, Joe. Miss Mary Burwell's Instruction Book for the Lute by Thurston Dart (book review). Mus Q v 46 n 3 p 393-5 Jl '60

LUTOSLAWSKI, WITOLD, 1913-, composer
Première: Musique funèbre; Venice Festival review. Mus Q v 46 n 1 p 86-7 Ja '60
--- ---(commentaire). GDC n 291 p 356 D 2'60
---Warsaw note; "Funeral Music for String Orchestra" (1958). WM n 2 p 28 Ap '60

LYAPUNOV, SERGEI, 1859-1924, composer
Davis, Richard. Sergei Lyapunov. (with check-list of piano solo compositions). MR v 21 n 3 p 186-206 Ag '60

LYMPANY, MOURA, 1916-, pianist
Por ph. MD v 50 n 7 cover Ja'60

LYON, RAYMOND. Editorial: ces Semaines Musicales de Paris. GDC n 287 p 213 N 4'60
--- ---Un électrophone mono-stéréophonique de bonne qualité. GDC n 289 inset N 18'60
--- ---Livres sur la musique, serie. GDC 1960
--- ---A propos d'une prochaine "Lakmé". GDC n 293-4 p 454 D 16'60
--- ---Les Semaines Musicales de Paris 1960. WM n 6 p 122-3 D '60
--- ---Le théâtre: le Théâtre de la Cité de Villeurbanne; La Comédie de l'Est (and other Paris notes). GDC n 278 p 851 Je 24'60

LYON
Gravier, Albert. Le Chevalier à la Rose. GDC n 255-6 p 305 Ja 15'60

LYRIC OPERA OF CHICAGO

Repertory; debuts. MC v 162 n 4 p 16 O '60
---Op v 11 n 10 p 683 O '60
---Reviews: Der fliegende Holländer; La Gioconda (Page); Thaïs. il Op v 11 n 2 p 134, 136 F '60
--- ---Le Nozze di Figaro; Aïda. MC v 162 n 6 p 22-3 D '60
--- ---The Flying Dutchman with Birgit Nilsson, Lovro von Matacic, conducting; A Masked Ball; Thais. il MC v 161 n 1 p 21 Ja '60
---Seventh season: Don Carlo; review; Boris Christoff, Tito Gobbi. MC v 162 n 5 p 20 N '60
---Stedman, Jane W. 1960 season. ON v 25 n 7 p 28 D 24'60
---Ten productions, 29 performances; summary 1960 autumn. Op v 11 n 12 p 817 D '60
---Four AP phs: Sorenson. Op v 11 n 2 p 135 F '60
---Jenufa, two ens AP wl phs: Nancy Sorensen. Th Arts v 44 n 3 p 30-1 Mr '60
---Portfolio of 7 singers, AP phs. Op v 11 n 1 p 27-8 Ja '60

THE LYRIC REPERTORY THEATRE
Newark notes. ON v 24 n 21 p 3 Mr 26'60

LYSISTRATA, play
Phoenix Theatre, NYC; review. PlM v 36 n 6 p 137 Mr '60

LYSY, ALBERTO, violinist
Frias, Leopoldo. Buenos Aires. MC v 161 n 3 p 47 F '60

M

MAAZEL, LORIN, 1930-, conductor
Career notes;b. Neuilly, France. por Am M v 8 n 10 p 3-4, 9 N'60
---Florence notes. MC v 161 n 6 p 33 My'60
---London criticism. Am M v 8 n 11 p 12 D'60
---La Société des Concerts review. GDC n 287 p 227 N 4'60
---Vienna criticism. MC v 161 n 5 p 30 Ap'60
---Por ph. Am M v 8 n 10 cover N'60
---With William Glock and Maureen Forrester, hl ph:London. Am M v 8 n 11 p 7 D'60

MacARDLE, DONALD W. Beethoven and the Philharmonic Society of London. MR v 21 n 1 p 1-7 F'60

--- ---Minor Beethoveniana II (eight items discussed). Mus Q v 46 n 1 p 41-55 Ja'60

MACBETH, play
Cambridge Drama Festival;Siobhan McKenna, two AP phs:1959. Th Arts v 44 n 3 p 41 Mr'60

---Cleveland, 1957, ens AP wl ph: Frank A. Muth. WT v 9 n 2 p 191 Summer'60

---Karamu Theatre;in masks, ens AP hl ph:Cleveland, Ohio. Th Arts v 44 n 1 p 75 Ja'60

MACBETH, opera
Barker, Frank Granville. London review. ON v 25 n 3 p 20 N 19'60

---Bloch;American première at University of California. MC v 162 n 1 p 25 Jl'60

--- ---review. il Op v 11 n 6 p 410 Je'60

---Cincinnati Summer Opera;notes. MC v 162 n 1 p 21 Jl'60

---Covent Garden review. il MC v 161 n 7 p 13 Je'60; same. Op v 11 n 8 p 580 Ag'60

--- ---Tito Gobbi and Amy Shuard; cast. portfolio Op v 11 n 5 p 369-371 My'60

---Hughes, Spike. An introduction to Verdi's Macbeth. portfolio Op v 11 n 4 p 247-256 Ap'60

---Metropolitan Opera cast;the story of Verdi's opera;bibliography;décor;discography;portfolio. ON v 24 n 9 Ja 2'60

--- ---intermission broadcast by Boris Goldovsky and Siobhan McKenna. Th Arts v 44 n 3 p 38-9 Mr'60

--- ---notes;Daniele Baroni as Macduff. MC v 161 n 3 p 23 F'60

---Stedman, Jane W. A good word for a bad pair (history contrasted with plays and librettos). ON v 24 n 9 p 4-5 Ja 2'60

---Warnke, Frank J. Macbeth demoted (Shakespeare's concept; that of Verdi). ON v 24 n 9 p 10-1 Ja 2'60

---Banquet scene, ens AP wl ph:Covent Garden. WM n 4 p 82 Ag'60

---Goltz, Cristel, e Nicola Rossi Lemeni, AP hl ph:Teatro alla Scala. LaS n 124 p 30 Mr'60

---Portfolio:Louis Melançon. ON v 24 n 9 Ja 2'60

---La Scala, two ens AP wl ph:Piccagliani;also Covent Garden's Macbeth, a portfolio. Op v 11 n 5 p 351 My'60

---Shuard, Amy, and Tito Gobbi, AP hl ph:Houston Rogers. MC v 161 n 7 p 13 Je'60

---Shuard and Gobbi, AP hl ph:Houston Rogers; several other scenes, Covent Garden production. Op v 11 n 5 cover, p 369-371 My'60

---Tintori, Silvano. Macbeth di Bloch, 4 bozzetti. LaS n 122 p 51-4 Ja'60

---Verdi;first production:Felice Varesi, Marianna Barbieri-Nini, por phs; some original costume designs. Op v 11 n 4 p 247-252 Ap '60

---Verdi in Lübeck, ens Ap ph: Wassner. Op v 11 n 9 p 625 S '60

MACAULEY'S THEATRE
Hill, West T., Jr. Famous American theatres, series; Macauley's Theatre in Louisville. il Th Arts v 44 n 2 p 92-5 F '60

---Exterior view; interior from the stage, 2 phs: Louisville, Kentucky. Th Arts v 44 n 2 p 92 F'60

McCLEERY, ALBERT (1912-). Theatre's debt to television. WT v 9 n 4 p 318-324 Winter '60

McCLURE, THERON R. (On the present need of new operas and how to get them written.) ON v 24 n 12 p 12-3 Ja 23'60

McCORMACK, JOHN, 1884-1945, singer
Robinson, Francis. John McCormack, a memoir. ON v 25 n 4 p 28-9 D 3'60

---As Don Ottavio, AP hl ph. MC v 161 n 3 p 11 F '60

---As Edgardo in Lucia, AP hl ph: 1909-10, Hammerstein's. ON v 25 n 4 p 29 D 3'60

McCRACKEN, JAMES, 1927?-, singer

Peltz, Mary Ellis. Otello promoted. il ON v 24 n 18 p 28 Mr 5'60

MACDOWELL, EDWARD, 1861-1908, composer
In Hall of Fame of New York University; first serious American composer chosen. IM v 59 n 6 p 27 D '60

McDUNN, MARK, trombonist
Por ph: Chicago. IM v 58 n 10 p 17 Ap '60

McELROY, GEORGE. Most unhappy fella; II (heroes in tales about Tristan, Launcelot Paola). ON v 24 n 11 p 4-5 Ja 16'60

--- ---The fortunes of fate (analysis of "fate stories" from the Greeks into 19th century opera). ON v 24 n 19 p 4-7 Mr 12'60

--- ---The unhappy fella; I (heroes in the tales about Tristan, Launcelot, Paola). ON v 24 n 10 p 4-5, 29 Ja 9'60

--- ---(Verdi and Wagner, comparison.) ON v 25 n 8 p 17-20 D 31'60

MACERO, TEO, composer
Premières: Density In Space (NYC 1960); Polaris (NYC 1960). ACAB v 9 n 3 p 33 1960

MACHA, OTMAR, 1922-, composer
Notes; b. Ostrava. Mus Q v 46 n 4 p 512 O '60

UN MACHO!, play
Mexico; Edmundo Baez. WP v 11 n 5 p 14 Mr '60

McINTYRE, PAUL, composer
Amor Triumphans, five songs; notes. CMJ v 4 n 2 p 39 Winter'60

McKEE, J. N. The symphonic elements in opera. MR v 21 n 1 p 30-37 F '60

MACKENZIE, GISELE, 1927-, singer
Cerulli, Dom. (Career sketch; b. Winnipeg, Canada.) IM v 58 n 12 p 20-1 Je '60

---Two por phs; IM v 58 n 12 cover, p 20 Je '60

MACKENZIE, MARY, 1931-, singer
Winner of Metropolitan Opera Audition;notes. por MC v 161 n 5 p 4 Ap '50

MACKERNESS, E. D. Music and moral purity in the early Victorian Era. CMJ v 4 n 2 p 14-24 Winter '60

MACKERRAS, CHARLES (1926-). How music fares in Australia ("Fonteyn, Kubelik and Menuhin just a bunch of incompetent amateurs" according to the "scurrilous" critics). MD v 50 n 12 p 15 Je '60

---Australian to conduct for ABC. por MD v 50 n 9 p 17 Mr '60

---Career sketch. por MD v 50 n 8 p 28 F '60

---Unwin, Arthur. (London Philharmonic under Mackerras at Holland House.) MD v 51 n 3 p 13-4 S '60

---Congress of the International Federation of Musical Youth, ph: Berlin. WM n 5 p 108 O '60

---Right profile ph. MD v 50 n 9 p 17 Mr '60

---Right profile por ph. MD v 50 n 12 p 15 Je '60

MACLEARY, DONALD, dancer
With Lynn Seymour in Le Baiser de la Fée, AP wl ph: Covent Garden. MD v 50 n 11 p 27 My'60

MacLEISH, ARCHIBALD (1892-). "J. B. " (complete text of play with portfolio and notes). Th Arts v 44 n 2 p 29-64 F '60

MacMILLAN, SIR ERNEST (1893-). Novello's new Messiah (criticism). CMJ v 4 n 2 p 57-60 Winter '60

--- ---(On Canada's music festivals.) CMJ v 5 n 1 p 30-2 Autumn '60

MacMILLAN, KEITH. Making the most of your tape recorder. CMJ v 4 n 2 p 25-32 Winter '60

McMULLAN, FRANK. (On his work in founding theatre 1959 at the University of Panama; Fulbright lecturer at Chile's University.) Th Arts v 44 n 6 p 68-9 Je'60

MacNEIL, CORNELL, 1924?, singer
Interview on his career. por ON v 24 n 13 p 15 Ja 30'60

---As Nabucco, AP hl ph: Melançon. ON v 25 n 4 p 20 D 3'60

(MacNEIL)
---As Rigoletto, AP hl ph: James Abresch. ON v 25 n 8 p 21 D 31'60
---Por ph; ON v 25 n 1 p 28 O 8'60; ON v 25 n 8 p 1 D 31'60
MacNUTT, R. P. S. A storm over the royal hunt (in Berlioz's Les Troyens à Carthage). Op v 11 n 5 p 332-3 My '60
MACRAE, HEATHER, 1941-, dancer
Melbourne; winner of Moomba Ballerina Quest 1958; now HSV 7 program. il MD v 50 n 10 p 29 Ap '60
McWILLIAM, G. H. Interpreting Betti. TDR v 5 n 2 p 15-23 D '60
MADAMA BUTTERFLY, opera
Melbourne; Joan Hammond and Ken Neate, both Australian singers; review. MD v 50 n 11 p 10 My '60
---Metropolitan Opera cast; story; background and décor notes; bibliography; discography; portfolio. ON v 24 n 24 Ap 16'60
--- ---NYC review. MC v 162 n 6 p 15 D '60
---Vancouver review; "more Kabuki than Puccini". ON v 25 n 2 p 22 O 29'60
---Act I, the presentation, ens AP wl ph: L'Opéra-Comique. OpP n 19 p 51 1960
---Portfolio: Melançon. ON v 24 n 24 Ap 16'60
MADAME, JE VOUS AIME, revue
Paris notes; Serge Veber. WP v 11 n 9 p 8 Jl '60
THE MADCAP, opera
Mankova, Lilyana. Sofia; review of Parashkev Hadjiev's new opera. Op v 11 n 6 p 415 Je '60
MADO MAVROGENOUS, play
Athens; Georges Roussos; notes. WP v 11 n 4 p 8 F '60.
MADRAS MUSIC ACADEMY
Thirty-third annual Conference and Music Festival; notes. WM n 1 p 9 F '60
LE MADRIGAL DE BUDAPEST
Castil. Paris review. GDC n 278 p 850 Je 24'60

MAGDALENO, YVETTE, pianist
Paris review. GDC n 293-4 p 459 D 16'60
MAGGI, ANGIOLINA
Letter from Puccini to his cousin, Angiolina Maggi, 1900: facsimile. La S n 128 p 16-7 Jl '60
THE MAGIC FLUTE, opera
Budapest; review. il La S n 124 p 38 Mr '60
---Budapest; Mihaly Szekely quale Sarastro; Radnai e Hazy, ens AP wl ph. La S n 124 p 38 Mr '60
MAGGIE, DINAH. (Letter on Mlle. Geneviève Mallarmé and Théâtre d'Essai de la Danse.) TD n 96 p 33 S-O '60
MAGGIO MUSICALE FIORENTINO
Opere, balletti, teatro drammatico, concerti sinfonico-corali, concerti sinfonici, concerti di musica da camera: 10 Maggio -30 Giugno 1960. LaS n 126 inset My '60
---Reviews. MC v 162 n 3 p 22 S'60
---Selden-Goth, Gisella. Cherubini's Elisa and Peri's Euridice; other notes. ON v 25 n 1 p 22 O 8'60
---Twenty-third festival; calendar. La S n 125 Ap '60; La S n 128 p 28-9 Jl '60; La S n 124 inset Mr '60
---Weaver, William. (Opera reviews: Elisa; Fidelio; Jenafu; l'Italiana in Algeri; Peri's Euridice and short modern triple bill.) il Op v 11 p 17-21 Autumn '60
---Five ens AP wl phs. La S n 128 p 28-9 Jl '60
---Opera scenes, four ens AP wl phs: Marchiori. Op v 11 p 18-20 Autumn '60
MAGNARD, ALBÉRIC, 1865-1914, composer
Chamfray, Claude. Fiche biographique. GDC n 276 p 794 Je 10'60
MAGON, JERO. Projected scenery. PlM v 36 n 7 p 164 Ap '60
--- ---Puppet stages. PlM v 37 n 2 p 35 N '60
--- ---The combination stage (puppets, shadow figures, marionettes, hand puppets, all in juxtaposed scenes). PlM v 37 n 3 p 51 D '60

MAHLER, GUSTAVE (1860-1911).
Symphonie No. I "Titan": analyse
par Pierrette Mari. GDC n 257-8
p 369-370 Ja 29'60
---Barford, Philip T. Mahler: a
thematic archetype. MR v 21 n 4
p 297-316 N '60
---Berges, Ruth. Mahler and the
great god Pan. por MC v 161 n 1
p 10-1, 37 Ja '60
---Chamfray, Claude. L'anniver-
saire; fiche biography. por GDC
n 259-60 p 414-6 F 12'60
---Marsh, Robert C. Mahler on
microgroove, a selective discography. por HF v 10 n 7 p 34-5,
75 Jl '60
---Pringsheim, Klaus. Gustav
Mahler. CMJ v 5 n 1 p 17-22
Autumn '60
---Roddy, Joseph. Mr. Mahler in
Manhattan. il HF v 10 n 7 p 30-3
Jl '60
---Selden-Goth, Gisella. La "de-
cima" di Mahler. por La S n 127
p 18-21 Je '60
---Sorell, Walter. For art's sake
(Mahler's philosophy). por ON
v 24 n 18 p 12, 32 Mr 5'60
---Left profile por; three facsimile
pages of music. La S n 127 p 19-
21 Je '60
---Por ph. MC v 161 n 1 p 10 Ja'60
---Two por phs. GDC n 259-60
p 415 F 12'60
---Two snapshots, USA visit. HF
v 10 n 7 p 30 Jl '60
MAHRENHOLZ, CHRISTHARD,
1900-
Thirty-five contributions by Mah-
renholz on organ, art of carillon
music, church music and such.
WM n 5 p 106 O '60
LE MAI MUSICAL DE BORDEAUX
Parisot, Raoul. (Reviews.) GDC
n 281-2 p 63-4 S 30'60
MAINBRAY (b. ?-d. ?)
Bergman, G. M. La grande mode
des pantomimes à Paris vers
1740 et les spectacles d'optique
de Servandoni (1695-1766). Th R
v 2 n 2 p 71-81 1960
MAINZ
Steyer, Ralf. Festival Gutenberg;

opera. Op v 11 n 11 p 765-6 N'60
MAIONE, RINO. Franco Alfano.
por La S n 122 p 48-9 Ja '60
--- ---La "quarta" di Schubert. por
La S n 128 p 38-9 Jl '60
--- ---Toscanini, artista e critico.
il La S n 132 p 17-23 N '60
MAISTRE, AMAN (1903-). Bilan et
projects. OpP n 19 p 3 1960
---His influence upon the Paris
Opéra. il Th Arts v 44 n 3 p 42-3
Mr '60
---Left profile as he talks with
Jane Rhodes, hl ph: Paris Opéra.
Th Arts v 44 n 3 p 44 Mr '60
MAJOR BARBARA, play
Belgrade Theatre, Coventry, ens
AP wl ph: P. W. A. L. Thompson.
NTM v 1 n 1 O '59
A MAJORITY OF ONE, play
Spigelgass, Leonard. A Majority
of One (complete text and NYC cast).
il Th Arts v 44 n 9 p 19, 26 S '60
MAKE UP
Barton, Lucy. Costumes for the
face. PlM v 37 n 3 p 62 D '60
---White, Melvin R. How much
make-up? (as little as possible).
PlM v 36 n 4 p 80 Ja '60
--- ---Make up for Mark Twain
(with portrait photographs before
and after). PlM v 37 n 1 p 8 O '60
IL MALATO IMMAGINARIO, opera
San Carlo, Naples; Jacopo Napoli;
review. La S n 127 p 56 Je '60
MALBIN, ELAINE, 1932-, singer
As Sara in Tobias and the Angel,
AP wl ph: BBC-TV. AmM v 8
n 5 p 7 Je '60
---With Charles Mackerras and
singer, Bernard Turgeon, hl ph:
London. AmM v 8 n 11 p 9 D '60
MALEK, ASDULLAH
Playing Kamantché, AP ph: Ray-
mond Burnier, WM n 1 cover F'60
LES MALHEURS D'ORPHEE, opera
British première: Group Eight re-
view, St. Pancras Hall. Op v 11
n 5 p 363 My '60
---Bruyr, José. Paris review. GDC
n 284 p 127 O 14'60
---Jacobs, Arthur. Two operas new
to London. Op v 2 n 3 p 182-3
Mr '60

(Les Malheurs)
---Ens AP wl ph: Boys, London.
Op v 11 n 5 p 366 My '60
MALIBRAN, MARIA FELICITA
GARCIA 1808-1836, singer
Por ph. ON v 24 n 17 p 9 F 27'60
---Por engr: J. C. Armytage. Op
v 11 n 10 cover O '60
MALKO, DR. NICOLAI(1888-).
(On critics, on what makes a
music critic, on cultural respon-
sibility of newspapers; "I envy
the sports pages".) MD v 51 n 2
p 9, 11 Ag '60
---Por ph: Sydney. MD v 51 n 1
p 23 Jl '60; MD v 51 n 2 cover
Ag '60
MALRAUX, ANDRÉ, 1901-, author
His plan for the French theatres.
Th Arts v 44 n 12 p 61 D '60
---Minister of Cultural Affairs,
France, on the Paris Opéra's
decadence, now over under A. M.
Julien. Th Arts v 44 n 3 p 42-3
Mr '60
---Minister of State for Cultural
Affairs (France), por ph: Max
Waldman. Th Arts v 44 n 12
p 60 D '60
MALTA
Opera notes. Op v 11 n 1 p 45
Ja '60; Op v 11 n 9 p 630 S '60
MAMA, KIJK ZONDER HANDEN,
play
Brussels notes; Hugo Claus. WP
v 11 n 7 p 2 My '60
---Brussels, 1960; ens AP wl ph:
José Billen. WT v 9 n 1 p 55
Spring '60
MAM'ZELLE NITOUCHE, operetta
Reims; also Rigoletto reviewed.
GDC n 263-4 p 482 Mr 11'60
A MAN FOR ALL SEASONS, play
London notes; Robert Bolt. WP
v 12 n 1 p 13 O '60
MANDELLI, PIERO. A Salisburgo
un nuovo gran Teatro d'Opera.
il La S n 128 p 20-2 Jl '60
THE MAN-EATERS, play
Bristol notes; Annie Piper. WP
v 11 n 4 p 13 F '60
LE MANÈGE, play
de V. Trojan; ens ph: Czechoslo-
vakia. WP v 11 n 8 p 1 Je '60

MANEY, RICHARD (1892-). Chivalry
set to music ("Camelot" and its use
of Arthurian material). Th Arts
v 44 n 12 p 25-6 D '60
THE MANGER, oratorio
Première of Pablo Casals work on
the birth and death of Christ in
Mexico under the composer. MC
v 162 n 4 p 24 O '60
MANGUEL, JOSE, jazz drummer
Cuban; bongo expert; note. IM v 58
n 9 p 21 Mr '60
MANHATTAN SCHOOL OF MUSIC
Brownlee, John. Making the opera
workshop work. MC v 162 n 4 p 8
O '60
MANN, HERBIE, 1930-, jazz musician
Notes; b. Brooklyn. IM v 58 n 9
p 21, 34 Mr '60
---Por ph. IM v 58 n 9 p 21 Mr '60
MANN, ROBERT. Convocation,
Juilliard, address (his own student
days at Juilliard, costs of living
21 years back; need of perspective
stressed). J Rev v 7 n 1 p 8, 26-7
Winter 59-60
MANN, THOMAS, 1875-1955, writer
His novel, Doktor Faustus, and his
consultations with musicians as
preparation; criticism by Murray
Schafer. CMJ v 4 n 3 p 29-34
Spring '60
MANN, WILLIAM (1924-). Burt's
Volpone at Stuttgart. Op v 11 n 7
p 461-2 Jl '60
DE MANN IN DE TRAPEZE (van
MANEN), ballet
Ostend; music, Britten. WP v 11
n 3 p 10 Ja '60
MANNES, LEOPOLD DAMROSCH,
1899-, composer
Por ph: Karsh. MC v 162 n 5 p 35
N '60
MANON LESCAUT, opera
Covent Garden; de los Angeles
André Turp; Jean Morel, con-
ducting; criticism. il Op v 11 n 8
p 576-8 Ag '60
---Metropolitan Opera cast; notes
on composer, history, décor, bib
liography, story with two scenes,
and the play bill 1912 of Lucrezia
Bori's debut. ON v 25 n 5 D 10'60
---NYC review. MC v 162 n 6 p 14 '60

---Ross, A. G. On television. CMJ v 4 n 3 p 47-9 Spring '60
---Zenginov, Dimiter. Review of Mihaïl Hadji-Mischev production; Sofia Op v 11 n 9 p 617 S '60
---Covent Garden, four scenes, phs: Donald Southern. Op v 11 n 8 p 577 Ag '60
---Metropolitan, two ens AP wl ph: Melançon. ON v 25 n 5 p 16, 20 D 10'60
MANUEL, MICHAEL, stage manager
Freeman, F. J. (Career sketch of Metropolitan stage manager.) por ON v 24 n 9 p 12-3 Ja 2'60
---and Aida cast, honoring super, Al Furman, ens wl ph: Louis Melançon. ON v 24 n 14 p 2 F 6'60
MANUEL, PHILIP, ?-1959, harpsichordist
Obituary notes; d. Chicago. MC v 161 n 1 p 6 Ja '60
MANUSEVITCH, VICTOR E., 1906-, conductor
Boston notes. MC v 161 n 3 p 41 F '60
MANZONI, ALESSANDRO, 1785-1873, playwright
Legnani, Emilio Sioli. Raro cimelio manzoniano. facsimiles La S n 122 p 44-6 Ja '60
MAR e WHISKY, musical
Milan notes; Guido Rocca; music by Piero Umiliani and Fiorenzo Carpi. WP v 11 n 5 p 12 Mr '60
MARAIS, MARIN, 1656-1728, composer
Thompson, Clyde H. Marin Marais's pieces de violes. Mus Q v 46 n 4 p 482-499 O '60
---Title page of Pièces de Violes. (1686), facsimile; also facsimiles of medallions struck in honor of Marais and Michel Delande. Mus Q v 46 n 4 p 484 O '60
MARCEAU, MARCEL, 1923-, director
In The Overcoat, AP wl ph. Th Arts v 44 n 11 p 11 N '60
MARCEL, ROBERT, actor
In DeHeld van Talavera, ens

AP hl ph: Reussens, 1958 WT v 9 n 1 p 28 Spring '60
MARCHETTI, ARNOLDO (1908?-). A dieci anni dalla sua scomparsa (Francesco Cilia). il La S n 133 p 78-9 D '60
--- ---Convenevoli dell'autore di "Manon". La S n 124 p 44-5 Mr '60
--- ---Lettere inedite di D'Annunzio a Zacconi. La S n 129-30 p 49-55 Ag-S '60
MARCHING SONG, play
Bohle, Bruce. (Review.) Th Arts v 44 n 3 p 14 Mr '60
MARCOUX, VANNI, 1879-, singer AP wl ph: 1932. ON v 24 n 11 p 11 Ja 6'60
MAREK, GEORGE R. (1902-). Live opera vs. recorded opera (pro and con). ON v 25 n 3 p 9, 30 N 19'60
MARGAT, YVES. Piano mon violon d'Ingres; les petits secrets de l'improvisation. GDC n 275 p 759 Je 3'60
MARI, PIERRETTE. Trio pour flûte, alto et harpe (études musicales analytiques). GDC n 273 p 699 My 20'60
MARIE TUDOR, play
Outdoors, Festival d'Avignon 1955, small ph: Agnès Varda. WT v 9 n 2 p 153 Summer '60
MARIKE WEIDEN, opera
Griesbach at Weimar; scene from Act 3, ens AP wl ph: National theater Weinser. Op v 11 n 12 p 836 D '60
MARIO 1810-1883, singer
Il marchese Giovanni de Candia, por. La S n 125 p 31 Ap '60
MARIO,e il MAGO (BLANK), ballet
Décor de J. P. Ponnelle, ens AP wl ph: Hamburg. TD n 89 p 7 Ja '60
MARION, JACQUES, 1903-, composer
Film, Le Bossu; criticism. GDC n 261-2 p 444 F 26'60
MARION, MADELEINE, actress
With Nathalie Nerval and Nelly Borgeaud in Chekhov's Three Sisters, AP hl ph: Paris, 1960.

175

(Marion)
Spec n 1 p 21 1960
MARIONETTES
Congress, 7th, in Bochum; 37
nations; notes. WP v 12 n 2 p 3
N '60
---US; Reed Marionettes of Wis-
consin booking for Childrens
Theatres. PlM v 37 n 2 p 28
N '60
MARKER, CHRIS. Un film blanc:
Moranbong. Spec n 1 p 70 1960
MARKOV, PAVEL. New trends
in the interpretation of Chekhov.
il WT v 9 n 2 p 101-110 Summer
'60
MARLBORO
Vermont; School of Music; tenth
anniversary celebration, Pablo
Casals; review. MC v 162 n 2
p 10 Ag '60
MARMIROLI, RENATO (1893-).
Artisti, soprani e maghi nel rid-
otto di Reggio Emilia. il La S
n 127 p 36-9 Je '60
MAROS, RUDOLF, 1917-, com-
poser
Notes. Mus Q v 46 n 4 p 532 O'60
MAROUF, opera
Lisbon; Marcel Lamy's production,
ens AP wl ph: Mendes. Op v 11 n 6
p 431 Je '60
MARPLE, HUGO D. The challenge
of the Conant report to music ed-
ucation (US schools and curricula
recommendations that affect mu-
sic). MEJ v 47 n 2 p 35-6, 96
N-D '60
MARQUES, LIA, ballerina
And Decio Otero in Les Indes Ga-
lantes, AP wl ph: Rio de Janeiro.
TD n 97 p 24 N '60
THE MARRIAGE OF FIGARO, opera
See Le Nozze di Figaro, opera
MARSCHALL, SIGURD von,
pianist
Paris review. GDC n 275 p 754
Je 3'60
MARSEILLE
A l'Opéra de Marseille: Galas de
Danse, Géo Stone et M. Lazzini.
TD n 93 p 20 My '60
---Abel, Jean. A l'Opéra: La
Fiance Vendue; Madame Butterfly;

Veronique. GDC n 255-6 p 305
Ja 15'60
--- ---Opera and operettas, a re-
port. GDC n 263-4 p 482 Mr 11'60
--- ---La Tétralogie; cast; review.
GDC n 265-6 p 520 Mr 25'60
---Réveil du Ballet de l'Opéra de
Marseille. il TD n 91 p 8-9
Mr '60
MARSH, OZAN
Por ph: Chautauqua Institute, New
York. MC v 161 n 4 p 43 Mr '60
MARSH, ROBERT C. Mahler on
microgroove . por HF v 10 n 7
p 34-5, 75 Jl '60
--- ---Music in the Midwest (the
roots, the present flowering). il
HF n 10 n 2 p 42-4 F '60
--- ---The Beethoven symphonies
in stereo. HF v 10 n 4 p 44-5,
85-7 Ap '60
MARSHALL, LOIS, 1924-, singer
Career notes b. Toronto. MD
v 50 n 8 p 30 F '60
---Por ph. MD v 50 n 8 cover F'60
MARSHALL, NORMAN (1901-). Are
stage plays suitable for TV? WT
v 9 n 4 p 301-312 Winter '60
MARSTELLER, ROBERT, tromb-
onist
Por ph. IM v 59 n 3 p 23 S '60
MARTELLI, HENRI (1895-). 2e
Quatuor à cordes (études musi-
cales analytiques). GDC n 255-6
p 322 Ja 15'60
--- ---Troisième Symphonie (ét-
udes musicales analytiques). GDC
n 261-2 p 445 F 26'60
---Première: La Divertissement
pour harpe; Lily Laskine, Paris.
GDC n 261-2 p 439 F 26'60
---Première: 3e Symphonie; à la
radio. GDC n 265-6 p 522 Mr 25'60
MARTHA, opera
Wiesbaden review; Herbert Esser;
Pohl production. Op v 11 n 4 p 281
Ap '60
MARTIN, FRANCES, singer
Bayreuth contract, b. Atlanta. ON
v 24 n 10 p 3 Ja 9'60
MARTIN FRANK, 1890-, composer
Création du Mystère de la Nativité;
Festival de Strasbourg. GDC n 286
p 201 O 28'60

176

---Salzburg; The Mystery of the Nativity, staged as a mystery play by Marguerite Wallmann and Helmut Juergens, "too cinematographic for the text". MC v 162 n 4 p 27 O '60

---Radio interview; wife, composer and interviewer, Mr. Matti Rautio, ph: Finland. WM n 5 p 108 O '60

MARTIN, MARY, 1913-, actress
Notes and two AP phs. Th Arts v 44 n 9 p 9 S '60

---In The Sound of Music; in Leave It To Me, two AP phs: Frissell. Th Arts v 44 n 9 p 9 S '60

MARTIN, NAN, actress
And others in "J. B"., ens AP wl ph: NYC. Th Arts v 44 n 2 p 41 F '60

MARTIN KORDA, D. P., opera
Holland Festival; Badings' work on refugees; Vesseur's projected décor; Fran Vroons. ON v 25 n 1 p 23 O 8'60

---Première by Henk Badings; other notes on the Holland Festival. MC v 162 n 3 p 23 S '60

---Ens AP (2) wl ph: Particam. ON v 25 n 1 p 24 O 8'60; Op v 11 n 9 p 634 S '60

---Holland, ens AP wl ph: Particam. Op v 11 p 25 Autumn '60

MARTINO, DON, composer
Première: Piano Fantasy (1958); chamber music 60 review. MC v 161 n 5 p 36 Ap '60

MARTINON, JEAN, 1910-, conductor
Düsseldorf orchestra appointment; note. WM n 3 p 56 Je '60

---Notes; b. Lyon. GDC n 277 p 799 Je 17'60

---Por ph. GDC n 277 cover Je 17'60

---Por ph: Chicago. MC v 162 n 4 p 17 O '60

MARTINS, JOSÉ-EDUARDO, pianist
Paris review; Brazilian. GDC n 291 p 360 D 2'60

MARTINU, BOHUSLAV, 1890-, composer
Première: Concerto No. 4

pour piano et orchestre; Théâtre des Champs-Elysées. GDC n 292 p 420 D 9'60

---Zanetti, Dina. Ricordo di Martinů. il La S n 131 p 42-3 O '60

---Two informal phs. La S n 131 p 42-3 O '60

MARTYN, LAUREL
Director of Victorian Ballet Guild, por ph. MD v 50 n 11 p 26 My '60

LE MARTYRE de SAINT SEBASTIEN
La Maschera, pseud. (Criticism.) La S n 126 p 29 My '60

MARY KAYE TRIO
Cerulli, Dom. The Mary Kaye Trio. il IM v 58 n 8 p 15, 43 F'60

MARY STUART, play
Phoenix Theatre 1957; Adrian, Le Gallienne and Campbell, AP hl ph: Friedman-Abeles. Th Arts v 44 n 1 p 72 Ja '60

MAS, MARGARET, singer
As Fidelio with Guy Chauvet as Florestan, Paris Opéra, AP wl ph. OpP n 19 p 34 1960

MASCAGNI, PIETRO, 1863-1945, composer
Matz, Mary Jane. The rustic cavalier; II. il ON v 24 n 13 p 4-6 Ja 30'60

---Ricci, Luigi. Un bauletto magico. facsimiles La S n 126 p 44-6 My'60

---Teatro dell'Opera di Roma: Le maschere. il La S n 126 p 34 My '60

---Left profile on gold medal 1940, ph: Bestetti. ON v 24 n 13 p 4 Ja 30'60

---Left profile por ph. La S n 133 p 57 D '60

---Por ph. La Scala n 122 p 30 Ja '60

---Two pages of music, facsimiles. La S n 126 p 44, 46 My '60

LA MASCHERA, pseud. Ridotto. La Scala 1960

A MASKED BALL, opera
See Un Ballo in Maschera, opera

THE MASS
Agricola, Alexander (1446-1506): comparison of his Mass with the first Gregorian cycle. Mus Q v 46 n 1 p 63 Ja '60

MASSELOS, WILLIAM, pianist
Chicago criticism. MC v 161 n 6

(Masselos)
p 27 My '60
---Left profile ph. AmM v 8 n 1
p 7 Ja '60
MASSENET, JULES (1842-1912).
Letter to author of "Manon".) il
La S n 124 p 44-5 Mr '60
---Por; Leoncavallo e Montecatini
in una foto del 1911; lettera auto-
grafa di Massenet. La S n 124
p 44-5 Mr '60
MASSEY, RAYMOND, 1896-, actor
As Lincoln, AP hl ph: 1938. Th
Arts v 44 n 9 p 20 S '60
---With Christopher Plummer in
"J. B." AP hl ph: NYC. Th Arts
v 44 n 2 p 35 F '60
MASSINE, LEONIDE, 1896-,
choregrapher
5e Festival de Ballets de Nervi.
por TD n 95 p 11 Jl-Ag '60
---Left profile, with Yvette Chau-
viré, hl ph: Nervi. TD n 95 p 11
Jl-Ag '60
MASSINE, TATIANA, dancer
And Angelo Pietre in "Laudes
Evangelii (Massine), AP hl ph:
Milan. La S n 128 p 26 Jl '60
THE MASTERPLAYERS OF LUG
ANO
NYC debut under Richard Schu-
macher; review. MC v 161 n 1
p 37 Ja '60
THE MATCHMAKER, play
Ohio State University; Ella Richey
Well as Mrs. Levi, ens ph. PlM
v 37 n 3 cover D '60
MATHIS DER MALER, opera
Munich; décor Helmut Jürgens;
Hans Hartleb producer; review.
il Op v 11 n 12 p 834-6 D '60
---Jürgens, Helmut, settings, two
phs: Rudolf Betz. Op v 11 n 12
p 834-5 D '60
MATSUDAIRA, YORITSUNÉ, 1907-,
composer
Por ph: Widmaier. WM n 6 p 136
D '60
MATTEIS, NICOLA (16?-d. ?)
violinist-composer
Tilmouth, Michael. Nicola Matt-
eis. Mus Q v 46 n 1 p 22-40 Ja'60
---Kneller, Sir Godfrey. Portrait
of Matteis, hl oil, ph: William

Barrow coll. Llandudno. Mus Q
v 46 n 1 p 28 Ja '60
MATTHEWS, CLIFTON, pianist
London debut; b. Kansas. AmM
v 8 n 11 p 6 D '60
MATHEWS, PAUL W. We need
superior music teachers. MEJ
v 46 n 6 p 31-2 Je-Jl '60
MATTHEWS, WILLIAM H. , JR.
Theatre collections: Big Top Am-
ericana. PlM v 36 n 5 p 116 F '60
MATZ, MARY JANE. A time for
the brave; II. ON v 24 n 9 p 6-7,
31 Ja 2'60
--- ---A year to die (Bellini and
Maria Felicità García Malibran).
il ON v 24 n 17 p 8-9, 30 F 27'60
--- ---First ladies of the Puccini
premières; 4. Claudio Muzio. il
ON v 24 n 24 p 10-1 Ap 16'60
--- ---Great opera houses: La
Fenice. il ON v 25 n 8 p 22-26
D 31'60
--- ---San Carlo. il ON v 25 n 7
p 22 D 24'60
--- ---The rustic cavalier; II.
Mascagni. il ON v 24 n 13 p 4-6
Ja 30'60
--- ---(Verdi.) il ON v 25 n 4 p 18-
9 D 3'60
LES MAUDITS, play
Havana; ens ph: Luis Crucet. WP
v 11 n 6 p 7 Ap '60
LE MAURE de VENISE (LIFAR),
ballet
Paris notes; music, Maurice
Thiriet. WP v 11 n 5 p 6 Mr '60
---Reviews; newspaper comments.
TD n 95 p 14 Jl-Ag '60
MAVRA, opera
Vincenzi, Edda, e Luigi Pontiggia,
AP hl ph: La Scala. La S n 124
p 28 Mr '60
MAXIMOWNA, ITA (1914-). Un
Ballo in Maschera, opera setting
Act III scene 3 for Wiener Staat-
soper 1958, ph. Ver v 1 n 2 Ag'60
A MAY NIGHT, opera
Zurich; ens AP wl ph: Baur. Op
v 11 n 4 p 288 Ap '60
MAYE, CAROLYN, singer
Career notes; b. NYC; Melbourne
review of the Music Man. por MD
v 50 n 11 p 25 My '60

---Por ph. MD v 50 n 9 p 25 Mr'60

MAYER, FRANCIS N. John Philip Sousa, his instrumentation and scoring. MEJ v 46 n 3 p 51-7 Ja '60

MAYER, PAULETTE, pianist
Paris review. GDC n 274 p 724 My '27-60

MAYER, SIR ROBERT (1879-). Student opera abroad. ON v 24 n 20 p 14, 32 Mr 19'60

---London; "Your Opera Nights", series for youth; notes. WM n 1 p 10 F '60

MAYERLING, opera
Composer, Barbara Giuranna; San Carlo notes. MC v 162 n 1 p 30 Jl '60

---San Carlo notes. La S n 125 p 51 Ap '60

---Weerth, Ernest de. Naples review. ON v 24 n 24 p 28 Ap 16'60

MAYUZUMI, TOSHIRO, 1929-, composer
Paris; "Mandala"; notes. GDC n 288 p 254 N 11'60

MAZEPPA, opera
Wiesbaden review. Op v 11 n 5 p 349 My '60

MECHEM, KIRKE, composer
San Francisco concert of his works; review. MC v 161 n 7 p 32 Je '60

MEDEA (CULBERG), ballet
Von Rosen, Elsa-Marianne, and Gerd Andersson, 1954, ens AP wl ph: Royal Swedish Ballet. Th Notbk v 15 n 1 plate 2 Autumn'60

LE MÉDECIN MALGRÉ LUI, opera
Aix-en-Provence; Gounod opera, The Mock Doctor, 2 AP phs: Serge Lido. Op v 11 p 32-3 Autumn '60

MEDEE, Tragedie
Corneille, M. T. Medée (libretto as it was published by Christophe Ballard, 1693, in French). Chrys v 13 nos 5-8 1960

MEDÉE, opera
Paris Opéra; Cherubini to be produced; Rita Gorr; José Beckmans' décor. portfolio OpP n 19 p 30-1 1960

MEDICI, MARIO (1899-). Editorials (Germany's recent performances of Verdi, statistics; a tribute to Dimitri Mitropoulos; list of writers welcoming the Verdi Institute; several language translations of this editorial). Ver v 1 n 2 Ag '60

--- ---Letters about King Lear (Verdi). Ver v 1 n 2 p 1039-1056 Ag '60

--- ---L'Instituto de Studi Verdiani. Ver v 1 n 1 p VII-XXII Ap '60

--- ---"Quel prete", che sposò Verdi; nota. (facsimile of marriage to Giuseppina Strepponi) Ver v 1 n 2 p 657-661 Ag '60

MEI LAN-FANG, 1894-, actor
Scott, A. C. Mei Lan-Fang, Leader of the Pear Garden. (book on Chinese dancer reviewed). Th Notbk v 15 n 2 p 70 Winter '60-61

MEIREI, play
The Command (Fuji Shun), ens AP ph: Tokyo. WP v 12 n 2 p 1 N '60

DIE MEISTERSINGER, opera
Munich review; Wolf Völker production. Op v 11 n 12 p 833 D '60

---Trilling, Ossia. The new Meistersinger production (Leipzig). Op v 11 n 12 p 810-11 D '60

---Mraz, Ladislav, as Sachs with Wilhelm Klemm as Beckmesser, AP hl ph: Helga Wallmüller; Act 3, scene 2 ens AP wl ph: same. Op v 11 n 12 p 809, 811 D '60

---Munich State Opera; closing scene, ens AP wl ph: Betz. Op v 11 n 11 p 767 N '60

--- ---ens AP wl ph: Rudolf Betz. Op v 11 n 12 p 834 D '60

---Quaglio's set for St. Katherine's Church 1868 in Munich; recent set under Wieland Wagner, 2 ens AP wl phs. Op v 11 n 11 p 734-5 N'60

---Tokyo; end of the church scene, ens AP wl ph: 1960. ON v 25 n 7 p 29 D 24'60

MEJORANA
Schaeffer, Myron. The mejorana: a typical song of Panama. CMJ v 4 n 3 p 4-22 Spring '60

MELBA, DAME NELLIE (Helen Mitchell), 1859-1931, singer
Hl ph: 1900. MC v 161 n 3 p 10 F'60

179

MELBOURNE
Music critics of newspapers
very harsh on visiting celebri-
ties; letters, press quotes, con-
troversy. MD v 50 n 12 p 10-13
Je '60
---National Theatre Movement
Festival; opera, ballet reviews.
il MD v 50 n 9 p 21, 24 Mr '60
---Phillips, Linda. 1960 "Sun aria
competition. MD v 51 n 5 p 15
N '60
MELCHIOR, LAURITZ, 1890-,
singer
Brooklyn concert. ON v 24 n 18
p 2 Mr 5'60
---As Tristan, AP hl ph. Th Arts
v 44 n 3 p 49 Mr '60
MELIKOVA, GENIA, dancer
La Fée Lilas, dans La Belle au
Bois Dormant, International Bal-
let, AP hl ph: Lido. TD n 98 p 10
D '60
---Posed, AP wl ph: Paris. TD
n 91 p 21 Mr '60
MÉLISSA, play
Ens AP wl ph: Bernand, 1960.
WT v 9 n 3 p 285 Autumn '60
MENASCE, JACQUES DE, 1905-
1960, composer
Goldman, Richard Franko. (Ob-
ituary.) Mus Q v 46 n 3 p 364-
367 Jl '60
---Notes. GDC n 259-60 p 368
F 12'60
---Obituary. MC v 161 n 3 p 20
F '60
MENCI, PIETRO, singer
Echternach concert; Pierre Ni-
max, pianist; review by Paul Ul-
veling. GDC n 285 p 167 O21'60
MENDEL, ARTHUR (1905-). A
brief note on triple proportion in
Schuetz. Mus Q v 46 n 1 p 67-70
Ja '60
--- ---Recent developments in
Bach chronology. il Mus Q v 46
n 3 p 283-300 Jl '60
MENDELSSOHN (BARTHOLDY),
Felix, 1809-1847, composer
Influence upon English taste.
CMJ v 4 n 2 p 21-3 Winter '60
---Ritratto. La S n 126 p 17
My '60

MENGELBERG, RUDOLF, 1892-
1959, composer
Obituary notes. MC v 161 n 1
p 6 Ja '60
MENGELBERG, WILLEM, 1871-
1951, composer
Amsterdam notes on radio con-
certs 1939-40; twelve documen-
tary LP records to be pressed.
HF v 10 n 9 p 30 S '60
MENOTTI, GIAN-CARLO, 1911-,
composer
Commission from NBC-TV, opera.
AmM v 8 n 10 p 10 N '60
---With Mietta Sighele, ph: Spoleto.
MC v 162 n 2 p 24 Ag '60
EL MENSAJE, play
Barcelona; Jaime Salom. WP v 11
n 5 p 3 Mr '60
MENTON
Mari, Pierrette. Le XIe Festival
de Menton (critiques). GDC n 281-2
p 66-7 S 30'60
MENUHIN, YEHUDI, 1916-, violin-
ist
and Hepzibah; Chicago review.
MC v 161 n 1 p 22 Ja '60
---and Hephzibah; sonates piano-
violon; Paris. GDC n 257-8
p 359 Ja 29'60
---Washington and Philadelphia
notes. MC v 161 n 3 p 40 F '60
MERELLI, BARTOLOMEO, 1793-
1879, impresario
Por: La Scala Museum. ON v 25
n 4 p 19 D 3'60
MERIAN, LEON, hornsman
Por ph. IM v 59 n 1 p 18 Jl '60
MERMAID THEATRE
Puddle Dock, the stage, ph.
NTM v 1 n 4 p 17 Jl '60
MERMAN, ETHEL, 1909-, actress
Keating, John. A marathon named Merman. Portfolio Th Arts
v 44 n 9 p 62-3 S '60
---Several phs: 1930s. Th Arts
v 44 n 9 p 64 S '60
MERRICK, DAVID, 1912-, pro-
ducer
Gehman, Richard. (Career ske-
tch.) il Th Arts v 44 n 11 p 15-7,
69 N '60
---Kulaway, Ronald. Drawing;
several phs: United Press.

Th Arts v 44 n 11 p 14, 16-7 N '60
MERRIE ENGLAND, operetta
Sadler's Wells review. Op v 11
n 9 p 645 S '60
---Sadler's Wells, ens AP wl ph:
Angus McBean. Op v 11 n 9
p 645 S '60
MERILL, ROBERT, 1919-, singer
Wilson, John S. (career notes;
"New Girl in Town".) Th Arts
v 44 n 1 p 81 Ja '60
---As Valentin, AP hl ph: LeBlang.
MC v 161 n 4 p 14 Mr '60
THE MERRY WIDOW, operetta
Melbourne; Garnet H. Carroll,
directing London stars using lo-
cal dance talent also. MD v 50
n 12 p 19 Je '60
---Vienna; Lotte Rysanek notes.
ON v 24 n 12 p 28 Ja 23'60
LE MERVEILLEUX ALLIAGE,
play
Pitoëff, ens AP wl ph: 1936.
Spec n 1 p 41 1960
MESPLÉ, MADY
La folie de Lucia, AP wl ph. OpP
n 19 p 24 1960
MESSEL, OLIVER (1905-). Le
Nozze di Figaro for the Metro-
politan, designs, portfolio: Mel-
ançon. ON v 24 n 12 Ja 23'60
MESSIAH
MacMillan, Ernest. Novello's
new Messiah. CMJ v 4 n 2 p 57-
60 Winter '60
MESSIEURS LES EMPLOYES,
play
Budapest; Imre Foldes; notes.
WP v 11 n 4 p 8 F '60
MESSINIS, MARIO. Teatro La
Fenice. il La S n 123 p 41 F '60
MESTRE, GLORIA, dancer
In Thais (Gallizia), opera at San
Carlo; notes. ON v 24 n 14 p 26
F 6'60
METROPOLITAN OPERA
Auditions for new talent; views
of Martha D. Wagner, of John
Gutman on the last ten years. ON
v 25 n 4 p 21 D 3'60
---Andrea Chénier: cast; story;
décor; bibliography; discography;
portfolio. ON v 24 n 21 Mr 26'60
---Benefits 1960-1; title date,

scale of prices, organization. ON
v 25 n 3 p 26 N 19'60
---Calendar: singers, operas, dates
in NYC. ON v 25 n 3 p 32 N 19'60
---Carmen: cast; story; décor;
bibliography; discography; portfolio. ON v 24 n 14 F 6'60
---Cavalleria Rusticana and Pagliacci: casts; décor notes; bibliography; discography; portfolio. ON
v 24 n 13 Ja 30'60
---Coleman, Emily. Mr. Bing's
Metropolitan. il Th Arts v 44
n 3 p 34-5 Mr '60
---Downes, Edward. Karl Böhm.
por HF v 10 n 3 p 54-5, 128 Mr '60
---L'Elisir d'Amore; cast notes;
story; criticism; pictures. ON v 25
n 7 D 24'60
---Fidelio: cast; story; criticism;
décor; bibliography; discography;
portfolio. ON v 24 n 15 F 13'60
---Der fliegende Holländer cast;
story; criticism; décor; bibliography;
discography and portfolio. ON v 24
n 18 Mr 5'60
---La Forza del Destino: cast; story;
background articles; décor notes;
bibliography; discography; portfolio. ON v 24 n 19 Mr 12'60
---Four new operas, notes; list of
others in repertory. AmM v 8 n 6
p 12 Jl '60
---Goth, Trudy. (Notes.) il La S
n 122 p 39 Ja '60
--- ---(Reviews.) La S n 125 p 53-
4 Ap '60
---Guarrera, Frank. (On preparing
Simon Boccanegra). il ON v 24 n 22
p 8-10 Ap 2'60
---Harrison, Wallace K. Steps to
the (new) opera house. il ON v 25
n 2 p 15-7 O 29'60
---Madama Butterfly cast; story;
notes; bibliography; discography;
portfolio. ON v 24 n 24 Ap 16'60
---Manon Lescaut; featured in notes and pictures; cast. ON v 25 n 5
D 10'60
---Nabucco; notes and pictures; the
cast. ON v 25 n 4 D 3'60
--- ---reviewed. MC v 162 n 5
p 14 N '60
---NYC reviews (9). MC v 162 n 6

(Metropolitan)
p 14-6 D '60
--- ---Andrea Chenier; Parsifal;
Aida with Lisitsian. MC v 161
n 5 p 14 Ap '60
--- ---La Forza del Destino; Die
Walkiere; Simon Boccandgra.
MC v 161 n 4 p 13-4 Mr '60
--- ---La Traviata; Pelléas et
Mélisande; Faust; Cavalleria and
Pagliacci. MC v 161 n 1 p 12-3
Ja '60
--- ---Tristan und Isolde; Mac-
beth; Der Rosenkavalier; Der
Fliegende Holländer; Don Giovan-
ni; Fidelio. MC v 161 n 3 p 23-4
F '60
--- ---Simon Boccanegra. MC
v 161 n 6 p 16 My '60
---Notes on Nabucco; on L'Elisir
d'Amore; ballet notes also. AmM
v 8 n 3 p 17 Mr '60
---Notes: younger singers visit
the New York schools in Così
fan tutte; gala list in welfare con-
cert. AmM v 8 n 11 p 8 D '60
---Le Nozze di Figaro: cast story;
décor; bibliography; discography;
criticism; portfolio. ON v 24 n 12
Ja 23'60
---Parsifal: cast; story; background and décor notes; bibliography; discography; portfolio.
ON v 24 n 23 Ap 9'60
---Pelléas et Mélisande: cast;
story; criticism; décor; bibliography; discography; portfolio.
ON v 24 n 11 Ja 16'60
---RePass, Richard. (Critical report; including death on stage of
Leonard Warren.) il Op v 11 n 5
p 336-8 My '60
--- ---Reviews. il Op v 12 n 3
p 198-200 Mr '60; same Op v 11
n 4 p 268-70 Ap '60
---Reviews and news, illustrated.
Op 1960
---Rigoletto cast; notes on Berman
décor; portfolio with facsimile of
1893 playbill with Melba. ON
v 25 n 8 D 31'60
---Season 1959-60 longest in 75
years; 189 performances of 24
operas; general estimate of the

events; Op v 11 n 6 p 407-8
Je '60
---Simon Boccanegra: cast; story;
historical notes; décor; bibliography;
discography; portfolio. ON v 24
n 22 Ap 2'60
---Spring tour; repertory listed and
cities. AmM v 8 n 4 p 16 Ap '60
---Summary 1960 fall season. Op
v 11 n 12 p 814 D '60
---Tannhäuser; cast; criticism,
portfolio. ON v 25 n 6 D 17'60
---La Tosca: cast; story; décor
notes; articles; bibliography; discography; portfolio. ON v 24 n 20
Mr 19'60
---Tristan und Isolde: cast notes;
story; décor; discography; portfolio. ON v 24 n 10 Ja 9'60
--- ---the 1886 story of US première. ON v 24 n 10 p 12-3 Ja 9'60
---Il Trovatore: cast; story; critical articles; décor notes; discography; bibliography; portfolio.
ON v 24 n 17 F 27'60
---Twelve regional auditions; details. IM v 59 n 5 p 53 N '60
---Die Walküre: cast; story; cri-
ticism; décor notes; bibliography;
discography; portfolio. ON v 24
n 16 F 20'60
---From the stage, Thomas Schippers on the podium, ph: NYC.
AmM v 8 n 11 p 9 D '60
---The National Council, 6 group
phs: Louis Melançon. ON v 25 n 5
p 26 D 10'60
METROPOLITAN OPERA AUDI-
TIONS
Lingg, Ann M. (Explanation of
present Regional Auditions to
prepare for final NYC contest.)
ON v 25 n 8 p 27 D 31'60
---Regional auditions 1961: list
MC v 162 n 4 p 10 O '60
THE METROPOLITAN OPERA
GUILD
Belmont, Eleanor R. A cause to
celebrate (25 years' survey). ON
v 25 n 1 p 9-13 O 8'60
---Fadiman, Clifton. Behind the
scenes. ON v 25 n 1 p 16-7
O 8'60
---Reports: Atlanta; Baton Rouge;

Birmingham;Los Angeles;Memphis;Mobile;Riverside-San Bernardino;Sacramento;San Diego; San Francisco;San Jose;Tucson. ON v 24 n 19 Mr 12'60
---Sixty-thousand members;types of membership. ON v 25 n 7 p 2 D 24'60
---The Speakers Bureau; how it operates. ON v 25 n 5 p 2 D 10'60
---Twenty-fifth anniversary program notes, backstage tours. il ON v 25 n 3 p 7 N 19'60
---Year's summary. ON v 24 n 24 p 1 Ap 16'60

METROPOLITAN OPERA MUSEUM
Mrs. Kathleen Hoover, viewing a wall cabinet of memorabilia, a beginning, ph: Taylor and Dull. ON v 24 n 19 p 15 Mr 12'60

METROPOLITAN OPERA NATIONAL COUNCIL
Hook, Howard J., Jr, chairman of Regional Auditions program; interview. por ON v 24 n 11 p 13 Ja 16'60

METROPOLITAN OPERA ORCHESTRA
Wagner, Martha D. Fanfare for orchestra, Metropolitan Opera, "finest in the business", under Felix Eyle. ON v 24 n 14 p 10-1 F 6'60

METZ
Le Festival (3e); report by Jean Abel. GDC n 284 p 131 O 14'60

METZENGER, EDWARD M.
Before his drums, Chicago Symphony, ph. MEJ v 46 n 4 p 1 F-Mr '60

MEXICO
Opera at Monterrey. Op v 11 n 12 p 837 D '60
---Pan American Festival, sponsored by Bellas Artes Institute; also opera reviews; Howard University Chorus on tour. MC v 162 n 3 p 26 S '60
---Poore, Charles. Music report. MC v 161 n 1 p 27 Ja '60; same. MC v 161 n 5 p 32 Ap '60; same. MC v 162 n 1 p 32 Jl '60; same. MC v 162 n 4 p 29 O '60
---Theatre report. WP v 11 n 8 p 8 Je '60

MEYER, JEAN, 1914-, director
Paris; notes. Th Arts v 44 n 12 p 61, 74 D '60

MEYER, KERSTIN, singer
Por ph. MC v 162 n 6 p 15 D '60

MEYERHOLD, VSEVOLOD (1874-).
From "On the Theatre", trans. Nora Beeson. TDR v 4 n 4 p 134-47 My '60

MIAMI OPERA GUILD
Career sketch of Arturo Di Filippi; and opera in Florida. ON v 24 n 21 p 26 Mr 26'60
---La Gioconda notes, Eileen Farrell, Frances Bible, Flaviano Lábò, Cesare Bardelli, Nicola Moscona; Carmen with Risë Stevens, Walter Cassell; Emerson Buckley conductor. Op v 11 n 6 p 411 Je '60

MICAULT, JEAN, pianist
Le Club des Amis des Arts et des Lettres: concert review. GDC n 273 p 689 My 20'60
---Louvet, Michel. Paris comment. GDC n 263-4 p 490 Mr 11'60
---Paris review. GDC n 278 p 848 Je 24'60

A MIDSUMMER NIGHT'S DREAM, play
Ens AP wl ph: Ontario. WP v 12 n 1 p 1 O '60

A MIDSUMMER NIGHT'S DREAM, opera
Holland Festival; Britten reviewed. Op v 11 p 29 Autumn "60
---Mitchell, Donald. In and out of Britten's "Dream". il Op v 11 n 12 p 797-801 D '60
---Première at Aldeburgh Festival; review by Noël Godwin of Britten work. MC v 162 n 2 p 22 Ag '60
---Aldeburgh, ens AP wl ph: allegro. Op v 11 n 7 p 495 Jl '60; same. 2 scenes, ens AP wl ph: allegro. Op v 11 p 23 Autumn '60

MIGGIANI, ANTONIETTA, 1937-, singer
Winner in Liverpool contest; Maltese. Op v 11 n 7 p 456 Jl '60

MIGNON, PAUL-LOUIS. France (theatre report). il WT v 9 n 2 p 158-160 Summer '60; same. WT v 9 n 3 p 282-5 Autumn "60; same. WT v 9 n 4 p 356-8 Winter '60

MIGOT, GEORGES, 1891-, composer
Mari, Pierrette. Musée des instruments, Paris. GDC n 287 p 237 N 4'60
---Strasbourg criticism of "Symphonie

(Migot)
pour Orchestre de cordes".
GDC n 281-2 p 65 S 30'60
MIHALY, ANDRAS, 1917-, composer
Critical notes. Mus Q v 46 n 4
p 532 O '60
MILA, MASSIMO (1910-). Problem
di filologia e d'interpretazione
intorno alla partitura del Ballo
in Maschera (English and German
translations p 458-493). Ver v 1
n 1 p 133-156 Ap '60
--- ---II. Ver v 1 n 2 p 720-731
Ag '60
---Parente, Alfredo. Difesa di un
mestiere. La S n 133 p 72-3 D'60
---Por ph. La S n 133 p 73 D '60
MILAN
Angelicum, XX stagione concertistica (ottobre 1960-aprile 1961):
concerti di Musica antica e contemporanea per orchestra di camera dell'Angelicum, Riccardo
Allorto. La S n 131   inset O '60
---Associazioni Riunite di Concerti: Teatro Nuovo e Sala Verdi
del Conservatorio: calendario dei
concerti, Ottobre 1960 al 4 Maggio 1961, XIII stagione. La S
n 131 inset O '60
---Castiglioni, Vittorangelo. Teatro Nuovo di Milano. il La S v 131
p 29, 59 O '60
---Gambetta, Rosario. Les Noces
de Figaro; Herbert von Karajan.
GDC n 276 p 784 Je 10'60
--- ---Othello; La Tosca; Hansel
et Gretel. GDC n 255-6 p 307
Ja 15'60
---Music report. La S n 122 p 64
Ja '60; La S n 123 p 67 F '60; LaS
n 125 p 77-9 Ap '60
---Sartori, Claudio, Opera report:
La Scala, La Piccola Scala, il
Op v 11 n 5 p 351-2 My '60
---Several illustrations to mark
the era of Francesco and Giovannina Lucea. La S n 128 p 6-15
Jl '60
MILANOV, ZINKA, 1906-, singer
As Amelia Grimaldi AP phs: Melançon. ON v 24 n 22 p 17 Ap 2'60
---As Floria Tosca, AP phs:

Melançon. ON v 24 n 20 p 17
Mr 19'60
MILHAUD, DARIUS, 1892-, composer
With Vronsky and Babin, hl ph:
Aspen. MC v 162 n 6 p 10 D '60
MILJOONAVAILLINKI, comedy
Helsinki notes; Mika Waltari. WP
v 11 n 4 p 5 F '60
MILLAR, GREGORY, 1924-, conductor
Career notes. por MD v 51 n 5
p 25 N '60
---NY Philharmonic review. MC
v 162 n 5 p 17 N '60
MILLER, ARTHUR, 1915-, playwright
Driver, Tom F. Strength and weakness in Arthur Miller. TDR v 4 n 4
p 45-52 My '60
MILLER, FRANK, conductor
Informal ph: Minneapolis. IM v 59
n 5 p 35 N '60
MILLER, HENRY (1859-1926).
Homère. WP v 11 n 8 p 1, 7 Je'60
MILLER, JAMES HULL. Why theatre architecture lags; Part I.
PlM v 37 n 1 p 6 O '60
--- ---Part II. PlM v 37 n 2 p 30
N '60
MILLER, MARY, 1944-, dancer
AP wl ph: Perth TV. MD v 51 n 1
p 28 Jl '60
MILLER, MILDRED, 1924-, singer
As Cherubino, AP wl phs: Melançon.
ON v 24 n 12 p 7 Ja 23'60
---Her family visiting her dressing
room, ph: Melançon. ON v 24 n 18
p 3 Mr 5'60
MILLER, MITCH, 1911-, oboist
Por ph. HF v 10 n 10 p 141 O '60
MILLER, PHILIP L. Leonard Warren, 1911-1960. portfolio Op v 11
n 6 p 397-403 Je '60
---Presiding at New York Public
Library's tribute to Edward Johnson. ON v 24 n 15 p 2 F 13'60
MILLER, ROBBIN, dancer
Notes; b. Reading, Pennsylvania.
MD v 51 n 6 p 25 D '60
---AP wl ph: Melbourne; also por
ph. MD v 51 n 6 p 25 D '60
MILLOSS, AUREL M., 1906-,
choreographer
Three new ballets for the Opera

at Cologne; notes. TD n 91 p 2 Mr '60

MILLS, MAJOR CLARENCE L.
An objective look at our music education program (US). MEJ v 46 n 5 p 80 Ap-My '60

MILLSTEIN, GILBERT. José Quintero (some quoted opinion on theatre directing), por Th Arts v 44 n 5 p 10-2 My '60
---Rudolf Bing. por Th Arts v 44 n 3 p 54-6 Mr '60

MILSTEIN, NATHAN, 1904-, violinist
Paris criticism. GDC n 278 p 850 Je 24'60

MILTON, JOHN R. The esthetic fault of Strindberg's "Dream Plays". TDR v 4 n 3 p 108-116 Mr '60

MILWAUKEE
Monfried, Walter. Theatre USA: Milwaukee. il Th Arts v 44 n 6 p 54-5, 66 Je '60

MIME
Paris; Mme. Zoya à alliance française. TD n 90 p 22 F '60

MIN ÄLSKADE ÄR EN FISKARE, play
Turku; Walentin Chorell. WP v 12 n 3 p 28 D '60

MINARDI, GIAN PAOLO. Frammenti Verdiani di Bruno Barilli. Ver v 1 n 2 p 790-798 Ag '60

MINGUS, CHARLES, 1922-, composer
Hentoff, Nat. Charles Mingus, jazz composer, bassist and leader (b. Arizona). IM v 59 n 6 p 24-5 D '60

THE MINNEAPOLIS SYMPHONY
Contemporary repertory under director, Stanislaw Skrowaczewski; guest conductors. AmM v 8 n 9 p 12 O '60
---Miller, Frank, on activities. IM v 59 n 5 p 35 N '60
---NYC review; Antal Dorati, conducting. MC v 161 n 4 p 17 Mr '60

MINSTREL SHOWS
Dr. Souchon Recalls Songs of Minstrel Days and Blues (New Orleans concert with spoken notes; Golden Crest recording. HF v 10 n 3 p 89

Mr '60

MINTON, YVONNE, singer
Winner of the Shell Aria prize (1000 pounds) at Canberra National Eisteddfod. MD v 50 n 12 p 20 Je '60

THE MIRACLE WORKER, play
NYC notes; William Gibson. WP v 11 n 4 p 3 F '60
---Richards, Stanley. NYC review. PlM v 36 n 5 p 107 F '60
---Helen Keller's life; Anne Bancroft and Patty Duke, 2 AP phs: Sheldon Secunda. Th Arts v 44 n 1 cover, p 26 Ja '60

THE MIRACULOUS MANDARIN, ballet
Ens AP wl ph: Catania. La S n 124 p 35 Mr '60

IL MIRAGGIO, a periodical
Saville, Eugenia. Italy; the Young Composers Experimental Group of Turin. Mus Q v 46 n 3 p 371-378 Jl '60

MIREILLE, opera
Reims review. GDC n 261-2 p 436 F 26'60

THE MIRROR OF LOVE, play
National Toneel, Antwerpen; ens AP wl ph: 1959. WT v 9 n 1 p 24 Spring '60

LE MISANTHROPE, play
Nelson, Robert J. The unreconstructed heroes of Molière. TDR v 4 n 3 p 28-35 Mr '60

MISKOVITCH, MILROAD, 1928?- danseur
AP wl ph: Lido. TD n 98 p 3 D'60
---With Dusna Sifnios and Wassili Sulich, AP wl ph: Lido. TD n 96 p 27 S-O '60

Mr. BROUCEK'S EXCURSIONS, opera
Janacek première, Munich, ens AP wl ph: Betz. ON v 24 n 23 p 3 Ap 9'60

MISTERO DELLA NATIVITA
Salsburg; Frank Martin's work, ens AP wl ph. La S n 131 p 68 O '60

MITCHELL, DONALD (1925-). In and out of Britten's "Dream". il Op v 11 n 12 p 797-801 D '60

MITHRIDATE, play

185

(Mithridate)
Bruxelles, 1956; ens AP wl ph:
O. V. Brugge. WT v 9 n 1 p 39
Spring '60
MITROPOULOS, DIMITRI, 1896-
1960, conductor
Debieve, Pierre. (Obituary.)
GDC n 289 p 288 N 18'60
---Medici, Mario. In memory
of Mitropoulos. Ver v 1 n 2
preface Ag '60
---Mina, Betty. A sonnet in mem-
ory of Dimitri Mitropoulos. MC
v 162 n 6 p 4 D '60
---Notes; US debut 1936. AmM
v 8 n 10 p 11 N '60
---Obituary. ON v 25 n 5 p 14
D 10'60
---Obituary. por IM v 59 n 6 p 16
D '60
---Pugliese, Giuseppe. (Notes.)
Ver v 1 n 2 p 981 Ag '60
---Toni, Alceo. Dimitri Mitro-
poulos (obituary). La S n 133
p 62-3 D '60
---AP ph. WM n 6 cover D '60
---Left profile ph: Herman Leo-
nard. ON v 25 n 5 p 15 D 10'60
MITTAG, EDWIN von. Vienna
report. ON v 24 n 12 p 28-9 Ja
23'60
MITTLEMANN, NORMAN, singer
As Prince Igor, Düsseldorf, AP
hl ph: Conti. ON v 25 n 4 p 4
D 3'60
MODERN DANCE
See Expressional dance
LE MODERN JAZZ QUARTET
Paris; "le succès commercial
est considérable"; l'idée bonne,
mais". TD n 94 p 5 Je '60
MODUGNO, DOMENICO, singer
Por ph. La S n 132 p 61 N '60
MODULATION
Woodham, Ronald. The meaning
of mudulation. MR v 21 n 4
p 265-281 N '60
MOFFO, ANNA, 1935?-, singer
Debut in La Traviata, Metropol-
itan; criticism. MC v 161 n 1
p 12 Ja '60
---Notes por ON v 24 n 24 p 3
Ap 16'60
---Philadelphia Grand Opera

notes. MC v 161 n 3 p 40 F '60
---AP wl ph: Roma. La S n 124 p 33
Mr '60
---As Violetta, AP hl ph: Italia.
Op v 11 n 9 p 616 S '60
---In Puritani, AP hl ph: Catania.
La S n 125 p 52 Ap '60
LA MOGLIE INGENUA e il MARI-
TO MALATO, play
Milan; Achille Campanile. WP
v 12 n 2 p 24 N '60
MOISEIWITSCH, BENNO, 1890-,
pianist
With Ramsi Tick and Josef Krips,
hl ph: Buffalo. MC v 162 n 1 p 21
Jl '60
MOLIERE, (JEAN-BAPTISTE PO-
QUELIN) 1622-1673, dramatist
As high school play material; a
practical article by Robert A.
Fahrner, College of Holy Names,
Oakland, California. PlM v 36 n 4
p 78 Ja '60
---Nelson, Robert J. The unrecon-
structed heroes of Molière. TDR
v 4 n 3 p 14-37 Mr '60
MOLINARELLA, opera
Naples review. La S n 132 p 46
N '60
---Two ens AP phs: Naples. La S
n 132 p 46 N '60
MONCILOVICH, MILAN, dancer
Notes; Belgrade. il La S n 127
p 31 Je '60
DER MOND, opera
Orff, ens AP wl ph: Hamburg,
1951. WT v 9 n 3 p 220 Autumn '60
IL MONDO DELLA LUNA, opera
Group Eight, London review; Mar-
cello Cortis good. il Op v 11 n 5
p 368-9 My '60
MONFRIED, WALTER. Theatre
USA: Milwaukee. portfolio Th
Arts v 44 n 6 p 54-5, 66 Je '60
MONICELLI, FURIO. Mazzini,
Giulia Grisi e Mario (del Risor-
gimento). il La S n 125 p 27-31
Ap '60
MONNA-VAUNA, opera
Rennes review. GDC n 265-6
p 519 Mr 25'60
THE MONOLITH, play
Montreal notes; Henry Hovenkamp.
WP v 11 n 7 p 3 My '60

MONSIEUR DE FALINDOR, play
Bruxelles, 1959; ens AP wl ph:
Cayet. WT v 9 n 1 p 44 Spring'60
MONTANDON, J. J., pianist
Paris notes. GDC n 287 p 228
N 4'60
MONTE CARLO
Berthoumieux, Serge. Reviews
of the festival; le chef, Pedro de
Freitas Branco; Pierre Fournier,
Rafael Kubelik, Lorin Maazel,
Christian Ferras. GDC n 284
p 130-1 O 14'60
---Christian, G. A l'Opéra de
Monte Carlo: La Tosca; Le Bar-
bier de Séville. GDC n 263-4
p 484 Mr 11'60
---Demarquez, Suzanne. Music
at Monaco. MC v 162 n 3 p 18
S '60
---Hiver 1959-1960, opera, ballets
comedies, la musique, concerts.
La S n 122 inset Ja '60
---Music report. MC v 162 n 1
p 34 Jl '60
---Opera di Stato Bavarese, Fes-
tival dell'Opera di Monaco 1961,
dal 7 agosto al 9 settembre 1960:
calendar. La S n 128 inset Jl'60
---Rocchia, G. La Saison lyrique:
Turandot; Don Juan; Don Quich-
otte; Manon Lescaut. GDC n 267-
8 p 553 Ap 8'60
---Turnbull, Patrick. (Opera re-
views.) Op v 11 n 5 p 355-7
My '60; same. Op v 11 n 7 p 490-
2 Jl '60
---Royalty and the orchestra, ph.
WM n 6 p 136 D '60
---Scene each: Salome; Don Qui-
chotte; Turandot, 3 ens AP wl
phs: Picedi. Op v 11 n 7 p 492
Jl '60
MONTEMEZZI, ITALO, 1875-
1952, composer
Por right profile ph. La S n 133
p 61 D '60
MONTEUX, PIERRE, 1875-, con-
ductor
Boston ovation; Beethoven's
Ninth. MC v 161 n 6 p 29 My '60
---Career notes. AmM v 8 n 4
p 7 Ap '60
---London concerts; one all Ravel;

Debussy's Pelléas et Mélisande.
MC v 161 n 7 p 13 Je '60
---Opening of Ravinia Festival, his
19th year; notes, MC v 162 n 2
p 12 Ag '60
---AP hl ph: Fred Fehl. IM v 58
n 10 back cover Ap '60
MONTEVIDEO
Goldberg, S. M. (Music report.)
MC v 161 n 3 p 46 F '60
MONTREAL
Saucier, Pierre. (Music report.)
CMJ v 5 n 1 p 45-7 Autumn '60
EL MONUMENTO, play
Buenaventura; ens AP wl ph: Bogota.
WP v 11 n 9 p 7 Jl '60
MONUMENTUM PRO GESUALDO
(BALANCHINE), ballet
Stravinsky score 1960; note. AmM
v 8 n 10 p 11 N '60
MOODY, JOHN. The Arts Council
and theatre finance. NTM v 1 n 1
p 21-3 O '59
THE MOON BESIEGED, play
Stanford Players, ens AP wl ph.
Th Arts v 44 n 3 p 61 Mr '60
MOON REINDEER(CULLBERG),
ballet
Ravn and Flindt, AP wl ph: Jack
Mitchell. Th Arts v 44 n 11 p 57
N '60
MOOR, EMANUEL, 1862-1931,
composer
Truscott, Harold. The piano con-
certos of Emanuel Moōr. MR v 21
n 2 p 121-129 My '60
MOOR, PAUL. Our operatic ex-
patriates (American singers ex-
ported). il HF v 10 n 11 p 50-2
N '60
MOORE, DALE, singer
NYC debut; all Hugo Wolf songs.
MC v 161 n 4 p 20 Mr '60
MOORE, DOUGLAS, 1893-, com-
poser
President of The American Aca-
demy of Arts and Letters. AmM
v 8 n 3 p 18 Mr '60
---Por ph: Blackstone. MC v 161
n 1 p 31 Ja '60
MOORE, JOHN R. (1890-) A fare-
well to something (implications in
Beckett's "Waiting for Godot").
TDR v 5 n 1 p 49-60 S '60

MORRE, LILLIAN (1917-). Un-
listed ballets by Jean Georges No-
verre. il Th Notbk v 15 n 1 p 15-
20 Autumn '60
MORANBONG, film
Marker, Chris. Un film blanc:
Moranburg. il Spec n 1 p 70 1960
---Several pictures, Ouan Djoeung
Ichi, Oeun Do Soun, phs. Spec
n 1 1960
MORAVIANS
Music criticism; Columbia re-
leases. HF v 10 n 6 p 57-8
Je '60
MORAWETZ, OSKAR, composer
Notes. CMJ v 4 n 2 p 41 Winter
'60
MOREHOUSE, WARD (1899). Br-
oadway had a building boom
(early 20th century theatre build-
ings with subsequent notes). Th
Arts v 44 n 1 p 79-80, 84 Ja '60
--- ---(US Theatre in the 1930s).
il Th Arts v 44 n 9 p 10-4 S '60
MOREL, FRANÇOIS, composer
Première: Boréal; Montreal
Symphony under Igor Markevitch;
symphonic poem as is "Rituel de
l'espace"; criticism. CMJ v 4
n 4 p 45-6 Summer '60
MOREL, JEAN, 1903-, conductor
Por ph. AmM v 8 n 5 p 7 Je '60
---With Victoria de los Angeles
and Gloria Davy, hl ph: London.
AmM v 8 n 7 p 7 Ag '60
MORELL, BARRY, 1927-, singer
As the Duke in Rigoletto, AP hl
ph: Louis Melançon. ON v 25
n 8 p 21 D 31'60
---As Lieut. Pinkerton, AP phs:
Melançon. ON v 24 n 24 Ap 16'60
MORENA, BERTA, 1878-, singer
As Elisabeth in Tannhäuser, AP
hl ph: Munich. ON v 24 n 16 p 10
F 20'60
MORGAN, MONA. Autobiographical
acting. PlM v 36 n 4 p 82-3 Ja '60
MORINI, MARIO (1925?-). Naso
fino di Giovannina (Strazza). LaS
n 128 p 7-15 Jl '60
--- ---Ojetti librettista per una
volta. il La Scala n 122 p 28-32
Ja '60
--- ---Simoni e Illica associati

per un libretto. il La S n 133
p 56-61 D '60
MORLAYE, GUILLAUME (b. ?-d. ?),
16th century lutenist-composer
Heartz, Daniel. Parisian music
publishing under Henry II (four re-
cently discovered guitar books).
Mus Q v 46 n 4 p 448-467 O '60
MORLEY, MALCOLM. Drama at
London Bridge (1833 opened; his-
torical notes on London Bridge
Theater). Th Notbk v 14 n 4 p 119-
122 Summer '60
MORLEY, THOMAS (1557?-1603?).
The First Book of Consort Lessons,
1599 and 1611 (book review by Er-
nest T. Ferand). Mus Q v 46 n 4
p 536-543 O '60
MORO, PETER. The new Notting-
ham Playhouse (with drawings).
NTM v 1 n 2 p 8-11 Ja '60
MORRIS, WILLIAM, 1834-1896,
poet
Stedman, Jane W. (His interest
in Arthurian and other legends;
his book, Sigurd the Volsung).
ON v 24 n 16 p 8-9 F 20'60
---Por age 23 ph. ON v 24 n 16
p 9 F 20'60
MORROW, BUDDY, trombonist
With instrument, hl ph: US. IM
v 58 n 10 p 17 Ap '60
MORROW, DORETTA, singer
As the Princess in "Aladdin",
AP hl ph: London. AmM v 8 n 1
p 7 Ja '60
MORSURE DE SERPENT, play
Budapest notes; Magda Szabo.
WP v 11 n 7 p 11 My '60
LA MORT D'AGRIPPINE, play
Ens AP wl ph: Bernand. WP v 11
n 9 p 7 Jl '60
LA MORT DE DANTON, play
TNP; Georg Buchner; Adamov,
the French version; review. GDC
n 255-6 p 321-2 Ja 15'60
MOSCHETTO, CORRADO, violinist
Louvet, Michel. Review; "J'admire
en tout cas, le pianiste Anne-Marie
Lavilléon". GDC n 269-70 p 599
Ap 22'60
MOSCONA, NICOLA, 1907-, singer
Athens homecoming; honors, il
ON v 24 n 13 p 2 Ja 30'60

188

---With royalty. ph: Athens. MC
v 161 n 7 p 38 Je '60
MOSCOW ART THEATRE
Markov, Pavel. New trends in
the interpretation of Chekhov. il
WT v 9 n 2 p 101-110 Summer'60
---Meyerhold, Vsevolod. On the
Theatre (excerpt trans. Nora
Beeson; the Naturalistic Theatre;
the Theatre of Mood). TDR v 4
n 4 p 134-47 My '60
MOSCOW STATE SYMPHONY
Boston review; " a good orches-
tra, the peer of Detroit or even
Cleveland but not of Philadelphia".
MC v 161 n 4 p 32 Mr '60
---Chicago reviews. MC v 161 n 4
p 28 Mr '60
---Los Angeles review. MC v 161
n 5 p 23 Ap '60
---NYC; two reviews; Constantine
Ivanoff. MC v 161 n 3 p 26-7
F '60
---San Francisco reception; "no-
thing but Russian music"; Val-
erii Klimov, violinist. MC v 161
n 6 p 29 My '60
MOSER, RUDOLF, 1892-1960,
composer
Notes; b. Niederuzeil. GDC
n 284 p 123 O 14'60
MOSES UND ARON, opera
Berlin review; Schönberg staged
by Gustav Rudolf Sellner. MC
v 162 n 6 p 31 D '60
---Schönberg's ideas. MR v 21
n 1 p 23 F '60
---Berlin Städtische Oper; the
Dance of the Golden Calf, ens
AP wl ph: Ilse Buhs. Op v 11
n 12 p 826 D '60
---Greindl, Josef, and Helmut
Melchert, ens AP wl ph: Berlin,
La S n 132 p 50 N '60
---Schoenberg, ens AP wl ph:
Heinz Köster, 1959. WT v 9 n 3
p 214 Autumn '60
MOSS, LAWRENCE, composer
Première: Sonata for violin and
piano; 1959 notes. ACAB v 9 n 2
p 22 1960
MOSSO, CARLO, composer
Turin; notes. Mus Q v 46 n 3
p 377-8 Jl '60

THE MOTHER, opera
Veroli, Donato di (1922-1945),
composer; A I DEM première
in Florence. MC v 161 n 1 p 26
Ja '60
MOTTE, CLAIRE, 1937-, dancer
In Giselle. TD n 95 p 12 Jl-Ag'60
---AP hl ph: Paris. OpP n 19
p 49 1960
---As Giselle, Act I, AP wl ph:
Nice. TD n 95 p 12 Jl-Ag '60
---In La Bacchanale Samson et
Dalila, Paris Opéra, ens AP ph:
OpP n 19 p 21 1960
LA MOUETTE, play
Moscow, 1898; Paris, 1939 ens
phs. Spec n 1 p 18-9 1960
MOUSSELINE, comedy
Paris; Louis Velle; notes. WP
v 11 n 3 p 9 Ja '60
MOVING-PICTURE MUSIC
See Film Music
MOVING PICTURES
Bergman, Ingmar (1918-); a
study by William S. Pechter.
TDR v 5 n 2 p 94-101 D '60
---Election 473-408 in Hollywood,
AFM to be the bargaining agent
for musicians; report. IM v 59
n 4 p 7 O '60
---Feature films (122), Warner
Brothers, to be transferred to
TV; re-use payments to musici-
ans stipulation by AFM. IM
v 59 n 4 p 7 O '60
---Film music, lifted from out-dated
foreign films; stored in US; avail-
able to be cut and fitted to US
films; editorial on Senator Wayne
Morse in US Senate speech. IM
v 58 n 7 p 6 Ja '60
---Frattini, Angelo. Frattini per
le riviste. il La S 1960
---Herrmann, Bernard. Compos-
ing for the screen. AmM v 8 n 4
p 12 Ap '60
---Ionesco, Eugène. (On present
cinema). TDR v 5 n 2 p 52 D '60
---Marker, Chris. Un film blanc:
Moranbong. il Spec n 1 p 70 1960
---Towarnicki, Frédéric de. Alain
Renais après "Hiroshima Mon
Amour". portfolio Spec n 1 p 60-
69 1960

(Moving Pictures)
---US; new contract between AFM and film producers; new milestones, one that Us films must have domestic musictrack. IM v 59 n 6 p 5 D '60
---producers circumventing immigration laws by using foreign tapes for films otherwise "American". IM v 58 nos 10, 11, 12 Ap, My and Je '60
---release of 1948-58 feature films involving agreement with musicians on TV rights written into original contracts; notes. IM v 58 n 12 p 16 Je '60
---Weigel, Hans. Twilight of the Cinema. WP v 11 n 7 p 1 My '60
---NYC filming of West Side Story Th Arts v 44 n 11 p 12-3 N '60
MOWE, HOMER G.
Por ph: J. Abresch. MC v 162 n 5 p 40 N '60
MOYNAGH, JOAN MARIE, singer Note. ON v 25 n 5 p 7 D 10'60
MOZART, WOLFGANG AMADEUS (1756-1791. Quatuor à cordes in si bémal majeur, K. 458: analyse par Pierrette Mari. GDC n 277 p 825-6 Je 17'60
--- ---Sérénade en sol majeur, Köchel 525 (Petite Musique de Nuit): analyse par Pierrette Mari. GDC n 273 p 697 My 20'60
---Broder, Nathan. Mozart operas on record; High Fidelity discography No. 49. HF v 10 n 11 p 56-7, 125-7 N '60
---Der Schauspieldirektor, one act comedy with music; notes on piano score, dialogue in German; Bärenreiter edition. MR v 21 n 2 p 162 My '60
---Slonimsky, Nicolas. The weather at Mozart's funeral. Mus Q v 46 n 1 p 12-21 Ja '60
MOZART AND SALIERI, opera Little Orchestra Society; Rimskykorsakov notes. ON v 24 n 19 p 28 Mr 12'60
MRAVINSKI, EUGEN, 1903-, conductor Prokofieff: la Sixième Symphonie; Paris review. GDC n 283

p 93 O 7'60
---Por ph. La S n 131 p 10 O '60
---Por ph: Leningrad. WM n 6 p 134 D '60
MULHOUSE
Ariel, Nick. Le Jongleur de Notre-Dame; Paillasse. GDC n 255-6 p 305 Ja 15'60
MULL, ISABELLA. Genoa's pride: Carlo Felice. il ON v 24 n 22 p 12 Ap 2'60
MULLIGAN, GERRY, 1927-, bandleader Cerulli, Dom. Gerry Mulligan. il IM v 59 n 4 p 18-9 O '60
THE MUMMERS
Kernodle, George R. Seven medieval theatres in one social structure. Th R v 2 n 1 p 28-36 1960
MUNCH, CHARLES, 1891-, conductor In the Music Shed at Tanglewood, ens ph. IM v 58 n 12 p 32 Je '60
---Vichy Orchestra podium, small ph. MC v 162 n 4 p 26 O '60
MUNICH
Bernheimer, Martin. A series of quality Strauss performances; Carl Orff's Trionfi choreographed by Heinz Roseu. MC v 162 n 5 p 26 N '60
--- ---(Opera notes.) ON v 25 n 2 p 18 O 29'60
---Ballets de Heinz Rosen; reviews. il TD n 92 p 26-7 Ap '60
---Festival de Ballets, Heinz Rosen, directeur du ballet de l'Opéra National Bavarois. TD n 96 p 11-2 S-O '60
---Opera reviews. Op v 11 n 12 p 833-4 D '60
---Opera reviews by The Editor; by Walter Davidson; by Lionel Dunlop. Op v 11 p 54-61 Autumn '60
---Spelman, Franz. (Theatre report.) portfolio Th Arts v 44 n 4 p 17-20 Ap '60
---Opera; six action pictures of summer opera: Betz. Op v 11 p 55-61 Autumn '60
MURDER IN THE CATHEDRAL, opera

Genoa; Pizzetti work at San Felice; review. il Op v 11 n 5 p 354 My '60

---Vienna review. MC v 161 n 7 p 16 Je '60

---Zuffi, Pietro. Setting for the Vienna Opera, ens ph: Fayer. MC v 161 n 7 p 16 Je '60

MURGIER, JACQUES (1912-). Le livre d'heures (études musicales analytiques). GDC n 273 p 699 My 20'60

MURPHY, JAMES F. Student conductors for high schools: a musical resource. MEJ v 46 n 5 p 47-8 Ap-My '60

MUSIC

Carter, Elliott. Shop talk by an American composer. Mus Q v 46 n 2 p 189-201 Ap '60

---Cercle Français de Musique Asiatique; Paris notes. TD n 90 p 19 F '60

---I Concerti dell'estate 1960 nello stadio di Domiziano; calendar. La S n 128 inset Jl '60

---Le cronache: Milan; Rome; Firenze; Certaldo; Bolzano; Trieste; Naples; Catania; Parma; Reggio Emilia; Pesaro; Spoleto; Palermo; Salerno. La S n 125 Ap '60

--- ---Milano; Roma; Firenze; Torino; Catania; Napoli; Trieste; Venezia; Bolzano; Salerno. La S n 126 My '60

--- ---Milan; Roma; Napoli; Torino; Venezia; Trieste; Bologna; Modena; Salerno. La S n 128 Jl '60

--- ---Milan; Roma; Firenze; Genova-Nervi; Napoli; Benezia; Ravello; Trieste; Spoleto; Verona; Siena; Lanciano; Bolzano. La S n 129-30 Ag-S '60

--- ---Milan; Roma; Trieste; Certaldo; Jesi; L'Aquila; Castell'Arquato; Reggio Emilia; Bolzano; Salerno. La S n 131 O '60

--- ---Milan; Roma; Venezia; Bergamo; Torino; Trieste; Reggio Emilia; Bolzano; Salerno; Jesi; Fano. La S n 132 N '60

--- ---Milan; Roma; Napoli; Fireuze; Bergamo; Spoleto;

Trieste; Ferrara; Reggio Emilia. La S n 133 D '60

--- ---Rome; Naples; Firenze; Catania; Torino; Genova; Venezia; Certaldo; Trieste; Bolzano; Salerno; Reggio Emilia. La S n 127 Je '60

---Curriculum to prepare teachers as evolved at Obelin; Karl Wilson Gehrkens looking back. MEJ v 47 n 2 p 31-4 N-D '60

---Daniélou, Alain. The importance of the preservation of the traditional musical culture in Oriental countries. WM n 1 p 2-4 F '60

---European news notes in regular column, "Oủ sont-ils? GDC 1960

---The House of Chester, music publishers; history 1860-1960. MD v 51 n 1 p 20-1 Jl '60

---Improvisation; Walter Stuart series on jazz improvising for all instruments. IM 1960

---Musique et médicine: Dr. A. Tomatis (de la voix). GDC n 257-8 p 349 Ja 29'60

---Oboist; Isai Belinsky on technique. IM v 59 n 4 p 34 O '60

---Published music reviewed under A. Piano, B. Piano (educational), C. Vocal; each issue CMJ 1960

---RAI (Italian radio): programmi sinfonici. La S 1960

---Recueils imprimes XVIe-XVIIe s. Ouvarage publiée sous la direction de François Lusure: Le RISM (critique). WM n 2 p 29 Ap '60

---Ricci, Luigi. Un bauletto magico (Mascagni). facsimile La S n 126 p 44-6 My '60

---Robertazzi, Mario. Un modo di raccontare la musica. La S n 132 p 58-61 N '60

---La Scala: stagione sinfonica 1960. La S n 129-30 inset Ag-S'60

---Scores reviewed each issue. MR 1960

---US scores available for loan at London's USIS office. AmM v 8 n 9 p 16-8 O '60

--- ---summer music, a survey. IM v 58 n 12 p 32-3, 35 Je '60

--- ---survey of jobs for professional musicians in summer.

(Music)

IM v 58 n 11 p 16, 18 My '60

---Verdi; the whole issue given to criticism of the composer with emphasis on Un Ballo in Maschera; recorded music also. Ver v 1 n 1 Ap '60

---Winters, Ken. Europe; opera, new instrumental and vocal, chamber music and young conductors. CMJ v 5 n 1 p 39-45 Autumn '60

MUSIC-ECONOMIC ASPECTS

American Federation of Musicians seeking "re-use payments to musicians who produced original sound tracks"; also cease of foreign tracks on US_made films. IM v 59 n 3 p 36 S '60

---AGMA's reply to proposed "united front" of US opera companies; objects to fees being disclosed, breach of contract, etc. being disclosed. MC v 162 n 1 p 36 Jl '60

---Beethoven offered fifty pounds for a symphony by the London Philharmonic, 1816, notes. MR v 21 n 1 p 3 F '60

---Canada; national subsidy of music; a survey. IM v 58 n 12 p 18-9 Je '60

---Conly, John M. Editorial on small companies, a return movement; notes on several. HF v 10 n 3 p 41 Mr '60

---Contract details American Federation of Musicians, NYC, and League of New York Theaters; $170 weekly for musicals, $119 dramatic shows. MC v 162 n 4 p 4 O '60

---Cost of symphony orchestra; need for subsidy; US examples of campaigns, comparable to museum and college subsidies. IM v 58 n 8 p 20-1 F '60

---Covent Garden Annual Report 1958-9: editorial; figures. Op v 11 n 1 p 6 Ja '60

---Elia, Joe, M. D. Trumpets and medicine (foreign music allowed in on our TV films "70 per cent of TV film for

commercial shows are using foreign made music"-and example given in the drug field also). IM v 59 n 6 p 14-5 D '60

---Europe; a "freeze" of copyrighted music due to dispute on returned merchandise royalties; Bureau Internationale de l'Edition Mécanique vs. Inter. Fed. of Phonographic Industry. HF v 10 n 5 p 28 My '60

---Goldin, Milton. Commerce, concerts and critics: the organized audience plan reviewed. MEJ v 46 n 6 p 37, 39, 42 Je-Jl '60

---International Federation of Musicians at conference, International Labour Office; points of discussion. WM n 4 p 76 Ag '60

---Jazz; employment and pay. IM v 59 n 6 p 13 D '60

---Kerr, Russell. What price a career in music? Steps in a career. MC n 162 n 1 p 7, 35 Jl '60

---Klees, Jay. Organizing an opera audience. Op v 11 n 10 p 671-3 O '60

---Labor agreement between Paramount Telemeter Division and American Federation of Musicians; The Consul, initial production. IM v 58 n 12 p 5 Je '60

---Los Angeles; "tracking" abuse caught: Hank Levine and 10 sidemen recorded music track separately from vocal planned; notes. IM v 59 n 5 p 9 N '60

---Managers of jazz bands and "combos": job opportunities. IM v 58 n 12 p 13 Je '60

---Metropolitan Opera deficit 1959-60 amounted to $40,547; other figures. MC v 162 n 6 p 9 D '60

---price schedule. ON v 25 n 3 p 26 N 19'60

---Morse, Senator Wayne. (Excerpts from his speech on foreign film music, lifted and used in US television films; live musicians at a disadvantage.) IM v 58 n 7 p 6, 8 Ja '60

---Music trends; managers interviewed on artistic and economic tides. MC v 162 n 1 p 12-19 Jl '60

---New York court injunction sought by AFM against Warner Brothers exhibition of 1948 feature films on TV unless contracts reaffirmed by court. IM v 59 n 3 p 9 S '60

---The New York Philharmonic Orchestra 1959: intake and deficit. AmM v 8 n 1 p 10 Ja '60

---Pension plans; George A. Clarke on plan of American Federation of Musicians. IM v 58 n 12 p 8 Je '60

---Rental of halls, NYC; other costs of a debut. MC v 162 n 1 p 35 Jl '60

---Richter, Sviatoslav, Russian pianist under Sol Hurok on US tour, recorded for RCA though Russia's Artia Records protested; notes on legal struggle. HF v 10 n 12 p 57 D '60

---Rockefeller, John D., 3rd. Financing the arts. il ON v 25 n 2 p 8-11 O 29'60

---Stoddard, Hope. Industry's aid to music (a survey). IM v 59 n 5 p 20-1 N '60

---Subsidies; George H. Kyme on procuring grants for research in music education (with 25 addresses of agencies). MEJ v 47 n 1 p 81-2 S-O '60

---US; coming NLRB television studio recording election; reasons listed for American Federation of Musicians as bargaining agent for the musicians. IM v 58 n 9 p 7, 44 Mr '60

---foreign tapes, made by those ineligible to play in USA at the time, imported, cut up, dubbed in from "music libraries" on US TV films; fight against this "illegal music" as led by American Federation of Musicians. IM '60

---organized audience field: United Audience Service; notes. MC v 162 n 4 p 5 O '60

---summer employment for professional musicians (a survey by Hope E. Stoddard). IM v 58 n 11 p 16, 18 My '60

---taxation via cabaret tax reduced to ten per cent from 20 per cent; review of the fight 1955-1960 by the American Federation of Musicians to protect live music. IM v 58 n 11 p 7 My '60

---"tracking abuse" drive in Los Angeles: Jerry Lewis recording 5 songs, "then same accompaniment without vocals", a violation of AFM contract, band leader Lou Brown, contractor Al Lapin. IM v 59 n 6 p 5, 7 D '60

---20 per cent music tax fight in 50 states; report. IM v 58 n 7 p 6 Ja '60

---Van Ess, Mary. What outlook for pianists? J Rev v 7 n 1 p 3-4 Winter 59-60

---Managers, portfolio, portraits of Ann Kullmer, Alfred A. Rossin, Nina Gordani, Felix W. Salmaggi, Michael Podoli, Lanham Deal, Ermine Kahn, James Sardos, Mary Bran, Wm L. Stein, Eliz. Crawford. MC v 162 n 1 p 17-9 Jl '60

---Clarence E. Cramer, Mildred Shagal, M. Bichurin, J. J. Vincent, Joseph Lippman. MC v 162 n 1 p 15 Jl '60

---Herbert Barrett, Henry and Ann Colbert, Cesar Saerchinger, Thea Dispeker and Edna Giesen. MC v 162 n 1 p 14 Jl '60

---Kurt Weinhold, F. C. Schang, Humphrey Doulens, Leverett Wright; of André Mertens, Arthur Judson, Ruth O'Neill, Wm Judd; of Sol Hurok; of Luben Vichey. MC v 162 n 1 p 12-3 Jl'60

MUSIC-HISTORY and CRITICISM
Abbiati, Franco. (Biography of Giuseppi Verdi discussed by Gino Roncaglia.) La S n 126 p 18-22 My '60

---Arvey, Verna. Famous authors and their love for music. MD v 50 n 8 p 18-20 F '60

---Balakirev's influence on the musical compositions of Sergei Lyapunov (1859-1924). MR v 21 n 3 p 187-189 Ag '60

---Bands in US; George Reynolds, a survey. MEJ v 47 n 1 p 59-62 S-O '60

193

(Music)

---Bennett, Rodney M. D. Collecting programmes and playbills. il Op v 11 n 7 p 463-7 Jl '60

---Broder, Nathan. History of Music in Sound series excludes Beethoven from The Age of Beethoven section; comments. HF v 10 n 3 p 62-3 Mr '60

---Capri, Antonio. La pianistica di Chopin. il La S n 126 p 9-17 My '60

--- ---Testimonianza di Pergolesi. il La S n 132 p 24-9 N '60

---Chancellor, Paul. British bards and continental composers. Mus Q v 46 n 1 p 1-11 Ja '60

---Eighty years of musical glamour: chronological survey of milestones with extensive portfolio. MC v 161 n 3 F '60

---Gary, Charles L. Vignettes of music education history: Charles Rice of Worcester, Massachusetts, speaks. MEJ v 46 n 3 p 48 Ja '60

---Harman, Alec, and Anthony Milner. Man and his Music. Late Renaissance and Baroque Music (book review) P. J. P. MR v 21 n 4 p 331-2 N '60

---Krems, Austria; report of Symposium on Old Music. WM n 2 p 31 Ap '60

---Landon, H. C. Robbins. It all began in Bonn (Beethoven's early years; Vienna study). il HF v 10 n 4 p 37-9 Ap '60

---MacArdle, Donald W. Beethoven and the Philharmonic Society of London. MR v 21 n 1 p 1-7 F '60

---Mackerness, E. D. Music and moral purity in the early Victorian Era. CMJ v 4 n 2 p 14-24 Winter '60

---Marais, Marin (1656-1728); his five books "Pièces de Violes" produced 1686 to 1725, criticism by Claude H. Thompson. Mus Q v 46 n 4 p 482-499 O '60

---Mari, Pierrette. L'Activité des Musigrains depuis vingt ans. GDC n 269-70 p 601 Ap 22'60

---Marmiroli, Renato. (The centenary of the theatre at Reggio Emilia; its past riches; present concert celebrations.) il La S n 127 p 36-9 Je '60

---Matteis, Nicola, his career in England as a violinist; his compositions discussed. il Mus Q v 46 n 1 p 22-40 Ja '60

---Mila, Massimo. Problem di filologia e d'interpretazione intorno alla partitura del Ballo in Maschera (English and German translations p 458-493). Ver v 1 n 1 p 133-156 Ap '60

--- ---II. Ver v 1 n 2 p 720-731 Ag '60

---Moór, Emanuel, 1862-1931; piano concertos discussed by Harold Truscott. MR v 21 n 2 p 121-129 My '60

---Music of the Polish Renaissance edited by Chominski and Lissa (criticism). Mus Q v 46 n 3 p 386-390 Jl '60

---Paris Opéra, sketch with pictures. ON v 25 n 6 p 22-7 D 17'60

---Picker, Martin. Three unidentified chansons by Pierre de la Rue. Mus Q v 46 n 3 p 329-343 Jl '60

---Porgy and Bess; the Gershwins and Dubose Heyward. il ON v 24 n 20 p 6-9 Mr 19'60

---Pratt, Ross. Chopin in Britain (1837 and in 1848). CMJ v 5 n 1 p 24-9 Autumn '60

---Sadie, Stanley. The chamber music of Boyce and Arne. Mus Q v 46 n 4 p 425-36 O '60

---Schafer, Murray. (On the novel, Jean Christoph by Romain Rolland, as a "history of music".) CMJ v 23-34 Spring '60

---Viviani, Alberto. Il Burchiello e la musica del suo tempo. il La S n 131 p 11-19 O '60

---Vötterle, Karl. The epoch of the complete edition. WM n 1 p 5 F '60

---Ward, John Owen. 300 years of music publishing (The Oxford

194

Press). il MC v 161 n 3 p 13, 47 F '60

---Young, Malcolm J. How to beat the trauma of the tympani (music played in Chicago Smyphony 1922-1940). MEJ v 46 n 6 p 67 Je-Jl'60

MUSIC-ORIENTAL

Phonograph records, seried "An Anthology of Music of the Orient" under Alain Daniélou for International Music Council; notes. WM n 6 p 131 D '60

---Van Khé, Tran. The emotional approach of the performer of Oriental music (a paper at 5-day Paris conference under International Music Council by Viet-Nam resident of Paris). WM n 6 p 127-8 D '60

---Five AP phs: Asian instruments and players. WM n 6 p 133 D '60

MUSIC-TWENTIETH CENTURY

Abbiati, Franco. Libera musica e musica di stato. il La S n 127 p 7-11 Je '60

---Alfano, Franco; criticism by Rino Maione. por La S n 122 p 48-9 Ja '60

---The amateur; Gerald Abraham at UNESCO music conference on the fact that "modern music is beyond the reach of amateurs, and even many professionals." WM n 6 p 124 D '60

---American composers, a discography (by Donald Jennings) with quoted reviews. ACAB v 9 n 2 p 13-7 1960

--- ---Part II. ACAB v 9 n 3 p 19-25 1960

---The American Music Centre with list of orchestras and composers commissioned. AmM v 8 n 10 p 12 N '60

---American orchestras with list of contemporary music in repertory: Los Angeles Philharmonic, San Francisco Symphony, Seattle Symphony, Houston Symphony. AmM v 8 n 2 p 14 F '60

---Arma, Paul; son concerto pour Bande Magnétique. GDC n 293-4 p 455 D 16'60

---Babbitt, Milton. Twelve-tone

invariants as compositional determinants. Mus Q v 46 n 2 p 246-259 Ap '60

---Basel Municipal Academy of Music; week of 12-tone and other contemporary trends; leader, Dr. Francis Travis. WM n 1 p 10 F '60

---Beckwith, John. Reviews: Claude Champagne's Altitude; François Morel's Boréal; Istvan Anhalt's First Symphony (analyzed). CMJ v 4 n 4 p 44-7 Summer '60

---Berthoumieux, Serge. Concert de musique contemporaine: Jean-Louis Belgrand; Jacques Murgier; Georges Hugon; Tersa H. de Amezaga; Marius-François Gaillard. GDC n 278 p 848 Je 24'60

---Blitzstein, Marc. (His story of producing with Orson Welles his opera, The Cradle Will Rock, Federal Theatre Project, NYC 1937.) por ON v 24 n 15 p 10-1 F 13'60

---Boston Symphony tour to the Far East; list of American composers in the repertory. MC v 161 n 6 p 29 My '60

---Broder, Nathan. Music for the age of calorie counters (today we "explore in both temporal directions", pre-Bach and electronic). HF v 10 n 8 p 29 Ag '60

---Bruyr, José. Concert Ondes Jenny; interprètes: Christiane Augustin, Jacques Casterède; premières: Cittanova; Casterède; Guinot; Dubois; Tournier. GDC n 275 p 752 Je 3'60

---Cage, John; estimate by Alfred Frankenstein, reviewing recording "Twenty-five Year Retrospective Concert" by Avakian, NYC. HF v 10 n 4 p 63 Ap '60

---Canada: composers to be heard in Paris: list. CMJ v 4 n 4 p 42 Summer '60

--- ---criticism of works released by BMl Canada: Harry Somers, Papineau-Couture, François Morel, Otto Joachim. CMJ v 5 n 1 p 62-7 Autumn '60

(Music-Twentieth Century)
---Canadian League of Composers International Conference of Composers at Stratford, Ontario; list of topics; list of speakers; report. WM n 6 p 131 D '60
---Capri, Antonio. Ildebrando Pizzetti (1880-). portfolio LaS n 129-30 p 9-17 Ag-S '60
---Carter, Elliott. Shop talk by an American composer. Mus Q v 46 n 2 p 189-201 Ap '60
---Chamfray, Claude. Musique contemporaine, le premier des trois concerts par la Fondation Belaieff à l'occasion de son 75e anniversaire. GDC n 285 p 165 O 21'60
---Cheltenham Festival of British Contemporary Music: report. WM n 3 p 56 Je '60
---Cologne opera, week of contemporary works; Wolfgang Nolter criticism of Prokofiev's Love of Three Oranges; Fortner's Blood Wedding. Op v 11 n 8 p 557-8 Ag '60
--- ---report of International Society For Contemporary Music. MR v 21 n 3 p 242-4 Ag'60
---Composers of 20th century: 41 per cent all composers listed in orchestral programs US 1959-60; and 64 per cent recorded discs. AmM v 8 n 8 p 10 S '60
---Concert Hall, a section: listing by composer, work and performance details the music of today; first performances indicated. ACAB 1960
---Cone, Edward T. Analysis today. Mus Q v 46 n 2 p 172-188 Ap '60
---Confédération Musicale de France: solistes; Milhaud, Ibert, Francaix, Condier, Bozza, Chas. Brown, Roger Calmen; Paris notes. GDC n 287 p 225 N 4'60
---Congress on "The Performer", Paris; UNESCO House. WM n 4 p 75 Ag '60
---The contemporary scene in music education: symposium

planned for Atlantic City meeting of US music educators (12 questions). MEJ v 46 n 3 p 24-26 Ja'60
---Contemporary works played by American orchestras: New York Philharmonic, National Symphony Cincinnati, Pittsburgh, Cleveland, Philadelphia. AmM v 8 n 1 p 11-12, 14 Ja '60
---Criticism. G. N. S. MR v 21 n 4 p 320-1 N '60
---Demarquez, Suzanne. Domaine Musical, "curieuse séance " dirige par Boulez. GDC n 259-60 p 410 F 12'60
--- ---Musique contemporaine; l'Orchestre Radio-Symphonique, P. M. Le Conte; Claude Rostand. GDC n 267-8 p 562 Ap 8'60
--- ---Vincent Gemignani et Alain Jacquest, vibraphone et marimba: les pages de H. Puig-Roget; P. Maurice; R. Planel M. Franck; M. Bitsen; Cl. Arrieu; G. Hugon; N. Gallon. GDC n 267-8 p 559 Ap 8'60
---Donaueschingen review. E. H. MR v 21 n 4 p 329-31 N '60
---Duchow, Marvin. The international conference of Composers at Stratford, Ontario. CMJ v 5 n 1 p 4-16 Autumn '60
---Festival of American Music (30th year) at Eastman School; review. MC v 161 n 7 p 6 Je '60
---Festival of Experimental Music in Paris; aspects of experimentation considered. WM n 4 p 76 Ag '60
---Ford Foundation $5,000 to 10 concert artists for commissions to 10 composers to be premiered by 10 American orchestras. AmM v 8 n 10 p 12 N '60
---France; report of April 28 meeting and quotations from the addresses on the musical situation in France; some of the speakers: Stéphane Wolff: René Nicoly; Manuel Recasens; Léon Algazi, Albert Ehrmann, Mme. Héline Jourdan-Morhange, Jacques Feschotte. GDC n 279-80 p 868-877 Jl 1'60
---Geddo, Angelo. L'umore dei decadenti nel solco dell'esperienza pittorica. portfolio LaS n 131

p 20-5 O '60
---Goldman, Richard Franko.
(On Stravinsky's recent compositions, heard in NYC: Double Canon; Movements for Piano and Orchestra, 1958-59; and Epitaphium). Mus Q v 46 n 2 p 260-264 Ap '60
---Gradenwitz, Peter. The religious works of Arnold Schönberg. MR v 21 n 1 p 19-29 F'60
---Great Britain; attention in the press; more interest shown in comtemporary music. MC v 161 n 5 p 31 Ap '60
---Il Gruppo Universitario per la Nuova Musica di Palermo; stagione. La S n 127 p 42 Je '60
---Hanson, Howard. Cultivating a climate for creativity (notes included on Festival of American Music, Rochester). MEJ v 46 n 6 p 28-30 Je-Jl '60
---Harrison, Lou, a critical study with check-list by Peter Yates. ACAB v 9 n 2 p 2-7 1960
---Helm, Everett. The dwindling racket (new composers; gatherings at Darmstadt, Donaueschingen, Kranichstein). HF v 10 n 8 p 43-4, 92 Ag '60
---Hungary; Kodály and present trends (a survey). Mus Q v 46 n 4 p 525-35 O '60
---Inter-American Music Festival (2nd), Washington 1961: list of composers commisioned. WM n 2 p 31 Ap '60
---International Society for Contemporary Music; Cologne festival 34th year; criticism. MC v 162 n 2 p 22-3 Ag '60
--- ---34th annual meeting, Cologne, 1960; notes. WM n 1 p 8 F '60
--- ---Cologne, 34th festival; list of composers. WM n 3 p 55 Je '60
---Jazz in the concert hall; "wrong milieu" says John H. Wilson. il HF v 10 n 5 p 34-7 My'60
--- ---Nat Hentoff on new directions in jazz. il IM v 59 n 3 p 14-5 S '60

---Jelinek, Hanns, 1901-; discussion of his "Anleitung"; "the first manifestation of an organic system of speculative thought"; twelve-tone. MR v 21 n 1 p 66-72 F '60
---Joachim, Heinz. (German composers today.) WT v 9 n 3 p 213-226 Autumn '60
---Jourdan-Morhanges, H. Paris review: Beatrice Berg and Gunnar Berg. GDC n 274 p 723 My 27'60
---Kahn, Erich Itor, 1905-; b. Rimbachim-Odenwald, Germany; a critical study with check-list by Russell Smith. ACAB v 9 n 2 p 8-12 1960
---Keller, Hans. Donaueschingen 1959. MR v 21 n 1 p 79-80 F '60
---Krenek, Ernst. Extents and limits of serial techniques. il Mus Q v 46 n 2 p 210-131 Ap'60
---Landau, Victor. Paul Hindemith, a case study in theory and practice. MR v 21 n 1 p 38-54 F '60
---(Lang, Paul Henry.) Introductory editorial for the issue which features, in signed articles, The Seminar In Advanced Musical Studies, Princeton. Mus Q Ap'60
---List of US composers and their scores on loan in London, USIS. AmM v 8 n 9 p 16-8 O '60
---Liviabella, Lino. Dove va la musica? portfolio La S n 124 p 20-5 Mr '60
---London conference on "Music in Britain, Today and Tomorrow." WM n 5 p 104 O '60
---London; notes on several new hearings. MC v 162 n 6 p 30 D'60
---Lowry, W. McNeil, reporting on 5-year survey by the Ford Foundation to a symposium of symphony men at the Waldorf under American Federation of Musicians; excerpts. IM v 59 n 3 p 40-1 S '60
---McClure, Theron R. Don't blame our composers (rules to produce the new operas we now seek). ON v 24 n 12 p 12-3 Ja 23'60
---Mamiya, M.   Enburi,

(Music-Twentieth Century)
2 tableaux pour orchestre; Paris notes. GDC n 288 p 254 N 11'60
---Managers interviewed; artistic and economic trends. MC v 162 n 1 p 12-19 Jl '60
---Mari, Pierrette. Musique contemporaine, Pairs concert (Trebinski, Gotkovsky, Soudères, Wissmer, Richer). GDC n 255-6 p 318 Ja 15'60
---NYC Composers' Forum; notes. MC v 161 n 7 p 39 Je '60
--- ---David Tudor, pianist, presenting "a new school of piano writing - - - lunatic-fringe explorers". MC v 161 n 7 p 26 Je '60
--- ---hearing of poets to music and original piano works; Carnegie Recital Hall review. MC v 162 n 1 p 40 Jl '60
--- ---recital of David Tudor, presenting piano music of John Cage and Christian Wolff; "a remarkable evening, ending 11:30. " MC v 161 n 7 p 26 Je '60
---News notes in two regular Juilliard columns: Faculty Activities; and Alumni News. J Rev 1960
---Papineau-Couture, Jean. Canadian composers at Hartt College Festival. CMJ v 4 n 2 p 35-7 Winter '60
---Paris; Carlheinz Stockhausen's Zyklas, a mixed reception; Pierre Boulez "Since some do not like this, we are going to play it again". HF v 10 n 4 p 11 Ap '60
--- ---concert by Domaine Musical; "not one in twelve of the experiments succeeded or was even interesting" (comments on Berio, Pousseur, Stockhausen, Boulez). CMJ v 4 n 4 p 43-4 Summer '60
--- ---concert of music for percussion (Varèse, Stockhausen, Kagel, Barraque). MC v 161 n 5 p 32 Ap '60
--- ---concert T. M. P-R. T. F. series: Sauguet's Les Trois Lys; Tadeusz Baird's Les Quatre Essais; Harsanvi's Pantins. GDC n 255-6 p 320 Ja 15'60

--- ---T. N. T. -R. T. F. :Nicolas Castiglioni; Jacques Bondon; Boucourechliev (commentaire). GDC n 259-60 p 410 F 12'60
---notes: René Herbin's Quatuor; J. Dumont's un Trio à cordes; Florent Schmidt's un quatuor peu joué. GDC n 292 p 422 D 9'60
---Palais de Chaillot series. MC v 161 n 6 p 33 My '60
---Société Nationale, musique contemporaine; Auclert's "Trio" et Wissmer's "Sonate pour piano", premières auditions. GDC n 255-6 p 317 Ja 15'60
--- ---Théâtre National Populaire, music chief, Maurice Jarre; list of contemporary composers. WM n 1 p 9 F '60
---Opera in US; 1985 performances of 150 contemporary works (from survey of opera expansion). ON v 25 n 3 p 12-15 N 19'60
---Opéra-bouffe: Jean Rivier's Vénitienne; Henri Martelli's Le Major Cravachon; Manuel Rosenthal's La Poule Noire; review. GDC n 295 p 491 D 30'60
---Riegger, Wallingford; articles, a check-list of works; a discography; short signed tributes. ACAB v 9 n 3 1960
---San Carlo, Naples; notes on Il vascello fantasma; La Luna (Orff); Il protagonista (Weill); Il malato immaginario (Jacopo Napoli). La S n 127 p 56 Je '60
---San Francisco; the Composers' Workshop: 2-hour rehearsals, various chamber groups play one or two scores; other programs. WM n 1 p 10 F '60
--- ---workshop in Contemporary American Music; Parrenin String Quartet; symposium, chaired by Alfred Frankenstein; report. MC v 162 n 2 p 15 Ag '60
---Schneider, Marcel. Le Théâtre lyrique et la musique contemporaine. il OpP n 19 p 52-4 1960
---Scores on exhibit, Unesco House, Paris; notes. WM n 5 p 104 O '60
---Séance April 28, 1960, on the music situation in France,

arranged by Guide du Concert and le Comité National de la Musique; speeches summarized. portraits GDC n 279-80 p 868-888 Jl 1'60

---Les Semaines Musicales de Paris 1960; 36 living composers; details of programs. WM n 6 p 123 D '60

---Sessions, Roger. Problems and issues facing the composer today. Mus Q v 46 n 2 p 159-171 Ap '60

---Some Twentieth Century American Composers. A selective bibliography. New York Public Library, 1959 (review). MR v 21 n 4 p 337 N '60

---Steinecke, Dr. Wolfgang, editor, Darmstadt "Beiträge zur neuen Musik 1960"; list of writers included. WM n 6 p 132 D '60

---Stoddard, Hope. Industry's aid to music. IM v 59 n 5 p 20-1 N'60

---Stratford, Ontario; list of composers to take part in conference; list of subsidies; of planned programs; Louis Applebaum, director. MC v 162 n 2 p 24 Ag '60

---Stravinsky, Igor, with Robert Craft and the Columbia Symphony Orchestra; Schonberg op. 34; Webern op. 6 and Le Sacre; criticism. MC v 161 n 3 p 26 F '60

---Survey by Broadcast Music, Inc. of US and Canada; report. WM n 5 p 104 O '60

---Szeryng, Henryk. Responsibility of the performer towards contemporary music. WM n 5 p 100 O '60

---Le Triptyque et le Madrigal de la R. T. F. ; Paris notes on Georges Hugon's Virgile; Manuel Rosenthal's La Belle Zélie; Messiaen; Daniel-Lesur. GDC n 287 p 225 N 4'60

---Trompeter, Lisa Roma. Editorial on managers as "bearers of culture". MC v 162 n 1 p 3 Jl '60

---Turin; a trittico: Rossellini's La Guerra; L'Iprocrita Felice by Ghedini; Viozzi's Allamistakeo; reviews. Op v 11 n 1 p 43-4 Ja '60

---Ussachevsky, Vladimir. Notes on "A Piece for Tape Recorder" (analysis, his method and sources). Mus Q v 46 n 2 p 202-209 Ap '60

---Valenti Ferro, Enzo. Contemporary music in Buenos Aires. WM n 5 p 104 O '60

---Verrall, John. Henry Leland Clarke (1907-); b. Dover, New Hampshire; check-list of works). ACAB v 9 n 3 p 2-8 1960

---Wagner, Alan. The new golden age of opera. il HF v 10 n 1 p 55-7, 120 Ja '60

---Walker, Alan. Back to Schönberg. MR v 21 n 2 p 140-147 My '60

---Warsaw concert; critical notes. WM n 2 p 28 Ap '60

---Wörner, Karl H. (Darmstadt report and estimate.) Mus Q v 46 n 2 p 270-5 Ap '60

--- ---(Living Czech composers; biographical and critical notes on twenty or more.) Mus Q v 46 n 4 p 509-17 O '60

---Zafred's Concerto per pianoforte e orchestra: RAI. TV. La S n 125 p 77 Ap '60

---Boulez, Pierre (1926-), Le marteau sans maître, facsimile of two bars. La S n 129-30 p 29 Ag-S '60

---Stockausen, Karlheinz, facsimile portion of Gesang der Junglinge. La S n 129-130 p 30 Ag-S'60

MUSIC CAMP ASSOCIATION Australia, 1949 founded by John Bishop; report of youth and top musicians over ABC. MD v 50 n 9 p 17 Mr '60

MUSIC EDUCATORS NATIONAL CONFERENCE, US
Collegiate newsletter; frequent reports from campus organizations, many group pictures. MEJ 1960

---Official directory 1960-1961. MEJ v 46 n 6 p 33-36 Je-Jl '60

---Performing groups at the March 1960 conference: a list. MEJ v 46 n 3 p 26 Ja '60

---Reports from sectional and national meetings; news. MEJ 1960

---Student chapters 1959-1960: list. MEJ v 46 n 6 p 61-3 Je-Jl'60

(Music Educators Natl. Conference)
---Washington convention 1961 schedule; publications; Southwestern Division notes. il MEJ v 47 n 1 S-O '60
---Atlantic City 1960; portfolio. MEJ v 46 n 6 Je-Jl '60

MUSIC FILMS
Good films and filmstrips for teaching and other forms of music work mentioned, usually rental fee and address given. MEJ 1960
---International Federation of Musical Youth; film by Canadians; another by German Section. WM n 1 p 9 F '60
---The Liszt Films (Teaching Film Custodians, NYC); "Virtuoso Franz Liszt as Composer": description of this film; objectives; teaching notes; discussion topics. MEJ v 47 n 2 p 45-6 N-D '60

MUSIC FORGOTTEN AND REMEMBERED
NYC series of concerts under Frederick Waldman. MC v 162 n 6 p 37 D '60

MUSIC IN UNIVERSITIES AND COLLEGES
L'Accademia Nazionale di Santa Cecilia e i suoi concerti. La S n 128 inset Jl '60
---Allen, Kenneth, manager, notes US colleges tend to emphasize "entertainment" when booking artists yet this is easily available elsewhere. MC v 162 n 1 p 15 Jl '60
---Australia; Trinity College of Music: Victorian Theory Medals 1959 list: Victorian Practical Medals 1959. MD v 50 n 10 p 21 Ap '60
---Boston University; Art Center Opera under Merle Puffer. ON v 24 n 20 p 3 Mr 1960
---Bradley University; King David, oratorio; review. MC v 161 n 5 p 43 Ap '60
---Brandeis University; La Salle Quartet. MC v 162 n 3 p 14 S '60

---Cambridge University Musical Society; review of The Damnation of Faust; analysis of the work. Op v 11 n 5 p 373-5 My '60
---Chatham College (Pittsburgh opera under Fredric Kurzweil. ON v 25 n 3 p 6 N 19'60
---College of the Pacific, Stockton, California: Faust. ON v 24 n 19 p 3 Mr 12'60
--- ---Outcasts of Poker Flat, music Stanworth Beckler; note. ON v 25 n 7 p 7 D 24'60
---Column, "College Campus and Conservatory". MC 1960
---Florida State University; Elena Nikolaidi, teaching. ON v 25 n 8 p 4 D 31'60
---France; recitals at the schools; several reviews. GDC n 277 Je 17'60
---Goodwin, Noel. College Operas: Royal College of Music in Orpheus and The Cairo Goose; Trinity College of Music in Le Villi and Arnell's The Petrified Princess. Op v 11 n 8 p 582-3 Ag'60
---Hofstra College, Opera Workshop: repertory. ON v 24 n 12 p 3 Ja 23'60
---Howard, Campbell. (Report on The University of New England, Armidale, New South Wales.) MD v 51 n 5 p 10 N '60
---Hunter College; Prima Donna; Sister Angelica; opera reviews. MC v 161 n 5 p 36 Ap '60
--- ---reviews: Prima Donna; and Sister Angelica. ON v 24 n 24 p 27 Ap 16'60
--- ---The Prima Donna; Sister Angelica. ON v 24 n 21 p 3 Mr 26'60
---Lake Forest College, Illinois; Hugo Distler's Weihnachtsgeschichte under choral director, Marvin C. Dilkey. WM n 6 p 131 D '60
---Los Angeles City College production of Boris Godunov. ON v 24 n 17 p 26 F 27'60
---Louisiana State University: A Game of Chance, opera by Seymour Barab; note. ON v 25

n 7 p 7 D 24'60
--- ---opera under Peter Paul
Fuchs. ON v 25 n 2 p 7 O 29'60
--- ---The Magic Flute. ON v 24
n 19 p 3 Mr 12'60
---Mannes College, NYC; A Hand
of Bridge by Barber; Milhaud's
Fiesta; Ibert's Angélique. Op v 11
n 7 p 472 Jl '60
---Moreau Fine Arts Center, Notre
Dame, Indiana; its plans and ac-
tivities. portfolio MC v 161 n 5
p 9 Ap '60
---Northern Illinois University;
Raya Garbousova, cellist; notes.
MC v 162 n 1 p 22 Jl '60
---Northwestern University: Roger
Sessions festival 1961. AmM v 8
n 10 p 14 N '60
--- ---Roger Sessions Festival;
notes. IM v 59 n 6 p 26 D '60
---Notre Dame University: 2nd an-
nual Collegiate Jazz Festival; report; north Texas State Band win-
ner. il IM v 58 n 11 p 9 My '60
---Ohio University: The Marriage
of Figaro. ON v 24 n 22 p 3 Ap 2'60
---Oxford; Khovanshchina; notes.
MC v 161 n 3 p 45 F '60
---Peabody Conservatory; The Turk
in Italy under Laszlo Halasz; re-
view. MC v 161 n 3 p 35 F '60
---Princeton seminar, sponsored
by the Fromm Music Foundation
of Chicago; notes. WM n 2 p 33
Ap '60
---Purcell's Fairy Queen, opera
at University of Nottingham; pro-
duction story, illustrated. Th Arts
v 14 n 3 p 92-99 Spring '60
---Purdue University: Industrial
Music Workshop. IM v 59 n 6 p 31
D '60
---Rollins College, Winter Park,
Florida; 25th annual Bach Festival:
review. MC v 161 n 5 p 20 Ap '60
---Schwartz, Will. The universities,
guardians of our musical heritage.
MEJ v 47 n 1 p 41-3 S-O '60
---Sessions, Roger; 3-day festival
of his music at Northwestern, Ev-
anston, Illinois. AmM v 8 n 8 p 4
S '60
---St. John's University (Minnesota)

première of a Haydn Concerto;
notes. AmM v 8 n 1 p 18 Ja '60
---San Francisco State College:
US première of A Tale of Two
Cities; note. Op v 2 n 3 p 200
Mr '60
---Southern Methodist Univer-
sity: song competition; $7, 200
over 3-year peroid, bonus $2, 500;
rules. IM v 59 n 5 p 53 N '60
---Tulane University: Ford Found-
ation $75, 000 to establish Ar-
chive of New Orleans Jazz; notes.
IM v 59 n 5 p 15 N '60
---University College, London;
Beatrice and Benedick, Berlioz
opera; criticism. Op v 11 n 4
p 304 Ap '60
---The University of Alabama;
Acis and Galatea, Handel note.
ON v 24 n 10 p 2 Ja 9'60
---University of Arizona, 7th Regional Music Festival (bands,
choruses, soloists in contests).
MC v 161 n 1 p 8 Ja '60
---University of Arkansas: Tri-
state opera festival with awards;
eleven high schools. ON v 24
n 12 p 3 Ja 23'60
---University of Buffalo: opera
productions 1959-60. ON v 24
n 11 p 2 Ja 16'60
--—University of California American première of Bloch's Macbeth
beth; notes. il Op v 11 n 6 p 410
Je '60
--- ---master class under Pablo
Casals; operas: Bloch's Macbeth and Britten's The Tale of
Two Cities. MC v 162 n 1 p 25
Jl '60
--- ---notable programs. MC
v 161 n 5 p 23 Ap '60
--- ---opera notes. MC v 161
n 3 p 38 F '60
--- ---opera, The Turn of the
Screw, directed by Jan Popper;
cast. MC v 161 n 4 p 31 Mr'60
---University of California, Los
Angeles: Festival of Oriental
Music and Related Arts. IM
v 58 n 11 p 23 My '60
--- ---Pélleas and Mélisande,
AP wl ph: Maria Jeanette. ON

202

---Hartt College of Music, Così
fan tutte, ens AP wl ph: Hartford,
Conn. MC v 162 n 3 p 17 S '60
---Inter-American University,
Puerto Rico; String Congress set-
ting, several phs. IM v 58 n 8
p 12-3 F '60
---Revelli, Dr. Wm. D. of Univ-
ersity of Michigan bands, por ph.
IM v 59 n 3 p 8 S '60
---Steber, Eleanor, at Adelphi
College, ens ph. MC v 162 n 2
p 26 Ag '60
--- ---with officials of the Univer-
sity of West Virginia, ens ph. MC
v 162 n 1 p 41 Jl '60
MUSIC PERFORMANCE TRUST
    FUND
Thayer Military Band (Canton,
Ohio) aided. IM v 59 n 1 p 32
Jl '60
---Notes in issues of IM 1960
MUSIC THERAPY
Brienholt, Verna, and Irene Sch-
oepfle. Music experience for the
child with speech limitations. MEJ
v 47 n 1 p 45-6, 48, 50 S-O '60
---Buker, Alden. The status of
music therapy. MEJ v 46 n 5 p 62,
64 Ap-My '60
---Guitars to children's hospital,
La Rabida Sanitarium; Chicago
notes. MEJ v 47 n 1 p 10 S-O '60
MUSIC USA, program seven days
a week; details of sound wave re-
ception; VOA. AmM v 8 n 4 p 11
Ap '60
MUSICA ABIERTA
Barcelona; founded by Juan Hid-
algo (1927-) and Jacques Bodmer.
WT n 4 p 76 Ag '60
MUSICA AETERNA
Under Frederic Waldman and Je-
rome Hines, bass; NYC review.
MC v 161 n 4 p 38 Mr '60
MUSICAE ANTIQUAE COLLEGIUM
    VARSOVIENSE
Warsaw concert; notes. WM n2
p 28-9 Ap '60
MUSICAL COURIER, periodical
Trompeter, Lisa Roma. Editorial
on 80 years of its publication. MC
v 162 n 6 p 3 D '60
MUSICAL INSTRUMENTS

Cardini, Maria Pimpanaro. Antonio Stradivari e le scuole musicali di Cremona. La S n 125 p 34-
8 Ap '60
---Cello; Theodore Salzman on
practical use of the instrument
(stringing and de-presswrizing).
il IM v 58 n 11 p 20-1 My '60
---Differences in conductors,
Toscanini (US) and Furtwängler
(Europe) partly the difference in
the brass choir instruments. HF
v 10 n 7 p 8 Jl '60
---Foster, Donald. The tourist in
musical Europe. MEJ v 46 n 6
p 69-70 Je-Jl '60
---Handbells, 4-octave; Fristen
Brothers, Deerfield, Illinois.
MEJ v 47 n 1 p 18 S-O '60
---Harmonica; Alan Schackner on
the chromatic harmonica as " a
new orchestral color". il IM v 58
n 10 p 12-3, 29 Ap '60
---Jackson, Robert. Clifford Hoing,
violin-maker of Wycombe since
1936 (with picture of him working). MD v 50 n 11 p 15-6 My '60
---Mari, P. Alejandro Barletta,
ce récital de bandonéon; Paris.
GDC n .255-6 p 313 Ja 15'60
---The melodica; notes. il MEJ
v 47 n 1 p 12 S-O '60
---Migot, Georges, musée des
instruments, Paris. GDC n 287
p 237 N 4'60
---New basses (York Band Instrument Company): E flat ro-
tary valve bass, the B flat, described. MEJ v 46 n 5 p 14
Ap-My '60
---Pastene, Joseph. Letter on
different trumpet used in orchestras under Toscanini and
Furtwängler, not merely conducting styles. HF v 10 n 7 p 8
Jl '60
---Roda, Joseph. Bows for mu-
sical instruments (book reviewed).
MEJ v 46 n 6 p 106 F-Mr '60
---Roddy, Joseph. Steinways and
Steinwayism (pianos). HF v 10
n 3 p 42-5 Mr '60
---The Tessin: old organs. (with
4 illustrations of the Baroque

(Musical instruments)
organs). La S n 128 p 36-7 Jl'60
---Vecchio-Verderame, Angelo.
Pianoforti. il La S n 125 p 39-41
Ap '60
---Africa; a koraplayer, Mali
Company, ph: Pic. WT v 9 n 4
p 346 Winter '60
---Asia; drummer of Sarawak; the
Khèrne, Thailand; anklung musi-
cians of Bandung; Thailand or-
chestra; gongs and drums of Sara-
wak, 5 AP phs. WM n 6 p 133
D '60
---Gajda player, Croatia, Yug-
oslavia, ph: Carner. WM n 4
p 84 Ag '60
---Guslar from Ljubovo, Yugos-
lavia, ph: Carner. WM n 4 p 84
Ag '60
---Kaval players with singers,
Macedonia, Yugoslavia, ph: Car-
ner. WM n 4 p 84 Ag '60
---Portfolio with notes, 16 AP
phs: US. MEJ v 47 n 1 p 94-5
S-O '60
---The Steinway grand piano: how
it is made. colored ph. La S
n 132 p 13 N '60
MUSICAL LIFE IN THE UNITED
STATES, program
Half-hour program, Voice of
America on Sunday. AmM v 8
n 4 p 11 Ap '60
MUSICALS
Cramer, Clarence E. (US de-
mand for attractive musical
show growing; ballet not a sub-
stitute.) MC v 162 n 1 p 14
Jl '60
---Engel, Lehman. The singer on
Broadway. MC v 162 n 1 p 9
Jl '60
---Griffith and Prince as Broad-
way producers: a profile. por
Th Arts v 44 n 10 p 20-1 O '60
---Hammerstein, Oscar, II. The
book had better be good. Th
Arts v 44 n 11 p 18-9, 70 N '60
---Indcox, John F. The new
Broadway musicals on record.
HF v 10 n 3 p 85-6 Mr '60
---Kanin, Garson; his jukebox
musical with Phil Silvers,

Nancy Walker; lyrics Betty Com-
den and Adolph Green; Jule Styne
music. Th Arts v 44 n 12 p 8
D '60
---Loewe, Frederick. (Interview.)
por MC v 162 n 1 p 8 Jl '60
---Martin, Mary. Once Upon a
Mattress (Layton); libretto. il Th
Arts v 44 n 7 p 21-4 Jl '60
---Melbourne première: The Music
Man; Ted Scott and Carolyn Maye;
notes. il MD v 50 n 9 p 25-6
Mr '60
---NYC notes on Valmouth; on Ir-
ma la Douce. Th Arts v 44 n 12
p 12 D '60
---Recordings criticized in the
section, World of Entertainment.
HF 1960
---Reviews of Rodgers-Hammerstein
musicals (Epic). HF v 10 n 8 p 70
Ag '60
---Saratoga; NYC notes. WP v 11
n 6 p 4 Ap '60
---The Sound of Music, based up-
on the Trapp family, starring
Mary Martin; notes. il Th Arts
v 44 n 1 p 65-9 Ja '60
---Todd, Arthur. What makes a
musical move. il Th Arts v 44
n 11 p 66-7, 72 N '60
---US list of musicals in process
of casting; data. MC v 162 n 5
p 9 N '60
--- ---data on each. MC v 162 n 6
p 9 D '60
---Wilson, John S. Musicals: the
old college try. il Th Arts v 44
n 8 p 48-52 Ag '60
---College shows, a US portfolio.
Th Arts v 44 n 8 p 48-50 Ag '60
---Show Boat rehearsal, Bruns-
wick, Maine, ens AP wl ph. Th
Arts v 44 n 6 p 19 Je '60
MUSIK FUR SAITENINSTRUMENTE
(WALTER), ballet
Ens AP wl ph: Wuppertal, 1957.
WT v 9 n 3 p 232 Autumn '60
MUSIQUE CONCRETE
See Concrete music
MUSY, LOUIS, singer
Notes. GDC n 274 p 703 My 27'60
---Por ph: Erlanger de Rosen.
GDC n 274 cover My 27'60

MUZIO, CLAUDIO 1889-1936,
 singer
Matz, Mary Jane. First ladies
of the Puccini premières; 4. Cl-
audio Muzio. por ON v 24 n 24
p 10-1 Ap 16'60
---As Tosca, 1932, AP hl ph:
Culver
MY FAIR LADY, musical
Moscow opening of tour; Franz
Allers, director. MC v 161 n 5
p 39 Ap '60
---Sweden; success. WT v 9 n 2
p 174 Summer '60
MY FRIEND KOLKA, play
Moscow, 1960; ens AP wl ph. WT
v 9 n 2 p 180 Summer '60
MYERS, GORDON. Organizing a
community chorus. MEJ v 46 n 4
p 68, 70 F-Mr '60
LE MYSTÈRE DE LA NATIVITÉ,
 opera-oratorio
Scenic première, Salzburg; Frank
Martin score under Ernest Anser-
met; description. WM n 3 p 56
Je '60
---Salzburg, ens AP wl ph: 1960;
Op v 11 p 53 Autumn '60
--- ---ens AP wl ph: Ellinger. WM
n 5 p 110 O '60
MYSTERY PLAYS
York cycle ; a summer festival of
3 weeks; cast of 200; the ruins of
St. Mary's Abbey. Th Arts v 44
n 5 p 20 My '60
---York Festival notes; the play of
Daniel notes. Th Arts v 44 n 12
p 16 D '60

N

NABOKOV, NICOLAS, 1903-, composer
Wangerin, R. H. (Letter on Holy
Devil as opera 1958 in Louisville;
later became Rasputin's End, enlarged version.) ON v 24 n 19
p 32 Mr 12'60
NABUCCO, opera
Historical notes. il ON v 25 n 4
p 10-1 D 3'60
---Metropolitan Opera cast; notes
on composer, Verdi; on décor;
pronunciation of the names; the

story; facsimile of original
playbill and other pictures. ON
v 25 n 4 D 3'60
--- ---review. MC v 162 n 5 p 14
N '60
---Ens AP wl ph: Athens. Op v 11
n 9 p 627 S '60
---Ens AP wl ph: Venice. La S
n 128 p 53 Jl '60
---Metropolitan, Act I, ens AP
wl ph: Louis Melançon. MC
v 162 n 5 p 14 N '60
--- ---Act II sc. 1; Act III, sc. 1.;
several Assyrian sculptures and
the Hanging Gardens of Babylon.
ON v 25 n 4 D 3'60
NABUCODONOSOR
See Nabucco, opera
NACHSAISON, comedy
Nürnberg; notes. WP v 11 n 3
p 2 Ja '60
NÁDASDY, KÁLMÁN, director
The Budapest Opera; notes ON
v 24 n 12 p 26 Ja 23'60
NAGLER, A; M. Hugo von Hof-
mannsthal and theatre. Th R
v 2 n 1 p 5-15 1960
NAÏS MICOULIN, opera
Bruneau from Zola's novel, end
of Act I, small AP wl ph. Op
v 11 n 9 p 599 S '60
NAKAMURA, HIROKO, 1944-,
 pianist
At the piano, ph. WM n 6 p 134
D '60
THE NAMING OF MURDERER'S
 ROCK, play
London notes; Frederick Bland.
WP v 11 n 9 p 14 Jl '60
NANCY
Baronnet, J. Trois mois d'ac-
tivité au Grand Théâtre. GDC
n 257-8 p 355 Ja 29'60
NANDRUP, AUDRE, singer
And Claude-Erik Nandrup, pi-
anist; Paris concert. GDC n 274
p 724 My 27'60
NAPLES
Benedetto, Renato Di. Teatro
di Corte: opera. il La S n 132
p 46-7 N '60
---Music report. La S n 122 p 73
Ja '60
NAPOLEON

(Napoleon)
David canvas, unfinished ph:
Bettmann Archive; also Vigée-
Lebrun's portrait of Caroline
Bonaparte, sister. ON v 24 n 20
p 4-5 Mr 19'60
NAPOLI, JACOPO, 1911-, com-
poser
Massimo Bellini di Catania: Mas
'Aniello. il La S n 126 p 35 My '60
DIE NASHÖRNER, play
Düsseldorf: Ionesco's Les Rhin-
océros. WP v 11 n 5 p 16 Mr '60
---See also Les Rhinoceros, play
NASREDDINE HODJA, play
Athens notes; G. Stavrou. WP
v 12 n 1 p 7 O '60
NAT, JEAN
Yves-Nat, Elise. Les yeux fer-
més. GDC n 293-4 p 447-452
D 16'60
NATIONAL ARTS ACADEMY
Interlochen, Michigan; plan
MEJ v 46 n 5 p 68 Ap-My '60
NATIONAL BROADCASTING CO-
MPANY OPERA
Opera telecast by NBC Opera
Theatre: Cavalleria Rusticana.
ON v 24 n 17 p 27 F 27'60
---Twelth season; première of
"Brigham Young" Nov. 12. AmM
v 8 n 6 p 13 Jl '60
THE NATIONAL COUNCIL OF
THE METROPOLITAN OPERA
Its work; relation to the older
Metropolitan Opera Guild. il ON
v 25 n 5 p 26-7 D 10'60
---See also Metropolitan Opera
NATIONAL CULTURAL CENTER,
WASHINGTON
Plans. il ON v 24 n 21 p 10-1
Mr 26'60
---Washington, D. C.; progress
report. Th Arts v 44 n 12 p 73
D '60
--- ---ten acres on the Potomac,
plans, halls; Edward Durrell
Stone, architect. AmM v 8 n 4
p 1-5 Ap '60
--- ---Views from New Hampshire
Avenue, from the air, floor plan,
the great salon, the theatre, phs.
AmM v 8 n 4 Ap '60
NATIONAL GRASS ROOTS, opera

Tour note. ON v 24 n 20 p 3 Mr 19
'60
NATIONAL MUSIC CAMP
Goth, Trudy. (Michigan; notes.)
il La S n 131 p 31-3 O '60
---Interlochen, Michigan; notes.
WM n 5 p 105 O '60
---French Horn students, ens AP
wl ph. WM n 5 p 108 O '60
---University Orchestra and Fes-
tival Choir presenting The Mess-
iah, ens ph: outdoors. WM n 5
p 108 O '60
NATIONAL MUSIC COUNCIL, US
Washburn, Robert, reporting on
his year as composer-in-residence
in Elkhart, Indiana, schools under
this Ford Foundation subsidy pro-
ject to 12 US young musicians.
MEJ v 47 n 1 p 108 S-O '60
NATIONAL MUSIC LEAGUE
Sending to Rio de Janeiro Joseph
Schwartz; will sponsor a Brazil-
ian for return tour. AmM v 8 n 8
p 10 S '60
THE NATIONAL OPERA CLUB
NYC; Waldorf-Astoria perfor-
mance. ON v 24 n 18 p 3 Mr 5'60
NATIONAL ORCHESTRAL ASSO-
CIATION
NYC; John Barnett, conducting,
Ryszart Bakst, pianist. MC v 161
n 1 p 14 Ja '60
NATIONAL SCHOOL OF OPERA
Cross, Joan, principal; London
notes. Op v 11 n 4 p 246 Ap '60
---Reviews: Il Maestro di Musica
by Pergolesi given by visiting
Swedes; Purcell's Dido and Aeneas
by the British. Op v 11 n 6 p 447
Je '60
THE NATIONAL SYMPHONY (US)
Concerts; Washington report.
MC v 161 n 3 p 40 F '60
---Highlights of the 29th season.
MC v 161 n 6 p 31-2 My '60
---Mexico; review. MC v 161 n 1
p 27 Ja '60
---NYC; criticism; Howard Mit-
chell conducting; Ellabelle Davis,
soprano. MC v 161 n 1 p 14 Ja'60
--- ---MC v 162 n 6 p 43 D '60
--- ---Howard Mitchell with Benno
Moiseiwitsch. MC v 161 n 5 p 16

Ap '60
NATIONAL SYMPHONY OF MEX-
ICO
Bellas Artes report. MC v 161
n 5 p 32 Ap '60
NATIONAL THEATRE OF BEL-
GIUM
Teirlinck, Herman. Two temper-
aments, two theatres. il WT v 9
n 1 p 23-34 Spring '60
NAVARRO, ARMANDO, dancer
AP wl ph: Cuevas Ballet. TD
n 95 p 25 Jl-Ag '60
NEEDHAM, GWENDOLYN B.
Mrs. Francis Brooke (1723-1789):
dramatic critic. Th Notbk v 15 n 2
p 47-52 Winter 60-61
LES NÈGRES, clownerie
Genêt, Jean; criticism; "disagree-
able and scabrid subject matter
about colonialism and race re-
lations. " il Th Arts v 44 n 12
p 67, 74 D '60
--- ---notes. Spec n 1 p 77 1960
---Paris; Genêt notes. WP v 11 n 3
p 6 Ja '60
---Several scenes au Théâtre de
Lutèce, phs. Spec n 1 p 76-8 1960
NEGROES
Frattini, Angelo. Lettere aperto
à Joséphine Baker. por La S n 132
p 70 N'60
---Hansberry, Lorraine. (On the
Negro in American theatre.) il
Th Arts v 44 n 10 p 9-11, 69 O'60
---The Negro theatre at the Théâtre
of the Nations, Paris; reports. il
WT v 9 n 4 p 344-351 Winter '60
---New York City Opera host to
300 Harlem school children; opera
program. ON v 24 n 19 p 3 Mr 12
'60
---Singers in opera; names and roles.
WM n 4 p 77 Ag '60
---Ewande, Lydia, and Bachir
Touré in the African troupe, the
Griots, playing "Les Nègres",
AP hl ph: Paris, Pic. Th Arts
v 44 n 12 p 66 D '60
---Laws, Hubert, Jr. of the Hous-
ton Symphony, with his piccolo,
ph. J Rev v 7 n 3 p 21 Fall '60
---Portfolio of American Negroes on
the stage. Th Arts v 44 n 10 O'60

---See also Les Nègres
NELSON, ROBERT J. (1925-). The
unreconstructed heroes of Mol-
ière. TDR v 4 n 3 p 14-37 Mr '60
NEMET, MARY, 1937-, violinist
Career notes; Australian. MD
v 50 n 9 p 15 Mr '60
NERVI BALLET FESTIVAL
See Il Festival di Nervi
NETHERLANDS
Theatre report. WP v 12 n 1 p 4
O '60; same. WP n 12 n 2 p 4
N '60; same. WP v 12 n 3 p 4
D '60
---Theatre report from I. T. I.
Center. il WT v 9 n 2 p 170-
174 Summer '60
---Van Dalsum, Albert (1890-)
notes; general theatre report
follows. WP v 11 n 3 p 1, 7 Ja '60
HET NEDERLANDS BALLET
Tassart, Maurice. Au Théâtre
des Nations. GDC n 274 p 720
My 27'60
---Théâtre des Nations; notes.
TD n 95 p 14 Jl-Ag '60
THE NETHERLANDS OPERA
Mindszenthy, Judith. Report;
Peter Maag's resignation. ON
v 24 n 20 p 26 Mr 19'60
NETTL, PAUL (1889-). On the
barricades (opera influenced by
"the struggle between human dig-
nity and arbitrayr powers"). ON
v 24 n 15 p 6-7 F 13'60
----Rich and strange (exoticism in
dramatic music) il ON v 24 n 24
p 4-7 Ap 16'60
NEULAND UNTERM PFLUG, play
Berlin notes; T. I. London. WP
v 11 n 4 p 12 F '60
---Ens AP wl ph: Berlin. WP v 11
n 4 F '60
NEVER HAD IT SO GOOD, play
Coventry, 1960, ens AP wl ph:
Richard Sadler. WT v 9 n 2
p 184 Summer '60
NEVEU, GINETTE 1919-1949,
violinist
L'Association Ginette Neveu;
Jacques Thiérac conte l'histoire.
GDC n 269-70 p 587 Ap 22'60
NEVILLE, JOHN (1925-(. The
actor's viewpoint (on theatre

(Neville, John
architecture). NTM v 2 n 1 p 7-
11 O '60
NEW ARTS ORCHESTRA
Boston; Howard Faberman. MC
v 162 n 6 p 27 D '60
NEW DRAMATISTS COMMITEE
Keating, John. A bridge for
young playwrights. WP v 12 n 3
p 1 D '60
--- ---(Michaela O'Harra and histo-
ry of this NYC organization). Th
Arts v 44 n 7 p 17, 20, 63-4 Jl '60
NEW ENGLAND OPERA THEATRE
Goldovsky, Boris, director; no-
tes on Rigoletto, on Cosi fan tutte.
Op v 11 n 8 p 545 Ag '60
---Notes. ON v 24 n 18 p 26 Mr 5
'60
---Repertory. MC v 162 n 4 p 16
O '60
---Rigoletto and Cosi fan tutte;
notes. MC v 161 n 4 p 32 Mr '60
NEW JERSEY
All-state High School Operatic
Festival; report. ON v 24 n 16
p 1 F 20'60
NEW MEXICO CHAMBER OR-
CHESTRA
Notes; founder, Norman C. Green-
berg. IM v 59 n 5 p 33 N '60
THE NEW MUSIC ENSEMBLE
Carewe, John, director; summer
school 1959 at Darlington. MR
v 21 n 1 p 81 F '60
NEW OPERA COMPANY
Sadler's Wells; The Nightingale;
and Oedipus Rex: reviews. Op
v 11 n 12 p 850 D '60
---See also Sadler's Wells
NEW ORCHESTRA OF NEW YORK
Franks, Dobbs, and Gregory
Millar, founders. por MD v 51
n 5 p 24-5 N '60
NEW ORLEANS
Aïda to mark 100th anniversary
of the old French Opera House.
Op v 11 n 2 p 138 F '60
---Lingg, Ann M. Great opera hou-
ses; New Orleans, the Théâtre
Américain. il ON v 25 n 5 p 22-5
D 10'60
---Myers, Sim. Opera reports.
MC v 161 n 1 p 24 Ja '60

---New Orleans Philharmonic,
25th year; New Orleans Opera
opened with La Gioconda; Bernstein
and NY Philharmonic debut; Cultural
attractions Fund started. MC
v 162 n 5 p 24 N '60
---Opera report. MC v 161 n 6
p 26 My '60
---Sublette, Bob. Theatre USA:
New Orleans. il Th Arts v 44
n 4 p 57-8 Ap '60
---Testimony before FCC on musicians losing out to canned music: "not a single instrumental
musician is employed as staff in
any of the 16 radio and TV stations
in New Orleans area". IM v 58
n 8 p 42 F '60
NEW ORLEANS PHILHARMONIC
Chicago review; Alexander Hils-
berg conducting, Grant Johanne-
sen, pianist. MC v 161 n 5 p 21
Ap '60
---Notes. IM v 59 n 4 p 22 O '60
NEW ORLEANS PLAYERS
Tracy, Ty, director; notes.
Th Arts v 44 n 4 p 57 Ap '60
NEW YORK
Piedmont; Rockland Lyric The-
ater operas. ON v 25 n 2 p 7
O 29'60
---Rochester Community Players;
notes on 37th season. Th Arts
v 44 n 12 p 69 D '60
NEW YORK CHAMBER SOLOISTS
Hillis, Margaret, director; re-
view. MC v 161 n 7 p 24 Je '60
NEW YORK CITY
The Academy of Music; Eman-
uele Muzio, conducting Verdi's
Un Ballo; notes. Ver v 1 n 2
p 947 Ag '60
---Balch, Jack. The openings.
Th Arts v 44 n 2 p 14-16 F '60
---Bohle, Bruce. (Plays; report.)
il Th Arts v 44 n 4 p 59-61 Ap'60
---Conference of Central Opera
Service and the National Opera
Association: report. ON v 24 n 24
p 13, 22 Ap 16'60
---Enseignements d'une saison à
Broadway, 1959-60. WP v 12
n 2 p 3 N '60
---Five premières in one week;

notes on Carnegie Hall. AmM
v 8 n 3 p 18 Mr '60
---Fund-raising theatre audiences
taken apart by John Keating.
Th Arts v 44 n 3 p 20, 22-4
Mr '60
---Goth, Trudy. A New York:
Balletti Filippini; Balletti Is-
raeliani; Balletti Polacchi. il
La S n 123 p 42-4 F '60
---John, Malcolm. New York, a
great cultural centre (with re-
port of Juilliard activities). MD
v 51 n 1 p 18-9 Jl '60
---Keating, John. (On the New
Dramatists Committee to aid
young playwrights.) WP v 12
n 3 p 1 D '60
--- ---The 1960-61 season on
Broadway. il Th Arts v 44 n 10
p 12-7 O '60
---Morehouse, Ward. Broadway
had a building boom (theatres of
the early 20th centruy). Th Arts
v 44 n 1 p 79-80, 84 Ja '60
---Music events. AmM v 8 n 10
p 10 N '60
---Radio station WBAI now under
Pacifica Foundation; details. HF
v 10 n 5 p 18 My '60
---Richards, Stanley. ON and off
Broadway (series of reviews).
PlM 1960
---Symposium of symphony play-
ers, Waldorf-Astoria July 28-9
1960: topics as central data sou-
rce, dismissal clause in a con-
tract, ratification of contracts,
pensions; reports. IM v 59 n 3
p 9, 40-1 S '60
---Watts, Richard, Jr. New York
play season 1959-60. Th Arts
v 44 n 7 p 13-5 Jl '60
---Worland, Tom. (Notes on
Broadway shows.) por MD v 51
n 1 p 30 Jl '60
---Central Park, distance view,
Henry V, ph. WP v 12 n 1 p 3
O '60
NEW YORK CITY BALLET.
(Balanchine)
Krokover, Rosalyn. (Report.)
MC v 162 n 6 p 12 D '60
---Report. MC v 161 n 6 p 9 My'60

NEW YORK CITY OPERA
Boston debut; criticism. MC
v 161 n 6 p 30 My '60
---Chicago criticism. MC v 161
n 5 p 22 Ap '60
---Cleveland criticism. MC v 161
n 5 p 24 Ap '60
---Eaton, Quaintance. (US opera
companies as well as the Ford
Foundation sharing the financial
risk of a 5-week tour with 4 Am-
erican operas.) ON v 24 n 17 p 14
F 27'60
---Goth, Trudy. Center Opera di
New York. il La S n 126 p 36, 70
My '60
---NYC reviews: Rigoletto; Car-
men. MC v 162 n 6 p 16 D '60
--- ---The Cradle Will Rock; The
Consul (2). MC v 161 n 4 p 14
Mr '60
---Notes on Orfeo (Joffrey as
choreographer), Gérard Souzay's
American debut; other notes. On
v 25 n 3 p 19 N 19'60
---Orfeo by Monteverdi, Gérard
Souzay; Christopher West, New
Regisseur, Leopold Stokoweski,
guest conductor; historical and
performance notes. MC v 162
n 5 p 14-5 N '60
---Repass, Richard. (Reviews.)
Op v 11 n 5 p 339-341 My '60
---Repertory notes; US cities
tour. AmM v 8 n 2 p 12 F '60
---Repertory plans. AmM v 8
n 11 p 8 D '60
---Third season of American
works; note. MD v 50 n 10 p 16
Ap '60
---US tour, repertory: Feb 23-
Mr 26 calendar. ON v 24 n 15
p 32 F 13'60
---Oedipus Rex, ens AP wl ph:
F. Fehl; and Carmina Burana,
ens AP wl ph: same. Th Arts
v 44 n 3 p 28-9 Mr '60
THE NEW YORK OPERA THEATRE
Repertory notes. ON v 24 n 16 p 3
F 20'60
NEW YORK PHILHARMONIC OR-
CHESTRA
At West Berlin Fesitval; notes.
AmM v 8 n 7 p 10 Ag '60

(Nre York Philharmonic)
---Contemporary repertory; list.AmM v 8 n 10 p 14 N '60
---Guest conductors 1960-61; other plans. MC v 161 n 4 p 4 Mr '60
---List of 7 guest conductors; notes. AmM v 8 n 5 p 12 Je '60
---NYC; reviews (3); Bernstein. MC v 161 n 1 p 13, 15 Ja '60
--- ---Bernstein and Aaron Copland, conducting. MC v 162 n 6 p 18 D '60
--- ---Bernstein(3) and Bruno Walter (1) concerts. MC v 161 n 6 p 17-19 My '60
--- --Bernstein (2), Thomas Schippers and Mitropoulos. MC v 161 n 3 p 25-6 F '60
--- ---Mitropoulos; Bernstein, two reviews. MC v 161 n 4 p 16, 18 Mr '60
--- ---Paul Hindemith, Leopold Stokowski, Fritz Reiner (2) MC v 161 n 5 p 14-6 Ap '60
---Subsidy for tour from Columbia Broadcasting Company; notes. MC v 161 n 6 p 6 My'60
NEW YORK PRO MUSICA (GREENBERG)
European tour, opened in Bath with The Play of Daniel; notes. WM n 4 p 77 Ag '60
---Founded 1952; notes on research of old scores; Play of Daniel criticism. il AmM v 8 n 5 p 3-4 Je '60
---A Royaumont, premières representations en France depuis le XIIe siècle, du "Jeu de Daniel" (notes). GDC n 278 p 844-6 Je 24'60
NEW YORK PUBLIC LIBRARY THEATRE COLLECTION
Matthews, William H. Jr. New materials. PlM v 36 n 7 p 168-9 Ap '60
--- ---reporting. PlM v 36 n 4 p 77 Ja '60
NEW YORK'S SETTLEMENT OPERA
Repertory notes. ON v 24 n 17 p 3 F 27'60
NEW YORK SIN FONIETTA

NYC; all-Vivaldi concert under Max Goberman; review. MC v 161 n 1 p 14 Ja '60
NEW YORK WOODWIND QUINTET
List of members. IM v 59 n 5 p 32 N '60
NEW ZEALAND
Wellington; Figaro, opera; notes. ON v 25 n 4 p 7 D 3'60
NEWAY OPERA THEATRE
NYC; notes on opening repertory. MC v 161 n 7 p 22 Je '60
NEWLIN, DIKA, composer
Première: Study in Twelve Tones; NYC 1959. ACAB v 9 n 2 p 22 1960
NEWMAN, ERNEST, 1888-1959, critic
(G. N. S.) Criticism of Newman's place as a music critic; one letter reproduced on Don Giovanni. MR v 21 n 1 p 77-8 F '60
NEWMAN, THEODORE, composer
Première: Hymn For Strings (1960); The Village Civic Symphony under Norman Masonson, NYC. J Rev v 7 n 2 p 22 Spring'60
NEWMAN, VERA. (Letter on her late husband, Ernest Newman; marriage 1919.) HF v 10 n 1 p 10 Ja '60
NEWMAN, WILLIAM S. (1912-). Letter: The Sonata in the Baroque Era (rebuttal from author). MR v 21 n 2 p 173-4 My '60
NHK Orchestra
NYC debut under William Schücter; review of Japanese visitors. MC v 162 n 6 p 17 D '60
NICE
L'Académie internationale d'été 1960; par Michel Lorin. GDC n 276 p 793 Je 10'60
---Ash-Moore, Denise. La saison lyrique de l'Opéra de-Nice. GDC n 279-80 p 898 Jl 1'60
---Demarquez, Suzanne. Fêtes du centenaire du Rattachement de Nice à la France. GDC n 263-4 p 473 Mr 11'60
---Festival on 100th anniversary of the annexation of the County of Nice to France; notes. MC v 161 n 7 p 15 Je '60

---International Summer Academy; Serge Lifar heading dance; staff of musicians listed. WM n 2 p 33 Ap '60

---Sous les toits de L'Académie de Nice. GDC n 284 p 129 O 14'60

---Turnbull, Patrick. (Aida reviewed and other notes.) Ap v 11 n 4 p 273 Ap '60

NICHOLLS, AUDREY
Career notes; b. Queensland. il MD v 50 n 7 p 28-9 Ja '60

---In five roles, AP phs. MD v 50 n 7 p 28-9 Ja '60

NICHTS NEUES, play
Cologne notes; Mario Pensa. WP v 11 n 9 p 10 Jl '60

NICKSON, NOEL, composer
Camerata Society, Melbourne; Sonata for Violin and Viola. MD v 51 n 1 p 17 Jl '60

NICOLESCO, STEFAN, composer
Premiere: Symphony No. I; Bucharest. WM n 5 p 104 O '60

NICOLOV, NICOLA, singer
British debut as Radamès; criticism of Bulgarian tenor. Op v 11 n 5 p 367 My '60

---Por ph: Ferri. Op v 2 n 3 p 195 Mr '60

NICOLS, MIKE, comedian
With Elaine May in sketches; "almost unmixed delight". Th Arts v 44 n 12 p 12 D '60

NIE MA NIEZNANYCH WYSP, play
Varsovie notes; Stanislaw Stampfl. WP v 11 n 8 p 10 Je '60

NIEDERMOSER, OTTO (1903-).
(On staging Chekhov; Austrian viewpoint.) il WT v 9 n 2 p 134-5 Summer '60

NIELSEN, CARL, 1865-1931, composer
Denmark recorded music notes. HF v 10 n 7 p 26 Jl '60

---Hedman, Frank. (Recordings.) HF v 10 n 7 p 26 Jl '60

NIES-BERGER, EDOUARD, organist
Beverly Hills, Episcopal Church concert for Dr. Albert Schweitzer's work; notes. MC v 161 n 4 p 30 Mr '60

NIGERIA
Banham, Martin. Drama in the Commonwealth: Nigeria. NTM v 1 n 4 p 18-21 Jl '60

NIGG, SERGE, 1924-, composer
Première: Le Concerto violon-orchestre; Christian Ferras. GDC n 277 p 820 Je 17'60

---Première at Aix-en-Provence: "Hieronymous Bosch Symphony" by Nigg; review. MC v 162 n 3 p 25 S '60

---Strasbourg cirticism of "Jérôme Bosch-Symphonie". GDC n 281-2 p 65 S 30'60

THE NIGHTINGALE, opera
London review; a jeweled fairy tale; history of the Stravinsky work. il Op v 11 n 6 p 441 Je '60

---New Opera Company; also The Rite of Spring (as a ballet by Maurice Béjart). MC v 161 n 7 p 13 Je '60

NIJINSKY, VASLAV, 1890-1950, dancer
Five AP wl phs: Paris. TD n 90 p 9 F '60

---Premier danseur, et Mlle. Anna Pavlova, prima ballerina du Théâtre Imperial Marie dans "Le Pavillon d'Armide", AP wl ph: St. Petersburg. TD n 90 p 5 F '60

NILSSON, BIRGIT, 1918?-, singer
Criticism of her debut at the Metropolitan; Isolde. MC v 161 n 3 p 23 F '60

---Cushing, Mary Watkins. New Swedish champion (b. Svenstad). ON v 24 n 10 p 14, 32 Ja 9'60

---In Un Ballo in Maschera; Stockholm Opera; criticism. Op v 11 n 10 p 710 O '60

---Jeffries, Walter. People; 41. Birgit Nilsson. il Op v 11 n 9 p 607-12 S '60

---Notes and hl ph. MC v 161 n 1 p 5 Ja '60

---AP hl ph: Th Arts v 44 n 3 p 48 Mr '60

---As Aïda, AP hl ph. La S n 127 p 24 Je '60

---As Brünnhilde, AP hl ph: Melançon. ON v 24 n 16 p 17 F 20'60

211

(Nilsson, Birgit)
---As Isolde, several AP phs:
Melançon. ON v 24 n 10 Ja 9'60
---Backstage after Metropolitan
debut, hl ph. ON v 24 n 11 p 2
Ja 16'60
---Hl ph. MC v 162 n 4 p 22
O '60
---In Fidelio, phs: Melançon.
ON v 24 n 15 F 13'60
---In six roles; several informal
phs also; por ph. Op v 11 n 9
cover, p 607-10 S '60
---Small ph. HF v 10 n 10 p 67
O '60
---With the three tenors of Tris-
tan Vinay (Act I), Liebl (Act II)
and Da Costa (Act III), Dec. 28,
1959 at the Metropolitan, ph.
ON v 24 n 13 p 3 Ja 30'60
NIMES
Operettas: Les Mousquetaires au
Couvent; Le Pays du Sourire;
La Veuve Joyeuse; La Vie Par-
isienne; par Raymond Teulon.
GDC n 257-8 p 353 Ja 29'60
---Teulon, Raymond. La Tosca;
Hérodiade; Manon. GDC n 255-
6 p 306 Ja 15'60
LAS NIÑAS TERRIBLES, play
Madrid notes; Alfonso Paso.
WP v 11 n 9 p 4 Jl '60
NO FOR AN ANSWER, opera
NYC; Circle in the Square;
"a morality play spotted with
songs". ON v 25 n 3 p 20 N 19
'60
NO RED CARPET, play
Ontario; Catherine Brickenden.
WP v 11 n 8 p 2 Je '60
NOH DRAMA
Kaula, David. ON Noh drama.
TDR v 5 n 1 p 61-72 S '60
---Traites de Zeami (Guillimard
in the UNESCO collection,"know-
ledge of the Orient"). WP v 12
n 1 p 2 O '60
LES NOCES
Stravinsky, Igor, on his Les
Noces. ON v 25 n 5 p 10-1
D 10'60
NOCES DE JEANNETTE, opéra-
comique
Massé, Victor; première notes.

OpP n 19 p 58-61 1960
---L'Opéra-Comique review.
GDC n 288 p 255 N 11'60
---Portfolio: Paris. OpP n 19
p 58-61 1960
NOCH ZEHN MINUTEN BIS BUF-
FALO, play
Ens AP wl ph: Ilse Buhs, Berlin,
1959. WT v 9 n 3 p 211 Autumn'60
NOGARA, ANNA, actress
Hl ph. La S n 124 p 52 Mr '60
NONO, LUIGI, composer
Paris; Extrait d'une Epitaphe
pour Garcia Lorca (critique).
GDC n 291 p 355 D 2'60
NORDICA, LILLIAN, 1859-1914,
singer
AP wl ph. ON v 25 n 8 p 13
D 31'60
NORMA, opera
Demos, Jean. Epidauros; Callas
and the setting. Op v 11 p 76, 78
Autumn '60
---Epidauros; Callas, ens AP wl
ph. Op v 11 p 78 Autumn '60
NORMAN, ELIZABETH. Schubert's
incidental music to Rosamunde.
MR v 21 n 1 p 8-15 F '60
NORTH CAROLINA
Brevard; The Mikado; notes. Th
Arts v 44 n 11 p 73 N '60
NORTON, ELLIOT (1903-). Barns
are a far cry from Broadway
("few new plays of quality in
summer circuit"; "damaged by
summer exposure"). Th Arts
v 44 n 6 p 18-20 Je '60
---Theatre USA: Boston. Th Arts
v 44 n 5 p 53-6 My '60
NORWAY, NEVIL SHUTE, 1899-1060
note. WP v 11 n 4 p 8 F '60
NORWAY
Bjarne, Ragnvald. (Music report.)
MC v 161 n 7 p 17 Je '60
---Theatre report. WP v 12 n 1 p 4
O '60
NORWEGIAN NATIONAL OPERA
Report. MC n 161 n 7 p 17 Je '60
---Axelsen, Doris Lanita. Report-
ON v 25 n 6 p 28 D 17'60
--- ---The Magic Flute. ON v 24
n 21 p 28 Mr 26'60
---Otello: Bjuntz and Nordmo Loev-
berg, AP hl ph: Sturlason. ON

v 25 n 6 p 28 D 17'60
NOT IN FRONT OF THE SER-
VANTS, play
Birmingham notes; Michael
Plant and Adrian Pryce-Jones.
WP v 12 n 1 p 13 O '60
LA NOTTE DI UN NEVRASTEN-
ICO, opera buffa
Rota, Nino, a one-act opera;
La Piccola Scala. il Op v 11
n 5 p 352 My '60
NOTTINGHAM PLAYHOUSE
Moro, Peter, architect, on
the new house. NTM v 1 n 2
p 8-11 Ja '60
---Willatt, Hugh. The new Nott-
ingham Playhouse. NTM v 1 n 1
p 13-6 O '59
---Model, ph: Mann Bros. and
plans. NTM v 1 n 2 p 14 Ja'60
NOVAK, BENJAMIN J. and
Gladys R. Barnett. Are music
and science compatible? MEJ
v 46 n 6 p 44, 46 Je-Jl '60
NOVÁK, JAN 1921-, composer
Notes; b. Moravia. Mus Q v 46
n 4 p 513 O '60
NOVARRO, ARMANDO, dancer
Notes. TD n 94 p 26 Je '60
NOVERRE, JEAN GEORGE, 1727-
1809, choreographer
Moore, Lillian. Unlisted ballets
by Jean Georges Noverre. il Th
Notbk v 15 n 1 p 15-20 Autumn'60
NOYES FLUDDE, opera
In Christ Church, Vancouver,
ens AP wl ph. MC v 162 n 5
p 26 N '60
--- ---ens AP wl ph: Graphic. Op
v 11 n 10 p 690 O '60
LE NOZZE DI FIGARO, opera
Brussels note on new regime.
Op v 11 n 1 p 30 Ja '60
---Chicago Lyric Opera, Act 2,
ens AP wl ph: Sorensen. Op v 11
n 12 p 818 D '60
---Metropolitan; NYC review. MC
v 162 n 6 p 15 D '60
--- ---cast; story; décor; bibliography; discography; criticism; portfolio. ON v 24 n 12
Ja 23'60
--- ---portfolio: Louis Melançon.
ON v 24 n 12 Ja 23'60

---Miller, Della Casa, Soeder-
strom, ens AP wl ph: Metropoli-
tan. La S n 122 p 39 Ja '60
---Warnke, Frank J. (Criticism.)
ON v 24 n 12 p 4-5 Ja 23'60
---Miller, Mildred, ens AP wl
ph: Metro. AmM v 8 n 1 p 13
Ja '60
---Tel-Aviv, two AP phs. La S
n 125 p 55 Ap '60
LA NUIT D'UN NEURASTHÉNI-
QUE, opera
Gambetta, Rosario. (Review.)
GDC n 263-4 p 485 Mr 11'60
NUITS DE SCEAUX 1960
Chamfray, Claude. (Programme;
Lycette Darsonval.) GDC n 274
p 726 My 27'60
NUKET, play
Helsinki notes; Paavo Haavikko.
WP v 12 n 3 p 28 D '60
NYS, ABBE CARL de (1917?-).
Le nouveau palais du Festival
de Strasbourg. GDC n 286 p 200-
1 O 28'60
---(On sacred music recordings.)
HF v 10 n 6 p 20 Je '60

O

O ERMITAO DA GLORIA, opera
Republicano, Assis; Brazil note.
Op v 11 n 5 p 344 My '60
O PAGADOR DE PROMESSAS,
play
Brazil notes; Dias Gomes. WP
v 12 n 2 p 19 N '60
OAKLAND SYMPHONY ORCHES-
TRA
Criticism; Gerhard Samuel. MC
v 161 n 5 p 24 Ap '60
---Samuel, Gerhard, director;
repertory; budget. MC v 162 n 6
p 25 D '60
OBITUARIES
Notes: Adam Fendt, 1915-1960;
Giorgio Polacco, 1875-1960;
David Allen ?-1960. Op v 11 n 6
p 434-5 Je '60
---Adam W. Stuebling 1876-1960;
Joseph A. Pipen 1885-1960. IM
v 59 n 3 p 34 S '60
---Albert A. Saunders; Hugh Com-
isky; Virgil Van Cleef,

---Linda Canetti, 1878-1960;
Armando Agnini, 1885-1960;
Siemen Jongsma, 1915-1960;
Joseph Farrington, 1882-1960;
Lucrezia Bori, 1888-1960. Op
v 11 n 7 p 496 Jl '60
---Louis Cahuzac, 1879-1960;
Louis Hillier, 1868-1960; Vasa
Prihoda, 1900-1960; Mark Ham-
bourg, 1879-1960; Alberto Bim-
boni, 1883-1960; Clarence Cam-
eron White, 1880-1960; Edward
Burlingame Hill 1872-1960;
Lawrence Tibbett, 1896-1960;
Désiré Defauw 1886-1960; Hans
Lange, 1894-1960; Oscar Ham-
merstein, 1895-1960; Rudolf
Moser, 1892-1960. GDC n 284
p 121-3 O 14'60
---Mack Harrell, 1909-1960;
Leonard Warren, 1912-1960;
Eduard Habich 1882-1960 (one
picture as Alberich). Op v 11
n 5 p 359 My '60
---Mario Lanza, 1921?-1959;
Fernanda Raspardi, 1862-1960,
Fernanda Raspardi, 1862-1960;
Mack Harrell, 1909-1960; Jac-
ques F. Renard, 1873-1960; Al-
exander Benois, 1870-1960. ON
v 24 n 18 p 29 Mr 5'60
---Mary D'Aneiro, 1871-1959;
Fernanda Rapisardi, 1861-1960;
Heinrich Köhler-Helffrich; An-
tenore Reali, 1898-1960; Ettore
Parmeggiani, 1896-1960; Al-
essandro Benois. Op v 11 n 4
p 292 Ap '60
---Paul Miche 1886-1960; Aline
Samat-Mikaelly, 1867-1960;
Jussi Bjorling, 1907-1960;
Dino Borgioli, 1891-1960; Ch-
arles Denizot, 1887-1960; Ketty
Lapeyrette, ?-1960. GDC n 286
p 187 O 28'60
---Ralph A. Pensyl 1896-1959;
Samuel S. Gelfer 1901-1959;
Otto K. Schill, 1863-1959; Har-
old Gibson Davidson, 1893-1959.
IM v 58 n 8 p 45 F '60
---Robert Bory, 1890-1960; Ida
Rubinstein; Fernand Warms,
1903-1960; Henri Crolla, 1920-
1960; Bonaventura Somma

1893-1960. GDC n 288 p 261
N 11'60
---Vasily Nebolsin, 1888-1959;
Hubert Marischka, 1881-1959;
Willi Wissiak, 1878-1960; Leila
Megane ; Ferruccio Negrelli, 1901-
1960; Constantin Joukowitsch,
1895-1960; Emma Romagnoli,
1872-1960. Op v 2 n 3 p 220 Mr'60
---Stuart M. Chambers 1888-1960;
Dino Borgioli, 1891-1960; Isaac
Louis Myers, 1898-1960; Joseph
Gregor, 1888-1960. ON v 25 n 4
p 33 D 3'60
OBERLIN, RUSSELL, 1928-,
  singer
  Notes; b. Akron, Ohio. AmM
  v 8 n 6 p 7 Jl '60
---As Prince in liturgical drama,
  The Play of Daniel, AP wl ph:
  Denis de Marney. AmM v 8 n 6
  p 9 Jl '60
OBRY, OLGA. Brazil (theatre
  report). il   WT v 9 n 4 p 352-4
  Winter '60
O'CASEY, SEAN (1884-). Letter
  on the Irish theatre (when during
  Irish Tostal Week, no O'Casey
  was to be played). Th Arts v 44
  n 2 p 8 F '60
--- ---"Out, Damned Spot" (on
  present "cry of isolation" of the
  playwright who conceitedly loves
  not an audience; on opinions in
  plays) por Th Arts v 44 n 5 p 20-2
  My '60
--- ---The drums of Father Ned
  (text of the play, cast of Lafayette
  Little Theatre, Indiana 1959).
  Th Arts v 44 n 5 p 23-52 My '60
---Coston, Herbert. Sean O'Casey:
  prelude to playwriting. TDR v 5
  n 1 p 102-112 S '60
---Por phs: W. Suschitzky. Th
  Arts v 44 n 5 cover, p 21 My '60
ODE, JAMES A. Army band oppor-
  tunities. IM v 58 n 7 p 18 Ja '60
ODETS, CLIFFORD, 1907-,
  playwright
  Por ph. Th Arts v 44 n 9 p 20
  S '60
O'DWYER, G. R. "GERRY",
  manager
  Australian notes. por MD v 51

215

(O'Dwyer)
n 3 p 29 S '60
OEDIPUS REX, play
Ankara, ens AP wl ph. WP v 11
n 6 Ap '60
---London, 1960, ens AP wl ph.
David Sim. WT v 9 n 2 p 185
Summer '60
OEDIPUS-REX, opera-oratorio
Paris; Jean Cocteau venir lui-
même présenter son Oedipus-
Rex; Janine Collard, Rèmi Cor-
azza, etc. GDC n 291 p 255-6
D 2'60
---Sadler's Wells review. ON
v 24 n 23 p 26 Ap 9'60
--- ---"brilliantly successful".
Op v 2 n 3 p 230 Mr '60
---Maurin, Louis, as Tiresias,
ens AP wl ph: Brussels, MC
v 161 n 7 p 15 Je '60
---Sadler's Wells, ens AP wl ph:
David Sim. Op v 2 n 3 p 230
Mr '60
---Sante Fe Opera review; Stra-
vinsky conducting, Paul Franke
and Mary MacKenzie. MC v 162
n 2 p 4 Ag '60
OEDIPUS DER TYRANN, opera
Stuttgart; Orff "rejected by the
influential German press";
review. Op v 2 n 3 p 209 Mr'60
---Orff; ens AP wl ph: Weizsäcker,
1959. WT v 9 n 3 p 221 Autumn
'60; same. Op v 2 n 3 p 210
Mr '60
OELLIG, YOLANDE, singer
Bruyr, José. Paris review.
GDC n 265-6 p 527 Mr 25'60
OF THEE I SING, musical
Ens AP wl ph: 1931. Th Arts
v 44 n 9 p 24 S '60
OGINSKI, PRINCE MICHAL KL-
EOFAS, 1765-1833, composer
Golos, George S. Some Slavic
predecessors of Chopin. Mus Q
v 46 n 4 p 437-447 O '60
OH, KAY! musical
NYC; 1926 revived by Bertram
Yarborough; notes. PlM v 37 n 1
p 10 O '60
---Phillips, Eddie, and the girls,
ens AP hl ph. Th Arts v 44 n 6
p 9 Je '60

OHANA, MAURICE, composer
Première: Llanto por Ignacio
Sanchez Mejias, d'apres F. Gar-
cia Lorca; récitant baryton et
ensemble vocal; Paris. GDC
n 265-6 p 525 Mr 25'60
O'HARRA, MICHAELA
As first director of New Drama-
tist's Committee; its structure,
1948 on. Th Arts v 44 n 7 p 17,
20, 63-4 Jl '60
OHEL THEATRE
Israel notes. WP v 12 n 3 p 4
D '60
OHIO COMMUNITY THEATRE
ASSOCIATION
Notes. PlM v 36 n 5 p 101 F '60
OISTRAKH, DAVID, 1908-, violinist
Berthoumieux, Serge. Orchestre
National de la Radio-diffusion
television française; David Ois-
trakh review. GDC n 267-8
p 556 Ap 8'60
---Los Angeles review. MC v 161
n 3 p 37 F '60
OJETTI, UGO, 1871-1946, librettist
Morini, Mario. Ojetti, librettista
per una volta. il La Scala n 122
p 128-32 Ja '60
---E Ottorino Respighi, wl ph:
1933. La Scala n 122 p 29 Ja '60
O'KEEFE CENTRE, TORONTO
Henderson, V. L. Acoustic con-
siderations at the O'Keefe Centre.
drawings CMJ v 4 n 4 p 25-32
Summer '60
OKINAWA play
Tokyo notes; Uchimura Nayoa.
WP v 11 n 9 p 9 Jl '60
OKLAHOMA CITY SYMPHONY
May, Louis. (Conductor, Guy
Fraser Harrison, and recent
programs.) MC v 161 n 3 p 35
F '60
OLEFSKY, PAUL, 1926-, cellist
London notes; b. Chicago. AmM
v 8 n 8 p 6 S '60
OLIVERO, MAGDA, 1914-, singer
Story of her replacing Tebaldi,
San Carlo's opening, in the role
of Adriana Lecouvreur. ON v 24
n 11 p 26 Ja 16'60
OLIVIER, SIR LAURENCE, 1907-,
actor

And Anthony Quinn in Becket,
AP hl ph: Friedman-Abeles.
Th Arts v 44 n 12 p 9 D '60
---And Charlton Heston in re-
hearsal of The Tumbler, hl
ph: Friedman-Abeles. Th Arts
v 44 n 3 p 13 Mr '60
---In Becket, ens AP wl ph:
Friedman-Abeles, 1960. WT
v 9 n 4 p 368 Winter '60
---Por ph: 1933. Th Arts v 44
n 9 p 61 S '60
OLIVER, play
Ens ph: A. Murray, 1960. WT
v 9 n 3 p 292 Autumn '60
OLSHANSKY, LUDWIG, pianist
Notes; b. NYC. AmM v 8 n 4
p 7 Ap '60
---Paris; "un peu prématuré".
GDC n 271 p 628 My 5'60
OLVIS, WILLIAM, 1928-, singer
As the Steersman in The Flying
Dutchman, AP ph: Melançon. ON
v 24 n 18 p 17 Mr 5'60
OMAHA SYMPHONY
Levine, Joseph, conductor; re-
port. MC v 161 n 7 p 32 Je '60
OMAHA YOUTH SYMPHONY
Levine, Joseph; notes. IM
v 59 n 5 p 24 N '60
OMBRES LUNAIRES (SKIBINE),
ballet
A l'Opéra-Comique; Maurice
Tassart notes. GDC n 277
p 812 Je 17'60
---L'Opéra-Comique; notes. MC
v 162 n 1 p 31 Jl '60
---Paris notes. WP v 11 n 10
p 3 Ag '60
ON YOUR TOES, musical
Bolger and Tamara Geva, AP
ph: 1936. Th Arts v 44 n 9 p 25
S '60
ONCE UPON A MATTRESS
(LAYTON), musical
Martin, Mary. (Its NYC and tour
history.) por Th Arts v 44 n 7
p 21-4 Jl '60
---Melbourne version; Joy Grisold
the Queen and Gloria Dawn the
Princess. MD v 50 n 8 p 28
F '60
---NYC cast; libretto; portfolio.
Th Arts v 44 n 7 p 25-50 Jl'60

---Three ens AP wl phs: Friedman-
Abeles. Th Arts v 44 n 7 p 31
Jl '60
ONE MORE RIVER, play
Cross, Beverly; London review.
PlM v 36 n 5 p 117 F '60
---London notes; Beverley Cross.
WP v 11 n 4 p 12 F '60
ONE THIRD OF A NATION, play
Federal Theatre 1938, ens AP
wl ph: NYC. Th Arts v 44 n 9
p 17 S '60
ONE WAY PENDULUM play
London; Royal Court Theatre re-
view. il Th Arts v 44 n 4 p 14
Ap'60
--- ---notes; N. F. Simpson. WP
v 11 n 6 p 12 Ap '60
O'NEILL, EUGENE, 1888-1953,
dramatist
Hofmannsthal, Hugo von. Eugene
O'Neill; trans. Barrett H. Clark.
TDR v 5 n 1 p 169-173 S '60
---Parks, Edd Winfield. Eugene
O'Neill's quest. TDR v 4 n 3
p 99-107 Mr '60
ONLY IN AMERICA, play
Golden, Harry, principal charac-
ter, as played by Nehemiah Per-
soff. PlM v 36 n 6 p 138 Mr '60
ONTWRICHT (FLIER), ballet
Pays-Bas; music, Henk Badings.
WP v 12 n 1 p 9 O '60
OPERA
Aix-en-Provence; 1960 reviews.
il La S n 129-30 p 40, 74 Ag-S '60
--- ---reviews. Op v 11 p 31-4
Autumn '60
---Aldeburgh Festival 1960. Op
v 11 Autumn '60
---Andersen, Rune (1946-). My
opera, Nightman's Children or
Nattmannens Barn. ON v 24 n 20
p 15, 32 Mr 19'60
---Anthony, James R., and Eugene
T. Conley. Readers Theatre ap-
proach to opera (University of
Arizona experiment in "operalo-
gues" in street clothes, piano and
props). MEJ v 46 n 4 p 64, 67
F-Mr '60
---Arundell, Dennis, on his re-
staging of La Tosca. il Op v 11
n 4 p 262-5 Ap '60

(Opera)
---Australia; Die Kluge by the
National Theatre and Fine Arts
Society of Tasmania and the
Elizabethan Theatre Trust.
MD v 50 n 8 p 14 F '60
---Un Ballo in Maschera: sev-
eral critics in an issue devoted
to this Verdi opera. il Ver n 1
n 1 Ap '60
---Bamboschek, Giuseppe. What
about televised opera? Cost
factor a brake. MC v 162 n 4
p 9 O '60
---Bauch, Jason Norman. (Am-
ahl and the Night Visitors, Me-
notti opera, used as school
project in Long Island, New
York.) MEJ v 47 n 1 p 112-4
S-O '60
---Bayreuth 1960; reviews. il
Op v 11 p 34-47 Autumn '60
--- ---The Ring; a review by
Edward Downes; an interview
with Wolfgang Wagner who was
responsible for the tetralogy.
por ON v 25 n 2 p 23-5 O 29'60
---Béatrice et Bénédict of Berlioz, a lovely condensation of
Much Ado; review of University
College, London. Op v 11 n 4
p 304 Ap '60
---Bergamo reviews. il La S
n 133 p 65, 99 D '60; same. LaS
n 132 p 45, 79 N '60
---Bing, Rudolf. (On inter-relation
of art and economics in today's
theatre.) por Th Arts v 44 n 3
p 54 Mr '60
--- ---Thoughts for a twenty-
fifth birthday (of the Metropolitan Opera Guild). ON v 25 n 1
p 14-5 O 8'60
---Bloch's Macbeth; analytical
review of University of California's American première
by Paul H. Little. Op v 11 n 6
p 411 Je '60
---Boll, André. France (short
report). WT v 9 n 1 p 74
Spring '60
---Bologna; Turandot; Lohengrin.
La S n 123 p 38 F '60
---Bortnyansky (1751-1825);

criticism. MR v 21 n 2 p 107-113
My '60
---Boston; expanding programs;
notes on Moriarty's new group,
The Boston Repertory Opera; and
others. MC v 161 n 5 p 24 Ap '60
---Bregenz; outdoor operas. Op
v 11 p 73-6 Autumn '60
---British 1960, summary: compan-
ies, new productions; finances
even tenth year of the periodical,
Opera, notes. Op v 11 n 12 p 796
D '60
---Britten's A Mid-Summer Night's
Dream; première reviewed. MC
v 162 n 2 p 22 Ag '60
---Brown, Tom, manager of opera
for the Elizabethan Trust: report.
por MD v 51 n 3 p 14 S '60
---Brownlee, John. Making the
opera workshop work. MC v 162
n 4 p 8 O '60
---Budapest; Opera di Stato. il
La S n 129-30 p 41, 77 Ag-S '60
---Buenos Aires report: Lucia di
Lammermoor, Rigoletto, La
Tosca, Norma. ON v 24 n 9 p 30
Ja 2'60
---Bulgaria; notes on singers and
roles over Europe. WM n 6 p 131
D '60
---Burke, Anthony. The Bartered
Bride on Australian TV; the Vic-
torian Symphony under Dr. Clive
Douglas; Elsie Morison, Victor
Franklin; choreographer, Rex Reid.
MD v 51 n 2 p 15 Ag '60
---Calendars for 1959-60 season:
La Scala, Milan; Naples, San Carlo;
Palermo, Teatro Massimo; Mon-
aco; Portugal. Op v 11 n 1 p 49-52
Ja '60
---The Canadian Opera Company,
1959-60; reviews. CMJ v 4 n 4
p 48-51 Summer '60
---Castiglioni, Vittorangelo. Tea-
tro alla Scala. portfolio La S
n 126 p 30-3 My '60
---Catania; notes on Elisir d'amore;
Puritani; Turandot. il La S n 125
p 52 Ap '60
---Chile; Italian works. ON v 24
n 9 p 28-9 Ja 2'60
---Cologne; week of contemporary

work reviewed by Wolfgang Nölter. Op v 11 n 8 p 557-8 Ag '60

--- ---Municipal opera; reviews by Everett Helm; MR v 21 n 3 p 243-4 Ag '60

--- ---Opera House; report. HF v 10 n 5 p 24 My '60

---Colón Theatre; reviews of Tannhäuser; Walkiria; Il Trovatore; Proserpina and the Foreigner. MC v 162 n 6 p 32-3 D '60

---Cushing, Mary Walkins. Mooncalves (Cherubino, Octavian, Frederick in Mignon, Oscar in A Masked Ball). ON v 24 n 12 p 6-7 Ja 23'60

--- ---The good companions (in librettos always a confidante or faithful servant). ON v 24 n 10 p 6-7 Ja 9'60

---Discography of operas and operettas, arranged by record companies. MC v 162 n 4 p 23 O '60

---The Dresden Opera, 1872-1913 under Ernst von Schuch. il Op v 11 n 1 p 7-15 Ja '60

---Dublin's Grand Opera Society; report. Op v 2 n 3 p 202 Mr'60

---East Berlin's Komische Oper under Walter Felsenstein. portfolio ON v 25 n 6 p 12-5 D 17'60

---Eckstein, Pavel. Spettacoli d'opera in Cecoslovacchia. il La S n 129-130 p 42, 78 Ag-S'60

---Edinburgh Festival 1960; opera reviews: I Puritani; Falstaff: La Voix Humaine; Arlecchino; Il Segreto di Susanna. Op v 11 p 62-4 Autumn '60

---Editorial on Covent Garden and Sadler's Wells; progress report. Op v 11 n 9 p 594 S '60

---Education; Metropolitan Opera Guild: the Speakers Bureau. ON v 25 n 5 p 3 D 10'60

---Eighteenth century Italian operas in la Piccola Scala, also on radio; Ricordi taping these; notes. HF v 10 n 6 p 14, 16 Je '60

---Electronic; notes on performance of "Stacked Deck", the first electronic opera. MC v 161 n 7 p 25 Je '60

---Le Fantôme de l'Opéra, pseud. (Commentaire). GDC 1960

---Festival dell'Opera di Monaco 1961; Opera di Stato Bavarese; dal 7 agosto al 9 settembre 1960; Rudolf Hartman; repertory. LaS n 127 inset Je '60

---Figaro polled at five Metropolitan performances: 6, 129 voted fpr Italian, 2, 952 for English, 22 for German. Op v 11 n 5 p 339 My '60

---The first High School Opera Festival, University of Arkansas; report. MC v 161 n 5 p 34 Ap'60

---Fleming, Shirley. Report on New York conference; regional production; future in US; Kansas City solution of costs. HF v 10 n 6 p 28 Je '60

---Fort Worth; Manon; review. MC v 161 n 6 p 30 My '60

---France: Paris; Enghien-les-Bains; Lyon; Mulhouse; Orange; Strasbourg; notes. Op v 11 n 11 p 762-4 N '60

---Gambetta, Rosario. Les sept chansons (Malipiero); La nuit d'un neurasthénique (Riccardo Bacchelli-Nino Rota); La Mavra (Stravinsky). GDC n 263-4 p 485 Mr 11'60

---Germany; reports and a forecast of 1960-61. Op v 11 n 9 p 619-626 S '60

--- ---reports from Augsburg; Düsseldorf; Mainz; Munich; Nuremberg; Stuttgart; Wiesbaden. Op v 11 n 11 p 764-7 N '60

--- ---Austria and Switzerland in German 1959-60: Verdi 2, 267 performances in 170 houses, Wagner 193 performances in 46 houses. Ver v 1 n 2 preface Ag'60

--- ---today. WT v 9 n 3 p 213-226 Autumn '60

---Glyndebourne 1960; reviews. il Op v 11 Autumn '60

--- ---week-end course: Opera-Classical, Romantic and Modern . Op v 11 n 6 p 403-6 Je '60

---Goldovsky, Boris. Touring the opera. por MC v 162 n 4 p 15 O'60

(Opera)
---Goodwin, Noël. England: New opera (Macbeth, The Trojans, Parsifal). MC v 161 n 7 p 13 Je '60
---Goth, Trudy. Center opera di New York. il La S n 126 p 36, 70 My '60
--- ---(Vienna Festival reviews.) il La S n 129-30 p 39 Ag-S '60
---Great Britain; notes on various coming events. Op v 11 n 8 p 544 Ag '60
---Grenoble; under M. Pierre Gerbal; repertory, casts. GDC n 263-4 p 481 Mr 11'60
---Grieg's Peer Gynt; story of unfinished opera. ON v 24 n 10 p 26, 28 Ja 9'60
---Hadjiev, Parashkev, composer, review of opera, The Madcap, Sofia, Bulgarian National Opera. Op v 11 n 6 p 415 Je '60
---Hamburg, State Opera House; selections of opera and other music for youth from the city's schools. WM n 1 p 9 F '60
---Haydn in the field of opera, critical study by Ronald Eyer. por ON v 24 n 12 p 10-1 Ja 23 '60
---Holland Festival 1960; reviews. Op v 11 p 25-29 Autumn '60
---In English; notes on EMI 3-year contract; notes. HF v 10 n 2 p 22 F '60
---The Italian houses with good illustrations. La S 1960
---Italy; each issue. La S 1960
--- ---reports by cities. Op v 11 1960
--- ---reports from Bergamo; Cagliari; Enna; Jesi; Leghorn; Lugano; Rome; Trapani. Op v 11 n 11 p 767-8 N '60
---Japan; report by Burton E. Martin; Japanese cast for Die Meistersinger. ON v 25 n 7 p 29 D 24'60
---Joint conference of the Central Opera Service and the National Opera Association; NYC report. ON v 24 n 24 p 13, 22 Ap 16'60

---Julien, A. M. Bilan et projets. OpP n 19 p 3 1960
---Kallman, Chester. (On bel canto; on opera buffa.) il ON v 25 n 7 p 9-13 D 24'60
---Klees, Jay. Organizing an opera audience. Op v 11 n 10 p 671-3 O '60
---Kodály's Háry János, first staged US performance at Juilliard School. portfolio J Rev v 7 n 2 p 26-7 Spring '60
---Korngold, Erich Wolfgang, 1897-1957; operas. ON v 24 n 20 p 13 Mr 19'60
---Larson, Orville K. Rolf Gérard's scene designs for opera. il PlM v 36 n 6 p 130-2 Mr '60
---Lausanne; 5th festival of Italian opera. Op v 11 n 1 p 45-6 Ja '60
---Ledain, Freddy. Théâtre Royal de Liège: L'Elixir d'Amour; Dialogues des Carmélites. GDC n 263-4 p 483 Mr 11'60
---Le Fon, James C. On opera singers of the past and the present as equated by Alan Wagner. HF v 10 n 4 p 22 Ap '60
---Leipzig; the new building in detail by Kunz Nierade; repertory; the new Meistersinger. Op v 11 n 12 p 802-11 D '60
---Lingg, Ann M. Opera manners (latecomers, conversation during music, inappropriate dress). ON v 25 n 7 p 30 D 24'60
---Lithuania; Kaunas Opera notes. Op v 11 n 4 p 286 Ap '60
---London calendar; last page each issue. Op 1960
--- ---Italian Opera at Adelphi Theatre: La Bohème; L'Elisir d' Amore ("best forgotten"). Op v 11 n 2 p 151-2 F '60
--- ---Princes Theatre, an Italian company; conductor, Franco Mannino; reviews. Op v 11 n 12 p 852-3 D'60
--- ---reports. MC v 161 n 3 p 45 F '60
--- ---reviews at Covent Garden and Sadler's Wells. MC v 162 n 6 p 29 D '60
--- ---series for youth, under

Sir Robert Mayer; "Your Opera Nights". WM n 1 p 10 F '60
---Los Angeles; report. MC n 161 n 6 p 28 My '60
---Lubiana; Il diario dalla casa morta; Il Revisore. il La S n 124 p 37 Mr '60
---McClure, Theron R. (How to get the new operas we need.) ON v 24 n 12 p 12-2 Ja 23'60
---McKee, J. H. The symphonic element in opera. MR v 21 n 1 p 30-37 F '60
---Maggio Musicale Fiorentino, eight works; review. Op v 11 p 17-21 Autumn '60
---Marek, George R. Live opera vs. recorded. ON v 25 n 3 p 9, 30 N 19'60
---La Maschera, pseud. Ridotto. La Scala 1960
---May Festival, Wiesbaden reviews. Op v 11 p 64-7 Autumn'60
---(Merkling, Frank.) The grass is greener (a survey of US opera growth; groups; television; premières). il ON v 25 n 3 p 12-5 N 19'60
---Metropolitan; notes on benefit evenings. ON v 25 n 6 p 2-3 D 17'60
--- ---NYC reviews. MC 1960
---Mezzadri, Ugo. Massimo Bellini di Catania. il La S n 126 p 35, 61 My '60
--- ---Teatro Massimo Bellini di Catania: Santa Giovanna al rogo (Honegger). La S n 124 p 35 Mr '60
---Milan; notes on Fedora; Mignon; La Bohème. il La S n 131 p 29, 59 O '60
---Montevideo; note on German Opera Group under A. Kranhals. MC v 161 n 3 p 46 F '60
---Moor, Paul. Our operatic expatriates. HF v 10 n 11 p 50-2 N '60
---Mozart discography. HF v 10 n 11 p 56-7 N '60
---Munich Festival 1960; reviews. Op v 11 p 54-61 Autumn '60
--- ---fifty years ago as described by Ernest de Weerth. ON

v 24 n 16 p 11, 23 F 20'60
---Naples, Teatro di Corte; reviews. La S n 132 p 46-7 N '60
--- ---Teatro San Carlo reviews. La S 1960
---National Theatre Silver Jubilee Festival; Aida with Jean Marks; Tosca, sung by Alwyn Smith; other Australian singers in the review. MD v 50 n 9 p 21 Mr '60
---Nettl, Paul. (Operas that deal with revolution; critical survey of librettos and composers inspired by liberty.) ON v 24 n 15 p 6-7 F 13'60
---New operas; list of completed and in process. AmM v 8 n 2 p 12 F '60
---NYC joint conference of Central Opera Service and National Opera Association; programs. MC v 161 n 5 p 38 Ap '60
---One-night revivals discussed by Alan Rich (for concert productions) and Robert Herman (production schedule forbids concert revivals). ON v 25 n 5 p 21 D 10'60
---Opinion (in letters) on (1) opera in English, pro and con; (2) imported singers in Covent Garden vs. homegrown. Op v 11 n 2 p 127-130 F '60
---Osborne, Conrad L. (The philosophy of Wagner's Ring: "man's most disastrous failing lies in his inability to accept himself".) ON v 24 n 16 p 4-5 F20'60
--- ---(why does America not have opera as does Europe?) HF v 10 n 11 p 45 N '60
---Pannain, Guido. L'Opera (Un Ballo in Maschera); II. Ver v 1 n 2 p 679-703 Ag '60
---Paris; account of the houses; cost of seats; audiences; poor programs for sale. ON v 24 n 14 p 13 F 6'60
---Parsifal; background articles. ON v 24 n 23 Ap 9'60
---Peltz, Mary Ellis. Festival diary. il ON v 25 n 1 p 20-1 O 8'60
---Petit, Pierre. Les droits du

221

(Opera)

répertoire. OpP n 19 p 48 1960
---Philadelphia; critical reports
from the Philadelphia Grand
and the Philadelphia Lyric. ON
v 25 n 8 p 29 D 31'60
--- ---Grand Opera; critical
notes. MC v 161 n 3 p 40 F '60
--- ---reviews. MC v 161 n 5
p 20 Ap '60
---Pittsburg; Civic Light Opera
under William Wymetal; repertory. MC v 161 n 7 p 34 Je '60
---Plinkiewisch, Helen. Opera
in the sixth grade (her productions). il MEJ v 47 n 1 p 96-7
S_O'60
---Poland trends. ON v 24 p 9 p 29
Ja 2'60
---Poulenc's La Voix Humaine;
criticism. il Op v 11 n 8 p 527-
534 Ag '60
---Preparation of a role; Frank
Guerra interview. il ON v 25
n 7 p 14-5 D 24'60
---Der Prinz von Homburg; analysis (with 4 pictures from Ham-
burg). Op v 11 n 7 p 457-461
Jl '60
---Proserpina and the Foreigner;
Buenos Aires review. MC v 162
n 6 p 33 D '60
---Puppet opera theatre at the
Kungsholm Scandinavian Res-
teraunt in Chicago. il ON v 24
n 17 p 12-3 F 27'60
---Purcell's Fairy Queen as pro-
duced at the University of Notting-
ham 1960; review by Percy J.
Hitchman, drawings and photo-
graphs. Th Notbk v 14 n 3 p 92-
99 Spring '60
---Reports: Marseille; Mulhouse;
Toulon; Rouen; Metz; Rennes.
GDC n 265-6 p 519-21 Mr 25'60
--- ---Nimes; Nice; Toulon; Reims;
Marseille and Rennes, operas
and operettas. GDC n 259-60
p 400-2 F 12'60
--- ---Reims; Rennes; Lyon; Mar-
seille; Dijon; Nice. GDC n 261-2
p 435 F 26'60
---Rinaldi, Mario. Teatro dell
'Opera di Roma. il La S n 126

p 34, 59 My '60
---Rio de Janeiro report. Op v 11
n 10 p 686-7 O '60
---Le Roi David à l'Opéra de Paris.
il OpP n 19 p 16-9 1960
---Rome; Teatro dell'Opera re-
views. La S 1960
---Rosamunde Floris; Blacher not-
es. WP v 12 n 2 p 23 N '60
---Rosenthal, Harold. Two Centuries of opera at Covent Garden; and
Hope-Wallace's A Picture History
of Opera (2 book reviews). PlM
v 37 n 2 p 38-9 N '60
---Rossellini, Renzo. (Opera in
Italy.) ON v 24 n 21 p 15, 32
Mr 26'60
---Sadler's Wells: Andrea Chénier,
La Cenerentola; Katya Kabanova,
reviews. ON v 24 n 13 p 26-7
Ja 30'60
---Saltman, Pauline. Phantoms
of the opera (singers' tales of
ghosts on stage). ON v 24 n 14
p 6-7 F 6'60
---Salzburg Festival 1960 in its
new opera house; reviews. MC
v 162 n 3 p 7 S '60
--- ---reviews. Op v 11 p 47-53
Autumn '60
---Saxe, Serge. Houston's Die
Walküre under Walter Herbert.
Op v 11 n 4 p 271 Ap '60
---La Scala; Joseph Wechsberg
in a behind-the-scenes tour; "a
well-run opera house can never
be a democracy". HF v 10 n 11
p 46-9 N '60
--- ---stagione lirica 1959-60
(maestri concertatori e direttori;
cantanti; primi ballerini). La S
1960
--- ---Stravinsky's Mavra Malipiero's Sette Canzoni and Rota's
La notte di un nevrastenico; notes.
il La S n 124 p 28-9 Mr '60
--- ---reviews. La S 1960
---Schoenberg's Erwartung; London criticism. Op v 11 n 6 p 439
Je '60
---Schultze, Friedrich. Crisis in
opera? Crisis in the repertory.
WP v 11 n 8 p 1 Je '60
---Spoleto Festival reviews. Op

v 11 p 30 Autumn '60

---Stedman, Jane W. A dose from Dulcamara (plots in opera that involve love portion and such.) ON v 25 n 7 p 17-9 D 24'60

---Supervia, Conchita, 1895-1936; career sketch. il Op v 11 n 1 p 16-23 Ja '60

---Taylor, Deems. What is American opera? ON v 25 n 6 p 9-11 D 17'60

---Teatro Sociale di Como; Aida; La Sonnambula; La scuola delle mogli. il La S n 125 p 50 Ap'60

---Tel-Aviv; Figaro review. Op v 11 n 4 p 282 Ap '60

---Tenth anniversary of periodical Opera; signed comment on the art, the influence of this periodical upon the art. Op v 11 n 2 p 85-103 F '60

---Toronto Opera Festival report. ON v 25 n 6 p 28 D 17'60

--- ---(12th); notes. MC v 162 n 5 p 29 N '60

---Toulouse, four reviews. GDC n 263-4 p 480 Mr 11'60

---Trieste; reviews. La S 1960

--- ---Teatro Verdi: Carmen (Gloria Lane); La Traviata (Rosanna Carteri). il La S n 124 p 36 Mr '60

---US; company by company, 1960-61 forecast both titles and singers. MC v 162 n 4 p 12-14 O '60

--- ---managers of Metropolitan, Chicago Lyric and San Francisco seek "protective group"; list of fields of co-operation. MC v 161 n 6 p 7 My '60

--- ---12 cities report on the Metropolitan Opera Guild activities. il ON v 24 n 19 Mr 12 '60

--- ---companies; notes on repertory. AmM v 8 n 9 p 14 O '60

--- ---companies, repertories and casts, Nov. 1960-Ap. 1961. ON v 25 n 2 p 30, 33 O 29'60

---Vancouver report. Op v 11 n 10 p 687 O '60

---Vaughan, Denis. Meeting Verdi on his own ground (the scores, manuscript changes not Verdi's own, necessity ot "manually copy" each score). Ver v 1 n 2 preface Ag '60

---Verdi on microgroove; opera by opera; criticism by Conrad L. Osborne. HF v 10 n 1 p 46-9, 95-7 Ja '60

---Verdi's Macbeth; criticism and portfolio. Op v 11 n 4 p 247-256 Ap '60

---Venice; opera in courtyard; Otello. Op v 11 p 72-3 Autumn '60

---Verona Arena: Aida; Cavalleria Rusticana, Pagliacci; La Fanciulla del West. La S n 129-30 p 37, 71 Ag-S '60

--- ---open-air; Aida and other reviews. il Op v 11 p 70-1 Autumn '60

---Vichy; operas, roles, comments. GDC n 283 p 97 O 7'60

---Vienna report. Op v 2 n 3 p 200-2 Mr '60

---La Voix Humaine, Denise Duval's US debut with the American Opera Society; review. MC v 161 n 4 p 19 Mr '60

---Wagner, Alan. The new golden age of opera. il HF v 10 n 1 p 55-7, 120 Ja '60

---Wagner at the Metropolitan, criticism. il Op v 11 n 4 p 268-9 Ap '60

---Warrack, John. Old Germany and new Bayreuth (Wagner characteristic of "heil'ge deutsche Kunst"; the new Bayreuth treatment). il Op v 11 n 11 p 729-737 N '60

---Washington, D.C.; open-air season, repertory, list of singers. Op v 11 n 8 p 546 Ag '60

---Weaver, William. Palermo report; Teatro Massimo as a building. HF v 10 n 11 p 12, 14 N '60

---Weinstock, Herbert. Paris Opéra (sketch with portfolio). ON v 25 n 6 p 22-7 D 17'60

---Winters, Ken. Europe (report). CMJ v 5 n 1 p 39-43 Autumn '60

---Wolff, Stéphane. Lucie de Lammermoor au Palais Garnier.

(Opera)
GDC n 271 p 622 My 5'60
---Yannopoulos, Dino. New ideas
in staging opera. MC v 162 n 4
p 6, 24 O '60
---Zagreb; reviews. La S n 123
p 45 F '60
---Bauernpassion, composer
Winfried Zillig, ens AP wl ph:
Bad Hersfeld. WM n 4 p 82
Ag '60
---Il diario dalla casa morta,
ens AP wl ph; La S n 124 p 37
Mr '60
---Photographs of contemporary
singers, interesting, frequently
not too clear photographically,
not listed but may be found in
La Scala 1960
---Ricci, Marco. The Rehear-
sal of an Opera, ens AP wl
pictures (6) with names of pre-
sent owners of each. Th Notbk
v 14 n 3 Spring '60
---Spoutnik di Berthe Di Vito-
DeLvaux, ens AP wl ph: Bel-
gium. La S n 125 p 91 Ap '60
OPERA, periodical
Tenth birthday issue; signed
messages from artists, offi-
cials, conductors, editors
Op v 11 n 2 p 85-103 F '60
OPERA BUFFA
Kallman, Chester. The beau-
tiful and sharp-witted (on bel
canto; on opera buffa.) ON v 25
n 7 p 9-13 D 24'60
L'OPÉRA DE PARIS
See Paris Opéra
L'OPÉRA DE PARIS, periodical
Della Cortd, A. In guesto mese
ha letto. La S n 129-30 p 44
Ag -S '60
OPERA DI STATO
di Lubiana e Zagabria. il LaS
n 128 p 31 Jl '60
OPERA FOR ALL
Great Britain; touring group
under Art Council; repertory-
Op v 11 n 11 p 752 N '60
THE OPERA GROUP
Caldwell, Sarah, Boston, in
third year; repertory. MC
v 162 n 4 p 16 O '60

OPERA GUILD OF GREATER
MIAMI
Florida; singers. Op v 11 n 10 p 648
O '60
OPERA NEWS, periodical
Re-designed format by Leo Lionni
of "Fortune". ON v 25 n 1 p 1
O 8'60
OPERA '59
See New York Opera Theatre
THE OPERA SOCIETY
Washington, D. C. ; Otello; fourth
season notes. MC v 161 n 6 p 32
My '60
OPÉRA-COMIQUE DE PARIS
Davies, Margaret E. (Bluebeard's
Castle and other Marcel Lamy in-
novations.) ON v 24 n 19 p 26
Mr 12'60
---Demarquez, Suzanne. Reprise
des Noces de Jeannette; création de
la Locandiera par M. Thiriet; cri-
tiques. GDC n 288 p 255 N 11 '60
---Repertory; premières. Op v 11
n 11 p 763 N '60
---Stein, Elliott. Report of opera.
Op v 11 n 8 p 551 Ag '60
---Wolff, Stéphane. Je ne Suis pas
convaincu . . . . . GDC n 274
p 717 My 27'60
---La mille et uniéme de "Butter-
fly". GDC n 259-60 p 399 F 12'60
---La petite histoire: Napoléon III
mélomane. GDC n 263-4 p 479
Mr 11'60
---Le répertoire de l'Opéra-Com-
ique. GDC n 269-70 p 589 Ap 22
'60
---Façade de la Salle Favart, ph.
OpP n 19 p 74 1960
---Scene from Bartók's Barbe
Bleue, AP wl ph: 1958. Th Arts
v 44 n 3 p 45 Mr '60
OPERA-GO-ROUND PLAYERS
Notes; Long Island. MC v 162
n 2 p 8 Ag '60
OPERA-HISTORY AND CRITICISM
Abbiati, Franco. Gli anni del
Ballo in Maschera. Ver v 1 n 2
p 631-656 Ag '60
---Cherubini, Luigi (1760-1842)
as"the first romantic"; criticism
by Margery Stomme Selden. por
ON v 24 n 15 p 12-3 F 13'60

---Gambly, Gavin. Opera in 19th
century life and literature. Op
v 11 n 11 p 738-741 N '60
---Gara, Eugenia. Il cammino
dell'opera in un secolo d'interpretazioni; II. Ver v 1 n 2
p 704-719 Ag '60
---Hamburg Opera; 1890, Pollini
paid damages for refusing ad-
mission to a critic. Op v 11 n 11
p 741 N '60
---Hughes, Spike. Verdi's Macbeth.
Op v 11 n 4 p 247-256 Ap '60
--New Orleans, 1808-1947. ON
v 25 n 5 p 22-5 D 10'60
---Opera, periodical, on its 10th
anniversary reprints criticism
1950-1960; a running comment
on the decade; a compact criticism. Op v 11 n 2 p 107-126
F '60
--- ---Part II; a commentary
on the decade. Op v 2 n 3 p 184-
194 Mr '60
---San Carlo in Naples il ON
v 25 n 7 p 22-7 D 24'60
---Warren, Dale. (Opera memories with a large portfolio of
singers.) ON v 25 n 8 p 8-13
D 31'60
---White, Eric Walter. The Re-
hearsal of an Opera (by Sebas-
tiano and Marco R icci; research
on similar scenes of 18th cen-
tury opera). il Th Notbk v 14
n 3 p 79-90 Spring "60
---Portfolio (16) past singers, in
private life and in stage roles.
ON v 25 n 8 p 9 D 31'60
OPERAS-IN-BRIEF, series
NYC; Town Hall schedule of the
Amato Opera Company. MC
v 162 n 4 p 14 O '60
OPERETTAS
Becq, M. Toulouse; notes.
GDC n 263-4 p 480 Mr 11'60
---Dijon; Bernard Laissus' re-
ports. GDC n 261-2 p 435 F 26'60
--- France; reviews from Nimes,
Marseille, etc. GDC 1960
---Indcox, John F. Reviews, 4
Angel recordings: The Merry
Widow; Lilac Time; Bitter
Sweet; White Horse Inn. HF

v 10 n 6 p 79 Je '60
---The Lady Was a Kitten, Ansonia
Opera Circle, NYC; Fredric Popper.
ON v 24 n 21 p 28 Mr 26'60
---Metz; La Vie Parisienne; La
Belle Hélène. GDC n 267-8 p 552
Ap 8'60
--Reims: Nina Rosa; No No Nan-
nette. GDC n 257-8 p 354 Ja 29'60
---Rennes; Symphonie d'Amour
(1946 casino du Luchon "Sur les
bords de la Garonne"). GDC
n 269-70 p 592 Ap 22'60
---Secret de Marco Polo, Théâtre
du Chatelet; review. MC v 161
n 3 p 44 F '60
OPPICELLI, AURELIO, singer
Metropolitan debut. MC v 161
n 6 p 16 My '60
OGUNQUIT PLAYHOUSE
Maine; exterior ph. Th Arts v 44
n 6 p 20 Je '60
ORATORIOS
Franchel, Blaise. Israel in Egypt
de Haendel; Amis de Mozart; Louis
de Froment, l'Orchestre Radio-
Lyrique; Paris. GDC n 257-8
p 358 Ja 29'60
---Leo, Leonardo, "La morte di
Abele"; della scuola napoletana;
Milano. La S n 124 p 59 Mr '60
---Melbourne; The Seasons of Hay-
dn: Victorian Symphony with the
Royal Melbourne Philharmonic
Society. MD v 50 n 7 p 17 Ja '60
---Nándor féhervár (Belgrade);
Father Aloysius Tamás; State
Opera in Budapest singing; his-
toric codices and florid folk
styles. HF v 10 n 10 p 91 O '60
THE ORCHESTRA OF AMERICA
Contemporary repertory; list.
AmM v 8 n 10 p 15 N '60
---Korn, Richard, director; sec-
ond season notes. AmM v 8 n 9
p 15 O '60
---NYC review; Richard Korn, con-
ducting; Eugene Istomin, pianist.
MC v 161 n 4 p 15 Mr '60
ORCHESTRATION
Stokowski, Leopold, on the un-
necessary complication of pre-
sent scores; "should use soprano
and bass clefs, not alto and tenor";

(Orchestration)
do away with old system of transposition for horns and trumpets. IM v 58 n 11 p 11 My '60

L'ORCHESTRE DES CONCERTS LAMOUREUX
Paris; Igor Markevitch; review. GDC n 276 p 785 Je 10'60

L'ORCHESTRE NATIONAL
Bruyr, José. Paris review; Manuel Rosenthal. GDC n 259-60 p 407 F 12'60
---Demarquez, Suzanne. Première biennale de la Recherche, sous la direction d'Hermann Scherchen. GDC n 278 p 847 Je 24'60
---Mari, Pierrette. Honegger's Antigone (singers listed); Le Roux, conducting. GDC n 287 p 194 O 28'60

L'ORCHESTRE PHILHARMONIQUE D'ISRAEL
Chamfray, Claude. Paris review; Carlo-Maria Giulini. GDC n 285 p 159 O 21'60

L'ORCHESTRE PHILHARMONIQUE DE PARIS
Notes on re-founding under Leon Barzin. MC v 161 n 6 p 33 My '60

L'ORCHESTRE SYMPHONIQUE DE LENINGRAD
Lyon, Raymond. Paris; premières. GDC n 283 p 93 O 7'60
---Mravinsky, Eugen, directeur; Semaines musicales de Paris. GDC n 281-2 p 21-2 S '30'60
---R odjestvenski, Gennadi, directing with Mstislav Rostropovitch, violinist, Paris review by Claude Samuel. GDC n 281-2 p 32-4 S 30'60
---Ens wl ph: Bergamo. La S n 133 p 99 D '60

ORCHESTRAS
Babitz, Sol. Problems of orchestra seating. IM v 59 n 5 p 40 N '60
---Canada; government grants. IM v 58 n 12 p 19 Je '60
---Sir Bernard Heinze's survey for Canade Canada: report. MD v 51 n 3 p 8-9 S '60
---Financial support from US industry: business subsidies

US and Canada: list. IM v 59 n 5 p 20 N '60
---New York City symposium on economic matters of symphony men; central information pool needed; pension as now set up; conditions of foreign government tours; present US conditions; W. McNeil Lowry reporting on Ford Foundation survey. IM v 59 n 3 p 40-1 S '60
---L'Orchestre de la Société Philharmonique de Paris; Léon Barzin; review. GDC n 271 p 628 My 5'60
---L'Orchestre des Cadets Pleyel; several reviews. GDC 1960
---L'Orchestre Lyrique de la R. T. F., dir. Ettore Gracis with Gaspar Cassado; Paris review. GDC n 281-2 p 49 S 30'60
--- ---dir. Manuel Rosenthal; Paris review. GDC n 281-2 p 29-30 S 30'60
---L'Orchestre National de Belgique, André Cluytens; renaissance. GDC n 287 p 233 N 4'60
---L'Orchestra National de L'Opéra de Monte-Carlo dir. Louis Fremaux; Paris review. GDC n 281-2 p 37-8 S 30'60
--- ---Paris review; Louis Frémaux; Stich-Randall; Yordanoff, violoniste. GDC n 285 p 159 O 21'60
---L'Orchestre National de Madrid; directeur, Rafael Fruhbeck de Burgos; Victoria de los Angeles; Paris review. GDC n 289 p 296 N 18'60
--- ---Paris review. GDC n 281-2 p 59 S 30'60
--- ---Paris review; Rafael Fruhbeck de Burgos, directing. GDC n 288 p 254 N 11'60
---L'Orchestre National et Choeurs de la R. T. F., dir. Maurice Le Roux; solistes; Paris review. GDC n 281-2 p 41-2 S 30'60
--- ---dir. Carlos Chavez, with Henryk Szeryng; Paris review. GDC n 281-2 p 31-2 S 30'60
---L'Orchestre Philharmonique de Leningrad, dir. Eugen Mravinsky; Paris reviews by Claude

Samuel. GDC n 281-2 p 21-4 S 30'60

---L'Orchestre Philharmonique d'Israel; directeur, Giulini. GDC n 286 p 194 O 28'60

--- ---dir. Carlo-Maria Giulini; Paris review. GDC n 281-2 p 39 S 30'60

---L'Orchestre Symphonique de Bamberg, dir. Joseph Keilberth; Paris review. GDC n 290 p 322 N 25'60

---L'Orchestre Symphonique de la N. H. K. (Tokyo), dir. Hirozuki Iwaki with Hiroko Nakamura; Paris review. GDC n 281-2 p 27-8 S 30'60

--- ---dir. Paul Klecki with Kietrich Fischer-Dieskau and Maurizio Pollini; Paris review. GDC n 281-2 p 55-6 S 30'60

--- ---Paris review; Hirozuki Iwaki, directing. GDC n 288 p 254 N 11'60

---Paris; under Richard Kraus, L'Opéra Municipal de Berlin-Ouest. GDC n 293-4 p 458 D 16'60

---Paris review of Cologne Orchestra under the Hungarian, Thomas Ungar: Siegerland Orchestra; Paris review. GDC n 275 p 752 Je 3'60

---Performance notes; L'Orchestre Pasdeloup; Lamoureux; Oubradous. GDC n 288 p 257 N 11'60

---Philharmonie de Sofia; Constantin Iliev, conducting; Paris review. GDC n 289 p 296 N 18'60

---Russia; 40-member group made up for Franz Allers for "My Fair Lady"; Rubato timing new, but soon learned; an orchestra inspector for discipline assigned. IM v 59 n 2 p 11 Ag '60

---Seventh Army Symphony; 1952 founded by Samuel Adler; story; methods used to keep sections filled. IM v 59 n 2 p 12-3 Ag '60

---"Symphonic Highlights", an occasional news column. IM '60

---US; Boston Symphony in Far East; tour plan. AmM v 8 n 1 p 17 Ja '60

---list of recipients of $210,000 commission project under American Music Center and Ford Foundation. IM v 58 n 8 p 40 F '60

---news notes in column, Symphony and Opera. IM v 59 n 1 p 18-9 Jl '60

---notes on many; repertory of 6 great orchestras, conductors. AmM v 8 n 9 O '60

---summer jobs; survey of arrangements made by professional musicians to play, sometimes en masse, at summer programs. IM v 58 n 11 p 16, 18 My '60

---Voss, Hermann. The problem of young talent for German orchestras. WM n 4 p 73-4 Ag '60

---Wolff, Stéphane. L'orchestre de l'Opéra de Paris. GDC n 265-6 p 517 Mr 25'60

---Kassel; Radio Frankfurt orchestra, ph: Lengemann. WM n 6 p 136 D '60

---US groups, ensemble phs. IM '60

ORDERING OF MOSES, oratorio
Dett, Nathaniel, composer; Eastman Festival. MC v 161 n 7 p 6 Je '60

ORDINI, periodical
Italy; notes on music and festival coverage; editors. WM n 2 p 33 Ap '60

OREGON SHAKESPEARE FESTIVAL
1960 attendance 42,978; 20th summer notes. PlM v 37 n 2 p 27 N '60

L'ORESTIE D'ÉSCHYLE, play
Théâtre grec de Monjuich, ens AP wl ph: Gausa, Barcelona. WP v 11 n 6 p 1 Ap '60

ORFEO, opera
New York City Opera; Monteverdi décor by Donald Oenslager in early Italiam baroque; Stokowski concucting; notes on cast. Op v 11 n 12 p 815 D '60

--- ---sung by Gérard Souzay; Robert Joffrey, choreographer; Stokowsku, conducting; review.

(Orfeo)
MC v 162 n 5 p 14-5 N '60
ORFEO ED EURYDICE, opera
Gluck under Karajan in Vienna;
criticism. ON v 24 n 12 p 29
Ja 23'60
---Vienna criticism; Parlic's
choreography "uninspired"; Kara-
jan unsatisfying. MC v 161 n 3
p 47 F '60
ORFF, CARL, 1895-, composer
Opera comment. WT v 9 n 3
p 219-20 Autumn '60
---Por ph. La S n 124 p 25 Mr '60
ORGAN
Berthoumieux, Serge. Marie-
Claire Alain; Orchestre de chamb-
re Paul Kuentz; Haerpfer Erman.
GDC n 257-8 p 358 Ja 29'60
---Biggs, E. Power. The Organ
in America (review of Columbia
release, 7 organs and 9 compositions, including Charles Ives'
"variations on America",). HF
v 10 n 11 p 101 N '60
---Convention Hall, Atlantic City
New Jersey; a description of the
two consoles, the larger 1477
stop controls, 1250 stop tablets
and 933 speaking stops. il MEJ
v 46 n 3 p 28 Ja '60
---Dupré, Marcel; Les Amis du
Guide visite de L'orgue de Marcel
Dupré. GDC n 275 p 746 Je 3'60
---Expansion of use: organs in
stratocruisers; return of cinema
theater organ, a trend; in US homes
rise to 500,000 sales a year. IM
v 58 n 7 p 19 Ja '60
---Jourdan-Morhange, H. Concert
d'orgue du Palais de Chaillot
(critique). GDC n 255-6 p 311
Ja 15'60
---Louvet, Michel. Palais de Chaillot; cinq concerts d'orgue; Nor-
bert Dufourcq. GDC n 293-4
p 460 D 16'60
---Periodical, L'Organo; Italian
board listed; twice a year, also
supplement of organ score; notes.
WM n 6 p 132 D '60
---Philadelphia; Academy of Music:
world's largest movable pipe organ; dedication. il MC v 162 n 5

p 20 N '60
---Semin, G. F. Fascino degli
Antichi organi Ticinesi. il La S
n 128 p 36-7 Jl '60
---US; old organs, notes and five
pictures. HF v 10 n 8 p 38-9
Ag '60
---Close-up of the console, Con-
vention Hall, Atlantic City, New
Jersey; interior views, 2 phs.
MEJ v 46 n 3 cover, p 28 Ja '60
---Dedication of new organ at
Academy of Music, Philadelphia:
Samuel Barber, Eugene Ormandy,
Mrs. Efrem Zimbalist, donor,
Paul Callaway, ph: Alan D. Hew-
ott. MC v 162 n 5 p 20 N '60
---Northwest Orient Airline:
playing for passengers 20,000
feet up, ph. IM v 58 n 7 p 37
Ja '60
ORGANISTS
de Tar, Vernon; NYC note. J
Rev v 7 n 1 p 12 Winter 59-60
ORIGINAL DIXIELAND JAZZ BAND
Allen, Edison B. (Its story). il
IM v 59 n 5 p 14-5 N '60
---NYC, ens AP ph: Apeda, 1917.
IM v 59 n 5 p 14 N '60
ORMANDY, EUGENE, 1899-, con-
ductor
Stoddard, Hope. The path of the
artist: Eugene Ormandy. por IM
v 59 n 4 p 20-1 O '60
---Por ph; small AP ph. IM v 59
n 4 cover, p 20 O '60
---Presenting triple-tie winners
with scholarships at the Inter-
national String Congress, spon-
sored by the American Federa-
tion of Musicians, ens ph: Puerto
Rico. IM v 58 n 12 p 11 Je '60
ORPHEUS IN THE UNDERWORLD,
opera
Sadler's Wells review (with 3
scenes, phs: Sim). Op v 11 n 7
p 506-7 Jl '60
ORQUESTA MUNICIPAL OF MON-
TEVIDEO
Estrada, Carlos, conductor; notes
also on the National and on AUCI
orchestras. MC v 161 n 3 p 46
F '60
ORVALHO-LABORDE, CATARINA

Et Charles Ludwig, deux jeunes artistes; commentaire. GDC n 295 p 493 D 30'60
---Winner of Vichy Festival contest; report. MC v 162 n 4 p 26 O '60

OSBORNE, CONRAD L. This above all (the theme of the Ring, its philosophy). ON v 24 n 16 p 4-5 F 20'60
---Verdi on microgroove (with portfolio of Verdi singers, small phs.) HF v 10 n 1 p 46-9, 95-7 Ja '60

OSBORNE, JOAN, dancer
Career notes; b. Australia; married to Norman Bicknell, Melbourne artist. por MD v 50 n 10 p 29 Ap '60

OSLO PHILHARMONIC ORCHESTRA
Notes. MC v 161 n 7 p 17 Je '60

OSSONA, PAULINA, dancer
Career notes; Paris review of expressional dance. TD n 94 p 6 Je '60

OSVATH, JULIA, singer
As Violetta, AP wl ph. La S n 125 p 57 Ap '60

OTANI, KIYOKO, singer
With James Vitale in Yu-Zuru, AP wl ph: Bascome, NYC. ON v 24 n 18 p 27 Mr 5'60

OTELLO, opera
Berlin's Komische Oper; Felenstein's production reviewed. Op v 11 n 2 p 143-4 F '60
---Covent Garden; Uzunov basing his Moor on Vinay. il Op v 11 n 8 p 574 Ag '60
---Gallini, Natale. Note sull'Otello. portfolio La Scala n 122 p 13-21 Ja '60
---La Scala; notes. il La S n 122 p 34 Ja '60
---Teatro la Fenice; Graf's use of the architectural décor, open-air. Op v 11 p 72-3 Autumn '60
---Zurich; cast. il La S n 131 p 30 O '60
---Covent Garden, Act II the Quartet, Uzunov, Maragliano Veasey and Taddei, ens AP wl ph: Donald Southern. Op v 11

n 8 p 575 Ag '60
---Doge's Palace; Act III, ens AP wl ph: Venice. MC v 162 n 3 p 22 S '60
---Komische Oper, Felenstein's production, ens AP wl ph: Simon. Op v 11 n 2 p 144 F '60
---La Scala; Del Monaco, and Tito Gobbi, AP wl ph: Piccagliani. Op v 2 n 3 p 213 Mr '60
---McCracken, James, and Maria di Gerlando, Washington, D. C. , AP wl ph: Finnigan. ON v 24 n 18 p 28 Mr 5'60
---Palazzo Ducale di Venezia; Nino Sanzogno, Erbert Graf; Marcella Pobbe, Mario Del Monaco Tito Gobbi (3 phs). La S n 129-30 p 34-5 Ag-S '60
---Portfolio: Venice. La S n 129-30 p 34-5 Ag-S '60
---L'ultima scena del IV atto, 1887 La Scala; interpreti principali (7). La Scala n 122 p 15-6 Ja '60
---Zurich; Herbert Graf production, ens AP ph: W. E. Baur. ON v 25 n 5 p 28 D 10'60
---See also Le Maure de Venise (Lifar)

OTT, BERTRAND, pianist
Louvet, Michel. Paris criticism. GDC n 267-8 p 564 Ap 8'60

OTTO, TED (1904-). Tristan sets, Metropolitan phs. ON v 24 n 10 p 22 Ja 9 '60

OUR TOWN, play
Interplayers, ens AP wl ph: San Francisco. Th Arts v 44 n 3 p 59 Mr '60

OVERTON, HALL, composer
Première: Sonata for Violin and Piano (NYC 1960). ACAB v 9 n 3 p 33 1960

OVIGNY, ANDRE, violinist
and Madeleine LaCandela; review by Michel Louvet. GDC n 295 p 494 D 30'60

OXENBERG, ALLAN SVEN
Infarmae ph. La S n 133 p 115 D '60

P

PABLO, DE, LUIS. Quatre

229

(Pablo)
inventions, op. 5 (études musicales analytiques). GDC n 285 p 174 O 21'60

PACE, ROBERT. Keyboard experience in the classroom. il MEJ v 46 n 4 p 44-5 F-Mr '60

PACHELBEL, JOHANN, 1653-1706
Owen, Robert, playing organ and harpsichord; Westminister record review. Mus Q v 46 n 3 p 405-7 Jl '60

PACHMANN, LIONEL de, composer-pianist
Criticism; Chopin. GDC n 271 p 627 My 5'60
---Notes. GDC n 295 p 493 D 30'60

PACIFICA FOUNDATION, 1949-
Aims; radio station WBAI, noncommercial, a gift to Pacifica from founder, Louis Schweitzer; listeners cheerfully send in $12 annual fee. HF v 10 n 5 p 18 My '60
---Cause of contemporary music; prizes offered. MC v 161 n 7 p 14 Je '60
---US; radio programs, San Francisco, now NYC. WM n 2 p 33 Ap '60

PACINI DE ALVEAR, REGINA, 1879-, singer
Jones de Schüller, Ana Celina. The Casa del Teatro, home for retired performers, in Buenos Aires, founded by Pacini. Op v 11 n 11 p 786 N '60

PADEREWSKI, IGNACE, 1860-1941, pianist
Chamfray, Claude. Fiche biographique. GDC n 283 p 105 O 7'60
---Notes on painting by Boleslaw Navrocki, preserved by the son; two photographs shown. GDC n 293-4 p 467 D 16'60
---Right profile por ph: Navrocki. GDC n 292 cover D 9'60

PAEAN (GOSOVSKY), ballet
Berlin; Gisela Deege and Klaus Beelitz, AP wl ph. La S n 132 p 51 N'60

PAGANINI, NICCOLO, 1782-1840, violinist

Berri, Pietro. Testimonianze e contributi elvetici su Paganini. il La S n 123 p 13-30 F '60
---Colombo, Gianluigi. Paganini pianista. por La S n 127 p 12-3 Je '60
---Mell, Albert. Review of Paganini's Cantabile and 6 Sonatas for violin and guitar, Boston Records B-213. Mus Q v 46 n 4 p 557-9 O '60
---Vyborny, Zdenek. Paganini as a music critic (trans. Willis Wager). Mus Q v 46 n 4 p 468-481 O '60
---Dantan, Jean-Pierre. Un gesso caricaturale. La S n 123 p 16 F '60
---Kersting, G. Paganini, AP wl ritratto, 1830 La S n 123 p 13 F '60
---Por drawing; and AP wl painting. La S n 127 p 13 Je '60

PAGANINI PRIZE
Genoa; rules for violin contest. MC v 161 n 7 p 14 Je '60

PAGANINI QUARTET
NYC notes; list. MC v 161 n 4 p 20 Mr '60

PAGE, GENEVIEVE, actress
With Gérard Philipe in Les Caprices de Marianne, AP hl ph: Avignon, 1958. Spec n 1 p 58 1960

PAGE, WILLIS, conductor
Career notes; b. Rochester, New York. por IM v 58 n 8 p 33 F '60

PAGENTS
Military Pageant in Madison Square Garden July 1960. AmM v 8 n 3 p 18 Mr '60
---The Procession of the Pénitents at Veure, ens ph: De Mayer. WT v 9 n 1 p 63 Spring '60
---See also Festivals

I PAGLIACCI, opera
Covent Garden; Geraint Evans "a fine Tonio" and Jon Vickers too restrained" a Canio. il Op v 11 n 2 p 154 F '60
---The final words in the original score of Leoncavallo given to Tonio; discussion. Op v 11 n 7 p 467 Jl '60
---Metropolitan cast; notes; décor; discography; portfolio. ON v 24 n 13 Ja 30'60

--- ---Nino Verchi, conducting; review. MC v 161 n 1 p 13 Ja'60

---Ens AP wl ph; also Mario Del Monaco with President Tito, 2 phs: Zagreb. La S n 126 p 37 My '60

PAGODA OF PROMISES, play Brazil; Dias Gomes, playwright. PlM v 37 n 3 p 58 D '60

PAIGE, NORMAN, singer Notes. ON v 25 n 5 p 4 D 10'60

---Hl ph. ON v 25 n 5 p 4 D 10'60

PAINTING Chapallaz, Gilbert. Ilse Voigt, à Lausanne. TD n 97 p 16 N '60

---Geddo, Angelo. L'umore dei decadenti nel solco dell'esperienza pittorica. il La S n 131 p 20-5 O '60

---Lederlé, Janick, peintre de la Danse; à la Galerie des Orfèvres, Paris. TD n 98 p 30 D '60

---Voigt, Ilse; London exhibit. TD n 90 p 21 F '60

---Lederle, Janick. Dancer, painting. TD n 96 p 17 S. O '60

--- Portfolio of color reproductions: Van Gogh, Giacomo Balla, Picasso, Braque, Sironi, Villon, Boccioni, Delaunay, Baumeister. La S n 131 p 20-5 O '60

---Tiepolo. Allegory of Africa, Milan 1740. ON v 25 n 7 p 13 D 24'60

---Venus of the Renaissance by a follower of Botticelli, ph: NYPL. ON v 25 n 6 p 19 D 17'60

PAISIELLO, GIOVANNI, 1740-1816, composer Osborne, Conrad L. First recording of Il Barbiere di Siviglia (Mercury). HF v 10 n 11 p 73-4 N '60

PAKISTAN Bokhari, Z. A. The composer in Pakistan faces new problems. WM n 1 p 4-5 F '60

PALAZZO DUCALE DI VENEZIA Messins, Mario. Otello. il LaS n 129-130 p 34-5 Ag-S '60

PALERMO Castiglioni, Vittorangelo. Musica nuova a Palermo. La S

n 127 p 42 Je '60

PALISCA, CLAUDE V. Vincenzo Galilei and some links between "Pseudo-monody" and monody. Mus Q v 46 n 3 p 344-360 Jl '60

PALLAS ATHENE WEINT, opera Krenek; ens AP wl ph: Peyer. WT v 9 n 3 p 226, Autumn '60

PALOCZ, LASZLO, singer E Maria Matyas in "Simon Boccanegra", AP hl ph: Budapest. La S n 125 p 57 Ap '60

PANAMA McMullan, Frank. Theatre, Panama. Th Arts v 44 n 6 p 66-8 Je '60

---The Mejorana; examples and criticism by Myron Schaeffer. CMJ v 4 n 3 p 4-22 Spring '60

---The Theatre Guild; tenth anniversary notes. Th Arts v 44 n 12 p 69 D '60

PANAMERICA (Balanchine), ballet NYC Ballet; review. MC v 161 n 4 p 46 Mr '60

---NYC notes. MD v 50 n 8 p 32 F '60

PANEGRIS (STRATOU) Au Théâtre des Nations; critique; la danse folklorique Grecque. il TD n 94 p 6 Je '60

PANNAIN, GUIDO (1891-). L'opera (Un Ballo in Maschera). Ver v 1 n 1 p 73-89 Ap '60

--- ---II. Ver v 1 n 2 p 679-703 Ag '60

PANTAGLEIZE, play de M. de Ghelderode, Montreal; ens ph: Henri Paul. WP v 11 n 8 p 1 Je '60

PAPINEAU-COUTURE, JEAN. Canadian composers at Hartford (Hartt College of Music, un premier festival de musique canadienne). CMJ v 4 n 2 p 35-7 Winter '60

LA PARADE, play Bucarest notes; Victor Eftimiu WP v 11 n 9 p 12 Jl '60

PARENTE, ALFREDO (1905-). Difesa di un mestiere; Massimo Mila. por La S n 133 p 72-3 D '60

PARIS Austin, D. W. S. Opera in Paris

(Paris)
(information on the houses, cost, audience and poorly made house programs on sale). ON v 24 n 14 p 13 F 6'60
---Concerts à Paris (regular calendar with the programs to be heard). GDC 1960
---Demarquez, Suzanne. Music report. MC v 161 n 3 p 44 F'60; same. MC v 161 n 5 p 31-2 Ap '60;same. MC v 161 n 6 p 33 My '60;same. MC v 162 n 6 p 31 D '60
---Dumesnil, René. Nostalgie de Montmarte. il LaS n 132 p 39-41 N'60
---Guest, Ivor. (French ballet; books.) MD v 51 n 2 p 26 Ag'60
---Heartz, Daniel. Parisian music publishing under Henry II: A propos of four recently discovered guitar books. il Mus Q v 46 n 4 p 448-467 O'60
---Lamare, Jean-Yves. Un mois de télévision musicale. GDC n 290 p 324-5 N 25'60
---Lenoir, Jean-Pierre. Paris: past, present, prospective. il Th Arts v 44 n 12 p 67, 74 D'60
--- ---Theatre, Paris. Th Arts v 44 n 1 p 24-5 Ja'60
---McMullen, Roy. Recording Brahms' Violin Concerto:Otto Klemperer, David Oistrakh and the Orchestre National de la Radio-diffusion française. HF v 10 n 9 p 26, 28 S'60
---Orchestras reviewed:the Leningrad;Israel Philharmonic; Orchestre National of Monte Carlo;NHK of Tokyo;National Orchestra of Madrid;list of conductors also. MC v 162 n 6 p 31 D'60
---Paris Music Weeks;notes. WM n 4 p 76 Ag'60
---Les Semaines Musicales de Paris 1960;Raymond Lyon's report. WM n 6 p 122-3 D'60; 27 Septembre-26 Octobre;critiques. GDC n 281-2 p 19-59 S 30'60
---Silvant, Jean. Une école de

danse à Paris (critique). TD n 96 p 3-5 S-O '60
---Towarnicki,Frédéric de. Quand Paris découvre Tchékhov. portfolio Spec n 1 p 12-21 1960
---Winters, Ken. The Paris music season 1959-60. CMJ v 4 n 4 p 41-4 Summer '60
PARIS OPERA
Les Amis du Guide: La visite de l'Opéra. il GDC n 259-60 p 394-5 F 12'60
---Durand, Lionel. (New regime; notes on its history, its present ambitions under A. M. Julien.) il Th Arts v 44 n 3 p 42-3 Mr '60
---Les examens de danse de L'Opéra par Jean Silvant. TD n 93 p 3, 20 My '60
---Examination results, a list. TD n 94 p 5 Je '60
---Law, Richard. Lucia di Lammermoor; Joan Sutherland's triumph. Op v 11 n 6 p 418-9 Je '60
---Ravel notes: L'Enfant et les sortilèges; L'Heure Espagnole; Daphnis et Chloé. TD n 92 p 15 Ap '60
---Stein, Elliott. Opera report. Op v 11 n 8 p 550-1 Ag '60; same. Op v 11 n 11 p 762-3 N '60
---Weinstock, Herbert. Great opera houses: Paris. ON v 25 n 6 p 22-7 D 17'60
---Wolff, Stéphane. Comparaisons: 1859, 1909, 1959. GDC n 257-8 p 351-2 Ja 29'60
--- ---Dernières représentations: liste; "Thais (Massenet), 683e et dernière le 20 août 1956", etc. GDC n 267-8 p 549 Ap 8'60
---Nouveaux Engagés, a portfolio. OpP n 19 p 70-1 1960
---Scenes of gala evenings; the exterior of the theatre; portfolios of recent productions OpP n 19 1960
PARIS OPERA HOUSE
Grand Foyer with audience of the last century chatting; and five other building phs: Duane Michaels. ON v 25 n 6 p 24-7

D 17'60
PARISE, GOFFREDO, playwright
La Moglie a Cavallo; Anna No-
gara. La S n 124 p 53 Mr '60
PARISOT, ALDO, 1919-, violin-
celliste
Machuel, Dominique. Paris
concert. GDC n 295 p 489 D 30
'60
PARK LANE OPERA GROUP
Repertory notes. Op v 11 n 5
p 334 My '60
PARKER, LOUISE, singer
London debut; notes; b. Phil-
adelphia. AmM v 8 n 5 p 9 Je'60
PARKS, EDD WINFIELD (1906-).
Eugene O'Neill's quest. TDR
v 4 n 3 p 99-107 Mr '60
PARNAS, LESLIE, 1930-, cellist
Por ph. AmM v 8 n 6 p 9 Jl '60
PARRAVICINI, ANGELO (1925-).
Un Ballo in Maschera, opera,
setting for Act III scene 1, La
Scala 1903, ph. Ver v 1 n 2
Ag '60
PARRIS, ROBERT, 1924-, com-
poser
Première: Trio-1959 (Washing-
ton 1960). ACAB v 9 n 3 p 33 '60
PARSIFAL, opera
Lawrence, Robert. Wagner's
eunuch (Kundry and Klingsor).
ON v 24 n 23 p 4-5 Ap 9'60
---Lingg, Ann M. Meet Titurel
(Parsifal) ON v 24 n 12 p 12-3
Ap 9'60
---Metropolitan Opera cast; story;
background and décor notes; bib-
liography; discography; portfolio.
ON v 24 n 23 Ap 9'60
---La Scala review. il La S n 127
p 24-5 Je '60
---Warrack, John. Bayreuth re-
view. Op v 11 p 39-40 Autumn'60
---Wörner, Karl H.Parsifal at
Bayreuth. CMJ v 4 n 4 p 19-24
Summer '60
---Joukowsky's set 1882; and
Wieland Wagner's production,
2 phs: Bayreuth. Op v 11 n 11
p 732-3 N '60
---Milan Act I scene 1, Sandor
Konya as Parsifal, Boris Chris-
toff as Gurnemanz, Rita Gorr

as Kundry, ens AP wl ph: Pic-
cagliani. Op v 11 n 8 p 561 Ag'60
PARTIE DU SPECTACLE DU "DO-
UZIÈME RIDEAU"
Athens; notes. WP v 11 n 7 p 9
My '60
PARTOS, OEDEON, 1907-, compo-
ser
Première: Maqamat; Israel. MC
v 161 n 7 p 20 Je '60
PAS DE DIEUX, (KELLY), ballet
Paris notes; George Gershwin
music. WP v 12 n 1 p 4 O '60
---Portfolio, two in color, a doz-
en ens AP wl phs: Lido, Paris
Opéra; Maquette originale du rid-
eau par André François, inset in
color. OpP n 19 1960
PAS DE QUATRE, 1845, ballet
Guest, Ivor. (Notes on this fam-
ous dance occasion and other
divertissements of four dances.)
Th Notbk v 15 n 2 p 70-1 Winter
'60-61
PAS DE TROIS (CHAZOT), ballet
Lafon, Madeleine, Jacques Chazot
et Mona du Château, AP wl ph:
Michel Petit. TD n 95 p 19 Jl-Ag
'60
PASCAL, CLAUDE, 1927?-
Première: Concerto pour violon-
celle; André Navarra, Besançon.
GDC n 283 p 95 O 7'60
PASO A NIVEL, play
Madrid notes; Jaime de Armiñan.
WP v 11 n 7 p 7 My '60
PASSANI, EMILE, 1905-, composer
Por ph: Arriat. GDC n 279-280
p 881 Jl 1'60
PASTA, GIUDITTA, 1798-1865,
singer
As Rossini's Desdemona, AP hl
lithograph: La Scala Museum. ON
v 25 n 8 p 25 D 31'60
PATACHOU, chanteuse
See Billon, Henriette, 1918-,
singer
PATERSON, RUSSELL
Kansas City Lyric Theater; how
opera is financed. HF v 10 n 6
p 28 Je '60
PATHETIC PROLOGUE, play
Sastre criticism. TDR v 5 n 2
p 117 D '60

PATOUCHAS, play
Athens notes; Auguelos Nicas.
WP v 12 n 1 p 7 O '60
PATTERSON, TOM (1911-). Strat-
ford and the Canadian theatre.
PIM v 36 n 5 p 103-4 F '60
PAUL, TIBOR, conductor
Notes; Australian. il MD v 50
n 10 p 17 Ap '60
PAYNE, DONALD, 1936-, bass
player
Notes; b. Texas. IM v 58 n 9
p 34 Mr '60
PAYZANT, GEOFFREY. (On
Canada's music festivals.) CMJ
v 5 n 1 p 37 Autumn '60
--- ---The competitive music fes-
tivals (Canada). CMJ v 4 n 3
p 35-46 Spring '60
PEABODY ART THEATRE
In Il Turco in Italia, ens AP wl
ph: Blakeslee-Lane. ON v 24
n 16 p 2 F 20'60
PEASE, JAMES, 1916-, singer
As Hans Sachs, Covent Garden
notes. AmM v 8 n 2 p 8 F '60
LA PEAU DE CHAGRIN (VAN
DIJK)
Paris, à l'Opéra-Comique. TD
n 93 p 23 My '60
LES PECHEURS DE PERLES,
opera
Sadler's Wells; June Bronhill
and Charles Craig; review. Op
v 11 n 4 p 299 Ap '60
PECHTER, WILLIAM S. The
light is dark enough (on Ingmar
Bergman). TDR v 5 n 2 p 94-101
D '60
PEDERZINI, GIANNA, 1904-,
singer
In Menotti's Medium; Rome Op-
era review. por La S n 127 p 27
Je '60
PEER, RALPH S. 1893-1960,
publisher
Obituary. MD v 50 n 9 p 18
Mr '60
PEER GYNT, play
Phoenix Theatre, NYC; Fritz
Weaver in the title-role; notes.
Th Arts v 44 n 3 p 14 Mr '60
---Nottingham Playhouse, ens
AP wl ph: Arnold-Allen. NTM

v 1 n 1 p 15 O '59
PEER GYNT, opera
Egk; set, Munich 1952, ph: Betz.
WT v 9 n 3 p 218 Autumn '60
PEERCE, JAN, 1904-, singer
Chicago review. MC v 161 n 3
p 36 F '60
PEIRCE, JOHN, 1894-1960, choral
director
Notes. MC v 161 n 6 p 37 My '60
THE PELICAN, play
Strindberg, August. The Pelican;
trans. Evert Sprinchorn. (text).
TDR v 4 n 3 p 117-143 Mr '60
PELLÉAS ET MÉLISANDE, opera
Ashbrook, William. A study in
estrangement (the composer's own
life intertwined with loss as in
Mélisande's). por ON v 24 n 11
p 8-9 Ja 16'60
---Griffith, Katherine. (Criticism.)
ON v 24 n 11 p 24 n 11 p 6-7, 28
Ja 16'60
---Metropolitan Opera: cast; story;
décor by Armistead; bibliography;
discography; criticism; portfolio;
ON v 24 n 11 Ja 16'60
--- ---review. Op v 11 n 2 p 134 F '60
--- ---de los Angeles and Uppman.
il MC v 161 n 1 p 12 Ja '60
---Opéra-Comique, 1905, under
Albert Carré; Mary Garden as
Mélisande; notes by Kathleen Hoo-
ver. ON v 24 n 11 p 14 Ja 16'60
---Washington, D. C. première;
John Reardon, Pélleas; Adele Add-
ison, Mélisande; Paul Callaway,
conducting ; notes. ON v 24 n 11
p 27-8 Ja 16'60
---Weerth, Ernest de. Scenes from
an enchanted life; 6. Baritone
(Vanni Marcoux) and Mélisande.
il ON v 24 n 11 p 10, 32 Ja 16'60
---Metropolitan portfolio: Louis
Melançon. ON v 24 n 11 Ja 16'60
PELLÉAS ET MÉLISANDE (ETCH-
EVERRY), ballet
Final scene, ens AP wl ph: Paris.
OpP n 19 p 67 1960
PELLETIER, WILFRID (1896-).
L'Orchestre Symphonique de
Quebec (notes on government sub-
sidy of ninety musicians beginning
1959). IM v 58 n 12 p 18 Je '60

---Hl ph. MEJ v 47 n 1 p 107
S-O '60
PELTZ, MARY ELLIS (1896-).
Festival diary (Nabucco in Herod-
es Atticus Theatre; Spoleto; Carmen at Pierrelatte; Aix-en-Pro
vence; Salzburg; Bayreuth; Glyn-
debourne's Cenerentola and
Magic Flute). il ON v 25 n 1
p 20-1 O 8'60
--- ---La Bohème by Opera
Guild Theatre Company; Am-
erican première of Leoncallo
work. ON v 24 n 17 p 27 F 27'60
--- ---Otello promoted (James
McCracken). il ON v 24 n 18
p 28 Mr 5'60
--- ---The magic of the Opera;
a memoir of the Metropolitan
(book review.) ON v 25 n 4 p 3
D 3'60
---Commentator on Walter Her-
bert's opera tour of European
festivals. ON v 24 n 20 p 3
Mr 19'60
PELZ, ANTONIN, 1890-, singer
As schoolmaster Benda in Dvor-
ak's Jakobin, AP hl ph: Brno.
ON v 25 n 8 p 5 D 31'60
PENBERTHY, JAMES. Festival
of Perth (program). MD v 51
n 6 p 9 D '60
PENDLETON, EDMUND
Mari, Pierrette. Paris con-
cert: Pendleton and Ida Presti-
Alexandre Lagoya; le Choeur
Philharmonique de Paris also.
GDC n 277 p 818 Je 17'60
PENN, ARTHUR
Directing The Miracle Worker,
ens ph. Th Arts v 44 n 7 p 53
Jl '60
PENNSYLVANIA
Norristown; campaign for live
music; details of newspaper use.
IM v 59 n 6 p 16 D '60
PERCUSSION MUSIC
Perry, Charles. Modern drum-
ming. IM v 58 n 8 p 29 F '60
---Rich, Buddy. (Interview on
drumming technique.) por IM
v 58 n 12 p 29-30 Je '60
---Stone, George Lawrence.
Technique of percussion, series.

IM 1960
---Ulano, Sam. Approach to
practical drumming. IM v 58 n 9
p 20, 23 Mr '60
PERELMANN, DORA, conductor
Career sketch; b. Leningrad. MC
v 161 n 6 p 12 My '60
---Two phs. MC v 161 n 6 cover,
p 12 My '60
PERGOLESI, GIOVANNI BATTISTA,
1710-1736, composer
Capri, Antonio. Testimonianza di
Pergolesi. La S n 132 p 24-29
N '60
---Hoover, Kathleen. Pergolesi:
a brief life. por ON v 24 n 12
p 9 Ja 23'60
---Left profile; and 4 scenes "sett-
ecentesca". La S n 132 p 24-8
N '60
PERIODICALS
Périodiques des arts du spectacle
dans le monde: France; Belgium.
Th R v 2 n 1 p 60-2 1960
PERKINS, ANTHONY, 1932-,
actor
And Zeme North in the musical,
Greenwillow, AP wl ph: Friedman-
Abeles. Th Arts v 44 n 3 p 9
Mr '60
PERLE, GEORGE (1915-). Germany
(contemporary music; meaning of
avant-garde today; the 34th World
Music Festival of the International
Society for Contemporary Music,
Cologne). Mus Q v 46 n 4 p 517-525
O '60
PERLEMUTER, VLADO, pianist
Jourdan-Morhange, Hélène. Paris
concert review. GDC n 255-6
p 309 Ja 15'60
PERRAS, JOHN, flautist
NYC review. MC v 162 n 6 p 35
D '60
PERRIN, JOE, trumpeter
Small por ph. IM v 58 n 12 p 11
Je '60
PERRY, CHARLES. Modern
drumming. IM v 58 n 8 p 29 F '60
---AP wl ph. IM v 58 n 12 p 43 Je '60
DIE PERSER, play
Berlin notes; Mattias Braun. WP
v 11 n 10 p 12 Ag '60
---Ens AP wl ph: Ilse Buhs, Berlin.

(Die Perser)
WT v 9 n 3 p 212 Autumn '60
PERSICHETTI, VINCENT, 1915-,
composer
Notes. J Rev v 7 n 3 p 20 Fall'60
---Première: Seventh Symphony,
St. Louis Symphony. J Rev v 7 n 1
p 13 Winter 59-60
PERU
Theatre report. WP v 12 n 2 p 4
N '60
---Lima; El Gesticulador (Usigli),
ens AP wl ph. WP v 12 n 2 p 1
N '60
---Scene from "Collacocha", ph:
Mayguel. WT v 9 n 3 p 271
Autumn '60
---Volpone (Johnson), play, ens
AP wl ph: Lima. WP v 12 n 3
D '60
PERUGIA, NOEMIE, singer
Chamfray, Claude. Paris review.
GDC n 291 p 359 D 2'60
PESCADORES, play
Monterrey; Jesus Lopez Floren-
cio. WP v 11 n 5 p 14 Mr '60
PETER GRIMES, opera
Decca release; detailed review
of LXT 5521-3. MR v 21 n 3
p 260-2 Ag '60
---Ferra, Giampaolo de. Teatro
Verdi. il La S n 125 p 47 Ap '60
---Frankenstein, Alfred. Peter
Grimes, recorded complete, com-
poser in command (London re-
cording). il HF v 10 n 3 p 59-60
Mr '60
---Wiesbaden; Georg Paskuda;
review. il Op v 11 n 5 p 349
My '60
---Cincinnati; trial scene, small
ens AP wl ph: Grauman Marks.
MC v 162 n 4 p 6 O '60
---Wiesbaden; end of Act II scene
1, ens AP wl ph: Harth. Op v 11
n 5 p 350 My '60
PETER IBBETSON; Opera
Empire State Music Festival; re-
view. Op v 11 n 11 p 752-3 N '60
---Albanese, Licia, Deems Taylor,
Wilfred Pelletier and others, ens
ph: Firedman-Abeles. Op v 11
n 11 p 753 N '60
PETER OG ULVEN (LARSEN),
ballet

Denmark notes; music, Serge
Prokoviev. WP v 11 n 6 p 2
Ap '60
PETERS, ROBERTA, 1931-,
singer
With Governor Wakehurst of
North Ireland, ph: Melançon. ON
v 24 n 15 p 3 F 13'60
PETERSON, ELWOOD, singer
Paris; "negro-spirituals"; notes.
GDC n 295 p 494 D 30'60
PETERSON, OSCAR EMMANUEL,
1925-, pianist
At the piano, ph. IM v 59 n 3 p 6
S '60
PETERSON, P. G. Sweden
(theatre report). WT v 9 n 2 p 174-
178 Summer '60
PETIT, FRANÇOISE
Paris criticism. GDC n 279-80
p 890 Jl 1'60
PETIT, PIERRE. Les droits du
répertoire (Paris, Théâtres Ly-
riques Nationaux). OpP n 19 p 48
1960
---Première: Toccata; Ida Presti
et Alexandre Lagoya à Gaveau.
GDC n 293-4 p 459 D 16'60
LE PETIT THEATRE DU VIEUX
CARRE, 1916-
New Orleans; Cyrano de Bergerac
notes. Th Arts v 44 n 4 p 57
Ap '60
LA PETITE MOLIÈRE, play
Paris; musique, Damase; dialogue
Anouilh. WP v 11 n 3 p 8 Ja '60
PETROVA, MARIA, singer
London debut; b. California. AmM
v 8 n 9 p 10 O '60
---Por ph. AmM v 8 n 9 p 9 O '60
PETROVICS, EMIL, 1930-, com-
poser
Criticism. Mus Q v 46 n 4 p 534
O '60
PEUS, MICHEL, pianist
Perpignan notes. GDC n 290 p 326
N 25'60
PFISTER, FRANÇOISE, violinist
Et Jacques Casterede; Paris re-
view. GDC n 292 p 424 D 9'60
PHAETON, opera
Dessau; Heinz Rottger, composer,
conducting. Op v 11 n 8 p 558
Ag '60
PHELPS, ROGER P. (1920-).

Research in music and music education. MEJ v 46 n 6 p 51-3 Je-Jl '60

PHILADELPHIA
Financial plan back of the Robin Hood Dell concerts, 1948 to date; Fredric R. Mann, President, reporting to symposium of symphony men, NYC. IM v 59 n 3 p 41 S '60
---Opera reviews: Philadelphia Lyric Opera (La Bohème, Madama Butterfly); Philadelphia Grand Opera (Suor Angelica, Pagliacci). ON v 24 n 16 p 27-8 F 20'60
---Schauensee, Max de. (Comments on Gloria Davy, Leontyne Price, Irene Kramarich, Irene Dalis, John Reardon.) ON v 25 n 8 p 29 D 31'60
---Singer, Samuel L. Music report. MC v 161 n 5 p 20 Ap '60; same. MC v 161 n 6 p 26 My '60; MC v 162 n 6 p 24-5 D '60
---Theatre; both home-grown shows and New York tryouts; scope discussed by Wayne Robinson. il Th Arts v 44 n 2 p 73-7 F '60

THE PHILADELPHIA GRAND OPERA
Bamboschek, Giuseppe, director; repertory. Op v 11 n 10 p 685 O '60
---Notes. MC v 161 n 3 p 40 F '60

THE PHILADELPHIA ORCHESTRA
An annual commission established at $5,000; Walter Piston first award. MC v 161 n 5 p 4 Ap '60
---Contemporary selections under Eugene Ormandy; guest conductors. AmM v 8 n 9 p 11 O '60
---Engagements: Robin Hood Dell six weeks; soloists; 10 concerts NYC. AmM v 8 n 6 p 13 Jl '60
---Kincaid, William, flutist for 39 years with the Philadelphia Orchestra; at 65 retirement compulsory; interview. opinions on conductors, on his famous pupils at the Curtis Institute. por IM v 58 n 11 p 12-3 My '60
---NYC; Eugene Ormandy, conducting; Guiomar Novaes

(1899-) pianist. MC v 161 n 1 p 13 Ja '60
--- ---Ormandy; Anshel Brusilow, violinist, and Lorne Munroe, cellist. MC v 161 n 3 p 26 F '60
--- ---review. MC v 162 n 6 p 17 D '60
--- ---review; Ormandy. MC v 161 n 6 p 18 My '60
--- ---reviews (2); Eugene Ormandy and Leopold Stokowski; Eugene Istomin, pianist; second, Shirley Verett-Carter, singer; MC v 161 n 4 p 16, 18 Mr '60
---Reviews; "its discipline far and above any American orchestra of today"; "Ormandy a keen designer of programs." MC v 162 n 5 p 17 N '60
--- ---Stokowski; Eugen Jochum. MC v 161 n 5 p 20 Ap '60
---University of Michigan Festival for 25th year; program notes. AmM v 8 n 4 p 17 Ap '60

PHILEMON UND BAUCIS, play
Rosar, Anni, und Carl Wery, AP hl ph: H. Steinmetz. WT v 9 n 3 p 207 Autumn '60

PHILIPE, GERARD, 1922-1959, actor
Cocteau, Jean. Hommage à Gérard Philipe. Spec n 1 p 44 1960
---Lebesque, Morvan. Les rendevous de Gérard Philipe (France, en U.R.S.S., aux Etats-Unis, au Canada ou au Japon . . .). Spec n 1 p 47-52 1960
---Dans le Prince de Hambourg, Avignon, AP hl ph: 1951; with Jean Vilar à Suresnes, hl phs: 1951; 1958; Le Cid, 1951; Le Figurant de la Gaité, 1948; Les Epiphanies de Pichette, 1947; La Calandria, 1951; Lorenzaccio, 1952; Les Caprices de Marianne, 1958, etc. Spec n 1 1960
---Three AP phs: Bernand; Agnès Varda. WP v 11 n 3 p 1 Ja '60

PHILIPPART, RENÉ. Noël feerique (études musicales analytiques). GDC n 292 p 430 D 9'60

PHILIPS, THEA,?-1960, singer
Career notes; b. Bournemouth. MD v 51 n 6 p 8 D '60

237

PHILLIPINE DANCING
Two AP phs; New York City.
La S n 123 p 42 F '60
PHILIPPINES
Philippine Music Educators
Group; report on arts. MEJ
v 46 n 3 p 6 Ja '60
---Manila; workshops, one week,
for elementary school music
teachers; 1959 beginning; suc-
cess. portfolio MEJ v 47 n 2
p 56-7 N-D '60
THE PHOENIX THEATRE, NYC
Funke, Lewis. A Phoenix with
personality (seventh season of
Phoenix under T. Edward Ham-
bleton and Norris Houghton). il
Th Arts v 44 n 1 p 72-3, 84 Ja'60
---In Henry IV, Part I, AP ph:
Avery Willard, NYC. Th Arts
v 44 n 5 p 58 My '60
A PHOENIX TOO FREQUENT,
play
Bibliography. TDR v 4 n 3 p 96
Mr '60
PHONOGRAPH RECORDS
See phonorecords
PHONORECORDS
American composers, a discog-
raphy by (Donald Jennings) with
quoted reviews. ACAB v 9 n 2
p 13-7 1960
--- ---Part II. ACAB v 9 n 3
p 19-25 1960
---Billiet, Jacques. Danse (11
commentaires). GDC n 285 in-
set O 21'60
---Bournay, Jean de. La Musi-
que en Registrée, serie. TD
Je '60
---Broder, Nathan. Mozart op-
eras; High Fidelity discography
No. 49. HF v 10 n 11 p 56-7, 125
N '60
---Chávez, Carlos: 3 symphonies
(review). Mus Q v 46 n 3 p 396-
8 Jl '60
---Composers Recordings, Inc.
(Seven discs reviewed by Richard F. French, including works
by Franchetti, Ruggles, Homer
Keller, Robert Ward, Billy Jim
Layton and others.) Mus Q v 46
n 4 p 548-556 O '60

---Conly, John M. (collected opinions of what recordings should
be made next.) HF v 10 n 1 p 42
Ja '60
---Coverage each issue, some
long signed reviews, of classical,
popular, spoken-all types of recordings. HF 1960
---Cowan, Edward A. (Letter from
Texas complaining that "complete"
recording   seldom so.) Op v 11
n 11 p 785 N '60
---Daniélou, Alain, director, of
UNESCO Collection-A Musical
Anthology of the Orient; notes on
series from Bärenreiter-Musica-
phon, Kassel. WM n 6 p 131 D '60
---De la Halle, Adam. Rondeaux
Polyphoniques; commentaires pour
la 6e leçon par J. Rollin. GDC
n 293-4 inset D 16'60
---Disques classiques; disques
parlés (critiques). GDC 1960
---Each issue, new recordings in
column, publications. WM n 2
p 33 Ap '60 or WM 1960
---Folk Music from Wisconsin,
Helene Stratman-Thomas Blotz;
notes. MEJ v 47 n 1 p 16 S-O '60
---Folkways, 700 discs; Moe Asch.
il HF v 10 n 6 p 42-4 Je '60
---German imports; notes. HF
v 10 n 3 p 30 Mr '60
---Goldman, Richard Franko. Arias,
Anthems and Chorales of the Am-
erican Moravians, 1760-1860 (a
review of a Columbia recording).
Mus Q v 46 n 4 p 547-8 O '60
---Griffiths, Joan. Shakespeare
recorded under George Rylands
(Cambridge); actors anonymous,
homogeneity of style; Decca. HF
v 10 n 5 p 33 My '60
---International Records Company
McGill University; "to promote
Canadian artists." CMJ v 4 n 2 p 51-2
Winter '60
---Janequin, Clément (1490?-1560?).
Le chant des Oiseaux (critique par
J. Rollin). GDC n 295 inset D 30'60
---Japanese traditional music; Du-
cretet-Thomson under André Cala-
buig, assisted by Hisao and Hideo
Tanabe; notes. WM n 6 p 132 D '60

---Labor Day to Christmas, releases scheduled are discussed.
HF v 10 n 9 p 59-60 S '60
---Legge, Walter, of EMI; his
various new releases. HF v 10
n 11 p 24, 26 N '60
---Library of Congress releasing
book "Preservation and Storage
of Sound Recordings" by Pickett-
Lemcoe, review. MR v 21 n 3
p 255-6 Ag '60
---Lista des Disques recomman-
dés; par composers; recitals;
musique spirituelle; folklore;
pour enfants; les meilleurs dis-
ques en 1960. GDC n 292 p 401-
16 D 9'60
---Locatelli, Pietro. Concerti
Grossi released by I Musici;
review. Mus Q v 46 n 3 p 399-
405 Jl '60
---Louvet, Michel. Inauguration
de la"Discothèque Marigny".
GDC n 265-6 p 514 Mr 25'60
---Machaut, G. De. Messe "Notre-
Dame" (critique par J. Rollin).
GDC n 292 inset D 9'60
---Marek, George R. Live opera
vs. recorded. ON v 25 n 3 p 9, 30
N 19'60
---La Maschera. Ridotto. La S '60
---Mode de classement des dis-
ques microsillons, utilisé par la
"Discothèque de France". GDC
n 292 p 398-9 D 9'60
---Moussorgsky, Modeste. Une
Nuit sur le Mont Chauve (Jean
Rollin's commentaire pour la
42e leçpn). GDC n 287 inset
N 4'60
---New company: Stand Records;
Eleanor Steber. por ON v 24 n 22
p 3 Ap 2'60
---NYC; $3, 900 collected for a
"warmed-over" disc, original
1956; notes. IM v 59 n 5 p 9 N'60
---New York Pro Musica in Eliza-
bethan and Jacobean Ayres, Mad-
rigals and Dances (review by F.
Mark Siebert). Mus Q v 46 n 3
p 397-8 Jl '60
---Opera discographies in issues
of Opera News; seek by title of
opera featured. ON 1960

---Opera; 18th century Italian
released by Ricordi, and by
Cetra; notes. HF v 10 n 6 p 14, 16
Je '60
---Opera review by Harold Rosenthal and others. Op 1960
---Paganini. Cantabile and 6 Sonatas for violin and guitar (reviewed by Albert Mell). Mus Q
v 46 n 4 p 557-59 O '60
---Pension plan for musicians; I.
Trust Agreement, trustees both
union and employer members; II.
Pension Plan, all definitions and
benefits; American Federation of
Musicians, January 1959 on. IM
v 58 n 12 p 8 Je '60
---Performers' rights; International Federation of Musicians;
notes. WM n 4 p 76 Ag '60
---Pour enseigner L'Histoire de
la Musique, serie; commentaires par J. Rollin. GDC 1960
---Présence de la musique contemporaine, Véga series, under Lucien Adés; notes. HF v 10 n 4 p 12
Ap '60
---Pugliese, Giuseppe. Brahmsiana
di Bruno Walter. por La S n 132
p 66-7 N '60
--- ---Il "Macbeth" di Verdi. il
La S n 133 p 68-9 D '60
--- ---La discografia (Verdi's operas,
in particular Un Ballo). Ver v 1
n 1 p 157-208 Ap '60
--- ---(Un Ballo in Maschera; Mit-
ropoulous; Marian Anderson; Mae-
stro Loibner, Vroons, Brouwen-
stijn.) Ver v 1 n 2 p 989-1007 Ag'60
---Purcell played by New York Pro
Musica Antiqua; review by Henry
Leland Clarke. Mus Q v 46 n 3
p 408-410 Jl '60
---Questionnaire: Pour vos achats
de disques- -etc. GDC n 295 inset
D 30'60
---Records in Review, regular sec-
tion; reviewing panel:Paul Affelder,
Nathan Broder, O. B. Brummell,
R. D. Darrell, Ray Ericson, Al-
fred Frankenstein, John F. Indcox,
Robert C. Marsh, Conrad L. Os-
borne, and John S. Wilson. HF '60
---Rehearsal records of La Traviata,

239

(Phonorecords)
comparison of Toscanini and
Tullio Serafin. HF v 10 n 10
p 65 O '60
---Reviews each issue, some
careful and lengthy discussions
of music. MR 1960
---Reviews of Recorded Music, a
regular, comprehensive column.
MC 1960
---Reviews in regular column
"Gramophone Records". Op 1960
---Rimsky-Korsakoff. La grande
Paque russe (commentaires par
Jean Rollin pour la 46e leçon).
GDC n 283 inset O 7'60
---Schwann Catalogue, 10th year;
19, 830 recordings; further an-
alysis. AmM v 8 n 2 p 17 F '60
---Shaw-Taylor, Desmond. A
"Puritani" discography. il Op
v 11 n 6 p 387-395 Je '60
---Slocumb, Paul. Players on
record (reviews not only of
plays but musicals, operettas,
etc.) PlM 1960
---Stravinsky's Firebird Suite;
Capriccio; Vox ST-PL 511, 020
reviewed. MR v 21 n 2 p 168-9
My '60
---Supplement 1961 au Guide de
l'amateur de microsillon. GDC
n 292 p 385-8 D 9'60
---Swiss; deux disques, Associa-
tion des Musiciens Suisses: Stur-
zenegger; Suter; Marescotti;
Schibler; criticism. GDC n 274
p 715 My 27'60
---Titcomb, Caldwell. Review of
Westminister release of Johann
Pachelbel (1653-1706). Mus Q
v 46 n 3 p 405-407 Jl '60
---Turner, Robert. Five Ameri-
can operas (critical reviews of
Barber's Vanessa; Blitzstein's
Regina; De Banfield's Lord By-
ron's Love Letter; Weisgall's
The Tenor). CMJ v 4 n 2 p 44-51
Winter '60
---Victoria:Missa pro defunctis,
sung by Portland Symphonic
Choir under C. Robert Zimmer-
man;review of RCA Victor by

Robert Stevenson. Mus Q v 46 n 3
p 414-5 Jl'60
---Wagner. Prèlude de Lohengrin;
commentaires pour la 35e leçon
(serie); utilisation pédagogique par
Jean Rollin. GDC n 285 inset O 21'60
---Warren, Leonard;his best noted by
Philip L. Miller. Op v 11 n 6 p 402
Je'60
---Williams, Verdon G. Record re-
views (series;two or more pages
of criticism of serious music, re-
corded). MD 1960
---Wilson, John S. Theatre on discs.
Th Arts v 44 n 1 p 81-3 Ja'60;same.
Th Arts v 44 n 2 p 80-1 F'60;same.
Th Arts v 44 n 3 p 62-4 Mr'60;same.
Th Arts v 44 n 9 p 66 S'60;same. Th
Arts v 44 n 11 p 80 N'60;same. Th
Arts D'60
---Yugoslavia;report. HF v 10 n 3
p 34 Mr'60
---Bjoeling and Nilsson in a record-
ing session, ens ph:Rome. ON v 25
n 3 p 9 N 19'60
---Vienna;Herbert von Karajan re-
cording Aïda, 6 phs:Hans Wild. HF
v 10 n 1 p 50-1 Ja'60
See also   Stereo
PHOTOGRAPHY
Melançon, Louis. Portfolios of Met-
ropolitan Opera productions. See
title of opera; see Metropolitan Op-
era.
PIAM. Musica in Francobolli. La S
1960
PIAMONTE, GUIDO. Radio-TV. LaS
1960
PIANISTS
Billard, Marie-José, et Julien Az-
ais;Paris review. GDC n 288 p 258
N 11'60;same. GDC n 295 p 495 D
30'60
---Boschi, Hélène, and Germaine
Mounier;Paris notes. GDC n 261-2
p 441 F 26'60
---Chicago reviews, including Claudio Arrau, Witold Malcuzynski. MC
v 161 n 4 p 28-9 Mr'60
---Conter, Lydia, et Mario, duo;Paris
review. GDC n 267-8 p 556 Ap 8'60
---Fleming, Shirley. Malcolm Frager,
1935-. HF v 10 n 12 p 24 D'60

---Hughes, Edwin. (Rebuttal of Davis article on group piano lessons now "displacing private teacher", on practice "as outdated as the private lesson" from head of National Music Council, NYC.) MEJ v 46 n 5 p 82 Ap-My '60
---Lee and Makanowitzky, duo;Paris review. GDC n 267-8 p 559 Ap 8'60
---NYC reviews: Eleanor Schreiber;Daniel Gutoff;Melvin Ritter-Jane Allen;Lydia Ryvicher;Ray Lev;Joel Rosen. MC v 162 n 5 p 31-2 N'60
--- ---Eugen List;Ernest Ulmer;Robert Mueller;Reginald Stewart;George Reeves;Peter Cook;others. MC v 161 n 5 p 17, 35 Ap '60
--- ---Jeaneane Dowis;Beveridge Webster;Jeanette Haien;Marisa Regules;Ralph Votapek;Zita Carno. MC v 161 n 1 p 17, 28, 34 Ja '60
--- ---Michel Block;David Goldberger;Louis Kentner;David Pollack;Ruth Geiger;Malcolm Frager;Ania Dorfmann;Nikita Magaloff;Claudio Arrau;Enid Dale; Samson François;John Cowell; Charles Rosen;Friedrich Gulda;Jorge Bolet. MC v 162 n 6 p 34-7, 43 D'60
---Paganini pianista. por LaS n 127 p 12-3 Je'60
---Roddy, Joseph. Steinways and Steinwayism. il HF v 10 n 3 p 42-5 Mr'60
---Van Ess, Mary. What outlook for pianists? J Rev v 7 n 1 p 3-4 Winter 59-60
---Vronsky-Babin marking 25th anniversary in America;notes. por MC v 162 n 6 p 10 D'60
---American judges at the Chopin Competition in Warsaw, Beveridge Webster, M. Horszowsky, Artur Rubinstein and Witold Malcuzinski, small ph. MC v 161 n 5 p 30 Ap'60
---Pastorelli, Chiaralberta, at the piano, ph:Salerno. LaS n 125 p 89 Ap'60

PIANO
Davis, Marilyn Kornreich. What's been happening to piano lessons? (Growth of group teaching). MEJ v 46 n 3 p 62-4 Ja'60
---Pace, Robert. Keyboard experience in the classroom. il MEJ v 46 n 4 p 44-5 F-Mr'60
---Vecchio-Verderame, Angelo. Pianoforti. il LaS n 125 p 39-41 Ap'60
---Several phs. LaS n 125 p 39-41 Ap'60

PIASTRO, MISHEL(1892-). The concertmaster as conductor. por IM v 58 n 7 p 22 Ja'60
---AP hl ph. IM v 58 n 7 p 22 Ja'60

PIAT, RENÉE
And Naudy, acrobats;"Danse et Culture" evening. il TD n 90 p 15 F'60

PICASSO, PABLO (1881-). Ma jolie (1914), color ph. LaS n 129-30 cover Ag-S'60

THE PICCADILLY BUSHMAN, play Melbourne;Ray Lawler. WP v 11 n 3 p 4 Ja'60

IL PICCOLO SPAZZACAMINO, opera Three ens AP wl ph:Zagreb. LaS n 132 p 49 N'60

IL PICCOLO TEATRO di MILANO
In The Servant of Two Masters, AP hl ph:NYC. Th Arts v 44 n 2 p 84 F'60

PICHAUD, MARIE-CLAIRE, singer Paris;Armand Lanoux, the guitar. GDC n 267-8 p 560 Ap 8'60

PICKER, LAURENCE. 13th annual conference of the International Folk Music Council held in Vienna. WM n 5 p 101-102 O'60

PICKER, MARTIN. Three unidentified chansons by Pierre de la Rue in the "Album de Marguerite d'Austriche". Mus Q v 46 n 3 p 329-343 Jl'60

PICTET, MARIE-ANTOINETTE, pianist
With L'Orchestre de la Société Philharmonique de Paris;review. GDC n 275 p 753 Je 3'60

PIÈCES BRILLANTES (BRIANSKY) Première notes;Anvers. TD n 92 p 23 Ap'60

241

LES PIEDS NICKELES,
operetta
Nougaro;Rennes commentaire.
GDC n 257-8 Ja 29'60
PIÈGE POUR UN HOMME SEUL,
play
Paris notes;Robert Thomas. WP
v 11 n 6 p 6 Ap'60
PIERWSZY DZIEN WOLNOSCI,
play
Varsovie notes;Leon Kruczkow-
ski. WP v 11 n 6 p 9 Ap'60
IL PIGMALIONE, opera
Bergamo notes. La S n 132 p 45
N'60
---Donizetti, ens AP wl ph:Ber-
gamo. LaS n 132 p 45 N'60
THE PILGRIM'S PROGRESS,
opera
BBC; Dennis Arundell, producer;
cast; review. Op v 11 n 12 p 855
D'60
PINAFORE, opera
Guthrie, Tyrone, director, ens
AP hl ph:Peter Smith, NYC. ON
v 25 n 3 p 13 N 19'60
PING-PONG, play
de A. Adamov, ens AP hl ph:Fin-
land. WP v 11 n 7 p 8 My'60
PINKHAM, DANIEL, composer
Première:Angelus ad Pastores;
Boston 1959. ACAB v 9 n 2 p 23
1960
---Première:Angeles ad pastores;
Boston notes. MC v 161 p 25 Ja'60
PIPER'S OPERA HOUSE
Virginia City, Nevada;article by
Wendell Cole. Th Notbk v 15 n 2
p 52-5 Winter'60-61
PIPKOV, LUBOMIR(1904-). Prem-
ière Symphonie (études musica-
les analytiques). GDC n 284 p 142
O 14'60
PIRIE, PETER J. A reprieve for
romanticism (music discussed).
HF v 10 n 10 p 48-50 O'60
--- ---Toscanini and Furtwängler,
an empire divided (Beethoven
symphonic canon). HF v 10 n 4
p 37-9 Ap'60
PISTON, WALTER, 1894-, composer
Career sketch;b. Rockland, Maine.
por Am M v 8 n 6 p 11 Jl'60
---Première:Second Violin Con-

certo;Pittsburg under William Stein-
berg. MC v 162 n 6 p 27 D'60
---Symphony No. 7, première by the
Philadelphia Symphony. Am M v 8
n 11 p 10 D'60
PITOËFF, GEORGES. (A 1939 comment on Tchékhov.) Spec n 1 p 5
1960
---Jouve, Pierre Jean. Mémoire de
Pitoëff. il Spec n 1 p 22-4 1960
---Les Pitoëff inconnus: Rainer-
Maria Rilke a Charles Vildrac,
1920;Joseph Kessel;Jean Prévost;
Michel Lassalle;Roger Martin du
Gard, 1925;et commentaires et
Témoignages sur les spectacles
présentés dan le chapitre. il Spec
n 1 p 27-42 1960
---Dans le rôle d'Hamlet, AP wl ph:
1926; dans le rôle de Joe; Paque-
bot Tenacity, Genève 1920; La Dame
aux Camélias, 1921;Voyageur sans
bagage;Les Hommes, 1931;Joe et
Cie; Brand; Tu ne m'échapperas
jamais, 1936;Sainte Jeanne, 1925;
La Ronde;Le Merveilleux Alliage,
1936;Liliom, 1923 and other phs.
Spec n 1 1960
PITOËFF, LUDMILLA, 1900?-1951,
actress
And Georges;Voyageur sans bagage, AP hl ph. Spec n 1 p 31 1960
---As Ophelia, AP wl ph:Paris. Spec
n 1 p 25 1960
---Dans La Mouette de Tchékhov, AP
wl ph:1922. Spec n 1 p 11 1960
PITOËFF, SACHA(1920-). La confidance en l'homme de Tchékhov. WP
v 11 n 3 p 1, 7 Ja'60
PITTSBURGH
Lewando, Ralph. Music report. MC
v 161 n 3 p 42 F'60; same. MC v 162
n 6 p 27 D'60
---Opera and concert report. MC v 162
n 1 p 23 Jl'60
THE PITTSBURGH OPERA
Repertory notes 1960-1. ON v 25
n 3 p 6 N 19'60
THE PITTSBURG SYMPHONY
Steinberg, William, director: soloists;conductors;premières. MC
v 162 n 4 p 18 O'60
---Thirty-third season notes. MC
v 161 n 7 p 34 Je'60

PIZZETTI, ILDEBRANDO(1880-).
Giuseppe Verdi Maestro di Teatro. Ver v 1 n 2 p 751-766 Ag'60
---Capri, Antonio. Ottant'anni di Ildebrando Pizzetti. portfolio LaS n 129-30 p 9-17 Ag-S'60
---And Maestro Alberto Curci, hl ph; Bologna award, ens ph. LaS n 133 p 93, 103 D'60
---Several photographs, including scenes from "Figlia di Jorio". La S n 129-30 p 10-5 Ag-S'60
---With Elena Zaniboni, harpist, hl ph. LaS n 127 p 56 Je'60
PLANCHON, ROGER, 1930-, director
Director of the People's Theatre in Villeurbanne (an American's view of his style of directing, of Marxist twists to interpretations alleged, "reminiscent of Brecht", "resembled sketches by Daumier". PlM v 37 n 3 p 56 D'60
---His position in the French theatre. Th Arts v 44 n 12 p 63 D'60
---Paris notes. TDR v 5 n 1 p 92 S'60
PLATÉE, opera
(Lang, Paul H.). Criticism of Rameau, recorded under Hans Rosbaud for Pathé. Mus Q v 46 n 1 p 127-30 Ja'60
PLATONOV, play
Gli Amori di Platonov, Teatro Stabile, Torino, 1958, set by Guglielminetti, ph:Trevisio Erminio. WT v 9 n 2 p 136 Summer '60
---Moskva, 1960;ens AP wl ph. WT v 9 n 2 p 107 Summer'60
---Théâtre National Populaire, Paris, 1956;Jean Vilar and Georges Wilson, AP hl ph:Agnès Varda. WT v 9 n 2 p 147 Summer'60
---Three actors in Chekhov attitudes, Den Haag 1958, 3 phs: Lemaire en Wennink. WT v 9 n 2 p 139 Summer'60
---Wien, 1959, ens ph:Hausmann. WT v 9 n 2 p 136 Summer'60
PLAUTUS IN NONNENKLOSTER, opera
Leipzig;Kurt Seipt, 3 ens AP wl phs:Wallmuller. Op v 11 n 1

p 40-1 Ja'60
PLAY OF DANIEL, music-drama
Cathedral of Wells in England, produced by New York Pro Musica; notes. Th Arts v 44 n 5 p 18 My'60
---Demarquez, Suzanne. Le Jeu de Daniel;Royaumont review. GDC n 281-2 p 61 S 30'60
---Maggio Musicale;notes. MC v 162 n 3 p 22 S'60
---New York Pro Musica Ensemble, Royaumont;articles on the work. GDC n 278 p 844-6 Je 24'60
--- ---notes. Am M v 8 n 3 p 17 Mr '60
--- ---a twelfth-century Bibical play in Latin "as an example of American culture";notes. Th Arts v 44 n 12 p 16 D'60
--- ---under Noah Greenberg;notes on 12th century work, Abbey of Beauvais;present scoring. Am M v 8 n 5 p 3-4 Je'60
--- ---Westminster Abbey;based on original Beauvais manuscript now in the British Museum;instrumentation by Noah Greenberg;medieval instruments used;staged after Lincoln Kirstein production; Auden's narration over-long. Op v 11 n 8 p 573-4 Ag'60
---Robinson, J. W. The Play of Daniel produced by the New York Pro Musica. Th Notbk v 15 n 1 p 33-4 Autumn'60
---New York Pro Musica, ens AP wl ph:Denis deMarney. Op v 11 n 8 p 573 Ag'60
THE PLAYERS, 1911-
Detroit men's group. Th Arts v 44 n 10 p 78 O'60
--- ---productions. Th Arts v 44 n 12 p 69 D'60
PLAYWRIGHTS
Decker, Hermine D. The author? Who's that? PlM v 37 n 1 p 7 O'60
---Germany today. WT v 9 n 3 p 203 Autumn'60
---In Belgium;the whole issue devoted to Belgian and Dutch schools. WT Spring'60
---List of playwrights able to translate foreign works:language, name, country of the translator (list of

18 nations). WP v 11 n 3 p 2
Ja'60

PLAYWRITING

Holloway, Sister Marcella M.
Playwriting can be fun. PlM v 36
n 5 p 102 F'60

---Valency, Maurice. Flight into
lunacy ("stories, no matter how
fantastic, must make sense"). Th
Arts v 44 n 8 p 8-9 Ag'60

---Ward, Winifred. Children's
theatre:help wanted. il Th Arts
v 44 n 8 p 53-8 Ag'60

THE PLEASURE of his COMPANY,
play
Taylor, Samuel, with Cornelia
Otis Skinner. (Text of play, NYC
cast, pictures). Th Arts v 44 n 4
p 22-52 Ap'60

PLINKIEWISCH, HELEN. Opera in
the sixth grade? il MEJ v 47
n 1 p 96-7 S-O'60

PLOWRIGHT, JOAN, actress

Por ph:Alfredo Valente. Th Arts
v 44 n 10 p 13 O'60

POPKIN, HENRY(1924-). The plays
of Tennessee Williams. TDR v 4
n 3 p 45-64 Mr'60

POETRY

Riva, Ubaldo. La musica nelle
poesie di Salvatore Di Giacomo.
il LaS n 133 p 48-55 D'60

---Viviani, Alberto. Cecco Angiolieri, a doomed disciple of the
dodecuple scale. il LaS n 133
p 31-41 D'60

--- ---Il Burchiello e la musica
del suo tempo. LaS n 131 p 11-19
O'60

THE POET'S THEATRE

In Mrozek's The Police, AP ph:
Cambridge, Mass. Th Arts v 44
n 5 p 55 My'60

POLACCO, GIORGIO, 1873-1960,
conductor
Obituary;b. Venice. MC v 161 n 6
p 37 My'60

POLAND

Brennecke, Wilfried. Chopin and
Polish music;impressions of a
visit to Warsaw. WM n 2 p 26-8
Ap'60

---Golos, George S. Some Slavic

predecessors of Chopin. Mus Q
v 46 n 4 p 437-447 O'60

---Music of the Polish Renaissance
(previously published as "Muzyka
Polskiego Odrodzenia"); review
by Jerry S. Golos. Mus Q v 46
n 3 p 386-390 Jl'60

---Schiller, Irena. Les exposi-
tions théâtrales en Pologne. Th
R v 2 n 3 p 188-192 1960

---Ungerer, I. D. (Opera report.)
ON v 24 n 9 p 29, 31 Ja 2'60

---Two dance, ens AP phs: NYC.
La S n 123 p 44 F '60

POLIFEMO, opera
Berlin; ens AP wl ph. La S n 132
p 51 N '60

POLIUTO
Notes. La S n 133 p 64 D '60

POLLAK, ANNA, 1915-, singer
As Queen Elizabeth in "Merrie
England", AP wl ph: Angus
McBean. Op v 11 n 9 p 647 S'60

POLLINI, MURIZIO, 1942-, pianist
Notes. HF v 10 n 8 p 18 Ag '60

---Warsaw; Sixth International
Chopin Competition winner;
notes. por MD v 50 n 10 p 16
Ap '60

---Warsaw, 1960; 6th International
Competition for Pianists: winner,
small ph. WM n 2 p 27 Ap '60

---Por ph. La S n 125 p 77 Ap '60

POLYEUCTE, play
Ens AP wl ph: Comédie-Française.
WP v 11 n 8 Je '60

PONFERRADA, JUAN-OSCAR.
Argentina theatre report. WT
v 9 n 1 p 68-70 Spring '60

PONSELLE, ROSA, 1897-, singer
As Giulia in La Vestale, AP wl
ph: Lumiere. ON v 24 n 19 p 13
Mr 12'60

POPESCO, TRAJAN, 1920-,
choral conductor
Career sketch; b. Roumania.
GDC n 276 p 767 Je 10'60

---Demarquez, Suzanne. Orchestre
et Choeurs Trajan Popesco. GDC
n 284 p 127 O 14'60

---Lorin, Michel. Rencontre avec
Trajan Popesco. GDC n 275
p 745 Je 3'60

(Popesco)
---Paris, en L'Eglise Saint-Germain-des-Prés: orchestre et choeurs Trajan Popesco; review. GDC n 281-2 p 25-8 S 30'60
---Por ph: Harcourt. GDC n 276 cover Je 10'60
POPOVA, KATYA, singer
As Manon; Sofia criticism. Op v 11 n 9 p 617 S '60
POPOVICH, VLADA, singer
Hl ph: Belgrado. La S n 122 p 41 Ja '60
POPOVICI, DORU, composer
Première Two Symphonic Sketches; Bucharest. WM n 5 p 104 O '60
POPPY'S THREE WISHES, play
Aslani, L., author; AP ph: Canada. WP v 12 n 3 D '60
PORGY AND BESS, opera
Grunfeld, Fred. The great American opera (so far only produced incompletely; Heyward and Gershwin two months on South Carolina coast and other notes). il ON v 24 n 20 p 6-9 Mr 19'60
---Davis-Breen production; Cab Calloway as Sportin'Life, ens AP wl ph: ANTA. ON v 24 n 20 p 7 Mr 19'60
---Theatre Guild 1935, ens AP wl ph: NYC. Th Arts v 44 n 9 p 25 S '60
PORGY AND BESS, film
Six stills from Samuel Goldwyn production. MD v 50 n 12 p 16-7 Je '60
PORRAS, JUANITA, singer
US debut; Peruvian soprano, very promising. MC v 161 n 3 p 28 F '60
PORT TOWN, opera
Première; Tanglewood, Jan Meyerowitz work. Op v 11 n 9 p 615 S '60
---Première at Berkshire Music Festival. AmM v 8 n 6 p 14 Jl'60
PORTER, ANDREW. An introduction to "La Sonnambula". il Op v 11 n 10 p 665-70 O '60
--- ---Bellini's last opera (I Puritani). il Op v 11 n 5 p 315-321

My '60
--- ---Cenerentola, Glyndebourne. Op v 11 p 16-7 Autumn '60
PORTER, E. G. (1889-). Der Doppelgänger. MR v 21 n 1 p 16-18 F '60
PORTER, QUINCY, 1897-, composer
Sketch; b. New Haven. por AmM v 8 n 8 p 11 S '60
LE PORTEUR DE NOUVELLES, play
Ens AP wl ph: Athens. WP v 11 n 7 My '60
IL PORTO DI CASA MIA, play
Notes. il La S n 125 p 71 Ap '60
PORTUGAL
Portugaliae Musica, collection covering mid-sixteenth to mid-nineteenth centuries; Gulbenkian Foundation. WM n 1 p 10 F '60
---Music report. La S n 123 p 75 F '60
---Saviotti, Gino. Music report. La S n 124 p 74 Mr '60;same. La S n 126 p 68 My '60; same. La S n 127 p 68 Je '60; same. La S 1960
POSTAGE STAMPS
Piam. Musica in francobolli. il La S n 122 p 56 Ja '60
POULENC, FRANCIS 1899-, composer
(Merkling, Frank.) Criticism of Les Mamelles de Tirésias; La Voix Humaine. ON v 24 n 20 p 28 Mr 19'60
---And Duval, hl ph: NYC. La S n 133 p 113 p 113 D '60
---E Polignac, ph. La S n 122 p 35 Ja '60
POUSSEUR, HENRI, 1929-, composer
Darmstadt; notes. Mus Q v 46 n 2 p 274-5 Ap '60
---Première: Repons pour 7 musiciens (Paris critique). GDC n 291 p 355 D '60
---Première: Rimes pour différentes sources sonores (1958-59); criticism, Donaueschingen. MR v 21 n 1 p 79 F '60
La POUVIGNÉ

(La Pouvigné)
Ballerina dell'Opéra di Parigi nella parte della statua in "Pigmalione", AP wl drawing. La S n 129-30 p 25 Ag-S '60

PRADES FESTIVAL
Tenth; notes. WM n 3 p 56 Je'60

PRAGUE
Lenoir, Jean-Pierre; Theatre, Prague. portfolio Th Arts v 44 n 8 p 57-60 Ag '60
---Spring Festival 1960; a report. MD v 50 n 1 p 18 Je '60
---Scenes from six plays. Th Arts v 44 n 8 p 58-9 Ag '60

PRATT, ROSS (1916-). Chopin in Britain. CMJ v 5 n 1 p 24-9 Autumn '60

PRAUSNITZ, FREDERICK, 1920-, conductor
Notes. J Rev v 7 n 1 p 13 Winter 59-60
---Notes; b. Cologne; American citizen. AmM v 8 n 11 p 6 D '60

PRAXMAIR, TONY, singer
Groupe Tyrolien de Tony Praxmair; commentaire. GDC n 293-4 p 460 D 16'60

PRAYER TO THE MOON, play
Ens AP wl ph: China. Th R v 2 n 1 p 25 1960

PREGUNTAN POR JULIO CESAR, play
Zaragoza; Alfonso Paso. WP v 11 n 5 p 3 Mr '60

THE PRESIDENT'S SPECIAL INTERNATIONAL PROGRAM FOR CULTURAL PRESENTATIONS
In six years, 3,500 American artists sent to 102 countries at cost of $12,600,000;5 percent administration. AmM v 8 n 7 p 10 Ag '60
---Schnitzer, Robert C. ANTA program aids U. S. abroad. MC v 161 n 7 p 9 Je '60

PRESTON, ROBERT, 1918-, actor
Notes on his role in the Music Man. Th Arts v 44 n 8 p 6 Ag '60

PREUSSISCHES MÄRCHEN, opera
Blacher; ens AP wl ph: Enkel-

mann, 1952. WT v 9 n 3 p 219 Autumn '60

PREY, HERMANN, singer
As Wolfram, AP hl ph: Metropolitan. ON v 25 n 6 p 21 D 17'60

PRICE, LEONTYNE, 1927-, singer
Berlin notes. MC v 162 n 6 p 31 D '60
---Career notes; b. Laurel, Mississippi. AmM v 8 n 2 p 18 F '60
---Detroit review. MC v 161 n 6 p 31 My '60
---European notes. AmM v 8 n 9 p 8 O '60
---As Donna Anna, AP hl ph: Ellinger, Salzburg. WM n 5 p 110 O'60
---As Thaïs, AP hl ph: Chicago. Op v 11 n 2 p 135 F '60
---Por ph. MC v 162 n 4 p 21 O'60

PRIHODA, VASA, 1900-1960, violinist
Notes; b. Vodnany. GDC n 284 p 121 O 14'60

PRIM, JEAN. A Royaumaumont: Jeu de Daniel (critique). GDC n 278 p 844-6 Je 14'60

PRIMAVERA (HARKAVY), ballet
Pays-Bas; music, Cimarosa. WP v 11 n 10 p 9 Ag '60

PRINCE, HAROLD S. (1928-), producer
And Robert E. Griffith, as Broadway musical producers. por Th Arts v 44 n 10 p 20-1 O '60
---Career notes. por Th Arts v 44 n 10 p 73-4 O '60

LE PRINCE DE L'ESCURIAL, play
Besci work, AP wl ph: Paris. WP v 11 n 6 Ap '60

PRINCE IGOR, opera
Dusseldorf review; dances arranged by Werner Ulbrich, "the only visual relief". Op v 11 n 5 p 347 My '60
---Vienna; uncut, 4 hours; notes. ON v 24 n 22 p 26 Ap 2'60
---Vienna Staatsoper review. Op v 11 n 5 p 342 My '60
---Vienna State Opera revival; Lovro von Matacic arranged the score, retaining Act III. MC v 161 n 5 p 30 Ap '60

THE PRINCE OF HOMBURT,opera

Berlin review; Hans Werner Henze, music; "success convincing".MC v 162 n 6 p 31 S'60
See also DER PRINZ
LA PRINCESSE DE BABYLONE, opera buffa
Arrieu, Claude; Reims notes. Op v 11 n 5 p 345 My '60
---Reims notes; music Claude Arrieu. WP v 11 n 9 p 7 Jl '60
---Reims, ens AP wl ph. Op v 11 n 5 p 345 My '60
PRINCETON UNIVERSITY
Fromm, Paul. The Princeton Seminar: its purpose and promise (followed by other signed articles). Mus Q v 46 n 2 Ap '60
IL PRINCIPE IVO DI SEMBERIA, opera
Belgrade review. il La S n 122 p 41 Ja '60
PRINGSHEIM, KLAUS. Gustav Mahler. CMJ v 5 n 1 p 17-23 Autumn '60
LE PRINTEMPS PARFUME
Une histoire d'armour en Corée, Théâtre des Nations. TD n 95 p 21 Jl-Ag '60
DER PRINZ VON HOMBURG, opera
Henze, Hans Werner; criticism; serial manner; cast notes. MC v 162 n 2 p 23 Ag '60
---Warrack, John. (Analysis of Ingeborg Bachmann's libretto from Heinrich von Kleist; of Henze who in forsaking German nationalism is "unresolved" as yet.) il Op v 11 n 7 p 457-461 Jl '60
---Ens AP wl ph: Hamburg. WM n 4 p 82 Ag '60
---Two scenes and two sets by Alfred Sïercke. Op v 11 n 7 p 457-9 Jl '60
THE PRISONER, opera
Dallapiccola by NYC opera; sung in English; symbolic of modern man. MC v 162 n 5 p 15 N '60
PRISONER'S COUNTRY, play
Melbourne notes; Vance Palmer. WP v 11 n 7 p 1 My '60
PRITCHARD, ROBERT, pianist

London debut; notes. AmM v 8 n 9 p 6 O '60
---Paris review. GDC n 287 p 228 N 4'60
PRO MUSICA DE NEW YORK
Paris review. GDC n 279-80 p 891 Jl 1'60
THE PRO MUSICA SOCIETY
Chicago chamber music group (once the trio); review. MC v 161 n 5 p 22 Ap '60
PROCLEMER, ANNA, actress
With Giorgio Albertazzi, AP hl ph: Italy. Th Arts v 44 n 4 p 55 Ap '60
THE PRODIGAL, play
Ens hl ph: Avery Willard, NYC. Th Arts v 44 n 5 p 58 My '60
THE PRODUCER'S JOURNAL, periodical
NYC; Charles Mandel; Jack Graham, editor. Th Arts v 44 n 11 p 76 N'60
PRODUCTION
Arena-style Tales of Hoffmann by John Price, Cleveland's Musicarnival. ON v 25 n 1 p 7 O 29'60
---Brustein, Robert. Scorn not the proscenium, critic. Th Arts v 44 n 5 p 8-9 My '60
---Camus, Albert. Why I work in the theatre ("the collective studios of painting during the Renaissance _experienced the kind of exaltation known to those who work on a big show"). Th Arts v 44 n 12 p 70 D '60
---Chain mail; how to knit chain mail by Edmund Chavez. il PlM v 37 n 2 p 34 N '60
---Chekhov; 23 producers reply to questions on how to stage Chekhov plays. il WT v 9 n 2 p 111-148 Summer '60
---Concert opera; Alan Rich for and Robert Herman against Metropolitan concert evenings of nonstandard repertory. ON v 25 n 5 p 21 D 10'60
---Johnston, Denis. That's show business (methods or lack of them in dealing with playwrights). Th Arts v 44 n 2 p 82-3 F '60
---Managers interviewed; artistic and economic angles. MC v 162 n 1

(Production)
  p 12-19 Jl '60
---Moscow Art Theatre, the Theatre Studio's method of "Stylized Theatre", from Vsevolod Meyerhold's book "On the Theatre": excerpt trans. Nora Beeson. TDR v 4 n 4 p 134-47 My '60
---O'Neill, Eugene. (Quoted on sound effects, to be introduced in early rehearsals.) PlM v 37 n 2 p 34 N '60
---Open-air; Yves Bonnat on lighting open-air performances. portfolio WT v 9 n 2 p 149-157 Summer '60
---Puppet theatre combination: by juxtaposed sets switching from string to hand puppets, to marionettes and shadow figures in one show. PlM v 37 n 3 p 51 D '60
---Scene technician; book by A. S. Gilette "Stage Scenery: its construction and rigging"; review. PlM v 37 n 1 p 17 O '60
---Shakespeare at Oak Ridge Tennessee; steps in the production of Julius Caesar. PlM v 36 n 4 p 78 Ja '60
---Todd, Arthur. What makes a musical move. il Th Arts v 44 n 11 p 66-7, 72 N '60
---Van Druten, John. The job of directing. Th Arts v 44 n 7 p 51, 54, 68 Jl '60
---Walker, Robert J. Producing a melodrama: Tom Cobb by Wm. S. Gilbert. il PlM v 37 n 2 p 33 N '60
---Wilson, John S. Griffith and Prince (a profile of Broadway musical firm; "prefer to produce without stars"). por Th Arts v 44 n 10 p 20-1, 73 O '60
PROKOFIEV, SERGE, 1891-1953, composer
  Italy; recent productions of Prokofiev operas; The Love of Three Oranges at Teatro San Carlo, review. Op v 2 n 3 p 215 Mr '60
---Nölter, Wolfgang. (The writing of The Love of Three Oranges; its staging under Oscar Fritz

Schuh in Cologne.) Op v 11 n 8 p 557 Ag '60
PROKOWSKY, ANDRÉ
  Dans le rôle du "Marchand", AP wl ph: Lido. TD n 98 p 9 D '60
PROMETHEAN FANTASY, opera
  Koegler, Horst. Dortmund; Gerhart von Westerman's work "failure". Op v 11 n 5 p 346 My'60
PROMÉTHÉE ENCHAÎNÉ, play
  Festival de Lyon-Charbonnière 1945; outdoor lighting, ens AP wl ph: Bernand. WT v 9 n 2 p 153 Summer '60
PROMETHEUS, opera
  Hessian State Theatre; première of Rudolf Wagner-Regeny one-act opera, Prometheus, producer Hermann Schaffner. MC v 161 n 3 p 47 F '60
---Kassel; Wagner-Regeny, d'après Eschyle. WP v 11 n 3 p 1 Ja '60
PRONKO, LEONARD C. The "Revolutionary Theatre" of Alfonso Sastre. TDR v 5 n 2 p 111-120 D '60
THE PROPOSAL, play
  Sofia, 1960, Chekhov, ph. WT v 9 n 2 p 141 Summer '60
PORSERPINA AND THE FOREIGNER, opera
  Buenos Aires review; Juan Jose Castro, music, libretto by Omar del Carlo. MC v 162 n 6 p 33 D '60
---Teatro Colón notes; Castro, composer. La S n 132 p 86 N '60
THE PROTAGONIST, play
  Kaiser, Georg (1878-1945). The Protagonist (text trans. H. F. Garten). TDR v 5 n 2 p 133-144 D '60
PROVINCETOWN PLAYHOUSE
  Reviews: Krapp's Last Tape; and The Zoo Story (one-act plays). PlM v 37 n 1 p 10 O'60
PRYCE-JONES, ALAN. (1908?-).
  Play reviews. Th Arts 1960 or v 44 n 12 D '60
---Por ph: Lotte Meitner-Graf. Th Arts v 44 n 11 p 8 N '60
PRYMA, ROMA, dancer
  Notes; b. Poland; worked in US with Martha Graham. AmM v 8

n 10 p 6 N '60

PUBLICATIONS
Dans l'édition musicale (frequent reviews of new music). GDC 1960
---Music; list of 51 state music education journals, editors, addresses. MEJ v 47 n 1 p 80 S-O '60

PUBLICITY
Hurok Attractions; complaint that publicity easy for newcomers; not enough articles on good musical artists. MC v 162 n 1 p 13 Jl '60
---Klees, Jay. Organizing an opera audience. Op v 11 n 10 p 671-3 O '60
---Plea for local newspapers to review artists well, to provide ahead for a serious critic; a great US need. MC v 162 n 1 p 14 Jl'60

PUCCINI, GIACOMO, 1858-1924, composer
Berri, Pietro. Puccini e il "mal della pietra" (his brick bug or love of houses). il La S n 128 p 16-9 Jl '60
---Schauensee, Max de. Puccini and Paris. ON v 25 n 5 p 17-9 D 10'60
---Por ph. signed; caricatura signed. La S n 128 p 19 Jl '60
---Por right profile ph: 1896. La S n 133 p 56 D '60

PUERTO RICO
Inter-American conference on music education; sponsors. WM n 3 p 57 Je '60
---The Inter-American Music Centre (CIDEM); conference. WM n 4 p 76 Ag '60
---Second International String Congress; notes. MC v 161 n 3 p 51 F '60
--- ---scholarship summer school; plans. il IM v 58 n 8 p 12-3 F'60
--- ---second annual training period; notes. portfolio IM v 59 n 3 p 10-1 S '60
--- ---supported by American Federation of Musicians; program. WM n 3 p 57 Je '60

PUGLIESE, GIUSEPPE. La discografia (Verdi; Un Ballo in Maschera) Ver v 1 n 1 p 157-208 Ap '60

--- ---II. Ver v 1 n 2 p 732-750 Ag '60

PULCINELLA
Stravinsky on his "recomposition of Pergolesi. " ON v 25 n 5 p 9 D 10'60

PUPPETS
Chramer, Fredrik A. ; his puppet opera theatre in Chicago. il ON v 24 n 17 p 12-3 F 27'60
---Derby, Marian. Lilliputian Players, Lewis Mahlmann. il PlM v 36 n 8 p 189-190 My '60
---Detroit; adult series, list of puppeteers. PlM v 36 n 5 p 97 F '60
---International relations in the puppet theatre. Th R v 2 n 1 p 47-8 1960
---The Lilliputian Players of San Francisco in Ravel's Enfant et les Sortilèges, live singers. ON v 25 n 5 p 7 D 10'60
---Magon, Jero. Puppet stages. PlM v 37 n 2 p 35 N '60
--- ---The combination stage. PlM v 37 n 3 p 51 D '60
---The Puppeteers of America; 25th annual festival; Detroit report by Rod Young. PlM v 37 n 1 p 9 O'60
---Two international organizations: UNIMA; CIPEMAT; notes. Th Notbk v 14 n 3 p 77 Spring '60
---Mahlmann, Lewis, with puppets, ph: San Francisco. PlM v 36 n 8 p 189 My '60

PUPPO, MAIRA, singer
And Mario Basiola, Jr. in "Molinarella" of Piccinni, AP hl ph: Teatro di Corte. La S n 132 p 46 N '60

PURCELL, HENRY, 1659-1695, composer
Goldman, Richard F. A review of essays on Purcell, edited by Imogen Holst. J Rev v 7 n 1 p 25 Winter 59-60
---New York Pro Musica Antiqua playing ode to St. Cecilia's Day, 1683, and other works; record review by Henry Leland Clarke. Mus Q v 46 n 3 p 408-410 Jl'60

PURGATORY, opera
Weisgall, Hugo, composer; review

249

(Purgatory) of score. P. J. R. MR v 21 n 4 p 344-5 N '60

I PURITANI, opera
Porter, Andrew. Bellini's last opera (I Puritani). il Op v 11 n 5 p 315-321 My '60
---Shawe-Taylor, Desmond. A discography. il Op v 11 n 6 p 387-395 Je '60
---Glyndebourne review; Bryan Balkwill, conducting. MR v 21 n 3 p 247-8 Ag '60
---Glyndebourne Opera at Edinburgh, ens AP wl ph: Gravett. ON v 25 n 2 p 21 O 29'60
---Glyndebourne, Act I, Act 3 two ens AP wl phs: Guy Gravett. Op v 11 p 10, 12 Autumn '60
---Portfolio of famous interpreters, Maria Callas, de Luca, Carosio, Barrientos and Lazaro, Alessandro Bonci, Luisa Tetrazzini, Hempel, Sembrich, phs. Op v 11 n 6 p 388-393 Je '60
---Scenes from the opera, Lane engravings; Jenny Lind and Lablache (1848); a rehearsal (1863). Op v 11 n 5 p 319-321 My '60

Q

QUARANTE ET, play
Athens; Sakellarios and Yannakopoulos. WP v 11 n 7 p 9 My'60
QUARTETTO CARMIRELLI
Smith, Carleton Sprague, flutist; NYC review. MC v 161 n 1 p 16 Ja '60
QARRTSILUNI (HARALD LANDER), ballet
Notes on Paris Opéra production. il OpP n 19 p 44 1960
---Paris Opéra review. MC v 161 n 5 p 31 Ap '60
--- ---review. il TD n 91 p 12 Mr '60
LES QUATRE FILS AYMON, play
Ens AP wl ph: Cayet. WT v 9 n 1 p 30 Spring '60
QUATUOR DE ZAGREB
Paris review. GDC n 263-4 p 487 Mr 11'60
QUATUOR HONGROIS

Paris review. GDC n 257-8 p 361 Ja 29'60
QUATUOR MICHELE MARGAND
Paris; et Jacqueline Dussol. GDC n 295 p 492 D 30'60
QUATUOR PARRENIN
Paris review; with pianist, Marcelle Mercenier, concert du "Domaine Musical". GDC n 281-2 p 43 S 30'60
QUATUOR VEGH
Menton; with George Solchany; review. GDC n 281-2 p 67 S 30'60
(QUÉANT, GILLES). Introductory remarks: a "new series" of the periodical, Spectacles. Spec n 1 p 4 1960
QUEEN ELIZABETH COMPETITION, 1961
Brussels; rules; musical composition. MD v 50 n 10 p 17 Ap '60
THE QUEEN OF SPADES, opera
Geneva; cast. Op v 11 n 7 p 493 Jl '60
---Geneva, ens AP wl ph: Joller. Op v 11 n 7 p 493 Jl '60
THE QUEENS REVELS
NYC; group at Columbia University. Th Arts v 44 n 11 p 73 N '60
QUEROL, LEOPOLDO, pianist
Paris criticism. GDC n 278 p 849 Je 24'60
QUÉVAL, MICHEL, pianist
Por ph: Paris Opéra. OpP n 19 p 40 1960
QUINTERO, JOSE
Interview of directing opera, NYC. il ON v 24 n 13 p 10-1 Ja 30'60
---Millstein, Gilbert. José Quintero (some quoted opinion of this Panama-born theater director). por Th Arts v 44 n 5 p 10-12 My'60
---Por ph: Roger Prigent. Th Arts v 44 n 5 p 11 My '60
QUINTETTE A VENT FRANÇAIS
Wtih Quintette de Cuivres de la Garde; Paris review. GDC n 281-2 p 53 S 30'60
QUINTETTE INSTRUMENTAL A VENT DE PARIS
Paris review. GDC n 281-2 p 33-4 S 30'60

R

RADAMISTO, opera
Kehl, Sigrid, as Zenobia, AP wl
ph:Helga Wallmüller, Leipzig.
Op v 11 n 12 p 807 D'60
---Handel Opera Society, two ens
AP wl phs:Allegro. Op v 11 n 9
p 641, 643 S'60
RADIĆ, DUŠAN, 1930-, composer
Jugoslav notes. Mus Q v 46 n 1
p 91 Ja'60
RADIO
Complete coverage of radio
programs to be heard by cate-
gories in each issue. GDC 1960
---Dean, Winton. Third Program-
me:Anna Bolena. Op v 11 n 8
p 584 Ag'60
---Detroit WJR, "Scope";cultural
media of European nations. Am
M v 8 n 4 p 17 Ap'60
---Ford Foundation grant for exchange of educational and cultural programmes;since 1958, progress notes. WM n 4 p 78 Ag'60
---RAI;programmi sinfonici: programma nazionale; secondo programma, terzo programma; II.
Opera Liriche: nazionale, secondo, terzo. La S n 124 inset Mr '60
--- ---programmi sinfonici, opere
liriche, programma nazionale e
secondo e terzo programma La S
1960
---Opera in Us; Texaco's broadcast
network; an inset each issue giving operas, dates, map with stations; statistics on listening. ON
v 25 1960-61
---Plessis, Dominique, entretien.
GDC n 276 p 782-3 Je 10'60
---Poland: un grand concours,
1960: VIe concours International,
Radio-Varsovie. GDC n 259-60
p 389 F 12'60
---Radio and Television, regular
news column. IM 1960
---Rostrum of Composers; how
broadcasts are selected from
22 countries; Paris meeting report of competition; winner, "Diary of a Madman " by Humphrey
Searle. WM n 3 p 55 Je '60

---US; the Pacifica Foundation
sponsoring programs in San Francisco and New York along the lines
of BBC's Third Programme. WM
n 2 p 33 Ap '60
---Voice of America; notes on
programs: Musical Life in USA;
and Music USA. AmM v 8 n 4
p 11 Ap '60
---WBAI station given to the Paci-
fica Foundation by the founder,
Louis Schweitzer; notes from NYC.
HF v 10 n 5 p 18 My '60
RAE, JOHNNY, 1934-jazz musician
Notes; b. Saugus, Massachusetts.
IM v 58 n 9 p 21 Mr '60
RAGLE, LUEANNE ROSA, 1943-,
singer
Winner 1960 Metropolitan Opera
Guild Vocal Scholarship. MC
v 161 n 5 p 44 Ap '60
---With Metropolitan jury, ens ph:
NYC. ON v 24 n 23 p 1 Ap 9'60
RAHIER, ALBERT 1895-violinist
Por ph. and notes on his retire-
ment from Pro Arte Quartet. IM
v 59 n 5 p 25 N '60
THE RAINMAKER, play
Martin, Denis. Stage setting for
Le Faiseur de Pluie, Bruxelles,
1958, ph: Cayet. WT v 9 n 1
p 33 Spring '60
A RAISEN IN THE SUN, play
Hansberry, Lorraine. (Text,
cast, portfolio.) Th Arts v 44
n 10 p 27-58 O '60
THE RAKE'S PROGRESS, opera
La Fenice; the composer, Stravin-
sky and Schwarzkopf in curtain
call at 1951 première, ph: Gia-
comelli. ON v 25 n 8 p 25 D 31'60
---Sante Fe comment. ON v 25 n 1
p 25 O 8'60
---Venice; artists before curtain
1951, ph: Piccagliani. Op v 11 n 2
p 115 F '60
RAKIETA "PIORUN", play
Cracow; Marian Prominski. WP
v 12 n 3 p 35 D '60
RAMBAUD, EDMOND, ?-1960,
singer
Debievre, Pierre. (Obituary.)
GDC n 289 p 303 N 18'60
RAMEAU, JEAN-PHILIPPE,

(Rameau)
1683-1764, composer
Koerner, Michael. Barenreiter:
Pièces de Clavecin. v 4 n 3
p 75-6 Spring '60
---Mellers, Wilfrid. Review of
BBC performance of Dardanus
under Anthony Bernard; baroque
criticism. Op v 11 n 4 p 303-4
Ap '60
IL RAMPOLLO (LEE SHERMAN),
musical
Scarnicci e Tarabusi; costumi
di Monteverde; scenari di Vec-
cia. il La S n 131 p 55 O '60
RANDALL, J. K. Haydn: string
Quartet in D major, op. 76,
no. 5. MR v 21 n 2 p 94-105
My '60
RANKIN, NELL, 1926-, singer
Notes. ON v 25 n 2 p 4 O 29'60
---Notes on Mme. Lorraine
(pseud.) her first voice teacher
in Alabama. ON v 24 n 13 p 14
Ja 30'60
---As Dorabella, San Francisco
Opera, AP hl ph: Seawell. ON
v 24 n 13 p 14 Ja 30'60
---Por ph: Farabola. ON v 25 n 2
p 4 O 29'60
RANKL, DR. KARL, 1898-,
conductor
Europe; year of auditioning for
1962 Elizabethan Trust season.
MD v 51 n 3 p 9 S '60
RAPAPORT, EDA, composer
Première: Cantilena; Staccato;
NYC 1959. ACAB v 9 n 2 p 23
1960
---Première: Two Pieces for
Unaccompanied Violin (NYC
1960). ACAB v 9 n 3 p 34 1960
RAPER, WAYNE, oboist
Notes; Texas. IM v 59 n 5 p 36
N '60
RASCADAS
Buenaventura, Enrique. Bird's-
eye view of the Latin American
theatre. WT v 9 n 3 p 265
Autumn '60
RASCHER, SIGURD, saxophonist
Por ph. MEJ v 46 n 6 p 3 Je-
Jl '60
---Por ph: US. IM v 58 n 9

p 43 Mr '60
RASHOMON, play
Bruxelles; ens AP wl ph: Cayet,
1959. WT v 9 n 1 p 34 Spring '60
---Cleveland Play House, ens AP
wl ph. Th Arts v 44 n 1 p 74
Ja '60
---de Akutagawa, ens ph: Bruxelles.
WP v 11 n 5 p 1 Mr '60
RASKOLNIKOFF, play
Berlin notes; Leopold Ahlsen.
WP v 12 n 2 p 22 N '60
RASPUTIN'S END
Cologne review; historical notes.
Op v 11 n 1 p 32 Ja '60
RATHBONE, BASIL, 1892-, actor
In "J. B." with Frederic Worlock,
AP wl ph: NYC. Th Arts v 44 n 2
p 38 F '60
RATTI, EUGENIA, 1935?-, singer
Weaver, William. La Figlia from
Palermo's Teatro Massimo. HF
v 10 n 11 p 10 N '60
DIE RAUBER, opera
Klebe, ens AP wl ph: E. Hess,
1957. WT v 9 n 3 p 222 Autumn'60
RAVEL, MAURICE (1875-1937).
Quatuor (études musicales analy-
tiques). GDC n 288 p 269 N 11'60
---Guadagnino, Luigi. Teatro Rav-
eliano. il La S n 126 p 24-8
My '60
---Paris Opéra; L'Enfant et les
Sortilèges, décor François Gan-
neau, Manuel Rosenthal, directing;
and L'Heure Espagnole with Mal-
clès décor; criticism. MC v 161
n 6 p 33 My '60
--- ---Ravel program reviewed.
Op v 11 n 8 p 550 Ag '60
---Composing, ph: 1926; piano di
Ravel, Luc-Albert Moreau; let-
tera autografa. La S n 126 p 25,
27, 28 My '60
THE RAVEN, play
Sastre criticism. TDR v 5 n 2
p 130 D '60
RAVET, JACQUELINE
Illustrating relationship of danse
and sport, 6 AP wl phs: Paris.
TD n 93 p 6-9 My '60
RAVINIA FESTIVAL
Devries, Dosha. Twenty-fifth
anniversary programs. MC

v 162 n 2 p 12 Ag '60
---Summer music notes. MC
v 161 n 7 p 30 Je '60
RAYET, JACQUELINE, dancer
Et Peter Van Dijk, deux artistes
de la Danse. TD n 96 p 7-8 S-O
'60
---In Daphnis et Chloé, Paris
Opéra review. por TD n 94 p 8
Je '60
---Et Peter Van Dijk dans le "Pel-
léas et Mélisande", AP hl ph:
Peyet. TD n 96 p 7 S-O '60
---In Le Peau de Chagrin (Van
Dijk), AP wl ph: Paris. OpP n 19
p 65 1960
---Two AP wl phs: Michel Petit.
TD n 92 p 29, 30 Ap '60
RAYMOND, PAUL. Diary of a
violin teacher. MD v 50 n 7 p 16
Ja '60; same. MD v 50 n 8 p 17
F '60
RAYNE, MICHEL, dancer
In Ombres Lunaires (Skibine),
AP wl ph: Petit. TD n 95 p 25
Jl-Ag '60
REALI, VITO. Caselliana (4 let-
ters, Alfredo Casella). por La S
n 123 p 24-5 F '60
THE REBEL PLAYERS
Illinois; notes on high school
group, annual tours, self-sup-
porting. PlM v 36 n 5 p 101 F '60
REBORA E JAELE
Criticism of Pizzetti work of
1922. La S n 129-130 p 9-17
Ag-S '60
RECORDER
New music for the recorder re-
viewed by Hugh Orr. CMJ v 4
n 4 p 58-61 Summer '60
RECREATIONAL DANCING IN-
STITUTE
US; aims; notes. IM v 59 n 2 p 8
Ag '60
RED EARTH, play
Sastre criticism. TDR v 5 n 2
p 118 D '60
REDLICH, HANS F. (1903-). Hanns
Jelinek(1901-). MR v 21 n 1 p 66-
72 F '60
REES, LESLIE. Australia (the cur-
rent drama). WT v 9 n 3 p 272-6
Autumn '60

REESE, GILBERT
Notes; b. California. AmM v 8
n 8 p 9 S '60
REGGIO EMILIA
Marmiroli, Renato. Artisti, so-
prani e maghi nel ridotto di Reg-
gio Emilia. il La S n 127 p 36-9
Je '60
REGNER, OTTO FRIEDRICH. The
ballet (in Germany today). WT v 9
n 3 p 227-232 Autumn '60
REICH, GEORGES, dancer
Ballets Ho (Reich) à l'Olympia.
TD n 92 p 14 Ap '60
REID, CHARLES. London (a fre-
quent report on recorded music).
HF 1960
REIMS
Hannigsberg-belle. La Mascotte;
Valses de Vienne; Les Ballets
Modernes de Paris (reviews).
GDC n 255-6 p 304 Ja 15'60
REINAGLE, ALEXANDER, 1756-
1809, composer
Notes; b. Portsmouth, England.
AmM v 8 n 1 p 10 Ja '60
REINE, BELLA, actress
Deux spectacles de mimodrames;
Paris. TD n 90 p 23 F '60
REINKING, WILHELM. Stage set-
ting since 1945 (in Germany). il
WT v 9 n 3 p 249-258 Autumn '60
RELIGIOUS DRAMA
Betti, Ugo (1892-1953). Religion
and the theatre. TDR v 5 n 2 p 3-12
D '60
---Kernodle, George R. Seven med-
ieval theatres in one social struc-
ture. Th R v 2 n 1 p 26-36 1960
---Union Theological Seminary,
NYC; playwriting contest notes.
Th Arts v 44 n 12 p 70 D '60
RENAIS, ALAIN, film director
Towarnicki, Frédéric de. Alain
Renais après "Hiroshima Mon
Amour". Spec n 1 p 60-69 1960
---Por ph. and a portfolio of his
film colleagues, signifigant pic-
tures, a portfolio. Spec n 1 1960
RENARD, burlesque dance scene
Little Orchestra Society; Stravin-
sky criticism. ON v 24 n 19 p 28
Mr 12'60
RENAULT, MICHEL, 1927-, dancer

253

(Renault)
And Liane Daydé in Russia, 2
travel phs. ṬD n 97 p 12-3 N'60
RENNERT, GÜNTHER (1911-).
Glyndebourne and its future. Op
v 11 p 7 Autumn '60
---Career notes; quoted on pro-
duction of opera. il ON v 25 n 4
p 14-5 D 3'60
---Vienna praise for his Ceneren-
tola; choreographer Parlic. Op
v 11 n 1 p 29 Ja '60
---AP ph: Guy Gravett. Op v 11
p 6 Autumn '60
---In rehearsal of Nabucco at the
Metropolitan, ph: Louis Melan-
çon. ON v 25 n 4 p 15 D 3'60
REPERTOIRE LITTLE THEATRE
Toledo, Ohio; notes. PlM v 36
n 7 p 155 Ap '60
REQUIEM POUR UNE NUN, play
Firenze, 1959; ens AP wl ph:
Bosio. WT v 9 n 1 p 86 Spring '60
---Piscator; Théâtre des Nations,
ens AP wl ph. Th R v 2 n 1 p 25
1960
RESCUED BY A COQUETTE,
opera
The Wushih opera company, ens
AP wl ph. Th R v 2 n 1 p 25 1960
RESIDENTIE ORCHESTRA OF THE
HAGUE
Otterloo, Willem Van, conductor;
program notes. MC v 161 n 5
p 33 Ap '60
LA RESISTIBLE ASCENSION D'AR-
TURO UI, play
Lyon, Raymond. Au T. N. P. ;
Brecht. GDC n 290 p 323 N 25'60
RESNIK, REGINA (1923-)
Interview on her career. por ON
v 24 n 12 p 15 Ja 23'60
---Notes; informal por ph: Ellinger.
ON v 25 n 1 p 5 O 8'60
---And small son, Michael, hl ph:
Whitestone. ON v 24 n 12 p 15
Ja 23'60
RESTOUT, DENISE. Manusia; vig-
nettes of Wanda Landowska. il
HF v 10 n 10 p 42-47, 136 O '60
RESZKE, de, EDOUARD, singer
Por ph: Nadar. ON v 25 n 5 p 25
D 10'60
RESZKE, de, JEAN 1855-1916,

singer
As Tristan, AP hl ph. MC
v 161 n 3 p 10 F '60
REUTTER, HERMANN, 1900-,
composer
Hl ph: Stuttgart. MC v 162 n 3
p 18 S '60
REV, LIVIA, pianist
Paris review. GDC n 286 p 197
O 28'60
RÊVE de VALSE, opera
Genève; Strauss review. GDC
n 267-8 p 554 Ap 8'60
UN REVEILLON TROP COP-
IEUX, play
Prague notes; Vratislav Blazek.
WP v 12 n 1 p 16 O '60
REVELLI, DR. WILLIAM D.
Director of Bands, University
of Michigan, por ph. MEJ v 47
n 1 p 53 S-O '60
IL REVISOR
See The Inspector-General, opera
REVIVAL OPERA COMPANY
London's Scala Theatre; reviews:
La Favorita; Oberon. Op v 11 n 7
p 510-1 Jl '60
EL REY HA MUERTO, play
Madrid notes; José Antonio
Gimenez-Arnau. WP v 11 n 9
p 4 Jl '60
REYES, ALFONSO, 1889-1960
Note. WP v 11 n 4 p 8 F '60
REYNA, FERDINANDO (1899-).
La Barberina, croce e delizia
(Barbara Campanini). il La S
n 124 p 9-13 Mr '60
--- ---Un dio della danza: Gaetano
Vestris. il La S n 129-30 p 18-25
Ag-S '60
REYNOLDS, GEORGE. You can't
beat the band (US historical
growth). il MEJ v 47 n 1 p 59-
62 S-O '60
RHINOCEROS, play
Ionesco notes. Th Arts v 44 n 8
p 69 Ag '60
---Lyon, Raymond. A l'Odéon.
GDC n 259-60 p 413 F 12'60
---de Ionesco, ens AP wl ph:
Bernand. WP v 11 n 4 p 1 F '60
---Ens AP hl ph: Witkowski, 1959.
WT v 9 n 1 p 79 Spring '60
---Paris, 1960, ens AP wl ph:

Bernand. WT v 9 n 2 p 159
Summer '60
---Three productions, 3 phs. Th
Arts v 44 n 10 p 19 O '60
---See also Die Nashörner
RHODES, JANE, 1932-, singer
Metropolitan; NYC review of
Carmen. MC v 162 n 6 p 16 D'60
---Metropolitan note. ON v 25 n 5
p 4 D 10'60
---In Carmen, opera, hl several
phs: Paris Opéra. OpP n 19 p 9
1960
---With Director Bing, hl ph: Mel-
ançon. ON v 25 n 5 p 4 D 10'60
RIABINKINA, ELENA
AP wl ph: Moscow. TD n 96 p 9
S-O '60
RICCI, MARCO (1676-1729). The
Rehearsal of an Opera (six cop-
ies of this picture with names of
present owners). Th Notbk v 14
n 3 Spring '60
RICE, ELMER (1892-). The Liv-
ing Theater (book review by
Richard Findlater). Th Notbk
v 15 n 1 p 37 Autumn '60
RICH (BUDDY) BERNARD(1917-).
Modern drumming;an interview.
IM v 58 n 12 p 29-30 Je'60
---Small por ph. IM v 58 n 12 p 29
Je'60
RICHARDS, STANLEY. On and
off Broadway, commercial thea-
tre (review section). PlM v 36
n 4 Ja'60
--- ---On and off Broadway (re-
views). PlM v 37 n 1 p 9-10 O'60
--- ---Theatre in Brazil. PlM
v 37 n 3 p 57-8 D'60
--- ---Theatre in Chile. il PlM
v 36 n 8 p 186-7 My'60
---Chile;International Educational
Exchange Service. PlM v 36 n 6
p 121 Mr'60
RICHARDSON, MRS. A. E. V.
President of the Guild of Aus-
tralian Composers, por ph. MD
v 50 n 11 p 19 My'60
RICHARDSON, SIR RALPH(1902-).
Foreword (to New Theatre Magazine, begun by Bristol University students interested in repertory theatre). NTM v 1 n 1 p 3 O'59

RICHART, RAFAEL. (On staging
Chekhov;Spanish viewpoint.) il
WT v 9 n 2 p 137 Summer'60
RICHTER, SVIATOSLAV
See Rikhter, Sviatoslav Feofil-
ovich, 1915-, pianist
RICORDI, TITO, 1840-1912, composer
E Giacomo Puccini, hl ph:1900.
LaS n 133 p 58 D'60
RIDDLE, NELSON, conductor
And Ella Fitzgerald, hl ph. Th Arts
v 44 n 2 p 78 F'60
RIEFLING, ROBERT, pianist
NYC review. MC v 161 n 4 p 36
Mr'60
RIEGGER, WALLINGFORD, 1885-,
composer
Becker, John J. Wallingford Rie-
ger. ACAB v 9 n 3 p 13 1960
---Check-list of works with pub-
lishers; a discography. ACAB v 9
n 3 p 16-9 1960
---Cowell, Henry. A note on Wall-
ingford Riegger. ACAB v 9 n 3
p 14-5 1960
---Criticism;short signed com-
ments. ACAB v 9 n 3 1960
---Goldman, Richard Franko. The
music of Wallingford Riegger.
ACAB v 9 n 3 p 15-6 1960
---Notes. GDC n 292 p 420 D 9'60
---Notes. J Rev v 7 n 2 p 20 Spring
'60
---Notes. por J Rev v 7 n 1 p 15
Winter 59-60
---Première:Cooper Square;NYC
1959. ACAB v 9 n 2 p 23 1960
---Première:Sinfonietta;Orchestra
of America;b. Albany, Georgia;
notes. por IM v 59 n 6 p 26 D'60
---Texas fête;report. MC v 161 n 6
p 30 My'60
RIEMENS, LEO. Belgium; opera
reports. Op v 11 n 1 p 30-2 Ja'60
RIGOLETTO, opera
Melbourne; Robin Lovejoy, pro-
ducer; review. MD v 50 n 11
p 10 My '60
---Metropolitan Opera cast; notes;
portfolio. ON v 25 n 8 D 31'60
---Metropolitan cast, 6 AP hl phs:
Melançon and others; Act I ens
AP wl ph; Leblang; two nineteenth
century scenes. ON v 25 n 8

(Rigoletto)
D 31'60
RIGOTTI, DOMENICO. Cechov
librettista mancato. il La S
n 129-30 p 26-7 Ag-S '60
RIKHTER, SVIATOSLAV FEO-
FILOVICH, 1915-, pianist
American debut; Chicago re-
view. MC v 162 n 5 p 21 N '60
---Career notes. GDC n 265-6
cover Mr 25'60
---Ericson, Ray. (Various re-
cordings reviewed.) por HF
v 10 n 6 p 56 Je '60
---Goldsmith, Harris. Rich-
ter's first Beethoven and others.
por HF v 10 n 11 p 74-5 N '60
---Philadelphia criticism. MC
v 162 n 6 p 24 D '60
---US notes. HF v 10 n 12 p 57
D '60
---Por ph. HF v 10 n 4 p 68
Ap '60
---Por ph: Deutsche Grammo-
phon. GDC n 265-6 cover Mr
25'60
---Right profile keyboard ph.
MC v 162 n 4 p 4 O '60
RINALDI, MARIO (1903-). Tea-
tro dell'Opera. il La S n 123
p 34-5 F '60
DER RING DES NIBELUNG,
opera
Bayreuth cast; Australian
Broadcasting Commission notes.
MD v 51 n 6 p 13 D '60
---Covent Garden review. il Op
v 11 n 11 p 775-779 N '60
--- ---review;? Stockholm opera,
R. L. J. MR v 21 n 4 p 325-6
N '60
---Downes, Edward. Bayreuth
criticism. ON v 25 n 2 p 23
O 29'60
---Bayreuth, Act II of Die Walk-
üre; Act I of Siegfried; Act III
scene 1 of Götterdammerung;
Windgassen; Hines five AP
phs. Op v 11 p 37-8 Autumn'60
---Covent Garden 1960, port-
folio of singers: Southern. Op
v 11 n 11 p 776-7 N '60
RING ROUND THE MOON, play
Ens ph: Stadium Theatre,

Ohio State. PlM v 36 n 4 cover
Ja '60
RIO DE JANEIRO
Building theatres; notes on plans.
WP v 11 n 6 p 1, 7 Ap '60
---Construction Théâtrale; manual
in prepartion; notes. WP v 11 n 3
p 7 Ja '60
---Lander, Harald; au projet de
M. Murillo Miranda; critique; les
Indes Galantes; Iara (Lander-Villa
Lobos); Etudes. TD n 97 p 24, 29
N '60
---Opera report by Antonio José
Jaro. Op v 11 n 10 p 686-7 O '60
---Vieira, Silvio, in Tosca; honor-
ed by the Carlo Gomez medal. Op
v 11 n 9 p 616 S '60
---Théâtre d'Art Populaire in Gim-
ba, play by Guarnieri, ens AP wl
ph: Pic. WT v 9 n 4 p 352 Winter
'60
RIOTON, MARTHE, singer
In "Louise", AP hl ph: Paris. LaS
n 132 p 41 N '60
RISTIC, MILAN, composer
Première: Symphonic Variations;
Belgrade Philharmonic. WM n 2
p 32 Ap '60
---Por ph. La S n 133 p 109 D '60
RITA, opera
Australian National Theatre; cast.
MD v 51 n 1 p 21 Jl '60
RITCHARD, CYRIL, 1898-, actor
And Cornelia Otis Skinner and
Dolores Hart in The Pleasure of
His Company, ens AP hl phs: Van-
damm. Th Arts v 44 n 4 p 29
Ap '60
RITES (AKESSON), ballet
Stockholm notes. WP v 11 n 9
p 15 Jl '60
RITTER, THELMA, 1905-, actress
Por ph. Th Arts v 44 n 12 p 1
D '60
RIVA, UBALDO. La musica nelle
poesie di Salvatore Di Giacomo.
il La S n 133 p 48-55 D '60
RIVERA, CHITA, dancer
In Bye Bye Birdie, musical, ens
AP wl ph: Sheldon Secunda. Th
Arts v 44 n 7 p 15 Jl '60
RIVIER, JEAN (1896-). Concerto
pour clarinette et orchestre à

cordes (études musicales analytiques). GDC n 290 p 334 N 25'60
--- ---VIe Symphonie en mi (études musicales analytiques). GDC n 261-2 p 445 F 26'60
---Notes; b. Villemomble. GDC n 290 p 304 N 25'60
---Première: Concerto pour clarinette (chez Oubradous). GDC n 292 p 421 D 9'60
RIVIERE, JEAN-PIERRE, composer
Ricordi International Competition: one-act opera, Pour un Don Quichotte, winner; notes. MD v 51 n 5 p 9 N '60
ROACH, J. TATIAN, ?-1960
Obituary notes. MEJ v 46 n 4 p 14 F-Mr '60
ROACH, MAX, 1925-, drummer
With his drums, ph. IM v 59 n 2 p 15 Ag '60
ROBARDS, JASON NELSON, JR. 1922-, actor
Keating, John. Theatre Arts gallery, series: Jason Robards, Jr. Th Arts v 44 n 4 p 10-2 Ap '60
---Por ph: Max Waldman. Th Arts v 44 n 4 p 11 Ap '60
ROBOTHAM, BARBARA 1940-, singer
Winner Liverpool contest. Op v 11 n 7 p 456 Jl '60
ROBERT MASTERS QUARTET
Notes. AmM v 8 n 2 p 6 F '60
ROBERTAZZI, MARIO. Un modo di raccontare la musica. La S n 132 p 58-61 N '60
ROBERTA, musical
Ens AP wl ph: NYC. Th Arts v 44 n 9 p 67 S '60
ROBERTSON, LEROY, 1896-, composer
Passacaglia (1955); NYC comment. MC v 161 n 6 p 18 My '60
ROBESON, PAUL, 1898-, singer
Australia; first tour. MD v 51 n 5 p 8 N '60
ROBIN, MADO, 1919-1960, singer
Obituary notes. OpP n 19 p 50 1960
---As La Reine de la Nuit, AP hl ph: Paris Opéra. OpP v 19

p 50 1960
ROBIN HOOD DELL
Mann, Fredric R. reporting as President to a symposium of symphony men at the Waldorf, NYC; excerpts. IM v 59 n 3 p 41 S '60
---Singer, Samuel L. Wilfrid Pelletier and Arthur Fiedler, Franz Allers for the D'Oyle Carte; other notes. MC v 162 n 2 p 14-5 Ag'60
---Mann, Frederic R, as president of the concerts, accepts award for 31 summers of concerts from American Federation of Musicians' president Mr. Kenin, ens ph: Philadelphia. IM v 59 n 2 p 7 Ag '60
ROBINSON, EDWARD G. 1893-, actor
Por ph. Th Arts v 44 n 9 p 81 S '60
ROBINSON, FRANCIS (1799-1872)?
Hl ph: Wagner. ON v 25 n 8 p 4 D 31'60
ROBINSON, JACQUELINE, dancer
Michel, Marcelle J. Chez Jacqueline Robinson. TD n 90 p 25 F'60
ROBINSON, J. W. The Play of Daniel produced by the New York Pro Musica. Th Notbk v 15 n 1 p 33-34 Autumn '60
ROBINSON, WAYNE. Theatre, Philadelphia (home-grown showmen as well as New York tryouts). il Th Arts v 44 n 2 p 73-77 F '60
ROCCHIA, GEORGES, 1913-1960
Obituary. GDC n 288 p 270 N 11'60
ROCKABILLY
Miscegenation of rock'n'roll, hill-billy and Tin-Pan alley idioms; Johnny Horton Makes History", ballad-type record reviewed. HF v 10 n 10 p 102 O '60
ROCKEFFER, JOHN D. , 3rd (1906-). Financing the arts. ON v 25 n 2 p 8-11 O 29'60
RODDY, JOSEPH. Mr. Mahler in Manhattan. il HF v 10 n 7 p 30-33 Jl '60
--- ---Steinways and Steinwayism. HF v 10 n 3 p 42-5, 126 Mr '60
RODGERS, MARY. (On the musical, Once Upon a Mattress, music

(Rodgers)
Mary Rodgers, choreography
Joe Layton; its NYC and tour
story.) por Th Arts v 44 n 7 p 21-
4 Jl '60
---Por ph: Friedman-Abeles. Th
Arts v 44 n 7 p 21 Jl '60
RODGERS, RICHARD, 1902-?
composer
With Oscar Hammerstein II, hl
ph. AmM v 8 n 3 p 13 Mr '60
RODRIGO, (JOAQUIN, 1902-).
composer
Première: le Concerto-Sérénade
pour harpe; played at Besançon
by Nicanor Zabaleta. GDC n 283
p 95 O 7'60
---Première: Tonadilla; Ida Pres-
ti et Alexandre Lagoya à Gaveau.
GDC n 293-4 p 459 D 16'60
ROESGEN-CHAMPION, MARGUE-
RITE, 1895?-, harpsichordist
Machuel, Dominique. Paris re-
view. GDC n 278 p 848 Je 24'60
ROGGERO, MARGARET, singer
As Suzuki, AP ph: Melançon.
ON v 24 n 24 p 17 Ap 16'60
LE ROI DAVID (CHARRAT), opera
Davies, Margaret E. Paris notes.
ON v 25 n 5 p 30 D 10'60
---Paris Opéra; Arthur Honegger
music to René Morax; notes,
also on previous performances.
MC v 162 n 6 p 30 D '60
--- ---1958 Toulouse sous la
direction Louis Izar; critique.
il TD n 98 p 21 D '60
--- ---review. GDC n 287 p 226
N 4'60
---Rostand, Claude. Le Roi David
à l'Opéra. il OpP n 19 p 16-9
1960
---Portfolio: Paris Opéra 1960.
OpP n 19 p 16-9 1960
LE ROI D'Ys, opera
Lalo's use of the legend (De-
bussy's use in "La Cathédrale
engloutine"); New Orleans prem-
ière 1890. ON v 24 n 14 p 8, 31
F 6'60
LE ROI FOL (GUELIS), opera
Jaque-Dupont; "historical fres-
co", disjointed life of Charles VI;
Rouen review. Op v 11 n 5

p 345 My '60
---Mennesson, Félix. Première
mondiale à Rouen; Jacque Du-
pont; cast. GDC n 255-6 p 303
Ja 15'60
---Rouen; notes. il TD n 91 p 10
Mr '60
--- ---music, Jacques Dupont.
WP v 11 n 5 p 8 Mr '60
LE ROI LÉPREUX, play
Ens AP wl ph: Verhassel. WT
v 9 n 1 p 5 Spring '60
LE ROI MALGRÉ LUI, opera
Wolfe, Stéphane. A l'Opéra-
Comique. GDC n 255-6 p 301-2
Ja 15'60
ROLAND-MANUEL, ALEXIS, 1891-,
professor
Notes. GDC n 287 p 208 N 4'60
---Por ph. GDC n 287 cover N 4'60
ROMAN, JOSETTE, pianist
And Yvette Roman, duo-pianists,
right profiles, ph. MC v 161 n 3
p 20 F '60
ROMAN CANDLE, play
Sheldon, Sidney. A journey to
our minds (extra sensory per-
ception) il Th Arts v 44 n 3 p 18
Mr '60
ROME
Music report. La S n 122 p 65
Ja '60
---Rinaldi, Mario. Teatro dell
'Opera: Ballo in maschera; Il
Vortice (Rossellini). il La S
n 123 p 34-5 F '60
--- ---Teatro dell'Opera di Roma.
il La S n 126 p 34, 59 My '60
---Selden-Goth, Gisella. Music re-
port. MC v 161 n 3 p 44 F '60
---Teatro dell'Opera: programma
della stagione 1959-1960. La S
n 122 inset Ja '60
---The Theatre Club, director
Mrs. Anne Guerrieri; notes. PlM
v 37 n 1 p 9 O '60
RONCAGLIA, GINO (1883-). Gius-
eppe Verdi cosi com'era. il La S
n 126 p 18-22 My '60
--- ---Gli avversari di Verdi.
caricatures La S n 131 p 38-41
O '60
--- ---Riccardo or Gustave III?
(Un ballo in maschera: music

neither Swedish, English nor American and" the music makes the drama"). Ver v 1 n 2 preface Ag '60

LA RONDE, play
Schnitzler; Georges Pitoëff revival, AP wl ph. Spec n 1 p 40 1960

LE RONDEAU DE PARIS
Paris; jeune ensemble féminin; review. GDC n 295 p 492 D 30'60

LA RONDINE, operetta
Philadelphia Grand Opera revival; Licia Albanese; review. MC v 131 n 5 p 20 Ap '60
--- ---review. il ON v 24 n 22 p 26 Ap 2'60

THE ROOM AND THE DUMB WAITER, play
London notes; Harold Pinter. WP v 11 n 8 p 12 Je '60

ROOSEVELT, ELEANOR (1884-).
On right-to-work laws, quoted. IM v 58 n 12 p 8 Je '60

ROOSEVELT, FRANKLIN DELANO, 1882-1945
Washington Records release 33 Roosevelt speeches; Mrs. Roosevelt in NYC presides with Robert Bialek over the press conference. HF v 10 n 7 p 47 Jl '60

THE ROPE DANCERS, play
Wishengrad, Morton. (Complete text of the play; 1957 NYC cast and portfolio). Th Arts v 44 n 1 p 33-64 Ja '60

ROSA LA ROSE, play
Paris notes; Ange Bastiani. WP v 11 n 5 p 7 Mr '60

ROSADA, LUCIANO
Notes. La S n 125 p 44 Ap '60

ROSAMUNDE, play
Norman, Elizabeth. Schubert's incidental music to Rosamunde. MR v 21 n 1 p 8-15 F '60

ROSAMUNDE FLORIS, opera
Berlin; review of Blacher's opera. il Op v 11 n 12 p 828 D'60
--- ---notes; Boris Blacher. WP v 12 n 2 p 23 N '60
--- ---review; Boris Blacher, music; Erwin Piscator, staging; Stina Britta Melander and Thomas Stewart. MC v 162 n 6 p 31 D '60

--- ---ens AP wl ph: Ilse Buhs. Op v 11 n 12 p 829 D '60

ROSBAUD, HANS, 1895-, conductor
Chicago criticism. MC v 162 n 6 p 23 D '60

ROSE ET COLAS, radio opera
Monsigny; critical comments on the score, compared to Mozart its "doggedly cheerful airs are dispiriting." Op v 11 n 5 p 376 My '60

THE ROSE TATTOO, play
Bruxelles; ens AP wl ph: 1952. WT v 9 n 1 p 37 Spring '60

ROSEN, CHARLES, 1927-, pianist
Notes. AmM v 8 n 4 p 6 Ap '60
---Right profile, at the piano, ph. MC v 161 n 4 p 18 Mr '60

ROSEN, HEINZ
Munich; Joan de Zarissa (Maudrick-Rosen). TD n 92 p 26 Ap'60

ROSENFELD, SYBIL. A Sadler's Wells scene book, (seven designs included). Th Notbk v 15 n 2 p 57-62 Winter'60-61
--- ---(Correction of an illustration from the engraver Iasper Isac, attributed wrongly by Dubech to a performance of Mitton's Comus.) Th R v 2 n 3 p 179 1960
--- ---Report on two Georgian theatres: Richmond (Yorks) Theatre; Stockton-on-Tees Theatre. Th Notbk v 14 n 3 p 100-101 Spring '60

DER ROSENKAVALIER, opera
Barker, Frank Granville. Covent Garden (Rosenkavalier with Schwarzkopt; Salome and Carmen). ON v 24 n 16 p 28-30 F 20'60
---Catania; cavaliere della Rosa di Riccardo Straus. La S n 127 p 57 Je '60
---Covent Garden review. Op v 11 n 1 p 65-7 Ja '60; same. Op v 11 n 12 p 849 D '60
---Glyndebourne 1960; review. MR v 21 n 3 p 250 Ag '60
---Karajan's opening of Salzburg's new Festspielhaus. Op v 11 p 47-8 Autumn '60
---Metropolitan; criticism. MC v 161 n 3 p 24 F '60
--- ---review; Graf "at his most

(Der Rosenkavalier)
inventive. " Op v 11 n 4 p 269
Ap '60
---NYC Opera review; James
Pease, Frances Bible, Anne Mc-
Knight; Joseph Rudel, conducting;
Ralph Herbert, new stage direc-
tor. MC v 162 n 5 p 16 N '60
---Osborne, Conrad L. The 1933
recording, newly re-issued, top
of the list; Lotte Lehmann. por
HF v 10 n 5 p 61 My '60
---Salzburg's new Festspielhaus;
cast. ON v 25 n 2 p 18 O 29'60
---Berlin Staatsoper, ens ph: Ma-
rion Schöne. Op v 11 n 10 p 692
O '60
---Covent Garden; 3 ens AP phs;
Kurt Böhme as Ochs, Jurinac as
Octavian, 5 AP phs: Houston
Rogers. Op v 11 n 1 p 65-7 Ja'60
---Salzburg, 1960; ens AP wl ph:
Ellinger. WM n 5 p 110 O '60
ROSENKER, MICHAEL, violinist
Notes; b. Russia. IM v 59 n 5
p 36 N '60
ROSENTHAL, HAROLD. Londres:
la saison lyrique. GDC n 257-8
p 357 Ja 29'60
ROSENTHAL, LAURENCE (1927-).
Wanted: a real musical theatre
in the United States. MC v 162
n 5 p 7 N '60
---At his desk, with his family,
two phs. MC v 162 n 5 cover,
p 7 N '60
ROSENTHAL, EMMANUEL (MANU-
EL) ,1904-, composer
Musique de Table (commentaire).
GDC n 291 p 356 D 2'60
ROSMERSHOLM, play
Dignam, Peggy Ashcroft and
Potter, AP ph: Guy Gravett. Th
Arts v 44 n 4 p 15 Ap '60
---London, 1960, Peggy Ashcroft
and Mark Dignam, AP wl ph:
Guy Gravett. WT v 9 n 2 p 183
Summer '60
ROSOWSKY, SOLOMON (1878-).
The Cantillation of the Bible; The
Five Books of Moses (review by
Israel Rabinovitch. CMJ v 5 n 1
p 77-8 Autumn '60
ROSS, DAVID. (On staging

Chekhov; US viewpoint.) il WT
v 9 n 2 p 138 Summer '60
ROSS, HERBERT, 1926?-, chor-
eographer
Spoleto; notes. TD n 95 p 7
Jl-Ag '60
ROSS, play
London notes; Terence Rattigan.
WP v 11 n 11 p 16 Ag '60
---Rattigan, Terence; notes. WT
v 9 n 3 p 291 Autumn '60
---Guiness, Alec, AP wl ph: An-
gus McBean, 1960. WT v 9 n 3
p 290 Autumn '60
ROSSELLINI, RENZO (1908-). It-
alian renaissance (opera in Italy).
ON v 24 n 21 p 15, 32 Mr 26'60
ROSSI-LEMENI, NICOLA, 1922-,
singer
As Eurito (Fedra), AP wl ph:
La Scala. La S n 123 p 31 F '60
---In L'assassinio nella catted-
rale, AP hl ph: La Scala, 1958.
La S n 129-30 p 14 Ag-S '60
ROSSINI, GIOACCHINO 1792-1868,
composer
Hughes, Patrick Cairns. The
swan who could laugh. HF v 10
n 7 p 38-40, 84 Jl '60
---Hughes, Patrick Cairns. The
swan who could laugh. HF v 10
n 7 p 38-40, 84 Jl '60
---Seracini, Giuliano. Lettere
sconosciute di Rossini. il La S
n 123 p 48-50 F '60
---Por print. La S n 123 p 49 F'60
ROSTAND, CLAUDE. Le Roi
David a l'Opéra. il OpP n 19 p 16-
9 1960
ROSTROPOVITCH, MSTISLAV,
1927-, cellist
Por ph. MD v 51 n 1 cover Jl '60
THE ROTH QUARTET
Los Angeles, U. C. L. A. review;
speaker at intermission "dubious
fad". MC v 161 n 5 p 23 Ap '60
ROTTERDAM PHILHARMONIC
Flipse, Eduard, conductor; pro-
gram notes. MC v 161 n 5 p 33
Ap '60
ROUBAKINE, BORIS. (On Cana-
da's music festivals.) CMJ v 5
n 1 p 34 Autumn '60
ROULEAU, JOSEPH, singer

And Jeannette Sinclair, AP hl
ph:London. Op v 11 n 12 p 848
D'60
LA ROULOTTE aux POUPÉES,
play
Montreal notes;Marie-Claire
Blais. WP v 12 n 3 p 27 D'60
ROUSSELOT, LÉONE, singer
Chamfray, Claude. Entretien
avec Léone Rousselot (Le chant,
acte réflexe). GDC n 291 p 339
D 2'60
ROYAL ACADEMY of DANCING,
LONDON
Hammond, Paul. What is the Roy-
al Academy of Dancing? por MD
v 50 n 12 p 25 Je'60
THE ROYAL BALLET (BRITISH)
Several ens AP wl phs. MD v 50
n 11 p 22-3 My'60
THE ROYAL BALLET, film
Melbourne première;story of its
making;review. il MD v 50 n 11
p 22-3 My'60
ROYAL COMMAND(MARTYN),
ballet
Australia;based on old lithogra-
phs. MD v 51 n 2 p 24 Ag'60
ROYAL DANISH BALLET
NYC report. MD v 51 n 2 p 29
Ag'60
ROYAL OPERA HOUSE
Editorial on Covent Garden An-
nual Report 1958-9. Op v 11 n 1
p 6 Ja'60
ROYAL PHILHARMONIC ORCH-
ESTRA
Russian tour;Sir Thomas Bee-
cham. WM n 2 p 31 Ap'60
ROYAL STOCKHOLM OPERA
London criticism;Göran Gentele,
producer. Op v 11 n 10 p 709-12
O'60
---Report. il Op v 11 n 5 p 357 My
'60
THE ROYALTY, theatre
Notes on new London playhouse.
Th Arts v 44 n 11 p 77 N'60
RUBBRA, EDMUND(1901-). Coun-
terpoint(book review). MR v 21
n 2 p 148-150 My'60
RUBINSTEIN, ARTUR, 1886-,
pianist
NYC review;all-Chopin. MC v 161

n 4 p 15 Mr'60
---Por ph:Blackstone Studios. HF
v 10 n 4 p 66 Ap'60
RUBIO, CONSUELO, singer
Paris concert review;Jacqueline
Bonneau. GDC n 257-8 p 358 Ja
29'60
RUDIE, ROBERT, violinist
Notes;b. NYC. IM v 59 n 5 p 37
N'60
RUDOLF, MAX, 1902-, conductor
Cincinnati criticism. MC v 161
n 6 p 32 My'60
RUDOLF, ROBERT, conductor
Por ph:Lotte Meitner-Graf. Am M
v 8 n 4 p 9 Ap'60
RUEGGER, GUSTAV ADOLFO. Uru-
guay (theatre report). il WT v 9
n 2 p 186-8 Summer'60
RUIZ SOLER, ANTONIO, 1921-,
dancer
See Soler, Antonio Ruiz, 1921
RUMA ELSA (TUULOS), musical
Helsinki notes;Jorma Panula, mu-
sic. WP v 11 n 10 p 2 Ag'60
RUMANIA
Theatre report. WP v 11 n 6 p 7
Ap'60
RUSHMORE, ROBERT. Scenes thru
a Freudian glass (opera plots, es-
pecially Il Trovatore). ON v 24
n 17 p 6-7 F 27'60
RUSSELL, ANNA, 1911-, concert
comedienne
Itinerary in Great Britain. Am M
v 8 n 9 p 10 O'60
RUSSELL, SIR JOHN W. (1893-). A
Tory and the provincial theatre.
NTM v 1 n 2 p 11-3 Ja'60
RUSSIA
Allers, Franz, on musical impres-
sions of the U. S. S. R. MC v 162
n 1 p 11 Jl'60
--- ---report of visit as manager of
My Fair Lady. IM v 59 n 2 p 10-1
Ag'60
---Assenine, Serge. L'Ecole choregraphique de Moscou. il TD n 98
p 16-7 D'60
---Bolshoi Ballet soloists (16) in
London;"the virtuoso bravura
clouded by the banality of contem-
porary choreography". MC v 162
n 2 p 22 Ag'60

(Russia)
---Bolshoi Theater; Prokofiev's War and Peace displacing (after 185 years) Ivan Susanin as opening bill. Op v 11 n 11 p 768 N'60
---Boulimov, Vladimir. Le Ballet Berezka en Italie. il TD n 97 p 5 N'60
---The Chekhov Centenary in the U.S.S.R. WT v 9 n 2 p 100 Summer'60
---Les Choeurs et danses de l'armée soviétique; Paris note on performance at Alhambra. il TD n 94 p 3 Je'60
---Cultural exchange program with USA: visiting Russian groups to more US cities, with longer stay than USSR allows US groups; comment. MC v 161 n 1 p 5 Ja'60
---The Filial Theatre closed; dispersal of artists and of repertory discussed; economic effect upon the Bolshoi. Op v 2 n 3 p 218 Mr '60
---Films ballets Soviétiques; Paris. TD n 98 p 23 D'60
---How singers start an operatic career; questions by Mattiwilda Dobbs, answers by Galina Vishnevskaya. por ON v 24 n 18 p 10-1 Mr 5'60
---Question of royalties to the musical artist from foreign recordings. HF v 10 n 4 p 24 Ap'60
---New agreement with USA on expanded exchange of musicians; summary. WM n 1 p 8 F'60
---Opera reports: Kirghizia; and Kuibyshev. Op v 11 n 4 p 288-290 Ap'60
---Paris; les danseurs de l'armée soviétique. J.S. TD n 93 p 19 My'60
---Polyanovsky, Georgi. Baku opera report; historical sketch of Azerbaijan opera. il Op v 11 n 1 p 46-8 Ja'60
---Polyanovsky, Georgy. Opera reports. Op v 11 n 9 630-2 S'60
---Recordings no longer via Leeds but handled by Recording Artist Music Corporation; US arrangements. HF v 10 n 6 p 53 Je'60

---Rigotti, Domenico. Cechov librettista mancato. il LaS n 129-30 p 26-27 Ag-S'60
---Singermann, Boris. (Theatre report.) il WT v 9 n 4 p 358-362 Winter'60
--- ---U.S.S.R. (theatre report). il WT v 9 n 2 p 178-181 Summer'60
---Theatre Report. WP v 11 n 10 p 8 Ag '60; same. WP v 12 n 1 p 4 O '60
---Zavadski, Youri. Theatre in U.R.S.S. WP v 11 n 5 p 1, 7 Mr'60
---Composers; a delegation visiting the Juilliard School, seven phs: Impact, NYC. J Rev v 7 n 1 p 10-1 Winter 59-60
RUYSDAEL, BASIL, 1888-1960, singer
Obituary notes. Op v 11 n 12 p 839 D '60
RUZDJAK, V., singer
Por ph: Zagreb. La S n 128 p 65 Jl '60
RYAN, PETER J. Letter (comments on O'Casey and other contributors). Th Arts v 44 n 5 p 6 My '60
--- ---Letter (on the contents of Theatre Arts by its publisher). Th Arts v 44 n 2 p 8 F '60
--- ---(Letter to readers of theatre Arts from the publisher.) Th Arts v 44 n 1 p 8 Ja '60
RYSANEK, LOTTE
And Rudolf Christ in the Tales of Hoffmann, AP hl ph: Pflaum-Gebhardt. ON v 24 n 19 p 26 Mr 12'60
RYSANEK, LEONIE, 1928-, singer
As Abigaille, AP hl ph: Melançon. ON v 25 n 4 p 20 D 3'60
---As Elisabeth in Tannhäuser, AP hl ph: Fayer. ON v 25 n 6 p 21 D 17'60
---As Lady Macbeth, AP hl ph: Louis Melançon. ON v 24 n 9 p 17 Ja 2'60
---As Lady Macbeth, two AP wl phs: the Metropolitan. Th Arts v 44 n 3 p 40 Mr '60
---As Senta, AP phs: Melançon. ON v 24 n 18 Mr 5'60

SABATO, DOMENICA e LUNEDI,
play
Rome; Eduardo de Filippo; notes.
WP v 11 n 4 p 9 F '60
THE SABINE WOMEN, play
Décor by Milenko Serban, ens
ph: Beograd, 1959. WT v 9 n 4
p 371 Winter '60
SABOURET, MARIE, actress
With Paul-Emile Deiber in Le
Pain de Ménage, AP hl ph: Ber-
nand, 1960. WT v 9 n 3 p 284
Autumn '60
SABRAN, EDMEE, singer
Wolff, Stéphane. Paris review.
GDC n 273 p 690 My 20'60
UN SAC D'EMBROUILLES, farce
Billiet, Jacques. A la Gaîte-
Lyrique; commentaire. GDC
n 271 p 630 My 5'60
LE SACRE DE PRINTEMPS (BE-
JART), ballet
Guest, Ivor. (Criticism.) MD
v 50 n 12 p 28 Je '60
---Notes. il TD n 95 p 15 Jl-Ag
'60
---Paris review. GDC n 274 p 720
My 27'60
SADIE, STANLEY, The chamber
music of Boyce and Arne. Mus
Q v 46 n 4 p 425-436 O '60
SADLER'S WELLS OPERA
Littlefield, Joan. Andrea Ché-
nier "helped by Leslie Hurry's
décor"; La Cenerentola; Katya
Kabanova. ON v 24 n 13 p 26-7
Ja 30'60
---Opera notes. Op 1960
---Report. Op v 2 n 3 p 198 Mr'60
---Reviews: Hansel und Gretel;
The Merry Widow; Tannhäuser;
The Marriage of Figaro. Op
v 11 n 2 p 152, 155, 160 F '60
--- ---La Traviata; Tosca; Tann-
häuser. Op v 11 n 11 p 780-3
N '60
--- ---Les Pêcheurs de Perles;
Madama Butterfly; Don Pasquale;
Fidelio. Op v 11 n 4 p 299-302
Ap '60
--- ---Oedipus Rex; Duke Blue-
beard's Castle; La Cenerentola;

Tannhäuser; La Bohème. Op
v 2 n 3 p 230-233 Mr '60
---Season 1959-60; singers con-
ductors, producers and list of
works with casts. Op v 11 n 7
p 468-9 Jl '60
---Stravinsky double-bill: Oedipus
and Nightingale; notes. MC
v 162 n 6 p 29 D '60
---Two companies; figures on
government subsidy; repertory.
MC v 161 n 5 p 31 Ap '60
SADLER'S WELLS THEATRE
Rosenfeld, Sybil. A Sadler's
Wells scene book. il Th Notbk
v 15 n 2 p 57-62 Winter 60-61
SAERCHINGER, CEASAR (1884-).
Letter congratulating the Musi-
cal Courier on its 80th year. por
MC v 161 n 3 p 6 F '60
SAEVERUD, HAROLD, 1897-,
composer
US visit of Norwegian; his Peer
Gynt Suite. MC v 162 n 1 p 29
Jl '60
SAFARTY, REGINA, singer
Career notes; b. Rochester.
AmM v 8 n 5 p 6 Je '60
SAGOSPEL, play
Götheborg notes; Erland Joseph-
son. WP v 11 n 4 p 14 F '60
SAGRA MUSICALE UMBRIA
Perugia; report. MC v 162 n 5
p 42 N '60
SAGUER, LOUIS. Seis cantares
de Federico Garcia Lorca (étu-
des musicales analytiques).
GDC n 292 p 429 D 9'60
THE SAILORS OF CATTARO,
play
The Theatre Union, ens AP wl
ph: NYC. Th Arts v 44 n 9 p 17
S '60
SAINT-DENIS, MICHEL, pseud.
1897-, directeur
Goring, Maurice. (Criticism in
review of Saint-Denis' book,
Theatre: The Rediscovery of
Style .) Th Notbk v 15 n 2 p 63-
4 Winter'60-61
---With Colin Davis, conductor,
and Monica Sinclair, singer, hl
ph: London. AmM v 8 n 2 p 9
F '60

SAINT JOAN, play
Shaw in 1925; la Compagnie
Pitoëff, ens AP wl ph. Spec n 1
p 38 1960
ST. LOUIS
Band; Laclede Concert Band
notes. IM v 59 n 2 p 46 Ag '60
ST. LOUIS SYMPHONY
Prize competition; notes. IM
v 59 n 5 p 53 N '60
SAINT MARY'S COLLEGE
Moreau Fine Arts Center, 2 phs:
Indiana. MC v 161 n 2 cover
Ap '60
SAINTE JEANNE DE L'AMERI-
QUE, play
Argentina notes; Andrés Lizar-
raga. WP v 12 n 2 p 19 N '60
SALAD DAYS, play
Ens AP wl ph: Cayet, 1959. WT
v 9 n 1 p 41 Spring '60
SALISBURY ART THEATRE
Salberg, Reginald. Repertory
in Salisbury. NTM v 1 n 3 p 15-
7 Ap '60
SALMON, RAYMOND. Trois mél-
odies (études musicales analy-
tiques). GDC n 263-4 p 494
Mr 11'60
SALOME, opera
Covent Garden review. Op v 11
n 1 p 61 Ja '60
---Historical notes. ON v 25 n 4
p 11-2 D 3'60
---Phillips, Linda. Melbourne;
Joan Hammond. MD v 50 n 11
p 8-9 My '60
SALTMAN, PAULINE. Phantoms
of the opera (singers tell of see-
ing phantoms on and off stage).
ON v 24 n 14 p 6-7, 30 F 6'60
SALVADOR, SAL, guitarist
With instrument, ph. IM v 59
n 3 p 7 S '60
SALZBURG
Chapowalenko, Georges. 3 Fes-
tivals; Salzbourg. TD n 98 p 24-
6 D '60
---Mandelli, Piero. Salisburgo
un nuova gran Theatro d'Opera
il La S n 128 p 20-2 Jl '60
---Mellen, Constance, as well as
Edward Downes, contribute cri-
ticism of operas. ON v 25 n 2

p 18 O 29'60
---Wechsberg, Joseph. Salzburg's
new Festspielhaus. il Op v 11 n 8
p 535-40 Ag '60
---New Festival House, exterior
and interior phs WM n 4 p 81
Ag '60
---Opera; ten action photographs.
Op v 11 p 48-53 Autumn '60
SALZBURG FESTIVAL
Faulkner, Maurice. (new theatre;
programs reviewed.) il MC v 162
n 3 p 7 S '60
---Hofmannsthal, Hugo von, 1919,
co-founder; notes. Th R v 2 n 1
p 15 1960
---Opera reviews by Joseph Wechsberg and by the Editor. Op
v 11 p 47-53 Autumn '60
---Festival Theatre, architect
Clemens Holzmeister, from the
air, ph. and Jurinac and Edelmann
in Act III of Der Rosenkavalier,
AP wl ph: Fayer. MC v 162 n 3
p 7 S '60
SALZEDO, CARLOS, 1885-,
harpist-composer
Notes; 130 compositions. IM
v 58 n 7 p 37 Ja '60
SALZMAN, ERIC. (Electronic
music synthesizer at the Columbia-Princeton Electronic Music Center, NYC; historical notes on electronic instruments.) il
HF v 10 n 8 p 40-42 Ag '60
SALZMAN, THEODORE. Cello
chat (stringing the instrument;
on pressure easing). il IM v 58
n 11 p 20-1 My '60
SAM, THE HIGHEST JUMPER
OF THEM ALL, play
London; William Saroyan. WP
v 11 n 10 p 14 Ag '60
SAMAZEUILH, GUSTAVE (1877-).
La musique de chambre de Gabriel Fauré. GDC n 289 p 289-
291 N 18'60
SAMSON ET DALILA, opera
Paris Opéra review; José Beckmans production. Op v 11 n 11
p 763 N '60
---Ens AP wl ph: Athens. Op v 11
n 9 p 628 S '60
---Portfolio: Paris Opéra 1960.

264

OpP n 19 p 20-3 1960
SAN ANTONIO
Première: La Vidi de la Mision,
Carl Venth's opera; notes. Op
v 11 n 1 p 29 Ja '60
---Sixteenth Grand Opera Festival:
repertory and casts; Victor Ales-
sandro, conductor. Op v 11 n 7
p 473 Jl '60
SAN ANTONIO WOODWIND QUIN-
TET
List of members. IM v 59 n 6
p 40 D '60
SAN CARLO OPERA
Benedetto, Renato di. Martirio
di San Sebastiano; Il vascello
fantasma; La Luna di Karl Orff;
Il protagonista di Kurt Weill; Il
malato immaginario di Jacopo
Napoli. La S n 127 p 28, 56 Je '60
--- ---Mayerling; Racconti di
Hoffmann. il La S n 125 p 51
Ap '60
--- ---Teatro San Carlo (Adriana
Lecouvreur; Thaïs). La S n 122
p 37, 73 Ja '60
--- ---Teatro San Carlo di Napoli:
Otello; L'elisir d'amore. il LaS
n 124 p 34 Mr '60
---Matz, Mary Jane. Great opera
houses, series; Teatro San Carlo.
il ON v 25 n 7 p 22-7 D 24'60
---Weerth, Ernest de. (Opening;
Ernani.) ON v 25 n 30 D 31'60
SAN FRANCISCO
Biskind, Joseph. Music reports.
MC 1960
---Composers' Workshop, methods
used. WM n 1 p 10 F '60
---Eichelbaum, Stanley. Theatre
USA: San Francisco. il Th Arts
v 44 n 3 p 57-61 Mr '60
---Opera: Cosmopolitan Opera
Company, and the San Francisco
Opera; repertory and casts. Op
v 11 n 7 p 473 Jl '60
---Opera reports: San Francisco
Opera working for a spring-sum-
mer season; Dario Shindell work-
ing on a rival plan. MC v 162 n 4
p 18 O '60
---Unions amalgamate: Local 6
and 669 of AFM; report. il IM
v 58 n 9 p 9 Mr '60

SAN FRANCISCO OPERA
Kerman, Joseph. (Wozzeck;
Boccanegra; Girl of the Golden
West; La Sonnambula; Der Ros-
enkavalier; Cosí fan tutte.) ON
v 25 n 3 p 17-9 N 19'60
---Frankenstein, Alfred. (Autumn
1960.) il Op v 11 n 12 p 819-22
D '60
---List of operas to be presented.
AmM v 8 n 6 p 12 Jl '60
---Los Angeles reviews. MC v 162
n 6 p 22 D '60
---Repertory notes. IM v 59 n 4
p 23 O '60
---Die Frau Ohne Schatten; Edith
Lang, Costa and Feiersinger,
AP wl ph: Bill Cogan. Th Arts
v 44 n 3 p 33 Mr '60
---Portfolio of seven phs: C. M.
Jones. Op v 11 n 12 p 820-2
D '60
SAN FRANCISCO SYMPHONY,
ORCHESTRA
Biskind, Joseph. (Deficit; En-
rique Jorda praised as conductor.)
MC v 161 n 1 p 23 Ja '60
---Black and White Symphony Ball,
annual event; four music and décor
moods at four hotels, three name
bands. IM v 58 n 10 p 29 Ap '60
---Critical notes. MC v 161 n 6
p 28 My '60
---Notes. MC v 162 n 6 p 25 D'60
---Reviews. MC v 161 n 7 p 32
Je '60
SAN FRANCISCO'S COMPOSERS
FORUM
Second program; review. MC
v 161 n 5 p 23 Ap '60
SANCHEZ PEDRENO, JOSEFINA.
(On staging Chekhov; Spanish view-
point.) WT v 9 n 2 p 135 Summer
'60
SANROMA, JESUS MARIA, 1903-,
pianist
Notes; teacher at 2nd International
String Congress in Puerto Rico.
IM v 58 n 9 p 37 Mr '60
SANT' AGATA
Verdi's home; notes by Ildebrando
Pizzetti. Ver v 1 n 2 p 1016-8
Ag '60
SANTA CRUZ, DOMINGO, 1899-,

(Santa Cruz, Domingo)
Composer; por ph. MC v 162
n 6 p 39 D '60
SANTA FE OPERA
Fourth season: Oedipus-Rex;
Gianni Schicci; La Traviata; The
Gondoliers under Martyn Green.
MC v 162 n 2 p 4 Ag '60
---Gianni Schicci, José Ferrer
in title role; Oedipus Rex con-
ducted by Stravinsky; other no-
tes. AmM v 8 n 5 p 13 Je '60
---Notes. il ON v 24 n 17 p 2
F 27'60
---Opera report. Op v 11 n 11
p 757-8 N '60
---Powell, Llaurence. (Report.)
ON v 25 n 1 p 24-5 O 8'60
---Opera scenes: Tosca, Act I;
Oedipus Rex, ens phs: Tony
Perry. Op v 11 n 11 p 758 N'60
SANTA GIOVANNA AL ROGO,
opera
Catania, Teatro Massimo Bel-
lini review. La S n 124 p 35 Mr '60
SANTA MONICA CIVIC OPERA
Repertory notes; Mario Lanzo,
conductor. ON v 24 n 18 p 3
Mr 5'60
SANTELMANN, WILLIAM F.(1902-)
The art of band scoring. MC
v 162 n 2 p 21 Ag '60
SANTINI, GABRIELE, 1886-,
singer
Career notes; b. Perugia. Op
v 11 n 6 p 406 Je '60
SÃO PAULO
Plays, scene from Poil de Car-
otte, Compagnie Cacilda Beck-
er; O Pagador de Promessas,
Teatro Brasileiro de Comédia;
Revolução na América do Sul,
Teatro de Arena, 3 phs: 1960.
WT v 9 n 4 p 352-4 Winter '60
SAPPHO, play
Hamburg notes; Lawrence Du-
rell. WP v 11 n 6 p 10 Ap '60
SARABELLE, SUZANNE
Paris sketch. il TD n 91 p 22-3
Mr '60
SÁRAI, TIBOR, 1919-, composer
Critical notes. Mus Q v 46 n 4
p 533 O '60
SARATOGA (BEAUMONT),

musical; NYC notes. WP v 11
n 6 p 4 Ap '60
---NYC press comments. Th
Arts v 44 n 2 p 16 F '60
---Beaton, Cecil. Sets and cos-
tumes for "Saratoga" portfolio.
Th Arts v 44 n 1 p 17-20 Ja '60
---Beaton's designs and one ens
AP wl ph. Th Arts v 44 n 1
p 17-21 Ja '60
SARDANAPALE, opera
Monaco contest winner, Jean-
Jacques Grunenwald, composer;
$6,000. ON v 25 n 2 p 7 O 29'60
---Monte Carlo; Grunwalder,
Jean-Jacques, composer; lib-
rettist, René Dumesnil, from
Byron's Sardanapalus. Op v 11
n 10 p 696 O '60
SARFATY, REGINA, 1934-,
singer
Career; roles; b. Rochester.
AmM v 8 n 6 p 3 Jl '60
---As Octavian, AP hl ph: Glyn-
debourne. Op v 11 n 8 p 543 Ag'60
---Por ph. AmM v 8 n 6 cover
Jl '60
SARGENT, SIR MALCOLM, 1895-,
conductor
Por ph. MD v 50 n 10 cover
Ap '60
---Por ph. MD v 51 n 6 p 16 D'60
SAROYAN, WILLIAM, 1908-,
playwright
Por ph. Th Arts v 44 n 9 p 21
S '60
SARROCA, SUZANNE
And Mario Cavaradossi in La
Tosca, AP hl ph. OpP n 19
p 14 1960
SARTRE, ANA RAQUEL, singer
Paris review; Jacqueline Bon-
neau, accompanist. GDC n 286
p 196 O 28'60
SARTRE, JEAN-PAUL (1905-).
Un texte inédit: la conférence
sur le Théâtre, Paris, 1960,
por WP v 11 n 9 p 1,7 Jl '60
---Por ph. WP v 11 n 9 p 1 Jl'60
SASTRE, ALFONSO. Drama and
society. TDR v 5 n 2 p 102-110
D '60
---De Coster, Cyrus C. Alfonso
Sastre. TDR v 5 n 2 p 121-132

D '60
---Group for Theatrical Realism formed; Sastre and José Maria de Quinto; Spanish report. WP v 12 n 3 p 4 D '60
---Pronko, Leonard C. The "Revolutionary Theatre" of Alfonso Sastre. TDR v 5 n 2 p 111-120 D '60
SATAN'S TRAP, opera
Actors Opera; note. Op v 11 n 11 p 756 N '60
THE SATIN SLIPPER, play
Ens AP wl ph: Catholic University Theatre. Th Arts v 44 n 12 p 23 D '60
SAUGUET, HENRI, 1901-, composer
Première: l'Oiseau avait vu cela, sur un poème de Jean Cayol; Besançon. GDC n 283 p 95 O 7'60
SANUDERS, RICHARD D. Life with music (long practice hours; competition inevitable). MD v 50 n 7 p 7 Ja '60
--- ---Life with music. MD v 50 n 8 p 16 F '60
--- ---Life with music (Los Angeles report). MD v 51 n 6 p 15 D '60
SAUT PAR LA FENÊTRE, play
Budapest; Istvan Kallai. WP v 11 n 7 p 11 My '60
SAVAGE, GEORGE. American colleges and universities and the professional theatre. NTM v 1 n 1 p 8-12 O '59
SAVILLE, EUGENIA. Italy (report of Young Composers Experimental Group of Turin). Mus Q v 46 n 3 p 371-378 Jl '60
SAYRE, ROBERT, cellist
Career notes; b. Pittsburgh. IM v 58 n 8 p 30 F '60
SAZANOVA, JULIE (?-1957) et Jean Laurent. Serge Lifar renovateur du ballet français (1929-1960). TD n 97 p 9 N '60
SCALA, DELIA, actress
Por ph. La S n 127 p 51 Je '60
LA SCALA
Castiglioni, Vittorangelo. Teatro alla Scala. il La Scala n 122 p 34-6 Ja '60;

same. La S n 127 p 23-5 Je '60; same. La S n 128 p 26-7, 51 Jl '60
--- ---Fedra di Pizzetti; Andrea Chénier di Giordano. il La S n 123 p 31-3 F '60
---Gambetta, Rosario. La saison lyrique au Théâtre de la Scala de Milan. GDC n 269-70 p 590 Ap 22'60
---Lingg, Ann M. Great opera houses. il ON v 25 n 4 p 22-7 D 3'60
---Opening night's Otello with Del Monaco; 14, 000 red carnations framed the tiers. ON v 24 n 12 p 26 Ja 23'60
---Parsifal; review. GDC n 275 p 751 Je 3'60
--- Porter, Andrew.) Opera reviews: Fedra; Andrea Chénier. il Op v 2 n 3 p 211-5 Mr '60
---Repertory notes. ON v 24 n 11 p 3 Ja 16'60
---Reviews: Turandot; Le bourgeois gentilhomme, comédie-ballet; Doctor Faust. il La S n 126 p 30-2 My '60
---Sartori, Claudio. La Scala: Otello with Nicola Benois' décor; Tosca with Tebaldi. Op v 11 n 2 p 146-7 F '60
---Secci, Lia. Ballet de La Scala de Milan. il TD n 92 p 16-7 Ap'60
---Stagione 1959-60. La S inset Ja '60; same. La S n 126 inset My '60
---Stagione Lirica 1960-61; calendario. La S inset D '60
---Stagione sinfonica 1960: direttori, solisti, esecuzioni per soli coro e orchestra; calendario. La S n 128 inset Jl '60; same. La S n 129-30 inset Ag-S '60; same. La S n 131 inset O '60; same. La S n 132 inset N '60
---Wechsberg, Joseph. Inside La Scala, il HF v 10 n 11 p 46-9, 149 N '60
---Exterior view; from the stage; Pizzetti and manager, Dr. Ghiringhelli, phs. HF v 10 n 11 p 47, 49 N '60
---Inganni, Angelo. La Scala, Milan

267

(La Scala)
(exterior view 1852 painting),
ph: La Scala Museum. ON v 25
n 4 p 23 D 3'60
SCANDALE AU MOULIN ROUGE,
play
Athens notes; Stefanos Fotiadis.
WP v 11 n 6 p 7 Ap '60
SCARLINO, ERIBERTO, 1895-,
composer
Première: Le Villi, il poema
sinfonico. La S n 133 p 116
D '60
SCHACKNER, ALAN. Chromatic
harmonica, a new orchestral
color. il IM v 58 n 10 p 12-3, 29
Ap '60
---AP hl ph; hands holding harmonica; facsimile excerpts "chromatic harmonica". IM v 58 n 10
p 12-3 Ap '60
SCHAEFFER, MYRON. The Mejorana: a typical song of Panama.
facsimiles CMJ v 4 n 3 p 4-22
Spring '60
SCHAFER, MURRAY. Two musicians in fiction: Jean Christoph
by Romain Rolland; Doktor Faustus by Thomas Mann. CMJ v 4
n 3 p 23-34 Spring '60
SCHANNE, MARGRETHE,
ballerina
With Flemming Flindt in La
Dame aux Camélias. AP wl ph:
Copenhagen. TD wl ph: Copenhagen. TD n 94 p 14 Je '60
SCHARLEY, DENISE, singer
As Dalila, AP hl ph. OpP n 19
p 23 1960
---In Carmen, AP ph. OpP n 19
p 11 1960
SCHAROFF, PETER. (On staging
Chekhov; Netherlands viewpoint.)
il WT v 9 n 2 p 139-40 Summer
'60
SCHAUENSEE, MAX DE. Passion-
ate believer: Fernando Delucia,
1860-1925 (rival of Caruso). por
ON v 24 n 20 p 10-1 Mr 19'60
--- ---Puccini and Paris. ON
v 25 n 5 p 17-9 D 10'60
SCHEIN, ANN, pianist
Hl ph: London. AmM v 8 n 1
p 7 Ja '60

SCHEMERING (GORE), ballet
Rotterdam; music, Frank Mar-
tin. WP v 11 n 10 p 10 Ag '60
SCHERMAN, THOMAS, 1917-,
conductor
With Rose Bampton and Gloria
Davy, hl ph: Impact. ON v 25
n 3 p 5 N 19'60
SCHILDE, KLAUS, pianist
Jourdan-Morhange, H. (Paris
criticism.) GDC n 289 p 297
N 18'60
SCHILLER, IRENA. Les expo-
sitions théâtrales en Pologne.
Th R v 2 n 3 p 188-192 1960
SCHLOB WEIKERSHEIM
Chamber music ensemble; Klaus
Bernbacher, conducting, 2 phs.
WM n 5 p 109 O '60
SCHMID,DR. ERNST FRITZ 1904-
1960, musicologist
Death of editor of new Mozart
edition. WM n 6 p 132 D '60
SCHMIDT, ANNLIES, violinist
Paris review. GDC n 293-4
p 463 D 16'60
SCHMIDT, FRANZ, 1874-1939,
composer
Notre Dame, opera, based on
Hugo's novel; review of the score.
P. T. B. MR v 21 n 4 p 354 N'60
SCHMIEDEL, GOTTFRIED. Ernst
von Schuch and the Dresden Opera.
portfolio Op v 11 n 1 p 7-15 Ja '60
--- ---Fritz Busch and the Dresden
Opera. il Op v 2 n 3 p 175-181
Mr '60
--- ---Karl Bohm and the Dresden
Opera (with 15 photographs). Op
v 11 n 5 p 324-330 My '60
SCHNEIDER, LISE, 1937-, pianist
Career notes; b. NYC. AmM v 8
n 8 p 9 S '60
---Por ph: London. AmM v 8 n 8
p 7 S '60
SCHNEIDER, MARCEL. Le Théâtre
lyrique et la musique contempor-
aine. il OpP n 19 p 52-4 1960
SCHNEIDER WIBBEL, opera
Nuremberg; notes. Op v 2 n 3
p 209 Mr '60
SCHNITZER, ROBERT C. 1906?-,
ANTA program aids U. S. abroad
(survey). il MC v 161 n 7 p 9 Je'60

LA SCHOLA CANTORUM, 1896-
Chamfray, Claude. A la Schola
Cantorum; innovations. GDC
n 288 p 253 N 11'60
---Orchestra d'Enfants; Alfred
Loewenguth, le chef; Paris notes.
GDC n 283 p 102 O 7'60
---Paris; directors, teachers.
GDC n 281-2 p 60 S 30'60
SCHOLL, JENNIFER, 1942-, dancer
Winner of "Sun" cup in Australia.
por MD v 50 n 12 p 26 Je '60
SCHÖNBERG, ARNOLD, 1874-1951,
composer
Boulez, Pierre; Suite, op. 29 of
Schönberg with the composer's
durations beside those of Boulez,
1959 at Donaueschingen. MR v 21
n 1 p 79 F '60
---Gradenwitz, Peter. The re-
ligious works of Arnold Schönberg.
MR v 21 n 1 p 19-29 F '60
---Selden-Goth, Gisella. Schön-
berg's life a struggle as shown in
letters. por MC v 161 n 5 p 19
Ap '60
---Walker, Alan. Back to Schön-
berg. MR v 21 n 2 p 140-147
My '60
---Zipper, Herbert, conductor,
of the 21 poems for musical re-
citation; list of instrumentalists,
Chicago. MC v 161 n 7 p 31 Je'60
---Por ph. La S n 127 p 9 Je '60
THE SCHOOL FOR SCANDAL, play
Birmingham Rep, produced by
Margaret Webster, ens AP wl
ph: Lisel Haas. Th Arts v 44 n 11
p 24 N '60
SCHRADE, ROBERT, pianist
London debut; b. NYC. AmM v 8
n 9 p 8 O '60
---Right profile, small ph. MC
v 161 n 6 p 17 My '60
SCHRADE, WILLIAM, pianist
Por ph. AmM v 8 n 9 p 9 O '60
SCHRODER-DEVRIENT, WILHEL-
MINE, 1804-1860, singer
Lingg, Ann M. Queen of tears
(her career; influence upon Wag-
ner). por ON v 24 n 18 p 8-9
Mr 5'60
---Por print: Bettmann Archive.
Op v 24 n 18 p 8 Mr 5'60

SCHUBERT, FRANZ, 1797-1828,
composer
Brown, Maurice J. E. Schubert,
a critical biography (book review
and criticism by Konrad Wolff)
Mus Q v 46 n 1 p 95-102 Ja '60
---Maione, Rino. La "quarta" di
Schubert. por La S n 128 p 38-9
Jl '60
---Norman, Elizabeth. Schubert's
incidental music to Rosamunde.
MR v 21 n 1 p 8-15 F '60
---Porter, E. B. Der Doppel-
gänger. MR v 21 n 1 p 16-8 F'60
--Ritratto. La S n 126 p 12 My'60
SCHUCH, ERNST VON, 1846-1914,
conductor
Schmiedel, Gottfried Ernest von
Schuch and the Dresden Opera.
por and portfolio Op v 11 n 1
p 7-15 Ja '60
---Por ph signed; with a portfolio,
illustrating his career. Op v 11
n 1 p 7-14 Ja '60
SCHULBERG, BUDD WILSON, 1914-,
and Harvey Breit. The Disenchant-
ed (text; NYC cast and 6 illustra-
tions). Th Arts v 44 n 8 p 21-47
Ag '60
SCHULHOF, ANDREW, 1895-1960,
concert manager
Obituary; b. Hungary. MC v 161
n 4 p 7 Mr '60
SCHULLER, GUNTHER A. (1926?)
John Lewis on the modern jazz
beachhead. por discography HF
v 10 n 10 p 54-56, 134 O '60
---Career notes. AmM v 8 n 2
p 15-6 F '60
---Seven Studios on Themes of
Paul Klee, NYC notes; also première "Concertino for Jazz Quartet and Symphony Orchestra". WM
n 2 p 32 Ap '60
---Por ph. AmM v 8 n 2 p 15 F '60
SCHULTZE, FRIEDRICH (1900-).
Crisis in opera? Crisis in the re-
pertory. WP v 11 n 8 p 1 Je '60
--- ---(on the Dramaturg; the
"Buhnenverlag" in the German
theatre.) WT v 9 n 3 p 195-8
Autumn '60
SCHULZ, GISA. A Northern legend: Edouard Lalo, 1823-1892.

(Schulz)
por ON v 24 n 14 p 12, 31 F 6'60
SCHUMAN, WILLIAM, 1910-,
composer
Composers Showcase concert;
NYC review. J Rev v 7 n 1 p 13
Winter 59-60
---Première: Seventh Symphony
by the Boston Symphony; criti-
cism. MC v 162 n 6 p 27 D '60
---With Eric Day, hl ph: London.
AmM v 8 n 8 p 7 S '60
SCHUMANN, ROBERT, 1810-1856,
composer
Berges, Ruth. Schumann in Vie-
nna. MC v 162 n 5 p 10-2 N '60
---Portrait drawing by Kniehuber,
also portrait of Clara Wieck, and
view of Zwickau, birthplace, engr.
MC v 162 n 5 p 10-1 N '60
SCHUMANN-HEINK, 1861-1936,
singer
Chay, Marie. (On Schumann-
Heink). por ON v 24 n 23 p 14-5
Ap 9'60
SCHÜTZ, HEINRICH, 1585-1672,
composer
Mendel, Arthur. A brief note on
triple proportion in Scheutz. il
Mus Q v 46 n 1 p 67-70 Ja '60
SCHWARTZ, WILL. The Univer-
sities, guardians of our musical
heritage. MEJ v 47 n 1 p 41-3
S-O '60
SCHWARZ, ALFRED (1925-). The
allegorical theatre of Hugo von
Hofmannsthal. TDR v 4 n 3
p 65-76 Mr '60
SCHWARZKOPF, ELISABETH,
1915-, singer
Detroit Symphony; critical note
on Strauss. MC v 161 n 6 p 31
My '60
---In Cosi fan tutte, Chicago re-
view. il Op v 11 n 1 p 28 Ja '60
---Interview. il ON v 24 n 23
p 10-1 Ap 9'60
---NYC review; all Hugo Wolf
program; "whole evening of the
same monotonous". MC v 161
n 5 p 35 Ap '60
---Paris review. GDC n 283 p101
O 7'60
---As Alice Ford, San Francisco,

AP wl ph:Lackenbach. ON v 24
n 23 p 11 Ap 9'60
---As Fiordilgi, small ph:Ellinger.
Op v 11 n 10 p 701 O'60
---As the Marschallin, AP hl ph:
Houston Rogers. Op v 11 n 1 cover
Ja'60
---In Così fan tutte with Christa
Ludwig, AP hl ph:Wiesbaden May
Festival. WM n 4 p 83 Ag'60
SCHWETZINGEN FESTIVAL
Steyer, Ralf. The Fairy Queen in
a modern setting. Op v 11 p 69
Autumn'60
SCIUTTI, GRAZIELLA, 1931?-, singer
Notes on Virtuosi di Roma;"the
frighteningly lovely Graziella
Sciutti, note-perfect as Rosina. "
Op v 11 n 8 p 552 Ag'60
---As Despina in Così, AP hl ph:
Ellinger. ON v 25 n 1 p 21 O 8'60
---E Badioli nel "Barbbiere" di
Paisiello, AP hl ph. LaS n 125 p 46
Ap'60
SCOTT, GEORGE C. , 1928-, actor
Balch, Jack. (Sketch of Broadway
star in his Greenich Village apart-
ment.) Th Arts v 44 n 6 p 10-2 Je
'60
---Por ph:Carl Perutz. Th Arts v 44
n 6 p 11 Je'60
SCOTT, JEAN CALVERT. Lecture
series for young listeners. MEJ
v 46 n 3 p 31-2 Ja'60
SCOTT, NORMAN, 1918-, singer
As Pietro in Simon Boccanegra, AP
ph:Melançon. ON v 24 n 22 p 17 Ap
2'60
SCOTT, TED, singer
In The Music Man;b. Wayne, Indi-
ana;Melbourne review. por MD v 50
n 11 p 25 My'60
---Por ph. MD v 50 n 9 p 25 Mr'60
SCOTT, WINFIELD TOWNLEY(1910-).
Opera at Santa Fé, fourth summer.
Op v 11 n 11 p 757-9 N'60
SCOTTO, RENATA, 1934-, singer
As Gretel, ens AP wl ph:Piccagli-
ani. ON v 24 n 14 p 27 F 6'60
---In La Sonnambula, AP hl ph. LaS
n 125 p 44 Ap'60
SCULPTURE
Gunnis, Rupert. Dictionary of Brit-
ish Sculptors, 1660-1851 (extracted

list of works having theatre interest). Th Notbk v 14 n 4 p 123-126 Summer'60

---Constantin le Grand, buste, ph. WP v 11 n 5 p 8 Mr'60

---Damer, Mrs. Bust of Elizabeth Farren, ph:coll. of Mr. Rupert Gunnis. Th Notbk v 14 n 4 Summer'60

---Donatello. Particolare della Cantoria, 2 phs. LaS n 131 p 13, 15 O'60

---Szymanowski, Waclaw. The Chopin monument in Warsaw. WM n 2 cover Ap'60

THE SEAGULL, play
Chekhov, Anton Pavlovich(1860-1904). Remarks on the Seagull as produced at the Alexandrinski Theatre. Th R v 2 n 1 p 11 1960

---Barcelona, 1959, ens AP wl ph: Gansa. WT v 9 n 2 p 137 Summer '60

---Malmö 1953, ens AP wl ph: Skäne. WT v 9 n 2 p 133 Summer '60

---Teatro La Cometa, Rome, set by Chiari, ph:1960. WT v 9 n 2 p 130 Summer'60

---Teatr Polski, Warsaw, 1959, ens AP wl ph:Myszkowski. WT v 9 n 2 p 143 Summer'60

---Various theatres, portfolio. WT v 9 n 2 p 108-110 Summer'60

SEAL, ELIZABETH, 1934?, dancer
AP wl ph:Friedman-Abeles. Th Arts v 44 n 10 p 13 O'60

---AP wl ph:Murray Laden. Th Arts v 44 n 11 cover N'60

SEAMAN, GERALD. D. S. Bortnyansky (1751-1825). MR v 21 n 2 p 106-13 My'60

SEARLE, HUMPHREY, 1915-, composer
Première:Third Symphony;Edinburgh criticism;"unites serial technique with subjective musical impressions of Mediterranean scenes". MC v 162 n 4 p 26 O'60

---(Warrack, John.)Diary of a Madman, Sadler's Wells review.

il Op v 11 n 6 p 442-4 Je'60

---Winner of competition of Rostrum of Composers, Paris, with opera, the Diary of a Madman. WM n 3 p 55 Je'60

SEATTLE SYMPHONY ORCHESTRA, 1903-
Contemporary repertory under director, Milton Katims;guest conductors. Am M v 8 n 9 p 12 O'60

---History, 1903 to date; Family Neighborhood Concert Series;finances;notes on conductor, Milton Katims. Am M v 8 n 11 p 3-4 D'60

---Patterson, D. Music report. MC v 161 n 3 p 39 F'60

---Two phs and por of conductor, Milton Katims. Am M v 8 n 11 cover D'60

SEBOK, GYORGY, pianist
And Janos Starker;Paris concert review by D. Machuel. GDC n 255-6 p 310 Ja 15'60

---Mari, Pierrette. Review. GDC n 267 p 557 Ap 8'60

---Notes. GDC n 261-2 p 423 F 26'60

---Por ph:Jean-Pierre Leloir. GDC n 261-2 cover F 26'60

LE SECRET de MARCO POLO, operetta
Importance du ballet au Châtelet. TD n 90 p 11 F'60

---Paris notes;music, Francis Lopez. WP v 11 n 5 p 6 Mr'60

---Théâtre du Châtelet;music of Francis Lopez and Paul Bonneau; ballet notes also. MC v 161 n 3 p 44 F'60

---Le Ballet des Oiseaux, au Châtelet, ens AP wl ph:Lido. TD n 90 cover F'60

---Ens AP wl ph:Lipnitzky. WP v 11 n 8 Je'60

LA SECTION INTERNATIONALE des Bibliothèques et Musées des Arts du Spectacle de la Fédération Internationale des Associations de Bibliothécaires: IVe Congrès, Varsovie, 1959. Th R v 2 n 1 p 53-5 1960

SECRETO A VOCES, play
Mexico notes;Rosa Margot Ochoa. WP v 11 n 10 p 9 Ag'60

SEDWICK, FRANK. Love and ven-

play
London;John Arden;notes. WP
v 11 n 3 p 13 Ja'60
---London review. Th Arts v 44
n 4 p 14 Ap'60
SERGI, ARTURO, singer
Notes;b. NYC. Am M v 8 n 10 p 5
N'60
SERIAL MUSIC
Cologne;34th year of festival of
the Society for Contemporary
Music;notes, names, comment.
MC v 162 n 2 p 22-3 Ag'60
---Forte, Allen. Bartok's "serial"
composition (3rd movement of
Fourth String Quartet, analysis).
Mus Q v 46 n 2 p 233-245 Ap'60
---Krenek, Ernst. Extents and
limits of serial techniques. il
Mus Q v 46 n 2 p 210-232 Ap'60
---Rochberg, George, on the prob-
lem of serialism vs. randomness;
Stratford conference of compo-
sers. CMJ v 5 n 1 p 13-6 Autumn
'60
---Sessions, Roger. Problems and
issues facing the composer today.
Mus Q v 46 n 2 p 159-171 Ap'60
SERKIN, PETER, 1947-
NYC debut. Am M v 8 n 1 p 18 Ja
'60
SERKIN, RUDOLF, 1903-, pianist
Japanese tour report. MC v 162
n 6 p 29 D'60
---NYC review. MC v 161 n 3 p 25
F'60
---O'Hara, Richard. (Interview.)
por MC v 161 n 6 p 10-1 My'60
---With New York Philharmonic;
Bartók's First Piano Concerto.
MC v 161 n 5 p 16 Ap'60
---At the piano, hl ph. HF v 10
n 7 p 60 Jl'60
---With Steinway's technician,
Oscar Ekberg, en route to the Far
East, ph. MC v 162 n 6 p 29 D'60
SERLY, TIBOR, 1900-, viola player
Cello Concerto from unfinished
Bela Bartók's Viola Concerto;
notes on this derivation score. Am
M v 8 n 10 p 13 N'60
SEROCKI, KAZIMIERZ, 1922-,
composer
Warsaw note on "Sinfonietta for

two String Orchestras". WM n 2
p 28 Ap'60
SERVANDONI, JEAN JEROME,
1695-1766, painter
Bergman, G. M. La grande mode
des pantomimes à Paris vers
1740 et les spectacles d'optique
de Servandoni. Th R v 2 n 2 p 71-
81 1960
THE SERVANT of TWO MASTERS,
play
NYC;Piccola Scala di Milano;re-
view. il MC v 161 n 4 p 15 Mr'60
SESSIONS, ROGER(1896-). Problems
and issues facing the composer
today. Mus Q v 46 n 2 p 159-171
Ap'60
---Notes;b. Brooklyn. Am M v 8 n 2
p 10 F'60
---Première:Quintet;NYC review.
Mus Q v 46 n 1 p 71-2 Ja'60
---Por ph. MC v 162 n 5 p 33 N'60
SETTE CANZONI, opera
Malipiero;La Piccola Scala. il Op
v 11 n 5 p 352 My'60
SETTIMANE MUSICALE SENESE,
opera
Siena review;"something pre-Mo-
zartian about its neat, delicate
cantilena". Op v 11 n 10 p 695 O'60
SEVENTH ARMY SYMPHONY
Underwood, Rex. (Story of 1952
founding;90 per cent college men;
example of Ramon Scavelli of the
Houston Symphony.)IM v 59 n 2
p 12-4 Ag'60
---Ens ph:US. IM v 59 n 2 p 12 Ag'60
SEVERANCE HALL
The façade, ph:Cleveland. IM v 59
n 4 p 13 O'60
SEVERO BALLET, INC.
Detroit;15th anniversary repertory.
MC v 161 n 1 p 23 Ja'60
SEVILLE, opera
Baku;ens AP wl ph. Op v 11 n 1 p 47
Ja'60
LE SEXE et le NÉANT, play
Paris notes;Thierry Maulnier. WP
v 11 n 7 p 8 My'60
SEXTUOR de CLARINETTES de
PARIS
Castil. Paris review. GDC n 283 p 100
O 7'60
SHAFFER, PETER. Labels aren't for

(Shaffer)
playwrights (with comments
on the play, Five Finger Exer-
cise). Th Arts v 44 n 2 p 20-1
F'60
SHAFRAN, DANIEL, 1923-,
violoncellist
NYC review. MC v 161 n 5 p 15
Ap'60
SHAKESPEARE, WILLIAM, 1564-
1616, dramatist
As an influence upon continental
composers, part of a study of
inter-relations by Paul Chan-
cellor. Mus Q v 46 n 1 p 1-11
Ja'60
---Complete recordings under
George Rylands of Cambridge;
Decca;details. HF v 10 n 5 p 33
My'60
---Hodges, C. Walter. (Review of
Martin Holmes'Shakespeare's
Audience;"thesis that Shakes-
peare was continually cutting
his dramatic coat according to
his audience's cloth".)Th Notbk
v 15 n 2 p 64-6 Winter '60-61
---Kawatake, Toshio. Shakespeare
in the Japanese theatre. Th R
v 2 n 2 p 82-7 1960
---Kellet, Brian. (Playing in India.)
WP v 12 n 2 p 1, 4 N'60
---Larson, Orville K. Robert Ed-
mund Jones' Henry VIII (with 8
designs, phs.) PlM v 37 n 3
p 52-4 D'60
---Mitchell, Donald. In and out of
Britten's "Dream"(A Midsum-
mer Night's Dream, opera). il
Op v 11 n 12 p 797-801 D'60
---Osborne, Conrad L. Four Shakespeare tragedies (recorded by
Marlowe Society of Cambridge
and the Dublin Gate Theatre).
HF v 10 n 8 p 57-8 Ag'60
---The Players' Shakespeare,
Twelth Night, first of the new
"school" series, reviewed by O.
E. B. Youngs. Th Notbk v 15 n 1
p 38 Autumn'60
---Phoenix Theatre, NYC;Henry
IV Parts 1 and 2;Stuart Vaughan,
directing;cast superb. PlM v 37
n 1 p 10 O'60

---Richards, Stanley. (Comment on
Shakespeare at American and
Canadian Stratford Festivals.)PlM
v 37 n 2 p 46 N'60
---Six recent books on Shakespeare;
notes. Th R v 2 n 2 p 115-6 1960
---Survey on dates and plays first
performed, report by countries.
WP v 12 n 3 p 4 D'60
---Zbierski, Henryk. Shakespeare
in Poland:a survey. Th R v 2 n 3
p 136-140 1960
---Pitoëff, Ludmilla, as Ophelia, AP
wl ph:Paris. Spec n 1 p 25 1960
---The Tempest, NBC-TV; several
scenes;NYC. Th Arts v 44 n 2 p 65-8
F'60
SHAKESPEARE BIRTHPLACE
TRUST
Editorial:plans for a library build-
ing, Stratford-on-Avon. Th Notbk
v 15 n 1 p 2 Autumn'60
---Fox, Levi. Proposed new library
and headquarters at Stratford-on-
Avon (with view of the scale mo-
del). Th Notbk v 14 n 3 p 90-91
Spring'60
SHAMUS O'BRIEN, opera
Jacobs, Arthur. B. B. C. Club
Operatic Society (review). Op v 11
n 11 p 784 N'60
---Shapey, Ralph, 1921-, composer
Première:Movements for Wood-
wind Quintet (Virginia 1960). ACAB
v 9 n 3 p 34 1960
SHAPIRO, NORMAN R. Suffering
and punishment in the theatre of
Georges Feydeau (1862-1921). TDR
v 5 n 1 p 117-126 S'60
SHARAN, SHIVA(1907-). The impor-
tance of the preservation of the
traditional musical culture in Or-
iental countries. WM n 1 p 2-4 F'60
SHARP, WILLIAM L. (1924-). A play:
scenario or poem. TDR v 5 n 2
p 73-84 D'60
---Sharrow, Leonard, bassoonist
Career notes;b. NYC. por IM v 58
n 8 p 30 F'60
SHAW, GEORGE BERNARD, 1856-
1950, dramatist
Bentley, Eric. The making of a
dramatist. TDR v 5 n 1 p 3-21 S'60
---Weintraub, Stanley. Bernard

Shaw, actor (1880's). il Th Arts v 44 n 10 p 66-7 O'60

SHAW, ROBERT, 1916-, conductor
Washington, D. C. notes on chamber-orchestra version of Bach's B Minor Mass. MC v 161 n 6 p 32 My'60

SHAW-TAYLOR, DESMOND(1907-). A gallery of great singers;10. Conchita Supervia (1895-1936). il Op v 11 n 1 p 16-23 Ja'60
--- --- A "Puritani" discography. il Op v 11 n 6 p 387-395 Je'60

SHAWN, TED(1891-). Letter on Jacob's Pillow. il MD v 50 n 8 p 2 F'60
---On Florida beach, wl ph. MD v 50 n 8 p 2 F'60

SHEARER, TOM. Bel Strepito (audience crudities at the opera separately stylized). Op v 11 n 12 p 812-14 D'60

SHEARING, GEORGE, 1920-, jazz leader
Australian tour with quintette. MD v 51 n 3 p 15 S'60

SHEEAN, VINCENT(1899-). The Bible and opera. ON v 25 n 4 p 9-12 D 3'60

SHELDON, SIDNEY. A journey to our minds (extra-sensory perception and his play, Roman Candle). il Th Arts v 44 n 3 p 18, 69 Mr'60

SHELTER, NORMAN, pianist
Notes;b. Philadelphia. Am M v 8 n 9 p 7 O'60
---Por ph. Am M v 8 n 9 p 9 O'60

SHELTON, ROBERT. The Weavers, America's folk-song group (history, criticism). il HF v 10 n 12 p 48-50 D'60

SHERIFF, NOAM(1935-). Psaume (études musicales analytiques). GDC n 283 p 106 O 7'60
---Career notes;his "Psaume" in Paris program 1960. GDC n 281 p 40 S 30'60

SHIRANUI KENGYO, Kabuki Tokyo;Uno Nobuo. WP v 11 n 8 p 8 Je'60

SHORE, DINAH, 1917-, singer
Review of ballads, Capitol

St 1247;"one of the finest albums by any female singer over the past year". HF v 10 n 1 p 81 Ja'60
---Por ph. HF v 10 n 1 p 81 Ja'60

SHOSTAKOVITCH, DIMITRY(1906-). Concerto pour violon (1955):analyse par Pierrette Mari. GDC n 271 p 633-4 My 5'60
---Rabinovich, D. Dimitry Shostakovich (book reviewed). MR v 21 n 4 p 338-9 N'60

SHOWBOATS
The theatre of the Southern United States from the beginnings through 1865, a bibliographical essay by O. G. Brockett. Th R v 2 n 3 p 163-174 1960

SHUARD, AMY, 1925-, singer
Critical sketch;b. South Africa. portfolio Op v 11 n 4 p 257-262 Ap'60
---Portfolio: in 10 roles;working with Eva Turner, phs. Op v 11 n 4 p 257-261 Ap'60

SHUTE, NEVIL
See Norway, Nevil Shute, 1899-1960, author

SI LA FOULE NOUS VOIT ENSEMBLE, play
Paris notes;Claude Bal. WP v 11 n 5 p 7 Mr'60

SI ON VOUS DEMANDAIT, play
Bucarest notes;Dorel Dorian. WP v 11 n 7 p 16 My'60

SIBBRITT, GERARD, 1942-, dancer-choreographer
Perth notes. por MD v 51 n 1 p 28 Jl'60
---Por ph:Australia. MD v 51 n 1 p 29 Jl'60

SIBELIUS, JEAN, 1865-1957, composer
Johnson, Harold E. Sibelius(1960 Faber;book reviewed). MR v 21 n 4 p 343-4 N'60

SICILIANO, TELLO, 1934-, singer
Note. MD v 50 n 8 p 12 F'60

SIDNEY MYER MUSIC BOWL
Fiddian, Paul, manager;concert for the 12th International Congress of Scientific Management delegates by the Victorian Symphony under Joseph Post. MD v 50 n 9 p 13 Mr'60

(Sidney Myer Music Bowl)
---Melbourne;Australian Symphony under Hector Crawford; soloists, Carolyn Maye and Ted Scott. MD v 50 n 9 p 17 Mr'60
SIENA
LaMorgia, Manlio. XVII Settimana Senese (annualmente). il LaS n 129-30 p 38, 72 Ag-S'60
SIEPI, CESARE, 1923-, singer
As Figaro, AP hl ph:Melançon. ON v 24 n 12 p 17 Ja 23'60
---As Mephistopheles, AP hl ph: LeBlang;and Bjoerling as Faust, same. MC v 161 n 1 p 13 Ja'60
---As Zaccaria in Nabucco, AP hl ph:Melançon. ON v 25 n 4 p 20 D 3'60
SIGHELE, MIETTA, 1936-, singer
Spoleto;Bohème, "an authentic star". Op v 11 p 30 Autumn'60
SIGISMONDO BATHORY, opera
Horusitzky;ens AP wl phs:Budapest. LaS n 129-30 p 41 Ag-S'60
SILAS MARNER, opera
Cape Town;John Joubert's work. Op v 11 n 9 p 632 S'60
SILBERTA, RHEA, 1897-1959, composer
Obituary. MC v 161 n 1 p 6 Ja'60
SILENT NIGHT, LONELY NIGHT, play
NYC notes;Robert Anderson. WP v 11 n 6 p 3 Ap'60
SILJA, ANJA, singer
As Senta, AP wl ph:Bayreuth. ON v 25 n 1 p 20 O 8'60
SILVANT, JEAN(1908-). Chronique du mois, serie. TD 1960
--- ---La Belle au Bois Dormant (Daydé et Golovine) chez Cuevas. il TD n 98 p 12-3 D'60
--- ---La danse en Allemagne (a survey). il TD n 89 p 6-15 Ja'60
--- ---La danse et le sport. il TD n 93 p 6-12 My'60
--- ---(On agreement between Maîtres de Danse Classique and Haut Commissariat à la Jeunesse et aux Sport;points of interest.) TD n 97 p 3 N'60
--- ---Place de la danse dans la vie au XXme siecle. TD n 97 p 14-15, 18 N'60

--- ---Une ecole de danse à Paris (L'Ecole Supérieure d'Etudes Chorégraphiques). il TD n 96 p 3-5 S-O'60
SILVANT, YVES. Luisillo et son théâtre de la danse espagnole. il TD n 98 p 19 D'60
SILVERSTEIN, JOSEPH, 1932-, violinist
Awarded the Walter W. Naumberg Foundation Award;details of the large biennial contest. Am M v 8 n 10 p 12 N'60
---Wins first Naumberg Award; details. MC v 162 n 5 p 4 N'60
SILVESTRI, CONSTANTIN, 1913-, conductor
American debut at Ravinia Festival;criticism. MC v 162 n 2 p 12 Ag'60
SIMIONATO, GIULIETTA, 1916-, singer
Career notes. ON v 24 n 17 p 14-5 F 27'60
---Kupferberg, Herbert. They opened her mouth with a corkscrew. il HF v 10 n 2 p 49-50 F'60
---As Amneris, AP wl ph. LaS n 127 p 24 Je'60
---As Azucena, AP hl ph. LaS n 122 p 39 Ja'60;same. AP hl ph:Melançon. ON v 24 n 17 p 17 F 27'60
---As Santuzza, AP hl ph:Louis Melançon. Th Arts v 44 n 3 p 27 Mr'60
SIMON, ERIC, 1908-, director
Third Annual Festival of Music, Town Hall, NYC notes. IM v 59 n 6 p 40 D'60
SIMON BOCCANEGRA, opera
Ashbrook, William. A single fatherland (unification of Italy;the opera Simon Boccanegra). ON v 24 n 22 p 11, 32 Ap 2'60
---Budapest notes. il LaS n 125 p 57 Ap'60
---Ferra, Giampaolo de. Trieste. LaS n 133 p 66 D'60
---Gerken, Eva. A Doge's life (Simon Boccanegra, historical notes). il ON v 24 n 22 p 7, 30 Ap 2'60
---Metropolitan Opera;Anselmo Colzani. MC v 161 n 6 p 16 My'60
--- ---cast;story;historical notes; décor;bibliography;discography.

portfolio ON v 24 n 22 Ap 2'60
--- ---review;Frederick Fox sets.
MC v 161 n 4 p 13 Mr'60
--- ---review (with 2 scenes). Op
v 11 n 5 p 336-7 My'60
---Act I scene 1, Act I scene 2, two
ens AP wl phs:Melançon. Op v 11
n 5 p 337 My'60
---Portfolio:Melançon. ON v 24
n 22 Ap 2'60
---Washington, Ferrari, Dondi
and Parutto, ens AP wl ph:Trieste.
LaS n 133 p 101 D'60
SIMONI, RENATO, playwright
Morini, Mario. Simoni e Illica
associati per un libretto. il LaS
n 133 p 56-61 D'60
SIMS, EZRA, composer
Première:String Quartet(NYC
1960). ACAB v 9 n 3 p 34 1960
SINCLAIR, JOHN. Adelaide Arts
Festival(reviews). MD v 50 n 10
p 12-3 Ap'60
SINGER, SAMUEL L. Philadelphia
music reports. MC 1960
SINGERMANN, BORIS. U. S. S. R.
(theatre report). il WT v 9 n 2
p 178-181 Summer '60
SINGERS
Boston concerts; notes on Marian
Anderson, on Galina Vishnevskaya,
Elisabeth Schwarzopf and Roberta
Peters. MC v 161 n 5 p 24 Ap '60
---Engel, Lehman. The singer on
Broadway. MC v 172 n 1 p 9
Jl '60
---Kolodin, Irving. Including the
Scandinavian (Copenhagen and
Stockholm, source of opera sin-
gers). portfolio Th Arts v 44 n 3
p 46-8 Mr '60
---Native countries after the cast
names, Metropolitan Opera each
issue. ON 1960
---NYC reviews: Betty Allen;
Laurel Hurley; McHenry Boat-
wright; Dorothy Hepburn; Richard
Goodlake; Esther Comas; Cesare
Valletti; Vera Lowry Ernst;
Helen Vanni; Miklos Gafni; Ker-
stin Meyer. MC v 162 n 6 p 34-7,
43 D '60
---Denise Duval; Roberta Basnett;
Elisabeth Schwarzkopf; John

Hornor; others. MC v 161 n 5
p 35-6 Ap '60
--- ---Galina Vishnevskaya; Juanita
Porras; Sophia Steffan; Matti-
wilda Dobbs; Mady Metzger-Zieg-
ler. MC v 161 n 3 p 27-32 F '60
--- ---Paolo Polaro and Josanne
Manche; Eleanor Steber; Ben
Cutler; William Shores; Robert
Fairfax Birch and others. MC
v 161 n 6 p 18-21 My '60
--- ---Wallace Thompson; Theresa
Greene; Doris Yarick; Hoté Cas-
ella; Velta Stott-Meilhuber; Mar-
got Rebeil. MC v 162 n 5 p 31-2
N '60
--- ---William Aubin; Ksenia Bid-
ina; Lois Hartzell; Theodora An-
drews; Paul Gavert; Joan Brain-
erd; Nan Merriman; Kum Hee
Mah. MC v 161 n 1 p 17, 28, 37
Ja '60
---Paris comment on Lisolette
Kostraki et Pierre Ligonesch.
GDC n 293-4 p 462 D 16'60
---Phonorecords reviewed: The
Best of Caruso; Giuseppe de
Luca; Berganza singing Rossini
and Elsa Cavelti singing Brahms
and Wolf. MR v 21 n 2 p 170
My '60
---Supervia, Conchita, 1895-1936;
career sketch; b. Barcelona; 1931
married Ben Rubenstein; died in
England. portfolio Op v 11 n 1
p 16-23 Ja '60
---Bayreuth; a number of small
action photographs of 1960 sin-
gers. Op v 11 Autumn '60
---The Dresden Opera; a port-
folio of singers in the era of Ernst von Schuh, phs. Op v 11 n 1
p 7-14 Ja '60
---Portfolio of contemporary singers, 16 por phs. ON v 25 n 4
p 30 D 3'60
---Scott, Helena, Jack Delon and
Gloria Lane, hl ph: London.
AmM v 8 n 11 p 7 D '60
---Small photographs of Verdi
singers, including Milanov, Merrill, Stella, Tozzi, Rysanek,
Peerce, Moscona, Callas, Tebaldi
and de Monaco. HF v 10 n 1

(Singing)
p 48-9 Ja '60
---Phillips, Linda, adjudicator on
City of Sydney Eisteddfod; report.
MD v 51 n 5 p 14-5 N '60
---Swanson, Frederick J. When
voices change; an experiment in
Junior High School music. MEJ
v 46 n 4 p 50, 53-4 F-Mr '60
SINGSPIEL
See The Cradle Will Rock
SION, GEORGES. Belgium, theat-
rical radar receiver (French
section). il WT v 9 n 1 p 35-47
Spring '60
THE SIRE DE MALETROIT'S
DOOR, opera
The Manhattan School of Music;
notes. ON v 24 n 18 p 27 Mr 5'60
SIRE HALEWYN, play
Sleyp, Paula, and Jan Moonen,
AP wl h ph: Reussens, 1956. WT
v 9 n 1 p 14 Spring '60
SISTINE CHOIR
Salaries raised, mandatory pra-
ctice, 25 men and 30 boys; notes.
MEJ v 46 n 3 p 8 Ja '60
SIVE, play
Dublin; criticism. Th Arts v 44
n 2 p 24 F '60
SIX CHARACTERS IN SEARCH OF
AN AUTHOR, opera
Criticism; Hugo Weisgall's mu-
sic "abrasive"; New York City
Opera review. Op v 11 n 5 p 341
My '60
---NYC Opera, ens AP wl ph. Op
v 11 n 5 p 341 My '60
SIX WINGS FOR EVERYBODY,
play
Tel Aviv, 1958; ens AP wl ph:
Mirlin-Yaron. WT v 9 n 1 p 82
Spring '60
SKINNER, H
See Laing, Hugh, 1914-, dancer
SKOPNIK, GUNTER (1907-). An
unusual person (the dramaturg
in German theatre). WT v 9 n 3
p 233-238 Autumn '60
SKORIK, IRENE, 1928-, dancer
Choreographing "Poème"; notes.
TD n 96 p 28 S-O '60
---Munich triomphe. TD n 94
p 26 Je '60
---With Peter Appel, AP wl ph.
TD n 96 p 28 S-O '60

SKULNIK, MENASHA, 1892-,
actor
Notes. Th Arts v 44 n 12 p 8
D '60
SKROWACZEWSKI, STANISLAW,
1924?-, conductor
Career notes; b. Lwow; music
director of the Minneapolis Sym-
phony. IM v 58 n 9 p 8 Mr '60
---Career sketch; b. Lwow, Po-
land. por IM v 59 n 3 cover, p 16
S '60
SKYGGEN, ballet
Copenhagen notes. WP v 11 n 8 p 4
Je '60
SLASK
NYC review of Polish State Folk
Ballet. PlM v 36 n 4 p 86 Ja '60
A SLEEP OF PRISONERS, play
Bibliography. TDR v 4 n 3 p 96
Mr '60
THE SLEEPING BEAUTY
Recorded by Orchestre de la
Suisse Romande under Ernest
Ansernet; criticism. HF v 10 n 5
p 79 My '60
THE SLEEPING BEAUTY (Petipa),
ballet
Royal Ballet (British), ens AP wl
ph: Houston Rogers. Th Arts
v 44 n 11 p 60 N '60
THE SLEEPING BEAUTY, ballet
See also La Belle au Bois Dormant
SLEZAK, WALTER, 1902-,
actor
AP wl ph. Th Arts v 44 n 6 p 17
Je '60
---In The Gypsy Baron, AP hl ph:
Louis Melançon. Th Arts v 44 n 3
p 26 Mr '60
SLOCOMB, DON B. Make way for
music (a Texas superintendent on
money and time for music to be
culturally important). MEJ v 47
n 2 p 70 N-D '60
SLOCUMB, PAUL. Players on Re-
cord (column of drama and musi-
cals including operettas on discs).
PlM 1960
SLONIMSKY, NICOLAS (1894-).
The weather at Mozart's funeral.
Mus Q v 46 n 1 p 12-21 Ja '60
HET SLOT, play
Ens AP wl ph: Reussens, Ant-
werpen, 1954. WT v 9 n 1 p 27
Spring '60

SMETERLIN, JAN, 1892-, pianist
Paris review. GDC n 271 p 629
My 5'60
SMIT, LEO, 1900-1934?, com-
poser
With Fred Hoyle, hl ph: London.
AmM v 8 n 8 p 7 S '60
SMITH, ETHEL, organist
Cerulli, Dom. Ethel Smith (b.
Pittsburgh). IM v 59 n 6 p 22-3
D '60
--- Por ph; in Disney's "Melody
Time", ens AP wl ph. IM v 59
n 6 cover, p 23 D '60
SMITH, JULIA, composer
With Jack O. Evans, conductor,
and Louis J. Diercks, choral
leader in "Our Heritage" by Smith,
hl ph: Ohio State Univ. MC v 161
n 4 p 33 Mr '60
SMITH, LEONARD B. (1918-). De-
veloping high register, the pro-
fessional's goal. por IM v 59 n 6
p 20-1 D '60
--- ---The professional's goal in
practice (his routine as a pro-
fessional trumpeter). IM v 58 n 12
p 14-5 Je '60
---AP hl ph. IM v 58 n 12 p 14
Je '60
---Por ph. IM v 59 n 6 p 20 D '60
SMITH, RUSSELL (1897?-). A fan-
fare for Piotr Ilyich (Tchaikovsky).
HF v 10 n 3 p 48-9 Mr '60
--- ---Erich Itor Kahn (with check-
list of compositions). ACAB v 9
n 2 p 8-12 1960
---Première: Can Can and Waltz;
1959 notes. ACAB v 9 n 2 p 24
1960
SMITH, WILLIAM R. 1924-, con-
ductor
Career notes; b. Haddon Heights,
New Jersey. por IM v 58 n 9 p 36
Mr '60
SMITH-BRINDLE, REGINALD.
Italy 3 dozen new works at 1959
Venice Festival. Mus Q v 46 n 1
p 83-88 Ja '60
SOBEL, BERNARD (1890-). Saga
of the one-man show. portfolio
Th Arts v 44 n 10 p 24-6 O '60
LA SOCIETA CORELLI
Australian tour. MD v 51 n 1
p 16 Jl '60

---Notes. MD v 50 n 9 p 17 Mr'60
SOCIÉTÉ DE MUSIQUE D'AUTRE-
FOIS
Chamfray, Claude. Paris re-
view. GDC n 277 p 818 Je 17'60
SOCIÉTÉ DES MIRACLES, play
Athens notes; Demetre Psathas.
WP v 11 n 6 p 7 Ap '60
SOCIÉTÉ PHILHARMONIQUE DE
PARIS
With Raquel Satre, singer; Paris
review. GDC n 281-2 p 47 S 30'60
SOCIETIES
American String Teachers Asso-
ciation; 1960 report. il MEJ v 47
n 2 p 79 N-D '60
---Amis des Arts et des Lettres,
Salle Berlioz: Concert, Trio
Viaudey, Pierre Jonneret, Jean
Micault. GDC n 291 p 358 D 2'60
---Les Amis du Bel Canto d'Agde;
report by Joseph Mai. GDC
n 269-70 p 592 Ap 22'60
---L'Association Française des
Maîtres de Danse Classique;
bulletin mensuel. TD n 92 p 2
Ap '60
---L'Association Française des
Maîtres de Danse Classique vient
de recevoir l'agrément du Haut
Commissariat à la Jeunesse et
aux Sports. TD n 97 p 3 N '60
---Australia; the Commonwealth
Society of Teachers of Dancing;
history. MD v 50 n 10 p 3 Ap '60
---Cercle Musicale de Paris; Geo-
rges de Lausnay présents les
artistes. GDC n 269-70 p 594
Ap 22'60
---review. GDC n 267-8 p 561
Ap 8'60
---Chicago; G. B. Shaw Society.
notes. PlM v 36 n 7 p 153 Ap '60
---Chicago meeting of Rudolf Bing,
Kurt Herbet Adler and Carol Fox
to consolidate opera management
by mutual association; results. Op
v 11 n 7 p 474 Jl '60
---Cincinnati Matinee Musicale club;
note. MC v 161 n 1 p 24 Ja '60
---The College Band Directors Asso-
ciation; notes. MEJ v 46 n 4 p 80
F-Mr '60
---Danse et Culture; 437 séance;
Jean Dorcy. TD n 98 p 23 D '60

(Societies)
---France; music "Calendrier des Organisateurs", each issue. GDC 1960
---Guild of Australian Composers (Victoria); report. MD v 51 n 2 p 18 Ag '60
---Les Heures Alpines; le president, Aimé Sainson, ?-1960; Grenoble music loss. GDC n 283 p 106 O 7'60
---An International Association of Museums and Collections of Musical Instruments; list of countries and aims; WM n 4 p 76 Ag'60
---International list of societies devoted to theatre history. Th Notbk v 14 n 4 p 114 Summer '60
---Johnen, Louis John. (The 15th annual convention of the National Association of Teachers of Singing, Cincinnati report; MC v 161 n 3 p 17 F '60
---The Leschetizky Association; report. MC v 161 n 1 p 35 Ja '60
---Mari, Pierrette. Société des Concerts, Eglise de la Madeleine; Mattiwilda Dobbs, Geneviève Macaux, etc; dir. Constantin Silvestri. GDC n 289 p 297 N 18'60
---Music and teaching: news, projects, meetings, equipment in the front pages each issue. MEJ 1960
---Music Critics Association (US); Chattanooga meeting; officers. MC v 162 n 6 p 18 D '60
---The Music Supervisors Conference; founded 1907, Iowa; notes with gavel pictured. MEJ v 46 n 5 p 29, 35 Ap-My '60
---The National Association for Music Therapy; notes; founded US, 1950. MEJ v 46 n 5 p 62 Ap-My '60
---National Collegiate Players and Junior Collegiate Players: officers with addresses, followed by chapter list and founding dates. PlM 1960
---New society in New York "a self-help program of musicians-for-musicians"; Michel Piastro, president. MC v 161 n 1 p 5 Ja'60

---New York Federation of Music Club; Manhattan conclave. MC v 161 n 7 p 10 Je '60
---Le Nouvel Ensemble Ars Redivia; directeur, Fernand Caratgé; concert. GDC n 274 p 724 My 27'60
---L'Offrande Musicale, Jean de Rohozinski, directeur: XIe concert, Paris. GDC n 273 p 692 My 20'60
---Opera; joint NYC conference under Central Opera Service (unit of Metropolitan's National Council) and the National Opera Association: program. ON v 24 n 20 p 1 Mr 19'60
---Paris; Société de Musique d'Autrefois; review. GDC n 269-70 p 597 Ap 22'60
---Paris concert: Fiori Musicali, Robert Dalsace; solistes. GDC n 269-70 p 596 Ap 22'60
---Radio organizations from 22 countries in Paris: the International Rostrum of Composers. WM n 3 p 55 Je '60
---Reggio Emilia; Società del Casino and Famiglia Artistica Reggiana: concerts to mark centenary. Teatro Municipale di Reggio Emilia. il La S n 127 p 36-9 Je'60
---Sigma Alpha Iota, 1959-1960 achievements. MC v 161 n 5 p 40 Ap '60
---Sindacato Autori, Roma. La S n 132 p 69 N '60
---Syndicat des Artistes choregraphiques; bulletin no. 1. Michel Gevel, secrétaire général. TD n 95 p 31 Jl-Ag '60
---Toronto Bach Society; notes. MC v 161 n 1 p 27 Ja '60
---Le Triptyque; frequent concerts. GDC 1960
---Union des Femmes Artistes Musiciennes; Paris concert. GDC n 276 p 785 Je 10'60
---L'Union Professionelle des Maitres du Chant français: concert review. GDC n 267-8 p 564 Ap 8'60
---US, Recreational Dancing Institute; officers; aims. il IM v 58 n 8 p 8 F '60
--- ---The National Federation of Music Clubs; convention plans

and awards. MC v 161 n 5 p 34 Ap '60

--- ---what the professional artist joins; other debut notes. MC v 162 n 1 p 35 Jl '60

---Universal Symphony Orchestra and Music Institute; Pablo Casals, chairman; aim. MC v 162 n 5 p 33 N '60

---Victorian Music Teachers Association; report. MD v 51 n 5 p 9 N '60

---Young, John Wray. (The American Community Theatre Association: history.) PlM v 36 n 8 p 184 My '60

SOCIETY FOR INTERNATIONAL CULTURAL EXCHANGE
Tokyo, 1961; East-West music "confrontation" planned. WM n 4 p 76 Ag '60

THE SOCIETY FOR THEATRE RESEARCH
Bulletin No. 47. Th Notbk v 14 n 3 p 76-78 Spring '60

---Bulletin No. 48. Th Notbk v 14 n 4 p 112-114 Summer '60

---Bulletin No. 49. Th Notbk v 15 n 1 p 3-6 Autumn '60

---Buletin 50; publication, The Early Manchester Theatre; other reports. Th Notbk v 15 n 2 p 44-5 Winter 60-61

SOEDERSTROEM, ELISABETH
As Susanna in Figaro, AP phs: Melançon. ON v 24 n 12 Ja 23'60

---In Figaro with Siepi, AP hl ph: Metropolitan. Th Arts v 44 n 3 p 37 Mr '60

LES SOEURS BOGA, play
de Lovinescu, AP ph: Bucarest. WP v 11 n 5 p 1 Mr '60

THE SOFA, opera
Maconchy, Elizabeth, composer, Ursula Vaughan Williams the libretto. Op v 11 n 2 p 150 F '60

SOFIA
Opera; National Opera; notes also on Drzhaven Muzikalen Teater's repertory. Op v 11 n 8 p 549 Ag'60

SOIRÉE DE DANSES EN L'HONNEUR DE COULA PRATSICA
Athens notes. WP v 11 n 10 p 4 Ag '60

SOIRÉES MUSICALES SOCIETY
List of players with Philippe Entremont, pianist in Melbourne debut. il MD v 50 n 12 p 19 Je'60

---Melbourne; 10 years; notes. founder Mischa Kogan. il MD v 50 n 7 p 12-3 Ja '60

SOLCHANY, GEORGES, 1922-, pianist
Mari, Pierrette. Paris review. GDC n 267-8 p 559 Ap 8'60

SOLEIL DE MINUIT, play
Paris; Claude Spaak; notes. WP v 11 n 3 p 7 Ja '60

SOLER, ANTONIO,1729-1783
Blaukoff, Kurt. (Sonatas to be released.) HF v 10 n 11 p 30 N '60

SOLER, ANTONIO, RUIZ 1921-, dancer
Notes. il TD n 97 p 20-2 N '60

---Jugando el toro, ens AP wl ph. La S n 132 p 83 N '60

---Torero, 2 phs. TD n 97 p 20 N '60

LES SOLISTES DE COLOGNE
Paris review; Helmut Müller-Bruhl. GDC n 273 p 690 My 20 '60

SOLISTI DI ZAGREB
NYC review. MC v 162 n 5 p 30 N '60

SOLOV, ZACHARY, 1923-, choreographer
Ballet ensemble to tour. ON v 24 n 9 p 3 Ja 2'60

SOLTI, GEORG, 1912-, director
Career notes on his German success. Op v 11 n 8 p 526 Ag '60

---Notes; b. Budapest. por MC v 161 n 6 p 4 My '60

---San Francisco Symphony; career notes; b. Budapest. IM v 59 n 5 p 23 N '60

SOMES, MICHAEL, 1917-, dancer
Career sketch. MD v 50 n 11 p 23 My '60

SOMMA, ANTONIO
Flora, Francesco. The libretto (Verdi's Un Ballo In Maschera). Ver v 1 n 1 p 305-353 Ap '60

SOMMER, VLADIMIR, 1921-, composer
Critical notes. Mus Q v 46 n 4

(Sommer)
p 512-3 O '60
LA SONATE DE L'ANGOISSE
(Milloss), ballet
Cologne Opera; "absolute music
used as the basis for ballets of
a descriptive character"; Tides,
a ballet to Stravinsky's Symphony
In Three Movements, also. MR
v 21 n 3 p 244 Ag '60
LA SONATE DU DIABLE, play
Athens notes; Georges Vicas.
WP v 12 n 1 p 7 O '60
LE SONGE, play
Strindberg; ens AP wl ph: Hel-
sinki, 1959. WT v 9 n 3 p 281
Autumn '60
SONGS
L'Abandonnée, musique de G.
Verdi, paroles de M. L. E. fac-
simile and notes Ver v 1 n 2
p 1068-1076 Ag '60
---Burchiello, Domenico; e la
musica del suo tempo. il La S
n 131 p 11-19 O '60
---Canadian composers; critical
notes by Chester Duncan on new
releases. CMJ v 5 n 1 p 67-73
Autumn '60
---Castil. Les chinois d'outre-
mer: Simone Genin, soprano,
Sieglind Rebeyre; Sylive Assael,
soprano; mélodies de Raymond
Salmon; Henri le Droumaguet;
Nicolaou. GDC n 267-8 p 562
Ap 8'60
---Charpentreau, Simone, et Jacques. La Chanson (book review
by Raymond Lyon). GDC n 290
p 331 N 25'60
---Copyright lifted by Bill on the
song, "Pledge of Allegiance to
the Flag", composer Irving Caesar. MC v 162 n 4 p 24 O '60
---Orr, C. W. Five Songs from
A Shropshire Lad (tenor voice);
review. MR v 21 n 3 p 259 Ag '60
---Porter, E. G. Der Doppelgänger. MR v 21 n 1 p 16-18 F '60
---Riva, Ubaldo. La musica nelle
poesie di Salvatore Di Giacomo.
il La S n 133 p 48-55 D '60
---Rousselot, Léone. Le Chant,
acte réflexe (entretien). GDC

n 291 p 339 D 2'60
---US; "How the West Was Won",
panorama in song (RCA Victor
review). HF v 10 n 7 p 66 Jl '60
LA SONNAMBULA, opera
Covent Garden review. Op v 11
n 12 p 848 D '60
---Porter, Andrew. An introduc-
tion to "La Sonnambula". il Op
v 11 n 10 p 665-70 O '60
---La Scala notes. il La S n 125
p 45 Ap '60
SORBELLO, UGUCCIONE RANI-
ERI DI.
Italy (theatre survey). il Th Arts
v 44 n 4 p 53-6 Ap '60
SORDELLO, ENZO, 1927-, singer
Por ph. MC v 162 n 6 p 33 D '60
SORELL, WALTER. For art's
sake (sketch of Gustav Mahler).
por ON v 24 n 18 p 12, 32 Mr 5
'60
THE SORROWS OF ORPHEUS
See Les Malheurs d'Orphée
SOUND ENGINEERING
Audio unit created at Wartburg
College, Iowa: doubled music
theory classes without a teacher
added; described. MEJ v 46 n 4
p 92 F-Mr '60
---Conn Corporation's Dynalevel,
electronic measure of sound; use.
MEJ v 46 n 6 p 73 Je-Jl '60
---Crowhurst, Norman H. Can
loudspeakers be tested? HF
v 10 n 4 p 46-9 Ap '60
---Fidelman, David. (Amplifiers.)
HF v 10 n 9 p 47-8 S '60
---Fowler Charles. Mozart as you
motor (tape machine in trunk, car's
battery, remote control). il HF
v 10 n 6 p 40-1 Je '60
---Gorman, Robert. The sound of
ambiophony (acoustics of any
space can be manipulated). HF
v 10 n 12 p 43-4 D '60
---Live Tone Concert Earphones;
described by Keith MacMillan.
CMJ v 4 n 3 p 61-2 Spring '60
---Lyon, Raymond. Un électrophone, mono-stéréphonique de
bonne qualité. GDC n 289 inset
N 18'60
---Osborne, Conrad L. High

fidelity; 2. amplifier wattage; how high an out put level? ON v 25 n 7 p 3 D 24'60

---Plays; Eugene O'Neill quoted; also Stevens Institute report of 1937. PlM v 37 n 2 p 34-5 N '60

---Preservation and Storage of Sound Recordings by A. G. Pickett and M. M. Lemcoe; Library of Congress publication (reviewed). HF v 10 n 1 p 27 Ja '60

---Women (US) and high fidelity equipment; discussion on fallacy of manufacturers that women care less for quality than the decorative side. HF v 10 n 1 p 111, 116 Ja '60

---Beersheba's theatre pit equipped with acoustic suspension boxes in place of orchestra, ph. ON v 25 n 1 p 31 O 8'60

THE SOUND OF MUSIC, musical Notes and portfolio. Th Arts v 44 n 1 p 65-9 Ja '60

---Ens AP wl ph: Friedman-Abeles, 1959. WT v 9 n 1 p 95 Spring '60

---Martin, Mary, in wedding dress, ens AP wl ph: NYC. AmM v 8 n 1 p 13 Ja '60

---Portfolio. Th Arts v 44 n 1 p 65-8 Ja '60

SOUND RECORDING AND REPRODUCTION
Chamfray, Claude. Un entretien avec Raymond Lyon sur la stéréophonie. drawings GDC n 292 p 390-3 D 9'60

---Clancy, Russell. (His home istallations with pictures.) HF v 10 n 3 p 50-3 Mr '60

---Crowhurst, Norman H. Big bass from small boxes. chart HF v 10 n 2 p 45-8 F '60

---Eisenberg, Norman. Do you need a phantom channel? charts. HF v 10 n 8 p 36-7, 88 Ag '60

---Equipment reports, a regular illustrated section. HF 1960

---Fleming, Shirley. Getting the twain (audiophile and the music lover) to meet. HF v 10 n 10 p 14 O '60

---Fowler, Charles. (Speakers.) charts HF v 10 n 9 p 40-42 S'60

---Freas, Ralph. The change in record changers. HF v 10 n 7 p 36-7, 83 Jl '60

--- ---The coming break-through in tape (interview Dr. Peter Goldmark). HF v 10 n 3 p 46 -7, 122 Mr '60

---HF Reports, section prepared by Hirsch-Houck Laboratories on current equipment. HF 1960

---Saunders, Scott J. Mounting a ceiling speaker. il HF v 10 n 7 p 82 Jl '60

---Whyte, Bert, of Everest on comparative costs of production England and US; halls with good acoustics numerous in England and union fees smaller. HF v 10 n 4 p 16 Ap '60

LES SOURIS DANSENT, operettas Coquatrix, Bruno; revival in Reims. GDC n 257-8 p 354 Ja 29'60

SOUDÈRES, VALÉRIE, composer Por ph: Guillemard. GDC n 263-4 cover Mr 11'60

SOUSA, JOHN PHILIP, 1854-1932, composer
Eastman Wind Ensemble under Dr. Frederick Fennell; huge audience; review of Sousa program. MC v 161 n 7 p 6 Je '60

---Mayer, Francis N. John Philip Sousa, his instrumentation and scoring. MEJ v 46 n 3 p 51-57 Ja '60

---And band leaders, Interlochen, Michigan, ph. MEJ v 47 n 1 p 60 S-O '60

SOUTH AMERICA
Dallas Symphony Orchestra holding auditions in SA for soloists. AmM v 8 n 8 p 10 S '60

THE SOUTH AUSTRALIAN BALLET THEATRE (Collis)
Note. MD v 50 n 11 p 26 My '60

SOUTH CAROLINA
Play script contest, $1000; The Columbia Town Theatre. Th Arts v 44 n 10 p 81 O '60

SOUTHERN, RICHARD. A university theatre (University of Southampton). NTM v 1 n 4 p 21-4 Jl'60

SOUZAY, GERARD, 1919? -, singer

(Souzay)
Menton criticism. GDC n 281-2
p 66 S 30'60
---Paris review. GDC n 275
p 755 Je 3'60
---Por ph. MC v 162 n 6 p 14
D '60
SPACE
Sound to satellites to man; im-
pact on "Music Around the Wor-
ld" program; editorial. MC v 162
n 5 p 3 N '60
---"Wave length used in space
program right next to the FM
band" - - -HF v 10 n 6 p 97
Je '60
SPAETH, ARTHUR. Theatre,
Cleveland (and the area round).
Th Arts v 44 n 1 p 76-7, 83 Ja'60
SPAETH, SIGMUND (1885-). Letter-
saluting the Musical Courier's
80th birthday. por MC v 161 n 3
p 8 F '60
---Por ph. MC v 161 n 3 p 8 F'60
SPAIN
Bilboa; opera notes. Op v 11
n 12 p 837 D '60
---Brookings, Jack. The damp
theatre of Spain. PlM v 36 n 7
p 160-1 Ap '60
---Dance festivals at Santander,
at Seville; notes. TD n 95 p 9-
10 Jl-Ag '60
---Langhi, Ugo Ramellini. Music
report. La S n 124 p 73-4 Mr'60;
same; La S n 125 p 92 Ap '60;
same. La S n 126 p 67 My '60;
same. La S n 128 p 59 Jl '60;
same. La S n 127 p 66 Je '60;
same. La S n 133 p 107 D '60
---Music at Compostella, under
Oscar Espla; 3rd summer school
notes. Wm n 5 p 105 O '60
---Music notes: "Musica in Com-
postela", fondato 1958; Granada; Santander; L'Orfeó Lau-
date, diretta dal maestro Angel
Colomer del Romero. La S
n 131 p 72 O '60
---Music report. La S n 122
p 81 Ja '60;
same. La S n 123 p 76 F '60
---Report on festivals, with
list of visiting companies;

dance; opera; drama; award win-
ners listed. WP v 11 n 3 p 1 Ja '60
---Theatre report. WP v 11 n 10
p 8 Ag '60; same. WP v 12 n 1 p 4
O '60; same. WP v 12 n 2 p 4 N'60
---Camerino Sin Biombo (Zabalza
Enrazquin), small AP ph: Madrid.
WP v 12 n 2 p 4 N '60
SPANISH DANCING
Agnes, Soledad; notes. il TD
n 93 p 23 My '60
---Antonio Ruiz Soler; notes. il
TD n 97 p 20-2 N '60
---Burke, Anthony. Carimina and
company; review. il MD v   51
n 2 p 25 Ag '60
---Carimina. An introduction to
Spanish dancing. MD v 50 n 8
p 31 F '60
--- ---II. MD v 50 n 9 p 32 Mr '60
--- ---III. MD v 50 n 11 p 29 My'60
---Gran Ballet Espagnol; Australian
tour. MD v 51 n 3 p 29 S '60
---Nantes; José de la Vega et sa
troupe. GDC n 289 p 299 N 18'60
---Paris; un Festival Espagnol,
organisé par le Comité des Fes-
tivals d'Espagne. TD n 89 p 30
Ja '60
---Silvant, Yves. Antonio Cortes,
authentique gitan. il TD n 92
p 22-3 Ap '60
---Sydney; Gran Ballet Espagnol;
also Melbourne, Carimina and
company of ten. MD v 50 n 12
p 28 Je '60
---Théâtre des Champs-Elysées;
Zamba troupe from Madrid. MC
v 161 n 3 p 44 F '60
---Antonio and Rosita Segovia;
Mariemma, 2 AP wl phs: Spain.
TD n 95 p 10 Jl-Ag '60
SPARRERS CAN'T SING, play
Lewis, Stephen, the playwright,
in an interview by Birgit Rommel.
il NTM v 2 n 1 p 12-5 O '60
---London notes; Stephen Lewis.
WP v 12 n 1 p 15 O '60
SPEAIGHT, GEORGE. Chinese
shadows. Th Notbk v 15 n 1 p 35
Autumn '60
SPECTACLES DE DANSES (ZOU-
ROUDI), ballet
Athens notes. WP v 12 n 1 p 6 O'60

284

SPELMAN, FRANZ. Germany; much ado in Munich (theatre report). il Th Arts v 44 n 4 p 17-20 Ap '60

LE SPEZIALE, opera
Brussels, ens AP wl ph: Ghizzoni di Scotti. Op v 11 n 1 p 31 Ja '60

SPIGELGASS, LEONARD. A Majority of One (complete text, NYC cast), il Th Arts v 44 n 9 p 19, 26 S '60

SPISAK, MICHAL (1914-). Concerto Giocoso pour orchestre (études musicales analytiques). GDC n 288 p 266 N 11'60
---Première: Concerto Giocoso; Paris review. GDC n 290 p 321 N 25'60

SPITZMÜLLER, ALEXANDRE, 1894?-, composer
Chamfray, Claude. Hommage à Sptizmüller. GDC n 267-8 p 566 Ap 8'60

SPIVAK, ELIE, 1902-1960, violinist
Sumberg, Harold. (Obituary.) CMJ v 5 n 1 p 51 Autumn '60

SPOLETO
Festival of Two Worlds; opera reviews La Bohème and Der Prinz von Homburg. Op v 11 p 30 Autumn '60
---Faulkner, Maurice (Spoleto review.) MC v 162 n 2 p 24 Ag '60
---Goth, Trudy. (Reviews.) il LaS n 129-130 p 36, 70 Ag-S '60
---Selden-Goth, Gisella. Review of events: The Prince of Homburg, opera; Cherubini's Missa Solennelle out doors; public "not as smart looking ss in the last two years"; American dancers. MC v 162 n 3 p 22 S '60
---Third year; notes. WM n 3 p 56 Je '60
---Wood, Peggy. Festivals: true and false. Th Arts v 44 n 12 p 17 D '60

SPONTINI, GASPARO LUIGI PACIFICO, 1774-1851, composer
Weinstock, Herbert. Spontini waiting (career; compostions; La Vestale). il ON v 24 n 19 p 12-3

Mr 12'60
---Por print: Bettmann Archive. ON v 24 n 19 p 12 Mr 12'60

SPOOK IN KWADRAAT, play
Antwerpen, 1956; ens AP wl ph: Reussens. WT v 9 n 1 p 52 Spring '60

SPORTS
La Danse et le sport, serie. TD n 92 p 29-30 Ap '60
---Silvant, Jean. La danse et le sport (discipline, equivalences, repercussions sur le sport). il TD n 93 p 6-12 My '60
---Ravet, Jacqueline, illustrating relationship of dance and sport, 6 AP wl phs: Paris. TD n 93 p 6-9 My '60

SPYCKET, SYLVIE, ?-1960
Debieve, Pierre. Hommage à Sylvie Spycket. GDC n 275 p 756 Je 3'60

SQUARZINA, LUIGI, actor
Notes "La congiura". il La S n 127 p 49 Je '60

STACKED DECK, electronic opera
Maxfield, Richard, composer; review. MC v 161 n 7 p 25 Je '60

THE STAG KING, opera
Henze's largest composition; review. Op v 11 n 8 p 553, 556 Ag'60

STAGECRAFT
Brustein, Robert. Scorn not the proscenium, critic. Th Arts v 44 n 5 p 8-9 My '60
---Opera; Dino Yannopoulos, new ideas. MC v 162 n 4 p 6, 24 O '60
---Young, D- Palmer. A rainmaker (with pictures). PlM v 36 n 6 p 136 Mr '60
---Mirror curtains; Looking Glass Curtain from the Queen's Theatre, Manchester; same from Surrey Theatre, phs: Bligh coll. and the Stone Coll. Th Notbk v 15 n 2 Winter '60-61

STAHLMANN, SYLVIA, singer
Brussels notes. Op v 11 n 1 p 30 Ja '60

STALAG XVII-B, play
Ens AP ph: Philadelphia, 1949. Th Arts v 44 n 2 p 75 F '60

STALLAERT, ALPHONSE. Sinfonia da Requiem (études musicales

285

(Stallaert)
analytiques). GDC n 292 p 430
D 9'60

STANAC, opera
Première in Zagreb;composer,
Jakov Gotovac. WM n 2 p 32 Ap
'60
---Ens AP wl ph:Zagreb. LaS
n 123 p 45 F'60

STANGER, RUSSEL, 1930-,
conductor
NY Philharmonic notes. MC
v 162 n 5 p 17 N'60

STANISLAVSKI, KONSTANTIN,
1863-1938, director
And Nemirovitch-Dantchenko
and others, ph. Spec n 1 p 7 1960

STANKOVITCH, NADIA, pianist
Paris criticism. GDC n 263-4
p 488 Mr 11'60

STAPLETON, MAUREEN, 1925-,
actress
Millstein, Gilbert. (Interview;car-
eer in NYC as an actress.)Th
Arts v 44 n 7 p 10-1 Jl'60
---Por ph:Roger Prigent. Th Arts
v 44 n 7 p 11 Jl'60

STARER, ROBERT , composer
Première:Fantasia Concertante,
for piano four-hands;notes. J Rev
v 7 n 2 p 13, 14 Spring'60

STARKER, JANOS, 1924-, cellist
Career notes;b. Budapest. Am M
v 8 n 5 p 6 Je'60

STARLIGHT THEATRE
Pawling, New York, 28th season,
stage being readied, ph. Th Arts
v 44 n 6 p 15 Je'60

STARTZ, DRAGO, singer
AP hl ph:Belgrade. LaS n 122
p 85 Ja'60

STATE MUSIC EDUCATORS
ASSOCIATIONS:USA
Activities calendar 1960-61, arranged by states. MEJ v 47 n 1
p 67-8, 70, 72, 74 S-O'60

STATISTICS
Cost of 12 symphony orchestras in US, eighty-piece, budget
broken into first chair men, 63
musicians, etc. ;excerpt from
Overture Dec. 1959. IM v 58 n 10
p 29 Ap'60
---Covent Garden 1959-60:list

of singers with number of appearances;list of producers;repertory
with casts. Op v 11 n 8 p 540-1
Ag'60
---Hindemith's music;studied by
Victor Landau and a chart made
of exceptions and violations. MR
v 21 n 1 p 38-54 F'60
---(Merkling, Frank.)The grass is
greener;opera expansion in US;
titles by popularity with total of
performances. il ON v 25 n 3 p 12-5
N 19'60
---Metropolitan deficit only $40, 547;
notes. ON v 25 n 4 p 7 D 3'60
---Opera in Germany, 1958-59. Op
v 11 n 9 p 627 S'60
---Paris theatre:40 houses, over
100 plays each season;other notes.
Th Arts v 44 n 12 p 65 D'60
---Philadelphia Orchestra:60 years;
1, 315, 600 miles. IM v 58 n 10 p 28
Ap'60
---Les Semaines Musicales de Paris
1960: 80 works, 36 living composers,
16 premières:list. WM n 6 p 123
D'60
---Stoddard, Hope. Industry's aid to
music (a survey). IM v 59 n 5 p 20
N'60
---Summer theatres, US: 80 of 150
Equity summer theatres belong to
one of these four:Council of Resi-
dent Theatres, Council of Stock
Theatres, Musical Arena Theatres,
Association of Civic Musical Theatres. Th Arts v 44 n 6 p 14-6 Je'60
---Theatre in Germany;1959-60
season;number of theatres, of seats.
WT v 9 n 3 p 242 Autumn'60
---US;adults who dance 20 million;
spend 40-50 million dollars. IM
v 59 n 6 p 9 D'60
---US music;groups, expenses for
equipment, box office;many figures,
money and participation. Am M
v 8 n 6 p 7 Jl'60
---US music employment;airing
before Federal Communications
Commission on broadcasters' use
of "foreign-produced background
music"; 502 out of 537 stations
"employ not a single musician, re-
maining 37 employ 27 regularly".

IM v 58 n 8 p 8 F'60
STEBER, ELEANOR, 1916-,
  singer
  Career sketch. Am M v 8 n 1 p 3
  Ja'60
---Career sketch. MC v 162 n 4
  p 7 O'60
---Founder of Stand Records:"the
  more unusual vocal repertoire".
  HF v 10 n 1 p 59 Ja'60
---Portfolio of eleven roles, one
  color ph. MC v 162 n 4 cover, p 7
  O'60
---Por ph. Am M v 8 n 1 front
  cover Ja'60;same. MC v 161 n 6
  p 18 My'60
STEDMAN, JANE W. A dose from
  Dulcamara (criticism with men-
  tion of other love-potion plots).
  ON v 25 n 7 p 17-9 D 24'60
--- ---A Victorian in Iceland
  (William Morris, 1834-1896). por
  ON v 24 n 16 p 8-9 F 20'60
--- ---(Macbeth and Lady Macbeth
  historical account;use of their
  story on stages.)ON v 25 n 9
  p 4-5 Ja 2'60
STEINER, DIANA, violinist
  With Ivan Davis, pianist;both
  winners 1959 National Federa-
  tion of Music Clubs fellowships,
  ph. MC v 161 n 5 p 10 Ap'60
STEINWAY, FREDERICK
  Por ph. and pictures of pianos.
  HF v 10 n 3 p 43-5 Mr'60
STELLA, ANTONIETTA, 1929-,
  singer
  As Cio-Cio-San, AP phs:Mor-
  rison;Melançon. ON v 24 n 24
  p 17 Ap 16'60
---As Leonora in Il Trovatore,
  AP phs:Melançon. ON v 24 n 17
  F 27'60
---Quale Amelia, AP wl ph. LaS
  n 127 p 23 Je'60
STENBERG, DONALD, singer
  And wife, Jo Ann Crossman, a
  pianist;NYC debut. MC v 161
  n 1 p 16 Ja'60
STEPHENSON, ROBERT C. (1893-)
  Farce as method. TDR v 5 n 2
  p 85-93 D'60
STERBA, SUSAN
  Music Queen 1960 of Music

Industry, por ph:Chicago. IM v 59
  n 2 p 36 Ag'60
STERCKX, PIET(1925-). New trends
  in the Flemish theatre. WT v 9 n 1
  p 51-7 Spring'60
STEREO
  Burstein, Herman. How to explain
  stereo to your friends. HF v 10
  n 1 p 52-4 Ja'60
---Chamfray, Claude. Un entretien
  avec Raymond Lyon sur la stéréophonie. drawings GDC n 292 p 390-3
  D 9'60
---Conly, John M. (On stereo, "worth
  all the trouble".)HF v 10 n 2 p 37
  F'60
--- ---Stereo without gigantism:
  chamber music. HF v 10 n 6 p 33
  Je'60
---Eisenberg, Norman. Stereo integration steps up. il HF v 10 n 10
  p 51-3 O'60
---Ferrier, Kathleen, voice (mono-
  phonic recording of Bach-Handel)
  attached to a stereo orchestral accompaniment;London. HF v 10 n 9
  p 24 S'60
---Freas, Ralph. (Comparison of
  trade fairs:New York High Fidelity
  Music Show, London Audio Fair,
  Paris Haute Fidélité et Stéropho-
  nie.) HF v 10 n 9 p 105 S'60
--- ---Towards stereo compatibil-
  ity;Design company began press-
  ing a stereo-mono disc. HF v 10
  n 6 p 45-6 Je'60
---Gorman, Robert. The sound of
  ambiophony. HF v 10 n 12 p 43-4
  D'60
---Lyon, Raymond. La stéréophonie.
  GDC n 292 p 389 D 9'60
---Mallory, Laurence. Hi-Fi and
  Stereophonic Sound (book reviewed
  with historical notes and nostalgia
  for 1938 Telefunken). MR v 21 n 4
  p 332-4 N'60
---Marsh, Robert C. Beethoven
  symphonies in stereo: a discogra-
  phy. HF v 10 n 4 p 44-5, 85-7 Ap'60
---La pratique de la stéréophonie.
  GDC n 292 p 394-7 D 9'60
---Reid, Charles. London Audio
  Fair. HF v 10 n 7 p 20, 22 Jl'60
---Reuling, Karl F. (Warns on con-

(Stereo)
fusing advertising in phonograph
field as "3-channel stereo".)
ON v 24 n 15 p 23 F 13'60
---Three-dhannel stereo;notes
on meaning of this term. HF v 10
n 3 p 111 Mr'60
---Zide, Larry. Stereo cartridges
have personalities. HF v 10 n 5
p 41-3 My'60
STERLING, ELEANOR. (Exper-
ience as night club singer.) por
IM v 59 n 6 p 34 D'60
STERN, ISAAC, 1920-, violinist
Career sketch;b. Russia but
San Francisco before one year
old. Am M v 8 n 7 p 3 Ag'60
---Paris review. GDC n 283 p 102
O 7'60
---Russian tour;"most extensive
an American artist has made".
MC v 162 n 1 p 10 Jl'60
---Left profile ph. Am M v 8 n 7
cover Ag'60
STEVENS, HALSEY, 1908-,
composer
Premières (2) in California 1959;
notes. ACAB v 9 n 2 p 23 1960
STEVENS, INGER, actress
With Robert Sterling in Roman
Candle, AP hl ph:Friedman-Ab-
eles. Th Arts v 44 n 2 p 19 F'60
STEVENS, RISË, 1913-, singer
Career notes. Am M v 8 n 4 p 8
Ap'60
---As Carmen, AP phs:Bender.
ON v 24 n 14 F 6'60
STEWART, THOMAS, singer
Lingg, Ann M. (Bayreuth inter-
view with Texas-born American
singer.) por ON v 25 n 8 p 15
D 31'60
---Por ph. Am M v 8 n 10 p 7 N'60
---Por ph:Willy Saeger. ON v 25
n 8 p 15 D 31'60
STICH-RANDALL, TERESA,
singer
As Donna Anna in Don Juan with
Maurice LeRoux, backstage at
Paris Opéra, ph. OpP n 19 p 29
1960
STOCK, GAIL, dancer
AP wl ph:Melbourne. MD v 51
n 2 p 24 Ag'60

STOCKAUSEN, KARLHEINZ,
composer
Ambesi, Alberto Cesare. Compo-
sitori di Punta. LaS n 129-30 p 28-
30 Ag-S'60
---Cologne;criticism of "Contacts".
MR v 21 n 3 p 242 Ag'60
---Facsimile "studio". LaS n 127
p 8 Je'60
STOCKHOLM OPERA SCHOOL
Cross, Joan. (Foundation;curricu-
la;limited to nine singers.) Op
v 11 n 4 p 266 Ap'60
STOCKHOLM ROYAL OPERA
Dahlin, Göran. Report. Op v 11 n 8
p 565 Ag'60
---Kolodin, Irving. Including the
Scandinavian (singers from Swed-
en). il Th Arts v 44 n 3 p 46-8 Mr
'60
---McCredie, Andrew. Le Nozze di
Figaro. Op v 11 n 1 p 45 Ja'60
STODDARD, HOPE. Eugene Orman-
dy;the path of the artist. por IM
v 59 n 4 p 20-1 O'60
--- ---Industry's aid to music. IM
v 59 n 5 p 20-1 N'60
--- ---What's right with subsidy
for music. IM v 59 n 6 p 18-9 D'60
STOHR, MIRA, singer
As Elsa in Lohengrin, AP hl ph:
Opera di Sarajevo. LaS n 132 p 85
N'60
STOKOWSKI, LEOPOLD(1882-). The
future of music in the United States
(also career notes on Stokowski as
a "pioneer"). IM v 58 n 11 p 11 My
'60
---Criticism of his program as
guest conductor of the New York
Philharmonic. MC v 161 n 5 p 15
Ap'60
---Dallapiccola's Il Prigioniero;
NYC note. WM n 5 p 104 O'60
---Guest conductor, Philadelphia
Orchestra;criticism;contract for
recording, Columbia. HF v 10 n 4
p 59 Ap'60
---Robin Hood Dell after 27 years;
31, 000 audience;notes. MC v 162
n 3 p 13 S'60
---Left profile por ph;also AP hl
ph. IM v 58 n 11 cover, p 11 My'60
---Por ph. MC v 161 n 3 p 6 F'60

STONE, EDWARD DURELL,
1902-, architect
Washington, D. C. ;National Cul-
tural Center;note. WM n 1 p 9
F'60
STONE, GEORGE LAWRENCE.
Technique of percussion, series.
IM v 58 n 7 p 30-1 Ja'60
STONE, GÉO, choreographer
Marseille criticism. GDC n 271
p 623 My 5'60
STORACE, ANNA SELINA, 1766-
1817, singer
Por:Mozarteum, Salzburg. ON
v 25 n 8 p 26 D 31'60
STORDAHL, AXEL, composer
Review of quasi-Oriental music,
recorded by Stordahl's orches-
tra, Jasimine and Jade. HF v 10
n 9 p 85 S'60
STRADIVARI, ANTONIO, 1644?-
1737
Cardini, Maria Pimpanaro. Ant-
onio Stradivari e le scuole musi-
cali di Cremona. LaS n 125 p 34-8
Ap'60
STRASBOURG
Dance report. TD n 92 p 28 Ap'60
---Festival 1960;contemporary
works under Charles Brück;re-
view. GDC n 281-2 p 65 S 30'60
---Nys, Carl de. Le Nouveau Pal-
ais du Festival de Strasbourg.
GDC n 286 p 200-1 O 28'60
---Premières listed;conductors
and groups, music and ballet. WM
n 3 p 55 Je'60
STRATAS, TERESA, singer
As Cio-Cio-San, ens AP wl ph:
Vancouver. ON v 25 n 2 p 21 O
29'60
---Signing for Cio-Cio-San in Van-
couver, ph. ON v 24 n 14 p 3 F 6'60
STRATFORD (ONTARIO) SHAKES-
PEAREAN FESTIVAL
Patterson, Tom. Stratford and the
Canadian theatre. PlM v 36 n 5
p 103-4 F'60
---Strauss, Johann, 1825-1899,
composer
Soirée Johann Strauss au Théâtre
des Champs-Elysées;Hans Löwlein,
directeur;solistes. GDC n 274
p 719 My 27'60

STRAUSS, PAUL, conductor
Florence notes. MC v 161 n 6
p 33 My'60
STRAUSS, RICHARD, 1864-1949,
composer
Joachim, Heinz. The composers
(Germany). WT v 9 n 3 p 213-5
Autumn'60
STRAVINSKY, IGOR (1882-) and
Robert Craft(1923-). Two for
the theater, a dialogue (on Pul-
cinella, on Les Noces). ON v 25
n 5 p 9-11 D 10'60
--- ---Firebird's first flight. il
HF v 10 n 6 p 34-6 Je'60
---American TV debut;notes. Am
M v 8 n 2 p 18 F'60
---French première:Mouvement
pour Piano et Orchestre;Marg-
rit Weber, l'exécution, Concerts
Lamoureux. GDC n 291 p 356
D 2'60
---Goldman, Richard Franko. New
York (critical report of three
compositions:Movements for Pi-
ano and Orchestra;Double Canon;
Epitapium). Mus Q v 46 n 2 p 260-
264 Ap'60
---Goth, Trudy. Stravinsky ser-
iale;New York City. il LaS n 124
p 39-41 Mr'60
---Kasemets, Udo. Recent works
(Canticum Sacrum, Agon, Threni);
criticism. CMJ v 4 n 2 p 63-70
Winter'60
---London;The Nightingale by the
New Opera Company;The Rite of
Spring(Béjart), ballet;and the
Royal Ballet in The Fairy's Kiss
(MacMillan). MC v 161 n 7 p 13
Je'60
---NYC;third concert under Col-
umbia Records;list of singers;
Robert Craft and Stravinsky con-
ducting;"Movements" criticized.
MC v 161 n 3 p 29 F'60
---NYC concert;with Robert Craft;
review. MC v 161 n 3 p 26 F'60
---NYC concert under Columbia
Records;Les Noces(1923), a wed-
ding cantata;review. MC v 161 n 3
p 29 F'60
---Première:Epitaphium (18 sec-
onds duration);Donaueschingen, 59.

(Stravinsky)
MR v 21 n 1 p 80 F'60
---Première "Gesualdo Monumentum";notes on Venice Festival where he conducted his
work. MC v 162 n 5 p 41 N'60
---Schafer, Murray. (Observa-
tions on "Conversations" with
Robert Craft.) CMJ v 4 n 4
p 69-72 Summer'60
---Venice Festival;notes. WM n 4
p 76 Ag'60
---Work habits;Craft and Stra-
vinsky in "Platonic-dialogue
technique". ON v 24 n 11 p 30
Ja 16'60
---Conducting, AP hl ph;with Mar-
grith Weber, hl ph. LaS n 124
p 39, 41 Mr'60
---Informal ph:1911. HF v 10 n 6
p 36 Je'60
---Por ph. ON v 25 n 5 p 8 D 10
'60
---Rehearsing "Symphony of
Psalms" in Cathedral of St.
Francis, ph:Sante Fe, N. M.   MC
v 162 n 2 p 4 Ag'60
STRAZZA, GIOVANNINA
Morini, Mario. Naso fino di
Giovannina(Lucca). por LaS
n 128 p 7-15 Jl'60
A STREETCAR NAMED DESIRE,
play
Ens ph:Chicago City College
System. PlM v 36 n 5 cover F'60
STREPPONI, GIUSEPPINA, 1815-
1897, singer
DeAmicis, Edmondo. Giuseppina
Verdi-Strepponi. Ver v 1 n 2
p 1057-1068 Ag'60
---Por 1943. Ver v 1 n 2 Ag'60
STRINDBERG, AUGUST, 1849-
1912, playwright
Milton,John R.The esthetic fault
of Strindberg's "Dream Plays".
TDR v 4 n 3 p 108-116 Mr'60
---The Pelican;trans. Evert Sp-
rinchorn. TDR v 4 n 3 p 117-143
Mr'60
STROMEYER, MARGUERITE,
pianist
Et Paul Bedouin, violin;Théâtre
Montensier, Paris. GDC n 292
p 422 D 9'60

STRZELECKI, ZENOBIUSZ. (On
staging Chekhov;a Polish viewpoint.) il WT v 9 n 2 p 142 Sum-
mer'60
STUART, WALTER. Jazz improvis-
ing for all instruments (several
installments). IM 1960
STUDHOLME, MARION
As Olympia, AP hl ph:Houston
Rogers. Op v 2 n 3 p 231 Mr'60
SUBLETTE, BOB. Theatre USA:
New Orleans. il Th Arts v 44 n 4
p 57-8 Ap'60
SUBSIDIES
Abbiati, Franco. Libera music e
musica di stato (Italian conditions).
LaS n 127 p 5-11 Je'60
---American manufacturers: gift
of 700 mouth pieces to music students in Israel who must share instruments. MEJ v 46 n 3 p 8 Ja'60
---American Society of Composers,
Authors and Publishers $500 each
to 10 major symphony orchestras
to present contemporary works.
MEJ v 46 n 5 p 6 Ap-My'60
---Australia;Elsa Stralia Scholarship for girl singers;notes. MD
v 51 n 2 p 19 Ag'60
---Boston Symphony to Australia,
US State subsidy;"more than 30
thousand for 7 concerts stipulated"
hence the Olympic Swimming Sta-
dium selected instead of better
acoustics. MD v 50 n 9 p 9 Mr'60
---Calouste Gulbenkian Foundation
at National Gallery of Art:Wash-
ington concerts (the first example
of such European aid?). IM v 59
n 4 p 22 O'60
---Caluste Gulbenkian Foundation
grants:list. Op v 11 n 1 p 23 Ja'60
---Detroit News, aid to the Detroit
Puppet Theatre. PlM v 36 n 5 p 97
F'60
---Florists Telegraph Delivery
Association sponsor colour TV,
Cavalleria Rusticana;also Don
Giovanni;cast. Am M v 8 n 2 p 17
F'60
---Ford Foundation fellowships to
12 young composers to write for
high-school ensembles;$5, 000
plus other funds. Am M v 8 n 5

p 14 Je'60
--- ---for 18 American operas,
$950, 000. MEJ v 46 n 3 p 6
Ja'60
--- ---grant for operas by American composers. Op v 11 n 1
p 29 Ja'60
--- ---grants ($5, 000 each) to
get new works for soloists and
orchestras;list of those ready.
Am M v 8 n 10 p 12 N'60
--- ---to 3rd group of 6 US composers;commissions list. Am M
v 8 n 5 p 14 Je'60
--- ---to Young Audiences, Inc.
which brings ensemble music
to US schools. Am M v 8 n 2 p 17
F'60
---Government subsidy of music
as important as stocking trout
streams;and other reports of
Kentucky Tri-State Conference
on music. IM v 58 n 12 p 16 Je'60
---Grants for the theatre in Belgium, 1958 season;detailed. WT
v 9 n 1 p 29 Spring'60
---Great Britain;Patron of Music
Fund allocations. Op v 11 n 4
p 268 Ap'60
--- ---23 percent increase in
subsidy of the arts;details. MC
v 161 n 5 p 30 Ap'60
---Hackenberg, Kurt. (German
theatre support.) WT v 9 n 3
p 199-202 Autumn'60
---Kentucky commonwealth to the
Louisville Orchestra $53, 000
annually for two years;notes. MC
v 161 n 5 p 44 Ap'60
---Kulas Foundation underwriting
2 fellowships under George Szell,
Cleveland Orchestra, for conductors under 40;details. Am M
v 8 n 6 p 10 Jl'60
---Kyme, G eorge H. Procuring
grants for research in music education (list of 25 agencies with
addresses). MEJ v 47 n 1 p 81-2
S-O '60
---Labor unions, US list, con-
tributing to the Congress of
Strings, Puerto R ico 1960; list.
IM v 58 n 11 p 9 My '60
---Moody, John. The Arts Council and theatre finance. NTM

v 1 n 1 p 21-2 O '59
---The National Music League,
Inc. from The Avalon Founda-
tion $15, 000; purposes. MC
v 161 n 1 p 35 Ja '60
---New York Philharmonic in
West Berlin sponsored by Ford
Motor Company. AmM v 8 n 8
p 10 S '60
---Philadelphia Orchestra $10, 000
from The Presser Foundation.
AmM v 8 n 3 p 18 Mr '60
---Phoinix Theatre, NYC; aid
from the Avalon and the Old Dom-
inion foundations. Th Arts v 44
n 1 p 72-3, 84 Ja '60
---Piston, Walter, $5, 000 for a
symphony for the Philadelphia
Orchestra. AmM v 8 n 5 p 13
Je '60
---Presser Foundation $10, 000:
to seat school children at Philadelphia Orchestra concerts. IM
v 58 n 8 p 40 F '60
---Riegger, Wallingford. For a
department of fine arts. ACAB
v 9 n 3 p 12 1960
---Rockfeller, John D. 3rd.
Financing the arts; (US) "this
laissez-faire attitude is beginning
to change". por ON v 25 n 2
p 8-11 O 29'60
---Sponsors listed for secind annual International String Congress; portfolio of scholarship
groups. IM v 59 n 4 p 10-1 O '60
---Stoddard, Hope. Industry's aid
to music IM v 59 n 5 p 20-1 N '60
--- ---National subsidy of music in
Canada. IM v 58 n 12 p 18-9 Je'60
--- ---What's right with subsidy
of music. IM v 59 n 6 p 18-9
D '60
---Symphony and opera to live
or die? US survey on costs; examples of budgets; compared to
museums and colleges in need
for subsidy. IM v 58 n 8 p 20-1
F '60
---Theatre, state aid; Argentina,
Colombia. WP v 12 n 3 p 2 D '60
---Thompson, Frank, Jr. Gov-
ernment aid to the arts. IM v 58
n 12 p 9, 42 Je '60
SUCHON, EUGEN, 1908-, composer

(Suchon, Eugen)
Critical notes. Mus Q v 46 n 4
p 509-10 O '60
SUCK, FRIEDRICH. Memorial
editions (definition of such music publications, description of
modern practice, resulting ad-
vance in criticism; particular
collections discussed). WM n 3
p 52-3 Je '60
SUGAR, REZSO, 1919-, composer
Critical notes. Mus Q v 46 n 4
p 532 O '60
SUIKER, play
Ens AP wl ph: Reussens, 1958.
WT v 9 n 1 p 18 Spring '60
SUK, JOSEF, 1874-1935, violinist
Trio Suk; Paris review. GDC
n 274 p 723 My 27'60
SULLAVAN, MARGARET (1911-
1960). Interview with John Kea-
ting). Th Arts v 44 n 2 p 26, 28
F '60
---Hl ph: Elliott Erwitt. Th Arts
v 44 n 2 cover F '60
SULLIVAN, ARTHUR 1842-1900,
composer
Hughes, Gervase. The music
of Arthur Sullivan (book reviewed).
MR v 21 n 2 p 155 My '60
LA SULTANE D'HURREM, play
Asena, Orhan; ens AP ph: O.
Darcan, Ankara. WP v 11 n 9
p 1 Jl '60
SUNSHINE, ADRIAN, conductor
Career notes; University of
California 1956; founded San
Francisco Chamber Orchestra
1956. por AmM v 8 n 3 p 9 Mr
'60
SUOR ANGELICA, opera
Palo Alto, California; West Bay
Opera, ens AP hl ph. ON v 25
n 3 p 15 N 19'60
SUPERVIA, CONCHITA (1895-
1936). singer
Letter to Covent Garden 1935
on casting for La Cenerentola.
ON v 24 n 14 p 9 F 6'60
---Fitzgerald, Gerald. Carmen
for posterity. ON v 24 n 14 p 8-9
F 6'60
---Shawe-Taylor, Desmond. A
gallery of great singers; 10.

Conchita Supervia (b. Barcelona).
portfolio Op v 11 n 1 p 7-15 Ja'60
---In the role of Carmen, AP
hl ph: Brown Brothers. ON
v 24 n 14 p 9 F 6'60
---In other roles. Dalia, etc.
portfolio. Op v 11 n 1 p 16 Ja'60
SUR, WILLIAM R. (1903-). Music
for teenagers. MEJ v 47 n 2 p 62,
64 N-D '60
SURINACH, CARLOS, 1915-, com-
poser
Notes; b. Barcelona; to US 1951.
AmM v 8 n 3 p 10 Mr '60
SUSANNAH, opera
Curtin, Phyllis. On being Susan-
nah. AmM v 8 n 3 p 11-12 Mr '60
---Walker, John. Letter on ova-
tion in Washington. MC v 162
n 1 p 39 Jl '60
SUTHERLAND, JOAN, 1928-,
singer
Career notes; London as Lucia;
Venice in Alcina. MD v 50 n 10
p 19 Ap '60
---Covent Garden roles. il Op v 2
n 3 p 228, 236 Mr '60
---Dallas; in Alcina; review. ON
v 25 n 8 p 28 D 31'60
---Dunlop, Lionel. People; 42.
Joan Sutherland. Op v 11 n 10
p 675-682 O '60
---In Alcina; criticism. il Op
v 11 n 4 p 284-5 Ap '60
---In Glyndebourne's I Puritani;
criticism. MR v 21 n 3 p 248
Ag '60
---Law, Richard. Her Lucia di
Lammermoor at the Paris Opéra.
il Op v 11 n 6 p 418-9 Je '60
---Notes. HF v 10 n 10 p 32 O '60
---Palermo; in Lucia di Lammer-
moor; review. Op v 11 n 5 p 355
My '60
---And Blanc in I Puritani, Glynde-
bourne, ph: Guy Gravett. Op v 11
n 7 p 494 Jl '60
---As Alcina at La Fenice, AP
phs: Giacomelli. Op v 11 n 4
cover, p 284, 286 Ap '60
---As Amina, Lazzari as Elviro,
small AP ph. Op v 11 n 12 p 848
D '60
---As Lucia de Lammermoor

with Alain Vanzo as Edgardo, AP
wl ph. OpP n 19 p 24 1960
---As Violetta AP hl ph: Houston
Rogers. Op v 2 n 3 p 229 Mr '60
---In eight roles, 8 AP hl phs.
Op v 11 n 10 p 677-681 O '60
SUTERMEISTER, HEINRICH,
1910-, composer
Première: Romeo and Juliet;
Linz notes. ON v 24 n 24 p 3
Ap 16'60
---Première: Seraphine; Eva-
Maria Rogner. MC v 161 n 7 p 16
Je '60
SUZUKI, SHINICHI, string teacher
Szigeti, Joseph. Between Nagoya
and Tokyo (account of youth en-
semble playing Bach and Vivaldi
under Suzuki). MC v 161 n 1 p 29
Ja '60
SVATOPLUK, opera
Bratislava notes. WP v 11 n 9
p 15 Jl '60
SVOBODA, JOSEF. (On staging
Chekfov; Czechoslovakia view-
point.) il WT v 9 n 2 p 144
Summer '60
SWAN LAKE
See LeLac des Cygnes
SWARTHOUT, GLADYS, 1904-,
singer
Florence home; interview with
Mr. and Mrs. Frank Chapman.
il ON v 25 n 3 p 16, 31 N 19'60
---And Frank Chapman in garden,
hl ph: Italy. ON v 25 n 3 p 16
N 19'60
SWEDEN
McCredie, Andrew. Gothenburg
centenary; history of its opera;
current notes. Op v 11 n 4 p 287
Ap '60
---Nordic music by the Associa-
tion of Swedish Composers; list
of composers at Stockholm. WM
n 4 p 76 Ag '60
---Peterson, P. G. (Theatre re-
port.) il WT v 9 n 2 p 174-178
Summer '60
---Theatre report. WP v 11 n 6
p 7 Ap '60; same. WP v 11 n 9
p 8 Jl '60
SWEENEY TODD (Cranko), ballet
Guest, Ivor. Report from England.

MD v 50 n 8 p 32 F '60
SWITZERLAND
Prix de composition musicale
"Reine Marie-José": Giorgio
Ferrairi, 1925-, Turin; André
Casanova, 1919-, Paris; Armin
Schibler, 1920-, Zurich. GDC
n 295 p 502 D 30'60
---Recordings by the Swiss Na-
tional Music Committee, list.
WM n 2 p 33 Ap '60
---Theatre report. WP v 11 n 8
p 8 Je '60
THE SWORD OF DAMOCLES, play
Moscow, 1959, ens AP wl ph.
WT v 9 n 2 p 181 Summer '60
SYDNEY
Morton, Helen C. Sydney (Music)
diary. MD v 50 n 8 p 14 F '60
---Petrouchka, adapted by James
Upshaw for TV; cast. MD v 51
n 6 p 29 D '60
SYDNEY OPERA HOUSE
Cost 4, 800, 000 pounds; notes.
MD v 50 n 7 p 15 Ja '60
LA SYLPHIDE (Bournonville),
ballet
Guest, Ivor. (Notes on Ballet
Rambert revival.) MD v 51 n 3
p 27 S '60
---Lami, Eugenio. Costume de-
sign for "uno scozzese". La S
n 132 p 33 N '60
SYMPHONY FOR FUN (Burke),
ballet
Music by Don Gillis; Australian
performance. MD v 51 n 2 p 24
Ag '60
THE SYMPHONY OF THE AIR
European tour, sponsored by the
American International Founda-
tion. AmM v 8 n 5 p 12 Je '60
LES SYNTHÉTISTES
Brussels "7", much like the
French "6": Rene Bernier, Gas-
ton Brenta, Théo de Jonckère,
Robert Otlet, Marcel Poot, Mau-
rice Schoemaker, Jules Strens;
notes. GDC n 290 p 329 N 25'60
SZABO, FERENC, 1902-, composer
Notes. Mus Q v 46 n 4 p 527 O'60
SZEKELY, ENDRE, 1912-, compo-
ser
Notes. Mus Q v 46 n 4 p 533 O'60

wl ph. Th R v 2 n 2 p 65 1960
TAMIRIS, HELEN (1905-) and
Daniel Nagrin. The Spartan Life
of Modern Dance. il Th Arts v 44
n 11 p 61-5, 72 N '60
---With José Limon, AP wl ph:
Barbara Morgan, Th Arts v 44
n 11 p 61 N '60
TANCHELIJN, play
Amsterdam notes; Harry Mulisch.
WP v 11 n 8 p 9 Je '60
---Amsterdam, 1960, ens ph: Le-
maire en Wennink. WT v 9 n 2
p 172 Summer '60
TANNHAUSER, opera
Heyworth, Peter. (Review of
Sadler's Wells.) Op v 11 n 11
p 783 N '60
---Metropolitan cast, criticism,
composer, décor; the story; port-
folio. ON v 25 n 6 D 17'60
---Sadler's Wells; Anthony Besch's
production, review. il Op v 11
n 2 p 155-6 F '60
--- ---review; Judith Pierce "gran-
dly in the old manner" others in
"People's Opera style". Op v 2
n 3 p 233 Mr '60
---Weerth, Ernest de. Rome review. ON v 24 n 23 p 26-7 Ap 9
'60
---Bayreuth, staged by Wieland
Wagner; Act II taken from above
the Hall of Song, ens AP wl ph:
Lauterwasser, ON v 25 n 6 p 16
D 17'60
---Metropolitan Opera, ens AP
wl ph: Sedge Leblang; and 5 Ap
hl phs. ON v 25 n 6 D 17'60
---Sadler's Wells: The Venusberg,
the Hall of Song, the Valley of
the Wartburg, 3 ens AP wl phs:
David Sim. Op v 11 n 2 p 157 F'60
TANSMAN, ALEXANDRE (1897-).
Cantate et Prologue (études musicales analytiques). GDC n 275
p 756 Je 3'60
---Notes; b. Lodz, Poland. AmM
v 8 n 9 p 8 O '60
TAPE-RECORDER MUSIC
Luening-Ussachevsky's "Con-
certed Piece for Tape Recorder
and Orchestra; notes on NY Philharmonic concert. MC v 161

n 6 p 18 My '60
---See also Concrete Music Electronic Music
TAPES
Darrell, R. D. A bandwagon at
7.5 ips. HF v 10 n 7 p 29 Jl '60
--- ---The Tape Desk, a review
section of all sorts; 4-track listed separately. HF 1960
---Decca-London 1960 to release
on tape; notes. HF v 10 n 1 p 59
Ja '60
---Foreign sound track from out-
dated cinema cut into "component
parts as bridges, cues, mood,
emotions", sold to makers of US
television film; further notes. IM
v 58 n 8 p 41 F '60
---Freas, Ralph. The coming break-
through in tape; home service 1970.
por HF v 10 n 3 p 46-7, 122 Mr '60
---MacMillan, Keith. Making the
most of your tape recorder. CMJ
v 4 n 2 p 25-32 Winter '60
---Murphy, Donn B. Turn on the
tape (use of theatre tapes for teaching). PlM v 36 n 6 p 133 Mr '60
---New cartridge system, CBS
laboratories: 3-track, 64 minute
play; 5 cartridges in player. HF
v 10 n 5 p 57 My '60
---Reuling, Karl F. Stereo on tape
(comparison with discs; progress
since 1947). ON v 24 n 18 p 23
Mr 5'60
--- ---Stereo Tape II. ON v 24 n 21
p 13 Mr 26'60
---"Robot tapes" snipped from foreign sound tracks; Senator Wayne
Morse and AFL-CIO oppose use in
US television films; report. IM
v 58 n 9 p 7 Mr '60
---Tape cartridge player developed
by CBS labs; Zenith in US and
Grundig tooling up; notes. HF
v 10 n 2 p 95 F '60
---US; fight against "illegal" foreign
tapes; example, "Sea Hunt", a non-
network adventure story "with foreign music dubbed into its sound-
track background"; details. IM
v 58 n 10 p 5 Ap '60
See also   Concrete Music, Electronic Music

TAPPAN ZEE PLAYHOUSE
Nyack, New York, readied for
3rd year, ph. Th Arts v 44 n 6
p 15 Je '60
TARADASH, DANIEL. (There
was a Little Girl, play adapted
from Lost Summer; directed by
Joshua Logan.) il Th Arts v 44
n 3 p 10-1 Mr '60
TARDOS, BÉLA, 1910-, composer
Notes. J Rev v 7 n 3 p 4 Fall'60
TARTINI, GIUSEPPE, 1539-1580,
composer
Boyden, David D. The missing
Italian manuscript of Tartini's
Traite des Agremens. il Mus Q
v 46 n 3 p 315-328 Jl '60
---Left profile portrait from en-
graving by Carlo Calcinoto,
1745; 3 pages from his Treatise,
facsimiles. Mus Q v 46 n 3
p 326 Jl '60
LE TARTUFFE, play
Nelson, Robert J. The unrecon-
structed heroes of Molière.
TDR v 4 n 3 p 14-9 Mr '60
---Ens AP wl ph: Finland. WP
v 11 n 7 p 1 My '60
---Helsinki, ens AP wl ph: 1960.
WT v 9 n 3 p 280 Autumn '60
TASSART, MAURICE. Six con-
certs à "L'Atelier de la Danse",
Bella Reine. GDC n 277 p 820
Je 17'60
IL TASSILONE
Della Corte, A. In questo mese
ha letto. La S n 133 p 70 D '60
A TASTE OF HONEY, play
NYC review; Joan Playwright
and Andrew Ray. Th Arts v 44
n 12 p 11 D '60
---Richards, Stanley. (NYC re-
view.) PlM v 37 n 3 p 68 D '60
TAUHERT, RUDOLPH. Letter
congratulating the Musical
Courier on 80th year. por MC
v 161 n 3 p 8 F '60
TAXATION
Managers interviewed on ec-
onomics of music. MC v 162
n 1 p 12-19 Jl '60
---Theatre survey; Argentina;
Belgium; Poland; Czechoslova-
kia; protective laws; price of

theatre seats. WP v 11 n 8
Je '60
--- ---Australia. WP v 12 n 3
p 2 D '60
--- ---Austria., Chile, Denmark,
Spain, France, Iceland, United
Kingdom: 1. theatre tax 2. other
tax 3. exonerations 4. total; pro-
tective laws. seat prices. WP
v 11 n 4 p 2 F '60
--- ---Brazil; Bulgaria; Colom-
bia; theatre seats, ballet seats.
WP v 11 n 10 p 2 Ag '60
--- ---Finland, Sweden, East
Germany, Greece; protective
laws; prices of theatre seats.
WP v 11 n 5 p 2 Mr '60
--- ---Korea; USA; Netherlands;
Yugoslavia; Russia; protective
laws; prices of theatre seats. WP
v 11 n 6 p 2 My '60
--- ---West Germany; Canada;
Hungary; Italy; Japan; Rumania;
Turkey; protective laws; prices
of theatre seats. WP v 11 n 6 p 2
Ap '60
---US; Bill H. R. 2164 to reduce
the cabaret tax from 20 percent
to 10 percent; details of discrim-
ination against live music. IM
v 58 n 10 p 8 Ap '60
--- ---Cabaret tax now at 10 percent, passing of the Forand Bill;
review of American Federation
of Musicians campaign 1955-1960.
IM v 58 n 11 p 7 My '60
--- ---individual income tax for
musicians; aid in finding out professional deductions. IM v 58 n 9
p 15 Mr '60
--- ---cut of cabaret tax to 10 percent producing 16, 445 more man-
hours of music work per week;
notes. IM v 59 n 6 p 5 D '60
TAYLOR, DEEMS(1885-). What is
American opera? ON v 25 n 6
p 9-11 D 17'60
---With conductor Pelletier and
director Defrère at Empire State
Festival, ph: Friedman-Abeles.
ON v 25 n 6 p 9 D 17'60
TAYLOR, SAMUEL(1912-). The
Pleasure of His Company (text
of play, NYC cast 1958, pictures).

Th Arts v 44 n 4 p 22-52 Ap'60
TCHAIKOVSKY, PETER ILYICH,
1840-1893, composer
Smith, Russell. A fanfare for
Piotr Ilyich. HF v 10 n 3 p 48-9
123 Mr '60
TCHEMERZINE, MONIQUE, 1924-,
dancer
Notes on "Nana" from Emile
Zola. TD n 96 p 34 S-O '60
---Russia; notes and pictures.
TD n 90 p 16-7 F '60
---San Carlos, Naples; notes. TD
n 92 p 8 Ap '60
---Dans le Martyre de Saint-Se-
bastien, AP wl ph: Naples, San
Carlo. TD n 92 p 9 Ap '60
---In Le Martyre de Saint Sébas-
tien, AP hl ph. TD n 96 p 34
S-O '60
TCHEREPNINE, ALEXANDRE
(1899-). Oraison symphonique
(études musicales analytiques).
GDC n 288 p 266 N 11'60
---Notes. MC v 161 n 4 p 25 Mr'60
---Première of "Bagatelles" at
Lucerne Festival; pianist, Marg-
rit Weber. MC v 162 n 5 p 25 N '60
---Première: Oraison Symphoni-
que; Igor Markevitch, conducting,
Paris review. GDC n 290 p 321
N 25'60
TCHERINA, LUDMILLA
See Tchemerzine, Monique 1924-,
dancer
THE TEACHER, play
Stratford, Canada; John Gray.
WP v 12 n 1 p 3 O '60
TEACHING
Accompanists; Sergius Kagen on
Juilliard program of training.
por J Rev v 7 n 1 p 5, 14 Winter
59-60
---Audio unit devised at Wartburg
College, Iowa, which doubled
music theory classes; description.
MEJ v 46 n 4 p 92 F-Mr '60
---Belinsky, Isai. The oboist looks
at his problems. IM v 59 n 4 p 34-
5 O '60
---Brienhalt, Verna, and Irene
Schoepfle. Music experience for
the child with speech limitations.
MEJ v 47 n 1 p 45-6, 48, 50 S-O'60

---Connecticut ninth graders
1903: demonstration of sight
reading; test re-told by Charles L.
L. Gary. MEJ v 47 n 1 p 56 S-O '60
---Creative potential, clues to look
for in children: list. MEJ v 46 n 3
p 67 Ja '60
---Double bass; Bertram Turet-
sky on teaching this instrument
(Hartt College teacher). MEJ
v 47 n 1 p 105 S-O '60
---Editorial: attitude of dance and
music teachers toward pupils.
MD v 50 n 1 p 7 Ja '60
---End of the year dance specta-
cles:France. TD n 96 p 8 S-O'60
---Gehrkens, Karl Wilson. (The
characteristics of a good music
teacher). MEJ v 46 n 6 p 48 Je-Jl
'60
---Goodman, Paul Roe. Getting
through to the piano student. MC
v 162 n 5 p 34 N'60
---Guerreo, Alberto, 1886-1959, as
a piano teacher. CMJ v 4 n 2 p 33
Winter'60
---Hoffman, Mary. (On teaching
music appreciation or teaching
students.)MEJ v 46 n 4 p 94-5
F-Mr'60
---Junior high school choral teaching;Lee Kjelson reporting from
California. MEJ v 47 n 1 p 114
S-O'60
---Kincaid, William, flutist, on his
teaching at the Curtis Institute;
list of distinguished pupils. por
IM v 58 n 11 p 11 My'60
---Lawler, Vanett. Music education
as a profession. por IM v 58 n 9
p 18-9 Mr'60
---Lyon, Raymond. Le Solfège avec
joie:M. Amable Massis, une douz-
aine de garçons et filles, 7-12
ans. GDC n 271 p 632 My 5'60
---Matthews, Paul W. We need superior music teachers. MEJ v 46
n 6 p 31-2 Je-Jl'60
---Music education lacks discovered
in US Army band auditions:"poor
knowledge of chromatic scale,
much less fingering", frequent;
"concert pitch" not understood;
Kwal-Wasser-Dykema test used.

(Teaching)
IM v 58 n 7 p 20 Ja'60
---Music Educators National Conference, Atlantic City;technique
described of letter-writing to
inform teachers of the use in US
of "illegal" music via "wetback"
tapes in film sound tracks, a
fight to protect US musicians. IM
v 58 n 10 p 35 Ap'60
---Music in small liberal arts
college;Marian Haines Schap, Illinois report. MEJ v 47 n 2 p 87
N-D'60
---Music in US schools;many fine
reports, suggested techniques,
re-statement of aims in each
issue, signed teacher reports.
MEJ 1960
---Payzant, Geoffrey. The competitive music festivals (Canada). CMJ v 4 n 3 p 35-46 Spring
'60
---Plinkiewisch, Helen. Opera in
the sixth grade (her teaching
and production). il MEJ v 47 n 1
p 96-7 S-O'60
---Sight-reading;Floyd Heyden-
berg on sight-reading the vocal
score (in US schools). MEJ v 47
n 1 p 106 S-O'60
---Swanson, Frederick J. When
voices change;an experiment in
Junior High School music. MEJ
v 46 n 4 p 50, 53-4 F-Mr'60
---Sydney, Wahroonga School of
Pianoforte;"music money" used
to teach note values;explanation
to five-year-olds. MD v 51 n 5
p 12 N'60
---Trumpet;twenty signed technical suggestions from famous
trumpeters in the series by Dan
Tetzlaff. IM v 58 n 10 p 22-3
Ap'60
---Trombone;Yale H. Ellis on
teaching this brass instrument.
MEJ v 47 n 1 p 102 S-O'60
---US music teachers;notes each
issue, The Changing Scene column. MEJ 1960
---A Visit to the Metropolitan,
35mm slides;and other visual
aids. ON v 24 n 11 p 1 Ja 16'60

---What a dance teacher needs to
have in culture;the practical ex-
ercises, etc. by Marcelle Bourgeat. TD n 94 p 23-4 Je'60
---Second annual international
String Congress in Puerto Rico
1960;faculty portfolio, Roy Harris
director and 12 teachers, small
por phs. IM v 58 n 9 p 12-3 Mr'60
TEAGARDEN, JACK, 1905-,
trombonist
Cerulli, Dom. (Career sketch of
Texas-born Weldon John Teagar-
den.)il IM v 58 n 7 p 12-3 Ja'60
---AP hl ph;with his band, ens AP
wl ph. IM v 58 n 7 cover, p 13 Ja'60
TEATRO ARGENTINO
La Plata;Die Fledermaus under Mar-
tin Eisler. Op v 11 n 8 p 547 Ag'60
TEATRO COLÓN
Andrea Chénier singers:Tucker,
Previtali, Udovick, Sereni, hl ph:
Claros. ON v 25 n 3 p 21 N 19'60
---Arnosi, Eduardo. Buenos Aires
report. Op v 11 n 8 p 546 Ag'60
--- ---Opera report. Op v 11 n 9
p 616 S'60
---Un Ballo in Maschera, Act I, ens
AP wl ph:Buenos Aires. Op v 11
n 8 p 546 Ag'60
---Pascal, Marie. Notes on The Love
of Three Oranges. ON v 24 n 17
p 28 F 27'60
--- ---(Opera reviews.) ON v 25
n 3 p 21 N 19'60
---Tannhäuser after 18 years;Gre
Brouwentijn excellent;Marta Moedl
"lacked freshness";review. MC v
162 n 6 p 32 D'60
---Principali di "Andrea Chénier",
ph. LaS n 131 p 72 O'60
LE TEATRO del BALETTO
Carandente, Gianni. La Seule com-
pagnie de ballet independante ital-
ienne. TD n 91 p 26 Mr'60
TEATRO dell'OPERA
Di Roma;Il Medium;Salome, Lilian
Birkas. LaS n 127 p 27, 55 Je'60
--- ---reviews. il LaS n 128 p 30
Jl'60
---Rinaldi, Mario. (Reviews.)LaS
1960
TEATRO della PERGOLA
Di Firenze;"Elisa" di Luigi Cher-

ubini. il LaS n 127 p 26 Je'60

TEATRO FARNESE, PARMA
Fassett, James H. (This should
become the theatre of Verdi, its
productions nurtured by the Institute of Verdi Studies;restor-
ation physically not enough.)
Ver v 1 n 2 preface Ag'60
---Graf, Herbert. (Restoration
neglecting backstage area and
sides;likely to be of disadvantage to future operatic use.)
Ver v 1 n 2 preface Ag'60

TEATRO LA FENICE
Messinis, Mario. Alcina. il LaS
n 125 p 48 Ap'60
See also Venice

TEATRO LIRICO di BUDAPEST
Szollosy, András. (Reviews.) il
LaS n 128 p 32, 63 Jl'60

TEATRO MASSIMO BELLINI
Di Catania;Ugo Mezzadri re-
views. il LaS n 127 p 29, 57 Je'60
---Mezzadri, Ugo. Catania. LaS
1960
--- ---Stagione lirica ufficiale,
quaresima 1960. LaS n 122 inset
Ja'60
---Wiesbaden Festival after the
Vienna Staatsoper;reviews. Op
v 11 p 65 Autumn'60

TEATRO PICCALO SCALA
Castiglioni, Vittorangelo. (Reviews.) il LaS 1960

TEATRO POPOLARE ITALIANO
Notes on growth;Vittorio Gassman. WT v 9 n 2 p 170 Summer
'60
---Exterior view. WT v 9 n 2
p 168 Summer'60

TEATRO SOCIALE di COMO
Angelini, G. (Reviews.) il LaS
n 125 p 50 Ap'60

TEATRO VERDI
See Trieste

TEBALDI, RENATA, 1922-, singer
Rome;annual Tosca;notes. Op
v 11 n 8 p 563 Ag'60
---AP hl ph. MC v 162 n 4 p 22
O'60
---And Bacquier in La Tosca, AP
wl ph. OpP n 19 p 13 1960
---As Tosca, AP wl ph:Rome. LaS
n 128 p 30 Jl'60

--- ---hl ph:Melançon. ON v 25 n 1
p 4 O 8'60
--- ---notes and in costume phs:La
Scala. Th Arts v 44 n 3 p 51-3 Mr'60
---As Leonora di Vargas, AP hl ph:
Melançon. ON v 24 n 19 p 17 Mr 12
'60
---As Maddelena di Coigny, AP phs:
Melançon. ON v 24 n 21 Mr 26'60
---E Giuseppe DiStefano in "Tosca",
AP wl ph:La Scala. LaS n 122 p 35
Ja'60
---Por ph. ON v 24 n 21 p 29 Mr 26
'60
---With Corelli, San Carlos Adriana
Lecouvreur, AP wl ph:Naples. ON
v 25 n 7 p 24 D 24'60
---With Gobbi, curtain call, Chicago
wl ph:Nancy Sorensen. ON v 25
n 7 p 28 D 24'60

TECHNIQUE
American view of French acting
style. PlM v 37 n 2 p 31 N'60
---Bass player in orchestra;spec-
ial problems discussed by Warren
A. Benfield. por IM v 58 n 8 p 18-9
F'60
---Capri, Antonio. La pianistica di
Chopin. il LaS n 126 p 9-17 My'60
---Smith, Leonard B. Developing
high register, the professional's
goal. por IM v 59 n 6 p 20-1 D'60
--- ---The professional's goal in
practice (routine as a trumpeter
in nine phases). por IM v 58 n 12
p 14-5 Je'60
---Tetzlaff, Dan. Trumpet talk, a
series. IM v 58 n 8 p 26-7 F'60
---Violin;three attacks in use today;
Sol Babitz, series. IM v 59 n 1 p 30
Jl'60

TEEDRINKEN, play
Toneelstudio'50;ens AP wl ph:De
Backer. WT v 9 n 1 p 53 Spring'60

TEIRLINCK, HERMAN(1879-). Two
temperaments, two theatres (Belgian in French and in Dutch ton-
gue). il WT v 9 n 1 p 23-34 Spring
'60

TEL AVIV
Piattelli, Heinke. Teatro dell'Opera;
Le Nozze di Figaro. il LaS n 125
p 55 Ap'60

TELEMANN, GEORG PHILIPP,

(Telemann)
1681-1767, composer
Career notes as well as record review, playing by I Solisti di Zagreb, signed by Caldwell Titcomb. Mus Q v 46 n 3 p 410-12 Jl'60

THE TELEMANN SOCIETY
Schulze, Richard, conducting; NYC review. MC v 161 n 7 p 25 Je'60

TELL PLAY
Ruoff, Jakob. Wood-cut of apple shooting scene Zürich 1545. Th R v 2 n 3 p 129 1960

TEMPERLEY, NICHOLAS. Beethoven in London concert life, 1800-1850. MR v 21 n 3 p 207-14 Ag'60

THE TEMPEST, play
American Shakespeare Festival Stratford 1960, ens AP wl ph: Friedman-Abeles. WT v 9 n 3 p 295 Autumn'60

TEMPETES et BONACES, play
Athens notes; Traïforos-St. Fotiadis. WP v 12 n 1 p 8 O'60

TEN THOUSAND MILES, folk opera
DeMerchaut, John, composer; NYC performance notes. MC v 161 n 1 p 36 Ja'60

TENDERLOIN(LAYTON), musical
NYC; "a funny valentine of a show". PlM v 37 n 3 p 68 D'60
--- ---notes. WP v 12 n 3 p 37 D'60
--- ---review; Maurice Evans as Dr. Parkhurst; Beaton décor. Th Arts v 44 n 12 p 12 D'60

THE TENTH MAN, play
Criticism. WT v 9 n 2 p 188 Summer'60
---NYC notes; Paddy Chayefsky. WP v 11 n 5 p 5 Mr'60
---Ens AP wl ph:NYC. Th Arts v 44 n 1 p 89 Ja'60
---NYC 1959, ens AP ph. WT v 9 n 2 p 190 Summer'60

TERMON, M. L'atlas du monde Chrétien. il WP v 11 n 5 p 8 Mr'60

TERRASSE, CLAUDE, 1867-1923, composer

Chamfray, Claude. Fiche biographique. GDC n 295 p 504 D 30'60

TERRY, WALTER(1913-). American ballet. il Th Arts v 44 n 11 p 57-60 N'60

TÊTE d'OR, play
Barrault and Alain Cluny, AP hl ph. Th Arts v 44 n 1 p 22 Ja'60

TETZLAFF, DAN. Trumpet talk. IM v 58 n 8 p 26-7 F'60(series)

TEXACO-METROPOLITAN NETWORK
Opera in US; map, stations, news on inset each issue. ON 1960-61

TEXAS
A Cloud of Witnesses, drama of the Alamo; review of verse play by Ramsey Yelvington. PlM v 36 n 5 p 114 F'60
---Commission to compose new "music for Texas" to Louis Gordon of Houston, now at Eastman. IM v 59 n 6 p 27 D'60
---Hines, Jerome, first Wotan and other notes on Houston's Die Walküre. Op v 11 n 4 p 271 Ap'60
See also Dallas; Fort Worth, etc.

TEXAS BOYS CHOIR
Fort Worth review. MC v 161 n 3 p 39 F'60
---Ens ph:Fort Worth. MC v 161 n 7 p 35 Je'60

TEYTE, DAME MAGGIE, 1889-, singer
Schauensee, Max de. Review of Teyte's book, "Star On the Door". ON v 24 n 11 p 31 Ja 16'60

THAÏS, opera
San Carlo review. LaS n 122 p 73 Ja'60
---Weerth, Ernest de. (Review of Virginia Zeani at San Carlo; the ballet by Bianca Gallizia; Ettore Bastianini.)ON v 24 n 14 p 26 F 6'60
---Lyric Opera, ens AP wl ph:Sorenson. Op v 11 n 2 p 136 F'60

THEATRE
Bailey, Bryan. Building the young audience. NTM v 1 n 2 p 18-21 Ja '60
---Balch, Jack. The openings (on Broadway). Th Arts v 44 n 1 p 14-16 Ja'60

300

(Theatre)
Th Arts v 44 n 12 p 60-3 D'60
---Lestrud, Vernon. The playwright's the thing. PlM v 36
n 6 p 132 Mr'60
---Marshall, Norman. Are stage
plays suitable for TV? WT v 9
n 4 p 301-12 Winter'60
---Miller, Henry, et Jean Giono
voient Homère. WP v 11 n 8
p 1, 7 Je'60
---Nagler, A. M. Hugo von Hofmannsthal and theatre. Th R
v 2 n 1 p 5-15 1960
---NYC; the openings, survey by
Bruce Bohle. il Th Arts v 44
n 5 p 57-60 My'60
---Le Nô; introduction aux traites
de Zeami. WP v 12 n 1 p 2 O'60
---Norton, Eliot. (On summer
theatre in US). Th Arts v 44 n 6
p 18-20 Je'60
--- ---Theatre USA: Boston.
Th Arts v 44 n 5 p 53-6 My'60
---Notes and Queries, a column
of signed questions from scholars concerned with theatre history and actors. Th Notbk 1960
---Patterson, Tom. Stratford and
the Canadian theatre. PlM v 36
n 5 p 103-4 F'60
---Prague;survey by Jean-Pierre
Lenoir. portfolio Th Arts v 44
n 8 p 57-60 Ag'60
---Projet de réglement des éch-
anges internationaux entre les
bibliothéques et musées des
arts du Spectacle. Th R v 2 n 2
p 126-8 1960
---Report from the Secretary
General of ITI, Jean Darcante
(several translations). WP v 11
n 10 Ag'60
---Reports from International
Theatre Centers each issue.
WP 1960
---San Francisco;center of regional or "little" groups;report
by Stanley Eichelbaum. il Th
Arts v 44 n 3 p 57-61 Mr'60
---Sartre, Jean-Paul. Un texte
inédit (Conférence sur le Théâtre, Paris, 1960). por WP v 11
n 9 p 1, 7 Jl'60

---Shakespeare research underta-
ken:dates and titles of first per-
formances, arranged by countries.
WP v 12 n 3 p 2 D'60
---Spain;viewpoint, survey by Jack
Brookings. PlM v 36 n 7 p 160-1
Ap'60
---Stacey, Roy. Great Britain: the
amateur theatre. PlM v 36 n 8
p 192-3 My'60
---Teaching enriched by tapes;a
practical approach by Donn B.
Murphy of Georgetown University.
PlM v 36 n 6 p 133 Mr'60
---US; National Collegiate Players
and Junior Collegiate Players:of-
ficers with addresses, followed by
chapter list with each founding
date. PlM 1960
--- ---P. W. Wodehouse lightly at-
tacks the Broadway stage as not
being the poor critics' fault. Th
Arts v 44 n 6 p 8-9 Je'60
---Veinstein, André, et Cécile Giteau. Code de References et de
Catalogage de l'Iconographie thea-
trale. Th R v 2 n 2 p 120-5 1960
---Watts, Richard, Jr. That "shabby
season" in perspective (1959-60,
NYC). il Th Arts v 44 n 7 p 13-5
Jl'60
---Young, John Wray. A community
theatre quiz. portfolio Th Arts v 44
n 8 p 16-20 Ag'60
---Young audiences;Bryan Bailey
on drama for school children in
Coventry. NTM v 1 n 2 p 18-21 Ja
'60
---Kammerspiele, Munich;scenes
from Galileo;from Fiesco;from
Einen Jux will er sich machen, 3
AP phs. Th Arts v 44 n 4 p 18 Ap'60
---Large pictures of stages:Arena
Theatre in a tent for summer:
Lacey;Festival Theatre, Stratford,
Ontario; Library Theatre, Scarbor-
ough;Mermaid Theatre, Puddle
Dock. NTM v 1 n 4 p 4 Jl'60
THEATRE-ECONOMIC ASPECTS
Austria;subsidy notes. WP v 11 n 3
p 7 Ja'60
---Elman, Mischa. (Quoted on being
an "angel" to Broadway musicals;
how he picks investments.) Th Arts

(Theatre-Economic Aspects)
v 44 n 10 p 4 O'60
---Gravey, Fernand. Performers' rights. WT v 9 n 4 p 341-3 Winter'60
---Munich meeting:La Convention mondiale des droits d'auteurs. WP v 11 n 3 p 7 Ja'60
---NYC; blackout of theatres June 2, 1960; Actors' Equity vs. League of New York Theatres (126 producers);list of Equity demands. Th Arts v 44 n 7 p 6 Jl'60
--- ---100-seat off-Broadway centers;notes. PlM v 36 n 7 p 149 Ap'60
---State-aid:Argentina; Colombia. WP v 12 n 3 p 2 D'60
---Taxation: Argentina;Belgium; Poland;Czechoslovakia;protective laws;price of theatre seats. WP v 11 n 8 p 8 Je'60
--- ---Australia. WP v 12 n 3 p 2 D'60
--- ---Austria;Chile;Denmark; Spain; France;Iceland;United Kingdom;protective laws;cost of seats. WP v 11 n 4 p 2 F'60
--- ---Brazil;Bulgaria;Colombia; cost of theatre and ballet seats. WP v 11 n 10 p 2 Ag'60
--- ---Finland;Sweden;East Germany;Greece;protective laws; prices of theatre seats. WP v 11 n 5 p 2 Mr'60
--- ---Korea;USA; Netherlands; Switzerland;Uruguay;Yugoslavia;Russia;protective laws;seats. WP v 11 n 7 p 2 Ap'60
--- ---West Germany;Canada;Hungary;Italy;Japan;Rumania;Turkey;protective laws;prices of seats. WP v 11 n 6 p 2 Ap'60
---Wilcke, Joachim. The audience (Germany). WT v 9 n 3 p 259-61 Autumn'60
---Wilson, John S. (On summer theatre, US; associations controlling "big time" stock.)Th Arts v 44 n 6 p 14-6 Je'60
THEATRE-HISTORY and
    CRITICISM
Albach, Ben. Bibliographie raisonnée du théâtre neerlandais.

Th R v 2 n 2 p 88-98 1960
---Brockett, O. G. The theatre of the Southern United States from the beginnings through 1865: a bibliographical essay. Th R v 2 n 3 p 163-174 1960
---Byrne, M. St. Clare. The earliest Hamlet prompt book in an English library. facsimiles Th Notbk v 15 n 1 p 12-31 Autumn'60
---Chalaupka, Christl. Austrian theses on theatre research. Th R v 2 n 1 p 37-43 1960
---Chevalley, Sylvie. Recherches théâtrales:thèses de doctorat soutenues et en préparation dans les Universités de France 1944-1959. Th R v 2 n 2 p 99-108 1960
---Clurman, Harold. (The Theatre Group and other projects of the 1930's.)Th Arts v 44 n 9 p 15-8 S'60
---Cole, Wendell. Piper's Opera House, Virginia City, Nevada. Th Notbk v 15 n 2 p 52-5 Winter 60-61
---Corneille's Medée (in the French libretto published 1693 by Christophe Ballard, performed by the Academie Royale de Musique in Paris 1693). Chrys v 13 nos 5-8 1960
---Eddison, Robert. Capon and Goodman's Fields (description from a rough pencil sketch made by William Capon, being a "hypothetical reconstruction" of 1741 period). facsimile Th Notbk v 14 n 4 p 126-132 Summer'60
---Fogle, Richard Harter. Coleridge on dramatic illusion. TDR v 4 n 4 p 33-44 My'60
---Gunnis, Rupert. Dictionary of British Sculptors, 1661-1851 (list of works having theatrical interest). Th Notbk v 14 n 4 p 123-126 Summer'60
---Highfill, Philip H. Actors' wills. Th Notbk v 15 n 1 p 7-15 Autumn '60
---Kawatake, Toshio. Shakespeare in the Japanese theatre. Th R v 2 n 2 p 82-7 1960
---Kernodle, George R. Seven med-

(Theatre-History)
ieval theatres in one social
structure Th R v 2 n 1 p 26-
36 1960
---Kindermann, Heinz. Theater-
geschichte Europas, volume III.
The Baroque (book reviewed by
George W. Brandt). Th Notbk
v 15 n 2 p 66-8 Winter '60-61
---Lewis, Robert. (The Group
Theatre 1931-41, NYC.) Th
Arts v 44 n 4 p 62 Ap '60
---Miller, Arthur; Tom E. Driver on Arthur Miller. TDR v 4
n 4 p 45-52 My '60
---Morehouse, Ward. (Theatres
built in NYC early 20th century;
drama notes also.) Th Arts v 44
n 1 p 79-80, 84 Ja '60
--- ---(US theatre in the 1930s).
il Th Arts v 44 n 9 p 10-4 S '60
---Morley, Malcolm. Drama at
London Bridge. maps Th Notbk
v 14 n 4 p 119-22 Summer '60
---Paris, 1740; G. M. Bergman,
la grande mode des pantomimes
et les spectacles d'optique de
Servandoni. Th R v 2 n 2 p 71-
81 1960
---Recherches théâtrales: thèses
de doctorat soutenues et en préparation dans les Universités
de France, 1944-1959. Th R
v 2 n 3 p 141-162 1960
---Rosenfeld, Sybil. Report on
two Georgian theatres: Richmond (Yorks) Theatre; Stockton-
on-Tees Theatre. Th Notbk
v 14 n 3 p 100-101 Spring '60
---Valency, Maurice. Flight into
lunacy ("the loss of meaning in
art is a major disaster"). Th
Arts v 44 n 8 p 8-9, 68 Ag '60
---Weintraub, Stanley. Bernard
Shaw, actor. Th Arts v 44 n 10
p 66-7 O '60
---Wilson, Adrian. (Notes on
early playbills and project to
reproduce same). Th Notbk v 14
n 4 p 142 Summer '60
---Zbierski, Henry K. Shakespeare in Poland: a survey. Th R
v 2 n 3 p 136-140 1960
---See also Books

THEATRE-TWENTIETH CEN-
TURY
ANTA; NYC: Board of Standards
and Planning for the Living Theatre; also ANTA Theatre Assembly drawing people to NYC. Chicago: Chicago Community Theatre, Latin American survey. WP
v 11 n 3 p 1 Ja '60
---Australia; F. H. Mares' survey;
Elizabethan Theatre Trust aims
listed; last decade in detail. NTM
v 1 n 3 p 24-8 Ap '60
---Blum, Daniel. New faces become old favorites (1930s in US).
Th Arts v 44 n 9 p 58-9 S '60
---Broadway's habit of using critic's wards as advertising; John
Keating on this present phenomenon. Th Arts v 44 n 12 p 14-5
D '60
---Brock, James W. New trends,
1960 (US). PlM v 36 n 8 p 185
My '60
---Brown, Ivor, After Chekhov
(on present lack of emotion in
acting). WP v 11 n 9 p 1 Jl '60
---Cleveland, Ohio; Arthur Spaeth's survey community and college stages. Th Arts v 44 n 1
p 76-7, 83 Ja '60
---Coe, Richard L. Theatre Washington (survey of facilities and
trends in the District of Columbia).
il Th Arts v 44 n 12 p 21-4 D '60
---Derwent, Clarence. Has fun
gone from the theatre? WP v 11
n 5 p 7 Mr '60
---Freedley, George. Plays first
produced off Broadway, June 1,
1959-May 31, 1960; Part I. PlM
v 37 n 2 p 32-3 N '60
--- ---Part II. PlM v 37 n 3 p 54-
5 D '60
---Great Britain; the provincial
theatre: plan for new houses run
on a community basis, government aid to repertory, and tours
by national companies. NTM v 1
n 1 p 5-7 O '59
---Iglésis, Roger. First steps in
television for the stage producer.
WT v 9 n 4 p 325-336 Winter '60
---Ionesco, Eugene (1912-). The

avant-garde theatre. TDR v 5
n 2 p 44-53 D '60
---Kronenberger, Louis. The fifties: patchwork progress (US).
Th Arts v 44 n 1 p 10-11 Ja '60
---Sterckx, Piet. New trends in
the Flemish theatre. WT v 9 n 1
p 51-57 Spring '60
---US; student theatre; methods
of getting youth into the theatre.
WP v 12 n 1 p 1 O '60
---US community and campus
plays, regular listing in "Pro-
gram News". PlM v 36 n 4 p 93
Ja '60
---Webster, Margaret. Whither
bound? (Theatre in England; the
"reps".) Th Arts v 44 n 11 p 23-
4, 71 N '60
---Whitehead, Robert, on his ideas
for Lincoln Center's Drama Re-
pertory Theatre. por ON v 25 n 2
p 12 O 29'60
---Zavadski, Youri. Theatre in
U. R. S. S. WP v 11 n 5 p 1, 7
Mr '60
THEATRE ARTS CLUB, 1910-
Detroit note. Th Arts v 44 n 10
p 78 O '60
THEATRE ARTS WORLD CALEN-
DAR
Plays, musicals, etc. listed by
place with annotations. Th Arts
1960
THEATRE COLLECTIONS
Matthew, W. H., Jr. Queen's
College, NYC, theatre collec-
tion. PlM v 37 n 2 p 28 O '60
THÉÂTRE DE LA MONNAIE
Brussels (city) Opera; new me-
thods; report. MC v 161 n 7 p 15
Je '60
LE THÉÂTRE DES NATIONS,
PARIS
Le Ballet: liste 15 Mars-Ier
Juillet. il TD n 91 p 14 Mr '60
---Blanchart, Paul. Le Théâtre
des Nations et la recherche dra-
matique et scénique. il Th R
v 2 n 1 p 16-25 1960
---Brookings, Jack. (Comment.)
PlM v 37 n 3 p 56 D '60
---Fourth season notes. MC
v 161 n 6 p 33 My '60

---Julien, A. M., director;
1960 plans. MC v 161 n 7 p 14
Je '60
---The 1960 season; program no-
tes. WM n 2 p 31 Ap '60
---Opera notes. Op v 11 n 8 p 552
Ag '60
---Paris: Sadler's Wells Opera
and le Théâtre Royal de la Mon-
naie de Bruxelles: Oedipus-Rex;
Sacre du Printemps; reviews.
GDC n 274 p 720 My 27'60
---Season 1961; 64 companies
from 34 countries invited. WP
v 12 n 2 p 3 N '60
LE THÉÂTRE D'ESSAI DE LA
DANSE
Paris criticism of performance
before "Mlle. Eyquem, inspec-
trice générale". TD n 95 p 3
Jl-Ag '60
---Paris notes. TD n 91 p 26
Mr '60
LE THÉÂTRE DU CHATELET
L'Ecole de danse, ens AP wl
ph: Paris. TD n 96 p 20 S-O '60
LE THÉÂTRE DU VIEUX COL-
OMBIER
Notes. WP v 12 n 3 p 4 D '60
LE THÉÂTRE LYRIQUE EN
FRANCE
Chastenet, André. Considéra-
tions. GDC n 277 p 813 Je 17'60
THÉÂTRE MOGADOR
Law, Richard. Paris; la Belle
Hélène revived by Henri Varna;
Offenbach compared to Sullivan
and Straus. Op v 11 n 6 p 420
Je '60
THÉÂTRE NATIONAL POPULAIRE
Bermel, Albert. Jean Vilar: un-
adorned theatre for the greatest
number. TDR v 5 n 2 p 24-43
D '60
---Paris programs of contem-
porary music; list of composers;
Maurice Jarre, music chief. WM
n 1 p 9 F '60
---Survey of its ten years; history;
aims; activities; Jean Vilar; by-
laws. WP v 12 n 2 p 2, 3 N '60
---Vilar, Jean. S'instruire est
une conquête personnelle. WP
v 12 n 2 p 1-3 N '60

(Theatre National Populaire)
   Vilar, Jean; policies. Th Arts
   v 44 n 12 p 63 D '60
---Four productions and a portrait
   of Jean Vilar. WP v 12 n 2 N '60
THEBOM, BLANCHE, 1919-,
   singer
   Notes. il ON v 25 n 2 p 4 O 29'60
THERE WAS A LITTLE GIRL, play
   Taradash, Daniel. Little girl,
   large theme (his adaptation of
   Lost Summer, novel by Christo-
   pher Davis to the stage, under
   Joshua Logan). il Th Arts v 44
   n 3 p 10-1 Mr '60
THIERAC, JACQUES. Sonate pour
   violon et piano (études musicales
   analytiques). GDC n 261-2 p 444
   F 26'60
---Première: La Sonate piano-
   violon; Suzanne Plazonich at the
   piano, Jacqueline Arnaud, vio-
   linist; Paris. GDC n 265-6 p 524
   Mr 25'60
THINAT, FRANÇOISE, pianist
   Demarquez, Suzanne. Paris cri-
   ticism. GDC n 273 p 692 My 20'60
THIRIET, MAURICE (1906-). En-
   tretien par Claude Chamfray.
   GDC n 286 p 192 O 28'60
---Criticism of his ballet music
   for "Maure de Venise". GDC n 274
   p 720 My 27'60
---Por ph: Harcourt. GDC n 286
   cover O 28'60
THOMAS, RONALD, violinist
   Carl Flesch Medal 1959; b. Perth.
   MD v 51 n 1 p 17 Jl '60
THOMAS, THEODORE, 1835-1905,
   conductor
   Por ph. HF v 10 n 2 p 43 F '60
THOMPSON, CLYDE H. (1919-).
   Marin Marais's pièces de violes.
   il Mus Q v 46 n 4 p 482-499 O '60
THOMPSON, FRANK, JR. (1918?-).
   Government aid for the arts. por
   IM v 58 n 12 p 9, 42 Je '60
THOMPSON, KAY, 1912?-, enter-
   tainer
   Took her pug dog into La Bohème
   at Spoleto. Th Arts v 44 n 12
   p 17 D '60
THORBORG, KERSTEN, 1896-,
   singer

As Orrud, AP hl ph: Alfredo
   Valente. Th Arts v 44 n 3 p 48
   Mr '60
THE THREE SISTERS, play
   Ames, Barbara, Kathleen Wid-
   does and Carol Gustafson, AP hl
   ph: Friedman-Abeles. Th Arts
   v 44 n 2 p 18 F '60
---New York, 1955, ens AP wl ph.
   WT v 9 n 2 p 138 Summer '60
---Paris 1929; Moscow 1901 ens
   AP phs; also 1960 Paris ph.
   Spec n 1 p 16-17 1960
---Sets and scenes from produc-
   tions: Roma (1953); Helsinki
   (1955); Malmö (1950); Senften-
   berg (1957); Leipzig (1954); Ost-
   Berlin (1956). WT v 9 n 2 p 128-9
   Summer '60
---Wien, 1956; Martha Wallner
   and Otto Woegerer, AP hl ph:
   Völkel. WT v 9 n 2 p 135 Summer
   '60
THURBER, JAMES, 1894-, actor
   Notes on blindness and his role
   in "A Thurber Carnival". Th
   Arts v 44 n 12 p 8 D '60
---Right profile por: P. Halsman.
   Th Arts v 44 n 2 p 9 F '60
THYSSENS-VALENTIN, GER-
   MAINE, pianist
   Career notes; b. Maastricht.
   GDC n 271 p 607 My 5'60
---Quatuor Pro Arte; Gabriel
   Fauré criticism. GDC n 275
   p 753 Je 3'60
---Por ph: Harcourt. GDC n 271
   p 607 My 5_21 '60
TIBBETT, LAWRENCE, 1896-
   1960, singer
   Newall, Robert H. (A critical
   summary of his roles.) il Op
   v 11 n 10 p 697-9 O '60
---Obituary. Op v 11 n 9 p 653
   S '60
---Obituary; b. Bakersfield, Cal-
   ifornia. MC v 162 n 2 p 7 Ag '60
---Robinson, Francis. Lawrence
   Tibbett (obituary). por ON v 25
   n 2 p 26-7 O 29'60
---As Rigoletto, AP hl ph: Wide
   World; por ph. also. ON v 25 n 2
   p 27 O 29'60
---In four roles, small phs. Op

v 11 n 10 p 697-8 O '60
THE TIGER AND THE HORSE,
   play
London notes; Robert Bolt. WP
v 12 n 1 p 14 O '60
TIGER RAG
   La Rocca, Nick. On how Tiger
   Rag came about. IM v 59 n 5 p 12
   N '60
TILMOUTH, MICHAEL. Nicola
   Matteis. Mus Q v 46 n 1 p 22-40
   Ja '60
TITONE, ANTONIO, 1904-, pro-
   fessor
   Il presidente il Gruppo Universi-
   tario per la Nuova Musica di Pal-
   ermo, ens wh ph. La S n 127
   p 42 Je '60
DER TOD der BESSIE SMITH,
   play
   Berlin notes; Edward Albee. WP
   v 11 n 9 p 11 Jl '60
DER TOD des GRIGORI RASPUTIN,
   opera
   Carter, Elliott. (Review of Nico-
   las Nabokov's opera at Cologne.)
   Mus Q v 46 n 3 p 367-8 Jl '60
---Cologne notes; Nicolas Nabokov.
   WP v 11 n 6 p 10 Ap '60
TODD, ARTHUR. What makes a
   musical move. il Th Arts v 44
   n 11 p 66-7, 72 N '60
DIE TÖDLISCHEN WUNSCHE,
   lyric drama
   Düsseldorf; notes. WP v 11 n 3
   p 2 Ja '60
---Klebe, Giselher, 1925-; b. Man-
   nerheim; review. Mus Q v 46 n 1
   p 81-2 Ja '60
---Klebe; ens AP wl ph: E. Hess.
   WT v 9 n 3 p 224, Autumn '60
TOKATYAN, ARMAND, 1896-1960,
   singer
   Obituary. ON v 25 n 3 p 24 N 19
   '60
TOMASELLI, JOSEPH F. Discip-
   lined diva: Maria Caniglia. il ON
   v 24 n 21 p 9, 32 Mr 26'60
TOMASI, HENRI 1901-, composer
   Chamfray, Claude. Entretien
   avec Henri Tomasi. GDC n 274
   p 716 My 27'60
---Première: Le Tombeau de Mireille; work for galoubet and

tambourin against a chamber
orchestra. MC v 161 n 3 p 44
F '60
---Première: Le Triomphe de
   Jeanne; Paris cast and review.
   GDC n 277 p 820 Je 17'60
TONI, ALCEO (1884-). Convegno
   di tre alla RAI-TV. La S n 127
   p 34-5 Je '60
TÖPPER, HERTHA, 1924-, singer
   San Francisco debut. por ON
   v 25 n 7 p 5 D 24'60
DAS TOR (Tatjana Gsovsky), ballet
   Ens AP wl ph: Enkelmann, 1965.
   WT v 9 n 3 p 229 Autumn '60
TORINO
   Ambesi, A. C. Teatro Nuovo di
   Torino (ballet from Mexico; can-
   tata "Amarus"; concerts). il LaS
   n 132 p 48, 80 N '60
---Music report. La S n 122 p 66
   Ja '60
TORONTO
   O'Keefe Center; première of
   "Camelot", musical; review. MC
   v 162 n 5 p 29 N '60
---Schabas, Ezra. Music report.
   MC v 161 n 1 p 27 Ja '60
---Ubriaco, Rita. Opera report.
   ON v 25 n 6 p 28 D 17'60
THE TORONTO SYMPHONY
   In Massey Hall, ens AP ph: Can-
   ada. IM v 58 n 12 p 18 Je '60
LA TORRE DEI TESCHI, cantata
   Logar, Mihovil. Teatro dell'Op-
   era di Belgrado. La S n 133 p 67
   D '60
---Radich work, ens AP wl ph:
   Belgrade. La S n 133 p 67 D '60
TORTELIER, PAUL, 1914-
   and Maud Tortelier; pianist, Wil-
   lem Hielkema; review. GDC
   n 261-2 p 442 F 26'60
LA TOSCA, opera
   Arundell, Dennis. Tosca re-
   studied. il Op v 11 n 4 p 262-5
   Ap '60
---Historical background. il ON
   v 24 n 20 p 4-5 Mr 19'60
---Metropolitan Opera cast; story;
   critical articles; décor notes;
   bibliography;discography; port-
   folio. ON v 24 n 20 Mr 19'60
---Notes on revival, Paris Opéra.

(La Tosca)
OpP n 19 p 13 1960
---Paris Opéra notes. GDC n 278
p 851 Je 24'60
---La Scala notes. La S n 122
p 35 Ja '60
---The church in Rome, interior
view; portrait of Victorien Sar-
dou, of Sarah Bernhardt; play-
bill for the Rome première of the
opera, phs. Op v 11 n 4 p 263-4
Ap '60
---Portfolio: Paris Opéra, 1960.
OpP n 19 p 12-5 1960
---Sadler's Wells; Charles Craig
as Cavaradossi and Peter Glossop
as Scarpia, 2 AP phs: Rogers. Op
v 11 n 11 p 782 N '60
--- ---Glossop, Craig and Collier,
Act II ens AP wl ph: Houston Rogers. Op v 11 n 6 p 437 Je '60
---Tucker and Tebaldi in Act III,
ens AP wl ph: LeBlang. ON v 24
n 20 p 20 Mr 19'60
TOSCANINI, ARTURO, 1867-1957
Haggin, B. H. Conversations with
Toscanini (book review. "the pique
and disdain that set the book's tone
as a whole"). ON v 24 n 11 p 30
Ja 16'60
---His impact on opera. ON v 25
n 4 p 26-7 D 3'60
---Hughes, Spike. The Toscanini
legacy (book reviewed). MR v 21
n 2 p 156 My '60
---Maione, Rino. Toscanini, Artista e critico. il La S n 132 p 17-
23 N '60
---Marsh, Robert C. Toscanini's
last Eroica; Beethoven's symphony as played at various stages
of Toscanini's career. HF v 10
n 3 p 61-2 Mr '60
---Pirie, Peter J. Toscanini and
Furtwängler, an empire divided
(Beethoven symphonic canon). HF
v 10 n 4 p 37-9 Ap '60
---Son, Walter Toscanini, releasing
rehearsal excerpts, introduced
by Marcia Davenport, of Arturo
Toscanini and the NBC Orchestra; criticism. HF v 10 n 3 p 57
Mr '60
---Symphony of the Air under Leopold Stokowski touring four weeks

in Italy and Europe as a mem-
orial to Toscanini; notes. IM
v 58 n 11 p 23 My '60
---Portfolio (5). La S n 132 p 17-
20 N '60
---With Illica, hl ph: Milan. La S
n 133 p 59 D '60
TOTENBERG, ROMAN, 1913-,
violinist
Notes; b. Lodz. AmM v 8 n 4
p 11 Ap '60
TOULON
Opera repertory; par Francine
Olivero. GDC n 257-8 p 353
Ja 29'60
TOULOUSE
Beck, M. Rigoletto; Mireille;
Pays du Sourire. GDC n 255-6
p 304 Ja 15'60
TOURANGA ILA (Van Dijk) ballet
Ens AP wl ph: Hamburg. TD
n 97 p 16 N '60
TOURE, BACHIR, actor
Le Noir apeuré, AP hl ph: France.
Spec n 1 p 75 1960
TOWARNICKI, FREDERIC de.
Alain Renais après "Hiroshima
Mon Amour". il Spec n q p 60-69
1960
--- ---Quand Paris découvre Tch-
ékhov. il Spec n 1 p 11-21 1960
TOYS IN THE ATTIC, play
Ens AP hl ph: Friedman-Abeles.
Th Arts v 44 n 5 p 58 My '60
---Hellman; ens AP ph: NYC WP
v 11 n 9 p 1 Jl '60
---Rehearsal under Arthur Penn,
ens ph: NYC. Th Arts v 44 n 3
p 15 Mr '60
TOZZI, GIORGIO, 1923-, singer
Interview in his home. ON v 24
n 18 p 14 Mr 5'60
---Taping Verdi Requiem, Vien-
na note. por ON v 24 n 19 p 2
Mr 12'60
---As Arkel, AP hl ph: Melançon.
ON v 24 n 11 p 17 Ja 16'60
---As Daland in The Flying Dutch-
man, AP ph: Melançon. ON v 24
n 18 Mr 5'60
---As Jacopo Fiesco, AP ph: Mel-
ançon. ON v 24 n 22 p 17 Ap 2'60
---Receiving award of gold record-
ing for his South Pacific, ens ph:
NYC. MC v 161 n 7 p 22 Je '60

TOZZI, RENZO
Cataldo, Antonio. La cantina musicale di via Giambologna. il La S n 123 p 27-9 F '60
---E Torrebruno e Maazel, hl ph; il maestro Tozzi durante una prova con l'orchestra Monteverdi, ph. La S n 123 p 27-8 F '60
A TRAGEDIAN IN SPITE OF HIMSELF, play
Stockholm 1950, ph: Järlas. WT v 9 n 2 p 141 Summer '60
TRAÏLINE, HELENE, dancer
Et Juan Guiliano; notes. il TD n 92 p 10 Ap '60
THE TRAITOR (LIMÓN), dance
Ens ph. Th Arts v 44 n 11 p 62 N '60
TRAN VAN KHÉ. The emotional approach of the performer of Oriental music (a paper at the 5-day Paris conference under International Music Council). WM n 6 p 127-8 D '60
TRANNOY, BRIGITTE, pianist
Jourdan-Morhange, Helene. Review. GDC n 295 p 495 D 30'60
TRAUBEL, HELEN, 1903-, singer
Review of her career in the book, "St. Louis Woman"; "frontal attack on the Metropolitan". ON v 24 n 16 p 22 F 20'60
LA TRAVIATA, opera
Covent Garden review; Joan Sutherland criticism; and Virginia Zeani in the same role. Op v 2 n 3 p 228-9 Mr '60
---In English; "negative"; NYC Opera review. MC v 162 n 5 p 16 N '60
---Steyer, Ralf. Stad theater performance (list of tenors sought in emergency and where they were at the time). Op v 11 n 5 p 348 My '60
---Ens AP wl ph: Bergamo. La S n 133 p 65 D '60
---Hamburg; two ens AP wl phs: Peyer. Op v 11 n 4 p 279-80 Ap'60
---Sadler's Wells; Act I, ens AP wl ph: Rogers. Op v 11 n 11 p 780 N '60
---Trieste; Rosanna Carteri, ens AP wl ph. La S n 124 p 36 Mr'60

TREBINSKY, ARKADY. 3e Symphonie, op. 27 (études musicales analytiques). GDC n 267-8 p 565 Ap 8'60
A TREE GROWS IN BROOKLYN, play
Ens ph: Ohio State University. PlM v 36 n 6 cover Mr '60
TREWIN, JOHN COURTENAY (1908-). Great Britain (theatre). WT v 9 n 3 p 290-293 Autumn '60; same. WT v 9 n 2 p 182-186 Summer '60; same. WT v 9 n 4 p 364-6 Winter '60
TRICENTENAIRE du TRAITÉ des PYRENEES
Bayonne et Côte Basque; reviews. GDC n 277 p 821 Je 17'60
TRIESTE
De Ferra, Giampaolo. Teatro Verdi. il La S n 122 p 38, 69 Ja '60; same. La S n 125 p 47 Ap '60
---Music report. La S n 122 p 69 Ja '60
---Teatro Communale Giuseppe Verdi: opera repertory. ON v 25 n 7 p 7 D 24'60
--- ---stagione Lirica 1960-61, programma; opere, spettacdo di balletti. La S n 132 inset N '60
TRILLING, LIONEL (1905-). All aboard the Seesaw (on William Gibson's book, The Seesaw Log, an account of staging his play, Two For the Seesaw). TDR v 4 n 4 p 16-22 My '60
TRIO (CORELLI), ballet
Ens AP wl ph: Hanover. TD n 89 p 9 Ja '60
TRIO DE FRANCE
Paris; Benevièbe Joy, Jeanne Gauthier et André Lévy. GDC n 292 p 423 D 9'60
TRIO GORDON
Castil. Paris review. GDC n 276 p 787 Je 10'60
TRIO PASQUIER
Machuel, Dominique. Paris review. GDC n 288 p 258 N 11'60
LE TRIOMPHE de JEANNE
Demarquez, Suzanne. Première de Henri Tomasi, l'Orchestre National singers, chorus. GDC

(Le Triomphe de Jeanne)
n 277 p 820 Je 17'60
IL TRIONFO DELL'ONORE, opera
Morley College Opera Group; review. Op v 11 n 12 p 854 D '60
IL TRIONFO di AFRODITE
Munich criticism of Orff's "scenic concerto". Op v 11 p 57 Autumn '60
LE TRIPTYQUE
Dernier concert: musique hongroise; Paris review. GDC n 279-80 p 892 Jl 1'60
TRISTAN et YSEULT
Dapilly, Jacques. De Jean de Beer; Verley, Claudine Boris Jacqueline Danno; la Kevernn. GDC n 257-8 p 354 Ja 29'60
TRISTAN und ISOLDE, opera
Lingg, Ann M. Tristan arrives (story of NYC's first Tristan und Isolde, Niemann at 55 in 1886). ON v 24 n 10 p 12-3 Ja 9'60
---Metropolitan; Nilsson and Viney; notes. il La S n 125 p 53 Ap '60
--- ---cast; notes and articles; story; décor; discography; bibliography; ON v 24 n 10 portfolio. Ja 9'60
--- ---performance with 3 Tristans: Ramon Vinay, Act I, Karl Liebl, Act II and Albert Da Costa, Act III; Birgit Nilsson " a sweeping success". MC v 161 n 3 p 48 F '60
--- ---review; Birgit Nilsson; Karl Böhm, conducting. Op v 11 n 2 p 131 F '60
---NYC review; Birgit Nilsson's debut with the Metropolitan. MC v 161 n 3 p 23 F '60
---Vandenburg, Howard. (Why Tristan drops his sword allowing Melot to strike him down.) Op v 11 n 4 p 306 Ap '60
---Wagner, Wieland; Berlin debut; criticism. ON v 2 n 3 p 203 Mr '60
---Dalis, Irene, as Brangäne, ens AP wl ph: Metropolitan. Th Arts v 44 n 3 p 36 Mr '60
---Ens AP wl ph: Budapest. La S n 122 p 40 Ja '60
---Metropolitan portfolio: Melan-

çon. ON v 24 n 10 p 7, 15, 17 Ja 9'60
---Nilsson e Vinay, AP wl ph; Metropolitan. La S n 125 p 53 Ap '60
---Original setting 1886 and Wolfgang Wagner's production 1957, 2 phs: Bayreuth. Op v 11 n 11 p 736 N '60
---Tristan und Isolde carved on lid of 14th century ivory chest. ON v 24 n 10 p 5 Ja 9'60
IL TRITTICO, opera
Melbourne; three one-act operas of Puccini, staged by Stefan Haag, Karl Rankl conducting; review. MD v 50 n 11 p 8 My '60
TROFIMOVA, NATACHA, dancer
Two AP phs. TD n 89 p 19, 20 Ja '60
TROILUS AND CRESSIDA, play
Stratford-upon-Avon, 1960, two ens AP wl phs: Roger Wood. WT v 9 n 4 p 365 Winter '60
LE TROIS MOUSQUETAIRES, play
Ens AP wl ph: Bernand. WP v 11 n 8 p 1 Je '60
THE TROJANS, opera
Covent Garden review; notes on John Pritchard; John Vickers as Aeneas, Kerstin Meyer as Dido. il Op v 11 n 6 p 446-7 Je '60
---(Merkling, Frank.) Review; Carnegie Hall, The American Opera Society version under Robert Lawrence. ON v 24 n 16 p 26 F 20'60
---Carnegie Hall concert version, ens AP ph: NYC. ON v 24 n 16 p 27 F 20'60
---Rankin and others in a dress rehearsal in La Scala 1959, ens ph: Erio Piccagliani. ON v 25 n 4 p 26 D 3'60
---Milan; Act II scene 1, ens AP wl ph: Piccagliani. Op v 11 n 8 p 560 Ag '60
---See also Les Troyens à Carthage, opera
TROMPETER, LISA ROMA. Editorial on the 80th year of Musical Courier; competition in

310

the musical field. MC v 161 n 1
p 4 Ja '60
IL TROVATORE, opera
Metropolitan Opera cast; story;
décor notes; criticism; discogo-
raphy; bibliography; portfolio.
ON v 24 n 17 F 27'60
---Rushmore, Robert. Scenes
through a Freudian glass. ON
v 24 n 17 p 6-7 F 27'60
---Sedwick, Frank. Love and ven-
gance. ON v 24 n 17 p 4-5 F 27
'60
--- Parutto, Mirella, AP wl ph:
Naples. La S n 125 p 51 Ap '60
---Two ens AP wl phs: Melançon.
Op v 11 n 1 p 25 Ja '60
LES TROYENS à CARTHAGE,
opera
Berlioz; the Royal Hunt scene of
part III of Les Troyens. Op v 11
n 5 p 332-3 My '60
---Lecorcher, Pierre. La second
moitié. GDC n 285 p 173 O 21'60
TRUMPETS
Sargent, George. Letter of trum-
pets before valves and with them.
HF v 10 n 9 p 12 S '60
---Tetzlaff, Dan. Trumpet talk.
IM v 58 n 8 p 26-7 F '60
TRUSCOTT, HAROLD. Beetho-
ven's Fourth Piano Concerto
(analysis); his Violin Concerto
MD v 50 n 7 p 8-11 Ja '60
--- ---The piano concertos of Em-
anuel Moór. MR v 21 n 2 p 121-
129 My '60
THE TRUTH ABOUT BILLY NEW-
TON, play
Salisbury Art Theatre, ens AP wl
ph: F. Davies. NTM v 1 n 3 p 15
Ap '60
TRYPTIQUE (CATON), ballet
International Ballet of the Mar-
quis de Cuevas; inspired by Bot-
ticelli; music of Vincent d'Indy;
cast. TD n 92 p 8 Ap '60
TUCKER, DAVID, 1942-, singer
Son of Richard Tucker, a singer
also. por ON v 24 n 20 p 3 Mr 19
'60
TUCKER, RICHARD, 1914-, singer
Buenos Aires criticism. ON v 25
n 3 p 21 N 19'60

---Notes. ON v 25 n 5 p 5 D 10'60
---As Andrea Chénier, AP phs:
Leblang. ON v 24 n 21 p 17
Mr 26'60
---As Don Alvaro, AP hl ph: Mel-
ançon. Op v 11 n 4 p 270 Ap '60
--- ---AP phs: Melançon. ON
v 24 n 19 p 17 Mr 12'60
---As Don José AP phs: Leblang.
ON v 24 n 14 F 6'60
---Por ph. MC v 162 n 4 p 21 O'60
TUDOR, ANTONY, 1908-, choreo-
grapher
Metropolitan Opera progress re-
port; dance plans. ON v 24 n 20
p 2 Mr 19'60
TUDOR, DAVID, 1926-, pianist
NYC; three reviews, all "start-
ling"; Toshi Ichiyanagi in one con-
cert at a second piano. MC v 161
n 7 p 26 Je '60
HET TUINFEEST, play
Haarlem; Lo van Hensbergen.
WP v 11 n 7 p 13 My '60
TULANE DRAMA REVIEW, per-
iodical
Index to volume 4. TDR v 4 n 4
p 159-160 My '60
THE TULSA OPERA
Note. Op v 2 n 3 p 200 Mr '60
THE TUNNEL, opera
Cole, Hugo, composer; première
reviewed. Op v 11 n 12 p 854 D'60
TURANDOT, opera
Covent Garden review (singers
good, production worn). Op v 2
n 3 p 235 Mr '60
---Monte Carlo review; Franco
Corelli "had them in a frenzy".
Op v 11 n 5 p 356 My '60
---Osborne, Conrad L. Review of
RCA-Victor, Nilsson, Tebaldi,
Bjoerling. HF v 10 n 10 p 67-8
O '60
---La Scala review; Nilsson. il
La S n 126 p 30 My '60
---Two ens AP hl phs: Milan.
La S n 126 p 30 My '60
TURECK, ROSALYN, 1916-,
pianist
Detroit; all-Bach; criticism. MC
v 161 n 4 p 30 Mr '60
---NYC criticism of all-Bach con-
cert. MC v 161 n 3 p 29 F '60

TURECK BACH PLAYERS
Tureck, Rosalyn, director; 21
players; Glyndebourne Festival.
AmM v 8 n 2 p 18 F '60
TURIN
Rodden, Philip. (Gianna d'Angelo
in Conte Ory; Tullio Serafin con-
ducting.) ON v 24 n 12 p 29 Ja 23
'60
THE TURK IN ITALY, opera
Two ens AP wl phs: Peabody,
Baltimore. MC v 161 n 3 p 35
F '60
TURKEY
Figures on music subsidy (at the
time US alloted military aid of
half a billion dollars). IM v 59
n 5 p 9 N '60
---Theatre report. WP v 11 n 6
p 7 Ap '60
---Gökcer, Cuneyt, dans le rôle
d'Oedipe, AP hl ph: Ankara. WP
v 11 n 7 My '60
TURNAU OPERA PLAYERS
Florida's Ascolo Theatre; notes.
ON v 24 n 17 p 3 F 27'60
TURNER, CLARAMAE, 1920-,
singer
Notes. por ON v 25 n 7 p 5 D 24
'60
TURNER, EVA, 1898-. singer
With American pupils, Flori
Caprino and Paul Britton, ens
ph: London. AmM v 8 n 4 p 9
Ap '60
---With others, hl ph: London.
AmM v 8 n 9 p 9 O '60
TWELTH NIGHT, play
As lit in Central Park, NYC,
1958, ph. NY Times. WT v 9
n 2 p 156 Summer '60
---Old Vic; ens AP wl ph: McBean.
ON v 24 n 12 p 4 Ja 23'60
TWELVE-TONE SYSTEM
Babbitt, Milton. (Review of
Spinner's A Short Introduction to
the Technique of Twelve-Tone
Composition.) J Rev v 7 n 3 p 25
Fall '60
--- ---Twelve-tone invariants as
compositional determinants.
Mus Q v 46 n 2 p 246-259 Ap '60
---Cologne, I. S. C. M.; comments
on Dallapiccola and others.

MR v 21 n 3 p 242-3 Ag '60
---Composers conference at
Stratford, Ontario; report. CMJ
v 5 n 1 p 4-16 Autumn '60
---Czechoslovakia today; "composers who are so closely bound
up with their tradition will deny
this way. How long will they do
so?" Karl H. Wörner's survey of
contemporary composers. Mus Q
v 46 n 4 p 517 O '60
---Liviabella, Lino. Dove va la
musica? portfolio La S n 124
p 20-5 Mr '60
---Paris; Concerts de Midi; Jacques Chailley et Antoine Coléa
sur le dodécaphonisme. GDC
n 265-6 p 526 Mr 25'60
---Redlich, Hans F. Hanns Jelinek (critical discussion of "Àn-
leitung" as "the official textbook»
of Jelinek's artistic credo). MR
v 21 n 1 p 66-72 F '60
---Stein, Leonard, pianist; Los
Angeles concert all 12-tone;
review. MC v 161 n 7 p 32 Je '60
---Walker, Alan. Back to Schönberg. MR v 21 n 2 p 140-147 My'60
---Ziems, Harry; notes from Di-
vonne. GDC n 288 p 259 N 11'60
TWO FOR THE SEESAW, play
Trilling, Lionel. All aboard the
Seesaw. TDR v 4 n 4 p 16-22
My '60
TZIPINE, GEORGES, conductor
Por ph: Australia. MD v 50 n 12
cover Je '60
TZRY KOBIETY I JA, play
Cracovie notes; Anna Swirszcyn-
ska. WP v 12 n 1 p 10 O '60

U

L'UCCELLO di FUOCO (Kostich),
ballet
Belgrade; notes. il La S n 127
p 31 Je '60
UDOVICK, LUCILLE, singer
Career sketch; b. Denver. AmM
v 8 n 3 p 3 Mr '60
---Covent Garden debut in Aïda;
notes. Op v 11 n 5 p 367 My '60
---In Turandot, AP wl ph: Venice.
La S n 128 p 53 Jl '60

---Por ph. Am M v 8 n 3 cover
Mr'60

THE UGLY DUCKLING, play
Children's Theatre in Flanders,
1950;ens ph:Segers. WT v 9 n 1
p 59 Spring'60

UHDE, HERMAN, 1914-, singer
As Amfortas, AP ph:Melançon.
ON v 24 n 23 p 17 Ap 9'60

---As Don Pizarro in Fidelio, AP
phs:Melançon. ON v 24 n 15 F
13'60

---As Wozzeck with Eleanor Steber, Act 2, scene 1, AP wl ph:
BBC. Am M v 8 n 1 p 13 Ja'60

UHL, FRITZ, 1928-, singer
Career notes;Tristan to be re-
leased 1961. HF v 10 n 12 p 14
D'60

ULANO, SAM. Approach to practical drumming. IM v 58 n 9
p 20, 23 Mr'60;same. IM v 58 n 10
p 19 Ap'60;same. IM v 59 n 2 p 20
Ag'60;same. IM v 59 n 5 p 30 N
'60

ULLERN, JEAN, pianist
Notes. por GDC n 281-2 p 8
S 30'60

ULMER, ERNEST, pianist
At the piano, right profile ph:
Nydtskov. MC v 161 n 4 p 30 Mr
'60

UNCLE VANYA, play
Markov, Pavel. New trends in
the interpretation of Chekhov.
il WT v 9 n 2 p 106-110 Summer
'60

---Arts Theatre Club, London,
1952, ens AP wl ph:Angus Mc-
Bean. WT v 9 n 2 p 127 Summer
'60

---Moscow Art Theatre, 1947,
ens AP wl ph. WT v 9 n 2 p 103
Summer'60

---Moscow 1899, scene from Act
III; Paris 1921, Georges Pitoëff,
3 phs. Spec n 1 p 12, 14 1960

---One scene each from productions in Budapest (1952), Tokyo
(1951), Copenhagen (1953), Roumania (1959), 4 ens phs. WT v 9
n 2 p 122 Summer'60

---Teatro Eliseo, Roma, 1955;
Visconti-Tosi production: 3 sets,

phs:Bosio. WT v 9 n 2 p 120 Summer'60

---Théâtre National de Grèce, ens
AP wl ph:Emile, Athens. WT v 9
n 2 p 132 Summer'60

---West-Berlin, 1959, 3 ens AP wl
phs:Ilse Buhs. WT v 9 n 2 p 121
Summer'60

UNDER MILK WOOD, play
Ens AP wl ph:Heinz Köster, 1957.
WT v 9 n 3 p 249 Autumn'60

UNGER, ROSEMARIE, ice dancer
AP wl ph. TD n 97 p 27 N'60

UNINSKY, ALEXANDRE, pianist
Berthoumieux, Serge. Paris review. GDC n 261-2 p 439 F 26'60

UNITED NATIONS
Concert de Gala:Orchestre Sym-
phonique de la N. H. K. (Tokyo).
GDC n 281-2 p 55-6 S 30'60

---Orchestre Symphonique NHK de
la radio de Tokyo:Paris review;
Paul Klecki. GDC n 287 p 226 N
4'60

UNITED STATES
Americans at work, series shown
on TV; musicians part of the project reported. il IM v 58 n 8 p 5, 9
F'60

---American composers: a discography by Donald Jennings with
quoted reviews. ACAB v 9 n 2 p 13-7
1960

--- ---Part II. ACAB v 9 n 3 p 19-25
1960

---American National Theatre and
Academy, New York and Chicago
reports. WP v 11 n 3 p 1 Ja'60

--- ---and national notes. WP v 11
n 4 p 7 F'60

---Americana;disc by Carmen Dragon and Capitol Symphony Orchestra (review, "engaging, naïve, Hol-
lywoodian excesses"). HF v 10 n 7
p 67 Jl'60

---Brockett, O. G. The theatre of
the Southern United States from the
beginnings through 1865: a bibliographical essay. Th R v 2 n 3 p 163-
174 1960

---Cincinnati premières:Ellis Kohs,
Nikolai Lopatnikoff and Walter
Piston;also Ingvar Lindholm's
Ritornello. MC v 161 n 3 p 43 F'60

(United States)
Clurman, Harold. Actors:the image of their era. TDR v 4 n 3 p 38-44 Mr'60

--- ---(The Theatre Group and other projects of the 1930s.) Th Arts v 44 n 9 p 15-8 S'60

---Cologne, I. S. C. M. ;notes on Sessions' 4th Symphony;Gunther Schuller's Spectra;on Arthur Berger's String Quartet (1958). MR v 21 n 3 p 242 Ag'60

---Coming events (listing each month of American musicians to perform in England, notes on each). Am M 1960

---Composers commissioned:Stravinsky by CBS-TV; Henry Cowell, Kenneth Gaburo, Robert Gerhard, Francis Poulenc, four assignments by the Koussevitzky Foundation; G. Shirmer, Inc. to Samuel Barber, Easley Blackwood and Alex Wilder. WM n 6 p 131 D'60

---Composers awarded fellowships by the Ford Foundation to write music for ensembles of 12 high schools:list. IM v 59 n 4 p 39 O'60

---Composers Recordings, Inc. (Seven discs reviewed by Richard F. French;including works by Franchetti, Ruggles, Homer Keller, Robert Ward, Billy Jim Layton and others). Mus Q v 46 n 4 p 548-556 O'60

---Concert halls;Lincoln Center report;notes on Carnegie Hall saved for 70 more years;Chicago's Orchestra Hall;Philadelphia's Academy of Music;Symphony Hall, Boston;Kleinshans Hall, Buffalo;Ford Auditorium, Detroit and others. il IM v 59 n 4 p 12-3 O'60

---Contemporary Composers' Commission;list of charter members and aims. MC v 161 n 4 p 37 Mr '60

---Creative Arts Festival of Charleston, West Virginia:commission to a native composer annually;Theron Kirk, 1960, composer. IM v 59 n 4 p 41 O'60

---DePass, Richard. The Metropolitan;the City Center;opera reports. il Op v 11 n 1 p 24, 26 Ja'60

---Exchange of musical fare with Italy:a progress report;1961 Maggio Musicale plans an "American Fortnight". MC v 162 n 4 p 28 O'60

---Exchange program with Russia; "Inequities" observed;panel report. MC v 161 n 1 p 5 Ja'60

---Freedley, George. Plays first produced off-Broadway, June 1, 1959-May 31, 1960;Part I. PlM v 37 n 2 p 32-3 N'60

--- ---Part II. PlM v 37 n 3 p 54-5 D'60

---Gilder, Rosamund. (USA theatre notes.) il WT v 9 n 4 p 366-68 Winter'60;same. WT v 9 n 1 p 92-4 Spring'60;same. WT v 9 n 2 p 188-92 Summer'60

---Goldman, Richard Franko. Arias, Anthems and Chorales of the American Moravians, 1760-1860 (as recorded by Columbia, ML 5427). Mus Q v 46 n 4 p 547-8 O'60

---Goth, Trudy. Music report. LaS n 127 p 69 Je'60;same. LaS n 128 p 63 Jl'60;same. LaS n 133 p 113 D'60

---Hanson, Howard. (How he created a "climate for creativity" in Rochester;need to expand such efforts.) MEJ v 46 n 6 p 28-30 Je-Jl '60

---Helm, Everett. Letter on America (music in California, in the East). MR v 21 n 3 p 240-1 Ag'60

---Kenin, Herman D. (Testimony before Federal Communications Commission, Washington, D. C. on "deceptive use of foreign canned music" in US television films.) IM v 58 n 8 p 5, 41-2 F'60

---Kronenberger, Louis. The fifties: patchwork progress (theatre). Th Arts v 44 n 1 p 10-1 Ja'60

---Legislative attempt to aid live music;H. R. 11043 against foreign musicians entering to play at substandard fees and "wet back" tapes made by those ineligible to enter the US at all;H. R. 2164 to reduce cabaret tax from 20 to 10 percent.

IM v 58 n 10 Ap'60
---Letters quoted from TV sponsors who discover "illegal music" has been imported on tapes and dubbed into films announced as "American made";example, "Men Into Space"produced with technical advice of US Air Force". IM v 58 n 11 p 8 My'60
---McCleery, Albert. Theatre's debt to television. WT v 9 n 4 p 318-324 Winter'60
---Marsh, Robert C. Music in the Midwest (traditions and present music groups). HF v 10 n 2 p 42 F'60
---Merkling, Frank. The grass is greener (opera). ON v 25 n 3 p 12 N 19'60
---Metropolitan Opera Guild;12 reports. ON v 24 n 19 Mr 12'60
---Moor, Paul. Our operatic expatriates. HF v 10 n 11 p 50 N'60
---Morehouse, Ward. (US theatres in 1930s.)Th Arts v 44 n 9 p 10 S'60
---Music jobs in the summer. IM v 58 n 11 p 16, 18 My'60
---Opera reports:Metropolitan; Juilliard;Manhattan School of Music;University of California; Cincinnati;Miami;Philadelphia; Sante Fé. Op v 11 n 6 p 407-412 Je'60
---Parmenter, Ross. Two State Department programs send musicians abroad as specialists. IM v 59 n 6 p 8-9 D'60
---Pension plan for musicians;details of American Federation of Musicians and employers in joint trustee control. IM v 58 n 12 p 8 Je'60
---Queries to be answered by American music teachers at the Atlantic City meeting in March: the contemporary scene. MEJ v 46 n 3 p 24-6 Ja'60
---Regional theatre;list of 150 names with addresses who constitute the Editorial staff of Players Magazine. PlM v 37 n 1 p 2 O'60
---Resume of seventh (1959) annual survey by Broadcast Music, Inc. Am M v 8 n 6 p 7 Jl'60
---Rockefeller, John D., 3rd. Financing the arts ("an exciting, pioneering effort"). por ON v 25 n 1 p 8-11 O 29'60
---Schwartz, Will. The universities, guardians of our musical heritage. MEJ v 47 n 1 p 41-3 S-O'60
---State Music Educators Association:activities 1960-61 by states. MEJ v 47 n 1 p 67-74 S-O'60
---Stokowski, Leopold. The future of music in the United States. por IM v 58 n 11 p 11 My'60
---String players in major orchestras choose students for free training at String Congress (in 1959, 83 boys and girls), founded by A F of M and partly supported; other sponsors listed and 1960 plan. IM v 58 n 8 p 12-3 F'60
---Student theatre;plans used to attract youth. WP v 12 n 1 p 1 O'60
---Summer music:a survey. IM v 58 n 12 p 32-3, 35 Je'60
---Summer theatre;John S. Wilson on the four "elements": Council of Stock Theatres, Council of Resident Theatres, Musical Arena Theatre Association, Association of Civic Musical Theatres. il Th Arts v 44 n 6 p 14-6 Je'60
--- ---directory:where to go, where to buy, where to rent. PlM v 36 n 6 p 123 Mr'60
---Survey of presentations (125) sent abroad as "cultural ambassadors". MC v 161 n 7 p 9 Je'60
---Tax reduction from 20 to 10 per cent cabaret fee, increased bookings;report. IM v 59 n 3 p 15 S'60
---Taylor, Deems. (Definition of "American opera" with critical survey.) ON v 25 n 6 p 9-11 D 17'60
---Terry, Walter. American ballet; don't take its greatness for granted. il Th Arts v 44 n 11 p 57-60 N'60
---Theatre;Broadway plays and openings followed by other US theatre schedules. Th Arts v 44 n 3 p 4-6 Mr'60

315

(United States)
- --Theatre;listing by place of plays, musicals, etc. with dates; each issue. Th Arts 1960
- --- ---community and campus; regular listing of current productions in "Program News". PlM 1960
- --- ---new trends 1960 by James W. Brock. PlM v 36 n 8 p 185 My'60
- --- ---directory:name, place, director, names of staff. Th Arts v 44 n 8 p 62-4 Ag'60
- --- ---report. WP v 11 n 9 p 7 Jl'60
- --- Travelers' Guide to Live Music, regular section of pictures with names of music groups, the place and date of appearance. IM 1960
- --- Valency, Maurice. Flight into lunacy (on loss of meaning in art by this professor of Columbia University). Th Arts v 44 n 8 p 8-9 Ag'60
- --- Ward, Winifred. Children's theatre. il Th Arts v 44 n 8 p 53-6 Ag'60
- --- The Washington Opera Company, community group under Edward Albion, during World War I; story by Leopold Glushak. il ON v 24 n 14 p 14-5 F 6'60
- --- Where They Are Playing, a regular section on music ensembles and soloists, contract dates. IM 1960
- --- Whitehead, Robert. American festival fundamentals. portfolio Th Arts v 44 n 6 p 51, 63 Je'60
- --- ---on the Drama Repertory Theatre at Lincoln Center;quoted on theatre philosophy. por ON v 25 n 2 p 12 O 29'60
- --- William Hale Harkness Foundation: recordings of American music, series; first, Stokowski and Symphony of the Air recording Ernest Bloch. HF v 10 n 4 p 59 Ap '60
- --- Wilson, John S. Musicals; the old college try. il Th Arts v 44

n 8 p 48-52 Ag '60
- --- Young, John Wray. A community-theatre quiz. portfolio Th Arts v 44 n 8 p 16-20 Ag '60
- --- The Young Composers Project: 12 high schools, 12 composers with home addresses; notes. MEJ v 46 n 6 p 72 Je-Jl '60
- --- American musical ensembles abroad, government sponsored events, six ens phs. MC v 161 n 7 p 2, 9 Je '60
- --- Community theatres, scene from plays by the Mummers, Oklahoma City; Antrim Players, Suffern, New York; Colonial Players, Annapolis; Western Springs, Illinois; The Attic Theatre, Wisconsin, phs. Th Arts v 44 n 8 p 18-9 Ag '60
- --- Music; performing groups at Atlantic City, MENC 1960: portfolio. MEJ v 46 n 4 p 39-41 F-Mr '60
- --- Music camp, Interlochen, Michigan, students learning, 6 phs. La S n 131 p 31-3 O '60
- --- United Audience Service; aims; Harlowe F. Dean, head. por MC v 161 n 5 p 6 Ap '60

US ARMY
Krone, Max T. (As coordinator of music for 117 schools for army children in Europe, he surveys aims and groups.) portfolio MEJ v 46 n 3 p 21-23 Ja '60
- --- ---Guides to Musical Experience (adopted 1959 by US Army Dependents Schools in Europe). il MEJ v 47 n 2 p 48-9, 52 N-D '60

UNITED STATES NAVAL SCHOOL OF MUSIC
Its educational opportunities; US Army Element; auditions reveal educational lacks; trumpet test only one in seven pass. IM v 58 n 7 p 18-9 Ja '60

USA, play
Don Passos, John, and Paul Shyre. (Complete text; NYC cast and 3 pictures). Th Arts v 44 n 6 p 23-50 Je '60

UNIVERSITY OF ARIZONA
Operalogue, method of teaching
opera to students. il MEJ v 46
n 4 p 64, 67 F-Mr '60
UNIVERSITY OF BAHIA, BRAZIL
Richards, Stanley. Theatre in
Brazil (the drama school under
Martin Goncales and its methods).
PlM v 37 n 3 p 57 D '60
UNIVERSITY OF BRISTOL
Chair of Drama established;
notes. Th Notbk v 15 n 1 p 3
Autumn '60
---Trumpet voluntary (to intro-
duce the new theatre periodical,
New Theatre Magazine). NTM
v 1 n 1 p 4 O '59
UNIVERSITY OF INDIANA
School of music: a profile. il
AmM v 8 n 9 O '60
---School of Music, exterior view,
ph. and 5 activity phs. AmM v 8
n 9 O '60
UNIVERSITY OF NOTTINGHAM
Purcell's Fairy Queen, produced
1960; scenery. il Th Notbk v 14
n 3 p 92-99 Spring '60
UNIVERSITY OF SOUTHAMPTON
Southern, Richard. Nuffield The-
atre; Technical description of
the lecture-hall theatre (the stage,
the auditorium, backstage). il
Th Notbk v 14 n 4 p 117-8
Summer '60
---Spence, Basil. Nuffield Thea-
tre theatre in the Arts Building.
il Th Notbk v 14 n 4 p 115-116
Summer '60
---Theatre: sketches (3). NTM
v 1 n 4 p 23-4 Jl '60
UPPMAN, THEODOR, 1920-,
singer
As Pélleas, AP wl ph: Melançon.
ON v 24 n 11 p 17 Ja 16'60
URBAN, JOSEPH, 1872-1933,
designer
With Wilhelm von Wymetal Deems
Taylor and Serafin, hl ph: Carlo
Edwards, 1931. ON v 25 n 6 p 11
D 17'60
URUGUAY
Ruegger, Gustavo Adolfo. (the-
atre report). il WT v 9 n 2
p 186-8 Summer '60

---Theatre report. WP v 11 n 9
p 8 Jl '60
---El Gran Tuleque de Maurice
Rosencof, ens AP wl ph: Mus-
itelli. WP v 11 n 9 p 1 Jl '60
USSACHEVSKY, VLADIMIR. Notes on "A Piece For Tape Recorder". Mus Q v 46 n 2 p 202-
209 Ap '60
UTAEMON VI, actor
Kabuki, AP ph. Th Arts v 44
n 7 p 60 Jl '60
UZUNOV, DIMITER
Career notes; Bulgarian. Op
v 11 n 6 p 406 Je '60

V

THE VAGABOND PLAYERS, 1938-
North Carolina; citation. PlM
v 36 n 7 p 149 Ap '60
VAILLANT, GEORGES, singer
As Méphisto, Paris Opéra, AP
wl ph. OpP n 19 p 26 1960
LA VAISSEAU FANTÔME
Au Palais Garnier; review. GDC
n 273 p 686 My 20'60
VAJTA, FERENC
Colombia; theatre notes. WT v 9
n 3 p 269 Autumn '60
VAKHTANGOV, B
Gortchakov, Nicolai. Vakhtan-
gov, ?1883-1922 (et ses élèves).
WP v 11 n 7 p 1, 7 My '60
VALDES, BENJAMIN, 1935-,
pianist
Paris concert; Mexican making
his debut. GDC n 265-6 p 524
Mr 25'60
VALDEZ, CARLOS "POTATO",
jazz drummer
Cuban; note. IM v 58 n 9 p 21
Mr '60
VALENCY, MAURICE (1903-).
Flight into lunacy ("irrationality
elevated to the rank of an artis-
tic principle" in today's art). Th
Arts v 44 n 8 p 8-9, 68 Ag '60
VALENTI, FERNANDO, harpsi-
chordist
Notes; Yale '46. AmM v 8 n 4
p 6 Ap '60
VALENTI, LEONE, 1946-,
Port-au-Prince, Haiti, AP wl ph.

317

(Valenti, Léone)
TD n 97 p 19 N '60
VALENTI FERRO, ENZO .
Report on contemporary music
in Buenos Aires. WM n 5 p 104
O '60
VALMOUTH, play
Review. PlM v 37 n 3 p 68 D '60
VAN BARENTZEN, ALINE,
pianist
Paris review. GDC n 259-60
p 405 F 12'60
VANCOUVER
Docherty, Ian. Vancouver Opera
Association: Carmen. il Op v 11
n 7 p 476 Jl '60
---George, Graham. (Music report.)
CMJ v 5 n 1 p 47-9 Autumn '60
--- ---(Queen Elizabeth Theatre,
history of project 1954 to date.)
CMJ v 4 n 2 p 4-6 Winter '60
VANCOUVER INTERNATIONAL
FESTIVAL
Docherty, Ian. (Opera reviews.)
Op v 11 n 10 p 687, 691 O '60
---Halpern, Ida. General report;
finances better, 26 sellouts; opera
reviews; concerts. MC v 162 n 5
p 26-7 N '60
--- ---Third year reviews. MC
v 162 n 1 p 32 Jl '60
VANCOUVER OPERA ASSOCIA-
TION
Repertory plans under Irving Gut-
tman. ON v 25 n 2 p 7 O 29'60
VAN DER SLOOT, PIETER, dancer
AP wl ph. TD n 91 p 27 Mr '60
VANDEVILLE, SIMONE, harpist
And Jacques Vaudeville, hautbois;
criticism. GDC n 269-70 p 596
Ap 22'60
VAN DIJK, PETER, 1929-, dancer
À Pleyel. J. M. F. TD n 89 p 28
Ja '60
---Et Jacqueline Rayet, deux ar-
tistes de la danse; critique. TD
n 96 p 7-8 S-O '60
---Dans L'Oiseau Bleu, AP wl ph:
M. Petit. TD n 89 cover Ja '60
---Et Jacqueline Rayet, dans Sym-
phonie Inachevée AP wl ph: Pic.
TD n 97 cover N '60
---In Bourmeister's Swan Lake,
ens AP ph: Paris Opéra. OpP

n 19 p 47 1960
---In Le Peau de Chagrin (Van
Dijk) with Ninon Lebertre, AP
wl ph: Paris. OpP n 19 p 66 1960
VAN DRUTEN, JOHN (1901-1957).
The job of directing. Th Arts v 44
n 7 p 51, 54, 68 Jl '60
VAN ESS, MARY. What outlook for
pianists? J Rev v 7 n 1 p 3-4
Winter 59-60
VANNI, HELEN, singer
As Inez in Il Trovatore, AP hl ph:
Melançon. ON v 24 n 17 p 17
F 27'60
VAN PRAAGH, PEGGY, 1910-,
ballet director
Career notes; new director of the
Borovansky Ballet; notes. MD
v 50 n 8 p 26 F '60
---Melbourne interview. MD v 50
n 10 p 26 Ap '60
VAN VLAENDEREN, MICHAEL. A
children's theatre in Flanders. il
WT v 9 n 1 p 58-61 Spring '60
VAR TIDS HJALTE, play
Stockholm notes; Beppe Wolgers.
WP v 11 n 4 p 13 F '60
VARÈSE, EDGARD, 1885-, com-
poser
Frankenstein, Alfred. The "big
and spacious" music of Edgard
Varèse (record review). HF v 10
n 10 p 69 O '60
---Notes; b. Paris; US 1916. AmM
v 8 n 5 p 9 Je '60
---Por ph: Fred Plaut. HF v 10
n 10 p 69 O '60
VARIATIES OP EEN THEMA
(Carter), ballet
Amsterdam notes. WP v 11 n 4
p 11 F '60
---Amsterdam notes. WP v 11 n 8
p 9 Je '60
VARNAY, ASTRID, 1918-, singer
As Isolde, AP wl ph. Th Arts
v 44 n 3 p 48 Mr '60
VARSI, DINORAH, 1940-, pianist
Dallas Symphony Orchestra aw-
ard to Montevideo girl. MC v 162
n 4 p 34 O '60
IL VASCELLO FANTASMA
Metropolitan notes. La S n 125
p 54 Ap '60
VASSILIEV, ALEXANDRE (1920?-).

(On staging Chekhov;chief
designer of the Mossoviet Theatre.) WT v 9 n 2 p 145 Summer
'60
THE VATICAN
RAI Symphony under Massimo
Freccia before His Holiness, Pope
John XXIII, ens ph:Giordani. MC
v 162 n 1 p 30 Jl'60
VAUDEVILLE
Frattini, Angelo. Rinnovato l'Olimpia in una "Piogga di Stelle".
il LaS n 124 p 54-5 Mr'60
VAUGHAN, DENIS. Meeting Verdi
on his own ground (necessity to
"copy by hand a Verdi score to
understand what the composer had
in mind"; examples.) Ver v 1
n 2 preface Ag'60
VAUGHAN WILLIAMS, RALPH,
1872-1958, composer
Letter between Gustave Holst and
Vaughan Williams (book review).
MR v 21 n 2 p 154-5 My'60
---Lloyd, Norman. Review of Nat-
ional Music by Vaughan Williams;
of his letters to Gustav Holst. J
Rev v 7 n 2 p 19 Spring'60
---National Music (book review).
MR v 21 n 2 p 154-5 My'60
VAUSSARD, CHRISTIANE, 1923-,
ballerina
Notes;b. Neuilly. TD n 94 p 5
Je'60
---AP wl ph:Paris. TD n 94 p 5
Je'60
VAZSONYI, BALINT, 1936-, pianist
Notes;b. Budapest. Am M v 8 n 9
p 6 O'60
VECCHIO-VERDERAME, ANGELO.
Pianoforti. il LaS n 125 p 39-41
Ap'60
DIE VEILCHEN, comedy
Bochum;Georges Schehade. WP
v 12 n 2 p 23 N'60
VEILLONS au SALUT de l'EM-
PIRE, play
Paris;Charles Prost;notes. WP
v 11 n 3 p 5 Ja'60
VEINSTEIN, ANDRE(1916-) et
Cécile Giteau. Code de Refer-
ences et de Catalogage de l'Icon-
ographie Theatrale. Th R v 2 n 2
p 120-5 1960

VEISTÄJÄ, VERNERI. Finland (the
theatre). WT v 9 n 3 p 280-2 Aut-
umn'60
VEJRAZKA, VILEZSTAV. The stage
actor on television. WT v 9 n 4
p 337-340 Winter'60
VENEZUELA
Caracas opera report. Op v 11 n 9
p 632 S'60
VENICE
Brindle, Reginald Smith. Venice
Festival. Mus Q v 46 n 1 p 83-8
Ja'60
---Goodwin, Noel. (Opera reviews
of two-month winter season;Alcina
with press quotations on Joan Su-
therland.) il Op v 11 n 4 p 283-6
Ap'60
---International Federation for
Theatre Research:Casa Goldoni;
subsidies;course of study to be
set up. Th Notbk v 15 n 2 p 43
Winter'60
---Messinis, Mario. Teatro La Fen-
ice;notes. il LaS n 123 p 41 F'60
---Music report. LaS n 122 p 66 Ja
'60;same. LaS n 123 p 68 F'60
---Opera review by Gwyn Morris.
Op v 11 n 72-3 Autumn'60
---Vianello, Mino. Music report. MC
v 161 n 5 p 32 Ap'60
VENUS OBSERVED, play
Bibliography. TDR v 4 n 3 p 97-8
Mr'60
VERDI, GIUSEPPE(1813-1901). Let-
ter to Clarina Maffei. Ver v 1 n 2
p 816 Ag'60
---Bacchelli, Riccardo. Verdi (Eng-
lish and German translations page
593-615). Ver v 1 n 1 p 209-219
Ap'60
---Le ballet de Macbeth "en Ire
audition à Paris". GDC n 285 p 161
O 21'60
---Barilli, Bruno. Appunti inediti
di Bruno Barilli, presentati da
Gian Paolo Minardi. Ver v 1 n 1
p 220-28 Ap'60
--- ---(Excerpts on Sant'Agata,
Verdi's home for fifty years;ex-
cerpts of criticism.) Ver v 1 n 2
p 1079-89 Ag'60
---Benois, Alessandro, and Nicola
Benois. Designing Verdi operas

(Verdi)
and the LaScala productions of
Un Ballo in Maschera (German
translation also). Ver v 1 n 1
p 380-412 Ap'60
---Gallini, Natale. Note sull'Otel-
lo. portfolio La S n 122 p 13-21
Ja'60
---Klein, John W. Letter (on points
discussed with Mr. Frank Wal-
ker in open letters). MR v 21 n 2
p 175-6 My'60
---McElroy, George. (Comparing
Wagner and Verdi.) ON v 25 n 8
p 17-20 D 31'60
---Matz, Mary Jane. A time for
the brave;II Garibaldi days,
Verdi's interest.) il ON v 24 n 9
p 6-7 Ja 2'60
--- ---The climate of sadness. il
ON v 25 n 4 p 18-9 D 3'60
---Medici, Mario. "Quel prete"
(Abbot Mermillod) che sposò
Verdi. Ver v 1 n 2 p 657-661
Ag'60
--- ---The Institute of Verdi
Studies. Ver v 1 n 1 preface Ap
'60
---Osborne, Conrad L. Verdi on
microgroove. il HF v 10 n 1
p 46-9 Ja'60
---Pannain, Guido. The opera
(Die Oper, German translation
side by side the English;Un Ballo
analysis). Ver v 1 n 1 p 354-379
Ap'60
---Pizzetti, Ildebrando. Giuseppe
Verdi, man of the theatre. il
Ver v 1 n 2 p 1013-1038 Ag'60
---Roncaglia, Gino. Giuseppe Ver-
di cosi com'era. il LaS n 126
p 18-22 My'60
--- ---Gli avversari di Verdi
(illustrated with 8 caricatures).
LaS n 131 p 38-41 O'60
---Walker, Frank. L'Abandonnée,
a forgotten song (1882). facsim-
ile Ver v 1 n 2 p 785-789 Ag'60
--- ---Letter (largely on material
in Abbiati's four volume life of
Verdi). MR v 21 n 2 p 175 My'60
--- ---(Letter on Verdi;mistakes
in Grove corrected.) MR v 21
n 1 p 83-4 F'60

---Weaver, William. A visit to Verdi's Sant'Agata. il HF v 10 n 1 p 42,
124 Ja'60
--- ---New light on Verdi. il Op v 11
n 9 p 600-5 S'60
---At his desk (1841), ph:La Scala
Museum. ON v 25 n 4 p 19 D 3'60
---Delfico, M. Caricature. Ver v 1
n 1 p 208 Ap'60
---Marriage to Giuseppina Strepponi, facsimile of Parish Register
of Collonges-sous-Salève. Ver v 1
n 2 p 656 Ag'60
---Por;calco della mano. LaS n 122
p 13, 18 Ja'60
---Por:1859. Ver v 1 n 1 p 1 Ap'60
---Por ph. of biographer, Franco
Abbiati and several pictures from
his recent life of Verdi. Op v 11 n 9
p 601-5 S'60
---Ritratto (coll. Gallini), e facsim-
ile di una pagina autografa della;
un ritratto poco noto di Giuseppina
Strepponi (coll. Gallini);lettera
autografa 1848;l'ultimo biglietto
autografo di Verdi ottuagenario;
scena del Trovatore. La S n 126
p 18-23 My'60
---Sant'Agata, near Busseto, 5 scenes;
also Giuseppina Strepponi, por ph:
Bettmann. HF v 10 n 1 p 43-5 Ja'60
VERDI-STREPPONI, GIUSEPPINA
See Strepponi, Giuseppina
VERDI REQUIEM
Paris;Lorin Maazel aux Champs-
Elysées;solistes. GDC n 289 p 296
N 18'60
VERDY, VIOLETTE, 1931-, dancer
Dans "L'Oiseau de Neige", AP wl
ph. TD n 93 p 24 My '60
VERESS, SÁNDOR, 1907-, com-
poser
Notes. Mus Q v 46 n 4 p 528 O '60
VERGANI, ORIO, journalist
Abbiati, Franco. (Letter signed
Orio.) La S n 126 p 41 My '60
---Cenzato, Giovanni. Ricordi di
Orio. il La S n 132 p 54-7 N '60
---Por and 3 informal phs. La S
n 132 p 54-7 N '60
VERGEZICHT (Van Dantzig), ballet
Pays-Bas; Robert Schumann mu-
sic. WP v 11 n 9 p 10 Jl '60
VERHAGEN, ELLY, singer

Critical note. Op v 11 n 2
p 146 F '60
VERMAN, E. Tom Payot, maître-
dessinateur et décorateur de théâtre. WP v 11 n 5 p 8 Mr '60
VERMONT
Circus Americana at Shelburne;
at Pownal; notes. PlM v 36 n 5
p 116 F '60
---Marlboro, Music School and
Festival under Rudolph Serkin;
notes. WM n 3 p 57 Je '60
VERONA ARENA
Gennari, Piero. Aïda; Cavalleria
Rusticana, Pagliacci; La Fanciu-
lla del West. il La S n 129-30
p 37, 71 Ag-S '60
---Opera reviews: Aïda, Cavaller-
ica Rusticana and Pagliacci, La
Fanciulla del West. Op v 11 p 70-
2 Autumn '60
---Stagione Lirica (38a), 21 Luglio-
15 Agosto 1960; calendar; Oliviero
de Fabritiis, Giandrea Gavazzeni.
La S n 128 inset Jl '60
---Amphitheatre, night audience,
ph: Piccaglioni. WT v 9 n 3 p 288
Autumn '60
VERRALL,JOHN (1908-). Henry
Leland Clarke(1907-; b. Dover,
New Hampshire; a check-list of
works included). ACAB v 9 n 3
p 2-8 1960
VESPRI SICILIANI, opera
Städtische Oper; review. Op v 11
n 8 p 553 Ag '60
LA VESTALE, opera
History of the work; review of
Lyon-Fourvière performance of
Spontini. GDC n 277 p 811 Je 17
'60
---Notes on Spontini's greatest op-
era; suggested cast for a revival.
il ON v 24 n 19 p 12 Mr 12'60
VESTRIS, AUGUSTE, 1760-1842,
dancer
Dufresne. Caricatura. La S
n 132 p 30 N '60
---Romney. Un ritratto giovanile;
scena di balletto in un disegno di
Boquet (and other pictures). La S
n 129-30 p 20-24 Ag-S '60
VESTRIS, GAETANO, 1728-1808,
dancer

Reyna, Ferdinando. Un dio del-
la danza. il La S n 129-30 p 18-
25 Ag-S '60
---Caricatura italiana. La S
n 129-30 p 19 Ag-S '60
---In Jason et Médée, 1781, ens
AP wl ph: coll. Mr. Fernau Hall.
Th Notbk v 15 n 1 p 20 Autumn '60
VETRA, VIJA, dancer
Expressional dance group; list;
Australia. MD v 51 n 6 p 30 D'60
LA VIA DELLA COMMEDIA
Il dottore, AP hl ph: Metropolitan.
La S n 125 p 54 Ap '60
VICHY FESTIVAL
Berthoumieux, Serge. Autour du
Xe Festival de musique de Vichy.
GDC n 283 p 97-8 O 7'60
---Demarquez, Suzanne. Contests
and concerts. MC v 162 n 4 p
p 26 O '60
---Opera report. Op v 11 n 9
p 619 S '60
VICKERS, JON, 1926?-, singer
Career sketch; b. Saskatchewan;
Royal Conservatory scholarship.
por ON v 24 n 15 p 15 F 13'60
---In Parsifal; London criticism.
Op v 11 n 6 p 439 Je '60
---As Florestan in Fidelio, AP
phs: Melançon. ON v 24 n 15
F 13'60
---As Siegmund, AP phs: Melan-
çon. ON v 24 n 16 F 20'60
---In Fidelio, AP hl ph: Metropo-
litan. La S n 125 p 53 Ap'60
VICTORIAN BALLET GUILD
(MARTYN)
Hutton, Geoffrey. Russell Street
Theatre, review. MD v 51 n 3 p 28
S'60
---Program notes. MD v 51 n 2 p 24
Ag'60
VICTORIAN SYMPHONY ORCHES-
TRA
Rostropovich, Mstislav. (Praise
for the VSO.) MD v 51 n 3 p 11
S'60
VIDAL, GORE(1925-). Notes on "The
Best Man". il Th Arts v 44 n 7
p 8-9 Jl'60
VIDAL, ROBERT J. , guitarist
Notes. GDC n 285 cover O 21'60
---Por ph. R. Denizon. GDC n 285

321

(Vidal, Robert)
cover O 21'60
LA VIDI de la MISION, opera
San Antonio notes. Op v 11 n 1
p 29 Ja '60
VIENNA
Brunner, Gerhard. Music re-
port. MC v 161 n 1 p 26 Ja '60;
same. MC v 161 n 5 p 30 Ap '60;
same. MC v 162 n 1 p 30-1 Jl'60
--- ---Tenth Festival; Vienna
State Opera in "Twilight of the
Gods" and " Andrea Chenier";
"Jeanne au Bûcher" before the
church. MC v 162 n 3 p 22-3
S '60
---Goth, Trudy. Le settimane
del Festival di Vienna. il La S
n 129-30 p 39 Ag-S '60
---Mittag, Edwin von. (Jenufa;
Parsifal and Jephta into an op-
era; other notes.) ON v 24 n 12
p 28 Ja 23'60
--- ---Opera. ON v 25 n 5 p 29
D 10'60
---Music Festival 1960: "Jeanne
d'Arc at the Stake", under Mil-
tiades Caridis; Max Mell's "My-
stère de la Succession du Christ".
WM n 1 p 9 F '60
---Music reports. MC 1960
---Opera: Staatsoper; Kammero-
per; Innsbruck Landes theater;
reviews by O. G. St. André.
Op v 11 n 6 p 412-5 Je '60
---Solomon, Seymour. (On Vien-
na not being a bargain basement
for the recording industry; and
Hans Herzog then correcting
Mr. Solomon on orchestra fig-
ures.) HF v 10 n 1 p 8 Ja '60
---Wechsberg, Joseph. (Opera
criticism.) Op v 2 n 3 p 200-2
Mr '60
--- ---Opera report. Op v 11 n 7
p 475 Jl '60; same. Op v 11 n 8
p 547-9 Ag '60
--- ---Schoenberg's Moses und
Aron (Michel Raffaelli's sets,
D oré Hoyer's choreography,
Hermann Scherchen conducting
the Berlin Städtische Oper). Op
v 11 n 12 p 823-4 D '60
--- ---The Staatsoper under Gü-
nther Rennert: Cenerentola.

Op v 11 n 1 p 29-30 Ja '60
--- Vienna Staatsoper (report). Op
v 11 n 11 p 760-1 N '60
---Recording Die Fledermaus, 8
informal phs. HF v 10 n 11 p 59
N '60
VIENNA ON PARADE
Deutschmeister Band, singers
and dancers from the Vienna
State Ballet; NYC review. MC
v 161 n 3 p 27 F '60
VIENNA WIND ENSEMBLE
NYC review; Friedrich Gulda,
pianist. MC v 162 n 6 p 35 D '60
DIE VIER TEMPERAMENTE
(Georgi), ballet
Ens AP wl ph: K. Julius. WT
v 9 n 3 p 231 Autumn '60
VILAR, JEAN (1912-). (On staging
Chekhov; French viewpoint.) il
WT v 9 n 2 p 146-8 Summer '60
--- ---S'instruire est une conquête
personnelle. WP v 12 n 2 p 1, 3
N '60
---Au T. N. P. concerts populaires
de musique contemporaine (com-
mentaire); Jean Cocteau venir
lui-même presenter son "Oedipus-
Rex". GDC n 291 p 355 D 2'60
---Bermel, Albert, Jean Vilar: un-
adorned theatre for the greatest
number. TDR v 5 n 2 p 24-43
D '60
---Paris survey by Jean-Pierre
Lenoir. Th Arts v 44 n 1 p 24-5
Ja '60
---As Robespierre in "La Mort de
Danton", ens AP hl ph: Agnes
Varda. Th Arts v 44 n 12 p 62
D '60
---Hl ph. WP v 12 n 2 p 1 N '60
---In "Arturo VI", AP ph: T. N. P.
WP v 12 n 3 p 4 D '60
VILLA-LOBOS, HEITOR, 1887-
1959, composer
Criticism of his film score for
"Vertes Demeures". GDC n 265-
6 p 521 Mr 25'60
THE VILLAGE WHICH NO LONGER
EXISTS, play
Ens AP wl ph: Reussens. WT v 9
n 1 p 22 Spring '60
VILLETTE, PIERRE. Blues (études
musicales analytiques). GDC n 271
p 631 My 5'60

VILMEISET KLUSAUKSET
PLAY
Tampere notes;Lauri Kokkonen.
WP v 11 n 5 p 6 Mr'60
VINAY, ROMAN(1913?-). An in-
terview, mostly on singing Wag-
ner. il ON v 24 n 10 p 15, 32 Ja
9'60
---As Parsifal, AP wl ph:Melan-
çon. ON v 24 n 23 p 9 Ap 9'60
---As Tristan, several AP phs:
Melançon. ON v 24 n 10 Ja 9'60
VINTAGE 60 (LUCAS), revue
NYC review. Th Arts v 44 n 9
p 76 S'60
VIOLANTA, opera
Notes on Korngold and Caruso.
ON v 24 n 20 p 13 Mr 19'60
VIOLIN
Babitz, Sol. The violin:views and
reviews (a series on technique,
literature on the violin and such
topics). drawings IM 1960
---Di Stradivari (several phs.)
La S n 125 p 36-8 Ap '60
VIOLINISTS
Kish, Anne L. The vanishing
violinist (survey of what a music
educator can find for one or two
violins, encouragement to a
school string program). MEJ v 46
n 3 p 68-9 Ja '60
---NYC reviews: Gerald Tarack;
Nathan Goldstein; Sonya Mono-
soff; Leonid Kogan (two); Johanna
Martzy; Murray Adler; Michel
Chauveton. MC v 162 n 6 p 34-7,
43 D '60
---Paris; Orchestre de Chambre
Sancta Coecilia; violinist Guy
Heifertz, etc. GDC n 267-8
p 560 Ap 8'60
---US; list of soloists and sym-
phony orchestras with date of
concert. IM v 58 n 7 p 32 Ja '60
LES VIOLONS de d'AUTOMNE,
play
Montreal notes; Jacques Lengui-
rand. WP v 11 n 9 p 3 Jl '60
VIOTTI, GIOVANNI BATTISTA,
1755-1824, composer
Quartets, played by the Baker
String Quartet, recorded for the
Society of Forgotten Music; re-
view. Mus Q v 46 n 1 p 130-2

Ja '60
VIRGINIA MUSEUM THEATRE
Richmond notes. PlM v 36 n 6
p 121 Mr '60
VIRTUOSI di ROMA
London; operas. Op v 11 n 11
p 779 N '60
---Salle Favart, Paris; review.
Op v 11 n 8 p 551 Ag '60
VISHNEVSKAYA, GALINA, 1927-,
singer
Career sketch; wife of 'cellist
Mstislav Rostropovitch. MD
v 51 n 1 p 4 Jl '60
---NYC concert. ON v 24 n 16 p 3
F 20'60
--- ---review. MC v 161 n 5 p 15
Ap '60
---Notes; wife of Rostropovich,
Russian cellist. MD v 50 n 8
p 12 F '60
THE VISIT, play
NYC review. PlM v 36 n 8 p 195
My '60
LA VISITE de la VIELLE DAME
Durrenmatt, ens AP wl ph: Mad-
rid. WP v 12 n 1 p 1 O '60
VIVA LA PAZ, play
Mexico notes; Alfonso Anaya B.
WP v 11 n 10 p 8 Ag '60
VIVALDI, ANTONIO, 1675-1741,
composer
Landon, H. C. Robbins. The Red
Priest of Venice. il HF v 10 n 8
p 30-35 Ag '60
---Portrait. WM n 1 back cover
F '60
VIVIANI, ALBERTO (1894-).
Cecco Angiolieri dodecafonico
maledetto. il La S n 133 p 31-41
D '60
--- ---Il Burchiello e la musica del
suo tempo. il La S n 131 p 11-19
O '60
VOICE OF AMERICA, radio series
New series, "Gift of Music"; Ed-
ward Sprague, narrator; notes.
AmM v 8 n 1 p 10 Ja '60
VOICOU, ION, violinist
Paris review. GDC n 292 p 423
D 9'60
LA VOIX d'OR de PARIS, contest
La première audition: Janine
Micheau et Vlado Perlemuter.
GDC n 259-60 p 405 F 12'60

LA VOIX HUMAINE, opera
American Opera Society; criticism of Poulenc score. Op v 11
n 7 p 471 Jl '60
---Goodwin, Noel. Edinburgh Festival; "trivial in conception".
MC v 162 n 4 p 26 O '60
---Lockspeiser, Edward. An introduction to Poulenc's "La Voix
Humaine". il Op v 11 n 8 p 527-
534 Ag '60
---McMullen, Roy. (Historical
notes on Poulenc work; on Ricordi's stereo, Mme. Duval and
the Opéra-Comique Orchestra;
comment.) HF v 10 n 2 p 22, 24
F '60
---Osborne, Conrad L. Review
of Denise Duval's 45 minute
farewell to her lover (RCA Victor). HF v 10 n 6 p 55-6 Je '60
---US première (NYC) by American Opera Society; Denise Duval, singer. WM n 2 p 32 Ap '60
---Cocteau, Jean, design for the
set; his design for cover of the
vocal score; portrait of Denise
Duval and several facsimile music excerpts. Op v 11 n 8 p 530-
4 Ag '60
LE VOLEURS de BLUES, revue
Paris notes; music by Jimmy
Loverman Davis. WP v 11 n 6
p 6 Ap '60
LA VOLEUSE de LONDRES, play
Amsterdam notes; Georges Neveux. WP v 11 n 10 p 9 Ag '60
VOLPONE, opera
Burt, Francis, 1926-, Londonborn composer; career notes;
analysis of the opera and its commedia dell'arte characters. Op
v 11 n 7 p 461-2 Jl '60
---Stuttgart notes; Francis Burt.
WP v 12 n 1 p 11 O '60
VOL de NUIT, opera
A l'Opéra-Comique; Luigi Dallapiccola (1904-) musique d'après
l'oeuvre de Saint-Exupéry;critique. GDC n 285 p 162 O 21'60
---Opéra-Comique;Dallapiccola,
20 years ago;review. MC v 162
n 6 p 30 D'60
---Saint-Exupéry;première

notes (four scenes). OpP n 19 p 54-5
1960
---Four phs: Paris, 1960. OpP n 19
p 54-5 1960
VOLTAIRE, pseud. (1694-1778)
Farmer, Henry George. Voltaire
as a music critic. MR v 21 n 4
p 317-9 N '60
VOORHEES, DONALD 1903-, conductor
Morton, Jon. (career sketch of
leader of the Bell Telephone Orchestra, 36th season.) MC v 162
n 3 p 8 S '60
---Por ph; and small AP ph: NBC.
MC v 162 n 3 cover, p 8 S '60
IL VORTICE, opera
Rome review. il La S n 123 p 35
F '60
VOSS, HERMANN (1910-). The
problem of young talent for German orchestras. WM n 4 p 73-4
Ag '60
VOTIPKA, THELMA, singer
Notes; b. Cleveland. por ON v 24
n 24 p 12 Ap 16'60
VOTTERLE, KARL (1903-). The
epoch of the complete edition.
WM n 1 p 5 F '60
VOTTO, ANTONIO, conductor
Chicago criticism. MC v 162 n 6
p 23 D '60
UN VOYAGE POUR UN RÊVE,
play
Buenos Aires notes; Carlos Carlino. WP v 11 n 5 p 1 Mr '60
VOYAGE TO THE MOON, opera
Caldwell, Sarah, directing; notes.
MC v 161 n 3 p 42 F '60
LE VOYAGEUR de FORCELOUP,
play
Ens AP wl ph: Bruxelles, 1952.
WT v 9 n 1 p 15 Spring '60
VOYAGEUR (MARTYN), ballet
Rodriques, Antonio, lead role in
Victorian Ballet Guild production,
MD v 51 n 2 p 24 Ag '60
VUILLERMOZ, EMILE, 1878-1960,
critic
Notes. TD n 92 p 11 Ap '60
VYBORNY, Z DENEK. Paganini as
music critic (trans. Willis Wager).
Mus Q v 46 n 4 p 468-481 O '60

W

WÄCHTER, EBERHARD, 1929-,
  singer
  In Tannhäuser, Rome note. ON
  v 24 n 23 p 27 Ap 9'60
WAGNER, ALAN. The new golden
  age of opera. il HF v 10 n 1 p 55-
  7, 120 Ja '60
WAGNER, FRIEDELIND
  And her protégée, Frances Martin, hl ph: Lammel. ON v 25 n 1
  p 5 O 8'60
WAGNER, RICHARD, 1813-1883,
  composer
  Dumesnil, René. Une profitable
  leçon de gout. por La S n 129-30
  p 32-3 Ag-S '60
---Garbato, Enzio. Una vita dolorosa. il La S n 129-30 p 46-8 Ag-S
  '60
---Janni, Guido. Wagner's idyl in
  the days of "Parsifal". La S n 127
  p 14-7 Je '60
---McElroy, George. (Comparison
  of Wagner and Verdi). ON v 25
  n 8 p 17-20 D 31'60
---Marsh, Robert C. By master
  hands, Wagner in concert form
  (3 new recordings compared).
  HF v 10 n 10 p 68 O '60
---Warrack, John. Old Germany
  and new Bayreuth. il Op v 11 n 11
  p 729-737 N '60
---Bust; print of Guglielmina Pla-
  ner (Minna); ritratto di Matilde
  Wesendonk; Cosima Liszt in un
  ritratto del 1870. La S n 129-30
  p 46-8 Ag-S '60
---Right profile por painting 1870;
  la villa di Tribochen; Riccardo
  Wagner con i suoi amici, ens picture; facsimile autografo 1882.
  La S n 127 p 14-7 Je '60
WAGNER, WIELAND, 1917?-,
  Warrack, John. Old Germany
  and new Bayreuth. il Op v 11 n 11
  p 729-737 N '60
WAGNER, WOLFGANG, 1919-,
  director
  Downes, Edward. The tetralogy
  of the Ring in "original and powerful stage designs"; criticism. ON
  v 25 n 2 p 23 O 29'60

---(Lingg, Ann M.) The younger
  Wagner (an interview on his Ring).
  por ON v 25 n 2 p 24 O 29'60
WAGNER OPERA COMPANY
  Fourth transcontinental tour; man-
  ager Felix W. Salmaggi; repertory.
  MC v 162 n 3 p 5 S '60
---US tour; repertory. ON v 24 n 22
  p 2 Ap 2'60
WAITING FOR GODOT, play
  Moore, John R. A farewell to
  something. TDR v 5 n 1 p 49-60
  S '60
WAITING IN THE WINGS, play
  London notes; Noel Coward. WP
  v 12 n 3 p 36 D '60
WAKHEVITCH, GEORGE (1907-).
  Un Ballo in Maschera, opera,
  setting for Act III scene 3, Teatro
  dell' Opera, Rome 1960, ph. Ver
  v 1 n 2 Ag '60
WALDMAN, FREDERIC, conductor
  Music Forgotten and Remembered,
  series; Myra Hess. MC v 161 n 5
  p 37 Ap '60
WALES
  Welsh National Opera; The Battle
  of Legnano, English version of
  Verdi by John Moody. MC v 162
  n 6 p 29 D '60
WALKER, ALAN. Back to Schön-
  berg. MR v 21 n 2 p 140-147
  My '60
WALKER, FRANK (1907-). L'Abandonnée, a forgotten song (Verdi).
  facsimile Ver v 1 n 2 p 785-789
  Ag '60
--- ---(Letter on Verdi.) MR v 21
  n 1 p 83-4 F '60
--- ---Unpublished letters: a contribution to the history of Un Ballo
  in Maschera (Italian and German
  translations also). Ver v 1 n 1 p 28-
  43 Ap '60
WALKER, ROBERT J. Producing a
  melodrama: Tom Cobb by Wm. S.
  Gilbert (with 2 scenes from a single
  set, phs.) PlM v 37 n 2 p 33 N '60
DIE WALKÜRE, opera
  Botley, Cicely M. The weather of
  their fate (in present weather vocabulary, the storm in Die Walkure;
  St. Elmo's Fire). ON v 24 n 16
  p 12-4 F 20'60

(Die Walküre)
---Lingg, Ann M. Meet Fricka.
ON v 24 n 16 p 6-7 F 20'60
---Metropolitan cast; story; criti-
cism; décor notes; bibliography;
discography; portfolio. ON v 24
n 16 F 20'60
--- ---review; Herbert Graf pro-
ducer, Karl Boehm conducting;
new singers. MC v 161 n 4 p 13
Mr '60
---Act III, Brünnhilde, sisters
and Sieglinde, ens AP wl ph: Bay-
reuth 1960. ON v 25 n 2 p 25
O 29'60
---Bayreuth; set used 1867; Wie-
land Wagner's production 1957,
2 phs. Op v 11 n 11 p 731 N '60
---Bayreuth, 1960; ens AP wl ph:
Lauterwasser. WM n 5 p 110
O '60
---Metropolitan, Act II: Nilsson,
Hines and Dalis, ens AP wl ph:
Melançon. Op v 11 n 4 p 269 Ap'60
THE WALL, play
NYC notes; Millard Lampell. WP
v 12 n 3 p 37 D '60
---Mitchell, Yvonne, ens AP wl
ph: Werner J. Kuhn. Th Arts
v 44 n 12 p 13 D '60
THE WALLACE, play
Edinburgh Festival notes. Th
Arts v 44 n 12 p 17 D '60
WALLENSTEIN, ALFRED, 1898-,
conductor
Chicago Symphony, guest con-
ductor; notes. MC v 161 n 3 p 36
F '60
---Los Angeles Philharmonic, the
Roger Wagner Chorale and soloists;
review of Messiah (Bärenreiter
edition). MC v 161 n 3 p 37 F '60
---Melbourne notes. MD v 50 n 7
p 15 Ja '60
WALTER, BRUNO, 1876-, con-
ductor
Pugliese, Giuseppe. Brahmsiana
di Bruno Walter. por La S n 132
p 66-7 N '60
---Conducting, ph. La S n 132
p 67 N '60
---Vienna, on podium, small ph.
La S n 129-30 p 39 Ag-S '60
WALTER, FRANZ. The growth

of international Festivals. WM
n 3 p 50-1 Je '60
WALTON, SIR WILLIAM, 1902-,
composer
Hughes, Patrick Cairn. Nobody
calls him Willie now. il HF n 10
n 9 p 43-6, 116 S '60
---Première of Second Symphony;
Edinburgh criticism. MC v 162
n 4 p 26 O '60
---Por ph. MC v 161 n 3 p 13 F'60
WAR AND PEACE, opera
The Bolshoi Theatre; review. Op
v 2 n 3 p 218 Mr '60
WARD, ROBERT, 1917-, composer
Career notes; b. Cleveland; quo-
ted. AmM v 8 n 3 p 15-16 Mr '60
---Por ph. AmM v 8 n 3 p 15 Mr '60
---With John Cruft and John Deni-
son, hl ph: London. AmM v 8 n 2
p 9 F '60
WARD, WINIFRED. Children's
theatre: help wanted. il Th Arts
v 44 n 8 p 53-56 Ag '60
WARGO, GEORGE, violist
Notes. IM v 58 n 7 p 37 Ja '60
THE WARM PENINSULA, play
NYC notes; Joe Masteroff. WP
v 11 n 4 p 3 F '60
---NYC review. PlM v 36 n 4 p 86
Ja '60
WARNKE, FRANK J. Macbeth de-
moted (Shakespeare and Verdi con-
cepts of the tragic hero). ON v 24
n 9 p 10-1 Ja 2'60
--- ---The happy ending (The Mar-
riage of Figaro). ON v 24 n 12 p 4-
5 Ja 23'60
WARRACK, JOHN. Old Germany
and new Bayreuth (Wagner then and
now). il Op v 11 n 11 p 729-737
N '60
--- ---Two new operas in Germany:
Henze's Der Prinz von Homburg
and Burt's Volpone at Stuttgart. il
Op v 11 n 7 p 457-462 Jl '60
WARREN, DALE. (Opera memories
with a large portfolio of past sing-
ers.) ON v 25 n 8 p 8-13 D 31'60
WARREN, LEONARD, 1911-1960,
singer
Career notes. AmM v 8 n 4 p 4
Ap '60
---Death scene during his role in

La Forza del Destino. MC
v 161 n 4 p 4 Mr '60
---Discography. por HF v 10 n 6
p 38 Je '60
---Gutman, John. (Obituary.) ON
v 24 n 22 p 5 Ap 2'60
---His death in the second act of
La Forza del Destino, Metropo-
litan. Op v 11 n 5 p 336 My '60
---Miller, Philip L. (Obituary;
b. NYC.) il Op v 11 n 6 p 397-
402 Je '60
---Notes on death in NYC. por
MD v 50 n 9 p 15 Mr '60
---Wagner, Alan. The life and
death of Leonard Warren. por
HF v 10 n 6 p 37-9 Je '60
---As Baron Scarpia AP ph: Sea-
well. ON v 24 n 20 p 17 Mr 19'60
---As Boccanegra; as Macbeth;
as Rigoletto and in nine other
roles, phs. Op v 11 n 6 cover,
p 396-401 Je '60
--- ---AP wl ph: Melançon. ON
v 24 n 22 p 4 Ap 2'60
---As Carlo di Vargas AP ph:
Leblang. ON v 24 n 19 p 17 Mr
12'60
---As Macbeth, AP hl ph. La S
n 133 p 68 D '60
--- ---AP hl ph: Louis Melançon;
2 other ens phs. ON v 24 n 9
Ja 2'60
WARTENSEE, XAVER SCHNYDER
VON
Irminger. Un disegno. La S n 123
p 15 F '60
WASHINGTON, D. C.
Coe, Richard L. Theatre Wash-
ington (a survey with pictures).
Th Arts v 44 n 12 p 21-4 D '60
---Mellen, Constance. Music re-
port. MC v 161 n 3 p 39 F '60;
same. MC v 161 n 6 p 31-2 My'60
---Smith, French Crawford. Opera
Society notes. ON v 25 n 7 p 29
D 24'60
THE WASHINGTON CATHEDRAL
View toward altar center aisle,
ph. MEJ v 47 n 1 p 98 S-O '60
THE WASHINGTON OPERA COM-
PANY
World War I days; community
opera; story by Leopold Glushak
with his picture in Don José

costume. ON v 24 n 14 p 14-5
F 6'60
WASHINGTON THEATRE CLUB
Wentworth, John B., founder;
notes. Th Arts v 44 n 12 p 24
D '60
WASOWSKI, ANDREZEJ, 1921-,
pianist
Berthoumieux, Serge. Paris
review. GDC n 289 p 296 N 18'60
WATSON, CLAIRE, 1933-, singer
Career; roles; b. NYC. AmM v 8
n 6 p 4 Jl '60
---As the Marschallin, AP hl ph:
Guy Gravett. Op v 11 p 13
Autumn '60
---In Peter Grimes: London press.
AmM v 8 n 11 p 11 D '60
---Por ph. AmM v 8 n 6 cover
Jl '60
WATSON, DON, ice-dancer
In Holiday on Ice; "un très grand
artiste". TD n 97 p 27 N '60
---And Liz Kaufmann in Holiday on
Ice, AP wl ph: Paris. TD n 97
p 26 N '60
WATTS, RICHARD, JR(1898-).
New York play season 1959-60.
Th Arts v 44 n 7 p 13-5 Jl '60
WAY, BRIAN. Plays for children
(by the director of the London
Children's Theatre Company).
NTM v 2 n 1 p 25-30 O '60
WAYSER, NATHALIE, 1948-,
pianist
Paris review. GDC n 279-80
p 892 Jl 1'60
WEAVER, CLARK. Notes and
News (regular column of short
items on publications, people,
plans, places concerned with
regional theatre). PlM 1960
WEAVER, FRITZ, 1926-, actor
And Edwin Sherin in Henry IV,
Part 2, AP hl ph: Phoenix, NYC.
Th Arts v 44 n 6 p 61 Je '60
WEAVER, WILLIAM. New light
on Verdi. il Op v 11 n 9 p 600-5
S '60
--- ---The pavilion of the open
sky, a visit to Verdi's Sant'Agata.
il HF v 10 n 1 p 42-3, 124 Ja '60
THE WEAVERS
Folk song group: Lee Hays, Ronnie
Gilbert, Fred Hellerman, Erik

(The Weavers)
Darling; notes on each. il HF
v 10 n 12 p 48-50 D '60
WEBER, BEN, 1916-, composer
Notes; b. St. Louis. AmM v 8
n 1 p 5 Ja '60
---Notes; b. St. Louis. AmM v 8
n 11 p 5 D '60
---Première: Chamber Fantasie,
in NYC 1959. ACAB v 9 n 2 p 24
1960
---Première: Fantasia; New Ad-
venture (NYC 1960). ACAB v 9
n 3 p 35 1960
WEBER, MARGRIT, pianist
Por ph: NYC. MC v 161 n 3 p 25
F '60
WEBSTER, BEVERIDGE, 1908-,
pianist
Berthoumieux, Serge. Paris cri-
ticism. GDC v 271 p 626 My 5'60
---Career notes; b. Pittsburgh.
AmM v 8 n 3 p 10 Mr '60
WEBSTER, MARGARET (1905-).
Whither bound? (Theatre in Eng-
land; the "reps".) Th Arts v 44
n 11 p 23-4, 71 N '60
WECHSBERG, JOSEPH (1907-).
Austria's new festival empire:
Vienna's Festwochen, Salzburg and
others. il Th Arts v 44 n 5 p 15-
7 My '60
--- ---Salzburg 50th Festival (re-
views of opera). il Op v 11 p 47-51
Autumn '60
--- ---Salzburg's new Festispiel-
haus (the building). il Op v 11 n 8
p 535-540 Ag '60
WEERTH, ERNEST de. Naples
drama (replacement of Tebaldi
by Magda Olivero on opening night;
Adrianna Lecouvreur). il ON v 24
n 11 p 26-7 Ja 16'60
--- ---Scenes from an enchanted
life; 4. A hat for Caruso. ON
v 24 n 9 p 8 Ja 2'60
--- ---5. Felia Litvinne and the
Gay Nineties. por ON v 24 n 10
p 9, 28 Ja 9'60
--- ---6. Baritone and Mélisande
(Vanni Marcoux). il ON v 24 n 11
p 10, 32 Ja 16'60
--- ---7. Venus of the boat train
(Lina Cavalieri). por ON v 24 n 13

p 6-7 Ja 30'60
--- ---8. Munich fifty years ago.
il ON v 24 n 16 p 11, 23 F 20'60
WEG IM NEBEL (JOOSS), ballet
Ens AP wl ph: Minos, 1952. WT
v 9 n 3 p 228 Autumn '60
WEIGEL, HANS (1908-). Twilight
of the cinema. WP v 11 n 7 p 1
My '60
---Por ph. WP v 11 n 7 p 1 My '60
WEIGEL, HÉLÈNE, actress
In Mère Courage, AP wl ph. WP
v 11 n 9 p 1 Jl '60
WEIGL, VALLY, composer
Première: Nature Moods (NYC
1960). ACAB v 9 n 3 p 36 1960
WEILL, KURT, 1900-1950, com-
poser
Review of his music recorded
under the title "Kurt Weill in Ber-
lin". PlM v 36 n 5 p 111 F '60
WEINSTOCK, HERBERT (1905-).
Great opera houses: Paris. il ON
v 25 n 6 p 22-7 D 17'60
--- ---Spontini waiting (career of
Italian composer 1774-1851). por
ON v 24 n 19 p 12-3 Mr 12'60
WEINTRAUB, STANLEY (1929-).
Bernard Shaw, actor. Th Arts
v 44 n 10 p 66-7 O '60
WEINZWEIG, JOHN, 1913-, com-
poser
Kasemets, Udo. John Weinzweig.
checklist CMJ v 4 n 4 p 4-18
Summer '60
---Por ph: Canada. CMJ v 4 n 4
p 5 Summer '60
WEISGALL, HUGO, 1912-, com-
poser
The Tenor, opera; notes on com-
poser; review of Westminster re-
cording. CMJ v 4 n 2 p 47-8
Winter '60
WEISSMAN, JOHN S. Hungary
(Budapest Music Weeks). Mus Q
v 46 n 4 p 525-35 O '60
WELSH NATIONAL OPERA
Financial report; plans. Op v 11
n 5 p 335 My '60
---Repertory under John Moody. Op
v 11 n 7 p 471 Jl '60
WERDER, FELIX, composer
Melbourne; notes. por MD v 50
n 10 p 18 Ap '60

WESKER, ARNOLD (1932-) (Interviewed on repertory theatre by Jill Pomerance.) NTM v 1 n 3 p 5-8 Ap '60

WEST, LUCRETIA, singer
Paris review. GDC n 263-4 p 491 Mr 11'60

WEST AUSTRALIAN BALLET (BOUSLOFF)
Penberthy, James. West Australian Ballet season 1960. il MD v 51 n 1 p 28-9 Jl '60

WEST SIDE STORY (ROBBINS), musical
Hutton, Geoffrey W. Melbourne review (singing not up to the Australian standard, otherwise good). MD v 51 n 5 p 23-4 N '60
---The story; critical comment. il MD v 51 n 6 p 24, 27 D '60

WEST SIDE STORY, film
Cast, ens ph: Hollywood. AmM v 8 n 10 p 7 N '60
---Several stills: NYC, United Artists; Russ Tamblyn, por. Th Arts v 44 n 11 p 12-3 N '60

WHAT EVERY WOMAN KNOWS, play
Old Vic, 1960, ens AP wl ph: Houston Roger. WT v 9 n 2 p 182 Summer '60

WHETSTONE, GEORGE A. Libretto by Zola (notes on his opera librettos). ON v 24 n 18 p 13, 30 Mr 5'60

THE WHIRLPOOL, opera
Bratislava review. Op v 11 n 9 p 618 S '60

WHITE, DOROTHY, harpichordist
With Vincent Sheppard and Peter Richardson; Australian notes. MD v 51 n 5 p 11 N '60

WHITE, EDNA(1898-). High cracked note (trumpet soloist before President Harding). IM v 59 n 4 p 24 O '60

WHITE, ERIC WALTER. The Rehearsal of an Opera (opera history brought to mind in this picture by Sebastiano and Marco Ricci, uncle and nephew, of an 18th century opera). il Th Notbk v 14 n 3 p 79-90 Spring '60

WHITE HOUSE CONFERENCE ON CHILDREN AND YOUTH 1960

Reports. MEJ v 47 n 2 p 81 N-D '60

WHITEHEAD, ROBERT (1916-). American festival fundamentals. portfolio Th Arts v 44 n 6 p 51, 63 Je '60
--- ---On Lincoln Center's Drama Repertory Theater "as a unique opportunity for theatrical cross-breeding". por ON v 25 n 2 p 12 O '29'60

WHITEMAN, PAUL, 1891-, conductor
And band, ens ph: 1924. HF v 10 n 5 p 35 My '60

WHITTALL, GERTRUDE CLARKE
In 1935, Whittall Foundation in the Library of Congress: instruments. IM v 59 n 6 p 40 D '60

THE WIDOW, play
Malmö, 1958; Gudrun Brost and Rune Turesson, AP wl ph: Alice Stridh. WT v 9 n 2 p 175 Summer '60

WIENANDT, ELWYN A. Das Licht scheinet; two settings by K. H. Graun. MR v 21 n 2 p 85-93 My'60

WEINER BLUT, opera
Bregenz, on the lake, ph. Elfie Mayerhofer and Peter Klein, two AP phs: Spang. Op v 11 p 73-4 Autumn '60

WIENER OKTETT
Chamfray, Claude. Paris criticism. GDC n 263-4 p 489 Mr 11 '60

WIENER SYMPHONIKER
Reviews; under Bruno Maderna; under Hans Swarowsky. MC v 161 n 5 p 30 Ap '60

WIESBADEN
May Festival; the Vienna Staatsoper; opera reviews. il Op v 11 p 64-7 Autumn '60

WIGGLESWORTH, FRANK, 1918-, composer
Première: Symphony No. 2 (NYC 1960). ACAB v 9 n 3 p 36 1960

WIJNBERG, NICOLAAS. (On staging Chekhov; Netherlands viewpoint.) WT v 9 n 2 p 148 Summer '60

WILCKE, JOACHIM. The audience (in German theatres). WT v 9 n 3 p 259-261 Autumn '60

WILDCAT (KIDD), musical

(Wildcat (Kidd)
Ball, Lucile, star; story of the
show. il Th Arts v 44 n 12 p 18-
9 D '60
WILDERMANN, WILLIAM
As Ferrando in Il Trovatore, AP
ph: Melancon. ON v 24 n 17 p 17
F 27'60
WILLAN, HEALEY, 1880-, com-
poser
Peaker, Charles. Works for or-
gan (criticism). CMJ v 4 n 2
p 60-2 Winter '60
WILLATT, HUGH. The new Nottin-
gham Playhouse. NTM v 1 n 1
p 13-5 O '59
WILLIAM TELL HAS SAD EYES,
play
Sastre criticism. TDR v 5 n 2
p 119 D '60
WILLIAMS, EDNA, singer
Chicago Negro soprano on John
Hay Whitney fellowship in Vienna.
MC v 162 n 3 p 29 S '60
WILLIAMS, HAROLD, 1893-, singer
Notes. MD v 51 n 6 p 14 D '60
WILLIAMS, JOHN,1942-, guitarist
Criticism; Asutralian. MD v 50
n 8 p 13 F '60
---Paris concert. GDC n 274 p 724
My 27'60
WILLIAMS, TENNESSEE, 1914-,
playwright
Paris; Théâtre de l'Alliance fran-
çaise: Quatre Pièces en un Acte;
review. GDC n 287 p 230 N 4'60
---Popkin, Henry. The plays of
Tennessee Williams. TDR v 4 n 3
p 45-61 Mr '60
WILLIAMS, VERDON G. Stars of
The Music Man (Melbourne pro-
duction). por MD v 50 n 11 p 25
My '60
--- ---Ten years' achievement in
chamber music: Micha Kogan and
his Soirees Musicales Society
(Melbourne). MD v 50 n 7 p 12-3
Ja '60
---Australia; notes. por MD v 50
n 7 p 32 Ja '60
---Perth notes. por MD v 51 n 3
p 13 S '60
---Por ph. MD v 50 n 7 p 32 Ja '60
WILLOUGHBY, ROBERT H. , 1921-,

flutist
Career notes; Iowa. por IM
v 58 n 8 p 31 F '60
WILLSON, MEREDITH, 1902-,
composer
Notes on The Music Man, musi-
cal. Th Arts v 44 n 1 p 82 Ja '60
WILSON, ANN, singer
Castil. Paris review. GDC
n 255-6 p 313 Ja 15'60
WILSON, BILLY, dancer
As Othello with Sonia Van Beers,
AP wl ph: Lido. TD n 95 p 14
Jl-Ag '60
WILSON, JOHN S. Griffith and
Prince (producers of Broadway
musicals). por Th Arts v 44 n 10
p 20-1 O '60
--- ---Is jazz too respectable? HF
v 10 n 5 p 34-7 My '60
--- ---Musicals: the old college try.
il Th Arts v 44 n 8 p 48-52 Ag'60
--- ---Scenic design and lighting
(interview with William and Jean
Echart). il Th Arts v 44 n 7 p 55,
67 Jl '60
--- ---The big time in straw hats
(US summer theatres). il Th Arts
v 44 n 6 p 14-16, 73 Je '60
--- ---Theatre on discs. Th Arts
v 44 n 1 p 81-3 Ja '60; same. Th
Arts v 44 n 2 p 80-1 F '60; same.
Th Arts v 44 n 3 p 62-4 Mr '60;
same. Th Arts v 44 n 9 p 66, 75
S '60
WINDSOR CAMP THEATRE
Lenox, Massachusetts, James
Hall and wife; aims and accom-
plishment in 3 years. il Th Arts
v 44 n 6 p 21-2 Je '60
WINGS OF THE DOVE, opera
Ayer, Ehtna, composing for NYC
Opera, Ford Foundation subsidy.
AmM v 8 n 5 p 13 Je '60
---Moore, Douglas, music; notes.
ON v 24 n 22 p 2 Ap 2'60
WISE, B. FRED, 1896-, singer
Por ph: Chicago. MC v 161 n 3
p 17 F '60
THE WISE MONKEYS (MORRICE)
Ballet Rambert; music Shostako-
vich, décor Ralph Adron: notes
by Ivor Guest. MD v 51 n 3 p 27
S '60

330

THE WISE WOMAN
See Die Kluge, opera

WISHENGRAD, MORTON. The rope dancers (complete text of play; NYC cast, 1957 and portfolio). Th Arts v 44 n 1 p 33-64 Ja '60

WISMEYER, LUDWIG. The Musical Youth of the World in Berlin (report of 15th Congress of the "Jeunesses Musicales"). WM n 5 p 98-100 O '60

WITHEY, J. A. Sound as environment (Eugene O'Neill quoted; Stevens Institute report of 1937 on problems of stage sound). PlM v 34 n 2 p 34-5 N '60

DE WITTE SALAMANDER (Taylor) ballet
Netherlands; music by Joop Stakkermans. WP v 12 n 3 p 34 D '60

WODEHOUSE, P. G. (1881-). What's wrong? (Broadway stage; critics.) Th Arts v 44 n 6 p 8-9 Je '60

WOESS, KURT, conductor
Melbourne notes. MD v 50 n 7 p 16 Ja '60

WOLDIKE, MOGENS, 1897-, conductor
AP hl ph: Vienna. HF v 10 n 3 p 105 Mr '60

WOLF, HUGO (1860-1903). Quatuor à cordes en ré mineur (études musicales analytiques). GDC n 293-4 p 468-9 D 16'60

---Berges, Ruth. The tragic star of Hugo Wolf (b. Windsichgraz, now in Yugoslavia). por MC v 161 n 4 p 10-2 Mr '60

---Osborne, Conrad L. In belated commemoration, 3 albums of Hugo Wolf Songs (Angel and Deutsche Grammophon). HF v 10 n 7 p 49-50 Jl '60

---Vienna celebrations. MC v 162 n 1 p 31 Jl '60

---Por ph. HF v 10 n 7 p 49 Jl'60; same. MC v 161 n 4 p 10 Mr '60

WOLFE, IRVING. Rural school music missionary (Charles A. Fullerton of Iowa). por MEJ v 46 n 5 p 26-28 Ap-My '60

WOLFF, ALBERT, 1884-, composer

Première: Petit Divertissement Symphonique; chez Pasdeloup, review. GDC n 284 p 137 O 14'60

WOLFF, STEPHANE. L'entr'acte: chronique des Théâtres Lyriques, serie. GDC 1960

--- ---Louis Musy et le Roi Malgré Lui reviennent à l'Opéra-Comique. GDC n 255-6 p 301-2 Ja 15'60

WOLFING, SIEGMUND. Leipzig opera review of Falstaff. Op v 11 n 5 p 347-8 My '60

THE WOLOHAN ORCHESTRA
Wolohan, Maury, his wife and five children, ens AP wl ph: San Francisco. IM v 58 n 12 p 28 Je '60

WOLOVSKY, LEONARD, singer
As Boris; criticism of Frankfurt revival of Rimsky-Korsakov. Op v 11 n 10 p 694 O '60

WOMEN IN PARLIAMENT, play
Ostia; ens AP wl ph: Bosio. WT v 9 n 3 p 289 Autumn '60

WOOD, CYRIL. A playhouse in Cheltenham (to replace The Opera House). il NTM v 1 n 3 p 18-23 Ap '60

WOOD, PEGGY (1892-). Festivals: true and false. Th Arts v 44 n 12 p 16-7 D '60

THE WOOD DEMON, play
Teatr Mossoviet, Moskva, 1960, ens AP wl ph. WT v 9 n 2 p 145 Summer '60

THE WOODCARVER, play
Bristol notes; Morris Brown. WP v 11 n 10 p 14 Ag '60

WOODHAM, RONALD (1912-). The meaning of modulation. MR v 21 n 4 p 265-281 N '60

WORDLESS FUNCTIONAL ANALYSIS
Chart, nos. 1-9 of Hans Keller's FA (wordless functional analysis) as performed in BBC and German broadcasts. MR v 21 n 1 p 73-76 F '60

---Keller, Hans. Wordless functional analysis: the second year and beyond-II. MR v 21 n 3 p 237-239 Ag '60

WORLD MUSIC BANK
Olver, Michael. (History of the project under American Symphony

(World Music Bank)
Orchestra League; Igor Buket-
off; notes on contents of the bank.)
CMJ v 4 n 2 p 39-41 Winter '60
THE WORLD OF CARL SANDBERG,
theatre piece
Pryce-Jones, Alan. (Review.)
Th Arts v 44 n 11 p 10 N '60
WORLD THEATRE, periodical
Index volume VII-3 to volume
IX-2: authors, subjects, illus-
trations. WT v 9 n 4 p 376-392
Winter '60
WORLD WORTH MY WINNING,
play
Ontario notes; Robert Gardiner.
WP v 11 n 8 p 3 Je '60
WÖRNER, KARL H. Czechoslo-
vakia (creative musical activity
today). Mus Q v 46 n 4 p 509-517
O '60
--- ---Germany; Kranichstein at
Darmstadt (report of recent In-
ternational Vacation Courses for
New Music; and a general criti-
cism of trends). Mus Q v 46 n 2
p 270-275 Ap '60
--- ---(Giselher Klebe's opera,
Die tödlichen Wünsche.) Mus Q
v 46 n 1 p 81-2 Ja '60
--- ---Parsifal at Bayreuth. CMJ
v 4 n 4 p 19-24 Summer '60
WORTHINGTON, RANDALL. Am-
sterdam (reports on recorded
music). HF 1960
WOYTOWICZ, STEFANIA, singer
American debut at Ravinia; notes.
MC v 162 n 2 p 12 Ag '60
WOZZECK, opera
Metropolitan Opera; BBC Third
Program; cast. AmM v 8 n 1 p 6
Ja '60
---San Francisco Opera; in English
under Kurt Herbert Adler; Geraint
Evans and Marilyn Horne. il ON
v 25 n 3 p 17 N 19'60
---San Francisco Opera review.
il Op v 11 n 12 p 819 D '60
---San Francisco première; review.
MC v 162 n 5 p 22 N '60
THE WRONG SIDE OF THE PARK,
play
London notes; John Mortimer.
WP v 11 n 6 p 15 Ap '60

WUORINEN, CHARLES, com-
poser
Première: Concertante IV for
Violin and Piano (NYC 1960).
ACAB v 9 n 3 p 36 1960
WYBLE, JIMMY, guitarist
With Benny Goodman band, ens
ph. IM v 58 n 12 p 15 Je '60
WYNER, YEHUDI
Première: Concert Duo (1955-
57); Chamber Music 60 review.
MC v 161 n 5 p 36 Ap '60
---Two premières: Concert Duo,
March 13; and Passover Offer-
ing, April 19; NYC notes. J Rev
v 7 n 2 p 22 Spring '60

X

XENAKIS, JANIX, composer
Première: Achorripsis; Paris
notes. MC v 161 n 3 p 44 F '60

Y

YAGHJIAN, HAIG, 1924-, con-
ductor
Career notes; b. Detroit. por
IM v 58 n 8 p 33 F '60
YANKOFF, VENTSISLAV, pianist
Mari, Pierrette. Paris review.
GDC n 255-6 p 313 Ja 15'60
YANNOPOULOS, DINO. New ideas
in staging opera. il MC v 162 n 4
p 6, 24 O '60
YATES, PETER. Lou Harrison
(a critical study of the composer,
now living in Aptos, California;
check-list of compositions).
ACAB v 9 n 2 p 2-7 1960
YORK FESTIVAL
Notes; each third year, mystery
plays. Th Arts v 44 n 12 p 16
D '60
YOUNG, JOHN WRAY (1907-). A
community-theatre quiz. port-
folio Th Arts v 44 n 8 p 16-20
Ag '60
--- ---The birth of a national or-
ganization. American Community
Theatre Association. PlM v 36
n 8 p 184 My '60
YOUNG, ROD. Puppet festival 1960
(25th gathering of the Puppeteers

of America, in Detroit). PIM
v 37 n 1 p 9 O '60
YOUNG AUDIENCES, INC.
US; Ford Foundation 3-year
grant $180,000; officers. MC
v 161 n 1 p 35 Ja '60
YOUNG COMPOSERS EXPERI-
MENTAL GROUP OF TURIN
Saville, Eugenia. (Il Miraggio,
magazine; some of the leaders
and music being written.) Mus Q
v 46 n 3 p 371-8 Jl '60
YOUNG PEOPLE'S CONCERTS
Hamburg; State Opera House
notes. WM n 1 p 9 F '60
---London; series, Your Opera
Nights; Sir Robert Mayer. WM
n 1 p 10 F '60
---New York Philharmonic; re-
view. MC v 161 n 6 p 19 My '60
---Washington, D.C.; National
Symphony under Howard Mitchell;
Mrs. Herbert May, sponsor. MEJ
v 46 n 4 p 10 F-Mr '60
---US; Young Audiences, Inc.;
Ford Foundation grant; notes.
WM n 2 p 32 Ap '60
---Vienna; British and Dutch You-
th orchestras; notes. WM n 2 p 32
Ap '60
YU-ZURU, opera
American première; review of
Manhattan School of Music. Op
v 11 n 6 p 410 Je '60
---Manhattan School of Music,
NYC; notes. ON v 24 n 18 p 27
Mr 5'60
--- ---$17,342 cleared. MEJ
v 46 n 5 p 4 Ap-My '60
--- ---Ikuma Dan, composer, Ju-
nji Kinoshita, librettist. il MC
v 161 n 3 p 32 F '60
---Ens AP wl ph: Manhattan School
of Music. Th Arts v 44 n 3 p 16
Mr '60
YUGOSLAVIA
Andric, Dragoslav. (Theatre re-
port.) il WT v 9 n 4 p 371-3
Winter '60
---Biennial International Festival
of Contemporary Music; notes.
WM n 4 p 77 Ag '60
---Dubrovnik; International Meet-
ing of Composers and Music

Critics: report. WM n 5 p 104
O '60
---Logar, Mihovil. Opera di Za-
gabria, Serajevo, Lubiana. il
La S n 132 p 49, 85 N '60
---Toncith, Vora. Seventh Fes-
tival at Split; Belgrade report.
MC v 162 n 1 p 33 Jl '60
YVES-NAT, ELISE. Les yeux
fermés. GDC n 293-4 p 447-452
D 16'60

Z

Z PREZESELOSCI, play
Poland; Maria Kornopnicka. WP
v 12 n 1 p 10 O '60
ZABALETA, NICANOR, 1907-,
harpist
Bruyr, José. Paris review.
GDC n 291 p 358 D 2'60
---NYC review; all harp composi-
tions. MC v 161 n 4 p 20 Mr '60
---Beside his harp, ph: Tel Aviv.
La S n 124 p 74 Mr '60
ZACCONI, ERMETE
D'Annunzio, Gabriele. Lettere
inedite a Zacconi. La S n 129-
30 p 49-55 Ag-S '60
---Por ph. La S n 129-30 p 51
Ag-S '60
ZAMBRA
Aux Festivals d'Espagne au The-
âtre des Champs-Elysées; un
spectacle flamenco pur. il TD
n 90 p 12-3 F '60
ZANETTI, DINA. Ricordo di Mar-
tinů. il La S n 131 p 42-3 O '60
ZANLONGHI, GILBERT, violinist
Machuel, Dominique. Paris re-
view. GDC n 271 p 627 My 5'60
DER ZAR LASST SICH PHOTO-
GRAPHIEN, opera
Frankfurt, ens AP wl ph: Eng-
lert. Op v 11 n 7 p 480 Jl '60
ZAR und ZIMMERMAN, opera
Frankfurt; ens AP wl ph: Englert.
Op v 11 n 10 p 692 O '60
DER ZAUBERFISH (SCHILLING),
ballet
Dresden notes; Wilhelm Hübner.
WP v 12 n 1 p 11 O '60
ZAVADSKI, YOURI (1894-). Thé-
âtre en U.R.S.S. WP v 11 n 5

(Zavadski, Youri)
p 1, 7 Mr '60
ZBIERSKI, HENRYK. Shakespeare in Poland: a survey. Th R v 2 n 3 p 136-140 1960
ZECCHI, ADONE (1904-). Teatro comunale di Bologna: Turandot, Lohengrin: London's Festival Ballet. il La S n 123 p 28 F '60
ZEFFIRELLI, FRANCO, producer Opera notes; Covent Garden. MC v 161 n 3 p 44 F '60
ZILLIG, WINFRIED. Variationen Ueber Neue Musik (book reviewed by Everett Helm). Mus Q v 46 n 3 p 381-3 Jl '60
ZIMBLER SINFONIETTA
List of members; activities; founded 1945 by Josef Zimbler. IM v 59 n 5 p 32 N '60
---At Teatro Colón. ens ph: Buenos Aires. IM v 58 n 7 p 14 Ja '60
DIE ZIMMERWIRTIN, play
Koln; Jacques Audiberti. WP v 12 n 1 p 12 O '60
ZITO, JIMMIE, trumpeter
Small por ph. IM v 58 n 12 p 7 Je '60
ZLOTE RECE, play
Varsovie; Helena Skrobiszewska. WP v 11 n 8 p 10 Je '60
ZOLA, EMILE, 1840-1902
As a librettist. Op v 11 n 9 p 595 99 S '60
DIE ZOO-GESCHICHTE
Berlin notes. WP v 11 n 3 p 4 Ja '60
THE ZOO STORY, play
Daniels, William, and Mark Richman, AP hl ph: NYC. Th Arts v 44 n 7 p 14 Jl '60
---Ens AP ph: Ilse Buhs, 1959. WT v 9 n 3 p 235 Autumn '60
ZORINA, VERA, 1917-, dancer
At Ravinia Festival in new small theatre, reciting Edith Sitwell's poems to Walton's Façade. MC v 162 n 2 p 12 Ag '60
DIE ZUKUNFT LIEGT IN DEN EIERN, play
Cologne notes; Eugène Ionesco. WP v 11 n 6 p 10 Ap '60
ZURICH
Epstein, Eugene V. Opera report. il ON v 25 n 5 p 28 D 10'60

---Otello; cast. il La S n 131 p 30 O '60
ZURIGO, ALFREDO. Un Ballo in Maschera, opera, set for Teatro dell'Opera, Rome, 1930, Act II ph. Ver v 1 n 2 p 1012 Ag '60
ZUTA COMPANY
Israel notes. WP v 12 n 3 p 4 D '60
ZWEI ARZTE, play
Leipzig; Hans Pfeiffer. WP v 11 n 5 p 16 Mr '60
ZYKLUS, solo percussion
Stockhausen, Karlheinz, composer; Paris performance described. CMJ v 4 n 4 p 43-4 Summer '60

TELEVISION ARTS INDEX 1960

NOTE:
Television material from those magazines indexed in the front section of this volume has been supplemented by listings from the following (in most cases not complete indexing but suggestive of sources):

Ballet Today, Dance Digest, Dance Magazine, Dance News, Dissertation Abstracts, Educational Screen and AV, Film Quarterly, Film World and AV, Fund For the Advancement of Education, Harpers, Holiday, Impulse, Industrial Arts and Vocational Education, Inter-American Music Bulletin, Journal of Chemical Education, Journal of Personality, Journal of Projective Techniques, Journal of the Society of Motion Picture and Television Engineers, Movie Life, Musical America, New York State Education Bulletin, Printers Ink, Public Opinion Quarterly, Punch, Radio Times (British), Saturday Review, Screen Album, Screen World and TV, Telefilm, TV Age, TV Digest, TV Guide (all issues), Texas Outlook, Times Educational Supplement, UNESCO Newsletter, Variety, The Writer, Writer's Digest, World Almanac.

A

ABICAIR, SHIRLEY. singer
Note. por Radio Times p 4
S 23'60
ABC of the NORTH, series
North of England, interview ser-
ies, 20-minute under David Mah-
lowe, no commercials. Punch
p 738 My 25'60
ACADEMY OF MOTION PICTURE
ARTS AND SCIENCES
Eighth annual Oscar telecast;
arrangements, Jerry Lewis and
staff. TV Guide v 8 n 14 p 9
Ap 2'60
ACTING
Beginners Please, a BBC series
on breaking into the theatre; documentary. Radio Times p 4
My 27'60
---Editorial: actors on TV should
count their blessings. TV Guide
v 8 n 27 p 3 Jl 2'60
---Gravey, Fernand. Performers'
rights. World Theatre v 9 n 4
p 341-3 Winter '60
---The latest word on some old
favorites (5 years as a TV star
is "success"): list of artists and
their present occupations. port-
folio TV Guide v 8 n 25 p 12-4
Je 18'60
---The stage actor on television,
disadvantages and advantages by
Vilezstav Vejrazka. World The-
atre v 9 n 4 p 337-340 Winter '60
---On golf links, Yorba Linda
Country Club, California, TV
stars in a charity tournament, 5
AP phs. TV Guide v 8 n 38 p 12-3
S 17'60
---Principal actors (adventure, my-
stery, comedy, history) in the
first week-end of the season,
color phs; TV Guide v 8 n 39
S 24'60
ADAMS, NEILE, 1935-,
Career notes; b. Manila as Ruby
Neilan Salvador Adams. por TV
Guide v 8 n 19 p 20-1 My 7'60
ADAMS, NICK, 1931-, actor
Notes and signed por ph. Screen

Album p 59 N '60
---Whitney, Dwight. Career
sketch; born Nanticoke, Penn-
sylvania. TV Guide v 8 n 33
p 12-5 Ag 13'60
THE ADVENTURES OF ALICE,
series
Carroll, Lewis; BBC cast. il
Radio Times p 52 D 15'60
ADVERTISING
Adapting a print ad theme to
TV; notes and 12 pictures, Qua-
ker Oats film. Printers' Ink
p 29-31 S 23'60
---As a career, picking shows
for sponsors: editorial. TV
Guide v 8 n 37 p 3 S 10'60
---Championship Bridge, a low-
rated show, sponsored by North
American Van Lines: 5-7 percent
growth in business to this sponsor. TV Guide v 8 n 46 p 2
N 12'60
---Cohen, Arthur R. Communi-
cation discrepancy and attitude
change: a dissonance theory approach. Journal of Personality
p 386-96 S '59
---Deodorizing commercial TV.
Times Educ Supplement p 636
N 11'60
---Editorial on Hallmark greet-
ing card advertising via TV
drama; little attention paid by
Hallmark to their "rating"; good
drama stressed. TV Guide v 8
n 8 p 2 F 20'60
---Furuya, Kenji. Responses of
school children to human and
animal pictures. Journal of
Projective Techniques v 21
p 248-52 1957
---How a tooth paste firm arrived
at a show for five million the
season. TV Guide v 8 n 43 p 23-
5 O 22'60
---In-store advertising, closed-
circuit; US testing. Jr SMPTE
v 69 n 8 p 558 Ag '60
---Kelly, Gaines. Questions of
taste (Television Code Affairs
issue report on laxatives, deod-
orants, etc. Do's and Don'ts
summarized). TV Age p 27, 82-3

336

(American Ballet Theatre)
v 34 n 4 p 13 Ap '60
AMERICAN BANDSTAND, series
Haines, Aubrey B. Dick Clark
big brother to America's teen-
agers. il Dance Digest v 10 n 1
p 4-7 F '60
THE AMERICAN COWBOY, show
Notes on Max Liebman, producer.
il TV Guide v 8 n 6 p 12-3 F 6'60
AMERICAN FILM FESTIVAL
NYC report; lists. Film World
and AV p 193 My '60
---NYC 1961; new category to be
shown, films "made for love, not
money"; notes. Jr SMPTE v 69
n 12 p 918 D '60
--- ---notes. Jr SMPTE v 69 n 10
p 760 O '60
AMERICAN INDIANS
Ten regulars in TV; names and
notes; phs. TV Guide v 8 n 12
p 8-9 Mr 19'60
AMERICANS AT WORK, series
Washington, D. C. scene of filming musicians at work; notes on
sequences shown; American Federation of Musicians in AFL-CIO
project. il International Musici-
an v 58 n 8 p 5, 9, 36 F '60
AMIS, JOHN, 1923-, singer
Notes. por Radio Times p 5
My 6'60
ANDERS, MERRY, 1934-, actress
Notes. por TV Guide v 8 n 28
p 22-3 Jl 9'60
ANDES, KEITH, 1920-, actor
Johnson, Bob. (Career sketch;
b. John Charles Andes, Ocean
City, New Jersey; Philadelphia;
year at Oxford.) por TV Guide
v 8 n 32 p 8-12 Ag 6'60
ANDREWS, EAMONN, compère
Sketch; American and English
engagements. Radio Times p 13
Ap 1'60
THE ANGRY YOUNG PLUMBER,
play
BBC notes. Punch 434 Mr 23'60
ANIMALS
Bird Migration; Dr. Ernst Sutter
of Switzerland; on "Look", BBC.
Radio Times p 33 O 13'60
---BBC; Peter Scott in California.

Radio Times p 39 O 20'60
---Carthy, John, new series of
"Listen and Learn" programs,
BBC. Radio Times p 2 My 20'60
--- French films, seven, directed
by Marc de Gastyne; The Ani-
mal Man on BBC. Radio Times
p 14 O 20'60
---Good Companions, TV series;
BBC notes. il Radio Times p 27
Jl 22'60
--- ---Stanley Dangerfield and
Peter West, new programs.
Radio Times p 3 My 6'60
---The great horse, Fox hunter;
BBC tale. Radio Times p 4 S 23'60
---Molony, Eileen. Heinz Sielmann
film "Summer with the Storks"
on "Look", BBC. il Radio Times
p 3 My 27'60
---News from the Zoo; Basle Zoo
on BBC. Radio Times p 31
O 20'60
---News from the Zoos, 5-part
serial; BBC. Radio Times p 4
My 20'60
---The Return of the Osprey, BBC
film notes. Radio Times p 26
Jl 8'60
---Riverbank films; Hammy, a
hamster, and Roderick, a white
rat featured in one; Dave Ellison
and Paul Sutherland (1931-) with
Josef Secheresh, Austrian photo-
grapher; BBC. Radio Times p 27
Jl 1'60
---Scott, Peter, in 1953 in Ice-
land; the pink-footed goose film.
Radio Times p 39 N 10'60
---Serial on cat, Mompty, and dog,
Peckham, BBC Childrens Hour;
Martin Armstrong series. Radio
Times p 27 Je 10'60
---Summer with the Storks on the
series, "Look"; BBC notes. il Radio
Times p 27 S 30'60
THE ANIMALS' WORLD, series
Seven programs; background notes
given ahead, popular but scientif-
ic. Radio Times p 8 Ja 15'60
ANIMATION
Cost breakthru; motion added to
transparencies through a new
process by Technamation Films.

il Telefilm p 9-10 Jl-Ag'60
---Cristenfeld, Marvin D. Artists
are unique: 1. Unique labor problems;II. Standard Contract Clau-
ses;III. The Cartoonists as a model union (NYC). Telefilm v 9
n XI-B p 4, 38 Commercials'60
special issue
---Glossary of animation terms,
trade terms from Roger Man-
vell's book, The Technique of
Film Animation. Telefilm v 9
n XI-B p 12-3, 16-7, 37 Commercials'60 issue
---Hanna, Bill, and Joe Barbera.
TV hungry for new animations.
por Telefilm p 35, 47 Jl-Ag'60
---How an animation is made, step
by step. Telefilm p 46 Jl-Ag'60
·---Perils and rewards of anima-
tion:research findings. charts
Telefilm v 9 n XI-B p 18-9, 22
Commercials'60 issue

ANIMATION WORKSHOP
NYC; Arthur Florman and others;
report. il Jr SMPTE v 69 n 6
p 444, 446 Je'60
ANSARA, MICHAEL
As an American Indian in TV;
born in Lowell, Mass. il TV
guide v 8 n 18 p 28-9 Ap 30'60
ANY QUESTIONS, program
Grisewood, Freddy, as Question
Master;BBC notes. Radio Times
p 5 S 9'60
THE AQUANAUTS
Tors, Ivan, producer;review. TV
Guide v 8 n 46 p 16 N 12'60
ARCHARD, BERNARD, actor
BBC roles. Radio Times p 4 Mr
18'60
ARCHITECTURE
Program (BBC) "Building Mat-
ters"; attitude of building socie-
ties toward new designs. Radio
Times p 4 Mr 18'60
ARDEN, JOHN, playwright
BBC;"Soldier, Soldier";notes.
Radio Times p 4 F 12'60
AREN'T WE ALL, play
Lonsdale, Frederick, author;BBC
Twentieth Century Theatre. Radio
Times p 7 My 13'60
ARGENTINA

(Television Index)
Célébration de l'année Tchék-
hov;Radio-diffusion argentine,
L'Ours. World Premieres v 11
n 9 p 7 Jl'60
---Ember, Nid. Post-Peron era,
film making. Variety p 13 N 30
'60
ARMY-NAVY FOOTBALL
Durslay, Melvin. (ABC-TV; ac-
ademies net $500, 000 each;hist-
ory of the annual event.) TV
guide v 8 n 48 p 6-7 N 26'60
ARNESS, JIM, actor
Notes and ph. Screen Album p 78
N'60
ARQUETTE, CLIFF
Story of his Charlie Weaver
Show. il TV Guide v 8 n 3 p 17-9
Ja 16'60
ART
Attenborough, Richard, narrator
of program on art fakes. Radio
Times p 3 Ag 5'60
---Boston;Dr. Brian Doherty in
series, Invitation to Art. por
TV Guide v 8 n 1 p 16 Ja 2'60
---BBC's Painting of the Month,
by mail reproduction in color
before TV analysis. Punch
p 142 Ja 20'60
---The Christmas Story in great
paintings;Donald Hyatt, BBC.
Radio Times p 54 D 15'60
---Closed-circuit auction of 50
paintings; NYC, Chicago, Los
Angeles and Dallas; report. il
TV Guide v 8 n 22 p 14-5 My
28'60
---Film narration by 6 artists on
BBC; how they create; list for
"The Artist Speaks". Radio Times
p 2 Jl 8'60
---Fine Arts course, New York
University, Dr. Jane Costello. il
TV Guide v 8 n 26 p 20-2 Je 25
'60
---How a young artist feels get-
ting started;John Schlesinger's
film; notes. Radio Times p 5
My 6'60
---Moore, Henry, sculptor on his
work;BBC. por Radio Times
p 15 N 17'60

(Art)

---Nolan, Sidney, artist on "Monitor", BBC. Radio Times p 14 D 1'60

---Project 20, Christmas show "The Coming of Christ" made by showing art masterpieces. il TV Guide v 8 n 51 p 4-5 D 17'60

---The Sketch Club Exhibition; BBC. Radio Times p 54 D 29'60

---Televised auction of art;closed-circuit, four US cities; report. Jr SMPTE v 69 n 5 p 364 My'60

THE ARTIST and the MODERN WORLD

Associated-Rediffusion schools section; young people and modern music with a stage spectacle to clarify. Ballet Today v 12 n 12 p 8 Mr'60

ASIAN CLUB, series

Macdonald, Malcolm, guest;BBC notes. Radio Times p 38 D 1'60

THE ASSASSINS, play

BBC notes (one scene). Radio Times p 15 D 1'60

---Shaw, Irwin, author; BBC's Twentieth Century Theatre notes. Radio Times p 3 My 27'60

ASTAIRE TIME

NBC; Barrie Chase; "a typical corny and expensive TV show". Dance News v 37 n 3 p 12 N'60

ASTRONOMY

Moore, Patrick. "Seeing Stars", on BBC (telling the young how to start the hobby, build a telescope, etc.). Radio Times p 27 F 12'60

--- ---back from Russia talks of the Russian Sky at Night. Radio Times p 22 N 3'60

ATTENBOROUGH, DAVID, adventurer

Notes on his travel programs for BBC. Radio Times p 9 Ap 22'60

AUDIENCES

Barrett, Herbert, of Barrett Management in an interview; TV exposure by artists no hinderance to management; is creating new and musically discriminating audience. Musical Courier

(Television Index)

v 162 n 1 p 14 Jl'60

---Greene, Felice, business of providing studio audiences for trying out shows; from San Francisco; now in Hollywood as "Audiences Unlimited". TV Guide v 8 n 51 p 6-7 D 17'60

---Heiffrich, Stockton. (US viewers can control public taste to a large extent; applaud the good.) TV Guide v 8 n 44 p 5-7 O 29'60

---TV has changed the "sticks"; taste has been sharpened. TV Guide v 8 n 35 p 3 Ag 27'60

AUSTEN, JANE

BBC; Emma; unsuited for stage or TV. Punch p 402 Mr 16'60

AUSTRALIA

Boyer, Sir Richard, in charge of National (A. B. C.) stations; expansion note. Music and Dance v 50 n 9 p 13 Mr'60

---Opera, ABV2: The Bartered Bride, review by Anthony Burke. Music and Dance v 51 n 2 p 15 Ag'60

---Petrouchka, ballet, adapted by James Upshaw for TV; review Sydney's Channel 2. Music and Dance v 51 n 6 p 29 D'60

AVALON, FRANKIE, 1940-, actor

Notes and wl signed ph. Screen Album p 69 N'60

AVERY, PHYLLIS, actress

Demonstration of The Golden Door spa's routines, five phs. TV Guide v 8 n 44 p 20-2 O 29'60

AWARDS

Academy of Motion Picture Arts and Sciences:scientific or technical achievement list. Film World and AV p 148 Ap'60

---DuPont Awards:public service TV shows;notes on many "fair and accurate" presentations. TV Guide v 8 n 29 p 6-7 Jl 16'60

---Lewine, Richard I. of CBS-TV and George Judd, manager of the New York Philharmonic receiving Sigma Alpha Iota TV Awards 1960, ph. International Musician v 59 n 1 p 29 Jl'60

---Notes and portraits of BBC

winners 1960. Radio Times
p 23 D 8'60
---Radio and TV awards; Academy of Television Arts and Sciences. World Almanac p 583 1959, etc. annually
---Sigma Alpha Iota award to George Judd, manager of New York Philharmonic by Marilyn Maryland and Richard L. Lewine of CBS; ph. Musical Courier v 162 n 1 p 4 Jl'60
---US; duPont Awards, begun in 1942, administered by Washington and Lee University; examples of public service programs. TV Guide v 8 n 29 p 6-7 Jl 16 '60
---TV Guide Awards;the counting by Cassidy-Richlar under Price Waterhouse and Company. TV Guide v 8 n 6 p 2 F 6'60
--- ---final ballot;details. TV Guide v 8 n 11 Mr 12'60

B

BACHELOR BROTHERS
On Saturday Playhouse; BBC notes. Radio Times p 5 O 20'60
BAKER, ART, dancer
And Jerri Baker; Pasadena, California notes. Dance Digest v 10 n 3 p 32 Ap'60
BAKER, DIANE, 1938-, actress
Career notes; from Los Angeles. por TV Guide v 8 n 34 p 24-5 Ag 20'60
BAKER, JACK, choreographer
His methods in TV-movie work. Dance Magazine v 34 n 6 p 19 Je'60
BAKER, STANLEY, actor
BBC; The Squeeze, play. il Radio Times p 15 N 17'60
BALL, LUCILLE, actress
Interview. por TV Guide v 8 n 29 p 17-9 Jl 16'60
---Interview with Richard Gehman on TV and her Broadway musical, "Wildcat"; Desilu picking up the cost. Theatre Arts v 44 n 12 p 18-20 D'60
---Jenkins, Dan. (Interview.) por

(Television Index)
TV Guide v 8 n 29 p 17-9 Jl 16'60
---Por ph. Th Arts v 44 n 10 p 16 O'60
LA BALLADE du SOLDAT
Bernadac, Lucienne; "Musique pour vous"; chorégraphe, Juan Corelli; Wladimir Skouratoff et Joan Cazdov. il Toute la Danse n 96 p 29 S-O'60
BALLADINE, CAROL
On Spanish National TV in "Don Pasquale"; notes. Dance Digest v 10 n 9 p 37 N'60
BALLET
Associated-Rediffusion; second Gala dance program from the Hackney Empire; review. Ballet Today v 12 n 14 p 9 My'60
---Australia; Laurel Martyn; her work as ballet director ABV2. por Music and Dance p 26 My'60
---Balanchine and Stravinsky signed by CBS-TV for a ballet on Noah. Musical Courier v 161 n 6 p 7 My'60
---Ballade Para Três (Dixon) for the Portuguese Television, AP wl ph: J. Testa Santos. Ballet Today v 12 n 19 p 14 N'60
---Briane, Mireille, et son ballets d'enfants à la "Parade du Jeudi". Toute la Danse n 92 p 23 Ap'60
---Dale, Margaret, TV choreographer, on her "The Sleeping Beauty", BBC. Radio Times p 27 Ap 15'60
---Franks, A. H. Monitor, BBC programme; interview with Madame Marie Rambert with excerpts from the films. Dancing Times v 50 n 594 p 295 Mr'60
---Granada TV: Ashton's Cinderella with Margot Fonteyn; review. Ballet Today v 12 n 15 p 11 Je'60
---London's Festival Ballet; BBC notes. il Radio Times p 30 D 22'60
---Ross, Helen. The Sleeping Beauty by Petipa, re-produced by Margaret Dale for BBC and for Eurovision; review. Ballet Today v 12 n 11 p 7 F'60

341

Television ballet compared to ballet in the round. Ballet Today v 12 n 14 p 8 My'60
---TV-français:Le Rossignol et l'Empereur de Chine. il Toute la Danse n 92 p 12-3 Ap'60
BALLET NACIONAL de VENEZUELA
Asmus, Harry, ballet master; list of works on TV; 22 dancers. Dance News v 37 n 3 p 6 N'60
BALLROOM DANCING
Aragon Ballroom, Lawrence Welk(1903-); sketch; Teleklew; Aragon Ballroom. il TV Guide v 8 n 27 p 17-9 Jl 2'60
---Bridlington Festival, a thirty-minute BBC broadcast. Ballroom Dancing Times v 5 n 1 p 43 O'60
---Clark, Dick, and his American Ballroom, TV series. il Dance Digest v 10 n 1 p 4-7 F'60
---Programs on BBC and on ITV; Hugh Carter on time table difficulties and the effect on dancing. il Ballroom Dancing Times v 4 n 9 p 370-1 Je'60
---Wainwright, Lyndon B. Amateurs on television (dancing). Ballroom Dancing Times v 5 n 1 p 24-5 O'60
BANDS
America's greatest bands of 1930's and 1940's on Lawrence Welk's "Great Dance Bands on Parade". International Musician v 59 n 4 p 53 O'60
---Brass Band Festival;Harry Mortimer on 1960. Radio Times p 4 O 13'60
---British Open Championship in Manchester;BBC notes. Radio Times p 5 S 9'60
---Royal Festival Hall, London: Ted Heath (swing), Edmundo Ros (Latin-American), Chris Barber (traditional jazz) and the Shadows (rock-type);notes. Radio Radio p 5 Mr 18'60
BARCELONA
National competition of flamenco dancers and singers;judges;winners. Dance Magazine v 34 n 6

p 82 Je'60
BARDOT, BRIGITTE, actress
Notes and wl ph. Screen Album p 41 N'60
BARIONI, DANIELE, singer
In Italian TV, May 1960. right profile photo with small son. Opera News v 25 n 1 p 4 O 8'60
BARNABY RUDGE, serial
Voysey, Michael. Notes. Radio Times p 6 S 23'60
BARRETT, CLAUDIA, 1936-, actress
Notes. por TV Guide v 8 n 36 p 26-7 S 3'60
BARRIS, MARTI, 1938-, actress
On Howdy Doody Show; notes; parents, Harry Barris and Loyce Whiteman. por TV Guide v 8 n 32 p 28-9 Jl 30'60
BARRY, GENE, 1921-, actor
Career notes; born Eugene Klass in Manhattan. por TV Guide v 8 n 21 p 17-9 My 21'60
THE BARTERED BRIDE, opera
Australia; ABV2 under Christopher Muir. Music and Dance v 51 n 1 p 27 Jl '60
BARREL, ANN. Looking at television (dance criticism). Dance Magazine 1960
BAXTER, CYNTHIA, actress
Wife of actor, Patrick O'Neal; note. TV Guide v 8 n 35 p 6 Ag 27'60
BAXTER, STANLEY, actor
London notes. Radio Times p 4 Ja 15'60
BAYNE, THE REV. STEPHEN
On "The Brains Trust", BBC. por Radio Times p 47 O 20'60
BAZIN, ANDRE (?-1958). The ontology of the photographic image. por Film Quarterly v 13 n 4 p 4-8 Summer '60
BE MY GUEST, series
Regan, Joan, BBC notes. Radio Times p 30 O 20'60
BEAIRD, BARBARA, 1949-,
Note. il TV Guide v 8 n 9 p 12 F 27'60
BEATRICE AND BENEDICT, opera
Berlioz on Shakespeare theme,

notes by Geoffrey Dunn on BBC
program. Radio Times p 6 Mr 18
'60

BEAUTY AND THE BEAST
BBC; play form by Nicholas
Stuart Gray. Radio Times p 13
D 29'60

BEAUTY CONTESTS
US TV contests. TV Guide v 8
n 35 p 11 Ag 27'60

BEHAN, BRENDAN, playwright
BBC; The Quare Fellow. Radio
Times p 29 N 24'60

BELL TELEPHONE HOUR, series
Voorhes, Donald, conductor; opinions about music on TV and
radio by a veteran. por Musical
Courier v 162 n 3 p 8 S '60

THE BELLS OF ST. MARY'S,
film
BBC notes (scene). Radio Times
p 5 D 22'60

BERNADAC, LUCIENNE
Directeur la Télévision Française: oratorio, le composer,
Marcel Delannoy et le librettiste
le poète, Gilles Durieux. Toute
la Danse n 98 p 23 D '60

BERNARD, PETER, 1888-, singer
On "beat" music; por. Radio Times p 23 O 6'60

BENNY, JACK, comedian
Ten memorable gags. por TV
Guide v 8 n 46 p 6-7 N 12'60
---With Danny Thomas and others
on BBC. il Radio Times p 44
D 15'60

BERGMAN, INGRID
Notes and signed por. Screen
Album p 9 N '60

BERLE, MILTON, 1908-
Debut on BBC; notes. Radio
Times p 4 My 13'60
---New show; interview on bow-
ling. il TV Guide v 8 n 46 p 24-7
N 12'60

BERLIN FILM FESTIVAL
10th year; BBC cover age. Radio
Times p 4 Jl 1'60

BERRY, FRANK
As compère; BBC. Punch p 738
My 25'60

BEYOND OUR KEN, series
BBC notes; folksongs, Jimmy

(Television Index)
Fraser. Radio Times p 4 Je 24'60

BILLY BUNTER OF GREYFRIARS
SCHOOL, serial
Campion, Gerald. (On his role of
Bunter in British school serial.)
il Radio Times p 25 Jl 8'60

BINGHAM, WADE, 1926-, news
photographer
Career sketch by Norman Sklarewitz. TV Guide v 8 n 16 p 10-1
Ap 16'60

BISHOP, JOEY, 1918-, comedian
Career sketch; born Bronx, NYC.
brought up in Philadelphia. por
TV Guide v 8 n 51 p 24-5 D 17'60

BITTNER, BARBARA, dancer
London; partner, Witold Gruca,
also from Poland. Ballet today
v 12 n 11 p 6 F '60

THE BLACK AND WHITE MINSTREL
SHOW, revue
Thomson, Ernest. (George Mitchell;
BBC notes.) Radio Times p 6
Mr 25'60

BLACKPOOL NIGHT, variety
Annual BBC show; notes. Radio
Times p 5 Je 17'60

BLAIR, JUNE, 1936-, actress
Notes; b. San Francisco as Mar-
garet June Blair; orphan. por TV
Guide v 8 n 49 p 24 D 3'60

BLAKE, AMANDA, 1927? actress
Career sketch; b. Buffalo, New
York as Beverly Louise Neill.
por TV Guide v 8 n 50 p 25-7
D 10'60

BLAKE, JEAN, 1937-, actress
Notes; b. Blytheville, Arkansas,
as Jean Beachman. por TV Guide
v 8 n 47 p 21 N 19'60

BLOCKER, DAN, actor
Career sketch; b. Texas. il TV
Guide v 8 n 10 p 7-8 Mr 5'60

BLUE PETER, children's serial
Blair, John Hunter, producer,
on BBC 5-10 years serial. il
Radio Times p 27 Mr 18'60

BOB JONES UNIVERSITY
Master's degree in film production; awards; notes. Jr SMPTE
v 69 n 11 p 826 N '60

BOOBS IN THE WOOD, Christmas
pantomime

(Boobs in the Wood)
BBC cast (scene). Radio Times
p 22 D 22'60
BONANZA, western
Analysis; cast. il TV Guide v 8
n 26 p 16-9 Je 25'60
---Silver-rush in Nevada, now
London series; notes. Punch
p 702 My 18'60
BOND, WARD, ?-1960, actor
Obituary of wagon master in
"Wagon Train". TV Guide v 8
n 47 p A-1-2 N 19'60
BONEHEAD, serial
Sutton, Shaun. (Crime does not
pay done lightly.) Radio Times
p 29 S 23'60
BOOKS
Actors' books; notes on autobiog-
raphical publications like "Grou-
cho and Me", "Early Havoc", "I
Kid You Not". TV Guide v 8 n 10
p 12-15 Mr 5'60
---BBC; John Slater reading a nov-
el; improvement on radio, we can
actually see the book. May we have
someone beside him to listen for
us?" Punch p 702 My 18'60
---Cinema subjects each issue,
signed reviews. Film Quarterly
1959, 1960
---Serialised reading (BBC) in 10
installments of "Night Without
End", novel by Alistair MacLean.
Radio Times p 4 My 6'60
---Three library plays for the Chi-
ldren's Hour by Bertha Lonsdale;
BBC notes. Radio Times p 26
My 27'60
BOOKSTAND, series
BBC; contemporary flavour. Ra-
dio Times p 15 O 13'60
BOONE, RICHARD, actor-director
Notes. por TV Guide v 8 n 6 p 9-
11 F 6'60
BOOTHROYD, J. B. On the air;
reviews, Great Britain TV. Punch
1960
BORROWED PASTURE, TV film
Ormond, John, producer; BBC
notes on Polish farmers in Wales.
Radio Times p 3 My 13'60
BOSTON UNIVERSITY
Composers' Forum, tenth year;

report of "live" programs,
WBUR. Musical Courier v 161
n 4 p 2 Mr '60
BOTH SIDES OF THE LAW,
series
Judge and criminal, both sides
in BBC series. Radio Times p 4
Jl 8'60
BOUE, GEORGI, singer
And José Luccioni in Offenbach's
La Grande Duchesse de Gérol-
stein, ph: Radio TV Française.
Opera v 11 n 12 p 827 D '60
BOYD, STEPHEN, actor
Notes and signed por. Screen
Album p 8 N '60
BOYLE, KATIE
Her TV jobs in the last seven
years. por Radio Times p 6
Jl 22'60
BRAND, NEVILLE
Career notes; b. Kewanee, Illi-
nois. por TV Guide v 8 n 18
p 23 Ap 30'60
BRANDO, MARLON, 1925-,
actor
Knight, Charlotte. Oldest teen-
ager. il Screen World and TV
p 25, 68 O '60
BRANDT, HERR WILLY
Interview with mayor of West
Berlin; born Ernst Willy Frahm;
notes. por Radio Times p 4
Ap 29'60
BRESSON, ROBERT, director
List of his films; review of
"Pickpocket". por Film Quart-
erly v 13 n 3 p 4-10 Spring '60
BRITISH ARMY
Fleming, Douglas. Army School
of Physical Training, Aldershot;
TV visit. Radio Times p 29
Ap 22'60
BBC
Four who will introduce evening
television; notes on Nan Winton,
Judith Chalmers, Kenneth Ken-
dall and Michael Aspel. Radio
Times p 4 O 6'60
---The new Television Centre
near Wood Lane; charts, pictures,
text. Radio Times p 6-7 Je 24'60
BROWN, PETER LYNN, 1936-,
actor

Career notes; born in New York, name deLappe. por TV Guide v 8 n 36 p 16-19 S 3'60
BRYNNER, YUL, actor
In film on refugees "Mission to No-Man's Land"; notes. Radio Times p 4 Ja 8'60
BRYSON, LYMAN
Seldes, Gilbert. (Tribute to educator who was also a pioneer in television; "Invitation to Learning".) Sat Rev p 23 D 19'60
BUDKNELL, BARRY, 1912-, engineer
Do-It-Yourself expert on BBC program; notes. por Radio Times p 6 Ja 29'60
BURNETT, CAROL, 1934-, actress
Career notes; b. San Antonio. por TV Guide v 8 n 42 p 11 O 15 '60
---Seven facial expressions, ph. TV Guide v 8 n 21 p 8-9 My 21'60
BURROUGHS, JULIAN CARR, JR.
The effectiveness of television criticism in influencing viewers' judgements of programs in an educational TV series (Ph. D. University of Michigan) Dissertation Abstracts v 20 n 12 p 4751 Je '60
BYRNES, EDD, 1933-, actor
Career notes; born NYC as Edward Breitenberger. por TV Guide v 8 n 35 p 17-9 Ag 27'60
---Notes and signed por ph. Screen Album p 77 N '60
CABLEFILM
Between Great Britain and America; 1960 progress. Jr SMPTE v 69 n 5 p 330 My '60
CAESAR, SID
With Perry Como; BBC. Radio Times p 5 N 24 '60
CALHOUN, RORY, 1921-, actor
Career notes; b. Los Angeles as Francis Timothy Durgin. por TV Guide v 8 n 7 p 13-5 F 13'60
---Notes; signed family ph. Screen Album p 79 N '60
CALIFORNIA
Let's Dance TV Show, teen-age dancers; notes. Dance Digest v 10 n 9 p 35 N '60

(Television Index)
CALL FOR ACTION, series
Real people in live situations sought instead of actors; BBC production notes. Radio Times p 11 Ag 19'60
CANADA
Film Awards, 12th annual presentations; list. Film World and AV p 237 Jl '60
---Kemp, Hugh. Canadian television drama (a survey by the National script supervisor, CBC). Players Magazine v 36 n 4 p 81-2 Ja '60
---Reports; play TV; Motion pictures. Jr SMPTE v 69 n 5 p 317, 322 My '60
---Saskatchewan; Fred Holliday on AV. Ed Screen and AV p 540, 542-6 O '60
---They Always Get Their Man, series on Mounted Police; BBC notes. il Radio Times p 3 Jl 8'60
---Winner at Educational Film Library Association, NYC; lists. Ed Screen and AV p 285 Je '60
CANASTA, CHAN, magician
BBC notes. Punch p 370 Mr 9'60
CANDID CAMERA, series
Godfrey, Arthur, as emcee vs. Allen Funt. TV Guide v 8 n 51 p A-1 D 17'60
---Review; Arthur Godfrey and Allen Funt (the inventor). TV Guide v 8 n 51 p 27 D 17'60
CANNED LAUGHTER
CBS: "honest laughter" campaign; comment. TV Guide v 8 n 9 p 2 F 27'60
CANNES
Grenier, Cynthia. Ill-starred thirteenth Festival of Cannes. il Film Quarterly v 13 n 4 p 15-19 Summer '60
CANNON, DIANE, actress
Career sketch; born Tacoma, Washington, Camille Diane Friesen. por TV Guide v 8 n 48 p 28-9 N 26'60
CAPTAIN MOONLIGHT, serial
Sycamore, Stephen, actor; espionage weekly. il Radio Times p 25 Mr 4'60

CAPUCINE, actress
Notes; b. Toulon. por Screen Album p 32 N '60
CARAVAN
Geidt, Jeremy, the Showman; notes on variety show outdoors. il Radio Times p 25 My 27'60
---Notes on westher problems making Caravan; BBC. Radio Times p 25 S 2'60
CARMICHAEL, HOAGY
Notes; his big clock in color ph. TV Guide v 8 n 32 p 28 Ag 6'60
CARSON, JEANNIE, actress
Notes. por Radio Times p 12 N 24'60
CARTER, HUGH. Ballroom dancing and television (B. B. C. and I. T. V.). Ballroom Dancing Times v 4 n 9 p 370-1 Je '60
CARTOONS
Clutch Cargo by Clark Haas. il TV Guide v 8 n 52 p 28-9 D 24'60
---Huckleberry Hound by Bill Hanna and Joe Barbera; story of present success. il TV Guide v 8 n 4 p 20-2 Ja 23'60
---Huckleberry Hound (1958) by Bill Hanna and Joe Barbera; review. TV Guide v 8 n 26 p 23 Je 25'60
---Laugh Line, series; group of actors play out ideas sent in for a funny situation; producer Michael Wynne-Willson. Radio Times p 4 Ap 29'60
---Popeye; historical sketch of the character. il TV Guide v 8 n 35 p 8-10 Ag 27'60
---Thomson, Ernest. Captain Pugwash. il Radio Times p 28 F 19'60
CARTWRIGHT, ANGELA, 1953-
Note. il TV Guide v 8 n 9 p 11 F 27'60
CASE, ALLEN, 1935-, actor
Career notes; b. Dallas. por TV Guide v 8 n 25 p 22-3 Je 18'60
CASTLE, PEGGIE, singer-actress
Career sketch; b. Appalachia, Virginia as Peggie Thomas Blair. por TV Guide v 8 n 23 p 8-9 Je 4 '60
CASTRO, FIDEL
Hall, Lee, and Wilson. Cuba's

unsponsored TV star. por TV Guide v 8 n 26 p 6-7 Je 25'60
CATTON, BRUCE. The problem of General Grant. il TV Guide v 8 n 8 p 13-4 F 20'60
CATV SYSTEMS
Lackenbruch, Davis. Community antennas in US and Canada. TV Guide v 8 n 44 p 10-11 O 29'60
CAVALLERIA RUSTICANA, opera
NBC Opera; notes. Opera News v 24 n 17 p 27-8 F 27'60
CELEBRITY TALENT SCOUTS, series
Review (CBS). TV Guide v 8 n 38 p 23 S 17'60
CENSORSHIP
Shayon, Robert Lewis. (On US investigations into TV quiz shows; Television Information Office, "the industry's new image-maker". Sat Rev p 34 D 5'59
---US; progress report; editorial. Film Quarterly v 13 n 3 p 2-3 Spring '60
CENTRAL AMERICA
New network linking US; list of countries. Jr SMPTE v 69 n 1 p 50 Ja '60
THE CHAMPAGNE LADY
Welk, Lawrence, and Telekew committee; rules of choosing. il TV Guide v 8 n 44 p 9 O 29'60
---Rainey, Sue, Fran Ervin, Gina Genardi Laurie Johnson, Diane Berry, Judy Busch, ens color ph. TV Guide v 8 n 44 p 8 O 29'60
CHAMPIONSHIP BRIDGE, series
Goren, Charles; notes. TV Guide v 8 n 1 p 15 Ja 2'60
CHAN, JACQUI, actress
In Without the Grail, play. BBC. por Radio Times p 4 S 9'60
CHAN CANASTA, TV artist
Born in Poland as Chan Mifelew, educated in Europe, now on BBC as an "experimenter" on the psychology of choice (extra-sensory perception sort of thing). Radio Times p 3 Ja 8'60
CHARGE ACCOUNT, game
The Jan Murray Show, "daytime drollery" called Charge Account; review. por TV Guide v 8 n 42

346

p 16 O 15'60

CHARMOLI, TONY
And other Hollywood choreog-
raphers; TV spectaculars. Dance
Magazine v 34 n 7 p 6 Jl '60
CHARNEY, KIMM, 1945-,
Notes; b. San Diego. Screen Al-
bum p 33 N '60
CHASING THE DRAGON, play
Morris, Colin, author; BBC no-
tes. por Radio Times p 3 Ag 12
'60
CHECKMATE, series
Ambler, Eric; suspense show;
crime prevented a new twist. TV
Guide v 8 n 47 p 23 N 19'60
---Review. TV Guide v 8 n 47 p 23
N 19'60
CHEVALIER, MAURICE, 1889-,
actor
Career notes. por TV Guide v 8
n 17 p 10-1 Ap 23'60
CHICAGO
Board of Education TV courses
for junior college level; report.
Film World and AV p 346 S '60
CHILDREN AND TELEVISION
Thomson, R. J. Television crime-
drama; its impact on children and
adolescents (review of book by
University of Melbourne press).
Telefilm v 5 n 2 p 23 S-O '60
CHILDREN 'S HOUR, series
Changes discussed. Radio Times
p 28 S 30'60
---Finlay, Winifred, tale of Had-
rian's Wall; how she got children
living near it to help with the
tale. Radio Times p 27 Jl 1'60
---The Flight of the Heron, 6-part
serial from Catherine Barr's
story; notes. Radio Times p 26
Ag 26'60
---The New Girl, a school play;
BBC notes by Irene de Selincourt.
Radio Times p 28 Ag 5'60
---Ocean Junction, film on the
Panama Canal. il Radio Times
p 27 Ag 19'60
---Potter, Margaret, second ser-
ial "Return to Hindleford"; notes.
Radio Times p 28 S 9'60
---Program on international vil-
lage for children of refugees

(Television Index)
from camps in Europe: British
Pestalozzi Village Trust. il
Radio Times p 27 Jl 15'60
---Rome; preview for Olympics.
Radio Times p 26 Ag 12'60
CHILDRENS' PROGRAMS
Comments on US TV shows for
children; Howdy Doody to Lassie.
TV Guide v 8 n 15 p 23 Ap 9'60
---Hollywood; list of recent films
for children. Variety p 7 N 30'60
---How to include moral precept.
Film World and AV p 303 Ag '60
---Junior Radio Times, a special
section of listings of articles and
pictures for the young TV viewers.
Radio Times 1960
---Miller, Peggy, to Russia and
elsewhere to procure children's
films to show in Britain; her trip.
il Radio Times p 27 Ag 19'60
---Pulse study; questions asked.
TV Age p 34-5 My 16'60
---The Splendid Spur (BBC serial
for children); notes. Punch p 402
Mr 16'60
CHINA
Interview with Chou En-Lai; BBC
por Radio Times p 47 O 27'60
CHORUSES
Let The People Sing, British
finals by hook-up; not bringing
choirs to London as before; notes.
Radio Times p 5 Je 24'60
CHRISTMAS
Carols; BBC moves to St. George's
Chapel, to St. Denys; to Stuttgart;
to Brussels. il Radio Times p 4
D 22'60
---Christmas Night With the Stars
(portfolio), compère David Nixon,
BBC. Radio Times p 13 D 22'60
---The Dean of Westminister spea-
king on "The Infant and the Man".
por Radio Times p 3 D 22'60
---NBC's The Coming of Christ,
show of art masterpieces. il TV Guid
Guide v 8 n 51 p 4-5 D 17'60
---The Nativity (Pisk), Associated-
Rediffusion triumph of word, song,
dance; camera Ian Fordyce. Ballet
Today v 12 n 12 p 8-26 Mr '60
---Opera, Golden Child by Philip

347

(Christmas)
Bezanson (1916-) on Hallmark
Hall of Fame; review. il TV
Guide v 8 n 50 p 5-7 D 10'60
---St. Nicholas by Britten over
CBS-TV; William Lewis sang
title role. Opera News v 24 n 9
p 3 Ja 2'60
---US; special programs for old
and young. TV Guide v 8 n 52
D 24'60
--- ---TV shows; notes. TV Guide
v 8 n 52 p 6-8 D 24'60
A CHRISTMAS CAROL
Drake, Charlie, as Bob Cratchit;
BBC. Radio Times p 53 D 15'60
CHRISTMAS STARTIME
Ford Motor Company; list of ar-
tists. American Music v 8 n 10
p 13 N '60
CHURCHILL, SIR WINSTON, 1874-,
statesman
BBC; list of actors in the memoirs,
26 shows. TV Guide v 8 n 48
p 17-9 N 26'60
---Winston Churchill, the Valiant
Years, ABC; planned by Jack Le
Vien; details of the show. TV
Guide v 8 n 48 p 16-19 N 26'60
CILENTO, DIANE, actress
Notes; b. Australia. Radio Times
p 4 S 30'60
CINDERELLA (ASHTON), TV
ballet
Fonteyn and the Royal Ballet on
BBC; "ballet is not suitable TV
material"(?) Punch p 598 Ap 27
'60
---Granada TV; review. Ballet To-
day v 12 n 15 p 11 Je '60
THE CINEMA TODAY, series
Buñuel, Luis; career as producer;
interview BBC. Radio Times p 4
S 16'60
---How war is now, BBC. Radio
Times p 55 N 3'60
CIRCLE THEATRE, CBS
Dramatization of 1943 plane loss
in Libyan dessert; "Lady Be Good"
to be produced by Robert Costello.
TV Guide v 8 n 5 p 6-7 Ja 30'60
CIRCUS
Bertram Mills Circus; Royal
Performance; BBC. Radio Times

p 36 D 15'60
---Billy Smart's Circus; BBC.
il Radio Times p 15 D 22'60
---BBC's mobile unit on Billy
Smart's Circus en route. Radio
Times p 5 Jl 8'60
---Cirque Napoleon Rancy from
France on BBC. Radio Times
p 33 O 27'60
---Hungarian State Circus on BBC;
notes. Radio Times p 5 S 30'60
CITIZEN JAMES, serial
BBC; adult delinquents. Radio
Times p 47 N 17'60
CLARK, AUDREY, 1930-, actress
Career notes; born Audrey Clark-
Caire, New Orleans. por TV
Guide v 8 n 51 p 20-1 D 17'60
CLARK, DICK
American Bandstand leader; born
Mount Vernon, New York. por
TV Guide v 8 n 37 p 9-11 S 10'60
CLARK-CAIRE, AUDREY, 1930-,
actress
Career sketch; b. New Orleans.
por TV Guide v 8 n 51 p 20-1
D 17'60
See also Clark, Audrey
CLASH! series
England; public discussions be-
tween national figures; subjects:
the press; a World Government;
Trade Unions and Politics. Punch
p 402 Mr 16'60
CLOSED-CIRCUIT
Florida, Hialeah; banking service
via TV and pneumatic tube for
transaction. il TV Guide v o n 38
p 27 S 17'60
---For testing, 2,000 families in
a closed-circuit; notes on technique. Film World and AV p 69
F '60
---Handleman, Stanley D. A comparative study of teacher attitudes
toward teaching by closed-circuit
television. New York University
1960 Dissertation Abstracts v 21
n 5 p 1289 1960
---Hawaii-Kai; Kaiser Industries
close-circuiting whole city; report. Variety p 25 N 30'60
---Kenney, Malcolm Edward. Closed circuit television as a supple-

ment to the general chemistry program. Journal of Chemical Education p 256-7 My '60
---Parry, Ernest B. Try closed-circuit TV for better industrial education. Industrial Arts and Vocational Education p 18-9 D '60
---Protective TV system in NYC, cinema supply firm; details for detecting and holding burglar. Jr SMPTE v 69 n 10 p 762 O '60
---San Diego State College; closed circuit lab for teachers. il Ed Screen and AV p 72-4 F '60
---Thompson, Franklin James. Use of closed circuit Television in teacher education: relationship to prefessional attitudes and interests. University Minnesota 1960 Dissertation Abstracts v 21 p 819 1960

CLOWNS
Poliakoff, Nicolai, Known as Coco; BBC (picture). Radio Times p 46 D 8'60

CLYDE, ANDY, 1892-, actor
Career notes; one of the original Keystone Cops; born in Scotland. por TV Guide v 8 n 47 p 29-30 N 19'60

COE, BARRY, 1935-, actor
Notes and por. Screen World and TV p 34 O '60

COLOMBIA
Dramatist Chekhov featured on radio and TV, the press and stage. World Premières v 11 n 9 p 7 Jl '60

THE COLONEL, play
White, Jon Manchip, playwright; BBC (scene). Radio Times p 5 D 15'60

COLUMBIA BROADCASTING COMPANY
Commission dance work on Noah: Balanchine, choreographer and Stravinsky, composer. World Music n 6 p 131 D '60
---Sponsor of Young People's Concerts, New York Philharmonic: "finest TV contribution in the serious music field". International Musician v 59 n 1

(Television Index) p 29 Jl '60

CBS TELEVISION WORKSHOP
Criticism of experimental season. TV Guide v 8 n 20 p 4 My 14'60
---McCleery, Albert, director; graduating writers and directors by live weekly show. il TV Guide v 8 n 37 p 24-6 S 10'60
---Training directors and script writers, using experienced show business people; Albert McCleery, director. il TV Guide v 8 n 37 p 24-6 S 10'60

COME DANCING, series
Ballroom; B. B. C. ; also "Silvester Dance Club", series; notes. Ballroom Dancing Times v 4 n 7 p 269 Ap '60
---BBC Inter-Regional; notes. Radio Times p 5 Ap 15'60
---Silvester, Victor, on B. B. C. ; no star featured. Ballroom Dancing Times v 4 n 6 p 241 Mr '60

COMEDIANS
Morecambe and Wise on BBC; comment. Punch p 402 Mr 16'60
---Notes on clowns, on fully men; Danny Kaye, George Burns, Jack Benny and others. Dance Digest v 10 n 10 p 12-4 D '60

COMMERCIALS
Broadcast Advertisers Reports, Inc. (Darby, Pa.); the work done in monitoring 225 stations in America. TV Guide v 8 n 4 p 26-7 Ja 23'60
---Dichter, Er nest. The TV commercial is a pause; steps in the perceptive process. Telefilm v 9 n XI-B p 10-1 Commercials '60 issue
---Editorial: timing not number of commercials a bore. TV Guide v 8 n 33 Ag 13'60
---Get your Brand X here, folks (a take-off on the usual commercial). TV Guide v 8 n 13 p 13 Mr 26'60
---Kintner, Earl W. Art or fraud? (visual devices if no deception). por TV Age p 27-29 Ap 18'60
---McMahan, Harry Wayne. TV

(Commercials)
Tape Commercial (a how-to-do-it book, reviewed). PIM v 37 n 2 p 45 N '60
---NYC festival of best commercials of the last ten years under Wallace A. Ross; comment. TV Guide v 8 n 16 p 3 Ap 16'60
---Snyder, Kenneth. Thought starters on TV commercial creativity (suggestions given at First American TV Commercials Festival and Forum). Telefilm v 9 n XI-B p 7, 22 Commercials '60 issue
---Statistics US: yearly cost to viewer 35 hrs week viewing; cost to sponsor 10 minutes per hour advertising. TV Guide v 8 n 49 p 2 D 3'60
---TV Code of the National Association of Broadcasters; explanation, examples. TV Guide v 8 n 51 p 14-6 D 17'60
---Television Code, voluntary however, adopted 1952, National Association of Broadcasters; details. TV Guide v 8 n 51 p 14-16 D 17'60
---Timing; ABC's 40-second system; comment. TV Guide v 8 n 33 p 2 Ag 13'60
---Toronto, Canada, Video Print Recorder: due to revolutionize making TV commercials. il Telefilm p 3-6 Jl-Ag '60
COMMUNITY ANTENNA TELEVISION SERVICE
US; three million viewers use CATV, paying two to six dollars per month; notes. TV Guide v 8 n 44 p 10-11 O 29'60
COMO, PERRY, 1912-,
English visit; notes. il Radio Times p 5 Ap 29'60
---In Covent Garden street market, ph: London. Ballet Today v 12 n 15 p 17 Je '60
COMPETITIONS
Beauty; BBC's Miss World. il Radio Times p 31 N 3'60
---Britain; personality contest for telephone girls "Miss Interflora-G. P. O. "; judges, rules and portfolio. Radio Times p 3 Je 10'60
---BBC's Home-maker Competition; notes. Radio Times p 46

O 27'60
---Get Ahead, a News Chronicle contest, 8 heats and a final on BB BBC; how to develop an existing business or create a brand new one; rules. Radio Times p 2 F 12'60
---MacPherson, Robert B. Picking Miss America (rules). TV Guide v 8 n 37 p 5-7 S 10'60
---Musico-dramatic work for television, Bilthoven, Holland, competition notes. World of Music n 5 p 118 O '60
---Notes on games and quiz show: What's My Line; The Price is Right, To Tell the Truth and others. TV Guide v 8 n 40 p 23 O 1'60
---Radio panel versus TV panel on BBC. Radio Times p 5 Jl 15 '60
---Reviews of "Mrs. America", won by Rosemary Murphy, "Miss Universe" (CBS) won by Linda Bement of Utah. TV Guide v 8 n 35 p 11 Ag 27'60
---What Do You Know? eight-year-old quiz on BBC. Radio Times p 5 Jl 8'60
CONNELL, JOHN, actor
Notes. por TV Guide v 8 n 9 p 15 F 27'60
CONNELLY, PEGGY, comedienne
Career notes; born Shreveport, raised in Texas. por TV Guide v 8 n 42 p 24-6 O 15'60
CONNOR, WHITFIELD, actor
Notes; b. Ireland. por TV Guide v 8 n 9 p 15 F 27'60
CONNORS, CHUCK, 1922-, actor
Notes; b. Brooklyn. TV Guide v 8 n 11 p 21-2 Mr 12'60
CONNORS, MIKE, actor
Notes on "Tightrope" series; Connors real name Krekor Ohanian; b. Fresno, California. TV Guide v 8 n 11 p 12-4 Mr 12'60
THE CONQUERING HERO, play
BBC revival of Allan Monkhouse drama of 1924; scene. Radio Times p 3 F 26'60
CONRAD, BOB, 1935-, actor
Notes and hl ph. Screen World and TV p 35 O '60

---Notes and wl ph. Screen Album p 62 N '60
CONRIED, HANS, actor
Interview; b. Baltimore; friend of Paar. por TV Guide v 8 n 17 p 28-9 Ap 23'60
CONTINENTAL CLASSROOM
Notes. Film World and AV p 205 My '60
CONWAY, RUSS, singer
BBC popular music series; Geoff Love and orchestra with Conway and others. por Radio Times p 4 F 5'60
CORRI, ADRIENNE, actress
Notes on Don't Do It, Dempsey series, BBC. por Radio Times p 4 Ap 15'60
COSMETTO ARTIST MANAGEMENT
in interview: "TV in its present state is neither a help nor a hinderance to the concert business. It merely tends to lower the taste of those people who have bad taste". Musical Courier v 162 n 1 p 18 Jl '60
COSTA, SAM, disc jockey
BBC's Juke Box Jury notes; his "Record Rendevous". por Radio Times p 4 Mr 11'60
COSTUME
Loper, Don, designer; once a dancer, partnering June Havoc. Dance Digest v 10 n 10 p 29 D'60
---Squeg from Outer Space, a character in Anthony Hopkin's operetta, "Hands Across the Sky", Ap ph: BBC-TV. Opera v 11 n 4 p 298 Ap '60
COTTEN, JOSEPH
Shown surrounded by his collection of commedia dell'arte figurines, ph. TV Guide v 8 n 24 Je 11'60
COUNTRY QUESTIONS, series
To go on TV; notes. Radio Times p 4 Jl 22'60
THE COWBOY LEGEND, TV film
Real life of cowboy 1960; BBC. Radio Times p 26 My 20'60
CRACKERJACK, series
Content of new children's series: quiz, games, etc. Radio Times

(Television Index)
p 31 S 23'60
CRAIG, COL. JOHN D. 1903-,
Career sketch; Ohio-born; world traveled; ABC series "Expedition" notes. por TV Guide v 8 n 52 p 12-5 D 24'60
CRIME
"Maigret" series on BBC. Radio Times p 21 N 24'60
---Simenon's Maigret, starring Rupert Davies; BBC notes. il Radio Times p 20 O 27'60
---Six programs on crime in Britain; Derek Holroyde on how made. Radio Times p 2 Jl 22'60
---The Verdict of the Court, series on BBC; notes. Radio Times p 4 S 23'60
CRITICISM
Advertising the Rose Adagio as "The Sleeping Princess Ballet" (Well!); notes on the dancing; Bell Telephone Hour. Dance News v 37 n 3 p 12 N '60
---Britain; quoted opinion on commercials there, of violence on the screen. TV Guide v 8 n 20 p 3 My 14'60
---Davenport, William. English as she is spoke on TV. TV Guide v 8 n 27 p 10-1 Jl 2'60
---Davison, W. P. On the effects of communication. Public Opinion Quarterly p 343-60 Fall 1959
---Dickinson, Peter. (TV stretches the emotions; where are stretch-the-mind programs?) Punch p 176 Ja 27'60
---Diefenbach, Robert C. The power of TV in this campaign (summary of poll of US Congress members). TV Guide v 8 n 38 p 9-11 S 17'60
---Editorial on critics; on basis of criticism; "Tall Man" as example. TV Guide v 8 n 44 p 2 O 29'60
---Editorial: TV slashing old movies; plea to run in entirety. TV Guide v 8 n 45 p 3 N 5'60
---Ergas, Morris. (Comments on harm done by Hollywood's "popular junk"; his finances improved when he stopped making the

(Criticism)
allegedly popular film.) Variety p 5 D 14'60
---Foreign TV reviews. Variety
1960
---Friendly, Fred W. Television
can open America's eyes (a
window on reality). TV Guide
v 8 n 50 p 5-7 D 10'60
---Green, Charles, of Consoli-
dated Concerts; TV as an ob-
stacle to prosperity for the
manager is negligible; other
factors listed. Musical Courier
v 162 n 1 p 15 Jl'60
---Helffrich, Stockton. Television
from the inside;II. Don't sell
the viewer short. TV Guide v 8
n 44 p 4-7 O 29'60
---Hollywood not lessening "sex
and violence" in spite of criticism. TV Guide v 8 n 36 p 2
S 3'60
---Hutchins, Robert M. The gigantic task ahead (bettering our
TV fare). TV Guide v 8 n 20
p 6-7 My 14'60
---"Inside TV", a program of
opening mailed complaints and
replying, CBS notes. TV Guide
v 8 n 43 p 12-4 O 22'60
---Jakes, Frank Henry, Jr. A
study of standards imposed by
four leading TV critics with
respect to live television drama
(Ph. D. thesis, Ohio State University, 1960). Dissertation
Abstracts v 21 n 4 p 991 O'60
---Kaye, Danny. How does tele-
vision affect our children?
TV Guide v 8 n 13 p 7-9 Mr
26'60
---Kennedy, John F. (Address
on broadcasting March 1958
at the Second Conference in
Public Service Programming,
held at Westinghouse.) por
Telefilm v 4 n 10 p 12, 27 Ap'60
---List of 100 fine TV shows
on US networks this season,
September through May. TV
Guide v 8 n 23 p 5-7 Je 4'60
---Mayer, Martin. How good is
TV at its best? Part II. More

than plenty of drama. Harper's
p 85-90 S'60
---National Council of Churches on
FCC and TV industry; law not ob-
scure;weaknesses noted. Film World
and AV p 30 Ja'60
---Questions coming out of US government inquiry into content of
US television fare. TV Guide v 8
n 4 p 3 Ja 23'60
---Ratings; opinions quoted; Senate
investigating committee; electronic
gadgets in 1050 homes to measure
112, 000, 000 viewers? TV Guide
v 8 n 5 p 9-11 Ja 30'60
--Robinson, Hubbell. You, the public,
are to blame. TV Guide v 8 n 48
p 14-6 N 26'60
---Schwartz, Alvin. (On the "message"
film as offset to guilt feeling of
"wasting" time). Variety p 3 D 21
'60
---Schramm, Dr. Wilbur. What does
your child bring to television?
(Encourage them to write viewers'
letters and to choose). TV Guide
v 8 n 19 p 5-7 My 7'60
---Serling, Rod. Why is TV the
whipping boy? por TV Guide v 8
n 25 p 10-1 Je 18'60
---Television making more demand-
ing audience for other entertainment.
TV Guide v 8 n 35 p 2 Ag 27'60
---Television vunerable because it
uses a public facility, the radio
spectrum; its evils are those already developed in other communication media; an editorial. TV Guide
v 8 n 23 p 4 Je 4'60
---Turton, Henry. (On detective TV
plays.) Punch p 434 Mr 23'60
---Unnecessary violence; editorial
on public's disgust at "assorted
murder gimmicks that provide
vicarious kicks to a few morons".
TV Guide v 8 n 5 p 5 Ja 30'60
---US; broadcasters instituting
many salutary changes (list given)
as result of public opinion; now
how about taste? TV Guide v 8 n 10
p 2 Mr 5'60
--- ---less violence in films of the
future;FCC. TV Guide v 8 n 51
D 17'60

--- ---panel on films, distribution, criticism, audiences. Film
Quarterly v 13 n 4 p 19-34 Summer'60
--- ---shows: tracing their changes
to keep up with America's trends
and to freshen established groups.
il TV Guide v 8 n 12 p 5-7 Mr
19'60
---violence and sex; any difference
after all the protesting? TV Guide
v 8 n 36 p 3 S 3'60
---Viewer Service to forward
letters to correct officials of
TV shows, Box 800 Radnor, Pa.
TV Guide v 8 n 21 p 4 My 21'60
---Violence;Dr. Frederic Wertham on The Untouchables, crime
series; "conditioned to accept
violence"; explanation of the conditioning. TV Guide v 8 n 43
p 6-9 O 22'60
--- ---editorial on lessening of
violence;economic sanctions
show up. TV Guide v 8 n 51 p 2
D 17'60
---Voice of slick style not help-
ful to educational films;notes.
Film World and AV p 352 S'60
---Wainwright, Lyndon B. Tele-
viewing (comparing criticism
of a television dance program
already given with comments
on a play or a film--what is
the value?) Ballroom Dancing
Times v 5 n 2 p 76 N'60
CROESO, series
Welsh choirs, 7-weeks Sunday
afternoons; BBC notes. Radio
Times p 4 F 12'60
CROSBY, BING. My show. il
Radio Times p 39 N 3'60
---BBC notes. il Radio Times
p 37 N 24'60
---And Perry Como, hl ph. TV
Guide v 8 n 9 p 7 F 27'60
CROWLEY, PAT, actress
Career notes;b. Olyphant, Penn-
sylvania;husband a Los Angeles
attorney, Gregory Hookstratten.
por TV Guide v 8 n 5 p 24-6
Ja 30'60
CUMMINGS, BOB, 1911-, actor
The Aerocar, small auto with

(Television Index)
wings; notes. il TV Guide v 8 n 43
p 26-7 O 22'60
---Interview on diet. por TV Guide
v 8 n 12 p 13-5 Mr 19'60
CUMMINGS, SUSAN, actress
Career notes; born Suzanne Gerda
TaFel in Alsace-Lorraine. il
TV Guide v 8 n 7 p 24-6 F 13'60
CURTIS, TONY, 1926-, actor
Johnson, Bob. (Interview.) il TV
Guide v 8 n 13 p 17-9 Mr 26'60
CZECHOSLOVAKIA
Pesek dans Pseudolus, Plaute,
AP ph: 1960. World Theatre v 9
n 4 p 339 Winter'60

D

DAHLBERG, REV. EDWIN T.   Television as I see it: A power for
good or evil. TV Guide v 8 n 6
p 17-9 F 6'60
DALTON, ABBY, actress
Career notes;from Glendale, Cal-
ifornia, Marlene Wasden; Hen-
nesey show star. il TV Guide v 8
n 48 p 9-11 N 26'60
D'ALTON, HUGH, mandolinist
Notes; BBC's London Lights. Radio
Times p 4 F 26'60
DALY, JOHN CHARLES
Career sketch;born Johannesburg,
Boston schooling; ABC news man.
por TV Guide v 8 n 30 p 8-11 Jl
23'60
---Panel moderator, news expert;
notes. por TV Guide v 8 n 30
p 8-10 Jl 23'60
DAMON, MARK, actor
Notes and por. Screen World and
TV p 35 O'60
DANA, BILL, 1925-, comedian
Career notes;b. Quincy, Massa-
chusetts. por TV Guide v 8 n 35
p 24-6 Ag 27'60
DANCE
Alwin Nikolais Dance Company
on Canadian Broadcasting;pro-
gram notes. Dance News v 37
n 3 p 4 N'60
---Article by D. N. S. Russell on
dance in television. Musical America D'60

(Dance)

---Bedford, Paul. (On not re-
peating on television a good
dance routine but instead of
rushing into a new and mediocre
one.) Dancing Times v 50 n 594
p 311 Mr'60
---Bob Hope Show: list of dancers. Dance Magazine v 34 n 4
p 79 Ap'60
---BBC annual dance competition
which includes: Modern (waltz,
Foxtrot, Quickstep); Latin-American (Cha Cha Cha, Samba,
Paso Doble); Old Time (Fylde
Waltz). Ballroom Dancing Times
v 4 n 10 p 404 Jl'60
---Czinner, Dr. Paul, making in
London a film of Margot Fonteyn;
notes on his camera placement;
editing the film. Ballet Today
v 12 n 11 p 6 F'60
---Kidd, Michael, teaching Hugh
O'Brien his dances in "Destry
Rides Again". il TV Guide v 8
n 2 p 20-1 Ja 9'60
---Moore, Jack, Modern dancer;
career notes; b. Indiana. il
Dance Magazine v 34 n 8 p 52
Ag'60
---NBC-TV Ford Startime: list
under Hermes Pan. Dance
Magazine v 34 n 4 p 79 Ap'60
---Nervi Festival; notes on TV;
criticism by Guido Piamonte.
LaS n 129-130 p 61 Ag-S'60
---Paris Mireille(Briansky) as
trainer of children. il Dancing
Times v 50 n 595 p 373 Ap'60
---Teaching dance with televis-
ion as a tool;interview with
Rudy Bretz. Impulse p 51-53
1960
---Television Dancing Club,
Victor Silvester notes. Radio
Times p 20 D 8'60
DANCE BANDS
Memories For You, series;
Victor Silvester relieved by
Phil Tate's band; BBC. Radio
Times p 4 Jl 29'60
DARIEN, JAMES, actor
Color portrait   signed, ph.
Screen Album back cover N'60

DARIN, BOBBIE, 1936-
Christy, George. (On the Bronx
home, his mother's devotion, Polly
Cassotto). Movie Life p 42-3, 68-9
D'60
---Notes; signed ph. Screen Album
p 58 N'60
THE DARK MAN
BBC; playwright, N. J. Crisp (one
scene shown). Radio Times p 46
D 1'60
DARREN, JAMES, actor
Notes and a signed portrait ph.
Screen Album p 10 N'60
DAVIES, RUPERT, actor
Lucas and the Inspector, Maigret
series. Radio Times p 23 D 29'60
DAVIS, GAIL, 1925-, actress
Career notes; born Little Rock,
Arkansas, as Betty Jeanne Gray-
son; Annie Oakley role. TV Guide
v 8 n 43 p 10-1 O 22'60
DAVY, GLORIA, singer
Beethoven's Ninth Symphony from
United Nations by world-wide radio
and TV; Eugene Ormandy, conduc-
ting. il Opera News v 25 n 8 p 4
D 31'60
DAY, DORIS
Notes and signed portrait ph.
Screen Album p 61 N'60
DAYDÉ, LIANE
Avec Michel Renault; Los Ange-
les. il Toute la Danse n 89 p 22
Ja'60
DEAFNESS
Summary of TV plays available
to the deaf, London's National In-
stitute for the Deaf. Radio Times
p 5 Ja 15'60
DEAN, ISABEL, actress
Notes and portrait; in BBC's " A
Life of Bliss". Radio Times p 5
F 5'60
DEATH of a GHOST, serial
New BBC drama series by Mar-
gery Allingham (one scene). Radio
Times p 3 Je 24'60
DEATH VALLEY DAYS
Woodman, Ruth, creator; her his-
tory of the show. il TV Guide v 8
n 46 p 8-10 N 12'60
DEBATES
Turton, Henry. (On a series,

"Clash", discussions on un-
ions, world government, the
press, etc.) Punch p 402 Mr 16
'60
DÉCOR
Scenery Block of the Television
Centre, BBC notes. il Radio
Times p 8 O 20'60
---Lass, Darrell. Design for Cin-
derella's kitchen, Granada TV
production. Ballet Today v 12
n 15 p 11 Je'60
DEE, SANDRA, actress
Several phs. Screen Album
p 70-1 and back cover N'60
DEMONGEOT, MYLENE, 1936-,
actress
Notes; b. Nice. por Radio Times
p 4 Je 17'60
DENCH, JUDI, 1935-, actress
In An Age of Kings, series. por
Radio Times p 4 Jl 15'60
DENNING, RICHARD, actor
Halliday, Brett. The real Mi-
chael Shayne; Denning's role in
TV series. por TV Guide v 8
n 41 p 28-30 O 8'60
DENNIS the MENACE, cartoon
Review, CBS. TV Guide v 8
n 8 p 22 F 20'60
DENVER, BILL, 1935-, actor
Career sketch; NYC-Denver
Jesuit-educated actor. il TV
Guide v 8 n 8 p 8-10 F 20'60
DERBY DAY GRANDSTAND
On both TV and radio, BBC. il
Radio Times p 4 My 27'60
DESERET, opera
NBC-TV Opera Company; Leo-
nard Kastle, the composer; the
cast. American Music v 8
n 9 p 14 O'60
DESERT ISLAND DISCS, series
BBC 500th edition; Sir Alec
Guinness. Radio Times p 5
Je 24'60
D'ESTI, ROBERTA, actress
Career notes; b. London. Radio
Times p 4 Ag 26'60
DETECTIVE PLAYS
BBC; Raymond Chandler; com-
ments. Punch p 272 F 17'60
DIAGNOSIS: UNKNOWN
O'Neal, Patrick;career notes.

(Television Index)
por TV Guide v 8 n 35 p 4-7 Ag
27'60
---Review (CBS). TV Guide v 8
n 33 p 27 Ag 13'60
DISNEY, WALT
ABC's Walt Disney Presents, a
series, now to run "Daniel Boone"
(Dewey Martin); notes on his bus-
iness. TV Guide v 8 n 51 p 9-11
D 17'60
---Interview on "Daniel Boone".
TV Guide v 8 n 51 p 9-11 D 17'60
DIVING
BBC first sub-aquatic broadcast;
Devon coast, Johnny Morris notes.
Radio Times p 4 Je 10'60
DIXON and FAMILY, serial
BBC notes. il Radio Times p 5
D 15'60
DIXON of DOCK GREEN
Willis, Ted. Dixon in Paris. Radio
Times p 8 O 13'60
DO IT YOURSELF, series
Dividing a room, carpentry by
David Bucknell on BBC. Radio
Times p 38 N 10'60
DOBIE GILLIS, series
Shulman, Max, and Rod Amateau,
creators; Dwayne Hickman as
Gillis. por TV Guide v 8 n 42
p 22-4 O 15'60
DR. BRADLEY REMEMBERS, play
Young, Francis Brett; his 1937
play revived on BBC; notes. Radio
Times p 7 F 26'60
DR. DOOLITTLE, serial
Children's Hour serial, The Story
of Dr. Doolittle; notes. Radio Times
p 28 Ap 29'60
DOCTOR IN THE HOUSE, play
Willis, Ted. Richard Gordon's
novel on TV (BBC). Radio Times
p 3 Je 3'60
DOCUMENTARIES
Awards by Academy of Motion
Picture Arts and Sciences:list.
Film World and AV p 101 Mr'60
---British trains; BBC. Radio
Times p 55 N 17'60
---CBS Reports; interpretative
journalism; reviews. TV Guide
v 8 n 5 p 23 Ja 30'60
---The Lawyers on BBC; legal

(Documentaries)
profession shown. Radio Times
p 46 N 17'60
---The Road to Carey Street;
BBC on bankruptcy. Radio Times
p 49 N 3'60
---This Is the BBC. il Radio Times
es p 31 D 22'60
---The U2 Story;BBC. Radio Times
es p 22 D 29'60
DODD, KEN, 1930-, comedien
BBC notes;The Ken Dodd Show.
Radio Times p 4 D 8'60
---Notes. Radio Times p 4 Mr
25'60
---Notes;BBC. il Radio Times
p 5 N 10'60
DOLLS
Children's Hour; stories on
dolls read aloud by Hilda Car-
son. Radio Times p 27 Je 10 60
DONAHUE, ELINOR, 1938-,
actress
In Father Knows Best, series, as
Betty Anderson. il TV Guide v 8
n 2 p 17-9 Ja 9'60
DONEGAN, ANTHONY, 1932-,
actor
BBC notes. Radio Times p 4
Ag 5'60
DORAN, ANN, actress
Notes. por TV Guide v 8 n 48
p 12-3 N 26 60
---And her collection of ceramic
owls, ph. TV Guide v 8 n 48 p 12
N 26 60
DORS, DIANA, actress
Criticism;TV debut, ITV. Punch
p 702 My 18 60
DOUGLAS, JACK, gag writer
Notes; b. Staten Island. por TV
Guide v 8 n 11 p 6-7 Mr 12'60
DRAGON, CARMEN, conductor
Hollywood leader in BBC debut.
Radio Times p 4 Je 10'60
DRAKE, CHARLIE, actor
BBC series;type of his come-
dies. il Radio Times p 6 Jl 1'60
---In new series (6), The Take-
Over Bid. il Radio Times p 54
N 17'60
DRAMA
Barry, Michael. Twenty first-
nights (program of BBC drama).

il Radio Times p 3 S 23'60
---BBC Television Drama series;
Hugh Walpole s The Herries
Chronicle; notes. Radio Times p 3
Je 24 60
---BBC-TV drama series; plays
written 1900 to date; Galworthy's
Justice, notes. Radio Times p 2
Ja 3'60
---Comedy-thriller series, Hotel
Imperial (AR); review. Punch
p 208 F 3'60
---Hawes, William Kenneth, Jr.
A history of anthology television
drama through 1958 (Ph. D., Uni-
versity of Michigan) Dissertation
Abstracts v 20 n 13 p 175 '59-60
---Jakes, Frank Henry, Jr. A
study of standards imposed by
four leading television critics
with respect to live television
drama. The Ohio State University 1960. Dissertation Abstracts
v 21 n 4 p 991 1960
---MacNiece, Louis. Another Part
of the Se; how he wrote this play.
por Radio Times p 2 S 2'60
---Marshall, Norman. Are stage
plays suitable for TV? World
Theatre v 9 n 4 p 301.-12 Winter
'60
---Mayer, Martin. How good is
TV at its best? Part II. More
than plenty of drama. Harper s
p 85-90 S 60
---Notes, literary and performance,
each issue. Radio Times 1960
---Preview fall 1960. TV Guide
v 8 n 39 p 20 S 24'60
---Situation comedy, general criticism and "Don t Do It, Dempsey" BBC series; Tell It To The
Marines. Punch p 565 Ap 20'60
---Step by step, Roger Iglésis
gives the staging of a TV play;
order of business, time allow-
ances, producer s rights. World
Theatre v 9 n 4 p 325-336 Winter
'60
---Sturcken, Francis William. An
historical analysis of live network
television drama from 1938 to
1958 (Ph. D. thesis, University
of Minnesota, 1960). Dissertation

Abstracts p 269 Jl '60
---Theatre on television, the
theme of whole issue. World The-
atre v 9 n 4 Winter '60
THE DRUID CIRCLE, play
BBC; John Van Druten, por Radio
Times p 4 D 1'60
DRY ROT, play
BBC farce; cast. Radio Times
p 5 N 24'60
DUBBING
From English into Spanish; arti-
cle by Pedro A. Sanjuan. il Jr
SMPTE v 69 n 5 p 346-7 My '60
DUFFY TAKES A WALK
Scott, Harold,as Duffy; BBC. il
Radio Times p 5 N 24'60
DUGGAN, ANDREW, 1923-, actor
Career notes; grew up in Hous-
ton. por TV Guide v 8 n 16 p 22-
3 Ap 16'60
DUKE OF BEDFORD
In Perry Como Comes to London
(BBC); "I expect to watch his
television career with increasing
chagrin". Punch p 666 My 11'60
DU MONT TELEVISION NETWORK
Hess, Gary Newton. An historical
study of the Du Mont Television
Network (Ph. D. thesis, North-
western University, 1960). Dis-
sertation Abstracts v 21 p 1663
D '60
DUNCAN, ANN, 1925-, stunt woman
Career notes. il TV Guide v 8
n 12 p 28-9 Mr 19'60
DURSLAG, MELVIN. The Giants
at Candlestick Park, San Fran-
cisco. TV Guide v 8 n 32 p 14-6
Ag 6'60

E

AN EAGLE ON THE THATCH,
US AIR FORCE
England's base for US 20th Tac-
ticalFighter Wing; notes on BBC
program. Radio Times p 2 My 6
'60
EASTMAN KODAK COMPANY
A-V Center; notes. il Film Wor-
ld and AV p 426 N '60
EDITING FILM
Wiegand, John Lee. Cutting

(Television Index)
feature films for television (techniques). Jr SMPTE v 69 n 7
p 465-9 Jl '60
EDUCATION
Background facts for viewing
coming BBC programs; new section, "Learn while you Listen
and Look". Radio Times 1960
---Biology course in color available by American Institute of
Biological Sciences. Film World
and AV p 117 Mr '60
---BBC; painting by subscription
the reproduction arriving before
the lecture; The Nature of Drawing, similarseries; Russian for
Beginners, Network Three. Punch p 142 Ja 20'60
---Burger, Elizabeth. The use of
television for in-service teacher
training. University of Virginia
1960 Dissertation Abstracts v 21
n 8 p 2204 1960
---Denver; US airmen given 3
hours daily TV fare; report. il
Film World and AV p 337 S '60
---Earphones in classroom;
special groups work simultaneously
around film projectors. Ed Screen
and AV p 489 S '60
---Eshelman, Dr. Walter W. as
President of National Education
Association on influence of US
television on US youth; more cultural fare meeded. TV Guide v 8
n 3 p 3 Ja 16'60
---Hancock, Alan. King's Hill
Modern (example of Britain's new
secondary schools). Radio Times
p 8 Ag 12'60
---Junior Radio Times, a special
section of pictures and articles to
appeal to the younger viewers;
listings of TV and radio shows also. Radio Times 1960
---Language courses in American
colleges (26) to provide seldom
taught languages; lists and places.
Film World and AV p 118 Mr '60
---Stratovision; Midwest Council
on Airborne Television Instruction;
list; plan. Film World and AV
p 348 S '60

357

(Education)
Syracuse University setting up
the Newhouse Communications
Center; details. Film World
and AV p 70 F '60
---Television Teaching Aid, an
educational service provided
free by the Prudential Insurance
Company of America: analysis
of programs to be presented
with background information,
list of films and reading to carry
further the theme.
---US Army Signal School; use of
TV; report. Film World and AV
p 386-7 O '60
---US; film and TV study program
for US schools; list of leaders;
Britannica Films and National
Council of Teachers of English;
notes. Film Quarterly v 13 n 4
p 64 Summer '60
---US; National Education Association 13-week series" The
School Story". TV Guide v 8
n 15 p 15-6 Ap 9'60
---Wasserman, Burton. Pathways
to learning in art through tele-
vision. por New York State Ed-
ucation p 12-3 Je '60
EDUCATIONAL TV
Alabama; George W. Moorman,
Chief of Production; notes on
Alabama ETV Network. Players
Magazine v 36 n 5 p 101 F '60
---Britain; "schools television";
notes on science series, begun
under Prof. P. B. Medwar; Twe-
ntieth Century Theatre notes.
Radio Times p 4 Ja 15'60
BBC's Stories in Pictures; exam-
ple J. W. Taylor demonstrating
his art in humorous pictures and
cartoons; Peter Kneebone also.
Punch p 466 Mr 30'60
---California; notes on firms in-
stalling in schools of Anaheim.
Jr SMPTE v 69 n 10 p 762 O '60
---Edelman, Robert S. Southern
Indiana; description of 25 minute
telecasts. Players Magazine
v 36 n 7 p 161-2 Ap '60
---Fund for the Advancement of
Education; course in Humanites

to be set up for high schools;
$400,000 spent; support with-
drawn"; films for rent. Saturday
Rev p 42 N 14'59
---Handleman, Stanley D. A comparative study of teacher attitudes toward teaching by closed-circuit
television (Ph. D. New York University, 1960). Dissertation Abstracts
p 1289 N '60
---Haney, John, Benjamin. A study
of public attitudes toward tax-sup-
port for educational television activities in the Detroit Metropolitan
area (Ph. D. thesis, University of
Michigan, 1960). Dissertation Abstracts v 22 n 12 p 4753 Je '60
---Kelley, Gaylen B. A study of
teachers' attitudes toward audio
visual materials. il Ed Screen
and AV p 119-121 Mr '60
---New programs; funds; plans. TV
Digest 1960
---New York State; project in music
for grades 3-4, grades 5-6; notes.
Music Educators Journal v 46 n 5
p 2 Ap-My '60
---NY State Regents and Metropolitan Opera Guild: 5-program opera series to 5th and 6th grade children; notes. Opera News v 24 n 17
p 1 F 27'60
---Ohio, Marietta; speech fundamentals by TV. Players Magazine v 36
n 6 p 123 Mr '60
---Packer, Roddy Earle. An analysis of the degree of integration of
existing educational television stations with their particular communities (Ph. D. thesis, University of
Minnesota, 1960). Dissertation Abstracts p 992 O '60
---Purdue University, Indiana; 7-
million dollar RV experiment;
spectrum conservation one angle.
Jr SMPTE v 69 n 1 p 50 Ja '60
---Reports, plans, equipment each
issue. Film World and AV 1960
---Seldes, Gilbert. (Several references.) Saturday Review of
Literature 1959-1960
---US report on use in public schools
1958-59, Fund for the Advancement
of Education; free, 477 Madison,NYC.

---US; survey of the role of music in educational TV. Musical Courier v 161 n 4 p 2 Mr '60
---Zaitz, Anthony William. The history of educational television 1932-1958 (Ph. D. thesis, University of Wisconsim, 1960). Dissertation Abstracts p 271 Jl '60
EDWARDS, BLAKE, producer
Notes. TV Guide v 8 n 28 p 3 Jl 16'60
---Notes on "Peter Gunn" and "Mr. Lucky". il TV Guide v 8 n 7 p 17-9 F 13'60
EDWARDS, RALPH
Notes on This Is Your Life. TV Guide v 8 n 1 p 10-11 Ja 2'60
EGLEVSKY, ANDRÉ, dancer
And Melissa Hayden on Bell Telephone Hour. Dance News v 37 n 1 p 13 S '60
EISENHOWER, PRESIDENT. (An appeal for United Fund.) por TV Guide v 8 n 40 p 7 O 1'60
EISLEY, ANTHONY, 1925-, actor
Career notes; b. Philadelphia. TV Guide v 8 n 14 p 15 Ap 2'60
THE ELDER STATESMAN, play
BBC's Twentieth Century Theatre; T. S. Eliot; notes (scene). Radio Times p 3 My 20'60
ELLIOTT, SUMNER LOCKE. The cracked lens (Hopper). Harper's p 78, 81 D'60
ELWELL see EWELL
EMMA, serial
Tilsey, Vincent, on adapting Austen's Emma for BBC. Radio Times p 3 F 19'60
THE ENCHANTED APRIL, serial
On BBC. Radio Times p 4 S 23 '60
AN ENGLISH SUMMER, play
The Battle of Britain, revived on BBC. Radio Times p 5 S 16'60
EQUIPMENT
Chicago exhibitors, a list; National Audio Visual Association meeting. Film World and AV p 248, 250, 254-6 Jl '60
---Florman, Arthur. (Views on leasing instead of buying equipment; analysis of both in money.) Film World and AV p 196 My '60

(Television Index)
---Lachenbruch, David. (Remote control devices to change programs for viewers; how they work.) TV Guide v 8 n 42 p 14-5 O 15'60
---Lefkowitz, Louis J. Beware of the TV repair rackets. TV Guide v 8 n 30 p 22-3 Jl 23'60
---Mitchell, Horace. TV Repairman; skit on his troubles. TV Guide v 8 n 32 p 6-7 Ag 6'60
---Tanney, J. A. (For leasing rather than buying AV equipment; See rebuttal by Florman in May issue.) Film World and AV p 106 My '60
EUGENE ONEGIN, opera film
Bolshoi Theatre on BBC; notes. Radio Times p 4 Ap 29'60
EUROPE
Editorial; since we send our TV shows abroad, why not tape theirs so America can see European fare as it is consumed there? TV Guide v 8 n 12 p 2 Mr 19'60
---Progress reports by country. Jr SMPTE v 69 n 5 p 318-20 My '60
EUROVISION
Amsterdam saw The Sleeping Beauty (Dale) with Fonteyn and Swan Lake, the Amsterdam Ballet. Ballet Today v 12 n 13 p 23 Ap '60
EUROVISION SONG CONTEST 1960
British heats; Eric Robinson; producer Harry Carlisle on value of the contest; portfolio of contestants at Festival Hall. Radio Times p 3 Ja 22'60
---Sloan, Tom, BBC report (12 portraits); how a contest is mounted. Radio Times p 3 Mr 15'60
EVANS, EDITH, actress
Holt, Edgar. Three Restoration plays (BBC). Radio Times p 2 My 27'60
EWELL, TOM, 1909-, actor
Career notes; b. Owensboro, Kentucky, as Yewell Tompkins. TV Guide v 8 n 49 p 9-11 D 3'60
(Also spelled Elwell, Tom, 1908) Career sketch; b. Kentucky, as

(Elwell, Tom)
  Yewell Tompkins. por TV Guide
  v 8 n 49 D 3'60
EXPEDITION, series
  ABC's documentary films; notes.
  Film -World and AV p 302 Ag '60
EXPORT
  Competition stiff against US Equipment; report in detail of export
  situation. Film World and AV
  p 62 F '60
---Rizzie, Melvin L. (Why US
  equipment frequently can not compete abroad.) Film World and AV
  p 234 Jl '60
---Taboos; foreign sales. sensitive
  to many specific taboos; examples;
  15-20 percent gross now from ex_
  port of TV film. TV Guide v 8
  n 6 p 6-7 F 6'60
---US fugures on export of films.
  Film World and AV p 382 O '60

F

Fabares, Shelley, 1944-, actress
  Career notes. por TV Guide v 8
  n 25 p 25-6 Je 18'60
---Notes, signed por ph. Screen
  Album p 68 N '60
FABIAN, actor
  Signed por. Screen Album p 26
  N '60
FABRAY, NANETTE
  Modeling three evening gowns,
  phs. TV Guide v 8 n 6 p 20-2
  F 6'60
FACE TO FACE, series
  Burnett, Hugh. (Criticism.)
  Radio Times p 13 S 16'60
---Lord Reith of Stonehaven; BBC.
  por Radio Times p 12 O 27'60
FALK, CONRAD ROBERT, 1935-,
  Career notes; "Hawaiian Eye"
  notes. TV Guide v 8 n 14 p 15
  Ap 2'60
FALK, PETER
  Notes; b. NYC 1932. por Screen
  Album p 31 N '60
FALSTAFF, opera
  Glyndebourne Opera over BBC-
  TV; Noël Goodwin on Geraint
  Evans. Radio Times p 6 S 9'60
FAN CLUBS

Johnson, Bob. Facts behind the
  fan clubs (9, 000 in US with 12 to
  15, 000 members). TV Guide.
  v 8 n 4 p 9-11 Ja 23'60
THE FANATICS, play
  BBC's Twentieth Century Theatre
  series; notes (one scene). Radio
  Times p 7 Mr 11'60
FARGÉ, ANNIE
  Notes; "Angel". Movie Life p 18
  D '60
FARMING TODAY, program
  BBC 15-minute film on the Great
  Yorkshire Show. Radio Times
  p 4 Jl 15'60
---BBC new agriculture, at "high-
  est level". Radio Times p 8
  S 16'60
FASHIONS
  BBC show to push ready-to-wear,
  Top Mark for Fashion, notes.
  Radio Times p 5 F 12'60
---Marden, Janie, on BBC-TV;
  notes on her dress program. Ra-
  dio Times p 47 O 6'60
---NYC; Ziegfield Theatre, "Paris
  à la Mode", 15 models, several
  phs. with light review. TV Guide
  v 8 n 15 p 8-10 Ap 9'60
FATHER KNOWS BEST, series
  Rodney, Eugene B. , producer, on
  why production stopped after 6 years;
  for 2 years the best films will be
  repeated; Robert Young's comment.
  TV Guide v 8 n 22 p 9-11 My 28'60
FEDERAL COMMUNICATIONS
  COMMISSION, US
  Field staff to check on payola,
  plugola, public service programs'
  quota; quality still up to public's
  demand, however. TV Guide v 8
  n 25 p 3 Je 18'60
---Ford, Frederick W. Making
  television serve the public (summary of FCC report July 1960).
  TV Guide v 8 n 41 p 6-9 O 8'60
---Ford, Frederick W. , chairman,
  setting up a monitoring system;
  licenses renewable annyally. Musical Courier v 162 n 3 p 5 S '60
---Legislation discussed to inves-
  tigate all regulatory agencies regularly; notes. Variety p 31
  D 21'60

---On broadcast licenses; new
rules. Variety p 20 D 14'60
---Ten key questions asked film
producers and answers (portraits
and names of production execu-
tives). Telefilm v 5 n 2 p 7-14,
16-7 S-O '60
---Uncle Sam's Kilocycle Cops.
TV Guide v 8 n 48 p 22-3 N 26'60
FCC-FIELD ENGINEERING TV'60
BUREAU
Warren, Al. How the FCC keeps
traffic flowing on US electronic
highways. TV Guide v 8 n 48
p 22-3 N 26'60
FELLINI, FEDERICO, film direc-
tor
BBC notes. Radio Times p 36
N 24'60
FENCING
Beaumont, C. L. on BBC's Focus;
art of fencing. Radio Times p 29
My 13'60
FERRER, MEL
And Audrey Hepburn, notes and
signed por. Screen Album p 13
N '60
FESTIVALS
Cannes; report; winners. Film
World and AV p 425 N '60
---Florence; "Restival of Peoples":
documentaries of ethnological and
sociological interest; notes. Var-
iety p 11 D 21'60
---Industry sponsored film festival;
report from Michigan. Film World
and AV p 298 Ag '60
---Milan International Fair adding
in 1960 a film and documentary
fair; plans. Film World and AV
p 105 Mr '60
---San Francisco Film Festival;
report. Film World and AV p 468
D '60
---San Francisco International
Film Festival, 4th year report.
Film World and AV p 147 Ap'60
---Tours; Cynthia Grenier reporting Fifth Annual Short Film Festival (for film-makers and other
professionals mostly). Film Quarterly v 13 n 3 p 23-6 Spring '60
---Tours, France; report of short-
film festival. Variety p 7 D 14'60

(Television Index)
FIDELIO, opera
Sadler's Wells studio perfor-
mance; BBC notes. Radio Times
p 2 My 6'60
FIELDING, FENELLA, actress
BBC note. por Radio Times p 4
Mr 25'60
FIELDS, GRACIE
Notes. por Radio Times p 14
N 10'60
FILM MUSIC
Foreign films on TV, remarks of
Senator Wayne Morse in the US
Senate; methods of lifting music
track from outdated foreigh films
for US use. International Musician
v 58 n 7 p 6 Ja '60
FILM SHOWS
US; syndicated shows; list on local
stations. TV Guide v 8 n 39 p 25
S 24'60
FILMS
Australia; sale of pre-1948 Metro
films; report. Variety p 22 D 14'60
---Figures on selling old features
to TV. Variety p 23 D 14'60
---William and Mary, Williamsburg;
meeting of University Film Pro-
ducers Association. Film World
and AV p 303 Ag '60
FINK, HARRY JULIAN 1924-,
script writer
Notes on his Western scripts; b.
Georgia, grew up NYC. por TV
Guide v 8 n 9 p 20-2 F 27'60
FINN, CHRISTINE, actress
Career notes. por Radio Times
p 5 F 19'60
THE FISHERMAN AND THE DAN-
CER, dance film
BBC; film by Giorgio Moser pro-
duced for Italian TV; review; Bal-
inese dancing. Ballet Today v 12
n 15 p 11 Je '60
FIVE PAST EIGHT
Fulton, Rikki, 1924-; BBC show.
il Radio Times p 5 O 27'60
FLAGSTAD, KIRSTEN, singer
Cooke, Deryck. (A study.) il
Radio Times p 6 Mr 11'60
FLAMINGO TELEFILM SALES,
INC.
Foreign TV films; considered as

361

(Flamingo Telefilm Sales, Inc.)
American fare; causes of popularity in US. il TV Guide v 8 n 34 p 28-30 Ag 20'60

FLEET STREET, 1960
TV program on personal privacy, managerial influence, and such; BBC list of editors. Radio Times p 4 Ap 22'60

THE FLINTSTONES, adult cartoon
Johnson, Bob. (Review.) il TV Guide v 8 n 42 p 28-30 O 15'60

FLORIDA
Cypress Gardens; report of Esther Williams; career notes. TV Guide v 8 n 32 p 17-9 Ag 6'60
---Gainesville; Institute for Medical Educators; Teaching with Television. Ed Screen and AV p 478 S '60

THE FLYING YEARS, series
Sir Alan Cobham, 1949-1960; BBC notes. Radio Times p 30 O 20'60

FOCUS, series
BBC judo session; notes on the art; "the gentle way"; Senta Yamada. il Radio Times p 29 Mr 18 '60
---Neville, John. Exploring the theatre of today, 7 weeks of Focus devoted to making and producing plays; introductory notes. il Radio Times p 25 Ja 29'60

FONDA, HENRY, 1906-, actor
Interview on his roles. TV Guide v 8 n 4 p 13-5 Ja 23'60

FONTEYN, MARGOT, ballerina
On TV about the 3 films made by Dr. Paul Czinner, starring herself and the Royal Ballet. il Radio Times p 5 Ja 15'60

FOR LOVE OR MONEY
Turton, Henry. (Criticism of Bob Monkhouse; ABC.) Punch p 370 Mr 9'60

FOR THE RECORD, column
Whitney, Dwight. (Stories, comments, etc. too good to be lost to TV history.) TV Guide 1960

FORD, ERNEST JENNINGS. On special shows. por TV Guide v 8 n 14 p 17-9 Ap 2'60

FORD, FREDERICK W. Making

television serve the public (chairman of FCC airs his views). TV Guide v 8 n 41 p 6-8 O 8'60
---of the FCC quoted on evasion of immigration laws by "wet back" tapes being dubbed onto American Westerns, etc. His letter in full. International Musician v 58 n 11 p 10 My '60

FORD, JOHN, director
Whitney, Dwight. (Jack Ford in TV; his own comments.) TV Guide v 8 n 47 p 5-7 N 19'60

FORD, TENNESSEE ERNIE, 1919-, actor
Jenkins, Dan. His partial retirement plans; family and work on Portola Valley ranch; reminiscences. por TV Guide v 8 n 50 p 17-19 D 10'60

FORMATION BALLROOM, dancing
Groves, Bill. Old Time and television (with six photographs of teams). Ballroom Dancing Times. v 4 n 6 p 232-3 Mr '60
See also   Ballroom dancing

FORMBY, GEORGE, guitarist
On "Friday Show", BBC. por Radio Times p 55 D 8'60

FORMULA FOR DANGER, serial
ATV review. Punch p 434 Mr 23 '60

FORSYTHE, JOHN LINCOLN, 1918-, actor
Career notes; "Bachelor Father", his career also. TV Guide v 8 n 24 p 18-9 Je 11'60

FOUR STAR FILMS, INC.
Notes. il TV Guide v 8 n 45 p 24-5 N 5'60

FOUR STAR TELEVISION, INC
Founding; notes and 2 ens phs. TV Guide v 8 n 45 p 24-5 N 5'60
---Stock to be offered to the public; 60-61 harvest of films listed. Telefilm p 7, 42 Jl-Ag '60

FRANCE
Censorship of films; report; philosophy. Variety p 17 D 14'60
---Coquelle, Jean. Invitation a la Danse (unfavorable review; complaint most ballet bad on French TV). Ballet Today v 12 n 14 p 24 My '60

(George, Anthony)
---Interview; b. Rome, Italy. por
TV Guide v 8 n 51 p 17-9 D 17'60
GIBSON, GERRY, 1937-, actor
BBC notes. por Radio Times p 4
Jl 22'60
THE GINNY PACE SHOW
Houston; clearing house for teen-
age activity and opinion. il TV
Guide v 8 n 20 p 5 My 14'60
GLOBAL TV
Discussion of under the sea and
an aerial "pipeline. " Film World
and AV p 68 F '60
---First International Assembly of
the Academy of Television Arts
and Sciences NYC, November
1961. UNESCO Newsletter v 8
n 12 p 2 Je 26'61
---Lachenbruch, David. Putting
satellites to work for you. TV
Guide v 8 n 48 p 26-7 D 3'60
---Notes; Echo I. many issues in-
cluding TV Digest v 16 n 34 p 2-3
Ag 22'60
GLOCK, WILLIAM. Introducing
1960 Prom programmes. Radio
Times p 7 Jl 1'60
GOBBI, TITO, singer
Music For You, guest; notes.
Radio Times p 5 Mr 25'60
GODFREY, ARTHUR
Return as host of CBS's Candid
Camera. por TV Guide v 8 n 41
p 17-19 O 8'60
---Stahl, Bob. (New series; and
cancer research interests.) por
TV Guide v 8 n 41 p 18-9 O 8'60
---Travel notes. il TV Guide v 8
n 18 p 7-9 Ap 30'60
---Dinner for him; several pic-
tures. TV Guide v 8 n 7 p 10-1
F 13'60
THE GOLDEN CHILD, opera
Bezanson, Philip, composer;
Paul Engle, librettist; story of
the Nativity; Patricia Neway as
Mary. il TV Guide v 8 n 50 p 12-4
D 10'60
---Hallmark Hall of Fame; 90-
minute work by composer Philip
Bezanson, 1916-; review. il TV
Guide v 8 n 50 p 12-3 D 10'60
GOLLANCZ, VICTOR, publisher

Interviewed on Face to Face,
BBC. por Radio Times p 12 N 24'60
GOMBERG, SY, 1918-, producer
The Law and Mr. Jones, series
starring James Whitmore, 1921-.
TV Guide v 8 n 50 p 5-7 D 10'60
GOMEZ, THOMAS
Career notes; New Yorker. il TV
Guide v 8 n 18 p 22 Ap 30'60
GOREN, CHARLES, 1902-, bridge
expert
His bridge program (ABC). por
TV Guide v 8 n 2 p 10-1 Ja 9'60
GRANADA
Criticism; "most severe chal-
lenge to BBC in standards".
Punch p 242 F 10'60
THE GRAND NATIONAL
BBC debut 1960; steeplechase
notes. il Radio Times p 3 Mr 18
'60
---BBC review of live TV. Punch
p 498 Ap 6'60
THE GRANDEUR THAT WAS ROME,
TV films
Hearst, Stephen. Sir Mortimer
Wheeler to single out aspects in
3 programs. Radio Times p 3
My 6'60
GRANDSTAND, series
BBC; behind the scenes on Satur-
day afternoon. Radio Times p 6
D 1'60
GRAYSON, KATHRYN, singer
On Showtime, BBC. por Radio
Times p 12 D 15'60
GREAT BRITAIN
Anglo-American tension over im-
ports eased; report. Variety p 26
N 30'60
---Chataway, Christopher, M. P.
on present economic conditions;
BBC. Radio Times p 52 N 24'60
--- ---II. Radio Times p 55 D 1'60
---Film-making; comments by di-
rector, Tony Richardson; unions;
costs. Film Quarterly v 13 n 4
p 11-13 Summer '60
---Highlights of the Week, a TV
listing. il Radio Times 1960
---How the British deal with vio-
lence on television; children's
programs; adult. TV Guide v 8 n 31
p 22-3 Jl 30'60

---King George's Jubilee Trust; the Duke of Glouster on youth welfare and research (BBC). por Radio Times p 4 Ap 22'60

---Papers read at convention of the British Institute, University of Cambridge:list. Jr SMPTE v 69 n 5 p 366, 368 My'60

---Programs (BBC) to mark the tercentenary of the Restoration, by P. H. Newby, Controller. Third Programme. Radio Times p 9 Mr 25'60

---Turton, Henry. On the air:Deadline Midnight, ATV; The Days of Vengeance, BBC; Knight Errant '60, Granada;reviews. Punch p 924 Je 29'60

---Violence on TV; BBC Code excerpts. TV Guide v 8 n 32 p 22-3 Jl 30'60

GREAT CAPTAINS, series
Horrocks, Sir Brian;BBC series; plan. por Radio Times p 45 D 15 '60

GREAT EXPECTATIONS, TV serial
Brooking, Dorothea, on her BBC production (3 scenes). Radio Times p 29 Mr 25'60

THE GREY BIRD, serial
Children's Hour; George Ewart Evans, author, on his smugglers tale of the Suffolk coast. Radio Times p 29 Ap 29'60

GRIFFIN, MERV, 1926-
Career sketch;b. San Mateo, California. il TV Guide v 8 n 34 p 16-19 Ag 20'60

GRIFFITH, ANDY, 1926-
The Andy Griffith Show, CBS. por TV Guide v 8 n 40 p 28-30 O 1'60

---Interview;home, Roanoke Island, North Carolina. por TV Guide v 8 n 40 p 28-30 O 1'60

GUEDEL, JOHN, 1913-
Career notes. por TV Guide v 8 n 36 p 24-6 S 3'60

GULAGER, CLU, actor
Johnson, Bob. Billy the Kidder (career sketch of William Martin Gulager, Oklahoma). por TV Guide v 8 n 48 p 24 N 26'60

GUNSMOKE
Trio from Western, Gunsmoke, now in an "act" that audiences enjoy; Dennis Weaver, Amanda Blake and Milburn Stone. ilTV Guide v 8 n 1 p 20-3 Ja 2'60

GUTHERIE, TYRONE, producer
Interview on BBC; some productions. Punch p 778 Je 1'60

H

HAAS, CLARK
Invention of new technique for cartoon-like film; Clutch Cargo, series. TV Guide v 8 n 52 p 28-9 D 24'60

HABERS, TONY
Vogel, Nancy. (His career growing in TV writing;his use of plot graphs.) Writers Digest p 34-7 N'60

HALL, TERRY, ventriloquist
Lenny the Lion and how the show with the stage lion began. il Radio Times p 26 Ap 8'60

HALLIDAY, BRETT. The real Michael Shayne (played by Richard Denning on TV). por TV Guide v 8 n 41 p 28-30 O 8'60

HANDS ACROSS the CHANNEL, program
Folkstone and Boulogne;BBC program on new companionship of towns. Radio Times p 6 S 30'60

HANDS ACROSS the SKY, operetta
BBC-TV; Anthony Hopkins'comedy;review and one picture. Opera v 11 n 4 p 298-9 Ap'60

---Notes on BBC program;first at Cheltenham Festival;Antony Hopkins. ilRadio Times p 3 F 5'60

HANSEN, TOM, 1926-, choreographer
Career sketch;b. Watsonville, California. il Dance Magazine v 34 n 4 p 44-6 Ap'60

HAPPY, series
Notes. il TV Guide v 8 n 29 p 20-2 Jl 16'60

---Talking baby show, created by Carleton Brown and Frank Gill, Jr.

Leone Ledoux, reader of lines.
TV Guide v 8 n 29 p 20-2 Jl 16
'60
HARDIN, TY, 1930-, actor
British note. il Radio Times
p 4 F 19'60
---Career notes. il TV Guide v 8
n 29 p 12-3 Jl 16'60
---Interview;Orison Whipple
Hungerford, Jr. in private life;
star of "Bronco". il TV Guide
v 8 n 29 p 12-3 Jl 16'60
HARDY, ROBERT, actor
In An Age of Kings;note. il
Radio Times p 5 Jl 29'60
HARP
Grandjany, Marcel, harpist;
Canadian Broadcasting Corpor-
ation's Montreal program. Juil-
liard Review v 7 n 2 p 13 Spring
'60
HARRISON, SIDNEY, pianist
Ballroom and Battlefield, a pro-
gram on BBC; delight in imper-
sonations. Punch p 816 Je 8'60
HART, DOLORES, 1937-, actress
Career sketch;Chicago-born,
name Hicks. por TV Guide v 8
n 45 p 13-4 N 5'60
HARTFORD SYMPHONY
Mahler, Fritz, directing TV
series sponsored by Aetna Life
Insurance;$1,000 prize. Inter-
national Musician v 58 n 9 p 45
Mr'60
HASS, HANS, scientist
And Lotte Hass, under sea ser-
ies from yacht, Xarifa. il Radio
Times p 27 Mr 4'60
HAWAIIAN EYE, series
Review. TV Guide v 8 n 22 p 17
My 28'60
---Review;private-eye in Hon-
olulu. TV Guide v 8 n 7 p 23
F 13'60
HAYES, ELTON, guitarist
Notes. por Radio Times p 5 Je
10'60
HAYES, PETER LIND. Recipe for
a happy marriage (he and Mary
Healy). por TV Guide v 8 n 42
p 5-8 O 15'60
HAYWARD, SUSAN, actress
Notes, signed portrait. Screen

(Television Index)
Album p 51 N'60
HEALTH
The Debbie Drake Show;exercises.
il TV Guide v 8 n 34 p 20-1 Ag 29
'60
---Fowler, Eileen, "Keep Fit";BBC.
Radio Times p 22 O 27'60
HEALY, MARY
Hayes, Peter Lind. Recipe for a
happy marriage. il TV Guide v 8
n 42 p 5-7 O 15'60
HEARNE, RICHARD. On his created
character role, Mr. Pastry (with
AP ph). Radio Times p 25 My 6'60
HEATON, ANN, dancer
With Donald MacLeary in "The
Artist and the Modern World", AP
wl ph:A-R.   Ballet Today v 12
n 11 p 14 F'60
HELFFRICH, STOCKTON. Televis-
ion from the inside;II. Don't sell
the viewer short. TV Guide v 8
n 44 p 4-7 O 29'60
HELICOPTERS
"Whirlybirds", program on BBC
based on charter helicopters. il
Radio Times p 25 Ag 26'60
THE HEMINGWAY SPECIALS
Review. TV Guide v 8 n 17 p 27
Ap 23'60
HENDERSON, FLORENCE, 1935-,
singer
Career nd es; wife of Ira Bern-
stein. por TV Guide v 8 n 3 p 28-9
Ja 16'60
HERBERT, DON, scientist
Notes on "Mr. Wizard". por TV
Guide v 8 n 33 p 22-3 Ag 13'60
HERE LIVED---, a series
Glover, C. Gordon. Series at homes
of six great English writers;BBC.
Radio Times p 26 Ap 8'60
HEROES OF THE DEEP, film
Frogmen (USA) on the BBC. Radio
Times p 39 D 22'60
HERRMANN, BERNARD. Composing
for the screen. Am M v 8 n 4 p 12
Ap'60
HICKMAN, DWAYNE, actor
Dobie Gillis;new shape to the
show;notes. por TV Guide v 8 n 42
p 22-3 O 15'60
---Interview on Tuesday Weld, his

366

co-star in The Many Loves of
Dobie Gillis. il Screen World and
TV p 48, 50 O'60
HILL, MARIANNA, 1941-, actress
Career notes;born in Santa Bar-
bara, name Schwarzkopf. por
TV Guide v 8 n 41 p 20-1 O 8'60
HINTON, PAR, singer-dancer
Notes;"Parasol", musical. por
Radio Times p 4 Mr 18'60
HOLIDAY MUSIC-HALL
BBC, 15-part holiday spirit
show;cast. Radio Times p 5 My
27'60
HOLLIMAN, EARL, actor
Career sketch;born Louisiana.
por TV Guide v 8 n 27 p 25-6
Jl 2'60
HOLLYWOOD
Producers;a portfolio of 21 por-
traits, including Samual A.
Peeples, Peter Tewksbury, Frank
Telford, etc.   Telefilm Jl-Ag'60
HOPE, BOB. (Interview on politics,
claiming he can joke both sides
as long as he is "fair"). il TV
Guide v 8 n 43 p 14-6 O 22'60
---As a 300-pound comedian;
notes and ph. Radio Times p 4 Jl 1'
Jl 1'60
HORNE, KENNETH, actor
Notes on "Beyond Our Ken", the
third year, BBC series. Radio
Times p 7 My 20'60
HORROR FILMS
Davis, John. (London comment
on horror films keeping many
away;"54 per cent married
women stop cinema going". Var-
iety p 13 D 28'60
HORSE GUARDS PARADE
BBC notes. il Radio Times
p 27 Je 3'60
HOUSE ON HIGH STREET, series
DeBlois, Frank. (Review.) TV
Guide v 8 n 2 p 28-9 Ja 9'60
HOVHANESS, ALAN, composer
Commission from NBC-TV for
TV opera, The Blue Flame;
played 1959 by San Antonio
Symphony. International Musi-
cian v 58 n 7 p 34 Ja'60
HUCKLEBERRY HOUND, car-
toon series

Notes on the characters, created
by Bill Hanna and Joe Babera
(with illustrations in color and
portraits); 120 artists employed.
TV Guide v 8 n 4 p 20-2 Ja 23'60
---Review. TV Guide v 8 n 26 p 23
Je 25'60
HUDSON, HENRY
Film on the discoverer, his tragic
end;BBC. Radio Times p 27 Jl
29'60
HUDSON, ROCK, actor
Notes and hl ph, signed. Screen
Album p 7 N'60
HUGUENY, SHARON, 1944-, actor
Notes;b. Los Angeles. Screen Al-
bum p 33 N'60
HULBERT, JACK, dancer-actor
BBC notes. Radio Times p 4 Jl
1'60
HUNTER, TAB, 1931-, actor
Career notes;Arthur Gelien, real
name. TV Guide v 8 n 44 p 17-9
O 29'60
---Notes;ph. Screen Album p 63
N'60
HUTCHINS, ROBERT M. The gigan-
tic task ahead (suggestions for
bettering TV).   TV Guide v 8 n 20
p 6-7 My 14'60
HUTCHINS, WILL, actor
Tenderfoot notes;BBC. por Radio
Times p 8 N 17'60

I

ICE SKATING
European Ice Skating Champion-
ships 1960, Garmisch-Partenkir-
chen;list of British eleven;system
of marking new; Ice Dance Champ-
ionship also. Radio Times p 7 Ja
29'60
---Ice Fantasia;Liverpool, Silver
Blades Ice Rink;BBC show. Radio
Times p 4 My 20'60
IMPORTS
Flamingo Telefilm Sales, Inc. ; its
success with US viewers. il TV
Guide v 8 n 34 p 28-30 Ag 20'60
IN TOWN TONIGHT, series
Notes on 1001th show, BBC. Radio
Times p 3 Jl 29'60
INDUSTRY FILMS

367

on jazz; notes.) por Radio Times
p 28 F 5'60

JENCKS, RICHARD W.
Bernstein, Harry. (On bargaining
methods in the TV film industry.)
por Telefilm p 20-22 Jl-Ag '60

JOHNSON, BRYAN, singer
Winner of Eurovision Song Contest; career notes; Knight and
the Music", BBC show. Radio
Times p 5 Mr 4'60

JOHNSTON, DONALD. Radio and
TV (US coverage). il Musical
Courier p 33 F '60

JONES, EDGAR ALLEN, JR.,
1921-, actor-lawyer
Career notes; b. Brooklyn, New
York. por TV Guide v o n 10
p 10-11 Mr 5'60

JONES, MERLE SILAS, 1905-,
executive
His CBS position, career notes;
his belief in TV on a global basis,
world net work aims. por Printers' Ink p 46-7 Ag 12'60

JONES, CAROLYN, actress
Health troubles and ph Screen
Album p 52 N '60

JONES, SHIRLEY, actress
Notes and signed por. Screen
Album p 20 N '60

JORY, VICTOR, 1903-, actor
Career sketch; born in Dawson
City, the Yukon. por TV Guide
v 8 n 36 p 12-14 S 3'60

JOURNEY INTO MELODY
Farnon, Robert, composer-con-
ductor, 20 numbers; producer,
Charles Rogers, 2 studios; BBC.
Radio Times p 5 My 27'60

JOURNEY'S END, play
History of R. C. Sherriff's play
revived by BBC (one scene). Radio Times p 3 Mr 4'60

JOYCE, EILEEN, pianist
Her TV career. por Radio Times
p 4 S 16'60

JUKE BOX JURY, series
BBC notes. portfolio Radio
Times p 5 N 3'60

JULIUS CAESAR, play
BBC; in modern dress. Radio
Times p 31 N 3'60

K

KARLOFF, BORIS, 1887-, actor
Interview; born William Henry
Pratt, Dulwich, England. por TV
Guide v 8 n 42 p 17-9 O 15'60

KAVANAGH, JAMES FRANCIS. An
investigation of the most comfort-
able listening levels for speech
(Ph. D. thesis, University of Michigan, 1960). Dissertation Abstracts
v 20 n 11 p 4458 My '60

KAYE, DANNY (1913-). How does
TV affect our children. TV Guide
v 8 n 13 p 7-9 Mr 26'60

---Debut on TV; career notes. il
TV Guide v 8 n 44 p 13-5 O 29'60

KAYE, DANNY, 1913-, actor
Now on TV; Sylvia Fine Kaye and
Norman Jewison (1927-) producer
talk of Danny's debut. il TV Guide
v 8 n 44 p 12-5 O 29'60

KEHIET, NIELS, dancer
In Pierre et le Loup, Royal Danish
Ballet, ph. Toute La Danse n 93
p 21 My '60

KEMP, HUGH. Canadian TV drama.
Players Magazine v 36 n 4 p 81-2
Ja '60

KENNEDY, JOHN F. (On broadcasting, address March 1958 at
second conference in Public Service Programming at Westinghouse.)
por Telefilm v 4 n 10 p 12, 27 Ap'60

KENNEDY, LUDOVIC
And his new team for Panorama,
now in its fifth year as a weekly;
portraits and notes by Michael
Peacock. Radio Times p 5 Ja 29'60

KERR, DEBORAH
Notes on marriage to Peter Viertel
in Klosters, Switzerland. por
Screen Album p 6 N '60

KIMBROUGH, EMILY. Portrait of
a woman. il TV Guide v 8 n 6
p 20-2 F 6'60

KINSOLVING, LEE, 1938-, actor
Notes and por. Screen World and
TV p 33 O '60

KIRBY, DURWARD
Notes; on Garry Moore show. il

369

(Kirby, Durward)
TV Guide v 8 n 11 p 29 Mr 12'60
KIRK, LISA, singer
Notes; b. Brownsville, Pa. por
TV Guide v 8 n 16 p 8-9 Ap 16'60
KNIGHT, SHIRLEY, 1936-, actress
Roles; b. Goessel, Kansas. por
TV Guide v 8 n 9 p 24 F 27'60
KNIGHT ERRANT, series
Granada; comment. Punch p 304
F 24'60
KOREA
Sklarewitz, Norman. American
Forces Korea Network; 500-watt
station; mostly kinescope. TV
Guide v 8 n 52 p 10-11 D 24'60
KOVACS, ERNIE
Notes. il TV Guide v 8 n 20 p 28
My 14'60
KRALL, HEIDI, singer
Color telecast of Otello, BBC;
Krall as Desdemona. Opera News
v 24 n 9 p 3 Ja 2'60
KRUPA, GENE
Cerulli, Dom. (Career story.)
por International Musician v 58
n 10 p 10-1, 32-3 Ap '60
KULKY, HENRY, 1920-, actor
Notes; name Henry Kulkawich.
il TV Guide v 8 n 19 p 28-9 My 7
'60

L

A LADY WITH FRIENDS, play
BBC notes; Molly Lefebure. Ra-
dio Times p 45 N 24'60
LALANNE, JACK, gym actor
Interview on health building. il
TV Guide v 8 n 46 p 20-3 N 12'60
LAMARE, JEAN-YVES. La télé-
vision (notes). Guide du Concert
n 276 p 791 Je 10'60
LAND OF SONG, monthly series
Welsh, TWW; review. Punch
p 272 F 17'60
LANDON, MICHAEL, 1937-,
Career sketch; Eugene Orowitz,
1937-, Forest Hills New York;
mother Peggy O'Neil, father Eli
M. Orowitz, radio producer.
portfolio Movie Life p 44-8 D '60
---Notes and signed ph. Screen
Album p 73 N 60

LANGUAGE
Davenport, William. English as
she is spoke on TV. TV Guide
v 8 n 27 p 10-1 Jl 2'60
---Strainchamps, Ethel. TV talks
good like a medium should! TV
Guide v 8 n 8 p 5-7 F 20'60
LAPLAND
Lester, Susan, visits the Lapps
for BBC's Wednesday Magazine
series. Radio Times p 5 My 20'60
LARKIN, JOHN, actor
Notes; b. Oakland, California.
por TV Guide v 8 n 9 p 15 F 27'60
LASSIE
Vogel, Nancy. (On writing the
Lassie shows.) Writer's Digest
p 48, 50-2 D '60
LAUGHLINE
Notes, BBC and portfolio. Radio
Times p 31 D 29'60
LAWSON, LINDA, 1936-, actress
Career notes; b. Ann Arbor, Mi-
chigan as Linda Gloria Spaziani.
por TV Guide v 8 n 8 p 28-9
F 20'60
LAYNE, BRONCO, cowboy actor
BBC Viewing Theatre No. 4 at
Lime Grove; report. por Radio
Times p 23 Ja 8'60
LEAVE IT TO BEAVER, series
Review; ABC comedy series with
Hugh Beaumont. TV Guide v 8
n 41 p 27 O 8'60
LEGISLATION
Payola, pay-offs, penalties, in-
vestigations, news each issue.
TV Digest 1960
---Spectrum- control bill in Con-
gress again; news notes. TV
Digest v 16 n 18 p 11 My 2'60
LESEUER, LARRY
Kantor, Katherine Pedell. He
deals with diplomats (career ske-
tch). TV Guide v 8 n 4 p 18-9
Ja 23'60
LET THE PEOPLE SING, series
Beardsall, Charles. (1956 to date
on contest-of-choirs program
over BBC; production notes.)
Radio Times p 6 F 5'60
LET'S FIND OUT, series
Youngsters to question (unre-
hearsed) prominent people;

370

BBC list. Radio Times p 5 Jl 22
'60
LET'S GO RIDING
Latto, Bill. Dressage, show-
jumping and cross-country, BBC-
TV. il Radio Times p 26 Jl 29'60
LEVY, RAOUL J. (On film making.)
Variety p 11 D 21'60
LEWIS, SHARI, 1933-, puppeteer
Interview; father, Dr. Hurwitz of
Yeshiva University. por TV Guide
v 8 n 29 p 8-10 Jl 16'60
L PILOT, series
Dempster, Derek, former R. A. F.
pilot and Geoffrey Wheeler; BBC
series; grand finale air rally.
Radio Times p 25 My 20'60
LLANGOLLEN EISTEDDFOD
BBC coverage; 26 countries. Ra-
dio Times p 11 Jl 1'60
LIFE BEFORE BIRTH, biology
series
Five BBC-TV programs to com-
memorate the tercentenary of the
Royal Society. Radio Times p 2
Je 10'60
A LIFE OF BLISS, series
Actor, George Cole, as David
Bliss; notes on BBC. por Radio
Times p 5 Ja 15'60
---BBC; review. Punch p 272
F 17'60
LIGHTING
Levy, Walter A. New technology
in lighting control equipment. il
Jr SMPTE v 69 n 4 p 253-256
Ap '60
LINCOLN CENTER FOR THE PER-
FORMING ARTS
How TV will be of assistance.
Film World and AV p 202 My '60
LINKLETTER, ART
And wife Lois, on packing for
travel. il TV Guide v 8 n 29 p 14-
5 Jl 16'60
LIVING SCREEN
Ford Foundation grant Ralph Al-
swang designer. Film World and
AV p 437 N '60
LOCK UP, series
Carey, Macdonald, plays lawyer-
for-unfortunates. il TV Guide v 8
n 38 p 28-9 S 17'60
LOCKHART, JUNE

(Television Index)
Jenkins, Dan. (His account of a
visit to the Lockhart's home to see
"the mother of Lassie".) il TV
Guide v 8 n 18 p 17-9 Ap 30'60
LOGAN, JIMMIE
As a comedian. Punch p 434
Mr 23'60
LOLITA, film
BBC notes; James Mason on his
role. Radio Times p 31 N 10'60
LONDON
Covent Garden arrangements to
televise visit of de Gaulle; fan-
fare from the stage as Royal Box
is occupied; description of ballet
gala. il Ballet Today v 12 n 15
p 5 Je '60
---King and Queen of Thailand;
arrangements for the visit. por
Radio Times p 3 Jl 15'60
---Royal Tournament Arena: Bri-
gade of Gurkas; the Queen's Own
Nigeria Regiment; notes on TV
Radio Times p 11 Je 24'60
---The Serpentine, "A Lovely
Lake in London", BBC notes. il
Radio Times p 3 Jl 29'60
---Why London? film on decentra-
lization of firms. Radio Times
p 2 Ag 26'60
LONDON LIGHTS, series
Previews of people and programs
by Trafford Whitelock. Radio Ti-
mes p 5 Mr 25 1960
LONE RANGER
Cummings, Roy. BBC; Clayton
Moore the 5th actor in the role,
ABC production. Radio Times
p 28 Je 10'60
LONG, RICHARD, 1928-, actor
Notes; Hollywood youth. TV Guide
v 8 n 16 p 23 Ap 16'60
THE LONG WAY HOME, serial
German prisoner of war camps;
a tale by Shaun Sutton of a break
through. il Radio Times p 26 Ap 22
'60
LONGLAND, JACK, emcee
Notes. Radio Times p 5 S 16'60
LOOK, series
The seashore; notes. il Radio
Times p 25 Ag 5'60
LOOKING FOR GARROW, comedy

(Looking for Garrow)
Morgan, Elaine, playwright;
BBC notes. Radio Times p 12
O 27'60
LOOKOUT, series
A diary technique with Geoffrey
Wheeler's camera, all of Britain
open to the roving eye; Wednesday
evening program. por Radio Times
p 11 Ja 3'60
LORD, MARJORIE
Five pors. TV Guide v 8 n 17
p 20-1 Ap 23'60
LORNE, MARION, actress
Career notes; b. Wilkesbarre, Pa.
TV Guide v 8 n 42 p 10-1 O 15'60
THE LOST WORLD
Film from Oxford-Cambridge Ex-
pedition to South America 1957;
notes by J. H. Moore. il Radio
Times p 30 Mr 25'60
LOVE AND MARRIAGE, comedy
series
NBC-TV; Kay Armen, singer, of
popular songs. Sat-Rev-p 66
O 17'59
LOVE ON THE DOLE, play
BBC's Twentieth Century Theatre;
Walter Greenwood's play from his
novel; Billie Whitelaw as Sally
Hardcastle. por Radio Times p 8
Ap 22'60
LUNDIGAN, WILLIAM, 1915-,
actor
Career sketch. por TV Guide v 8
n 14 p 10-1 Ap 2'60
LYNLEY, CAROL, 1942-, actress
Notes. por Movie Life p 36 D '60
LYNN, JENNIE, 1954-
Note. il TV Guide v 8 n 9 p 11
F 27'60

M

MACADAM AND EVE, play
BBC's Twentieth Century Theatre
series; Roger MacDougall, 1951.
il Radio Times p 7 F 12'60
MACARTHUR, JAMES, 1937-,
actor
Notes and signed ph: NYC. Screen
Album p 22 N '60
MCBAIN, DIANE, 1941-,
Notes. por Movie Life p 37 D '60

---Interview on "Surfside". por
TV Guide v 8 n 50 p 28-9 D 10'60
MACBETH, play
Schaefer, George, producer;
Scotland the scene for "authentic"
Hallmark Hall of Fame production.
il TV Guide v 8 n 47 p 8-9 N 19'60
MACBETH, opera
Aprahamian, Felix. Macbeth
from Covent Garden. il Radio
Times p 6 Ap 1'60
MCCLURE, DOUG, actor
Career sketch; b. Pacific Pali-
sades, California. il TV Guide
v 8 n 30 p 28-30 Jl 23'60
MCDOWELL, PAUL, 1932-, com-
edian
And Piers Stephens, 1935-; notes
on BBC series: "one man off his
head and another going off his
head while talking to him". il
Radio Times p 4 Ja 29'60
MCGAVIN, DARREN, actor
Career notes; b. Spokane. por
TV Guide v 8 n 23 p 17-9 Je 4'60
MACGREGOR, JIMMIE, folk singer
And Robin Hall BBC's Tonight;
notes. il Radio Times p 4 F 26'60
MAGRUDER, JANE NOEL. Devel-
opment of the concept of public in-
terest as it applies to radio and
television programming (Ph. D.
thesis Ohio State University 1959).
Dissertation Abstracts v 20 n 9
p 3890 Mr '60
MCKAY, GARDNER, 1932-, actor
Johnson, Bob. (Career sketch;
b. NYC.) por TV Guide v 8 n 25
p 19-21 Je 18'60
---Notes and ph. Screen World and
TV p 30 O '60
MCKELLAR, KENNETH, singer
Career notes of singer on " A
Song For Everyone". por Radio
Times p 9 F 12'60
MCKENNA, SIOBHAN, 1924-,
actress
DeBlois, Frank. Siobhan McKenna
il TV Guide v 8 n 8 p 25-7 F 20'60
MACKENZIE, GISELE
Cerulli, Dom. (Career sketch;
b. Winnipeg.) International Musi-
cian. v 58 n 12 p 20-1 Je '60
MACKENZIE, JACQUELINE,

comedian
Series on Americans, "fun at America's expense" (AP ph). Radio Times p 4 My 27'60

MACKENZIE REPEATER
Machine for laughter and many sounds; Louis G. Mackenzie, 1915-, before his machine, ph. TV Guide v 8 n 41 p 24-5 O 8'60

MCLEAN, David, 1922-, actor
Notes on Tate role; b. Ohio. por TV Guide v 8 n 31 p 8-9 Jl 30'60

McLEAN, DONALD, 1922-, actor
Creating character, Tate, a Western hero. il TV Guide v 8 n 31 p 8-10 Jl 30'60

MACLEISH, ARCHIBALD
His first TV play, The Secret of Freedom. il TV Guide v 8 n 5 p 17-9 Ja 30'60

MACMURRAY, FRED, actor-musician
Career notes; b. Kankakee, Illinois. por TV Guide v 8 n 46 p 17-9 N 12'60

MACREADY, GEORGE
Career notes; b. Providence, Rhode Island. por TV Guide v 8 n 18 p 22 Ap 30'60

MADRID
American Festival Ballet under Renzo Raiss on TV; notes. Dance Magazine v 34 n 6 p 82 Je '60

MAGIC
British in London and Italians in Milan to compete, with Dutch jury. Radio Times p 4 Je 3'60
---Focus (BBC); president of Magic City Museum to bring to this program historic properties and tell how they were used in tricks. Radio Times p 29 Ap 29'60
---Harbin, Robert; "Magic, Music and Mystery", BBC. Radio Times p 54 D 22'60
---Programs by Koran (BBC). Radio Times p 4 Ap 15'60
---Scenic Effects men, Bernard Wilkie and Jack Kine; BBC notes. il Radio Times p 5 Ja 8'60

MAHLER, GUSTAVE, composer
Mann, William. Royal Albert Hall, Jascha Horenstein conducting Mahler's Eighth Sym-

(Television Index)
phony (a diptych: the church's view then a metaphysical humanist view of Goethe in the last scene of Faust). Radio Times p 6 Ap 22'60

MAIGRET, series
Simenon, author; BBC's Rupert Davies as the inspector, Maigret Radio Times p 23 D 1'60

MAKE MINE MUSIC, series
No gimmicks, straight singing by David Hughes; popular. Radio Times p 4 Ja 8'60

MAKE WAY FOR MUSIC, series
Clouston, George, conductor; BBC notes. Radio Times p 54 O 13'60

MAKE-UP
Diefenbach, Robert C. Some tips for beginners facing the camera. TV Guide v 8 n 17 p 22-3 Ap 23'60
---For color motion pictures and color TV; Seki and Kodama on "High-con". Jr SMPTE v 69 n 6 p 414-420 Je '60
---How to look younger, 9 phs. TV Guide v 8 n 27 p 28-9 Jl 2'60

THE MAN AND THE CHALLENGE
Review. TV Guide v 8 n 16 p 27 Ap 16'60

MAN BEFORE ADAM, series
Lutyens, David, on BBC introducing in first talk, Dr. Kenneth Oakley of the British Museum of Natural History. il Radio Times p ᴸ Ja 15'60

MAN FROM INTERPOL, series
Review; NBC. TV Guide v 8 n 27 p 23 Jl 2'60
---Review; Richard Wyler the police agent. TV Guide v 8 n 27 p 23 Jl 2'60

MANDAN, ROBERT, actor
Notes. por TV Guide v 8 n 9 p 14 F 27'60

MANN, HERBIE, 1930-, jazz musician
Career sketch; b. Brooklyn. International Musician v 58 n 9 p 21, 34 Mr '60

MANON, opera
Ross, A. G. Manon as produced

373

(Manon)
by M. Bernier in Canada. Canadian Music Journal. v 4 n 3 p 47-9 Spring '60

MANTOVANI
BBC notes on his particular style of orchestration. Radio Times p 4 Jl 1'60

MAPS
In "Pinpoint", map making explained; BBC. Radio Times p 28 My 27'60

MARIS, HERBERT, 1881-, lawyer
"Lock Up", series out of cases handled by Maris; Macdonald Carey as Maris. il TV Guide v 8 n 38 p 28-9 S 17'60

MARKOVA, ALICIA, ballerina
As handled by Eamonn Andrews on "This Is Your Life"; BBC report. il Ballet Today v 12 n 12 p 3 Mr '60
---BBC; "a natural" for TV reading and speaking, unaffected clear voice". por Ballet Today v 12 n 16 p 3 Jl '60
---BBC contract: "Markova's Ballet Call" program. DN v 37 n 1 p 8 S '60
---BBC notes. Radio Times p 4 S 30'60
---Markova's Ballet Call, series; note. Radio Times p 4 S 9'60
---On Light Music Festival, story of The Sleeping Beauty; notes. Radio Times p 5 Je 3'60
---Her first teacher, Dorothy Thorne, Margot, Fonteyn, Serge Lifar, Markova's sisters, protege Suzanne Abbott, all at "This Is Your Life" show, BBC. Ballet Today v 12 n 12 p 14 Mr '60

MARSHALL, NORMAN, producer
Luncheon talk in London on the Television Theatre, International Theatre Association host. World Premières v 11 n 3 p 7 Ja '60

MARTIN, DEAN
Notes; signed por. Screen Album p 50 N '60

MARTIN, MARY
Third telecast of "Peter Pan" (1955, 1956, now 1960); putting the show together. TV Guide

v 8 n 49 p A 1-2 D 3'60

MARTIN, QUINN (1923-). Interview on series, The Untouchables; Robert Stack plays incorruptible Treasury agent. il TV Guide v 8 n 9 p 17-9 F 27'60

MARTIN, ROSS, 1923-, actor
Career notes; b. Poland. TV Guide v 8 n 21 p 10-1 My 21'60

MARY OF MAGDALA, play
Milton, Ernest, playwright; notes on bibical material and handling on BBC. por Radio Times p 7 F 12'60

MARX, GROUCHO
Interview on his role in The Mikado. il TV Guide v 8 n 17 p 13-4 Ap 23'60

MARX, HARPO, 1893-? 1961, comedian
Career notes. il TV Guide v 8 n 51 p 28-9 D 17'60

MASON, TED, script writer
Notes on BBC detective series. Radio Times p 5 F 19'60

MASSACHUSETTS INSTITUTE OF TECHNOLOGY
Applegate, Joseph R. New lab. il Educational Screen and AV p 176-7 Ap '60

A MATTER OF DEGREE, serial
BBC; Elaine Morgan in 6-part drama. Punch p 738 My 25'60
---Morgan, Elaine, on her TV serial (6 parts) on South Wales girl going to Oxford; BBC. Radio Times p 7 My 13'60

MATTERS OF MOMENT, series
Dillon, Francis, program on private clubs and England's problem of unlicensed clubs. Radio Times p 4 Ag 26'60

MAY, ELAINE, comedian
With Mike Nichols; notes. portfolio Theatre Arts v 44 n 10 p 59-61 O '60

MAYER, MARTIN. How good is TV at its best? Part I. Public affairs; Part II More than plenty of drama. Harper's Ag and S'60

MEADOWS, AUDREY
Kantor, Katherine Pedell. (Interview.) por TV Guide v 8 n 24 p 20-2 Je 11'60

MEDARIS, MAJ. GEN. J. B. We must educate for survival of democracy. por Ed Screen and AV p 426-7 Ag '60

MEDICINE
Cologne; first international congress on Medical Photography and Cinematography. Jr SMPTE v 69 n 5 p 366 My '60
---Color abstractions on film correlate with hallucinations from drugs; work of Betty Scheyer; notes. Film World and AV p 380 O '60
---Film for children on going to the hospital; BBC. Radio Times p 31 S 16'60
---Hay fever on "Woman's Hour"; BBC notes. Radio Times p 5 Jl 1'60
---McIndoe of East Grinstead, a hommage to the late Sir Archibald McIndoe; notes. Radio Times p 4 Ap 29'60
---Matters of Medicine, series; scope given by John Furness, BBC. Radio Times p 2 Mr 4'60
---Replacements for Life; new graft operations on BBC. Radio Times p 30 N 17'60; same. Radio Times p 28 D 15'60
---US Medical schools to tape courses and exchange data; subsidy from Lilly Company. Film World and AV p 432 N '60
---University of Florida College of Medicine, Gainesville: Teaching with Television, an Institute for Medical Educators. notes. Ed Screen and Av p 478 S '60
---Voice of Medicine, prepared in Amsterdam, Holland; $25 year; also pharmaceutical houses to specialists to inquiring doctor, a new information plan. Film World and AV p 192 My '60

MEETING POINT, drama
American missionaries lost in Ecuador 1956; on BBC. Radio Times p 5 S 23'60

MEN INTO SPACE, series
Review TV Guide v 8 n 4 p 30 Ja 23'60

MENUHIN, YEHUDI
Kingsway studios, rush from recording at EMI's Abbey Road; notes. High Fidelity v 10 n 2 p 20 F '60

MESSTER, OSKAR, 1866-1943
Narath, Albert. (Survey of life of founder of German motion picture industry.) por Jr SMPTE v 69 n 10 p 726-734 O '60

METHODIST CHURCH
Survey of activity in Audio-visual and film. Film World and AV p 74-5 F '60

METROPOLITAN OPERA
New York Board of Regents "A Visit to the Metropolitan"; notes on educational program for schools. Opera News v 24 n 22 p 1 Ap 2'60
---On "Monitor", BBC notes. Radio Times p 4 Je 17'60

MEXICO
Films from US and into US; survey of Mexican business. Variety p 5 D 28'60
---Report on government purchase of Manuel Espinosa Iglesias chain; "monopoly or break up of monopoly" aim? Variety p 13 N 30'60
---Report on government buying film chains; and plans. Variety p 13 D 28'60
---Third World Review of Film Festivals; report. Variety p 11 D 28'60
---Tinoco, Carlos. (On impending "boom" of Hollywood picture-making in Mexico.) Variety p 18 D 14 '60

MEXICAN FIESTA
NBC; Janet Blair and others in Aztec costume, ph. TV Guide v 8 n 13 p 15 Mr 26'60

MIAMI
Renick, Ralph, news editor of WTVJ; his attack on crime; rating tripled, on TV. TV Guide v 8 n 17 p 5-7 Ap 23'60

A MID-SUMMER NIGHT'S DREAM, opera
Britten's work at Aldeburgh; its production told by Peter Pears. Radio Times p 2 Je 17'60

MIDWEST AIRBORNE

(Midwest Airborne)
Beamed to 6 states, a program in music, grades 1-6, Indiana, US. Music Educators Journal v 47 n 2 p 8 N-D '60

MILLAND, RAY, 1908-, actor
Interview. por TV Guide v 8 n 23 p 13-5 Je 4'60

MILLER, MARVIN
As Michael Anthony in The Millionaire; on his many voice roles. TV Guide v 8 n 9 p 8-10 F 27'60

MILLER, MAX
Notes; back on BBC. por Radio Times p 5 My 27'60

MIMIEUX, YVETTE, 1942-, actress
Notes. por Screen Album p 47 N '60

MINSTREL SHOWS
The Black and White Minstrel Show; BBC (scene). Radio Times p 55 D 15'60

THE MIRACLE WORKER: play
Wright, Teresa, and Patty McCormick, AP ph: CBS-TV. World Theatre v 9 n 4 p 321 Winter '60

MIRANDA, ISA, actress
BBC debut. por Radio Times p 4 Mr 11'60

MISS AMERICA CONTEST
MacPherson, Robert B. (Basis of judging, not beauty alone.) il TV Guide v 8 n 37 p 5-7 S 10'60

MR. GILLIE, drama
BBC's Twentieth Century Theatre; James Birdie, author; Alastair Sim, the star. Radio Times p 4 Je 10'60

MR. LUCKY, series
Created by Blake Edwards; review. TV Guide v 8 n 11 p 27 Mr 12'60

MR. MAGOO, cartoon show
Foreign-recorded musical sound track; notes on Kellogg Company withdrawal as sponsor. International Musician v 59 n 5 p 9 N '60

MITCHELL, GUY, singer
On BBC, notes for "the squares" about this American pop singer. Radio Times p 5 Ap 15'60

MOBLEY, MARY ANN, 1937-, actress
Career notes; b. Brandon, Miss. por TV Guide v 8 n 17 p 24-6

Ap 23'60

MONEY
Bank of England's Governor on BBC-TV. Radio Times p 4 Ap 22 '60
---My Word Is My Bond, a TV film on the stock exchange (BBC). Radio Times p 26 My 6'60

MONITOR, series
Wheldon, Huw. Twelve films shown on "Monitor" to be cast into a Film Festival, portfolio Radio Times p 3 Jl 22'60

MONTE CARLO RALLY
Plans for 1960 coverage by radio and TV for English viewers; notes on the contest: "a matter of secret checks, of seconds and metres", Radio Times p 11 Ja 15'60

MONTEVECCHI, LILIANE, 1934-, actress
Notes; b. Paris. por TV Guide v 8 n 10 p 16 Mr 5'60

THE MOON AND SIXPENCE
Shayon, Robert Lewis. (Review of Maugham's novel adapted by S. Lee Pogostin.) Sat-R-p 29 N 21'59

A MOON FOR THE MISBEGOTTEN, play
BBC; notes (scene). Radio Times p 47 O 20'60

THE MOONSTONE, film
Collins, Wilkie, tale discussed by Shaun Sutton (one scene, BBC). Radio Times p 25 Ag 12'60

MOORE, GARRY. You can't run scared (analysis of his shows, prices, artists). por TV Guide v 8 n 5 p 13-5 Ja 30'60

MOORE, JOANNA, 1935-, actress
Notes; from Americus, Georgia. por TV Guide v 8 n 43 p 30-2 O 22'60

MOORE, ROGER GEORGE, 1927- actor
Career notes. por TV Guide v 8 n 41 p 10-11 O 8'60
---Notes; The Alaskans. por TV Guide v 8 n 24 p 27 Je 11'60

MORGAN, ANITA, 1935-, actress
Serial, A Matter of Degree; BBC notes. Radio Times p 5 Je 10'60

MORLEY, PETER, TV director
British opera, The Turn of the

Screw, analyzed as Morley pro-
duced it. December 25 and 28th
1959, Ass-R. Opera v 11 n 2
p 162, 164 F'60
MORTIMER, JOHN, TV playwright
Notes on plays for BBC. Radio
Times p 4 Je 17'60
---Notes on TV plays;on "David
and Brocoli" coming. por Radio
Times p 2 Ja 22'60
MOSCOW TELEVISION CENTER
Poch, Waldemar J. (Report.)
Jr SMPTE v 69 n 5 p 348-50 My
'60
MOSES, CHARLES
General manager of Australian
Broadcasting Commission, por
ph. Music and Dance p 11 Je'60
MOTORIZED MOVEMENT
New technique to cut cost of
cartoon-type; background moves,
etc. Clutch Cargo, series. TV
Guide v 8 n 52 p 28-9 D 24'60
MOVING PICTURES
Brislin, Marge T. The technical
motion picture as a means of
communication. Journal SMPTE
v 69 n 1 p 45-6 Ja'60
---BBC's Film Club on the jobs
that people do in making a film.
Radio Times p 38 N 3'60
---Directors Guild asking TV
not to "butcher" old movies but
to present them as film classics.
TV Guide v 8 n 45 p 2 N 5'60
---Hollywood's lost splendor on
"Picture Parade"; "labour costs
have driven the film-makers to
Europe". Radio Times p 30
O 27'60
---Japan; Derek Prouse on film
making;BBC. Radio Times p 54
D 8'60
---Notes on the silent movies;
TV's use. il TV Guide v 8 n 38
p 20-3 S 17'60
MOWBRAY, ALAN, actor
Career sketch;b. London. por
TV Guide v 8 n 24 p 8-9 Je 11'60
MUNI, PAUL, 1898-, actor
Notes. por Movie Life p 28 D'60
MUSEUMS
Children's Hour visits museums
especially for children;BBC

(Television Index)
notes. il Radio Times p 27 Jl 8'60
MUSIC
ABC's Make a Date, series;Ernest
Maxin's Orchestra in gold lamé;
"marshmallow arrangements".
Punch p 532 Ap 13'60
---ABC's Wham; Jack Good's Fat
Noise:"streets behind East Africa
in rhythm";"uninhibited American
idols of rock". Punch p 629 My
4'60
---Bliss, Sir Arthur;his special mu-
sic for the Shakespeare cycle,
BBC-TV, "An Age of Kings". Radio
Times p 4 Ap 22'60
---Bradbury, Ernest. Three choral
occasions (BBC): Dvorak's Re-
quiem;Elgar's The Dream of Ger-
ontius;Brahms' Alto Rhapsody.
Radio Times p 8 Mr 25'60
---BBC Northern Dance Orchestra
in "Suddenly It's Swing". il Radio
Times p 46 D 29'60
---British programs:Music With
Sir Malcolm (on a particular work);
TV Concert Hall (soloists);Celeb-
rity Recitals;Opera. Radio Times
p 9 Ja 15'60
---Chicago's WNBQ, a color show-
case of young musical talent;Louis
Sudler, host. Musical Courier v 162
n 5 p 4 N'60
---Clark, Dick, and his American
Bandwagon:interview. por TV
Guide v 8 n 37 p 8-11 S 10'60
---Dickinson, Peter. (Music is an
aural delight, hence radio better
for music lover than TV.) Punch
p 176 Ja 27'60
---Drive against foreign sound
track in US films;Locals of American Federation of Musicians involved;Federal Communications Commission hearings report. il Inter-
national Musician v 58 n 8 p 5
F'60
---Goodwin, Noël. Music diary, BBC.
Radio Times p 6 My 13'60
---International Concert Hall;Lon-
don Mozart Players, BBC. Radio
Times p 30 D 29'60
--- ---notes;Henry Szergng. Radio
Times p 30 N 3'60

377

(Music)

--- ---Sir John Barbirolli and the Halle;BBC. Radio Times p 28 D 15'60

--- ---the BBC Symphony. Radio Times p 31 D 1'60

---Judd, William M. (On artists; "colossal fees paid by TV for talent, the amount into the artists' pocket scandalously small". Musical Courier v 162 n 1 p 13 Jl'60

---Labor agreement details of Paramount Telemeter Division and American Federation of Mucians. International Musician v 58 n 12 p 5 Je'60

---Light Music Festival, London; notes on BBC shows that feature light music. Radio Times p 7 My 27'60

---Liverpool Cathedral; a music program, BBC;how the far reaches are to be used. Radio Times p 5 My 20'60

---McLaren, Norman. (Music in films important when films sent to other countries;"Western" music unsatisfactory to the East which has its own classics.) Film World and AV p 66 F'60

---Music in Television, a listing of coming events. Radio Times 1960

---Orchestra BBC and Vilem Tausky on musical expedition to resorts, "Friday Night is Seaside Night". Radio Times p 5 Jl 1'60

---Pianist from Japan on BBC: Hiroko Nakamura. por Radio Times p 30 O 20'60

---Preview 1960 fall. TV Guide v 8 n 39 p 21 S 24'60

---Regular column, Radio and Television. International Musician 1960

---Robinson, Eric, in Music For You, series;BBC. por Radio Times p 31 O 13'60

---Salter, Lionel. International Concert Hall (list of orchestras over BBC). Radio Times p 30 O 6'60

---Song contest "Eurovision 1960", reported by Tom Sloan, BBC;how London show was mounted. il Radio Times p 3 Mr 25'60

---TV coverage of the Proms and Sir Malcolm Sargent; BBC plans. Radio Times p 7 Jl 15'60

---Tempo 60, series on modern music;BBC notes. Radio Times p 5 My 6'60

---US; the role of music in educational television (general survey of programs). Musical Courier v 161 n 4 p 2 Mr'60

---The Vienna Philharmonic Orchestra in "Waltzes From Vienna", New Years BBC. Radio Times p 12 D 29'60

---Voorhes, Donald, composer-conductor;career notes and his opinions about music on television; 18 years on radio, 2 on TV. por Musical Courier v 162 n 3 p 8 S'60

---University of Alabama;"Music Time" series under Dr. Ed Cleino, AP wl ph. International Musician v 58 n 7 p 34 Ja'60

MUSIC CORPORATION OF AMERICA
Schreiber, Taft. (Testimony in FCC investigation of film producers when "10 key questions" were asked.) Telefilm v 5 n 2 p 7-14, 16-7 S-O'60

MUSIC FOR a SUMMER NIGHT
ABC; review. TV Guide v 8 n 34 p 15 Ag 20'60

---Review (ABC). TV Guide v 8 n 34 p 15 Ag 20'60

MUSIC FOR YOU, series
Beriosova, ballerina, and Yehudi Menuhin, violinist;BBC. il Radio Times p 30 D 8'60

---BBC; Polovtsian Dances from Prince Igor;criticism. Ballet Today v 12 n 14 p 9 My'60

MUSIC ON ICE, series
Review;variety show on skates (NBC). TV Guide v 8 n 25 p 27 Je 18'60

MUSIQUE POUR VOUS
Piaf, Edith, director of this program on the French TV; review

of ballets. il Ballet Today v 12
n 11 p 25 F'60
THE MUSIC ROOM, film
Russian director, Satyajit Ray;
review. Film Quarterly v 13 n 4
p 42-3 Summer'60
MUSIC THEATRE, series
Sixty-four music lessons, Maine
and New Hampshire;primary
grades. Music Educators Journal v 47 n 2 p 14 N-D'60
MUSIC WHILE YOU WORK, series
20th year;BBC notes. Radio
Times p 4 Je 17'60
MVT-TV, company
LeVan, Ted, president;mobile
unit, a Videotape-equipped DC-4;
details. il TV Guide v 8 n 14
p 22-3 Ap 2'60
MY WORD, series
Bird, Kenneth. Tony Shrayne on
63 editions of "My Word , panel
game on BBC, broadcast regularly to 40 countries. Radio
Times p 6 Ap 22'60
MYSTERY FILMS
Dow Hour of Great Mysteries;
review. TV Guide v 8 n 23 p 29
Je 4'60
---"Mystery Show", series;re-
view. TV Guide v 8 n 29 p 23
Jl 16'60

N

THE NATIONAL ACADEMY of
TELEVISION ARTS AND SCI-
ENCES
NYC; 1961 festival;1962 Los
Angeles. Film World and AV
p 467 D'60
NATIONAL AUDIO-VISUAL
ASSOCIATION
US; report. Film World and AV
p 334 S'60
NATIONAL BROADCASTING
COMPANY OPERA
Cavalleria Rusticana, color
telecast, January 31, 1960;cast.
Opera News v 24 n 12 p 2 Ja
23'60
---Don Giovanni; W. H. Auden and
Chester Kallman version in
English "for the video audience"

(Television Index)
"not high-flown in diction"; re-
view. Musical Courier v 161 n 6
p 16 My'60
---Season 1960-61:list. Musical
Courier v 162 n 3 p 5 S'60
NATIONAL DEFENSE EDUCATION
ACT
The first year, 1959. Film World
and AV p 10 Ja'60
NATIONAL VELVET, serial
Review. TV Guide v 8 n 49 p 23
D 3'60
THE NATIVITY(PISK)
Associated-Rediffusion;dance,
mime, singing, instrumental music,
spoken word;movement based on
Romanesque sculpture;Ian For-
dyce, camera. Ballet Today v 12
n 12 p 8-26 Mr'60
NATURE NEWS, series
Not only newsy natural history but
linking naturalists and what each
is doing;BBC. Radio Times p 5
Ap 22'60
NEARER TO HEAVEN, play
BBC cast (scene). Radio Times
p 15 D 29'60
NELSON, RICK, 1940, actor
Notes and signed por. Screen Al-
bum p 23 N'60
NERINA, NADIA, ballerina
Partnered by Fadeychev;Giselle
note. Ballet Today v 12 n 12 p 4
Mr'60
NEW ORLEANS
The Maison Seignouret housing
WDSU-TV. il TV Guide v 8 n 42
p 12-3 O 15'60
NEW YEARS PARTY
At White Heather Club, Scotland;
cast. il Radio Times p 5 D 29'60
NEW YORK CITY
Fourth annual Industrial Film and
A-V Exhibition;report. Film World
and AV p 427 N'60
NEWHART, BOB, 1929-, actor
Career notes. por TV Guide v 8
n 36 p 8-10 S 3'60
NEWMAN, PAUL, actor
And wife, Joanne Woodward;Israel
notes. il Screen Album p 43-5 N
'60
NEWS

379

(News)
British news broadcasts;J. A.
Camacho on "Ten o'Clock". Ra-
dio Times p 3 S 16'60
---Dimbleby, Richard. The Royal
Wedding;arrangements by BBC
to cover H. R. H. Princess Mar-
garet and Mr. Antony Armstrong-
Jones' nuptials. Radio Times
p 3 Ap 29'60
---Foster, Hugh G. A group por-
trait of TV's commentators,
masters of the slanted story.
Holiday p 83-4 Ag'61
---Granada's series;What The
Papers Say; dishonest or du-
bious dodges;entertaining for
the worldly and disenchanted,
good for the young. Punch
p 466 Mr 30'60
---How the BBC covers South-
East England. Radio Times p 2
Jl 15'60
---Nixon and Khrushchev in Moscow;award for the broadcast.
TV Guide v 8 n 30 p 1 Jl 23'60
---Notes on US newsmen:Chet
Huntley, David Brinkley, Doug-
las Edwards, John Daly; and
article on Howard K. Smith. TV
Guide v 8 n 31 p 27 Jl 30'60
---Preview of news and documen-
tary fall 1960 in US. TV Guide
v 8 n 39 p 21 S 24'60
---TV editorializing; US exam-
ples. TV Guide v 8 n 17 p 5-7
Ap 23'60
---Stahl, Bob. Howard K. Smith
on CBS News;analyze don't
editorialize. por TV Guide v 8
n 32 p 25-6 Jl 30'60
---US programs;comments and
reviews. TV Guide v 8 n 32 p 27
Jl 30'60
---Washington "news hens";
Nancy Hanschman of CBS in
particular. por TV Guide v 8
n 24 p 5-7 Je 11'60
---What Goes On, a series for
young people by Stephen King-
Hall. Radio Times p 28 S 30'60
NICHOLS, BARBARA, actress
Interview; from Long Island. por
TV Guide v 8 n 30 p 25-7 Jl '60

NICHOLS, MIKE
And Elaine May, comedians;
notes and portfolio. Theatre Arts
v 44 n 10 p 59-61 O '60
NIGERIA
Notes to prepare viewer for the
new nation, Nigeria, an indepen-
dent sovereign State within the
Commonwealth. Radio Times
p 13 S 23'60
A NIGHT OUT, TV play
ABC; dramatist, Harold Pinter,
Philip Saville, directing; caviar.
Punch p 629 My 4'60
THE NIGHTWALKERS, play
BBC cast. il Radio T imes p 13
N 24'60
NIXON VS. KENNEDY
Historic TV meeting; questions
by 4 newsmen; notes on debate
series 1960. TV Guide v 8 n 38
p A 1-3 S 17'60
NO WREATH FOR THE GENERAL,
serial
BBC, 6-part by Donald Wilson;
notes. Radio Times p 4 S 16'60
NOAH, play
Harington, Joy, on her production
(BBC) of André Obey's play. Ra-
dio Times p 25 Ap 8 60
NORSTAD, GENERAL LAURIS
Supreme Commander of Allied
Powers in Europe on BBC. por
Radio Times p 5 Ap 1 60
NORTH, JAY, 1953-, actor
Johnson, Bob. (Sketch of polite
youngster playing Dennis the
Menace.) por TV Guide v 8 n 10
p 17-9 Mr 5'60
NORTON, CLIFF, comedian
Interview; Scarsdale, New York,
into a British-type comedian. il
TV Guide v 8 n 50 p 14-5 D 10'60
NOVAK, KIM, actress
Right profile ph. Screen Album
p 40 N '60
NURSERY SERVICE
Maine; Portland TV employs
nurse for 300 children weekly,
wervice for shopping mothers.
il TV Guide v 8 n 36 p 15-16
S 3'60

O

THE ODYSSEY, serial
BBC notes, half-hour translations. Radio Times p 9 S 23'60

O'BRIEN, EDMOND, actor
Notes. por TV Guide v 8 n 27
p 13 Jl 2'60

O'BRIEN, LOUISE, singer
Career sketch; b. Oklahoma.
por TV Guide v 8 n 3 p 20-2
Ja 16'60

O'BRIEN, WILLIAM JOSEPH
PATRICK, ? 1899-, actor
Career notes; b. Milwaukee. por
TV Guide v 8 n 52 p 17-9 D 24'60

OHIO STATE UNIVERSITY
Institute for Education by TV-
radio; awards; report. TV Digest v 16 n 19 p 14 My 9'60

OLD AGE
BBC series; Preparation for Re-
tirement. Radio Times p 47
N 10'60

THE OLD MAN AND THE SEA
Production notes by James Wong
Howe. Film World and AV p 310
Ag '60

OLD TIME BALLROOM DANCING
Groves, Bill. (Formation dancing, and team dancing on television, with six photographs).
Ballroom Dancing Times v 4
n 6 p 232 Mr '60
See also   Ballroom dancing

OLYMPICS 1960
The BBC team at the XVII Olym-
piad, Rome 1960. portfolio Radio Times p 3 Ag 19'60
---Durslag, Melvin. (Preview.)
il TV Guide v 8 n 34 p 4-6 Ag 20
'60

ON STAGE, EVERYBODY
Spectacular in sound, described by
Gale Pedrick; Evelyn Laye emcee.
por Radio Times p 7 Ap 1'60

ON THE BRIGHT SIDE, serial
Baxter, Stanley (1929-) and Betty Marsden in satire that is uni-
versally understood; BBC notes
on 2nd year. Radio Times p 3
Je 10'60
---BBC notes. Punch p 888

Je 22'60

ON THE EDGE, play
BBC adventure film by Donald
Campbell-Shaw; cloak and dag-
ger. Radio Times p 3 Jl 8'60

O'NEAL, PATRICK, 1928-, actor
Career notes; b. Ocala, Florida.
por TV Guide v 8 n 35 p 5-7
Ag 27'60

O'NEILL, EUGENE
Three short plays on BBC; El-
wyn Jones on these and on O'Neill
Radio Times p 7 S 23'60

OPERA
Cologne; Janácek's Jenufa; note.
Opera News v 25 n 8 p 7 D 31'60
---CBS-TV; Galuppi's Filosofo di
Campagna; notes. Opera News,
v 24 n 20 p 3 Mr 19'60
---Don Giovanni; review of NBC-
TV; "highest note in US tele-
vision". Musical Courier v 161
n 6 p 16 My '60
---Educational program, Board
of Regents, New York State with
the Metropolitan; notes. Opera
News v 24 n 22 p 1 Ap 2 60
---I Puritani, Glyndebourne Op-
era; Eric Mason prepares the
viewer. Radio Times p 2 Je 10'60
---The Metropolitan Opera Guild,
Educational Department and NY
State Regents Board, 5-program
series to 5th and 6th grade child-
ren; notes. Opera News v 24
n 17 p 1 F 27'60
---NBC Opera Company; season
notes. Musical Courier p 33
F '60
---NBC-TV commission for Gian-
Carlo Menotti; details. American
Music v 8 n 10 p 10 N '60
---Pagliacci on BBC; Polish Na-
tional Theatre. Radio Times.
p 45 N 24'60
---Palma and Bologna; notes on
opera; all'Eurovisione, d'Oltra-
lpe. La Scala n 123 p 57 F '60
---Pears, Peter. On the produc-
tion at Aldeburgh "of A Mid-
Summer Night's Dream", Britten's
new opera. Radio Times p 2
Je 17'60

(Opera)
---Piamonte, Guido. La RAI ha licenziato alle stampe il cartellone della sua stagione lirica. La Scala n 128 p 45 Jl '60
---Poleri and Copeland in Cavalleria, AP ph: NBC. Opera News v 25 n 3 p 15 N 19'60
---US in 1959-60; opera expansion; titles. Opera News v 25 n 3 p 14 N 19'60

OPERATION CICERO
BBC; Ricardo Montalban. por Radio Times p 5 D 8'60

OPERATION SKYWATCH, series
Midwest Council on Airborne TV Instruction; backers; costs; Purdue University and CBS. TV Guide v 8 n 7 p 28-30 F 13'60

ORATORIOS
Delannoy, Marcel, music and libretto by the poet, Gilles Durieux: Le Télévision française. Toute la Danse n 98 p 23 D '60

ORCHESTRAS
The Leningrad Symphony; BBC notes. il Radio Times p 8 S 16'60

THE ORDEAL OF GILBERT PINFOLD, play
Waugh's novel, adapted by Michael Bakewell at BBC's Radiophonic Studio. Radio Times p 5 Je 3'60

O'SULLIVAN, TERRY, actor
Notes; b. Kansas City. por TV Guide v 8 n 9 p 15 F 27'60

OUR AMERICAN HERITAGE, series
Catton, Bruce. The problem of General Grant. il TV Guide v 8 n 8 p 13-4 F 20'60
---Review of US history clashes, of people. TV Guide v 8 n 21 p 27 My 21'60

OUR BETTERS, play
Maugham's 1923 production revised for BBC; notes and one scene. Radio Times p 3 F 5'60

OUR STREET, series
AR; day-to-day happenings in a London street. Punch p 598 Ap 27'60

OUT OF DOORS, series
Mercer, Ian (1934-), chairman; 5-16 years outdoor contests; badges given to 7,000. Radio Times p 30 Ap 1'60

OUT OF THE BLUE, TV film
Bond, Roger, 12 years hero; BBC; Isles of Scilly. Radio Times p 28 Je 24'60

P

PAAR, JACK
BBC; Perry Como Music Hall. por Radio Times p 5 D 8'60
---Condon, Maurice. The predictable Jack Paar; why his NBC walkout was completely in character. TV Guide v 8 n 8 p A 3-4 F 20'60

PACIFICA FOUNDATION
Radio programs from WBAI, noncommercial station in NYC; notes on opera by Alan Rich. Opera News v 24 n 17 p 2 F 27'60
---Shayon, Robert Lewis. (Purpose of Pacifica, West Coast organization, operating in NYC.) Sat Rev p 26 D 26'59

PADDICK, HUGH, comedian
Beyond Our Ken, serial; BBC. Radio Times p 5 Je 10'60

PAGEANTS
Croydon; notes on local celebration; history 1000 years; BBC notes. Radio Times p 2 Je 17'60

PAINTING
Sketch Club, traveling exhibit by young British artists; notes. Radio Times p 25 Je 3'60
---Painting of the Month, new European series from the Renaissance to the 19th century, BBC; first talk on Ucello (1397-1475), Saint George and the Dragon by Sir Philip Hendy, Director of the National Gallery; 6 people for the year with background notes beforehand. Radio Times p 2 Ja 3'60

PALMER, BETSY, actress
DeBlois, Frank. (Career notes; born Chicago, Patricia Betsy Hrunek; husband, Dr. Vincent J. Merendino, Englewood, New Jersey; on "I ve Got a Secret" TV Guide v 8 n 34 p 9-11 Ag 20'60

PALMISANO, LEON
In Tokyo as TV director; notes

and pictures. Dance Magazine
v 34 n 6 p 38-9 Je '60
PANEL-GAMES
BBC; Laugh Line, review. Punch
702 My 18'60
PAMORAMA, series
Notes on American election on
Panorama. Radio Times p 7
S 2'60
PARADE, series
Melville, Alan. On the new series.
Radio Times p 7 S 30'60
---BBC notes. por Radio Times
p 38 D 22'60
PARACHUTE REGIMENT
Aldershot on BBC. il Radio Tim-
es p 30 S 23'60
PARASOL, musical
Brahms, Carol. (Malcolm Arnold;
from Schnitzler's "Anatol" Dia-
logues; on BBC's Musical Play-
house.) Radio Times p 7 Mr 18'60
PARIS
Lamare, Jean-Yves. Un mois
de télévision musicale (Paris).
Guide du Concert n 290 p 324-5
N 25'60
PARIS IN THE TWENTIES, film
Notes. Radio Times p 5 Ag 5'60
PARKER, SUZY
Notes and signed ph. Screen Al-
bum p 28 N '60
PARKS, BERT, 1915-,
Career notes; b. Atlanta. TV
Guide v 8 n 32 p 13 Ag 6'60
PARRISH, LESLIE
Career sketch; from Pennsylvania,
name, Marjorie Hellen. por TV
Guide v 8 n 38 p 25 S 17'60
PARRY, RON, comedian
Be my Guest; BBC. il Radio Tim-
es p 29 D 15'60
PAS DE QUATRE (DOLIN) ballet
Critical notes; Alonso as Taglioni,
Hayden, Kaye and Slavenska. il
Dance Magazine v 34 n 5 p 13
My '60
PASSION PLAY
Sleath, Alan. Oberammergau;
film, The Vow, first performance
1634 a year after the town's vow
to play the Passion each 10 years.
il Radio Times p 5 Ap 8'60
---The True Mistery of the Passion
by brothers Gréban, 15th century;

(Television Index)
BBC's Holy Week play by James
Kirkup. Radio Times p 4 Ap 8'60
PATTERSON, LEE
Notes. Movie Life p 16 D '60
PAUL OF TARSAS, serial
Filming on Crete; BBC. Radio
Times p 32 S 16'60
---Reed, Owen. (Notes.) il Radio
Times p 13 O 13'60
PAY TV
British producers in favor; notes.
Variety p 13 D 28'60
---Canada; Telemeter system re-
viewed. il TV Age p 32-3, 73
My 30'60
---Canada; Toronto system. Jr
SMPTE v 69 n 5 p 317 My '60
---Hartford, Connecticut; 3-year
trial of subscription TV via Pho-
nevision; notes. Film World and
AV p 158 Ap '60
---Hartford Phonevision; notes.
TV Digest v 16 n 49 p 2 D 5'60
---Progress report. Film World
and AV p 112 Mr '60
---Survey by Pulse, Inc. on US
market for pay TV: report. TV
Age p 42-3, 75 S 19'60
---Survey of income potential for
viewers' bill; charts. TV Age
p 25-7 My 16'60
PAYOLA
Testimony before FCC on "com-
mercial arrangements" of TV
film producers and manufacturers;
general survey of "10 key ques-
tions" by FCC. Telefilm v 5 n 2
p 33 S-O '60
---US Senate hearings; "plugola"
hidden plugs in TV shows; notes.
Music and Dance v 51 n 3 p 19
S '60
PEARS, PETER. A Mid-Summer
Night's Dream, opera by Britten
(how it was produced at Aldeburgh).
Radio Times p 2 Je 17'60
PECK, GREGORY
Notes and signed portrait. Screen
Album p 46 N '60
PEEPLES, SAMUEL, writer
Vogel, Nancy. (Peeples and his
script methods.) Writers Digest
p 52-3 Ag '60
THE PEN OF MY AUNT, play

(The Pen of My Aunt)
Dowling, Patrick, on BBC's
"light-hearted mystery". Radio
Times p 27 Ap 8'60
PEOPLE
British programs: Face to Face
(interviews); Press Conference
(journalists interview); Men of
Action (men who handle danger).
Radio Times p 9 Ja 15'60
THE PEOPLE OF PARADISE,
travel film
Attenborough, David, on his Ton-
ga visit; BBC. il Radio Times
p 25 Jl 22'60
---Series of his films made in the
South Seas. il Radio Times p 3
Ap 15'60
PEOPLE TODAY, series
BBC; Sir John Barbirolli and Ben-
jamin Britten. Radio Times p 5
Je 17'60
PEPPARD, GEORGE
Notes. por Screen World and TV
p 32 O '60
PERREAU, GIGI, 1941-,
And Richard Miles(1938-) who
play (and are) brother and sister;
the Perreau-Saussine Art Gallery
theirs. il TV Guide v 8 n 18 p 20
Ap 30'60
THE PERRY COMO MUSIC HALL
BBC notes. il Radio Times p 5
N 17'60
PERRY MASON, series
Burr, Raymond, in title role;
Ray Collins (1890-) as Lieuten-
ant Tragg; notes on all the cast.
il TV Guide v 8 n 12 p 24-7
Mr 19'60
PERSOFF, NEHEMIAH, 1920-,
actor
Career sketch; b. Palestine. por
TV Guide v 8 n 22 p 29 My 28'60
PERSON TO PERSON, series
Collingwood, Charles. Touring
Europe with TV camera. il TV
Guide v 8 n 32 p 25-7 Ag 6'60
---Sir Anthony Eden at home;
Charles Collingwood plans half the
programs in foreign countries;
technique. TV Guide v 8 n 3 p 6-
7 Ja 16'60
PERSUASION, play
Austen, Jane, in 4 parts,

producer, Campbell Logan;
cast, BBC (scene). Radio Times
p 55 D 22'60
PESTALOZZI CHILDRENS VIL-
LAGES
In BBC's "One Family", the
British type shown; general notes
on the project begun by Walter
Robert Corti. il Radio Times
p 25 Ja 22'60
PETERS, AUDREY
Notes; b. Maplewood, New Jer-
sey. TV Guide v 8 n 33 p 25-6
Ag 13'60
PHILHARMONIC TELETHON
Jessel, George, toastmaster;
Buffalo Philharmonic played;
simulcast earned $14,062 toward
drive to support the orchestra.
International Musician v 58 n 9
p 45 Mr '60
PHILIP MARLOWE, PRIVATE
EYE, series
History of the charactization;
Philip Carey now in the role.
Radio Times p 7 Ja 22'60
PHONOGRAPH RECORDS
BBC: Juke Box Jury, a panel con-
test; and Easy Beat, produced by
Brian Matthew. Radio Times
p 4 Mr 11'60
---Children's Favourites, disc
jockey Derek McCulloch; BBC
notes. por Radio Times p 27
Je 3'60
---Jackson, Jack, his disc jockey
program, "Record Roundabout".
Radio Times p 5 Ap 22'60
---Tricks used in recording, es-
pecially the teen-age voice: echo
chamber, tracking, changes in
frequencies, splicing. TV Guide
v 8 n 26 p 11 Je 25'60
PHOTOGRAPHY
Advance program, papers summarized, International Congress
on High-Speed Photography 1960
Washington. Jr SMPTE v 69 n 9
p 609-652 S '60
---Bazin, André (?-1958). The
ontology of the photographic image. por Film Quarterly v 13
n 4 p 4-8 Summer '60
---History and use of the camera
lucida. Educational Screen and

(Photography)
AV p 274-6 Je '60
---Kingston, Arthur on "Focus"
to show early movie equipment;
notes on his career and inventions. Radio Times p 27 My 20
'60
---Papers read at International
Congress on High-Speed Photography, Washington, D. C. Jr
SMPTE v 69 n 7 p 489-90 Jl '60
---Placing TV cameras: Granada
TV in Village Wooing, 1959; Sver-
iges Radio in Antigone, 1960,
e phs. World Theatre v 9 n 4
p 326 Winter '60
---Portfolio of camera position-
ing, various countries, various
TV angles in an issue devoted to
television drama. World Theatre
v 9 n 4 Winter '60
PIAMONTE, GUIDO. La RAI inten-
de procedere al rilancio della
filo-diffusione, da tempo in atto
a Milano, Torino, Roma e Nap-
oli e in via di estensione ad al-
tre otto città. La Scala n 126
p 49 My '60
---Radio-TV. La Scala n 122 p 59
Ja '60 (series 1960)
PICASSO, PABLO
On "Monitor", seen at work. por
Radio Times p 5 Jl 1'60
PICTURE PARADE, series
Robinson, Robert, new leader;
cinema criticism. por Radio
Times p 4 F 12'60
PINEAPPLE POLL, ballet
BBC viewers around 4 million
(Covent Garden audience in 2000
performances). Radio Times
p 5 Je 3'60
THE PLAY OF THE WEEK, series
No interference from sponsor,
Standard Oil; David Susskind and
Ely Landau, producing; how these
dramas are budgeted. TV Guide
v 8 n 12 p 18 Mr 19'60
PLAYBOX, series
Wiltshire, Gerald. Inter-Regional
Quiz "Playbox" (Danish vs. Bri-
tish youth team pictured). Radio
Times p 31 Ap 1'60
PLAYWRITING
TV play's dialogue more vital

than same play on stage; reasons.
World Theatre v 9 n 4 p 312
Winter '60
PLOTS
A machine that writes scripts at
Massachusetts Institute of Tech-
nology; Dr. Douglas Ross and
TX-O. il TV Guide v 8 n 43
p 28-9 O 22'60
PODOLI, MICHAEL, manager;
TV attracted to groups not the
single artist so much, unless
widely known; TV helps bookings.
Musical Courier v 162 n 1 p 16
Jl '60
POETRY
The Children's Hour, parody of
Longfellow by Bob Johnson. TV
Guide v 8 n 34 p 16 Ag 20'60
---Johnson, Bob. Invictus, par-
ody of William Ernest Henley.
TV Guide v 8 n 36 p 11 S 3'60
--- ---The children's hour (par-
ody of Longfellow). TV Guide
v 8 n 34 p 16 Ag 20'60
POLARIS
Murrow, Edward R., The Year
of the Polaris; BBC notes. Ra-
dio Times p 22 O 13'60
POLITICS
American election on Panorama;
notes. Radio Times p 23 N 3'60
---British local politics, M. P.
facing home folk on past week's
events; BBC chairman, Robert
Carvel. Radio Times p 5 F 12'60
---Cronkite, Walter. These are
the Democrats. il TV Guide v 8
n 28 p 17-20 Jl 9'60
---Debates: Nixon vs. Kennedy;
background notes. TV Guide v 8
n 38 p A 1-3 S 17'60
---de Gaulle Gala at Covent Garden; arrangements described, including fanfare from the stage as
the Royal Box is occupied; ballet
reviewed. il Ballet Today v 12
n 15 p 5 Je '60
---Democratic National Convention
as set up in Los Angeles: preview.
TV Guide v 8 n 28 p 8-11 Jl 9'60
--- ---description of TV coverage.
TV Guide v 8 n 28 p 6-11 Jl 9'60
---Diefenbach, Robert C. The power of TV in the campaign

(Politics)

(summary of poll taken on members of Congress). TV Guide v 8 n 38 p 9-11 S 17'60

---Editorial: debate by US presidential candidates forcing the public out of partisan viewing. TV Guide v 8 n 43 O 22'60

--- ---on watching the US political conventions. TV Guide v 8 n 28 p 3 Jl 9'60

--- ---urge all to watch election programs; not to do so "electronic Russian roulette". TV Guide v 8 n 28 Jl 9'60

---Edwards, Douglas. Facing the Republican Convention. il TV Guide v 8 n 30 p 17-9 Jl 23'60

---Edwin, Ed. A look at leading (US) candidates. il TV Guide v 8 n 28 p 12-4 Jl 9'60

---Equal time on TV to ALL candidates; Communications Act, US, under fire. TV Guide v 8 n 34 p 3 Ag 20'60

---Harris, Kenneth. The party conferences: the Liberals, the Labour Party, the Conservatives. Radio Times p 6 S 23'60

---Hope, Bob. Open season on politicians. il TV Guide v 8 n 43 p 14-18 O 22'60

---Howe, Quincy. Television: the new political weapon. por Telefilm v 5 n 2 p 3, 22 S-O '60

---Major party votes in all US Presidential elections, 1789-1956. TV Guide v 8 n 30 p 6-7 Jl 23'60

---Medium can swing an election; US examples, Florida, New York, Massachusetts, etc. TV Age p 30-1, 36- Je 27'60

---New series, financed by The Fund for the Republic, called "The American Republic; criticism by Robert Lewis Shayon. Saturday Review p 36 O 3'59

---News coverage, ABC's John Charles Daly; born in Johannesburg; career sketch, Boston youth. por TV Guide v 8 n 30 p 8-11 Jl 23'60

---The Nixon-Kennedy debate series; notes. TV Guide v 8 n 43 p 3 O 22'60

---Nixon-Khruschev debate in Moscow 1959: award from the Academy of Television Arts and Sciences to RCA and to Ampex. TV Guide v 8 n 30 p 3 Jl 23'60

---President de Gaulle in London; Godfrey Talbot on BBC's coverage. Radio Times p 3 Ap 1'60

---Presidential election: how to be your own expert; US laid out (map) by electoral votes. TV Guide v 8 n 45 p 5-8 N 5'60

---Questionaire answers from senators and representatives on TV in US politics; replies in percentages. TV Guide v 8 n 38 p 10 S 17'60

---Report to the People of Pennsylvania; Hugh D. Scott, Republican, and Joseph S. Clark, Democrat; review. TV Guide v 8 n 2 p 22-3 Ja 9'60

---Sen. Wayne Morse attacking Sen. John F. Kennedy as enemy of labor; film retaken as original worn by prints. Film World and AV p 60 F '60

---Television upon US politics; opinion of Senator Jacob K. Javits. TV Guide v 8 n 40 p 9-11 O 1'60

---US; election data. TV Guide v 8 n 45 p 5-9 N 5'60

--- ---las as it stands on free time to debates; suggested change. TV Guide v 8 n 15 p 2 Ap 9'60

--- ---law on donated time on TV; hence time is bought; comment. TV Guide v 8 n 34 Ag 20'60

--- ---notes on NBC's The Campaign, on CBS Presidential Countdown, on ABC Campaign Roundup. TV Guide v 8 n 45 p 23 N 5'60

--- ---president doesn't have to be the people's choice (the Electoral College explained). TV Guide v 8 n 30 p 14-5 Jl 23'60

---various shows: US election fare; notes. TV Guide v 8 n 45 p 23 N 5'60

POLLS

Gallup, Dr. George, 1901-; career sketch; methods. por Printers'

Ink p 53-5 Je 24'60
PONCE, PONCIE, 1933-, actor
In Hawaiian Eye; notes. il TV
Guide v 8 n 22 p 19 My 28'60
PONY EXPRESS
Mayne, L. Bruce. Pony Express
on Children's Hour, BBC. Radio
Times p 29 Ap 1'60
POPEYE, cartoon series
History of the cartoon created
by Segar. il TV Guide v 8 n 35
p 8-10 Ag 27'60
---Notes on new series. il TV
Guide v 8 n 35 p 8-10 Ag 17'60
PORT SUNLIGHT
Suction dregger at work, BBC
program. Radio Times p 23
F 26'60
PORTER, DON, 1917-, actor
Career notes; b. Miami, Oklahoma;
Ann Sothern show. por TV Guide
v 8 n 16 p 13-5 Ap 16'60
PORTLAND, MAINE
WGAN-TV; baby-sitting service;
notes. il TV Guide v 8 n 36 p 14-
6 S 3'60
PORTUGAL
Ballade for Three by Norman
Dixon for Portuguese Television.
Ballet Today v 12 n 18 p 29 O '60
POSTON, TOM
Notes; To Tell the Truth, series.
TV Guide v 8 n 37 p 17-9 S 10'60
POWELL, DICK
Notes on his collection of Wild
West relics. il TV Guide v 8 n 44
p 28-9 O 29'60
POWER, TYRONE, 1911-1958
Note. por Movie Life p 31 D '60
PRESLEY, ELVIS, 1935-, actor
Levy, Alan. Elvis comes marching
home. por TV Guide v 8 n 19 p 10-
2 My 7'60
---Notes; house in Bel Air. Movie
Life p 14 D '60
---Zucker, Herb. (Report on Mia-
mi, Florida, Hotel Fontaine Bleau
taping of Frank Sinatra (1916-)
show with Presley.) por TV Gui-
de v 8 n 19 p 15 My 7'60
PRIESTLEY, J B. On his play "I
Have Been Here Before", on BBC
in revival. Radio Times p 7
Mr 25'60

PRODUCTION
Ballroom; amateurs on TV; suggestions. Ballroom Dancing Times v 5 n 1 p 24-5 O '60
---Cost; breakdown of half-hour
film program budget by Nicholas
Archer and John Barnwell. Telefilm p 30-3, 40 Jl-Ag '60
---Cost of producing a TV special;
broken into details, $241,000. TV
Guide v 8 n 34 p 14 Ag 20'60
---Curtiz, Michael. (From Italy, his
comments on why producers are
going abroad; "Francis of Assisi"
discussed.) Variety p 4 N 30'60
---Dance choreographer for TV is
a good choreographer aware of two-
dimensional composition; other
pointers. Impulse p 43 1960
---Fights on TV; Terry Baker,
1930-, arranger of fights for junior programs, how they are done.
il Radio Times p 27 Ap 29'60
---Hollywood properties house,
Display Industries Cooperative Exchange: Dice, Inc. il TV Guide
v 8 n 26 p 28-9 Je 25'60
---Iglésis, Roger. First steps in
television for the stage producer.
il World Theatre v 9 n 4 p 325-
336 Winter '60
---Lachenbruch, David. Look, Ma,
no hands (explanation of electron-
ically run studio in Cincinnati,
WKRC-TV where a day's programs
are by "computer language" released automatically). TV Guide
v 8 n 24 p 10-1 Je 11'60
---McCleery, Albert, director of
CBS Television Workshop; now
directors are being made. il TV
Guide v 8 n 37 p 24-6 S 10'60
---The Mackenzie Repeater; discussion of sound-making on TV.
TV Guide v 8 n 41 p 24-5 O 8'60
---Mobile unit, Videotape-equipped, MVT leased, ready for world use. il TV Guide v 8 n 14 p 22-3
Ap 2'60
---Old automobiles, why needed and
hunting old models: ph: Desilu Studios. TV Guide v 8 n 21 p 24 My 21'60
---Production report, films from

(Production)
several countries besides US, each issue. Film Quarterly 1959, 1960

---Properties; notes on Cinema Mercantile; the First Street Furniture Store; House of Props; Hollywood Studio Furniture. il TV Guide v 8 n 35 p 12-3 Ag 27 '60

---They protect TV against anything except flops; insurance cases. TV Guide v 8 n 18 p 10-1 Ap 30'60

---Thomson, Ernest, on wardrobe and TV make-up; BBC. il Radio Times p 56 N 24'60

---Wray, Richard, on cutting film for 18 serials a week at Rebue Studio; techniques. por TV Guide v 8 n 23 p 24-5 Je 4'60

THE PROFESSOR'S LOVE STORY, play
BBC play to celebrate Sir James Barrie's centenary; notes. Radio Times p 5 Jl 22'60

PROGRAMS
Experts: E. K. Hartenbower, Charles A. Siepmann, Hendrick Booraem, Jr.; good and bad programs, trends. TV Age p 27-9, 69 Je 13'60

---Ford, Frederick W. Making television serve the public (legislation recommended for direct regulation of networks). TV Guide v 8 n 41 p 6-9 O 8'60

---The new season, Saturday thru Wednesday; sports and specials also listed and discussed. il TV Guide v 8 n 39 S 24'60

---Summer viewing; Nielsen ratings quoted; Pulse Inc. quoted; re-runs are viewed each summer. TV Guide v 8 n 17 p 3 Ap 23'60

---US; notes on "thinking man" programs; CBS Reports, World Wide 60 and such. TV Guide v 8 n 18 p 27 Ap 30'60

PROJECT 20, series
Hyatt, Donald B. (1924-) the producer; compiled from historic film footage and such. il TV Guide v 8 n 35 p 14-6 Ag 27'60

---Producer, Donald B. Hyatt; broadly, public service but entertainment also; historical digging into US heritage. il TV Guide v 8 n 35 p 14-6 Ag 27'60

PROPERTIES
Dice, Inc., a Hollywood firm of 10,000 items. il TV Guide v 8 n 26 p 28-9 Je 25'60

---Notes on US prop houses. il TV Guide v 8 n 35 p 12-3 Ag 27'60

PROVINE, DOROTHY, 1937-, actress
Notes; b. Seattle. TV Guide v 8 n 24 p 27 Je 11'60

---Notes; "I. Q. 165"; AP hl ph. Screen Album p 76 N '60

P. S. 4, series
High-school-level course; St Louis notes. Film World and AV p 162 Ap '60

PUBLICITY
Granada's publicity program for Cinderella: editors flown in, lunched, sets and costumes on display, dress rehearsal. Ballet Today v 12 n 14 p 3 My '60

---US; advice on getting tickets in NYC or Los Angeles to see TV shows in the studio. TV Guide v 8 n 26 p 26 Je 25'60

PUPPETS
BBC show of pig puppets: Pinky and Perky; Jan and Vlasta Dalibor; announcer, Roger Moffat. il Radio Times p 4 F 26'60

---Hank the Cowboy, invented by Francis Coudrill; notes and picture (BBC). Radio Times p 25 F 5'60

---Lewis, Shari (1933-); Lamb Chop, Charley Horse and Hush Puppy, each a facet of her personality as explained by Miss Lewis. il TV Guide v 8 n 29 p 8-10 Jl 16'60

---Puppets at Tokushima shown in "Safari to Asia"; BBC notes. Radio Times p 39 D 8'60

---Something In the Air, a BBC puppet play by Gordon Murray; space ship. il Radio Times p 23 F 26 '60

Q

QUINN, CARMEL, actress
Irish monologue on her US career. il TV Guide v 8 n 22 p 20-2 My 28 '60

QUINN, LOUIS, 19,15-, actor
Interview; born Louis Quinn Frackt, Chicago. por TV Guide v 8 n 33 p 16-9 Ag 13'60

QUIZ SHOWS
BBC; comment on The Charlie Green and others. Punch p 852 Je 15'60

---Playbox, Tony Hart, for boys and girls; Inspector Bruce; BBC notes. Radio Times p 46 O 13'60

---Reactions of quiz show winners now nervous over "perjury charges" before Frank Hogan, New York district attorney; quoted. TV Guide v 8 n 44 p A 1-2, 30 O 29'60

---Sporting Chance, sports quiz of teams by Brian Johnston; BBC notes. Radio Times p 5 S 23'60

---US; comment. Sat-Rev p 25 O 31'59

---US; news report of NYC grand jury investigation; Elfrida Von Nardoff, top winner, and others arraigned. TV Guide v 8 n 44 p A 1-2 O 29'60

---What Do You Know, series on BBC; Brain of Britain" prize. Radio Times p 4 Ja 8'60

R

RADIO
Music on BBC; orchestral concerts, chamber music and recitals; regular listings. Radio Times 1960

---Radio Link, a program; topical, live TV, nationals speaking from their own lands. Radio Times p 7 Ag 5'60

---Survey of US radio programs, and of some TV by Robert Wangermée, traveling in USA and recording impressions. Inter-American music bulletin March 1961

RADIO SHOW, LONDON
Report; BBC's place. Radio Times p 2 Ag 19'60

RAGOSIN, LYDIA, pseud.
Real name Lydia Kyasht, Jr.; TV scripts; The Magic Weathercock. Ballet Today v 12 n 16 p 4 Jl '60

THE RAGTIME ERA, series
Twelve programs, 1890-1920, notes. Music Educators Journal v 47 n 1 p 11 S-O '60

RAI-TV
Italy; opere liriche; concerti sinfonici (programma nazionale, secundo programma, terzo programma). La Scala 1960

---L'Orchestra A. Scarlatti diretta da Franco Caracciolo: Concerto per violino, pianoforte e orchestra di Roberto Gorini Falco. La Scala n 133 p 116 D '60

RANDALL, TONY. (Randall, the creator; zany shows that could enliven TV.) il TV Guide v 8 n 27 p 5-7 Jl 2'60

RATINGS
ABC as "number one network" in coast to coast rating; evidence summarized by National Nielsens. Variety p 23 N 30'60

---American Research Bureau ratings; information show has higher rating than supposed. TV Guide v 8 n 26 Je 25'60

---Moral ratings of films; service by phone in Newark New Jersey for Catholics. Film World and AV p 305 Ag '60

---New device, TVQ, to research on casting, on scripting etc. "if successful, should put TV back 10 years. " TV Guide n 41 p 2 O 8'60

---Stahl, Bob. Those ratings, TV's slave or master? TV Guide v 8 n 5 p 9-11 Ja 30'60

---TV ratings as a marketing tool; confusions aired. Printers' Ink p 26-7 S 2'60

TV Guide v 8 n 24 p 4 Je 11'60
---Smith, Don Crawmer. Levels
of attention given to television
by housewives of Tuscaloosa,
Alabama in 1955. (Ph. D. thesis
Ohio State University 1959). Dissertation Abstracts v 20 n 10
p 4218 Ap '60
---Social Research, Inc. survey of
TV Guide readers; editorial on
results. TV Guide v 8 n 32 p 3
Ag 6'60
---Swart, John Carroll. Auditory
threshold variability: frequency,
intensity step and descending
versus ascending series (Ph. D.
thesis, Indiana University, 1960).
Dissertation Abstracts p 702 S'60
---World survey of motion picture
theater facilities, US Dept. of
Commerce release (10 cents):
review. Jr SMPTE v 69 n 11
p 826 N '60
RESNAIS, ALAIN
Burch, Noel. Conversation with
Alain Renais. Film Quarterly
v 13 n 3 p 17-19 Spring '60
THE REVLON REVUE
Review. TV Guide v 8 n 14 p 27
Ap 2'60
REYNOLDS, DEBBIE, 1932-,
actress
Interview; career notes. il TV
Guide v 8 n 43 p 19-21 O 22'60
RICHARDSON, TONY, director
Young, Colin. Interview. il Film
Quarterly v 13 n 4 p 10-15
Summer '60
RIKKO, FRITZ
With Collegium Musicum on NBC-
TV, "Sunday Gallery"; Bach, Vi-
valdi, Mozart. Juilliard Review
v 7 n 3 p 20 Fall '60
RIVA, MARIO
Italy; criticism. La Scala n 131
p 51 O '60
RIVERBOAT, series
NBC; Darren McGavin as the
Captain; review. TV Guide v 8
n 2 p 27 Ja 9'60
RIX, BRIAN, actor-manager
Career notes; the Whitehall Thea-
tre in London 10 years; "the dri-
ving force behind this post-war

(Television Index)
revival of force". por Radio
Times p 7 F 19'60
ROBERTS, PERNELL, 1927-,
actor
Notes; b. Waycross, Georgia.
por TV Guide v 8 n 38 p 15
S 17'60
ROBINSON, HUBBELL. You, the
public, are to blame(need for view-
ers to help TV mature). TVGuide
v 8 n 48 p 14-6 N 26'60
ROBINSON, ROBERT
Picture Parade (BBC) on cinema.
Punch p 370 Mr 9'60
ROCKWELL, ROBERT, 1922-,
actor
Career sketch; b. Lake Bluff,
Illinois. il TV Guide v 8 n 5
p 21-3 Ja 30'60
ROGERS, ANNE, actress
Note por Radio Times p 4 Ap 8'60
ROGERS, HELEN JEAN
Career notes; b. Fond Du Lac,
Wisconsin. il TV Guide v 8 n 11
p 24-6 Mr 12'60
ROGERS, WAYNE
Notes; Princeton degree in busi-
ness management; Stage Coach
West, series. Movie Life p 18
D '60
ROOM SERVICE, play
BBC; Marx Brothers. Radio
Times p 5 Ag 12'60
ROSAY, FRANÇOISE, actress
British TV debut in "Colombo";
notes. il Radio Times p 3 Ja 15'60
ROYAL ASCOT
BBC coverage of racing and fashion.
Radio Times p 7 Je 10'60
ROYAL WEDDING
Brussels; King Baudouin of the
Belgians; BBC background. Radio
Times p 47 D 8'60
THE RUFFIANS, play
BBC notes. il Radio Times p 15
O 6'60
RULE, JANICE
Career notes; b. Cincinnati. por
TV Guide v 8 n 44 p 25-6 O 29'60
RUM
Under-sea TV camera for research;
notes. il TV Guide v 8 n 35 p 22-3
Ag 27'60

391

RUPPERT BREWERY
NYC; cancellation of "Sea Hunt" at discovery of foreigh tape used for sound. International Musician v 59 n 4 p 7 O '60

RUSSELL, JEANNIE, 1952-
Note. il TV Guide v 8 n 9 p 12 F 27'60

RUSSELL, JIM, dancer
Career notes. por Dance Magazine v 34 n 4 p 21 Ap '60

RUSSIA
Audio-visual in the schools; Millard Harmon report. il Ed Screen and AV p 18-9 Ja '60
---Cinematography; report. il Jr SMPTE v 69 n 5 p 339-343 My '60
---Government survey of radio and television; report. Film World and AV p 111 Mr '60
---Third in TV sets. Film World and AV p 377 O '60
---Williams, Don G. (Ten students in cinema and TV to each one training in US.) Ed Screen and AV p 320 Jl '60

S

SAFARI TO ASIA, series
BBC notes; Armand Denis. Radio Times p 39 D 1'60
---Denis, Armand; BBC notes on travel. Radio Times p 5 Jl 1'60

SAHL, MORT. (On his career as a comedian.) por TV Guide v 8 n 3 p 10-1 Ja 16'60

ST. IVES, serial
Tucker, Rex. His adaptation to TV of Stevenson's tale. (one scene). Radio Times p 25 Je 10'60

ST. NICHOLAS, Christmas opera
Britten's work over CBS-TV Dec. 20, 1959; William Lewis as St. Nick. Opera News v 24 n 9 p 3 Ja 2'60

SAN FRANCISCO
Opera telecasts, previews over KQED; stimulating. Opera News v 25 n 1 p 7 O 8'60

SATELLITE TV
Cortright, Edgar M. of the National Space Administration on Gloval TV via satellites. Film

World and AV p 156 Ap '60
---Lackenbruch, Davis. (Passive and active; notes.) TV Guide v 8 n 49 p 26-7 D 3'60
---Tiros; notes. il Jr SMPTE v 69 n 4 p 272, 274 Ap '60
---What advantages; RCA submitting to FCC proposals. Jr SMPTE v 69 n 8 p 556 Ag '60
See also   Global TV

SATURDAY NIGHT THEATRE
A repertory group, now in 21st year; history since 1939; "Carnival", play, notes. Radio Times p 3 Ag 26'60

SAXON, JOHN, actor
Notes and por. Screen World and TV p 34 O '60

SCHRAMM, DR. WILBUR. What does your child bring to TV? (His needs which TV like a cafeteria may satisfy). TV Guide v 8 n 19 p 5-7 My 7'60

SCHARY, DORE, 1906-, producer
Career notes. por TV Guide v 8 n 16 p 5-7 Ap 16'60

SCIENCE
ATV; It Can Happen Tomorrow; comment. Punch p 208 F 3'60
---BBC; Eye on Research, series; notes. Punch p 565 Ap 20'60
---Cockerell, Christopher, inventor of the Hovercraft principle, in program (BBC) "No Visible Means of Support." Radio Times p 5 Ag 17'60
---Eye on Research, series (BBC); the fellows of the Royal Society; honoring tercentenary of its founding. Radio Times p 7 Ap 1'60
---Insight, series of 11 programmes, Dr. Bronowski. por Radio Times p 9 S 9'60
---Lifeline (on psychological problems); The Sky at Night (astronomy), both BBC. Radio Times p 9 Ja 15'60
---Look, series; Dragonflies and Preying Plants; BBC program notes. Radio Times p 39 O 6'60
---Series: "Experiment" on BBC; Arthur Garratt on man-made fibres. il Radio Times p 27 My 6'60
---TV camera in "remote underwater manipulator", RUM;

explanation. il TV Guide v 8
n 35 p 22-3 Ag 27'60
---The Tercentenary of the Ro-
yal Society; programs on BBC
explained by Dr. D. C. Martin.
Radio Times p 2 Jl 15'60
SCIENCE COUNT-DOWN 1960
Boston, WBZ-TV for eighth
graders to compete; questions by
Lowell Technological Institute;
sample quiz given. TV Guide
v 8 n 16 p 18-9 Ap 16'60
SCIENCE FICTION
Films on BBC; list. Radio Times
p 5 Ag 12'60
SCOTLAND YARD, series
Barr, Robert. (Introducing the
new police series; "no guns but
plenty of action".) il Radio Times
p 3 Ap 8'60
---Documentary under Robert
Barr. Punch p 598 Ap 27'60
SCOTSMEN'S GOLD, play
Cameron, Audrey. New Zealand
gold rush of 1861 (notes on BBC;
cast.) Radio Times p 6 Ap 29'60
SCOTT, PIPPA, 1938-, actress
Career notes. por TV Guide v 8
n 14 p 28-9 Ap 2'60
SCRIPTS
Anatomy of a script; notes and
portions of The Twilight Zone.
TV Guide v 8 n 45 p 26-9 N 5'60
---Cartoon and gags on a writers'
conference. TV Guide v 8 n 25
p 8-9 Je 18'60
---A machine writes scripts, TX-
O, by Dr. Douglas Ross of Mass-
achusetts Institute of Techmology;
comments. il TV Guide v 8 n 43
p 28-9 O 22'60
---Elliott, Sumner Locke. The
cracked lens; notes on "Hedda
Hopper's Hollywood". Harper's
p 78, 81-3 D '60
---Massachusetts Institute of
Technology; new machine to write
Westerns; TX-O developed by Dr.
Douglas Ross. TV Guide v 8 n 43
p 28-9 O 22'60
---Reynolds, Paul R. The literary
agent. The Writer p 8-13 F '60
---Vogel, Nancy. (Need for a
writer to visit a set; example,

(Television Index)
Universal Studios.) Writers
Digest p 42, 44-5 Jl '60
--- ---(Series on scripts and
writers.) Writer's Digest 1960
THE SEA SHALL NOT HAVE
THEM, film
Year 1944, sea rescue on BBC;
cast. il Radio Times p 5 O 13'60
SEARCHLIGHT, program
Comments on Granada series
by J. B. Boothroyd. Punch 852
Je 15'60
SEARLE, PAMELA, actress
Notes. por TV Guide v 8 n 46
p 28 N 12'60
THE SECRET KINGDOM, play
Greenwood, Walter. Play from
TV serial in 8 parts from his
novel; Maureen Pryor as Paula
Byron. por Radio Times p 9
Ap 29'60
SELDES, GILBERT. The petulant
highbrow and TV. TV Guide v 8
n 1 p 17-9 Ja 2'60
SELLERS, PETER, 1925
Notes; b. Southsea. por Screen
Album p 30 N '60
SEVAREID, ERIC
The Freedom Explosion, his
Nigerian example of African
politics; film CBS on BBC. il
Radio Times p 5 Ap 15'60
SHAKESPEARE, WILLIAM
Barry, Michael. Fifteen parts
covering historical plays of
Shakespeare on alternate Thurs-
days: An Age of Kings. portfolio
Radio Times p 3 Ap 22'60
SHARPE, KAREN, 1935-, actress
Career notes; b. San Antonio,
Texas. por TV Guide v 8 n 27
p 8-9 Jl 2'60
SHEEP'S CLOTHING, serial
Rawlinson, A. R. on his mystery
serial (BBC). Radio Times p 29
S 16'60
SHELTON, ANNE, singer
On BBC's Friday Show. por Ra-
dio Times p 54 N 10'60
SHERLOCK HOLMES, series
Since Conan Doyle wrote 56
Holmes stories, why these "base
imitations" on AR? Punch p 816

(Sherlock Holmes)
Je 8'60

SHERMAN, ANDY, 1944-, actor
Note on "Laramie; b. Virginia.
Radio Times p 29 Mr 18'60

SHIPS
The Last of the Battleships, BBC
film on H. M. S. Vanguard; re-
miniscenes. Radio Times p 5 Jl
22'60

SHORE, DINAH, actress
Interview; Fanny Rose Shore
Montgomery, from Nashville,
Tenn. por TV Guide v 8 n 40 p 17-
19 O 1'60

SHOTGUN SLADE, western
Brady, Scott, notes. il TV Guide
v 8 n 8 9 10-12 F 20'60

SHOWTIME, series
Drake, Alfred, and others on
BBC. il Radio Times p 13 O 27'60

THE SIEGE OF CYRIL STREET,
play
BBC thriller; Charlie Drake.
Radio Times p 55 D 1'60

SIEPI, CESARE, singer
In Don Giovanni, NBC Opera;
notes. Musical Courier p 33
F '60

SIGNORET, SIMONE, actress
In BBC's Face to Face. por Radio Times p 13 N 10'60

SILENCE
Its place in learning; excerpt from
Cahier d'Etudes de Radio-Tele-
vision. Educational Screen and
AV p 179 Ap '60

SILENTS PLEASE, series
Killiam, Paul, collector of pioneer silent films, using them in
half-hour series. il TV Guide
v 8 n 38 p 20-22 S 17'60
---Re-run of old movies (ABC);
review. TV Guide v 8 n 37 p 27
S 10'60

SILHOUETTE FILMS
Reiniger, Lotte. How I make my
silhouette films; animation problems. il Radio Times p 27 Ja 15
'60

SILVERS, PHIL
And Polly Bergen; notes. il TV
Guide v 8 n 41 p 12-4 O 8'60

SILVESTER, VICTOR

Television Dancing Club on
BBC. por Radio Times p 23 O 27
'60

SIMMONS, JEAN, actress
Notes. por Screen Album p 39
N '60

SIMPSON, CHRISTIAN, director
BBC; Jazz A La Carte: "abstract
production" of "arty hullaballoo",
song, dance and Humphrey Little-
ton's Band. Punch p 888 Je 22'60

SINATRA, FRANK
Notes and signed ph. Screen Album p 58 N '60

SINCLAIR, MARY, actress
Her story of her comeback. por
TV Guide v 8 n 18 p 12-4 Ap 30
'60

SINGERS
Nilsson, Birgit with Perry Como
on Kraft Music Hall Feb. 3 and
Renata Tebaldi on Bell Telephone
Hour in Otello arias. Opera News
v 24 n 12 p 3 Ja 23 '60
---Stahl, Bob. Can they really
sing? Fabian Forte, Bobby Dar-
ian, Paul Anka, Frankie Avalon,
Edd Byrnes. Tricks at the mike,
tricks of recording young singers.
il TV Guide v 8 n 26 p 9-11 Je 25'60

SKATING
Ice Cocktail; Jacqueline DuBief.
Radio Times p 15 N 3'60
---US; notes on Ronny Robertson;
on Bobby Specht; Jacqueline Du-
Bief; Dorothy Keller. Dance Mag-
azine v 34 n 7 p 25 Jl '60

SKELTON, RED
Hollywood; report of new mobile
units. il Film World and AV
p 342 S '60
---Jenkins, Dan. (Interview.) il
TV Guide v 8 n 8 p 17-9 F 20'60

THE SLEEPING BEAUTY (PETI-
PA-DALE), ballet
BBC and Eurovision; review. Bal-
let Today v 12 n 11 p 7 F '60
---Dale, Margaret. (The story and
TV introduction, BBC production).
Radio Times p 27 Ap 15'60
---Review of BBC-TV by Alfred H.
Franks (two stills) Dancing Times
v 50 n 593 p 243 F '60

SLEZAK, WALTER, 1902-, singer

DeBlois, Frank. (career sketch; born Vienna.) por TV Guide v 8 n 26 p 12-15 Je 15'60

SLIPWAY 14, series
BBC; 6 programs on building a liner; "Canberra" taken as the program model. Radio Times p 27 F 5'60

SMALL WORLD, series
Murrow, Ed, in "inter-continental conversations"; notes. Radio Times p 5 Ja 15'60

---Murrow, Ed; comments on "intellectual conflict" show. Punch p 208 F 3'60

SMITH, HOWARD K., 1914-, news analyst
Notes. por TV Guide v 8 n 31 p 24-6 Jl 30'60

SMITH, ROGER. Live it up before you marry. il Movie Life p 32, 49 D '60

SOAP OPERA
Full Circle and The Clear Horizon; notes on CBS serials. TV Guide v 8 n 32 p 23 Ag 6'60

---Notes on Full Circle and on The Clear Horizon. TV Guide v 8 n 32 p 23 Ag 6'60

SOCIETIES
Girl Guides, play to celebrate 50 years; Carl Huson, author, tells of the play to be televised at Wembley Pool. Radio Times p 27 Jl 15'60

---News, conferences, leaders US and abroad, in the pages of the Journal of the Society of Motion Picture and TV Engineers.

SOCIETY of MOTION PICTURE and TV ENGINEERS
1960 convention, Los Angeles: background of 100 authors of papers to be given. Telefilm My'60

---Papers read at convention, Los Angeles, May 1960; list with annotations. Jr SMPTE v 69 n 3 p 184-190 Mr'60

THE SOLDIER'S TALE, play with music
BBC; Stravinsky's use of current jazz and ragtime; other notes. il Radio Times p 6 Ag 12'60

(Television Index)

SOMETHING TO SHOUT ABOUT, film
On advertising; BBC satire. Radio Times p 2 Jl 1'60

THE SONG of a MARCH HARE, play
BBC notes (scene). Radio Times p 13 D 8'60

THE SONG of CRAZY HORSE, serial
North America; Sioux on BBC; Chief Crazy Horse born 1844 the central character. Radio Times p 2 Je 10'60

SONGS
The illustrated song on TV; its history 1895-1913 by John W. Ripley, who collects old song slides; Project 20, the TV revival. TV Guide v 8 n 47 p 24-7 N 19'60

---Ripley, John W. Everybody sing (Project 20 re-introducing old songs). il TV Guide v 8 n 47 p 24-6 N 19'60

---The Top Ten; frequent notes on these. Radio Times 1960

---Trent, Bruce, song series "mezso voce", BBC notes. Radio Times p 4 Jl 8'60

SONS of the MUSKETEERS, play
Based somewhat on The Three Musketeers but these are the "next generation" and one a girl; BBC. Radio Times p 4 S 2'60

SOTHERN, ANN, 1912-, actress-producer
Career notes. por TV Guide v 8 n 16 p 13-5 Ap 16'60

SOUND EFFECTS
Editorial on TV sounds this season; speech drowned out, background music becomes foreground, etc. TV Guide v 8 n 48 p 2 N 26'60

---Laughter; Felice Greene and her company, Audiences Unlimited; notes. TV Guide v 8 n 51 p 6-7 D 17'60

---Radio Recorders, MP-TV Services, over 2200 sound effects in the catalog; cost to make; cost to buy. TV Guide v 8 n 47 p 14-6 N 19'60

SOUND ENGINEERING
Editorial; too many good songs and words now lost on TV. TV

(Sound Engineering)
Guide v 8 n 48 p 4 N 26'60
---Gardner, Loris M. Simultaneous theater reproduction of four languages. Jr SMPTE v 69 n 3 p 179-180 Mr '60
---Goodall, George B. Modern control of theater sound. il Jr SMPTE v 69 n 4 p 249-252 Ap '60
---MacKenzie, Louis G. (1915-), inventor of "The Multiple Channel Program Repeater"; use in TV; how it works. il TV Guide v 8 n 41 p 24-5 O 8'60
---Sinclair, Charles. How to improve your TV's audio (technical but practical). charts High Fidelity v 10 n 12 p 115-6 D '60

SPACE
Florida; report film safe in space; Cape Canaveral notes. Film World and AV p 101 Mr '60
---Issue devoted to space problems, some of which affect present TV thinking. Journal SMPTE Ja '60
---Lost Planet, serial, on Children's Hour; notes. Radio Times p 28 My 13'60
---Men Into Space, series; submitted to American Defense men and only what could happen included; William Lundigan as pioneer spaceman. Radio Times p 29 S 9'60
---Program: Into and Out of Space; notes on UFO (Unidentified Flying Objects) on BBC weekly. Radio Times p 26 Ja 29'60
---Spaulding, S. W. Television and lunar exploration. il Journal SMPTE v 69 n 1 p 39-43 Ja '60
---US; TV as a tool; notes. Film World and AV p 338-9 S '60

SPECIAL-EFFECTS CINEMATOGRAPHY
Fielding, Raymond. Bibliography, 1909-1959. Jr SMPTE v 69 n 6 p 421-4 Je '60

SPECIALS
Cost of TV special shows; some statistics. TV Guide v 8 n 34 p 14 Ag 20'60
---Preview of season's special TV shows. TV Guide v 8 n 39

p 20-1 S 24'60

SPECTRUMATTE
A process developed by Television Films, Inc.; infrared film and regular film in the camera; used in commercials since 1959. TV Guide v 8 n 8 p 23 F 20'60

SPEECH
Burak, Matt. The medium's use of English. TV Guide v 8 n 34 p 22-3 Ag 20'60

SPELLING, AARON
As producer of "Johnny Ringo"; story of the show, starring Don Durant. il TV Guide v 8 n 13 p 20-2 Mr 26'60

SPICER, DENNIS, ventriloquist
Talking to a cigarette package, etc. on "Make It Tonight", BBC. Radio Times p 4 Jl 15'60

THE SPLENDID SPUR, play
BBC; year 1642, Civil War; David Tutaev's adaptation from Sir Arthur Quiller-Couch (several scenes and cast). Radio Times p 25 F 26'60

SPLIT PERSONALITY, series
Poston, Tom, the star; contestants try to identify a celebrity. TV Guide v 8 n 3 p 27 Ja 16'60

SPONSORS
Advising sponsors, a new high level hob in picking shows to suit a product. TV Guide v 8 n 37 p 4 S 10'60
---Epstein, Donald K. Why sponsors buy (a fictitious typical tale of selling shows to sponsors, US). TV Guide v 8 n 43 p 23-5 O 22'60
---Fund of the Republic report on TV tactics; rebuttal by ad men that sponsors can change film very little if any, do very little harm to playwright. Printers' Ink p 13 Jl 29'60
---Involved in protest against use of foreign music in American films; details. International Musician v 59 n 3 p 9 S '60
---Sponsor interference; Rod Sterling on the subject. TV Guide v 8 n 46 p 12-5 N 12'60
---US; film track protest (against

foreign "wet-back" tapes) gets sponsors' aid; examples. International Musician v 58 n 11 p 8 My '60

---US; hands off policy (example Standard Oil's Play of the Week); responsibility taken by some sponsors (examples). TV Guide v 8 n 12 p 18-9 Mr 19'60

SPORTING CHANCE, quiz show Towns in Britain compete, sports information; finals to be a live show. Radio Times p 7 Ja 8'60

SPORTS

Army-Navy, annual football, ABC-TV; history. TV Guide v 8 n 48 p 6-7 N 26'60

---Auto racing, Ken Wharton Trophy on "Grandstand", BBC notes. Radio Times p 4 D 8'60

---The Badmington Horse Trials; notes on BBC coming review. Radio Times p 9 Ap 15'60

---Baseball; Candlestick Park, San Francisco; the Giants in action. TV Guide v 8 n 32 p 14-6 Ag 6'60

--- ---players who end up on TV, broadcasting: list. TV Guide v 8 n 21 p 22-3 My 21'60

---Behind the Name, series; Stanley Matthews. por Radio Times p 53 N 24'60

---Boxing; BBC notes (scene at the National Sporting Club). Radio Times p 39 D 22'60

--- ---on "Sportsview"; BBC notes. Radio Times p 47 O 13'60

--- ---on "Sportsview"; BBC. Radio Times p 39 N 17'60

--- ---notes on US fights. TV Guide v 8 n 22 p 23 My 28'60

---Britain's A.A.A. Champships to weed for the Olympics; notes on second and third strings new standards; BBC coverage. Radio Times p 7 Jl 8'60

---BBC-TV; notes on various programs. Radio Times p 7 Ag 12'60

--- ---Junior Sportsview; notes. Punch p 304 F 24'60

---Catamarans, small-boat sailing; BBC. Radio Times p 55

(Television Index) D 29'60

---Durslag, Melvin. Charlie Dressen and Fred Haney argue baseball on and off TV. TV Guide v 8 n 31 p 10-1 Jl 30'60

--- ---Football; NFL and AFL. TV Guide v 8 n 41 p 22-3 O 8'60

--- ---(Golf on TV "the most perplexing problem" to shoot; prize money soothes the pro.) TV Guide v 8 n 24 p 14-5 Je 11'60

--- ---Jackpot Bowling, show with Milton Berle, comedian, and Chick Hearn, sports announcer; review. TV Guide v 8 n 52 p 27 D 24'60

--- ---New league: American Football League; National Football League rival. TV Guide v 8 n 41 p 22-3 O 8'60

--- ---Professional football on TV; problems; NBC coverage 6 years. TV Guide v 8 n 50 p 22-3 D 10'60

--- ---Seeing CBS's Game of the week and ABC's Big League Baseball in Los Angeles; Walter O'Malley on subscription TV, Bill Veeck on free TV. TV Guide v 8 n 23 p 10-1 Je 4'60

--- ---The Olympics in Rome; TV plans. TV Guide v 8 n 34 p 5-7 Ag 20'60

--- ---The sorry state of tennis (open competition needed; TV has done nothing for tennis). TV Guide v 8 n 37 p 14-5 S 10'60

---England's National Hunt Meeting, BBC Midland reporting. Radio Times p 7 Mr 4'60

---Football film made from hydraulic operated boom, loaned by a tree surgeon; 50 feet up view; New Hampshire. Film World and AV p 482 D '60

--- ---Melvin Durslag on Army-Navy this year. TV Guide v 8 n 48 p 6-7 N 26'60

--- ---Melvin Durslag on recent seasons; "National League has enormous impudence telling viewers what they may see". TV Guide v 8 n 50 p 22-3 D 10'60

---Golf in Detroit. il TV Guide

(Sports)

v 8 n 49 p 6 D 3'60

--- ---"World Championship Golf"
with illustrated trouble shots. il
TV Guide v 8 n 27 p 14-6 Jl 2'60

---Goodwood, racing; TV coverage. Radio Times p 7 Jl 22'60

---Grandstand, sports series BBC;
106th University Boat Race, John
Snagge, commentator. Radio
Times p 13 Mr 25'60

---Hilton, Ronnie, singer and
centre-forward, on BBC's The
Friday Night Show. por Radio
Times p 55 N 3'60

---H. R. H. The Duke of Edinburgh
on "Grandstand"; notes. por Radio Times p 7 My 6'60

---Hollowood, Bernard. (Sports
neglected by ITA; reasons given
why commercial TV slights
sport.) Punch p 498 Ap 6 1960

---The Horse of the Year Show;
1949 to date; BBC notes on Wembley. Radio Times p 9, 29 S 30'60

---Horses; "Spotlight" given over
to recreational riding for the
young; The Pony Club. Radio
Times p 27 Ag 26'60

---Ice Skating (and Ice Dancing)
Championships 1960 at Garmisch-
Partenkirchen, West Germany-
notes. Radio Times p 7 Ja 29'60

---Junior Sportsview; list of awards 1956 to date; BBC notes.
Radio Times p 55 D 8'60

---Marathon motor-race at LeMans;
how BBC will cover. Radio Times
p 4 Je 24'60

---Merchant, Larry. (Television
upon baseball; new techniques; new
problems; effect on minor leagues.)
TV Guide v 8 n 15 p 5-7 Ap 9'60

---Moore, Reginald. Watching
sport on television. Radio Times
p 27 Je 24'60

---NBC to televise National Football League games; list of other
plans, also ABC sports list. TV
Guide v 8 n 39 p 17 S 24'60

--- ---World Championship Golf;
review. il TV Guide v 8 n 6 p 27
F 6'60 ; also Jl 2'60

---Open Golf Championship; one
hundred year old contest; BBC
coverage. Radio Times p 6
Jl 1'60

---Oxford vs. Cambridge; 79th
Rugby Union on BBC. Radio
Times p 30 D 1'60

---Plans for BBC coverage of
Wimbledon cricket at Edgbaston.
Radio Times p 2 Je 3'60

---Preview of TV sports programs.
TV Guide v 8 n 39 p 17-8 S 24'60

---Report on BBC's week of sports:
Boxing; motor racing; lawntennis;
cricket; swimming Radio Times
p 7 Ap 22'60

---Rosenthal, Harold. How the
World Series became the World
Series. TV Guide v 8 n 40 p 14-
5 O 1'60

---R. A. C. Rally 1960; 180 crews;
on "Grandstand", BBC. Radio
Times p 4 N 24'60

---The Royal International Horse
Show, pre-Olympic equestrian
events over BBC-TV. il Radio
Times p 6 Jl 15'60

---Rugby; Wales vs. South Africa;
BBC. Radio Times p 5 D 1'60

---San Francisco, Candlestick
Park; story; Horace Stoneham,
the Giants. TV Guide v 8 n 32
p 14-6 Ag 6'60

---Schmidt, Milt. How to watch
hockey (CBS ice show). TV Guide
v 8 n 3 p 24-6 Ja 16'60

---Shark hunting; Bob Fuller, Ka-
thy Nolan, Chuck Courtney. il
TV Guide v 8 n 44 p 16 O 29'60

---Slow-motion recorder for TV
pictures; Hiwatashi and Kitagawa
describe invention for sports pictures. Jr SMPTE v 69 n 4 p 261-2
Ap '60

---Sport on the Spot, series on BBC;
David Coleman. Radio Times
p 53 N 24'60

---Sports Review 1960; the award
of the year, BBC. il Radio Times
p 39 D 8'60

---Wimbledon; All England Lawn
Tennis Club; BBC plans. Radio
Times p 7 Je 17'60

---Winter Olympics at Squaw Valley, California; film to settle argument of Russian woman claiming a Swedish entrant tripped her; report. Film World and AV p 110 Mr '60

--- ---CBS story. il TV Guide v 8 n 7 p 5-7 F 13'60

---Wolstenholme, Kenneth. The F. A. Cup Final (Wolves vs. Blackburn Rovers). Radio Times p 7 Ap 29'60

SPY-CATCHER, series
Counter-intelligence; notes on the series by Lt. Col. Oreste Pinto. Radio Times p 3 F 12'60

---Moving from TV to radio; BBC. Radio Times p 3 S 2'60

STACK, ROBERT, actor
Johnson, Bob. Actual fate of gangsters caught on TV by Robert Stack; part I. il TV Guide v 8 n 28 p 24-6 Jl 9'60

---Por ph. TV Guide v 8 n 9 cover F 27'60

STAGECRAFT
Sound effects; MP-TV Services, Inc. (notes and il) TV Guide v 8 n 47 p 14-6 N 19'60
See also   Sound Effects; Production

STANDARDS
Progress report on TV magnetic tape standardization by C. E. Anderson. Jr SMPTE v 69 n 6 p 410-2 Je '60

---US; several given, as speed for 2-in video magnetic tape, dimensions same; theater screen luminance for indoor theaters, etc. Jr SMPTE v 69 n 4 p 269-271 Ap'60

STARBUCK, JAMES, choreographer
NBC; three decades of Hollywood songs with dancers. Dance Magazine v 34 n 5 p 13 My '60

STARER, ROBERT, composer
CBS commission for "The Story of Esther". Juilliard Review v 7 n 2 p 14 Spring '60

STARTIME, series
Editorial on failure of the fifteen-million budget show, sponsored by Ford; lack of time the cause. TV Guide v 8 n 22 p 6 My 28'60

(Television Index)

STATISTICS
Actors, etc. birthplace and date. World Almanac page 560-568 1959, also 1960 edition

---Cost per hour to US viewer; cost to watch commercials (free?). TV Guide v 8 n 49 p 1 D 3'60

---Growth of radio and TV in US: homes with sets; sets in the world, in the   US; and other figures. page 84 World Almanac 1959, see each edition

---Poll of members of Congress on the power of TV in the 1960 campaign; questions and statistics. TV Guide v 8 n 38 p 10-11 S 17'60

---US; expenditures on TV by the public 1959. TV Guide v 8 n 38 p 3 S 17'60

STEVENS, CONNIE, 1939-, singer
Notes. por TV Guide v 8 n 6 p 29 F 6'60

---Notes. por TV Guide v 8 n 29 p 28 Jl 16'60

---Notes and signed por ph. Screen Album p 54 N '60

---Notes on role of Cricket in Hawaiian Eye. TV Guide v 8 n 22 p 18-9 My 28'60

STEVENS, RISË, singer
On Telephone Hour; note. por Opera News v 25 n 6 p 5 D 17'60

STOCKWELL, DEAN, actor
Notes and signed por ph. Screen Album p 53 N '60

---Por. Screen World and TV p 31 O '60

STORM OVER THE NILE, film
BBC notes. il Radio Times p 5 O 27'60

STAINCHAMPS,   ETHEL. TV Talks good like a   medium should! TV Guide v 8 n 8 p 5-7 F 20'60

STRAVINSKY, IGOR
American TV debut with New York Philharmonic in "Firebird" excerpts. Musical Courier p 34 F '60

STUART, MARK
As producer for ITA of a full-length Cinderella with Margot Fonteyn. por Dancing Times v 50 n 595 p 349 Ap '60

STUART, MARY, actress
Stahl, Bob. Mary Stuart, star of
Search for Tomorrow, series.
por TV Guide v 8 n 47 p 18-20
N 19'60
A SUBJECT OF SCANDAL AND
CONCERN, play
BBC; John Osborne work. Radio
Times p 14 N 3'60
SUBMARINE STORY
Fleming, Douglas. (On past, pre-
sent and future of subs in British
Navy; inside latest model.) Radio
Times p 27 My 13'60
SUBSCRIPTION TV
Both sides: Walter O'Malley for
subscription TV for his baseball
and Bill Veeck for free TV; areas
of speculation by Melvin Durslag.
TV Guide v 8 n 23 p 10-1 Je 4'60
---Lackenbruch, David. CATV for
three million (US) viewers; costs.
TV Guide v 8 n 44 p 10-1 O 29'60
See also   Pay TV
SUBSIDIES
Ford Foundation list 1959. Film
World and AV p 58 F '60
SULLIVAN, BARRY
And small daughter, Patsy, watch-
ing Daddy's show, 6 phs. TV Gui-
de v 8 n 651 p 22-3 D 17'60
SUMMERHOUSE, series
BBC for juniors; Anthony Oliver,
relaxed garden observations with
guest speakers. Radio Times p 27
Jl 1'60
THE SUNDAY SPORTS SPECTACU-
LAR
Review of William MacPhail's an-
thology of sport. TV Guide v 8
n 10 p 22 Mr 5'60
SUNRISE SEMESTER, series
Fine Arts H-12 taught by Dr. Jane
Costello of New York University,
notes. il TV Guide v 8 n 26 p 20-2
Je 25'60
---New York University, WCBS-TV:
Peoples of Africa and Shakespeare's
Major Tragedies. Players Mag
v 37 n 2 p 1 N '60
SURVEYS
Social Research, Inc.; survey of
viewers (US). TV Guide v 8 n 32
Ag 6'60

SWAMP FOX, series
Disney Studios; Gen. Francis
Marion; comparison to Davy
Crockett's TV fame; Leslie Nie-
lsen, actor. il TV Guide v 8 n 1
p 8-9 Ja 2'60
SWEDEN
Development of TV; no adver-
tising. World Theatre v 9 n 2
p 174 Summer '60
SYKES, ERIC, actor
BBC series with Hattie Jacques.
il Radio Times p 39 D 29'60
---Comedy series on BBC; Hattie
Jacques and Richard Wattis. il
Radio Times p 4 Ja 22'60
---Domestic situation comedy
series; "no witless fooling".
Punch p 242 F 10'60

T

THE TAB HUNTER SHOW
BBC; cast (scene). Radio Times
p 47 D 29'60
---Review. TV Guide v 8 n 48
p 27 N 26'60
TAEGER, RALPH ADOLF(1936-).
Interview. por Movie Life p 10,
58 D '60
---Career sketch; born in Queens,
NYC. por TV Guide v 8 n 52
p 20-3 D 24'60
TALES OF THE VIKINGS, series
Brynaprod Company; list of
players. TV Guide v 8 n 1 p 13
Ja 2'60
TAPES
US fight against "illegal" tapes,
made abroad and dubbed in. In-
ternational Musician v 58 n 10
Ap '60
---Wiseman, Robert. Language
lab. Ed Screen and AV p 586-9
O '60
TAYLOR, BOB, 1912-, actor
Notes; wife, Ursula Theiss. por
Movie Life p 29 D '60
TAYLOR, JOYCE
Notes; from Taylorville, Illinois.
por TV Guide v 8 n 37 p 29
S 10'60
TAYLOR, LIZ, 1932-, actress

Chamm, Ron. (Health comments; father, Francis Taylor, art dealer, mother actress, Sara Sothern Taylor; married to Nicky Hilton, to Mike Wilding, to Mike Todd, to Eddie Fisher.) Movie Life p 20, 53-5 D '60

TCHAIKOVSKY, PETER ILYITCH
Bell Telephone Hour; dramatic and musical presentation of his life; Helen Hayes and Farley Granger; Donald Voohres, conducting. Musical Courier v 162 n 5 p 12 N '60

TEAGARDEN, JACK, 1905-, trombonist
Cerulli, Dom. (Career sketch of Texan-born Weldon John Teagarden.) il International Musician v 58 n 7 p 12-3 Ja '60

TEL-AVIV
Le Nozze di Figaro review. Opera News v 24 n 21 p 28 Mr 26'60

TELECLUB
NBC The Nation's Future; Irving Gitlin. por TV Guide v 8 n 49 p 1 D 3'60

TELECOACH
Schlihs, Robert B. (The idea, the device and its use in coaching.) Ed Screen and AV p 16-17 Ja '60

TELEPHONE TV
Telectrovision; NYC. Jr SMPTE v 69 n 5 p 372 My '60

TV-HISTORY
The decade of the fifties on US screens; high spots with pictures. TV Guide p 4-7 Ja 2'60
---Roberts, Louis. People since 1875 claiming it as their invention. TV Guide v 8 n 31 p 5-7 Jl 30'60

TV INDUSTRY
Dale, John L. Will Alliance of Television Film Producers merge with Association of Motion Picture Producers? Telefilm p 28-9, 42 Jl-Ag '60
---Labor negotiations: a summing up 1960 Hollywood by Richard W. Jencks. Telefilm p 22-3, 38 Jl-Ag '60
---Progress report on various phases: Networks; closed-circuit;

(Television Index) pay TV; world reports by country. Jr SMPTE My '60
---Wald, Jerry. (On the need in the entertainment industry of a World Court; piracy ceases to be enterprising.) por Telefilm p 37, 45 Jl-Ag '60

TV AND CHILDREN
Bumpass, Eugene. TV: school rival or school aid? por Texas Outlook p 12-3 Je '60
---Kaye, Danny. How does TV affect our children? TV Guide v 8 n 13 p 7-9 Mr 26'60
---Schramm, Dr. Wilbur. What does your child bring to TV? TV Guide v 8 n 19 p 5-7 My 7'60
---White House Conference on Children and Youth; suggestions to parents concerning TV. TV Guide v 8 n 18 p 3 Ap 30'60

TELEVISION ARCHIVES
University of California; notes. Jr SMPTE v 69 n 4 p 276 Ap '60

TV CODE REVIEW BOARD
Expansion; Hollywood and New York. TV Guide v 8 n 41 p 9 O 8'60
---National Association of Broadcasters; 559 US stations "back" the Code; no teeth in it; 3-year licenses by FCC might be made the stake? TV Guide p 2 Ja 2'60
---US industry-sponsored code; extent of its use. TV Guide v 8 n 13 p 2 Mr 26'60

TELEVISION ENGINEERING
Each issue Journal of Society of Motion Picture and Television Engineers.

TELEVISION IN EDUCATION
Aylward, Thomas James, Jr. A study of the effect of production techniques on a televised lecture (Ph. D. thesis, University of Wisconsin, 1960). Dissertation Abstracts v 21 p 1660 D '60
---Comment on findings in correlation of TV viewing and school work; Dr. Paul A. Witty of Northwestern, one researcher. TV Guide v 8 n 7 p 2 F 13'60
---Packer, Roddy Earle. An

(TV in Education)
analysis of the degree of integration existing educational television stations with their particular communities. University of Minnesota 1960. Dissertation Abstracts v 21 n 4 p 992 1960
---Pockrass, Robert Mandell. Effects on learning of continuous and interrupted exhibition of educational television programs. Stanford University 1960. Dissertation Abstracts v 21 n 4 p 870 1960
---Tadros, Samy Samaan. An investigation of the impact of television upon the maturing process of the adult. Indiana University 1960 Dissertation Abstracts v 21 n 3 p 536 1960
TELEVISION IN MEDICINE
Magid, Myra. The war against cancer (television's use). TV Guide v 8 n 10 p 19-21 Mr 5'60
---Seattle; KIRO-TV by hour-long color film, The Priceless Gift, arousing interest in the corneal-transplant operation; 37,000 have pledged to the eye Bank. TV Guide v 8 n 25 p 29 Je 18'60
TV FILMS
American Film Festival, NYC; list of TV films entered. Film World and AV p 104 Mr '60
---Capital requirements discussed by Bruce McKay, banker in Beverly Hills. Telefilm v 4 n 10 p 10-11 Ap '60
---Cost; analysis of half-hour film program's budget by Nicholas Archer and John Barnwell. Telefilm p 30-33, 40 Jl-Ag '60
---Economics of television film production: Bernstein Report 1960, summary. Telefilm v 4 n 10 p 7-9, 20 Ap '60
---Editorial: corporate image unavoidable, the responsibility of top management in Hollywood. Telefilm p 48 Jl-Ag '60
---Producers with portraits and quotes on their recent films for network programs: Frank Telford on "outlaws"; Boris Ingster on "Roaring 20's"; Aaron Ruben

on "Andy Griffith Show"; and 18 other criticisms by producers. Telefilm Jl-Ag '60
---Thirty-three new Hollywood produced-on-film programs, charted information. Telefilm p 26-7 Jl-Ag '60
---Wray, Richard, film cutter for Revue Studios; the work of editing 18 series a week, one and a half million feet a year. por TV Guide v 8 n 23 p 24-5 Je 4'60
THE TEMPEST, play
NBC, Hallmark Hall of Fame; notes and stills. Th Arts v 44 n 2 p 65-70 F '60
---Production scenes, performance scenes, NBC-TV. Theatre Arts v 44 n 2 p 65-68 F '60
TEMPLE, SHIRLEY, 1928-, actress
In TV; notes. por TV Guide v 8 n 49 p 17-9 D 3'60
---Mrs. Charles Alden Black now; return; broadening of the "Shirley Temple Show". TV Guide v 8 n 49 p 17-19 D 3'60
---Notes; Mrs. Charles Black. por Movie Life p 30 D '60
TEXAS
American re-broadcasts of BBC shows; Austin gave a 14-hr day to English programs on the fourth birthday of KHFI station. Radio Times p 5 Ap 15'60
THEATRE
Focus, for 7 weeks program to show how plays are made; "exploring the theatre"; introductory notes by John Neville. il Radio Times p 25 Ja 29'60
---Television as aid to theatres; Rockford, Illinois, report. TV Age p 38, 69 Jl 11'60
THEY MADE HISTORY, series
Begins with medicine, David Lister in London; then George III and loss of American Colonies. Radio Times p 9 Ja 15'60
THIS IS THE BBC, film
Cawston, Richard, director; criticism. il Radio Times p 5 Je 24 '60
THIS IS YOUR LIFE, series

Backward look; BBC. Radio Times p 22 D 29'60
---Markova, Alicia, ballerina on BBC, January 11, 1960; report. il Ballet Today v 12 n 12 p 3 Mr '60
THORNTON, SPENCER, 1930-, doctor
Ramsey, Sy. Quiz shows will be back (telepathy not yet tapped). por TV Guide v 8 n 12 p 10-1 Mr 19'60
THE THREE PRINCES, play
Tucker, Rex, playwright; BBC notes (scene). Radio Times p 30 D 15'60
THRILLER, series
Review; NBC, starring Boris Karloff. TV Guide v 8 n 44 p 27 O 29'60
TIGHTROPE, program
Whitney, Dwight. Story of production, its rise, its death; Mike Conners. il TV Guide v 8 n 32 p 17-9 Jl 30'60
TILSLEY, VINCENT, playwright
The Chopping Block; BBC. Radio Times p 15 O 20'60
TIME AND TIME AGAIN, serial
Children's Hour, BBC; John Keir Cross on his adaptation of Philippa Pearce's book "Tom's Midnight Garden". Radio Times p 28 Ap 29'60
A TIME TO DANCE, film
Nine half-hour programs on US TV; interview format not well-organized; Martha Myers, moderator; "cozy first names"; Antony Tudor the best. Dance Magazine v 34 n 6 p 22 Je '60
A TIME TO FIGHT, play
BBC; cast and notes. il Radio Times p 13 D 15'60
TO TELL THE TRUTH, series
Stahl, Bob. (How the show works; examples.) TV Guide v 8 n 33 p 9-11 Ag 13'60
TOBIAS AND THE ANGEL, TV opera
Bliss, Sir Arthur, composer; BBC-TV review. Opera v 11 n 7 p 514 Jl '60
---Sir Arthur Bliss' work over

(Television Index)
BBC-Tv; Rudolf Cartier producer. Opera v 11 n 5 p 334 My '60
---Story from the 8th century; cast and BBC production notes. Radio Times p 3 My 13'60
TOBIN, JUNE, actress
Roles on BBC. por Radio Times p 4 Mr 25'60
TODAY, series
Ninth year; "highly mobile"; under Dave Garroway; review. TV Guide v 8 n 24 p 23 Je 11'60
TOKYO
Palmisano, Leon, Jr. and others introducing American style presentations. il Dance Magazine v 34 n 6 p 38-9 Je '60
TOM SAWYER, serial
BBC; American Boys, Fred Smith, 1947-and Mike Strotheide, 1946-;other notes. il Radio Times p 25 Jl 22'60
TOMME, RONALD, actor
Notes; b. Chicago. por TV Guide v 8 n 9 p 14 F 27'60
TONG, SAMMEE, actor-singer
Career sketch. por TV Guide v 8 n 7 p 21-2 F 13'60
TONGA
Attenborough, David; films on Queen Salote and Tonga, a member of the Commonwealth; BBC. il Radio Times p 3 My 20'60
TONIGHT, series
Notes, BBC. Radio Times p 46 D 22'60
---Notes on BBC series, contents not determined until the afternoon before the telecast. Radio Times p 7 Ag 26'60
TOP TOWN, series
England; mayor arranges with BBC-TV to include local dance team; light numbers. Dancing Times v 50 n 595 p 369 Ap' 60
TOP TOWN TOURNAMENT
Annual amateur show, BBC; notes. Punch p 666 My 11'60
TORS, IVAN, 1917-, producer
Career notes; b. Budapest. por TV Guide v 8 n 15 p 20-2 Ap 9'60
TOWN AND COUNTRY, serial
BBC visits to interesting spots

403

(Town and Country)
as the observatory tower once at Greenich now in Sussex. Radio Times p 2 Jl 1'60

TOWN PLANNING
BBC; Angel in Need; Burslem redesigned by the Civic Trust. Radio Times p 15 O 20'60

THE TRAIN SET, play
BBC notes (scene). Radio Times p 47 D 29'60

TRAVEL
Dimbleby, Richard. Passport, a second series on possible holidays (how Dimbleby demonstrates possibilities). Radio Times p 7 F 5'60

---Morris, Johnny; notes on his jaunts in Europe; BBC. Radio Times p 2 Ag 12'60

---Morris, Johnny, series on his travels, BBC 15-minute programs. Radio Times p 4 Jl 22'60

---Travellers' Tales, new series; BBC notes on adventure constantly being shot. Radio Times p 3 Jl 1'60

THE TROJANS, opera
Keefee, Bernard. Royal Opera House program on BBC. il Radio Times p 2 My 6'60

TROOPING THE COLOUR
London; BBC-TV notes. il Radio Times p 4 Je 3'60

TUDOR, ANTONY, choreographer
Best in the film sequence, "A Time To Dance"; with Nora Kaye and Hugh Laing; Ann Barzel review. Dance Magazine v 34 n 6 p 22 Je '60

TUPPENCE IN THE GODS, play
BBC cast. il Radio Times p 14 D 22'60

THE TURN OF THE SCREW, TV opera
Associated-Rediffusion review; Peter Morley staging of Britten's work; ghost scenes less mysterious; "TV failed to make the most of its sleight of hand". Opera v 11 n 2 p 162 F '60

TURTON, HENRY. On the air; reviews BBC, Granada, ATV, mostly. Punch 1960

THE 20th CENTURY, series
CBS; producer, Burton Benjamin;

new format. il TV Guide v 8 n 40 p 24-6 O 1'60

---CBS, Sunday evening documentary; notes. TV Guide v 8 n 14 p 2 Ap 2'60

---Now "news in width, instead of news in depth"; plans. TV Guide v 8 n 40 p 25-6 O 1'60

---Plays on BBC; critical notes and background on the authors. Radio Times 1960

THE TWILIGHT ZONE, series
Serling, Rod, script writer; Buck Houghton, producer; series of "between science and superstition". TV Guide v 8 n 9 p 23 F 27'60

U

UNDERWATER CINEMATOGRAPHY
Barton, William R. San Clemente Island near Long Beach, California; US Naval filming; 10 illustrations. Film World and AV p 200-1 My '60

---Rebikoff, Dimitri I. and Paul Cherney. Mobility in underwater cinematography. il Jr SMPTE v 69 n 4 p 267-8 Ap '60

UNITED FAN MAIL SERVICE
Hollywood; 12-year old enterprise for setting up fan clubs (a star must impress the sponsor); costs. TV Guide v 8 n 4 p 11 Ja 23'60

UNITED NATIONS
Outline of film use around the world. Film World and AV p 431, 434 N '60

UNESCO
Publications: Television and Education in the United States 1953 ($1.50); Television and rural adult Education 1956 ($3.50); Television and Tele-clubs in rural communities 1955 ($ .40); Television, a world survey 1954 ($ 1.75) with a 1955 supplement ($ .50).

UNITED STATES
Armed Forces TV stations. il TV Guide v 8 n 20 p 10-1 My 14'60

---Comment on coming season in TV shows. TV Guide v 8 n 39

p 2 S 24'60
---Electoral College system; previous decisions; chart of major party votes in Presidential elections 1789-1956. TV Guide v 8 n 30 p 6-7, 14-5 Jl 23'60
---FCC: 10 key questions with the answers quoted, also protraits of TV film executives with charts of business relationships. Telefilm v 5 n 2 p 7-14, 16-7 S-O '60
---Film distribution and exhibition; panel: Shirley Clarke, experimental films; Edw. Harrison, importer; Bill Kenly, theater manager; Elodie Osborn, film society; Bill Bernhardt and John Adams. Film Quarterly v 13 n 4 p 19-34 Summer '60
---Informational programs in the evening hours; should not attempt too broad a theme for the time span. TV Guide v 8 n 47 p 2 N 19'60
---More "think" shows due to the FCC ruling (editorial comment also on previews for the whole season). TV Guide v 8 n 39 S 24'60
---Notes: What's My Line, series; Ive Got a Secret; The Price is Right. TV Guide v 8 n 40 p 23 O 1'60
---Presidential election film on BBC; Anthony de Lotbiniere. Radio Times p 54 O 27'60
---Russell, Dorothy N. S. (Survey o of 1960-61 TV programs; old and new films killing live performers; details.) Dance Magazine v 34 n 9 p 24 S '60
---Survey of radio and TV programs as seen by visitor, Robert Wangermée. Inter-American Music Bulletin March 1961
US ARMY
Mohr, Phillip Joe. The radio and television listening habits and program preference of Eighth U. S. Army personnel in Korea, autumn 1959. (Ph. D. thesis, Ohio State University 1960, Microfilmed University Microfilms, Inc.) Dissertation Abstracts v 21 p 3193 Ap '61

(Television Index)
THE UNTOUCHABLES, crime series
Johnson, Bob. What really happened (thumbnail sketches of gangsters from whom The Untouchables arose). il TV Guide v 8 n 28 p 24-6 Jl 9'60
---ABC show on gangsters. il TV Guide v 8 n 29 p 24-7 Jl 16'60
---Johnson, Bob. What really happened, Part II. il TV Guide v 8 n 29 p 24-6 Jl 16'60
---Martin, Quinn (1923-), producer for Desilu Playhouse; ABC release discussed. il TV Guide v 8 n 9 p 17-9 F 27'60
---Review of series on US Treasury agents. TV Guide v 8 n 13 p 27 Mr 26'60
---Wertham, Dr. Frederic. Do you really like "The Untouchables"? (Psychiatrist claims it is conditioning to enjoy violence) TV Guide v 8 n 43 p 6-9 O 22'60
UPGREEN AND AT'EM
All star vaudeville on BBC for National Playing Fields Association; notes on cast. Radio Times p 7 Je 3'60

V

VAN ORDEN, ROBERT, actor
As Slim Sherman in Laramie; stage name, John Smith. por Radio Times p 5 Mr 4'60
VAUGHAN, FRANKIE, 1928-
Notes; b. Liverpool. por Screen Album p 32 N '60
VAUGHN, ROBERT, 1934-, actor
Note. TV Guide v 8 n 7 p 19 F 13'60
VAUGHAN WILLIAMS, RALPH, composer
Vaughan Williams, Ursula. (On her late husband's opera, The Pilgrim's Progress; to be broadcast BBC.) por Radio Times p 2 Ap 8'60
THE VERDICT IS YOURS, series
CBS; no formal scripts; real lawyers battle; "it's rough enought to lose a case in a real court but I'll be doggoned if I'll do it if front of

(The Verdict is Yours)
4,000,000 people". TV Guide
v 8 n 15 p 29 Ap 9'60
VICTORY AT SEA, series
BBC; Richard Rodgers' score;
notes. Radio Times p 38 D 29'60
VIDEO VILLAGE, series
Review (CBS game show). TV
Guide v 8 n 36 p 23 S 3'60
VIEWER SERVICE
Radnor, Pennsylvania; the ser-
vice for views of viewers. TV
Guide v 8 n 38 p 3 S 17'60
VINCENT, J. J. on young artists;
could be helped by TV; that med-
ium makes it harder to book yo-
unger artists. Musical Courier
v 162 n 1 p 18 Jl '60
VISCONTI, LUCHINO
Poggi, Gianfranco. Visconti and
the Italian cinema. il Film Quar-
terly v 13 n 3 p 11-22 Spring '60
VIVYAN, JOHN,1924-, actor
Notes; b. Pittsburgh, grew up in
Chicago. TV Guide v 8 n 7 p 18-9
F 13'60
VOGEL, NANCY. (Series on TV
writers.) Writer's Digest 1960
THE VOICE, serial
BBC aeroplane adventure mystery
tale; Terence Longdon and others
in the new sequence. Radio Times
p 4 N 3'60
VOICES IN THE AIR, revue
Cleverdon, Douglas, producer;
BBC notes. Radio Times p 5 My
20'60
VOORHEES, DONALD, composer-
conductor
Morton, Jon. (Two years on TV
and 18 on radio; quoted on musical
taste on TV; Bell Telephone Hour.)
por Musical Courier v 162 n 3 p 8
S '60
VYVYAN, JOHN, actor
Notes; b. Australia. il Radio Times p 5 Mr 11'60

W

WAGNER, FRANK
Career on TV and other dance
work; trained in Katherine Dunham
school; commercial shows; wife,

Marsha, assists in staging
summer stock. por Dance Mag-
azine v 34 n 11 p 18 N '60
WAGNER, WENDY, stunt girl
Notes. il TV Guide v 8 n 33
p 6-7 Ag 13'60
WAKEY WAKEY TAVERN
Cotton, Billy; BBC. Radio
Times p 8 N 3'60
WALD, JERRY. (On need for a
World Court in entertainment
industry; rivalry has become as
uneconomic as piracy became.)
por Telefilm p 37, 45 Jl-Ag '60
WALES
Drana; Eynon Evans, actor-
playwright and Dafydd Gruffydd;
notes. Radio Times p 5 F 5'60
---National Eisteddfod; R. E.
Griffith, Director of the Welsh
League of Youth; Children's
Hour. Radio Times p 27 Je 3'60
---National Youth Orchestra on
BBC; notes. Radio Times p 27
Ag 12'60
---Over the Waves, a scenic trip
around Wales by Wynford Vaughan
Thomas; BBC. Radio Times p 5
Jl 15'60
WALKER, PAUL ATLEE, 1881-
Emery, Walter B. Champion of
the public interest (FCC official's
career sketch). por Telefilm v 5
n 2 p 19-20 S-O '60
WALLENSTEIN, ALFRED, con-
ductor
Comment on American TV's
attitude: only 21 million saw his
90 minute spectacular so it was
dubbed "a failure" officially, even
with Boris Christoff, Artur Rubin-
stein and Victoria de los Angeles.
Music and Dance v 50 n 7 p 15
Ja '60
WANGERMÉE, ROBERT. Impre-
ssions and reflections of a trave-
ler (in USA). Inter-American
Music Bulletin March 1961
WARNER, JACK, actor
BBC roles. Radio Times p 4
Mr 25'60
WARREN, CHARLES MARQUIS,
director
Interview on cattle driving in the

old days;making of Westerns. il
TV Guide v 8 n 37 p 21-3 S 10
'60
WATER
Program, "Enquiry"; Robert
Reid on water problems;BBC.
Radio Times p 55 O 20'60
WATER ALIVE
Singer, Burns, BBC film on her-
ring industry;notes. Radio Times
p 6 Mr 11'60
WAUGH, EVELYN, novelist
On Face to Face;por. Radio Times
p 4 Je 24'60
THE WAY OF THE CROSS
World Wide 60 project, The Way
of the Cross, Jesus' final jour-
ney, six scenes. TV Guide v 8
n 16 p 28-9 Ap 16'60
THE WAY OF THE WORLD,
comedy
Congreve on BBC;Edith Evans.
Radio Times p 2 Je 24'60
WAYNE, JOHN, 1908-, actor
Notes;first wife Josephine Saenz,
four children; third wife, Pilar
and daughter in Africa also. por
Movie Life p 28 D'60
WE ARE the MUSIC MAKERS
Telecast list by cities and time
and the day, station;under AFL-
CIO sponsorship. International
Musician v 58 n 8 p 36 F'60
WEATHER
BBC's Your Holiday Weather,
giving conditions for sport and
for sailing. Radio Times p 5
Ap 8'60
---Stierli, Joe. (Dialogue weather
man and station manager.) TV
Guide v 8 n 45 p 15 N 5'60
WELCH, JOSEPH N. , 1890-,
actor-lawyer
DeBlois, Frank. (Interview with
Boston lawyer acting in who dun-
its.) por TV Guide v 8 n 21
p 5-7 My 21'60
WELD, TUESDAY, 1944-, actress
Career notes. portfolio TV Guide
v 8 n 32 p 12-4 Jl 30'60
---Interview. il Screen Album
p 17-8 N'60
WELK, LAWRENCE, 1903-, dancer
Johnson, Bob. Candid portrait of

(Television Index)
Welk, his Aragon Ballroom and
TV show. il TV Guide v 8 n 27
p 17-9 Jl 2'60
WELLES, ORSON
Anderson, Lindsay. A study of
Orson Welles. il Radio Times
p 3 Mr 11'60
---BBC notes; revival of his "The
Magnificent Ambersons" (one
scene shown). Radio Times p 5
F 26'60
WERTHAM, DR. FREDERIC. Do
you really like The Untouchables
(program of violent killing)? TV
Guide v 8 n 43 p 6-9 O 22'60
WESTERNS
Assemblage of guns carried by
the leading actors; notes on each
and on studio regulations on their
custody. TV Guide v 8 n 18 p 26
Ap 30'60
---Bonanza; analysis of show. il
TV Guide v 8 n 26 p 17-9 Je 25'60
--- ---saga of the Cartright family;
notes. il TV Guide v 8 n 26 p 16-9
Je 25'60
---Boothroyd, J. B. ("The stories
deal only indirectly with guns;
they deal with the interplay of
character. ") Punch p 816 Je 8'60
---British notes on Dale Robertson
(b. Oklahoma City); "Wells Fargo".
Radio Times p 4 F 19'60
---British reaction; Robert Fuller,
1933- (b. Troy, New York) in La-
ramie. il Radio Times p 4 F 19'60
---Lynch, Jack. How Western heroes
would sound if they spoke real cowboy lingo. TV Guide v 8 n 22 p 26
My 28'60
---Note on Lone Ranger; on Jack Ma-
loney in "Range Rider", BBC. il
Radio Times p 4 F 19'60
---Notes on several series; Laramie,
Bonanza, Overland Trail, Bronco.
TV Guide v 8 n 19 p 23 My 7'60
---On BBC; Bronco back (Ty Hardin
pictured). Radio Times p 4 Ap 1'60
---The Range Rider, series; notes
on Jack Mahoney and Dick Jones
por Radio Times p 27 Jl 22'60
---Pearman, Bob. The Wild West
comes alive (many towns are

(Westerns)
constructing for tourists old buildings in replica, etc.) il TV Guide v 8 n 25 p 5-7 Je 18'60
---Rawhide and how Charles Marquis Warren creates the series. il TV Guide v 8 n 37 p 21-3 S 10'60
---Steiger, Rod, producer "A Town Has Turned to Dust"; BBC notes (scene). Radio Times p 3 Jl 1'60
---Tenderfoot, starring Will Hutchins, 1932-; BBC notes. Radio Times p 3 S 2'60
---Warren, Charles Marquis, on making Westerns; old style cattle-driving. il TV Guide v 8 n 37 p 21-3 S 10'60
---Wayne, John. Quoted on the cowboy in cinema. por Screen Album p 42 N '60
---Whitney, Dwight. The day it rained at "Laramie" (rain and the shooting must go on). il TV Guide v 8 n 17 p 17-9 Ap 23'60
WHACK-O, serial
Boys school, Chiselbury School in England; new scripts. Radio Times p 5 My 6'60
---Howard, Arthur; BBC notes. Radio Times p 31 D 8'60
WHAT DO YOU KNOW, series
Statistics: 200th program, 8th year; 12000 questions; 385 people. Radio Times p 5 Ja 22'60
WHAT'S MY LINE
Comments on 10-year show, producer Bob Bach. TV Guide v 8 n 20 p 13-5 My 14'60
WHELEN, CHRISTOPHER. On writing incidental music for TV. Radio Times p 4 My 6'60
WHERE ARE YOU NOW?
BBC series, lost friends brought together; Wilfred Pickles. Radio Times p 9 Mr 11'60
THE WHISTLE STOP, revue
BBC; local revue people and McDonald Hobley. Radio Times p 22 D 1'60
---Scotland; comic actors; BBC. Radio Times p 22 O 20'60
WHITE, JOSH, balladeer
BBC notes; "polished". Radio

Times p 38 O 6'60
WHITMORE, JAMES, 1921-, actor
In series, The Law and Mr. Jones; criticism. TV Guide v 8 n 50 p 9-10 D 10'60
WHO, ME?
BBC police questioning show. il Radio Times p 4 Mr 18'60
WICHITA TOWN, a western
McCrea, Joel, and his son, Jody McCrea (1935-); notes. il TV Guide v 8 n 2 p 13-5 Ja 9'60
WILD RIVER, film
Kazan, Eliz, director; review. Film Quarterly v 13 n 4 p 50-1 Summer '60
WILLIAMS, ESTHER, 1923., swimmer
Character sketch; born Los Angeles. por TV Guide v 8 n 32 p 17-9 Ag 6'60
---With Jeff Chandler, notes. and signed por. Screen Album p 16 N '60
WILLIAMS, ROY, script writer
Notes; b. Maidenhead. Radio Times p 5 F 19'60
THE WIND AND THE SUN, play
BBC; Colin Morris work; cast. Radio Times p 16 N 10'60
WINTERS, GLORIA
Penny on "Sky King" series; notes. il Dance Digest v 10 n 2 p 38 Mr'60
WITCH OF ENDOR (BUTLER), ballet
Notes. Dance Magazine v 34 n 4 p 13 Ap '60
WITHOUT THE GRAIL, play
Cooper, Giles, author; tea planter in Assam; BBC. Radio Times p 3 S 9'60
THE WOMAN IN WHITE, play
BBC conversion by Howard Agg of Wilkie Collins novel. Radio Times p 2 S 9'60
WOOD, NATALIE, actress
Notes on her work and her husband Robert Wagner. il Screen Album p 49 N '60
WOODING, program
Holland, Philip. (On his program on Forest Commission in England.) Radio Times p 6 Ap 1'60
WORDS AND MUSIC, series
In 30 minutes, writing orchestrating and presenting a song, BBC. Radio

Times p 5 My 20'60

THE WORLD OF APU, film
Review. Film Quarterly v 13 n 3
p 53-4 Spring '60

THE WORLD OF TIM FRAZER,
serial
Durbridge, Francis, author on
his BBC serial. por Radio Times
p 30 N 10'60

---Hedley, Jack, star; BBC notes.
por Radio Times p 31 D 1'60

WORLD WAR II
Hayes, Ira Hamilton, an American
Indian, one of the six marines in
flag-raising on Iwo Jima; notes on
TV re-creating. il TV Guide v 8
n 13 p 10-12 Mr 26'60

WRITE ME A LETTER, series
Thomas, Adrian; children's letters, individual and from class
groups; pointers on better letters;
Saturday show for youth. por Radio Times p 22 Ja 22'60

WYNN, ED
And his son, Keenan, play together, story of "Requiem for a
Heavyweight. " por TV Guide v 8
n 15 p 12-14 Ap 9'60

Y

YORK, JEFF, 1912-, actor
Notes. TV Guide v 8 n 24 p 28
Je 11'60

YORKY, series
BBC; modern country village,
Wilfrid Pickles series; comment.
Punch p 738 My 25'60

---Pickles, Wilfred, as village
school master; BBC notes. il
Radio Times p 5 My 13'60

YOUNG, LORETTA, 1913-, actress
Interview on keeping young. por
TV Guide v 8 n 45 p 17-9 N 5'60

---Notes and signed ph. Screen
Album p 80 N '60

YOUNG WOODLEY, play
BBC's Twentieth Century Theatre
notes (one scene) on John Van
Druten play. Radio Times p 5
Mr 18'60

YOUR OBEDIENT SERVANT, play
BBC cast and notes. il Radio
Times p 8 N 17'60

YOUTH

(Television Index)
Cowley Recreational Institute   in
program "In the South-East" (of London); activities. Radio Times p 2
My 27'60

Z

ZANE GREY THEATER, series
Powell, Dick; his use of relics of
Indians and the old West to introduce episodes. il TV Guide v 8 n 44
p 28-9 O 29'60

ZIMBALIST, EFREM, 1919-, actor
Career notes. por TV Guide v 8
n 15 p 17-19 Ap 9'60

ZIMBALIST, EFREM, JR.
Por signed ph. Screen Album p 35
N '60

LIBRARY OF MOUNT ST. MARY'S COLLEGE EMMITSBURG, MARYLAND
WITHDRAWN